PowerShell in Practice

PowerShell in Practice

RICHARD SIDDAWAY

MANNING

Greenwich
(74° w. long.)

For online information and ordering of this and other Manning books, please visit
www.manning.com. The publisher offers discounts on this book when ordered in quantity.
For more information, please contact

Special Sales Department
Manning Publications Co.
180 Broad Street
Suite 1323
Stamford, CT 06901
Email: orders@manning.com

Manning Publications Co.
180 Broad Street, Suite 1323
Stamford, CT 06901

Development editor: Sebastian Stirling
Copyeditor: Benjamin Berg
Cover designer: Leslie Haimes
Typesetter: Gordan Salinovic

ISBN 9781935182009
Printed in the United States of America
1 2 3 4 5 6 7 8 9 10 – MAL – 15 14 13 12 11 10

To Ann, for everything

brief contents

contents

11 Active Directory topology   321

14 SQL Server 414

preface

These are the last words that I am writing and perhaps the first words you will be reading. For me the journey is coming to an end, and for you the adventure just begins as you dive deeper into the world of PowerShell. Welcome!

There are a significant number of PowerShell books already, so why do we need another one? I wanted to produce a book that showed how to use PowerShell to solve the sorts of problems administrators face every day. PowerShell is a tool for automating the administration of your Windows-based systems, but there wasn't a book available that described how to use it to solve my problems. Now there is.

I've written this for system administrators who want to automate their administration tasks. The PowerShell language is covered in sufficient detail to explain everything you see in the book, but we're concentrating on providing solutions to the types of problems we continually face administering Windows, Exchange, Active Directory, and IIS, among others.

We'll look at how to automate our system administration, and equally importantly, we'll look at why we're doing these things. The book supplies a large suite of scripts that can be put to work in your environment immediately. Linked to the scripts is the background to the task we're solving, so you can put the script into the context of your needs. More than a cookbook or a description of the PowerShell language, this is your guide to automation through PowerShell.

As you read along, you'll also find my thoughts on best practices for administration in general, and automating those administrative tasks in particular. There's no point in automating bad practices—that just makes things go wrong more quickly.

Solutions to the problems faced by administrators of all levels of experience can be found in these chapters. Use the scripts to solve your problems, and if you find a better way to perform the task, please share it with the PowerShell community.

I've gained a number of things from working with PowerShell:

- A deeper understanding of the technologies I work with: I can't automate it until I understand what it's doing.
- Some wonderful opportunities, including the writing of this book.
- New friends who share my interest and passion for PowerShell.

If nothing else, I hope that you gain a sense of that interest and passion from reading the book. Use the techniques, join the PowerShell community, and most of all—enjoy what you do.

acknowledgments

This book wouldn't have been possible without the contributions of many other people. It isn't until you get involved in a project like this that you realize just how many other people contribute to any book before it gets published.

First and foremost is the Microsoft PowerShell team. The introduction of Power-Shell marks a huge change in the way we administer Windows systems. You guys don't get thanked enough for creating PowerShell and the time you spend with the Power-Shell community, so I'd like to record my thanks on behalf of that community.

The group of people at Manning who worked with me on this book have been superb. The level of support for a first-time author was outstanding. I couldn't have done this without you, so many thanks to Sebastian Stirling, Benjamin Berg, Elizabeth Martin, Michael Stephens, Marjan Bace, Steven Hong, Karen Tegtmeyer, Jamie Tara-toot, Mary Piergies, Gordan Salinovic, Dottie Marsico, Tiffany Taylor, and Gabriel Dobrescu. The book is much better thanks to your input and ideas. It's been a pleasure working with such a professional group.

There have been a number of reviews of this book during its development and production. The individual reviewers have taken time to read through and comment on the original manuscript, in some cases three times. Thanks are due to Jonathan Medd, Jonathan Noble, Jeffrey Snover, Peter Johnson, Andrew Tearle, Wolfgang Blass, Tomas Restrepro, Amos Bannister, Dave Corun, Lester Lobo, Anderson Patricio, Marco Shaw, Austin Osuide, Dmitriy Kopylenko, Bruce Payette, Michael Bain, Oliver Sturm, and Jeff Copeland. Special thanks to Marco Shaw for also performing the technical review of the manuscript and code. And I'd like to thank the readers who took the time to comment on the MEAP forum. I did read all of the comments and have corrected the manuscript as appropriate. Any errors of omission or commission are mine alone.

The PowerShell community is young but strong and enthusiastic. The ideas that I've included in this book aren't just the result of my work with PowerShell, but the fruit of numerous discussions, emails, and debates about how PowerShell should be used. The participants are too numerous to mention, but my heartfelt thanks to you all for the time you've put into the community and for graciously allowing me to quote your work. The UK PowerShell User Group deserves a special acknowledgment for putting up with me drilling down into the details during question times.

Finally, thanks must go to my family, friends, and colleagues who've supported me through the writing and production of this book.

about this book

This is a PowerShell book for administrators. It'll show you how to use PowerShell v1, PowerShell v2, and the PowerShell functionality introduced with products such as SQL Server, Exchange, and Windows Server 2008 R2. Third-party additions will also be used where appropriate. We'll see problems solved using scripts in version 1 with reference to cmdlets that were introduced in version 2. This is a deliberate decision to ensure that the book has the widest possible scope. PowerShell v1 isn't going to disappear overnight and we need to be able to work across both versions in the near future.

I've aimed at covering the breadth of PowerShell, in terms of showing the number of different aspects of the environment we can control, and the depth in terms of showing the detailed and practical techniques for performing administrative tasks.

When you read the book, it'll seem to be a hybrid. It lies somewhere between a cookbook of PowerShell recipes and an explanation of how to administer Windows-based systems. That's deliberate in that I believe you can't properly apply the automation techniques you'll gain from the book unless the underlying technologies are understood. The book is a PowerShell book, so the explanations aren't complete—just enough to explain why we're performing a specific task.

Most of all, it's a book to be used. Keep it on your desk and refer to it often. There are 205 techniques in the book, numbered consecutively and divided into sections called Problem, Solution, and Discussion. Techniques first appear in chapter 5. They should enable you to solve your particular problem. If not, a message on the Author Online forum will reach me and I may be able to supply some pointers. No promises, because I have a day job as well.

Who should read this book?

PowerShell in Practice is written for anyone interested in using PowerShell to automate the administration of her Windows environment. The obvious audience is administrators in a large enterprise environment, but the lone administrator in a smaller organization will gain as much if not more from the techniques described here.

The IT manager and IT architect audience will also benefit from viewing what it's possible to achieve using PowerShell. Microsoft is releasing a number of workbooks that cover the actions that need to be taken to ensure the reliability of various components of the infrastructure such as DNS, Active Directory, or IIS. Many of the actions can be performed by PowerShell scripts taken directly, or adapted, from the techniques shown in the book.

Above all, this book is written for people interested in PowerShell and what can be accomplished with it. It's not the last word on the subject—we'd need a book 5 or 10 times the size for that—but it does take you a long way on the journey to automation.

Roadmap

PowerShell in Practice is organized into three parts. The book opens with part 1, "Getting Started with PowerShell." This introductory section covers the installation and configuration of PowerShell, together with the background knowledge we'll need to work with other technologies such as WMI and Active Directory.

Chapter 1, "PowerShell fundamentals," covers some of the background to Power-Shell, including the major features of PowerShell such as cmdlets and providers, the PowerShell pipeline and the utility cmdlets we use for operations such as sorting and grouping. The chapter closes with an overview of the new features introduced in Pow-erShell v2.

Chapter 2, "Learning PowerShell," discusses the installation and configuration of PowerShell and how we can use PowerShell to discover information about PowerShell, including the help system. We'll also look at the language features we need to know, such as loops and branching. The use of scripts will be highlighted together with information on converting from other VBScript to PowerShell.

Chapter 3, "PowerShell toolkit," covers the other technologies we need to know. PowerShell on its own can't solve all of our administration problems. We need to use other technologies such as WMI, ADSI (for Active Directory), .NET to access functionality not built into PowerShell, and COM to work with applications such as Microsoft Office and Internet Explorer. How to use these technologies is covered in depth, with examples that are immediately usable.

Chapter 4, "Automating Administration," concludes part 1. After a look at the way our administration scripts can evolve through an ad hoc development process, we examine some PowerShell best practices. These aren't meant to dictate the way we work with PowerShell, but are more of a set of guidelines to help avoid major pitfalls. This chapter closes with an examination of how we can make our scripts secure, including how to use a code-signing certificate.

The three chapters of part 2, "Working with people," describe how we administer those aspects of our environment that directly impact the user population. The 205 techniques covered in this book can be found, numbered chronologically, in parts 2 and 3. The final technique is in appendix D

In chapter 5, we look at the management of user accounts and groups. This covers local accounts and Active Directory accounts. In the enterprise environment, we'll be mainly working with Active Directory, but there are a number of areas such as the DMZ where we still need local accounts.

In chapter 6, we turn our attention to Exchange mailboxes. The usual management functions for mailboxes and other mail-enabled objects are discussed together with mail protocols and quotas. We also discover how to report on mailbox statistics such as size and number of items.

Part 2 concludes with chapter 7, which discusses the administration of the user's desktop. This includes system configuration, printers, special folders, and Microsoft Office applications such as Word and Excel.

The third and final part of the book, "Working with servers," opens with chapter 8, "Windows servers," in which we find techniques for working with services, processes, the filesystem, registry, and event logs. This is a linking chapter between parts 2 and 3, as many of these techniques can be applied to the desktop environment.

DNS is the subject of chapter 9. It's a supporting technology for all modern Windows environments, and as such we need to be automate where appropriate. We can't work directly with DNS, but we can use WMI and the techniques we learned in chapter 3.

Active Directory is revisited in the next two chapters. In chapter 10, we concentrate on Active Directory structure and work with organizational units. This leads us to administering GPOs through PowerShell and protecting objects from accidental deletion. Chapter 10 concludes with a look at recovering objects that have been deleted from Active Directory.

The physical topology is visited in chapter 11, with an examination of domain controllers, global catalogs, and Active Directory sites and subnets. We close out Active Directory by examining how we can administer site links and replication.

The next three chapters demonstrate how we can use PowerShell to administer applications we'll commonly find in a Windows environment. Chapter 12 deals with Exchange 2007/2010, where we learn how to work with data stores, mail servers, and the mail organization as a whole. The creation and management of Exchange policies is also covered.

IIS 7 is the topic of chapter 13. We learn how websites and applications can be managed by PowerShell cmdlets, a PowerShell provider, and WMI or .NET classes. Working with XML files completes the chapter. PowerShell remoting is heavily featured in this chapter.

In chapter 14, our attention turns to SQL Server. PowerShell functionality is directly available in SQL Server 2008, but we can use .NET based techniques to work with earlier versions. A framework configuration database is presented that can be created and administered by PowerShell.

The final chapter looks at PowerShell innovations, including new features introduced with PowerShell v2 and Windows Server 2008 R2. Topics include PowerShell background jobs, Server Manager cmdlets, Hyper-V PowerShell library, and new Active Directory functionality. We close the book with a brief glance at the administration of cloud based applications.

Five appendices are supplied. They cover PowerShell reference material including format files, PowerShell modules and advanced functions, PowerShell events, reference data, and useful links to downloads and further information.

Code and typographical conventions

This is a book about using PowerShell and there are a lot of examples provided throughout the book. A `fixed-width font like this` is used for all source code, and major blocks of code are formatted as a specific listing as, for example, this listing from chapter 5:

Listing 5.12 Searching for a user account

```
$struser = "BOSCH Herbert"

$dom = System.DirectoryServices.ActiveDirectory.Domain]::GetCurrentDomain()
$root = $dom.GetDirectoryEntry()

$search = [System.DirectoryServices.DirectorySearcher]$root
$search.Filter = "(cn=$struser)"
$result = $search.FindOne()

if ($result -ne $null){$result.properties.distinguishedname}
else {Write-Host $struser " Does not exist"}
```

These listings are annotated with full explanations provided in the text. In many cases, the code statements have been split across multiple lines to fit the page correctly. These lines terminate with a back tick (`` ` ``), which is the PowerShell line continuation character.

Code examples are also be embedded in the text where they aren't long enough to warrant an explicit listing. They are presented as follows:

```
Search-ADAccount -AccountDisabled -UsersOnly |
select Name, distinguishedName
```

If the code has been typed directly at a PowerShell prompt, it'll be displayed like this:

```
PS> 1kb
1024
```

PowerShell has the ability to span multiple lines at the prompt, in which case the continuation lines will be prefixed by >>.

When discussing code examples, attribute names, cmdlet names, and all other PowerShell related items are displayed like this: `-Get-Help about_Arrays`.

Source code for the examples can be downloaded from the publisher's website at http://www.manning.com/PowerShellinPractice.

WARNING In my experience, any script obtained from the internet or any other source should be treated as suspect until proven otherwise. This includes the scripts in this book! I've tested them in my environment but I don't know and can't guarantee that they're 100% safe for your environment. It's your responsibility to test them in your environment.

In addition to the presentation conventions, I've also applied my own style to the code examples. I've used the following "rules":

- Full cmdlet and parameter names
- Avoid the use of aliases and partial parameter names
- Follow common usage for the names of the `*Object` cmdlets so `foreach` instead of `foreach-object`, `sort` instead of `sort-object`, `select` instead of `select-object`, and so on.
- For `select`, `sort`, and `format-table` or `format-list` code statements, just supply the property names rather than using the `-property` parameter.

My intention is to provide a balance between readability, conciseness, and completeness. Only you can tell if I've succeeded.

Author Online

Purchase of *PowerShell in Practice* includes free access to a private web forum run by Manning Publications where you can make comments about the book, ask technical questions, and receive help from the author and from other users. To access the forum and subscribe to it, point your web browser to http://www.manning.com/PowerShellinPractice. This page provides information on how to get on the forum once you are registered, what kind of help is available, and the rules of conduct on the forum.

Manning's commitment to our readers is to provide a venue where a meaningful dialog between individual readers and between readers and the author can take place. It is not a commitment to any specific amount of participation on the part of the author, whose contribution to the AO remains voluntary (and unpaid). We suggest you try asking the author some challenging questions, lest his interest stray!

The Author Online forum and the archives of previous discussions will be accessible from the publisher's website as long as the book is in print.

about the author

Richard Siddaway is a technical architect for Serco in the UK, working on transformation projects in the Local Government and Commercial arena. With more than 20 years of experience in various aspects of IT, Richard specializes in the Microsoft environment at an architectural level—especially around Active Directory (AD), Exchange, SQL Server, and infrastructure optimization.

Much of his recent experience has involved Active Directory migrations and optimizations, which often include Exchange. Richard has hands-on administration experience and is involved in implementation activity in addition to filling architectural and design roles. He has extensive experience specifying, designing, and implementing high-availability solutions for a number of versions of the Windows platform, especially for Exchange and SQL Server.

Richard is always looking for the opportunity to automate a process, preferably with PowerShell. Richard founded and currently leads the UK PowerShell User Group. Microsoft has recognized his technical expertise and community activities by presenting a Microsoft Most Valued Professional award. Richard has presented to the Directory Experts Conference, at various events at Microsoft in the UK and Europe, and for other UK user groups. Richard has a number of articles and technical publications to his credit.

about the cover illustration

The figure on the cover of *PowerShell in Practice* is a "Mufti, the chief of religion," or the chief scholar who interpreted the religious law and whose pronouncements on matters both large and small were binding to the faithful. The same figure appears in full-length on the cover of *PowerShell in Action, Second Edition* by Bruce Payette.

The illustration is taken from a collection of costumes of the Ottoman Empire published on January 1, 1802, by William Miller of Old Bond Street, London. The title page is missing from the collection and we have been unable to track it down to date. The book's table of contents identifies the figures in both English and French, and each illustration bears the names of two artists who worked on it, both of whom would no doubt be surprised to find their art gracing the front cover of a computer programming book...two hundred years later.

The collection was purchased by a Manning editor at an antiquarian flea market in the "Garage" on West 26th Street in Manhattan. The seller was an American based in Ankara, Turkey, and the transaction took place just as he was packing up his stand for the day. The Manning editor did not have on his person the substantial amount of cash that was required for the purchase and a credit card and check were both politely turned down. With the seller flying back to Ankara that evening the situation was getting hopeless. What was the solution? It turned out to be nothing more than an old-fashioned verbal agreement sealed with a handshake. The seller simply proposed that the money be transferred to him by wire and the editor walked out with the bank information on a piece of paper and the portfolio of images under his arm. Needless to say, we transferred the funds the next day, and we remain grateful and impressed by this unknown person's trust in one of us. It recalls something that might have happened a long time ago.

The pictures from the Ottoman collection, like the other illustrations that appear on our covers, bring to life the richness and variety of dress customs of two centuries ago. They recall the sense of isolation and distance of that period—and of every other historic period except our own hyperkinetic present.

Dress codes have changed since then and the diversity by region, so rich at the time, has faded away. It is now often hard to tell the inhabitant of one continent from another. Perhaps, trying to view it optimistically, we have traded a cultural and visual diversity for a more varied personal life. Or a more varied and interesting intellectual and technical life.

We at Manning celebrate the inventiveness, the initiative, and, yes, the fun of the computer business with book covers based on the rich diversity of regional life of two centuries ago, brought back to life by the pictures from this collection.

Part 1

Getting started with PowerShell

Welcome to *PowerShell in Practice*. PowerShell is the new command shell and scripting language from Microsoft. This book will enable you to use Windows PowerShell to administer your Windows servers and applications such as SQL Server, IIS 7, Exchange 2007, and Active Directory from the command line. PowerShell provides a more efficient and powerful mechanism for administration that'll save you time and effort in your daily job. Whether you're a PowerShell novice or a more experienced user, there'll be something for you in the many examples used to illustrate PowerShell based administration.

The book is divided into three parts. Part 1 begins with the fundamentals of working with PowerShell, including an explanation of what it is and how it works, as well as the new features of PowerShell v2.

Chapter 2 shows how to learn PowerShell with practical examples to speed the process. Chapter 3 covers the other technologies that are required to work with PowerShell—.NET, COM, ADSI, and WMI. The final chapter in this section, chapter 4, is concerned with the process of automation and best practice around writing scripts.

Part 2 shows how to perform administrative tasks that are concerned with people—managing user accounts in Active Directory and on local systems, managing Exchange mailboxes, and managing the user's desktop.

Part 3 looks at working with servers, starting with Windows, including the new Server Core install option in Windows Server 2008. Subsequent chapters consider Exchange 2007, SQL Server, IIS 7, DNS, and Active Directory, including the new features in Windows Server 2008 R2.

PowerShell fundamentals

This chapter covers

- Using cmdlets and providers
- PowerShell's building blocks
- Learning the pipeline

Microsoft seems to be always talking about PowerShell. Listen to a talk about Exchange Server 2007 or 2010, Windows Server 2008 R2 (release 2), or even SQL Server 2008, and PowerShell will be mentioned. PowerShell gets its own section on the Microsoft scripting center and there is a stack of books on the subject. So what's PowerShell and why are so many people excited about it? This chapter introduces PowerShell and answers some of those basic questions. It is formally known as Microsoft Windows PowerShell but that is too much of a mouthful so we will refer to it as PowerShell from now on. In this chapter you'll discover:

- The major features of PowerShell that make it stand out from other automation tools in the Windows arena
- The things that PowerShell is good at and the odd areas where you shouldn't use it
- What changes you can expect with version 2 of PowerShell

Installation and configuration of PowerShell we'll postpone until chapter 2. This chapter will provide an overview of PowerShell and why it's such an important tool for the administrator community.

Microsoft is building PowerShell into all of its major products. PowerShell v1 was released in November 2006 as a free download from the Microsoft website. Power-Shell v2 shipped with Windows 7 and Windows Server 2008 R2 in July 2009. It is also available as a download for older versions of Windows. This will give a consistent and coherent way to manage Windows and services such as Exchange and SQL Server. It'll save you time and administrative effort across your Windows-based servers and will amply repay the time spent learning it.

PowerShell has a number of unique features, such as *cmdlets* and *providers*. These features, which form the fundamentals of PowerShell, will be explained with examples. Underneath the covers the differences between PowerShell and other scripting tools become even more apparent. PowerShell is based on, and makes extensive use of, .NET objects. These provide the power to the shell.

Scripting languages need to be able to perform utility functions such as sorting, grouping, and comparing. PowerShell has a number of utility cmdlets to perform these roles. We'll discover how to use these cmdlets with practical examples relating to tasks that Windows administrators need to perform. Throughout the book, examples will be drawn from practical administrative tasks rather than demonstrating Power-Shell as a programming language.

PowerShell, like any tool, has a learning curve. It seems to be steep when you're first introduced to it, but this chapter and the next three will lay the foundations for us to dive into using it in our day-to-day administrative tasks. This will enable us to spend more time on other, potentially more interesting, tasks.

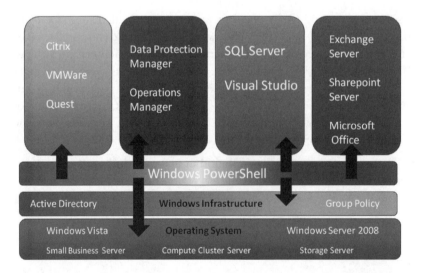

Figure 1.1   PowerShell is the automation and integration layer in a Microsoft environment. It can be used to administer Windows systems as well as an increasing number of Microsoft and third-party applications.

A number of PowerShell commands will be used in this chapter, including `Get-Member`, `Get-Command`, `Get-Help`, and `Get-PSDrive`. This chapter will provide sufficient information to explain examples as we work through them. A full explanation of these commands will have to wait until chapter 2.

At the end of the chapter, you'll understand what PowerShell is and more importantly what it isn't; what the major features are and how they work; and you'll understand the utility commands within PowerShell.

1.1 What's PowerShell?

Newcomers to PowerShell usually ask "What's PowerShell" and "What can I do with it?". This section will answer the first question. The second question takes the rest of the book to answer.

A simple answer to "What's PowerShell" would be that it's the new scripting language and command-line shell from Microsoft. It's better described as the automation engine that Microsoft is building into all major products, as shown in figure 1.1. The central position of PowerShell for administering our Windows-based environment will become even more entrenched with successive versions of Microsoft products.

We can think of PowerShell as a layer of automation functionality that connects the OS of our servers, the infrastructure applications such as Active Directory, Microsoft applications such as Exchange and SQL Server, and third-party products. PowerShell can be used to administer them all. This gives us a single method of automating our whole environment.

The shell and scripting language is the most visible implementation of PowerShell, but it can also be hosted in .NET applications. That aspect of PowerShell is outside the scope of this book. We'll be concentrating on using PowerShell at the command line and in scripts for administering Windows-based systems.

Windows administration is often viewed as a GUI-based occupation. One of the major failings of the Windows OS, at least according to UNIX and Linux administrators, is the inability to perform the powerful shell-based, command-line administration activities they traditionally use. PowerShell addresses that failing and provides a first-class command-line experience that makes administrators' lives easier. It's so good that an open source project called PASH was started to port PowerShell to the Mac and UNIX/Linux platforms. Unfortunately, that development is currently on hold. This book will show you how to get the most out of PowerShell on the Windows platform.

1.1.1 .NET—not necessarily

PowerShell is .NET-based and enables the .NET framework to be used in scripts and from the command line. This mixture of interactive and scripting use makes it easy to start using and building on what you already know. To paraphrase: "Great scripts from little cmdlets grow."

ADMINISTRATORS PLEASE READ THIS! You *do not* have to become a .NET programmer to be able to use PowerShell. It's perfectly possible to work with PowerShell and never use any .NET code. But there are a lot of examples of using .NET code within PowerShell that can be downloaded and reused.

PowerShell uses a syntax that's similar to C#. If you do any C# programming, you'll find it close enough to be confusing sometimes. It's not necessary to use a semicolon at the end of each line, though one can be used as a line separator if multiple PowerShell lines are combined. PowerShell isn't case sensitive like C#.

PowerShell commands produce .NET objects rather than the text output produced by other shells. The objects may not be "pure" .NET objects in that PowerShell creates a wrapper around the object. This wrapper controls the methods and properties in the output object. One of the great strengths of PowerShell is that extra properties called `noteproperty` and `scriptproperty` may be added to a PowerShell output object.

TYPE SYSTEM PowerShell has an Extensible Type System (ETS) so we can even define our own types and objects.

A `noteproperty` enables a new piece of data to be attached to the object, whereas a `scriptproperty` is a property whose value is determined by a PowerShell script block. A script block is a piece of PowerShell code surrounded by braces ({}). We will meet script blocks in a number of places throughout the book. They are one of the fundamental building blocks of PowerShell but in many cases we use without explicitly thinking about them as separate entities.

The relationship between PowerShell and .NET, together with how to use the .NET framework, are covered in chapter 3.

Now that we have an idea of what PowerShell is, we'll consider why it's worth learning.

1.2   *Why PowerShell?*

After asking "What's PowerShell?" the next question is often "Why should I bother with PowerShell?" (I'm assuming that if you're reading this book, you're interested in using PowerShell.) There are many parts to the answer to "Why PowerShell?" For one, I think it provides the best automation engine for the Windows platform and saves me lots of time. We will discover the breadth and depth of PowerShell's versatility in the subsequent chapters. Learning every new technology has some "Eureka!" moments where everything suddenly clicks. I'll share a few of those moments as we progress through the book.

PowerShell isn't the answer to every problem. There are a number of situations where PowerShell v1 is difficult to use or can't be used:

- Windows 2008 Server Core
- Logon scripts
- WinPe environments, because .NET isn't loaded

This still leaves the vast majority of the Windows environment for PowerShell. Power-Shell v2 addresses these issues, even to the extent of being installable on Server Core in Windows Server 2008 R2.

1.2.1 Eureka 1

I was once asked to look through a 12,000-seat Active Directory to find all of the users that didn't have Outlook Web Access enabled. Not the sort of task to perform using GUI tools! I wrote a script that has been reused several times since. It took much less time to write and test the script than it would've to perform the process manually. That extra time can be spent on other, more interesting tasks.

The original script was written in VBScript, as that was all I had available at the time. The script occupied 86 lines of code and took me about a day to conceive, write, and test.

When PowerShell became available in Exchange Server 2007, I converted the code to PowerShell. It took me about 30 minutes, most of which was starting the virtual machine (this was when Exchange Server 2007 was in beta) and looking up the appropriate cmdlets. Those 86 lines of VBScript condensed to one line of PowerShell that consisted of three cmdlets linked on the *pipeline*. A pipeline is a method of passing data from one command to another. It is covered in detail later in the chapter.

That drove home just how powerful PowerShell was and how much coding it was going to save me. Eureka! PowerShell rocks!

1.2.2 Importance to you

PowerShell is an important technology to you the administrator. It's a small download, but it has a large impact on the administration of a Windows environment. The way things are changing in the Microsoft world, if you can't do things at the command line—through PowerShell—you'll be stuck with the mundane jobs. PowerShell support is being built into all of the major Microsoft products, either as parts of the product or as an optional download, including:

- Windows Server 2008
- Exchange Server 2007
- SQL Server 2008
- IIS 7
- Members of the System Center family
- Small Business Server 2008 and Windows Essential Business Server 2008

Microsoft's Common Engineering Criteria for 2009 includes PowerShell. The one major omission from the list appears to be SharePoint, but it's possible to use the .NET APIs for SharePoint 2003 and 2007 within PowerShell. SharePoint 2010 includes built-in PowerShell support.

Using the same automation engine across all Microsoft products enables you to transfer skills across products. The MMC GUI tools have a (more or less) common look and feel. This has accelerated learning, as the tools are navigated and used in the same way. PowerShell brings this same concept to the command line. Product-specific add-ins building on a common language base mean that only the new commands need to be learned, rather than a whole new language. PowerShell also provides the common administration tools that VBScript has never had.

As PowerShell appears in more Microsoft (and third-party) products, it'll be the best way to automate the administration of your Windows' systems. PowerShell is already incorporated into products from Quest, IBM, Citrix, VMWare, Special Operations Software, and SDM Software, for example. Some of these we'll meet in later chapters. The ability to use the same basic language makes PowerShell the only way to integrate administration using these products.

1.2.3 *Designed for you*

PowerShell has been designed from the beginning for administrators. It has built-in access to a number of the most common things in which administrators are interested, including:

- Processes—what's running on the machine?
- Services
- Event logs—what's happening on the machine?
- ACLs for security
- WMI—much easier to use than in than VBScript
- Filesystem

One of the points that drive this home is that PowerShell understands GB, MB, and KB as gigabyte, megabyte, and kilobyte, respectively. In PowerShell v2, TB and PB are added to extend the coverage to terabyte and petabyte. In case you were wondering, 1 PB is 1,125,899,906,842,624 bytes. Presumably we'll see even more exotic extensions to this range as storage capacities increase. PowerShell isn't case insensitive, so gb, mb, and kb or any combination of case are equally understood. Listing 1.1 shows an example.

Listing 1.1   Use of GB, MB, and KB

```
PS> 1kb
1024
PS> 1mb
1048576
PS> 1gb
1073741824
PS> (1024*1024)/1MB
1
```

These terms can be used in a standalone manner or can be used in calculations, as shown in the listing.

PowerShell can access the full range of .NET, with a few exceptions that really concern developers more than administrators, as well as COM interfaces on products such as Office. This allows administrators to continue to work with known tools. These tools, and PowerShell, enable us to perform our routine administrative tasks in a shorter time and with a reduced error rate. The power of the command line is now yours.

1.2.4 Quicker and more powerful

There's a perception that the only way to administer Windows-based systems is through the GUI tools. In fact, Microsoft has been increasing the support for command-line administration through the various versions of Windows since Windows 2000. The use of command-line tools was emphasized at many technical events after the launch of Windows 2000. With each subsequent release, more command-line tools have been added. Microsoft has also promoted the use of scripting tools much more over the last five years or so.

If you need to perform an administrative action on a single user in Active Directory, it may be as fast to use the GUI as to use a script. If you have to perform that same action on 100 users, it'll definitely be quicker and easier to use a script. Once the script is written, it can be saved and used for the one-user or 100-user scenarios. The return on time spent writing the script is paid back every time you use it—plus it makes you look good. If you can script it, you must really understand this stuff. Right?

The venerable command file could be regarded as the first, if limited, scripting language on Windows. Command files have limited functionality and rely to a large degree on command-line tools to perform most tasks. These tools can't be integrated and only pass text between them, making processing difficult.

VBScript was introduced early in the life of Windows NT. At that time, scripting wasn't regarded as a mainstream activity by Windows administrators. That perception is slowly changing, but the majority of Windows administrators, in my experience, still prefer not to write scripts.

> **NOTE** I've found that UNIX administrators who become involved in administering Windows often adopt PowerShell much more quickly than administrators who've always worked with Windows.

VBScript is COM-based. This gives it access to a wide range of interfaces for administration. Unfortunately, they're often very different in the way they work and the way they're used. This makes VBScript difficult to use. There are gaps in the products that can be administered through VBScript, which reduces its potential.

PowerShell can be used interactively at the command line as well as in a script, which makes testing and development much easier. This isn't possible with VBScript native tools. The VBScript commands have to be in a file which is then executed, making testing and development a slower and more difficult task.

1.2.5 Extensible and flexible

PowerShell is easily extensible. Writing cmdlets is a fairly straightforward piece of development work, and though providers may be more complicated, there are examples available. Many commercial and open source PowerShell extensions are available. Some of these extensions will be covered in chapter 4.

PowerShell is a flexible system. There are often a number of ways to achieve the same task. This allows administrators to find a method with which they feel comfortable. It also means that it's more likely that someone will have a found a solution to your problem and posted the script on a blog or forum.

This flexibility can be a disadvantage. Many people have commented that a weakness of PowerShell is that there can be multiple methods of achieving the same end. I disagree that this is a weakness, but it can make life much more difficult for a newcomer. Let's say he has a problem to solve, so he searches the internet for a script to copy or alter. He may find three scripts that say they do the same thing but seem to be very different—which one should he use? This can be a difficulty, but the idea of this book is to present the information required to make an informed choice, or better still, for him to be able to write the script himself and share it with the wider PowerShell community. No doubt, some people looking at the examples will say, "He should've done it this way...." The examples I use are those that seem to me to be the most straightforward to use and learn. When it comes to PowerShell, the old saying "If you have three techies in a room, there are at least four opinions on how to do something" was never truer. All of those opinions will be good, though.

The more we use PowerShell, the more obvious the benefits of using it become. Our review of the benefits is now complete, and it's time to start learning about PowerShell. We'll start with the major features of PowerShell. These are the things that stick in your mind and make you realize it's different.

1.3   *Major features*

PowerShell has a number of features that combine to make it such a unique and powerful tool. We'll examine the language in more detail in the next chapter, but for now, the most obvious features will be covered. These include:

- Cmdlets
- Pipeline
- Providers
- Help system

Putting these things together will give us the basics of PowerShell that we can take into the rest of the book. I'll concentrate on the needs of the administrator who wants to know how to use these features, rather than looking at it purely from a programming viewpoint.

One of the great strengths of PowerShell is that it can be used interactively as well as in scripts. The same commands should, and usually do, work equally well from the command line and in scripts. This is useful when developing scripts, as you can work interactively to solve your problems. Alternatively, this could be viewed as a way to get to the head scratching and grumbling stage much faster.

1.3.1 *Cmdlets*

Cmdlets are probably the most obvious feature when comparing PowerShell to other scripting languages. A cmdlet (I always pronounce it "command-let") is a small, self-contained piece of functionality that does one specific job. A cmdlet is analogous to a shell command such as ping.exe. PowerShell v1 has 129 cmdlets. More than 100 extra cmdlets are added in PowerShell v2. One of the nice things about PowerShell is that it's easy to discover information like this using PowerShell itself. In this case, I used the following code:

```
(Get-Command | Where {$_.PSSnapin -like "Microsoft.P*"}).Count
```

`Get-Command` generates a list of PowerShell commands. That list is piped into a filter (`Where` is an alias or shorthand for `Where-Object`) that only accepts those commands installed by a PowerShell snapin (a method of extending PowerShell) whose names start *Microsoft.P*. We then count the number of commands in the filtered list, as shown in figure 1.2.

> **CASES AND OPERATORS** PowerShell isn't case sensitive. The code in figure 1.2 could have been written in all lowercase, all uppercase, or any random combination. I'll follow the style of PowerShell itself when capitalizing cmdlet names, properties, or methods.
>
> The operator `-like` is used to perform the comparison in figure 1.2. PowerShell operators are detailed in appendix A.

This one line of code, simple as it seems, demonstrates a number of PowerShell features. It starts with the cmdlet `Get-Command`. This, like all cmdlets, has a *verb-noun* syntax. It starts with a verb. The PowerShell team maintains a list of approved verbs. Their aim to ensure consistency—for example, any time you have a command that fetches information, the verb to use is *get*. The second part of the name is a noun that describes what the verb is acting on—in this case, the commands within PowerShell. The full list of standard verbs used in PowerShell is given in appendix A.

Cmdlet names should always be singular, so use `Get-Service` rather than `Get-Services`. This is one of the most common mistakes when writing PowerShell commands and to prove that PowerShell was designed for you it has a solution for this problem. Tab completion (and the IntelliSense functionality built into the editors

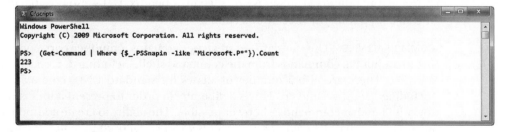

Figure 1.2   PowerShell shell used to count the number of cmdlets

covered in chapter 4) makes entering PowerShell commands quicker, easier, and less-error prone. Having said that, I'll give you one guess as to who still makes cmdlets plural from time to time.

`Get-Command` retrieves information regarding the installed cmdlets. We'll learn much more about `Get-Command` in the next chapter. Having generated a list of cmdlets, we pass that list onto the pipeline. I'll cover the pipeline in much greater detail in the next section.

The second cmdlet, `Where-Object`, which is one of the utility cmdlets covered in detail later, functions as a filter acting on the information moving along the pipeline—in this case on each command. The filter determines whether the `PSSnapin` property is like the string `Microsoft.P*`, where * is the usual wildcard character. Note the use of {} to enclose the script block that provides the filtering. By wrapping the cmdlets in (), we can treat the results as a collection of objects and use the `Count` property to determine the number of cmdlets present that match the filter.

TAB COMPLETION

When working at the command line, PowerShell demonstrates another feature that aids productivity: tab completion. If you type `Get-` at the command line, then press the Tab key, the PowerShell engine will complete the command with the first cmdlet that matches what's been typed so far. In this case, it's usually `Get-Acl`. If the Tab key is pressed again, the next Get- cmdlet will be displayed, and repeated pressing of the Tab key enables you to cycle through the list of relevant cmdlets. Tab completion can be invoked from any relevant part of the cmdlet name, so for instance `Get-C` followed by Tab starts cycling through the Get cmdlets whose noun part starts with C.

Tab completion also applies to parameters, in that typing—followed by the Tab key enables you to cycle through the parameter list. As with the cmdlet names, the more of the parameter name you give, the sooner the process brings the required parameter.

Though the in-built Tab completion works well, there are alternatives, including one from the PowerShell Guy (usually known as /\/\o\/\/) and the PowerShell Community Extensions. The download links for these are given in appendix E.

ALIASES

As an alternative to typing the full name of a cmdlet or parameter, it's possible to use an alias. An alias is shorthand for the command. Aliases can be used at the command line as well as in scripts. The use of aliases saves on typing, but at the expense of readability. The list of standard aliases is provided in appendix A. It's also possible to create your own aliases using the `Set-Alias` cmdlet.

> **COMMON ALIASES** The standard set of aliases contains a number corresponding to traditional commands from the command shell, including `dir`, `cd`, `copy`, and `del`. There are also a number of aliases for standard UNIX commands, including `ls`, `lp`, `mv`, and `cp`. This is deliberate, in order to present administrators with familiar commands wherever possible. The ability to create additional aliases means that the command line toolset can be tailored to match the way you want to work, rather than having to learn a new set of commands.

The following two examples show the use of aliases:

```
gwmi -cl win32_process
Get-WmiObject -Class Win32_Process
```

```
gps|?{$_.Handles-gt 500}|%{$_.Name}
Get-Process | Where-Object{$_.Handles -gt 500} | ForEach-Object {$_.Name}
```

The first example shows `Get-WmiObject` and one of its parameters being aliased. The second example shows a slightly contrived example of an aliased script. The use of `%` and `?` make this especially difficult to read. Heavily aliased scripts can be off-putting for newcomers to PowerShell, and should be avoided apart from when working interactively.

> **IN THE BOOK** In the rest of the book, I'll be using full cmdlet and parameter names to aid understanding and learning. I'm slightly inconsistent, in that I'll be using the aliases for the `*-Object` cmdlets, because `Select` and `Where` are more readable than `Select-Object` and `Where-Object`. This also matches common usage.

I strongly advise against using aliases in scripts: it makes them difficult to understand when you come back to them several months later.

Cmdlets and their aliases aren't used in isolation. Each has a number of parameters to further define and control its actions.

PARAMETERS

PowerShell cmdlets have parameters to define the input and possibly output, or to select various options. Examples of using parameters can be seen in code samples throughout the book. Parameters are always preceded by a hyphen. The parameters of a particular cmdlet can be viewed by using `Get-Help`. Using a command such as `Get-Help Get-WmiObject -full` will display the parameters of `Get-WmiObject` as well as the other help information. Typing `Get-Help  Get-WmiObject -parameter *` will display only the parameters. As an example, consider the `Class` parameter from `Get-WmiObject`:

```
-Class [<string>]
    Specifies the name of a WMI class. When this parameter is used, the
cmdlet retrieves instances of the WMI class.

    Required?                   true
    Position?                   1
    Default value
    Accept pipeline input?      false
    Accept wildcard characters? false
```

The parameter listing commences with the parameter name and the type of data that can be used with it. This is followed by a short description. The description may contain a list of acceptable values if the parameter is restricted as to the values it can accept. The `Required?` option indicates whether the parameter is considered mandatory for that cmdlet, with the value given as true or false. If the parameter is mandatory and isn't supplied, PowerShell will prompt for the value.

The `Position?` option indicates whether data can be passed to the cmdlet and be automatically allocated to the parameter. In this case, the first argument passed to the cmdlet is assumed to be the WMI class to retrieve. If the data doesn't represent a valid WMI class, an error will be thrown. If a value of named or 0 is given here, it means that the parameter name must explicitly be used. Default value indicates whether a default value has been set. If the data required by a parameter can be accepted from the pipeline, `Accept pipeline input?` will be set to true. The `Accept wildcard characters?` option will be set to true if wildcards can be used in the input.

There are a number of common parameters defined for all cmdlets, as listed in table 1.1.

Table 1.1   Common cmdlet parameters

Parameter	Meaning
-Debug	Displays detailed information useful to programmers.
-ErrorAction	Indicates how the cmdlet responds to a nonterminating error. Possible values are `SilentlyContinue`, `Continue`, `Inquire`, `Stop`.
-ErrorVariable	Stores information about errors in the specified variable.
-OutBuffer	Determines the number of objects to store before sending them onto the pipeline. This is usually omitted, which means that objects are sent onto the pipeline immediately.
-OutVariable	Stores error messages in the specified variable.
-Verbose	Displays detailed information about the operation.

If a cmdlet will modify the system, it has another two parameters, as listed in table 1.2.

Table 1.2   Safety parameters

Parameter	Meaning
-WhatIf	If present, this parameter causes PowerShell to output a list of statements indicating what would've happened if the command had been executed, without executing the command.
-Confirm	Prompts the user for confirmation before performing any action.

Further information can be found using `Get-Help about_CommonParameters`.

Having looked at cmdlets and their parameters, it's time to see how we can link them together using the PowerShell pipeline. The pipeline is what makes PowerShell a really powerful shell.

1.3.2   *Pipeline*

The ability to pipe data from one command to another has been a standard part of shells and command-line utilities for many years. DOS, the command shell in later

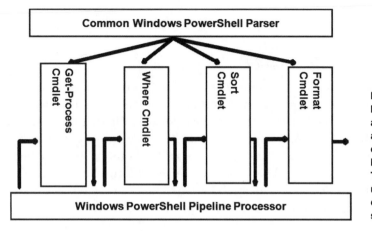

Figure 1.3 The PowerShell pipeline in action. The objects pass along the pipeline, which controls their processing by the individual cmdlets. The PowerShell parser uses the code to tell the cmdlets what actions should be performed.

versions of Windows, and most notably UNIX/Linux shells have all had this functionality. PowerShell also has this functionality, as we've seen in some of the examples earlier in the chapter.

If shells are expected to have this functionality, why is there such a fuss about the ability to pipe data from one command to the next in PowerShell? All other shells pipe text data, but PowerShell pipes .NET objects. This is one of the places where the power of PowerShell comes from:

```
Get-Process | Where-Object {$_.Handles -gt 500} |
Sort Handles | Format-Table
```

This example shows a `Get-Process` cmdlet passing data along the pipeline to a `Where-Object` cmdlet. The `Get-Process` cmdlet passes one .NET object for each process that's present on the machine. A filter is applied to only accept processes that use more than 500 handles. The objects representing the processes are sorted by the number of handles and finally displayed in a table. The interaction of the cmdlets and the pipeline is shown in figure 1.3.

.NET objects may sound complicated, but we can discover which particular .NET object is being passed by using `Get-Member`, as shown in listing 1.2.

Listing 1.2   Using `Get-Member` to view the .NET type

```
PS> Get-Process | Get-Member

   TypeName: System.Diagnostics.Process

Name                    MemberType      Definition
----                    ----------      ----------
Handles                 AliasProperty   Handles = Handlecount
Name                    AliasProperty   Name = ProcessName
.
.
Kill                    Method          System.Void Kill()
```

```
.
.
Id                      Property      System.Int32 Id {get;}
.
.
```

```
...Listing truncated for brevity
```

The use of Get-Member shows that the Get-Process cmdlet is producing, or emitting, .NET objects of type System.Diagnostics.Process. This .NET type has a property called Handles. The Where-Object cmdlet performs a filtering operation based on the value of the Handles property of each .NET object. Any object that has a value greater than 500 for the Handles property is passed. All other objects are filtered out.

The symbol $_ is used in PowerShell to refer to the current object being passed along the pipeline. We will see this symbol used in many of the scripts in future chapters. It functions as an object so we can refer to, and use, its properties and methods.

> **NOTE** As explained earlier, the .NET objects emitted by PowerShell objects aren't necessarily identical to an object of the same type produced by a .NET program. This can be seen if the output of listing 1.2 is compared to the list of properties and methods for the System.Diagnostics.Process that can be found at http://msdn.microsoft.com/en-us/library/system.diagnostics.process.aspx. More information on working with .NET can be found in chapter 3.

A number of cmdlets, including the Format- and Write- cmdlets, will terminate the pipeline in that the objects cannot be passed to another cmdlet. If a Foreach-Object cmdlet is used, it's perfectly valid to create a pipeline within the loop produced by that cmdlet.

The data that Get-Process produces is as of the time of execution. When investigating a set of data such as that referring to the running processes, it's sometimes necessary to ensure that all comparisons are performed on exactly the same data. Running variants of listing 1.2 won't suffice, as the data will change between runs. In this case, we can use a variable:

```
$proc = Get-Process

$proc | Where-Object{$_.Handles -gt 500}

$proc | Where-Object{$_.CPU -gt 100}

$proc | Sort-Object -Property WS -Descending |Select-Object -First 5
```

In this example, we start by setting a variable, $proc, equal to the output of Get-Process. A $ symbol is used in PowerShell to designate a variable ($_ is in effect a special variable used to refer to the current object on the pipeline). The result from piping $proc to Get-Member show that the variable is of type System.Diagnostics.Process. It's an array of such objects. When it's passed on to the pipeline, the array elements, or collection, are processed one at a time as they're passed along the pipeline.

The first use of $proc is a repeat of what we saw in listing 1.2. The second is a variant using the CPU property instead of the Handles property.

The third use is more interesting, in that we're sorting the data based on the WS (WorkingSet) property. The output of the sort is largest to smallest, as designated by the use of the –Descending parameter. The first five objects in the sorted output are then displayed. Select-Object discards the other objects.

Most cmdlets will accept input from the pipeline. There are some exceptions where this isn't possible. The help file for the cmdlet will show if this is the case. We will look at the help system in detail in the next chapter. The fact that the command will generate an error will also show this quickly!

NOTE For more information on the pipeline, type Get-Help about_pipeline at the PowerShell prompt.

This concludes our look at the pipeline. There will be many more examples throughout the book. Next we'll look at the utility cmdlets that have made brief appearances up to now.

1.3.3   *Utility cmdlets*

We've seen how cmdlets can be linked together on the pipeline and how .NET objects are passed along the pipeline. Utility cmdlets are used to supply the glue to join together the cmdlets performing the processing. They supply utility actions such as sorting, selecting, and filtering. Some of the utility cmdlets have been used in the previous examples. The utility cmdlets are listed in table 1.3. When we use these cmdlets, we normally don't include the -Object part of the name. This makes scripts more readable. Remember that aliases aren't case sensitive.

Table 1.3   Utility cmdlets and their purposes

Utility cmdlet	Alias	Purpose
Compare-Object	Compare or diff	Compares two sets of objects.
ForEach-Object	Foreach or %	Performs an operation against each of a set of input objects.
Group-Object	Group	Groups objects that contain the same value for specified properties.
Measure-Object	Measure	Calculates the numeric properties of objects, and the characters, words, and lines in string objects, such as files of text.
Select-Object	Select	Selects specified properties of an object or set of objects. It can also select unique objects from an array of objects, or it can select a specified number of objects from the beginning or end of an array of objects.
Sort-Object	Sort	Sorts objects by property values
Tee-Object	Tee	Saves command output in a file or variable and displays it in the shell.
Where-Object	Where or ?	Creates a filter that controls which objects will be passed along a command pipeline.

Common usage is to use the alias (though I do recommend avoiding % and ?) instead of the full cmdlet name, even in scripts! It is just one of those delightful quirks that seem to occur in computing.

You can generate this information from within PowerShell by using the following:

```
Get-Alias | Where {$_.definition -like "*-Object"} |
   Sort Definition
```

This is a good example of using PowerShell to discover more about PowerShell. Remember that PowerShell is not case sensitive so I could use $_.definition, $_.Definition or even $_.dEfInItIoN. I will mix the way I use case in the examples to help emphasize this point.

> **PERSONAL NOTE** I don't particularly like % and ? as aliases of foreach and where, respectively. They make scripts harder to read for people new to Power-Shell, so I tend to avoid using them. In this chapter, I'll mix and match the full name and alias for the *-Object cmdlets and only use the alias in subsequent chapters.

The best way to demonstrate the use of these cmdlets is with examples. We'll look at comparing files and their contents, filtering with Where-Object, followed by grouping and sorting the data. Examples of using Measure-Object and how to create calculated fields for use in select statements will also be shown. Full details on the syntax and use of these cmdlets can be found in the help system. Get-Help followed by the cmdlet name will supply the required information.

COMPARING

At some time when working in Windows administration, it'll be necessary to compare two files. They may be two different versions of scripts or configuration files, but it's almost certain that you'll spend a long time looking at them to spot the differences. They never seem obvious until you've stared at them for a long time. The time to discover the differences can be shortened dramatically by using Compare-Object as follows.

Listing 1.3   Comparing files

```
PS> Compare -ReferenceObject chap01v1.txt -DifferenceObject chap01v2.txt

InputObject                                          SideIndicator
-----------                                          -------------
chap01v2.txt                                         =>
chap01v1.txt                                         <=
```

Compare-Object is used for comparisons. PowerShell really is self-describing! In this case, I have two text files that I want to compare. The ReferenceObject parameter supplies the object against which comparisons will be made. DifferenceObject supplies the object to be compared.

In this example, the SideIndicator shows whether an object appears in the reference object (<=) or the difference object (=>). We can see that there are differences between the files, but we have no idea what they are and where they occur in the file. We need to modify our script slightly in order to discover that:

Listing 1.4 Comparing file content

```
PS> Compare -ReferenceObject $(Get-Content chap01v1.txt) `
>> -DifferenceObject $(Get-Content chap01v2.txt)
>>

InputObject                                            SideIndicator
-----------                                            -------------
This is line 6a                                        =>
This is line 6                                         <=
```

Notice the use of a backtick (`` ` ``) character at the end of the first line. This is the line continuation character. It's used here to split the line of code onto a continuation line to make it more readable. Here we've compared the individual lines within the files so we can see exactly where the differences occur. Of special interest is the use of `$(Get-Content chap01v1.txt)` and `$(Get-Content chap01v2.txt)` when supplying the objects to be compared. The structure `$()` is a sub-expression that tells PowerShell to evaluate what's between the parentheses and treat that as the variable to be used. All variables in PowerShell start with the `$` symbol.

Our command could also be written as:

```
$v1 = Get-Content chap01v1.txt
$v2 = Get-Content chap01v2.txt
Compare -ReferenceObject $v1 -DifferenceObject $v2
```

The choice of which to use is a matter of personal preference and really depends on your style of coding. I often use a multistep approach if I need to let other people use the script or if I am using it as a teaching example.

By default, only data that isn't equal is displayed in the output from `Compare-Object`. If matching data is required, use the `IncludeEqual` parameter. It'll generate a lot of output, though. Comparing files gives us some information about our filesystem, but we often need to determine the distribution of file types. We turn to the grouping and sorting cmdlets for this task.

GROUPING AND SORTING

Storage is relatively cheap, but no organization can afford to have an infinite amount of disk space. In order to make better use of the space, we need to know the distribution of files on the storage medium. Counting the number of files of each type can give a good indication of where the space is being used, especially if they're files that shouldn't be there. How many organizations have server disk space taken up by downloaded music or video files? In listing 1.5, we're grouping on the file type. Any suitable property can be used.

Listing 1.5 Counting the number of files in a folder by extension type

```
PS> Get-ChildItem -Path "c:\temp" | Where {!$_.PSIsContainer} |
>> Group -Property Extension | Sort Count -Descending
>>
```

```
Count Name                    Group
----- ----                    -----
   92 .tmp                     {AD~5D8C.tmp, artD5CD.tmp, artD5DE.tmp...}
   61 .cvr                     {CVR1162.tmp.cvr, CVR2463.tmp.cvr...}
   60 .od                      {12623912.od, 13136469.od, 13819442.od...}
   33 .txt                     {dd_depcheck_VS_PRO_90.txt...}
   14 .log                     {java_install_reg.log, jusched.log...}
    2 .xml                     {setup.xml, tmp713D.tmp.xml}
    2 .exe                     {msxml6-KB927977-enu-x86.exe...}
    2 .dll                     {fxdecod1.dll...}
    1 .sqm                     {wmplog00.sqm}
    1 .msi                     {Virtual_PC_2007_Install.msi}
    1 .psc1                    {powergui.script.editor.psc1}
    1 .fzip                    {ImageDecoder_2.0.2008.523.fzip}
    1 .bmp                     {INT+rsiddaway.bmp}
```

We'll be meeting `Get-ChildItem` again in chapter 8 when we examine the filesystem, but for now let's just say it's the PowerShell equivalent of `dir` or `ls` (both of these exist in PowerShell as aliases of `Get-ChildItem`). Use `ls`; it's less typing! It'll also impress the UNIX admins. The `Path` parameter tells `Get-ChildItem` the folder to examine. The output of `Get-ChildItem` is piped to `Where`, which applies a filter based on whether the object is a container (a folder in this case). PowerShell adds a property (`PsIsContainer`) to the output of `Get-ChildItem` which indicates whether the object is a folder. In this case, we want those objects that aren't folders-just the files. The "!" symbol means not, so `!PsIsContainer` means objects that aren't containers.

The results of the filter are piped to `Group`, which groups the files by extension. Finally, we use a `Sort-Object` to order the output by the number of files in each group. The output gives the number of files in each group, the name of the group (in this case, the file extension), and a partial list of the group membership.

> **NOTE** The PowerShell pipeline used in this example is actually a single line of code. It could be typed at the PowerShell prompt and allowed to wrap around. In order to make it more readable, the input has been split across multiple lines. When entering code, pressing the Enter key before the command is complete (in this case immediately after the pipe symbol) causes PowerShell to display a continuation line, as shown in listing 1.5. Once the extra code has been typed, pressing Enter twice will run the code. Code can also be split in this manner before a closing bracket or closing quote for a string value.

This script could be modified to read a folder tree by adding the `recurse` parameter. The script would then start `Get-ChildItem –Path "c:\temp" -recurse |` and so on. If you're not sure of the location of the temporary folder on your system, we can find it using `$env:temp`. If we want our scripts to be really portable, we could code it as:

```
Get-ChildItem -Path $env:temp -Recurse
```

Now that we've found our file distribution, we can see how much space is taken up by these files.

MEASURE

We used `Group-Object` to determine the number of files of each type earlier in this section. We can use `Measure-Object` to determine statistics for those files, including total number and the sum of their sizes.

Listing 1.6   Producing statistics on file sizes in a folder

```
PS> Get-ChildItem -Path "c:\temp" | Where {!$_.PSIsContainer} |
>> Measure -Property Length -Average -Sum -Minimum -Maximum
>>

Count     : 272
Average   : 366154.713235294
Sum       : 99594082
Maximum   : 29440512
Minimum   : 0
Property  : Length
```

As in the previous example, we use `Get-ChildItem` and `Where-Object` to produce a set of objects representing the files in a folder. This time, we pipe them into `Measure-Object`. If we use `Measure-Object` without any parameters, it'll return just the number of files—the `Count`. By telling the cmdlet which property to measure, and selecting the measurements to make, we can generate the average, minimum, maximum, and sum of the file length (size in bytes). The parameters indicating which statistics to measure can be used in any combination that you require. A count of the total number of items will always be produced.

   `Measure-Object` can be used with an array of numbers. It can be applied to any numeric property, but only numeric properties. `Where-Object` is the cmdlet that's used most of all. So far, we've seen single filters used. In some cases, we need to think about using multiple filters.

FILTERING

The `Where-Object` cmdlet is used for filtering. We've seen it being used in a number of the previous examples. Correct use of filtering can have a beneficial impact on your scripts, as they'll run faster because less data is being processed. Filtering can also make the output easier to understand.

> **WHERE TO FILTER**   It is generally better to filter as early as possible especially is you are manipulating large sets of data. Performance is not necessarily a number one criterion for administration scripts but your scripts will run faster if you reduce the amount of data being processed.

Think of the case where a problem has arisen on a server and you need to test whether the relevant service is actually running. You could run `Get-Service`, but that involves reading through a lot of output. A better solution is to filter on just the service or services in which you're interested. `Get-Service` does have a certain level of built-in filtering, as the parameters for service names accept wildcards. In listing 1.7, I'll only filter using `Where-Object` because I want to show how to combine filters. PowerShell supports the full range of logical operators.

Listing 1.7 Using multiple filters in `Where-Object`

```
PS> Get-Service |
>> Where{$_.Name -like "WM*" -and $_.Status -eq "Stopped"}
>>

Status    Name              DisplayName
------    ----              -----------
Stopped   wmiApSrv          WMI Performance Adapter
Stopped   WMPNetworkSvc     Windows Media Player Network Sharin...
Stopped   WMSvc             Web Management Service
```

Get-Service returns the list of Windows services installed on the system. This list is passed into `Where-Object`, which performs a filter on the first part of the service name and on the status of the service. This could be extended by making the service partial name an argument which is passed into the script. This will be covered in chapter 2.

An alternative form of filtering is supplied by the `Select-Object` cmdlet. This is used to limit the properties of the objects that are passed down the pipeline. It can also be used to add a calculated property or select a specific number of objects from the beginning or end of the list, as shown in listing 1.8.

Listing 1.8 Using a calculated property in `Select-Object`

```
PS> $now = Get-Date
PS> Get-Process | Where-Object{$_.StartTime} |
>> Select Name, @{Name="Run Time";
>> Expression={[int]($now - $_.StartTime).TotalMinutes}} |
>> Sort "Run Time" -Descending | Format-Table -AutoSize
>>

Name                         Run Time
----                         --------
svchost                           909
smss                              909
csrss                             909

- - output truncated

WUDFHost                          207
WINWORD                           202
Quest.PowerGUI.ScriptEditor       190
PowerShell Assistant              187
Foxit Reader                      169
notepad                           119
powershell                         12
```

This is the most complicated example we've seen so far. We start by using the Get-Date cmdlet to record the current date and time in a variable. Remember that variables always start with the symbol.

Get-Process retrieves a list of the running processes on the system. We filter out those processes that don't report a start time. If they're left in, the script will still work, but we get error messages for those processes that don't have a start time recorded. Select-Object is used to filter the properties. We're only interested in the process name and calculating the running time.

The calculated property is a hash table (see arrays in chapter 2). It's an array with two values separated by a semicolon. The first, known as the *key*, is the name of the property—in this case `Run Time`. The second item, known as the *value*, is an expression to calculate the property. This calculation will happen for every process coming along the pipeline.

Once the property is calculated, it can be manipulated in the same way as any other property and we can use it in a sort operation. We can see the longest-running processes by sorting in a descending direction.

The final step is to use `Format-Table` to output the results to screen. The `autosize` parameter is used to control the formatting of the columns onscreen.

> **HASH TABLES** Hash tables are also known as *associative arrays*. Details can be found in the help files about_associative_arrays (PowerShell v1) and about_ hash_ tables for PowerShell v2.

This concludes our look at the utility cmdlets (`Tee-Object` isn't used much, and its use is self-explanatory). They'll appear in many more scripts throughout the book. You've now learned enough about them to follow their use in future scripts, where they'll be referred to by their aliases. Having completed learning about cmdlets and the pipeline, it's time to turn our attention to another feature that gives us an alternative method of working in PowerShell: the providers. Once we've learned about the providers, we'll have a look at the help system before examining PowerShell v2.

1.3.4 Providers

Have you ever wanted a consistent method of working with multiple data stores such as the filesystem, Active Directory, SQL Server, IIS, and the Windows Registry? PowerShell can deliver a large part of that vision through the use of providers.

The provider feature in PowerShell gives us a way of treating data stores as if they were the filesystem. PowerShell demonstrations where we do a `dir` through Active Directory or the Registry always go down well. The provider exposes a data store as just another drive on your system. Listing 1.9 shows how to view the installed providers and the associated drives. Note that the cmdlet refers to them as *PSDrives* to differentiate them from physical drives.

Listing 1.9 Viewing the installed PowerShell drives

```
PS> Get-PSDrive | Format-Table -AutoSize

Name     Provider      Root            CurrentLocation
----     --------      ----            ---------------
Alias    Alias
C        FileSystem    C:\                     Scripts
cert     Certificate   \
D        FileSystem    D:\
E        FileSystem    E:\
Env      Environment
F        FileSystem    F:\
```

```
Feed      FeedStore
Function  Function
Gac       AssemblyCache     Gac
HKCU      Registry          HKEY_CURRENT_USER
HKLM      Registry          HKEY_LOCAL_MACHINE
IIS       WebAdministration \\PCRS2
OneNote   OneNote           OneNote
Variable  Variable
```

NOTE The following drives aren't part of the standard PowerShell install: Feed, Gac, IIS, and OneNote.

The list includes some drives that are specific to PowerShell, such as Environment, which exposes the environmental variables; Function, which exposes the PowerShell functions (see chapter 2) loaded into memory; and Variable, which contains the variables active in your session (mixture of system and user-defined variables). In PowerShell v2, the filesystem drives get another two columns, which supply used and free space in GB.

An alternative way of viewing the installed providers is to use Get-PSProvider, which will display the providers, associated drives, and some capabilities. Get-PSProvider will display all providers installed in the PowerShell session, but Get-PSDrive shows only the active providers. I have a provider for Active Directory installed on my laptop, but it's only active when I'm connected to the network and logged on to the Active Directory domain.

In theory, providers should supply access to a common set of cmdlets that enable navigation through and interaction with the data exposed by the provider. The full list can be seen by typing Get-Help about_Core_Commands at a PowerShell prompt. The list includes cmdlets with the following nouns: Item, ItemProperty, ChildItem, Content, Location, Path, PSDrive, and PSProvider.

NOTE Not all providers supply access to all of the core commands; for example, the SQL Server provider doesn't implement the New-Item cmdlet. The common cmdlets can have dynamic parameters added depending on the provider in which they are being used. Check help from within the provider for changes to parameters.

A provider is navigated in exactly the same way as the filesystem. The full cmdlet name is Set-Location, but I expect most people will be happier using the aliases cd or chdir depending on their background (it's also much less typing!). Aliases are good things when typing interactively, but should be avoided in scripts.

The core commands have aliases corresponding to DOS or UNIX commands. As a demonstration of navigating a provider, try typing the commands from listing 1.10 into PowerShell one at a time.

> **Listing 1.10   Navigating the Registry provider**

```
cd HKLM:
ls
chdir software
```

```
dir
cd microsoft
ls
cd ..
dir
cd c:
```

> **NOTE** cd and chdir are aliases of Set-Location; ls and dir are aliases of Get-ChildItem.

In this example, we start by navigating into the HKLM: drive (HKEY_Local_Machine). A directory listing is then produced. This process is repeated to view the software and Microsoft keys, respectively. It's also possible to work with the data exposed by a provider directly; for example, dir HKLM:\software\Microsoft.

We've now covered the basics of providers. We'll be working with the providers again when we examine the Registry, SQL Server, and IIS in more depth later in the book. The last feature I want to examine is something that's been mentioned several times: the help system.

1.3.5 Help system

PowerShell has a set of help files that are presented in the shell as text files when you use Get-Help. The help system will be covered in detail in chapter 2 when we look at learning PowerShell.

We've completed our introduction to PowerShell; all that remains is a look to the future by examining some of the new features we can expect in PowerShell v2. The examples of using PowerShell we've seen so far are all usable in v2. In these early chapters, we're learning how to use PowerShell. These techniques will see a lot of use in parts 2 and 3.

1.4 PowerShell v2

PowerShell v2 is available for download from the Microsoft website (http://support. microsoft.com/kb/968929) or is available as part of Windows Server 2008 R2/ Windows 7. The folder name is still v1.0 and we still use .ps1 for script extensions. Like PowerShell v1, it's also available through Windows Update. PowerShell v2 introduces a number of new features that extend its capabilities. If you like PowerShell, you'll love v2. Table 1.4 covers the major new features.

Other new features include:

- New parameters for existing cmdlets
- Improved tab expansion function
- Improvements to [ADSI] type accelerator (see chapter 4) and the introduction of [ADSISearcher] for searching Active Directory.

I don't intend to cover PowerShell v2 as a separate entity. Instead of having one or more chapters dedicated to PowerShell v2, I'll weave the new functionality into the appropriate chapters. For instance, the remoting functionality is covered in the chapter on

Table 1.4   New features in PowerShell v2

Feature	Explanation
Remoting	Enables PowerShell on the local machine to issue commands that'll be executed on a remote machine or machines. PowerShell remoting requires WinRm and PowerShell v2 to be installed on the local and remote machine(s). PowerShell must be started with administrative privileges to use for running remote commands.
Background jobs	Enables PowerShell to run commands asynchronously. This facility returns the PowerShell prompt immediately rather than waiting until the command has finished. The asynchronous command runs in the background. The status of the job can be viewed and the output data retrieved when the job has completed. Commands can be run against remote machines using background jobs.
Advanced functions	Cmdlets can now be written in PowerShell instead of needing to use a .NET language such as C#. Advanced functions accept parameters in the same way as a compiled cmdlet. These were known as *script cmdlets during the CTP process though this term* is no longer used officially.
Modules	A module is a method of loading additional functionality into PowerShell. A module can contain collections of functions contained in a .psm1 file that are loaded into PowerShell as a unit or a dll that provides functionality. Individual functions can be made visible to the shell or remain hidden and only be accessible from other functions within the module. The cmdlet `Import-Module` is used to add modules into PowerShell. It can also be used to load PowerShell snapins without registering them with PowerShell. Modules are an improved approach compared to the snapin functionality in PowerShell v1.
Transactions	When making a change via a provider, the change can be wrapped within a transaction so that it can be rolled back in the event of an error. PowerShell v2 only supports transactions on the Registry provider.
Eventing	PowerShell can access the eventing system to work with management and system events.
PowerShell startup parameters	New PowerShell startup parameters have been added, to run script files via a `File` parameter, run PowerShell as a single-threaded application, hide the console window, and pass complex commands into PowerShell that require using quotes or curly braces.
Try-Catch-Finally	PowerShell v1 uses the `trap` and `throw` commands to process .NET exceptions. A Try-Catch-Finally block is added to PowerShell v2 to bring it in line with the .NET languages. The command that may throw an exception is put in a `try{}` block, any exceptions are caught in the `catch{}` block, and a `finally{}` block executes regardless of whether an exception occurred.
Steppable pipelines	This makes it easier for developers to write cmdlets that call other cmdlets. It also enables finer control on how a script block executes.
Data language	Enables separation of data from code in a PowerShell script.
Script internationalization	Enables the internationalization of scripts by importing files of message strings into a data section. The file to be imported is controlled by the UI culture of the system.

Table 1.4 New features in PowerShell v2 *(continued)*

Feature	Explanation
Script debugging	The debugging facilities have been enhanced with new debugging cmdlets.
New operators and automatic variables	New operators for working with strings and new automatic variables for working with the PowerShell system have been added.
New cmdlets	New cmdlets have been added for remoting, adding, or converting types; ETW logs on Windows Server 2008 and Vista; script internationalization; modules; debugging; eventing; background jobs; transactions; WMI; and some miscellaneous actions.
PowerShell Integrated Scripting Environment	PowerShell Integrated Scripting Environment (ISE) is a GUI-based editor with an interactive shell. It requires .NET 3.5 SP1. ISE can support up to eight PowerShell tabs (instances), each of which can have multiple scripts open. ISE can execute the whole script or just the highlighted part.
Out-Gridview	Displays output in an interactive table that can be searched and filtered. This feature requires .NET 3.5 SP 1.

IIS (13), the event log cmdlets are covered in chapter 8, and there are sections in the appendix dealing with modules, advanced functions, and PowerShell events. I want to concentrate on using PowerShell, not describing its features.

The examples in this book will be based on PowerShell. As far as possible, the code will run on v1. PowerShell v2 examples will be supplied if new functionality makes the task easier to perform. There are some exciting features in v2 that have been thought about for a long time.

1.4.1 PowerShell 2 Eureka

In November 2007, at TechEd EMEA, I was talking to the CTO of a company that was busy building PowerShell into its products. We'd just been to a talk on PowerShell v2 and the new capabilities it would introduce. We were discussing how the new functionality could be utilized and had talked about remoting, which always seems to catch the headlines. The conversation moved to background jobs (see chapter 15) and how they could be used. We must've had the same thought because we just looked at each other and grinned. Background jobs provide a great way to kick off activities on the remote machine without disturbing the user.

Remoting may get the headlines, but I expect background jobs to be at least as useful. Having got all excited about PowerShell v2 and its capabilities, should we upgrade immediately?

1.4.2 Should I upgrade?

Whenever a new version of a product appears, this is always the killer question. For PowerShell v2, there are a number of scenarios where the answer is straightforward, as well as a few murky areas. Pretty standard for IT, really!

If Windows Server 2008 R2 is being used for the OS, then PowerShell v2 is installed by default (with the usual caveat about Server Core being an option rather than part of the default installation). If the application will install on R2, then it should be okay using PowerShell v2. For instance, SQL Server 2008 will happily install on R2 with PowerShell v2 (it does moan at the beginning that you need to apply SP1 post installation). Exchange 2007 won't install on Windows Server 2008 R2 until SP3 is available later in 2010. Exchange 2010 will only install on Windows Server 2008 R2 and use PowerShell v2.

For servers running Windows Server 2008 or Windows Server 2003 that have had PowerShell v1 installed, the upgrade scenario is dependent on the application. Power-Shell v2 will install over the top of v1 unless you have installed a Windows Service Pack on top of v1. In that case it will be necessary to uninstall the Service Pack, uninstall PowerShell v1 and reinstall the Service pack before installing PowerShell v2. If the application depends on PowerShell, it may accept the upgrade or it may not. Check with the vendors and test if possible. If in doubt, don't upgrade.

Workstations are in a similar position, in that if Windows 7 is being used, then PowerShell v2 is installed. If the Remote Server Administration Tools for Windows Server 2008 R2 are required, Windows 7 is mandatory. The case for upgrading Power-Shell v1 on Vista or XP is again dependent on applications. Possibly the only thing that might cause problems are the Exchange 2007 administration tools.

There's no hard and fast answer. My advice is that if you can safely upgrade then do so, but do remember to test.

1.5   *Summary*

This chapter introduced PowerShell and explained some of the fundamental concepts that are required for the following chapters.

PowerShell is the new automation engine for the Windows platform. It's available as a download or installable feature (Windows Server 2008 and later) that supplies a command shell and scripting language. It's .NET-based and has been designed for administrators. The PowerShell language contains more than 130 built-in commands, known as cmdlets, that enable administrators to work with the filesystem, Registry, event logs, processes, and services on a Windows machine.

PowerShell cmdlets can be linked via a pipeline. Unlike other shells, the pipeline passes .NET objects rather than text between cmdlets. A number of utility cmdlets to perform actions such as sorting, grouping, filtering, and measuring are available and provide the "glue" for joining cmdlets on the pipeline.

Shells can usually work with the filesystem. PowerShell extends the concept of drives to expose other data stores such as the Registry, Certificate Store, and the environment as if they were the filesystem. This functionality is supplied by a provider. The core cmdlets work on these providers generally in the same way they work with the filesystem.

The PowerShell help system is text-based, similar to the man pages in UNIX. Help is supplied on the individual cmdlets and on PowerShell language and environmental features.

The second version of PowerShell is available for download, adding more than 100 new cmdlets. New features in PowerShell v2 are briefly outlined; whether to upgrade is dependent your the OS and the applications using PowerShell.

The remainder of part 1 will look at learning PowerShell (chapter 2); other technologies used with PowerShell including ADSI, .NET, COM, and WMI (chapter 3); and automation, including best practices around writing scripts in chapter 4. Parts 2 and 3 consider working with PowerShell to perform administration tasks in a Windows environment.

Learning PowerShell

This chapter covers

- Installing and configuring PowerShell
- Self-discovery
- Language features
- Scripts

We'll have created an automation toolkit by the time we reach the end of the book. The core of that toolkit is PowerShell itself. We've looked at the fundamentals of PowerShell; now we learn how to use it. Think of it as unpacking a shiny new tool, putting the bits together, and learning how to use it.

When I downloaded the first beta of PowerShell, I remember installing it, clicking the icon to start it, then having one of those "What on Earth is this?" moments. I usually mention this when giving talks about PowerShell, and often someone comes up to me and says she had the same problem. I spent a lot of time working through the documentation, searching the internet, and experimenting through trial and (lots of) error to find out how this stuff worked. This chapter will be your shortcut to that learning process; I'll show you the self-discovery mechanisms in PowerShell as well as provide usable examples of how it works.

We start by discovering how to install and configure PowerShell. The main configuration item is the PowerShell profile, what you put in it, and where you store it. It's possible to have four profiles—though not recommended—and I'll explain which to use when. Once PowerShell is configured, we can start learning how to use it. This is done by using PowerShell's self-discovery mechanisms. We'll find four new friends along this journey.

The joy of learning continues as we dig further into the language features, such as loops, branches, and variables. These are what give us the ability to write scripts in PowerShell as well as work interactively at the prompt.

The chapter will close by looking at script development. (Though it's sometimes hard to justify calling a piece of PowerShell a script when it's one line of code!)

VBScript has been the main Windows-based administration scripting language for the last 10 years. There's a huge body of administrative scripting examples available on the internet through sites such as the Microsoft TechNet Scripting Center, which can be found at http://www.microsoft.com/technet/scriptcenter/default.mspx.

> **WARNING** As with any download from the internet, ensure that you understand what the script is doing before trying it in your production environment. Virtual machines are a good place to experiment with downloaded scripts.

Many administrators have created a library of scripts in VBScript that are used to perform daily administration tasks. I'll show how to convert VBScript into PowerShell by working through an example. It's not feasible to instantly convert to using PowerShell, especially if you rely on VBScript. I'll show you how to incorporate and run VBScript code in your PowerShell scripts. This enables you to use a phased approach when converting to PowerShell.

Now it's time to start learning PowerShell.

2.1 *Open the book—learn by doing*

Everyone has different ways of learning a new subject. I think learning a new technology is best achieved by a mixture of theory and practice, which is the approach I am going to adopt. When I give talks about PowerShell, they're always heavy on demonstrations, as I believe that seeing PowerShell working and solving problems explains more than a large set of PowerPoint slides. There's also the excitement for the audience of waiting to see how my demo sessions go wrong. If it can go wrong, I'll find a way!

This book will follow the same concept with lots of examples.

I recommend that you type in the scripts that are given as examples in the book. Most are short, and if you use one of the editors with IntelliSense (Microsoft's auto-completion technology that reduces the amount of typing you need to do) that are discussed in chapter 4, the code entry won't be onerous. The scripts are also available for download from the associated website if you prefer. I've always found that typing in the examples helps me learn.

The interactive nature of PowerShell means that we can experiment in the shell, then build what works into our scripts. One useful trick is *dot sourcing*. When a script is executed in PowerShell, all references to the variables in use are lost when the script finishes. As explained in section 2.2.4, we need to add a reference to the folder by typing .\script_name.ps1 when we want to run the script. If we dot source the script—if we type ..\script_name.ps1 and run the script—we find that the variables are left in memory. This means we can continue to work with them interactively. I find this particularly useful when I'm developing scripts and need to experiment how to perform a particular task, or when I'm trying to work out why a script doesn't work properly.

Having thought about how we're going to learn to use PowerShell, it's time to start the learning process. Starting at the beginning, we'll install and configure PowerShell.

2.2   *Installation and configuration*

PowerShell v1 can be installed on most modern Windows OSs:

- Windows 2003
- Windows XP Service Pack 2
- Windows Vista
- Windows Server 2008

Windows Server 2008 has PowerShell v1 as an optional installable feature. There are downloadable versions for the other OSs. In addition, PowerShell and .NET are available through Windows Update. PowerShell is available in 32- and 64-bit versions. It's not possible to install PowerShell on Windows 2000. It's also not supposed to be possible to install PowerShell on Windows Server 2008 Server Core, but as we'll see in chapter 8, there's a method of performing the installation.

PowerShell v2 is installed and enabled by default in Windows 7 and Windows Server 2008 R2 (except Server Core, where it's an optional install). On Windows Server 2008 R2, the ISE isn't installed by default; it's an optional install. PowerShell is buried in the Start menu: Start -> All programs -> Accessories -> Windows PowerShell. A download is available for these operating systems:

- Windows Server 2008 SP1 and SP2
- Windows Server 2003 SP2
- Windows Vista SP1 and SP2
- Windows XP SP3

The download is known as the Windows Management Framework and includes WinRM 2.0 which is required for remoting (this is covered in chapter 13).

2.2.1   *Installation*

The only prerequisite for installing PowerShell is that the .NET 2.0 framework is installed. .NET 2.0 is either installed as an optional feature or the framework is downloaded and installed. Some features of PowerShell v2 require .NET 3.5 SP 1.

.NET VERSIONS   Windows Vista and Windows Server 2008 have .NET 3.0 as the installable option. Windows 7 and Windows Server 2008 R2 use .NET 3.5. We are lucky that .NET 3.0 and 3.5 are supersets of .NET 2.0, so it's automatically installed.

Download links for the various .NET versions are given in appendix E. In both cases, the Windows Installer software must be at least version 3.0. Links to download the installer software are available on the appropriate download page. There are also links to the latest service pack for .NET 2.0. PowerShell can be downloaded from the Microsoft website, as detailed in the appendix E. Select the correct OS version to download.

On Windows 2003, XP, and Vista, PowerShell is installed via the update mechanism. It appears in the list of updates installed on the system rather than as an individual program in its own right.

NOTE   If you install PowerShell, then install a service pack, it may not be possible to remove PowerShell without uninstalling the service pack.

The actual install is a simple matter of double-clicking on the installation file and following the wizard. The 32-bit version of PowerShell is installed on 64-bit systems as well as the 64-bit version. Having successfully installed PowerShell, we now need to configure it to meet our requirements.

2.2.2   *Configuring PowerShell*

There are a number of configuration items we can perform on PowerShell. The most common are covered in this section.

EXECUTION POLICY

The PowerShell execution policy determines whether scripts can be run and if they need to be digitally signed. A full description of how to set execution policy can be found in section 2.2.4. This is one of the most common issues raised by people starting to use PowerShell.

The execution policy still confuses people who've been using PowerShell for a while. If you build a new machine and install PowerShell, don't forget to set the execution policy. It saves the muttering when you discover you forgot!

PROFILES

A PowerShell profile is a script that executes when PowerShell is first started. Profiles are used to configure PowerShell and load extra functionality automatically at startup. This could be done manually, but profiles make the application of a standard, repeatable configuration much easier. It's possible to use four separate profiles in PowerShell. In order of loading, the profiles are:

1 $pshome\profile.ps1
2 $pshome\Microsoft.PowerShell_profile.ps1
3 $home\My Documents\WindowsPowerShell\profile.ps1
4 $home\My Documents\WindowsPowerShell\ Microsoft.PowerShell_profile.ps1

where *$pshome* is a variable that points to the PowerShell install directory and *$home* contains the full path of the user's home directory. On Windows Vista and Windows Server 2008, My Documents is replaced by Documents. Variables are used to store objects and data. They are signified by having a $ symbol as a prefix.

> **NOTE** Profiles that are applied later in the sequence can override settings from earlier profiles. Avoid using multiple profiles if possible.

The first profile in our list applies to all users and all shells. Most PowerShell functionality can be added into the base shell that's the standard PowerShell install. The second profile applies to all users, but only to the Microsoft.PowerShell shell (an example of an alternative shell is PowerShell Analyzer—see the PowerShell Toolkit section in chapter 4). Profile 3 applies to the individual user, but across all shells, and the final profile applies to the individual user but is restricted to the Microsoft.PowerShell shell. The rationale behind the naming and location of the profiles can be found on Lee Holmes's blog (Lee is a member of the PowerShell team) at http://www.leeholmes.com/blog/ TheStoryBehindTheNamingAndLocationOfPowerShellProfiles.aspx.

> **RECOMMENDATION** I recommend using number 3 if you're the only person using the machine, for example on your personal workstation. If you want the same settings to apply to all users, then number 1 should be used, for example on a server where several administrators have accounts and you want them all to have the same settings. Whatever you do with profiles, remember the KISS principle and keep it simple.

The profile locations are summarized in table 2.1.

Table 2.1 Summary of PowerShell profile locations

	All shells	**Standard PowerShell**
All users	$pshome \profile.ps1	$pshome \ Microsoft.PowerShell_profile.ps1
Individual user	.. \My Documents\ WindowsPowerShell\profile.ps1	.. \My Documents\ WindowsPowerShell\ Microsoft.PowerShell_profile.ps1

$pshome is the path to the PowerShell installation folder. PowerShell doesn't create any profiles during the installation process. All profiles have to be created manually, though it's possible to store the profile centrally and reference it from a profile on the local machine.

Profiles can perform several actions, including:

- Loading additional functionality via PowerShell snapins
- Creating functions and storing in memory for future use
- Setting the PowerShell prompt
- Running scripts
- Setting environmental factors such as color schemes
- Changing the current folder

A folder containing an example profile is created when PowerShell is installed. On 32-bit machines, it can be found at C:\Windows\System32\WindowsPowerShell\v1.0\Examples. The folder contains a file called profile.ps1.

> **NOTE** If you copy the profile.ps1 file, ensure that you delete the lines at the beginning of the file that start Set-Alias. These aliases are automatically defined, and attempting to redefine them in a profile will cause a lot of error messages. This example hasn't been updated for PowerShell v2.

A sample profile is provided in listing 2.1 (part of my standard profile).

Listing 2.1 Sample profile

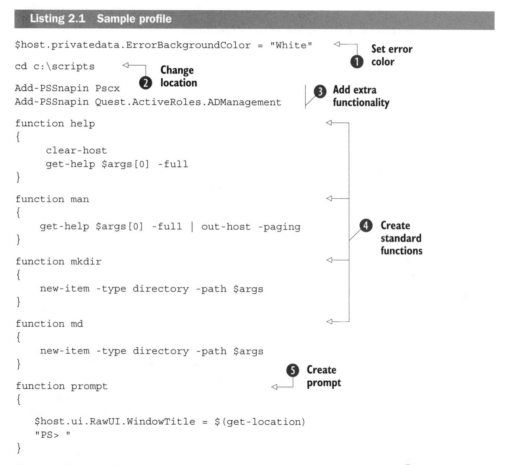

```
$host.privatedata.ErrorBackgroundColor = "White"        ⯇── ❶ Set error
                                                                color
cd c:\scripts    ⯇──┐ ❷ Change
                      location
Add-PSSnapin Pscx
Add-PSSnapin Quest.ActiveRoles.ADManagement    ❸ Add extra
                                                  functionality

function help                                   ⯇
{
    clear-host
    get-help $args[0] -full
}

function man                                    ⯇
{
    get-help $args[0] -full | out-host -paging          ❹ Create
}                                                          standard
                                                           functions
function mkdir                                   ⯇
{
    new-item -type directory -path $args
}

function md                                      ⯇
{
    new-item -type directory -path $args
}                                                ❺ Create
                                                   prompt
function prompt                                  ⯇──┘
{

    $host.ui.RawUI.WindowTitle = $(get-location)
    "PS> "
}
```

The profile starts by setting the background color for error messages ❶. Typing $host at a PowerShell prompt displays a number of PowerShell configuration items. $host.privatedata displays all of the foreground and background colors. These items can be changed.

NOTE Setting colors like this in your profile will generate an error when you open the Integrated Scripting Environment in PowerShell v2. It doesn't stop anything working, though.

The folder location is then changed ❷. One of the main uses for a profile is to load additional functionality into PowerShell using the Add-PSSnapin cmdlet ❸. The functions shown at ❹ create predefined commands, in this case mimicking standard commands from DOS and UNIX. The final function ❺ performs two tasks. It defines the PowerShell prompt to be PS> rather than the full path of the current folder. It also sets the title of the shell window to be the full path to the current folder. This will change as the location is changed in the filesystem or any other provider. A quick search on the internet will reveal other prompt functions.

CONSOLE FILES

An alternative method of configuring PowerShell is to use a *console file*. A number of products such as Exchange 2007, the IIS 7 PowerShell provider, and the Quest Active Directory cmdlets create console files as part of the installation process. It's also possible to create a console file for a PowerShell session using the Export-Console cmdlet. An example console file is shown in listing 2.2.

Listing 2.2 Sample PowerShell console file

```xml
<?xml version="1.0" encoding="utf-8"?>
<PSConsoleFile ConsoleSchemaVersion="1.0">
  <PSVersion>1.0</PSVersion>
  <PSSnapIns>
    <PSSnapIn Name="IIsProviderSnapIn" />
  </PSSnapIns>
</PSConsoleFile>
```

The working part of the console file is the line <PSSnapIn Name="IIsProvider-SnapIn" />, which causes the snapin to be loaded. PowerShell can be started using a console file for configuration like this: powershell.exe -PsConsoleFile MyConsoleFile.psc1.

   If you install one of the previously mentioned products, check the console file to see what you should add to your profile, check online or ask in the forums for advice if you are not sure. I prefer to put everything in the profile and only use the one "version" of PowerShell on a machine. It saves having to remember which console file you started with and what functionality you have available.

2.2.3 *Extending PowerShell*

PowerShell's extensibility is a major strength that helps third-party vendors and the PowerShell community thrive. There are an increasing number of PowerShell-related products available commercially and through community-based projects. It's preferable to have a single shell incorporating all of the functionality you require rather than spreading the functionality across a number of different PowerShell shells.

PowerShell is extensible in a number of ways:

- Create functions that are loaded at PowerShell startup
- Create new cmdlets in a PowerShell snapin
- Create a provider in a PowerShell snapin
- Create a new shell incorporating the extra functionality

We saw an example of creating functions in the previous section. New cmdlets or providers are created as PowerShell snapins in a .NET language and complied into a DLL. An installation package is created to install and register the DLL with PowerShell.

All registered snapins are visible by typing `Get-PSSnapin –Registered`. Snapins can be loaded using `Add-PSSnapin` as shown in the sample profile and removed using `Remove-PSSnapin`. To view the installed snapins, use `Get-PSSnapin`.

In v2, we also have the concept of *modules*. These can be libraries of functions or compiled DLLs analogous to snapins. There's a separate set of cmdlets for working with modules: `*-Module`. Modules are covered in detail in the appendix B.

2.2.4 *Potential issues*

You've now installed and configured PowerShell and want to start using it to solve your administration problems. You're at the keyboard ready to start working with PowerShell. What issues are we likely to meet?

EXECUTION POLICY

The first issue is that when you first install PowerShell, you can't run scripts. Even the profile scripts won't execute. You're permitted to work interactively at the PowerShell prompt. In some cases, you may want PowerShell left in that state, but most of the time you want to run scripts. The ability to execute scripts is controlled by the PowerShell execution policy. This is a deliberate design decision by the PowerShell team.

The rationale is that this makes PowerShell secure by default as part of Microsoft's Trustworthy Computing initiative. This policy allows admins to include PowerShell in their system images without fear of exposing their systems to a security risk. Only those machines that will actually do scripting will make this change. All the others can have PowerShell installed and have no security exposure.

> **THIS WILL BITE** You'll forget about execution policies at some stage. Everyone does.

The setting for the execution policy can be found in the Windows Registry key ExecutionPolicy at HKLM:\SOFTWARE\Microsoft\PowerShell\1\ShellIds\Microsoft.PowerShell. When PowerShell is first installed, it's set to Restricted. The possible values for ExecutionPolicy are shown in table 2.2.

The ExecutionPolicy value can be changed by editing the Registry and changing the value to the appropriate setting. A better way is to perform this task from PowerShell.

Table 2.2   Possible values for PowerShell execution policy

Value	Meaning
Restricted	This is the default setting. It doesn't allow profile scripts to be loaded or scripts to run.
AllSigned	All scripts and profiles must be digitally signed using a code-signing certificate from a trusted certificate authority. This also applies to scripts created and executed on the local system.
RemoteSigned	All scripts or profile files downloaded from the internet must be digitally signed. This also applied to scripts from network shares.
Unrestricted	All profile files and scripts will be executed regardless of origin.

NOTE   On Windows Vista, Windows 7, Windows Server 2008, and Windows Server 2008 R2, PowerShell must be started using the Run as Administrator feature-with elevated privileges—if you intend to change the execution policy. On Windows XP and 2003, the user who started PowerShell must have administrator privileges in order to change the execution policy. PowerShell can't request that an elevation of privileges be performed once it's running.

The setting for the execution policy can be viewed using the `Get-ExecutionPolicy` cmdlet. Only the value of the setting is returned. The setting can be changed using `Set-ExecutionPolicy`, as shown in listing 2.3.

Listing 2.3   Using `Set-ExecutionPolicy`

```
PS> Set-ExecutionPolicy -ExecutionPolicy RemoteSigned
PS> Get-ExecutionPolicy
RemoteSigned
PS>
```

Note that nothing is returned to indicate a successful change of execution policy. The `Get-ExecutionPolicy` cmdlet has to be used to view the setting. What's the recommended setting for execution policy? My recommendation would be to set the execution policy as high as possible without compromising the ability to perform required administrative tasks. The `UnRestricted` setting should be avoided. Ideally, `AllSigned` would be used, but if you don't have access to a code-signing certificate, use `RemoteSigned`. `Restricted` can be used if you want to allow a user access to run PowerShell interactively but not run scripts. Ensure that the user doesn't have Administrator-level privileges on the system; otherwise he'll be able to change the execution policy.

DOUBLE-CLICK

Many Windows executables can be started by double-clicking the file in Windows Explorer. This includes EXE files, batch files, and VBScript files. If a PowerShell file is double-clicked, it won't execute. The default behavior is for the file to be opened in Notepad.

RECOMMENDATION It's strongly recommended that this default behavior *not* be modified to allow a PowerShell script to be executed by double-clicking.

This default behavior may be overridden by applications such as PowerGUI. The settings are changed so that the files are opened in the PowerGUI editor rather than Notepad.

Blocking script execution by double-click is intentional behavior and is viewed as a security feature in PowerShell.

CURRENT FOLDER

In PowerShell, the current folder isn't on the search path. The contents of the search path may be viewed by typing `$env:path` at the PowerShell prompt. This means that a PowerShell script file in the current folder can't be executed simply by typing the name of the script.

In order to execute a PowerShell script in the current folder, use `.\script_name.ps1`. The option `./script_name.ps1` also works. This is the option I tend to use, as it's quicker to type at the prompt. One can remove the ".ps1" in this case. Tab completion in PowerShell v2 will complete script names in the current folder.

RECOMMENDATION It's strongly recommended that the current folder *not* be added to the search path.

This is another deliberate configuration decision by the PowerShell team to help prevent the accidental or malicious running of scripts that could have an adverse effect on your system.

.NET

PowerShell is .NET-based. It opens nearly the whole of the .NET framework for use in your scripts or from the command line. One small issue is that the whole of the .NET framework is *not* loaded into PowerShell by default.

There are a number of methods of loading .NET assemblies into PowerShell. These methods will be explored in chapter 3 when we look at .NET and PowerShell.

NOTHING RETURNED

Sometimes nothing appears to happen when you run a PowerShell cmdlet, as seen in the earlier example using `Set-ExecutionPolicy`. There could be for two reasons for this. First, there may not be any data to act upon, so the cmdlet may not be able to perform the designated action. Second, the cmdlet may not return anything.

The behavior can be frustrating at times. If this happens and you're unsure as to what's happening, try to perform an independent check on the data to make sure that the cmdlet did perform as expected. Also, check whether the cmdlet should actually return anything. This information can be found in the help file for the cmdlet.

This completes our look at configuring PowerShell. Using this information, you should be able to install and configure PowerShell to meet your requirements. It's time now to read the instructions and learn how to use our shiny new tool.

2.3   *Your four best friends*

We've looked at how to install and configure PowerShell, and now we'll discover how to get over the "What on Earth is this?" moment. The documentation delivered with PowerShell v1 (strangely it has been dropped from PowerShell v2, but can be found on the Microsoft download site) consists of:

- Getting Started Guide
- Quick Reference Guide
- User Guide
- Release Notes

The documentation is well worth reading. If, like me, you want to use the product and then read about it, the PowerShell discovery mechanisms are designed for just that purpose.

PowerShell has a built-in discovery mechanism—you can use PowerShell to discover how to use PowerShell. The way that this has been thought through and designed into the product is what makes a lot of people think that PowerShell rocks!

I've called this section "Your four best friends," and when using PowerShell, there are four tools that you'll come to rely on:

- Get-Help
- Get-Command
- Get-Member
- Get-PSDrive

We'll look at these in turn and discover how they help us learn PowerShell and how they continue to help us when we're working with PowerShell. When something isn't working or you can't work out how to do something, chances are that one of these tools will solve your problem or provide enough information to point you in the right direction.

There are a number of code snippets in this section. They're there for you to try and look at the results. PowerShell is best learned by doing. We'll keep meeting these friends in later chapters. I guarantee you'll use one of these commands at least once in any session when you're using PowerShell.

We'll visit each of our new friends in turn, starting with Get-Help.

2.3.1   *Get-Help*

The first stop when trying to discover how something works is the help system. Power-Shell supplies help in the form of files that are displayed as text in the shell. Help information is stored in either XML files related to the DLL containing the PowerShell cmdlets, or in text files stored (for the about topics) with the PowerShell binaries. Comment-based help can be used in PowerShell v2. We will see an example later in the book. The PowerShell help system is text-based and is analogous to the man files available on UNIX systems.

Two sets of help are available:

- Information specific to an individual cmdlet, accessed by Get-Help followed by the cmdlet name
- PowerShell language and environment information, accessed by Get-Help followed by about_topic_name.

Typing Get-Help returns the help file for Get-Help itself. If a cmdlet name is appended—for example Get-Help Get-Command—then a brief set of information is displayed, including:

- Name of the cmdlet
- Synopsis—a one sentence statement of what it does
- Syntax description—how we use it
- Detailed description
- Related links pointing to related cmdlets or about files
- Remarks—usually a reminder about the -full and -detailed parameters

Using Get-Help -detailed adds information on the parameters available for the cmdlet and examples of how to use it. The -full parameter returns more information on the cmdlet's parameters, notes on the cmdlet, information about the input and output data, and examples.

To see the range of about files available, type Get-Help about at the PowerShell prompt. The list of files includes language features such as the if statement and the looping commands, as well as information about the PowerShell environment such as variables and the pipeline.

The sample profile discussed in chapter 1 contains two functions that are worth copying into your profile. One defines a function called help and the other is called man. The functions as presented are identical, in that they take the output from a Get-Help call and pipe it into the Out-Host cmdlet, which uses the paging parameter to generate a paged output. Again, note the use of DOS and UNIX commands for the aliases.

> **NOTE** If you want to see the full help information, you'll need to change the code in these functions to read Get-Help $args[0] -full | out-host -paging. The example profile was produced during the beta process and not updated when the full and detailed parameters were added to Get-Help. Modified versions are shown in listing 2.1

Using the help system can be awkward when you're in the middle of working through a problem, especially if you want to keep the screen relatively clear. One solution is to use two PowerShell shells. The first is your working prompt where you're running scripts or working interactively. A second PowerShell instance is used to display help information as required.

An alternative method of accessing the help information is to download the graphical help file from the Microsoft Script Center at http://www.microsoft.com/technet/scriptcenter/topics/winpsh/pschm.mspx (it moves around a bit, so you may need to

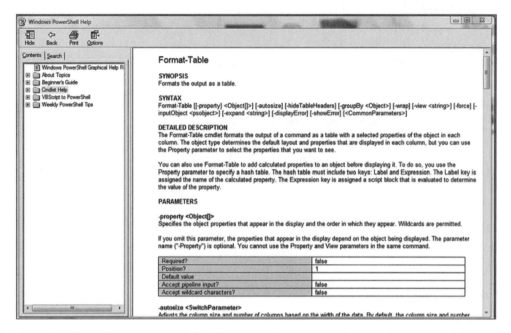

Figure 2.1 PowerShell graphical help file. The help topics are browsable using the tree control in the left pane. Also included are introductory documentation and a conversion guide.

hunt for it). After unblocking the downloaded file, if necessary, install the compiled help file into a folder of your choice and add the Get-GuiHelp function given on the web page to your profile. When you've restarted PowerShell, you'll be able to type Get-GuiHelp Format-Table at the PowerShell prompt and the graphical help system will open at the correct place, as shown in figure 2.1 If a nonexistent command is entered, the graphical help file will open and an error message will be provided. The help topics can be browsed using the controls in the left pane. The graphical help file contains the cmdlet and about file help documentation for PowerShell v1. In addition, there's a beginner's guide with articles from Microsoft's Scripting Guys plus information on converting VBScript to PowerShell and some of the early Weekly PowerShell Tips. Well worth the download time.

PowerShell v2 supplies a similar sort of graphical help system through the graphical editor. Another possibility is to use the help power pack in PowerGUI.

Get-Help gives us a lot of information about PowerShell and the cmdlets, but it's not the whole story. The next friend we need to visit is Get-Command.

2.3.2 *Get-Command*

Get-Command is complementary to Get-Help. If we type Get-Help Get-Command at the PowerShell prompt, the synopsis states "Gets basic information about cmdlets and about other elements of Windows PowerShell commands." So how is that different from Get-Help? Get-Help gives help for those things that have help files in Power-Shell. Get-Command gives data about those things that can be executed, including cmd-lets, functions, scripts, and even Windows executables. Enter Get-Command ipconfig.exe | Format-List and see what's returned.

Get-Command is useful in a number of ways. If you know you want to work with the processes on the computer but can't remember the cmdlets, then use:

```
Get-Command *process
```

If you want to retrieve the names of the cmdlets in a particular snapin:

```
Get-Command -PSSnapin IIsProviderSnapIn | Sort verb, noun
```

As I explained earlier I tend to use the alias for the utility cmdlets, such as sort, and also ignore the parameters. I find that the utility cmdlets tend to be used in the same way nearly every time so nothing is gained by using the full name. Common accepted usage is to use the aliases rather than the full cmdlet name.

> **POWERSHELL V2** In PowerShell v2, the -PSSnapin parameter is renamed -Module. An alias of -PSSnapin is defined so that existing code won't break. The v2 version also works with modules.

The last common use of Get-Command is to provide a quick reminder of the syntax used by a particular cmdlet:

```
Get-Command Get-Process -Syntax
```

Get-Help and Get-Command provide information about PowerShell and PowerShell commands. We're always dealing with objects in PowerShell. When we want to discover things about objects, we turn to Get-Member.

2.3.3 *Get-Member*

Get-Member is best described as the Swiss Army knife of PowerShell. It seems to be the one tool for which I'm always reaching. It would be worth reading the help file for Get-Member. Type Get-Help Get-Member to display it. Get-Member retrieves information about objects. PowerShell cmdlets return objects, so we can use Get-Member to view those objects.

If we use the Get-Process cmdlet to return information about the running processes whose names start with C:

```
PS> Get-Process c*

Handles  NPM(K)   PM(K)      WS(K) VM(M)   CPU(s)    Id  ProcessName
-------  ------   -----      ----- -----   ------    --  -----------
    820       6    1772       5352    96            620  csrss
    613      14    3180      19288   193            684  csrss
    372      10   11452      17344    98     1.53  5400  cssauth
    136       7    3604       6580    77           1724  cvpnd
```

Note that that only eight properties are shown for each process. If you've looked at processes in Task manager, you'll know there are a lot more properties available. We use Get-Member to view them. Objects and properties are covered in more detail in the next chapter but for now think of them as a piece of information that helps describe the object (e.g., "red" is the value of the property color for a red balloon).

Typing Get-Process c* | Get-Member will return more information than can easily be displayed on a page, so I'll leave that for you to try. We can use Get-Member to only display the property names as follows.

Listing 2.4 Using Get-Member to view object properties

```
PS> Get-Process c* | Get-Member -MemberType Property |
Format-Wide -Column 2
```

BasePriority	Container
EnableRaisingEvents	ExitCode
ExitTime	Handle
HandleCount	HasExited
Id	MachineName
MainModule	MainWindowHandle
MainWindowTitle	MaxWorkingSet
MinWorkingSet	Modules
NonpagedSystemMemorySize	NonpagedSystemMemorySize64
PagedMemorySize	PagedMemorySize64
PagedSystemMemorySize	PagedSystemMemorySize64
PeakPagedMemorySize	PeakPagedMemorySize64
PeakVirtualMemorySize	PeakVirtualMemorySize64
PeakWorkingSet	PeakWorkingSet64
PriorityBoostEnabled	PriorityClass
PrivateMemorySize	PrivateMemorySize64
PrivilegedProcessorTime	ProcessName
ProcessorAffinity	Responding
SessionId	Site
StandardError	StandardInput
StandardOutput	StartInfo
StartTime	SynchronizingObject
Threads	TotalProcessorTime
UserProcessorTime	VirtualMemorySize
VirtualMemorySize64	WorkingSet
WorkingSet64	

Get-Member will also display the methods on the object as well as properties specifically added by PowerShell.

There's a default formatter for each cmdlet that determines what will be displayed. Further information on working with format files can be found in appendix A. The utility cmdlet Select-Object that we saw in chapter 1 can be used when nondefault properties are to be displayed, or we want to reduce the amount of data . Alternatively, the Format-* cmdlets can be used to select what will be displayed.

Last but not least is Get-PSDrive, which gives us information about the PowerShell providers.

2.3.4   *Get-PSDrive*

`Get-PSDrive` displays information about the providers that are currently installed. Full details were supplied in chapter 1, where providers were discussed as part of the PowerShell feature set.

You can now install, configure, and learn how to use PowerShell, and you've learned to use it. Now you can start writing scripts. Oh... you don't know the Power-Shell language. We'll look at that next.

2.4   *Language features*

PowerShell works as a scripting language as well as an interactive shell. So far we've been using PowerShell interactively. In this section, we'll look at the major features of the language.

> **NOTE** This isn't a complete guide to the PowerShell language. This section will supply the information required to start scripting and to understand the scripts that will be presented later in the book. I recommend Bruce Payette's *PowerShell in Action, Second Edition* for complete coverage of the language.

All scripting languages need to be able to perform a common set of actions:

- Store data—variables and arrays
- Repeat actions—loops
- Control logic flow—branches
- Reuse sections of code—functions
- Output results

They also need to be able to accept input. Typing at the PowerShell prompt has been covered, and we'll see lots of examples of reading files later in the book, especially in chapter 8. We'll start by considering variables.

As we get into the loops and branching, you'll see that there's a common structure to many PowerShell commands:

```
command(condition){script block of actions}
```

A command is followed by a condition (a test of some kind), which causes a script block to execute.

2.4.1   *Variables*

A *variable* is a store for data that'll be used during the execution of a script. What can a variable store? Variables store .NET objects or a collection of objects.

PowerShell variables are typed; each variable stores a particular type of data based on the .NET object. Try the following code:

```
$a = 1
$a | Get-Member
$b = "1"
$b | Get-Member
```

We've defined two variables, $a and $b. PowerShell variables are designated by a $ symbol. Get-Member gives us information about the object, in this case the variables. It'll report that $a is TypeName: System.Int32 whereas $b is TypeName: System.String.

PowerShell will assign the type based on the data you input. The most common variables to deal with are integers and strings. If the type should change because of the code, then PowerShell will perform the change if it can based on the .NET rules for changing (casting). For example:

```
$a = $a * 2.35
$a | Get-Member
```

results in $a being TypeName: System.Double.

> **NOTE** Instead of writing $a = $a * 2.35, we could use $a *= 2.35. There are similar operators for performing addition, subtraction, and division. They're explained in the Operators section in appendix A.

PowerShell has a number of predefined variables. They can be viewed by using Get-ChildItem variable: (yes, variables can be accessed as a drive). Help information on variables changes slightly between PowerShell versions and can be gained from:

- About_Automatic_variables—variables created and maintained by PowerShell
- About_Environment_variables—Windows environment variables as used in batch files
- About_Preference_variables—variables that customize PowerShell (v2 only)
- About_Shell_variables (v1) or About_variables (v2)

One automatic variable that causes a lot of confusion is $_. It represents the current object coming down the pipeline. We saw it in the Where statements we used in chapter 1. Another example would be:

```
Get-ChildItem "c:\temp" | Where {$_.Length -gt 1MB}
```

We use Get-ChildItem to generate a directory listing of the c:\temp folder. The output from Get-ChildItem is an object of the System.IO.FileInfo class (type) for each file in the folder. We don't always need to consider that and will commonly refer to it as a file. Where-Object is then used as a filter to pass only those files whose length (size) is more than 1 megabyte, using MB, as discussed earlier.

Variable names can be composed of letters, numbers, and a few special characters, including the underscore character _.

A variable stores a single value. Sometimes we want to store multiple values, in which case we need an array, which is next on the menu.

2.4.2 *Arrays*

Arrays are used to store a collection of objects. In an earlier example, we saw an array that contained System.IO.FileInfo objects (the directory listing). Arrays can be created directly as follows:

```
$a = 1,2,3,4,5
$b = 1..5
$c = "a","b","c","d","e"
$a = @(1,2,3,4,5)
```

The first example creates an array containing the integers 1 through 5. The second example does the same, except we use the range operator (see appendix A) instead of typing each value. In the third example, we create an array containing strings. The final example shows a variation on the first example, in which @() is used to explicitly define the array. This leads to the possibility of creating an empty array and adding values to it:

```
$a = @()
for($i=1;$i-le5;$i++){$a += $i}
```

Here we create an empty array, then use a loop to populate the elements. Note the use of += to add the value. Assignment operators like this are explained in appendix A.

Array values can be accessed by the element number (index), which starts at 0, so the third element in our first example is $a[2].

> **NOTE** Starting an array at element 0 is a .NET feature. It can cause problems for users coming from scripting languages that start at 1. This is something to be aware of, so check this if you get unexpected problems with an array index.

A second type of array is the *associative array*, which is equivalent to the dictionary type object in VBScript. The associative array is normally referred to as a hash table in Power-Shell. Hash tables consist of key-value pairs. For example:

```
PS> $h =@{"one"=1;"two"=2;"three"=3}
PS> $h

Name                           Value
----                           -----
two                            2
three                          3
one                            1
```

Note that when we dump the values, they're not in the order in which they were input into the hash table. The hash table creates a hash index of the names so that it can search on the name:

```
PS> $h["two"]
2
```

This can make some activities such as sorting the hash table seemingly impossible. In this case, we need to use the GetEnumerator method to enable sorting to work:

```
$h.GetEnumerator() | sort value
```

The GetEnumerator method is discovered by using Get-Member on a hashtable object. It is also explained in the MSDN documentation for hash tables.

This gives us enough information on arrays to start working with them. Further information can be found in the help files about_array and about_associative_array (about_hash_tables in v2). Next on the menu is decision making and the branching statements in PowerShell.

2.4.3   *Branches*

Branching involves making a decision based on the relationship between two objects or an objects value. There are two PowerShell keywords used for branching. The if statement is used for situations when you want to create a test and perform actions based on the outcome of the test. The other branching command is the switch statement, which is a better statement to use when there are multiple outcomes, usually based on the value of a variable.

IF STATEMENT

An if statement is the simplest kind of branch. A test is performed and is evaluated to true or false. If the result is true, one set of actions is performed, but if it's false, another set of actions is performed. Listing 2.5 shows how a test of this sort could be used to delete the largest files in a folder if you needed to create free space quickly.

Listing 2.5   Using an if statement to test file size

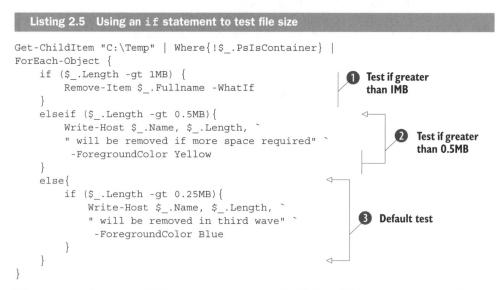

```
Get-ChildItem "C:\Temp" | Where{!$_.PsIsContainer} |
ForEach-Object {
    if ($_.Length -gt 1MB) {                                     ❶ Test if greater
        Remove-Item $_.Fullname -WhatIf                             than 1MB
    }
    elseif ($_.Length -gt 0.5MB){
        Write-Host $_.Name, $_.Length, `                         ❷ Test if greater
        " will be removed if more space required" `                than 0.5MB
         -ForegroundColor Yellow
    }
    else{
        if ($_.Length -gt 0.25MB){
            Write-Host $_.Name, $_.Length, `
            " will be removed in third wave" `                   ❸ Default test
             -ForegroundColor Blue
        }
    }
}
```

We start by using Get-ChildItem to generate a file listing. We're not interested in the subfolders for this example. If you want to include the subfolders, use the -Recurse switch with Get-ChildItem. The directory listing is piped to Where-Object, which filters out the containers. We're only concerned with files. We then use ForEach-Object to examine each file in the listing.

The first if statement ❶ checks whether the file is larger than 1MB. File size is stored in the length property. If the file is larger than 1MB we delete it with Remove-Item. Note that I've used the -whatif parameter (-whatif is one of the parameters common across many cmdlets—see get-help about_CommonParameters for details). This tells us which files will be removed without performing the action. That way, I can keep using the files for other examples. Once you're happy with the way the script works, remove the -whatif. It could be replaced by -confirm if you want to be prompted for each deletion.

Any file that's less than (or equal to) 1MB in size drops through to the elseif statement ❷. The elseif tests whether the file is more than half a MB in size and prints a warning that we'll get it next time around when we need more space.

Finally we drop into the else statement ❸. This is the catch-all for everything that doesn't get caught by the preceding tests. In this, we nest another check for a possible third wave of deletions.

It's possible to have multiple elseif statements, but it's usually better to use a switch statement instead, which is what we'll look at next.

SWITCH STATEMENT

The if statement that we used in the previous section is good when you have a small number of decision points. When there are a large number of decision points and the syntax of the if statement would get cumbersome, we can use a switch statement. Listing 2.6 shows a switch statement being used to check the size of a file so that the information can be printed to screen in the appropriate color.

Listing 2.6   Using a switch statement to display file size

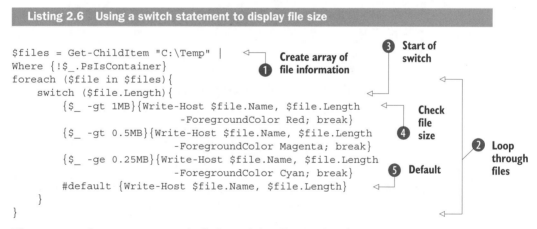

The output of Get-ChildItem (a listing of the files in the c:\temp directory) is stored in the variable $files ❶. $files is a collection of objects (array), so we can iterate through them using a foreach loop ❷. The switch statement uses a variable, in this case the file length property ❸, as its test. We define a number of tests in this case:

- Greater than 1MB ❹
- Greater than 0.5MB
- Greater than or equal to 0.25MB

When a file matches the particular criteria, the associated script block is executed. We use Write-Host to write the file name and size to screen and set text color based on the size. Note the ; symbol. This signifies that we've reached the end of a state-ment. We use it to concatenate multiple PowerShell commands on one line. The break command tells switch to terminate processing and not to perform any of the other tests.

A switch statement usually has a default clause ❺ to catch anything that hasn't been processed previously. In this case, we don't want to see the bulk of the files dis-played, so the line is commented out by a # symbol.

> **SWITCH**   The switch statement probably doesn't get used enough. Try using it in preference to lots of if statements.

We've mastered the use of variables and arrays, and have seen a number of loops in use. It's time to consider PowerShell's looping commands in more detail.

2.4.4   Loops

We often need to repeat the same code. We often need to repeat the same code. That's bad enough to read (never mind write), so what would it be like if we had to use the same piece of code 10 times, or 50, 100, or more? This is where loops come to our rescue. There are a number of looping mechanisms in PowerShell:

- Foreach-Object cmdlet
- Foreach loop
- For loop
- Do loop
- While loop

They serve slightly different purposes; I'll explain when it's best to use each one as we go along. When using the foreach, do, for, or while loop, you can use the break com-mand to jump out of the loop and the continue command to skip processing the script block and return to the start of the loop. Details can be found in the about_break and about_continue help files.

> **MISSING HELP**   The PowerShell v1 help system does *not* contain information on Do loops. The others are covered by about files. This is corrected in v2.

Foreach-Object is the odd one out among the looping mechanisms because it's a cmdlet rather than a PowerShell language feature. Just to show that we don't hold that against it, we will start with it.

FOREACH-OBJECT

Foreach-Object is used in a pipeline to perform some processing on each object coming along the pipeline. It may not be thought of as a loop but that's exactly what it does. As with all things PowerShell, the workings of this cmdlet are best shown by an example, shown in listing 2.7.

Listing 2.7   Using the `Foreach-Object` cmdlet to count file distributions

```
$Out1 = @"
 $count files are smaller than 1MB and occupy $total_size bytes
"@
$Out2 = @"
$count_big files are bigger than 1MB and occupy $total_size_big bytes
"@

Get-ChildItem "c:\Temp" |
    where {!$_.PSIsContainer} |   ForEach-Object   `
-Begin {
    $count = 0
    $total_size = 0
    $count_big = 0
    $total_size_big = 0
 } `
-Process {
    if ($_.Length -gt 1MB) {
        $total_size_big += $_.Length
        $count_big ++
    }
    else {
        $total_size += $_.Length
        $count ++
    }
} `
-End {

    Write-Host $out1
    Write-Host $out2
}
```

❶ Define here strings

❷ Start of loop

❸ Begin script block

❺ If-else decision block

❹ Start/end of process script block

❻ Start/ end of End script block

NOTE   The script is split across multiple lines using the ` continuation charac-
ter. This makes it more readable both in the book and when editing.

We start with two variables of special note—$out1 and $out2 ❶. These are known as
here strings. A here string has the following format:

```
$out1 = @"
$count files are smaller than 1MB and occupy $total_size bytes
"@
```

A here string starts with @", or alternatively @', which is immediately followed by
pressing the Enter key. The data in the here string can span multiple lines. The here
string is terminated by "@, or '@, which must be the first characters on the line.
Within a here string, quotes are interpreted literally, so they'll be displayed for example like this:

```
PS> @"
>> This string
>> spans multiple lines and contains
>> some quotes. Both double " and single
```

```
>> ' quotes will be displayed.
>> "@
>>
This string
spans multiple lines and contains
some quotes. Both double " and single
' quotes will be displayed.
```

If we use double quotes in the here string terminators, variables will be substituted as normal. Here strings terminated by single quotes do not perform substitution.

> **HERE STRINGS**   Here strings are another PowerShell item that don't get used enough. I'm as guilty of this as anyone.

Get-ChildItem is used to generate a directory listing ❷. This is piped into the Foreach-Object cmdlet. The Begin, Process, and End parameters are used to define script blocks that perform some actions before the first object is processed, as every object is processed, and after the last object is processed, respectively. Often, only a single script block is seen, and that is, by default, the process block.

> **SCRIPT BLOCK**   A *script block* is some PowerShell code surrounded by {} that can be used in loops or if statements, assigned to variables or other cmdlets, and even used directly in the pipeline.

The -Begin script block is used to set the initial value of some variables ❸. It's executed once, just before the first object enters the loop. In traditional scripting languages, this would have to happen outside of the loop. These variables are counters, so we set them to zero.

Each object coming down the pipeline goes through the -Process script block ❹. In this case, it goes through an if statement to decide whether the file is bigger than 1MB ❺. Depending on that outcome, the appropriate counter and total file size variables are updated.

After all of the objects have been processed, the -End script block is executed ❻. The results are written to screen using the Write-Host cmdlet, which is described in more detail in section 2.4.6.

Get-Help Foreach-Object -full will supply the help information for this cmdlet. Now we move on to the foreach loop, which has a similar name and does similar things. Confused? You won't be after reading the next section.

FOREACH LOOP

A foreach loop is similar in concept to the Foreach-Object we've already looked at. So why do we need two things that are nearly the same? Foreach is part of the PowerShell language rather than being a cmdlet. Its purpose boils down to doing the following script block to every object in a collection of objects. This is best explained by an example. We could use the previous example and just rewrite it, but we'll do something else because it'll be more interesting. If you want try to rewrite the script in the previous example, you can check your answer against the example on the companion website.

One of the unwritten rules of PowerShell is that if you can get your code down to one line—the "one-liner" of much discussion on blogs and forums—then you're a real PowerShell user. This leads to some horrible examples of the overuse of aliases, and in some cases inefficiencies. I've produced a one-line version of listing 2.8 to demonstrate how it can be done. The script spans three lines but that is just to get make it fit the lines of the book. It is really one continuous line of code.

```
dir "c:\test" | ?{!$_.PSIsContainer} |
% {if ($_.LastAccessTime -lt ((Get-Date).AddDays(-10)))
{rm $($_.Fullname) -wh} }
```

Though it does demonstrate the flexibility and strength of PowerShell, condensing your code into a one-liner isn't always the best answer for administrative scripting, as understanding and speed may be lost.

One important difference is that `Foreach-Object` will process objects as they come along the pipeline, but a `foreach` loop needs the objects to be already available in a collection. Testing has suggested that in PowerShell v1 a `foreach` loop is faster than using the cmdlet version, though the gap has narrowed in v2. If you have a huge number of objects, the cmdlet's ability to process the objects as presented will be a bonus. Listing 2.8 shows how to use a `foreach` statement to iterate through a set of files and remove files older than a certain date. This is a common technique for cleaning up sets of data that are created periodically.

Listing 2.8 Using a `foreach` loop

```
$date = (Get-Date).Adddays(-10)
$files = Get-ChildItem "c:\Temp" | Where{!$_.PSIsContainer}     Start loop
foreach($file in $files){
    if ($file.LastAccessTime -lt $date){
        Remove-Item -Path $file.FullName -WhatIf
    }                                                             End loop
}
```

This script loops through all of the files in the C:\Temp folder and checks whether they've been accessed in the last 10 days. If they haven't been accessed they're deleted. The script starts by using `Get-Date` to retrieve the current date. We then use the `AddDays` method to subtract 10 days from the current date. Yes, it does seem odd, but the alternative is more complicated. The next line is interesting, in that we create a variable called `$files` and set its value equal to the output from a pipeline consisting of:

```
Get-ChildItem "c:\Temp" | Where{!$_.PSIsContainer}
```

which is capable of being run as a standalone piece of PowerShell. Try it. In the pipeline, we start with `Get-ChildItem` producing a directory listing of the C:\Temp folder. That's piped into a `Where-Object` filter that looks to see whether the object is a container (a folder). Only objects that aren't folders are passed.

The `$files` variable contains all of the output from the pipeline, so it's actually a collection of objects rather than a single object. We can use the `foreach` loop as shown. The $files variable is completely arbitrary; it could've been $xxx. Usually, collection names are plural and object names are singular. If the names reflect the objects being processed, in this case files, it aids understanding and readability of the script, but this isn't mandatory.

> **OBJECTION**   If you do decide on a different convention in your foreach conditions, someone will moan at you. Ignore them. Write your code for the way you work. If you share with the community—you are going to share, aren't you?—expect that someone will change it.

Inside the loop, we check the LastAccessTime property of each file against the date we calculated at the beginning of the script. Note that we use less than (-lt) for the comparison. Dates are assumed to be increasing. If the file is older than 10 days, we use Remove-Item to delete it. Note that I have a -Whatif parameter on Remove-Item. This is a safety mechanism when developing and testing the script to prevent accidents and to leave the files available for further tests. When you're ready to move the script into production, remove the -WhatIf parameter. You could use the -Confirm parameter instead in production if you want to double check the files before deletion.

> **DOUBLE CHECK**   If you're working with critical files, the double check is a good idea. Double check or restore from backup—I know which I'd rather do. You do have a backup, don't you?

The Foreach-Object that we used in the previous section is an alias for the foreach loop that can be used in a pipeline. You can get full details on using foreach from Get-Help about_foreach.

Having looked at a couple of options for looping through a collection of objects, we'll now look at the straightforward coding loops.

FOR, WHILE AND DO LOOPS

The for loop is the classic "perform this set of code x number of times" type of loop that has been in programming languages since the year dot (since the beginning of programming in other words). The PowerShell syntax borrows heavily from the C# language. While and do loops keep repeating a script block until some condition is met. The example in listing 2.9 uses a simple for loop to create some test files.

Listing 2.9   Creating test folders and files with loops

```
$data = 1..57
$j = 1                                    1  Start while
while ($j -le 10){                           loop
    $foldername = "Testfolder_$j"
    New-Item -ItemType directory -Name $foldername
    $j++

    for ($i=0; $i -le 10; $i++){
        $filename = "file_$i.txt"         3  Start for loop
```

```
        Set-Content -Path "$foldername\$filename" -Value $data
    }
}       ⭘❷ End while loop          ❹ End for loop
```

We start by creating an array containing the values 1 to 57. This is arbitrary data that's easy to create. A variable $j is created to be a counter. An outer loop, using a while command, is used to create test folders ❶ ❷. New-Item is the standard cmdlet for creating objects. It's one of the core cmdlets that should be enabled to work in all providers, but this isn't always the case, as we'll see in chapter 14 when we look at the SQL Server provider.

> **POWERSHELL IMPLEMENTATIONS** The PowerShell team is responsible for the core PowerShell engine. How it's implemented in various products is down to the team producing that product. This leads to differing styles of implementation. I expect these to be smoothed out over time as PowerShell and the various implementations mature.

All we need to do is pass it the type of object and the name of the object, as shown. If you want to create the object anywhere but the current folder, the path needs to be defined as well. After creating the folder, we increment the counter by one.

We then use a for loop to create test files ❸ ❹. The part in () sets the conditions and counters for the loop:

- Starting point is $i=0
- End point is $i -le 10
- Counter increment is $i++

$i is an arbitrary counter. The fact that many people use $i is a hangover from FORTRAN, where i was automatically defined as an integer and was often used as a counter in loops. The initial value of $i is 0. We increment $i by one on successive iterations of the loop until we get to a point where $i is equal to 10.

> **NOTE** In a for loop or a while loop, the test occurs before the script block is executed. So in this case, when $i is 10, the block is executed, but at the next iteration, $i has increased to 11, so the condition is exceeded and the loop stops.

The script block is executed during each loop. A file name is created by substituting the counter variable into the file name, so we end up with file_0.txt, file_1.txt, and so on. We then use Set-Content to write the array into the file. One of the properties of Set-Content is that it'll create a file that doesn't exist. We can exploit that mechanism here to create and write the content to the file in one line.

Time now to turn our attention to another loop type—the do loop.

The do loop suffers a bit because there isn't any official documentation supplied for it in v1. All the other looping mechanisms get an about file, but not the poor do loop. Another reason for its underuse is that it can be awkward to use sometimes. Here's an example:

```
$i = 1
do {
    $name = "Testfolder_$i"
    New-Item -ItemType directory -Name $name
    $i++
}
while ($i -le 10)
```

We start our counter at 1 and create a new folder using the counter to supply a differentiator. All we need to do is pass it the type and name of the object as shown. If you want to create the object anywhere but the current folder, the path needs to be defined as well. After creating the folder, we increment the counter by one.

The script will create 10 folders named testfolder_1 to TestFolder_10.

As an alternative, we could replace the last line of the previous example with this:

```
until ($i -gt 10)
```

Note how the operator changes because of the difference between while and until.

> **RECOMMENDATION**   The do loop can cause problems in testing, as we've seen. If you know the number of times you'll traverse the loop, use a for loop; otherwise use a while loop.

That's enough on loops to make you an expert. We'll continue our look at the language features by working with functions, then look at how to output data before moving on to creating scripts.

2.4.5 *Functions*

The looping mechanisms that we've just looked at are one way to reuse code, or at least be more efficient in the way we use code. There are times when we want to run a set of code and get a result returned, or we want to separate a piece of code to make the main part of the script easier to understand. That's when we want to use a function. PowerShell, unlike VBScript for instance, makes no distinction between functions that return a result and those that don't. They're all functions. Functions get a huge boost in ability in PowerShell v2. Advanced functions are covered in appendix B.

Let's take listing 2.9 and use a function instead of the inner loop. That gives us the code shown in listing 2.10.

Listing 2.10   PowerShell script to create test folders and test files

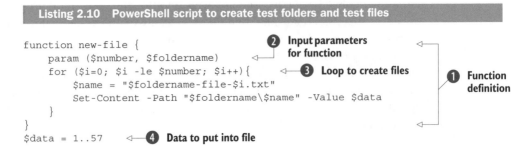

```
function new-file {
    param ($number, $foldername)              ❷ Input parameters
    for ($i=0; $i -le $number; $i++){            for function
        $name = "$foldername-file-$i.txt"     ❸ Loop to create files    ❶ Function
        Set-Content -Path "$foldername\$name" -Value $data                  definition
    }
}
$data = 1..57      ❹ Data to put into file
```

```
$i = 1
while ($i -le 10) {
    $name = "Testfolder_$i"
    New-Item -ItemType directory -Name $name
    new-file $i $name
    $i++
}
```

➎ Loop to create folders

➏ Call to function

The function has to be defined first and given a name ➊. It's considered best practice to use the PowerShell cmdlet naming conventions.

> **POWERSHELL NAMES** PowerShell has a *verb-noun* naming convention for cmd-lets and the functions that are supplied out of the box. We saw the list of verbs currently in use in chapter 1. The noun should be singular and related to the activity or object that's being accessed. A list of the nouns currently in use can be obtained using Get-Command | group noun.

The param statement is used to accept arguments passed into the function ➋. A data type can be assigned to the parameter. It's possible to use the $args automatic variable instead of the param statement. The param statement gives more flexibility and can be used to perform more checks on the parameters, including setting default values. The for loop we saw earlier is used to create the test files ➌. In this case, the number of files to create is based on the number passed into the function as its first parameter. The folder name is used as part of the file name and to define the path to the file.

The main body of the script follows the function. An array ➍ is created to provide data we can write into the files we create in the function. The folders are created by the while loop used earlier ➎. The only difference being that a call to the function used to create the files is put into the loop ➏. We could've nested the loops at this point instead of using a function, but then I'd have had to think of another example! Note how the function is called. The arguments to pass into the function are listed after the function name rather than using () to surround them as in other scripting languages. More information can be found in the about_function help file.

There are two things to notice about the way variables are used in this script. First, $i is used in the main body of the script and within the function as a counter. As far as PowerShell is concerned, these are two totally independent variables, even though they have the same name. Second, we define $data in the main body of the script, but use it in the function. This is an example of *variable scope*, which isn't as complicated as it seems.

SCOPE

Scope defines how scripts and functions work with variables. When PowerShell starts, it defines a top-level or *global* scope. When a script, script block, or function is started, a new scope is defined. A parent-child relationship is created between the original scope and the child scope. Similarly, when a function is called within a script, a scope is created that's a child of the script's scope.

Variables are defined with the scope of where they're created. In our function example, $data is created in the scope of the script, as is the $i used in the while loop. The $i used in the function is recreated every time the function is called and is created in the scope of the function. The function's scope is a child of the script's scope. The function can read and use the $data variable because it was created in the parent scope of the function.

PowerShell treats the $i independently because they're created in different scopes. The rule is that a variable can be read from a higher scope but not modified unless the scope of the variable is stated. A parent scope can't modify variables in a child scope.

The important thing to remember is that scope exists and that child scopes can access variables from the parent scope. Get-help about_scope gives more examples and is useful to check when troubleshooting your more scripts.

LIBRARY FILES

Functions can be loaded into memory at the start of a PowerShell session, as we saw when looking at profiles. The profile can become too big to manage if there are many functions defined within it, so the alternative is to use a library file. This is achieved by collecting the functions into a single file called Library*XXXX*.ps1, where *XXXX* is a suitably descriptive name. The library file can be dot-sourced from your profile to make the functions available within the PowerShell session. Alternatively, dot-source the library file from a script if you don't require the functions to be universally available.

> **MODULES** PowerShell v2 introduces the concept of modules, which give more flexibility and generally replace the concept of library files—see appendix B for more details.

The last of the language features is *output*. We've seen how to use variables and loops, how to make decisions, and the working of functions. Administrative scripts normally produce output of some kind. We'll close this section by looking at the output methods in PowerShell.

2.4.6   *Output*

Most administrative scripts produce output, even if it's only a message to say the script has completed. There are number of output methods available in PowerShell:

- Out-*—cmdlets that send the objects or formatting records to a specific destination
- Write-*—cmdlets that write data to a specific destination
- Format-*—cmdlets that convert the objects into formatting records and write them by default to the screen
- Export-*—cmdlets that export data to a file

Typing Get-Command Out-* or any of the other examples in the preceding list will generate a list of the cmdlets in that category. Get-Help can be used to view the help file. The commonly used output cmdlets are summarized in table 2.3.

Table 2.3 Common output cmdlets

Name	Purpose
Out-File	Sends output to a file. Data can be appended to a file.
Out-Null	Deletes output rather than displaying it. Use it to suppress messages, for instance when loading .NET assemblies.
Out-Printer	Sends output to the default printer, or an alternative printer if specified. It doesn't format the data so use only for simple text documents.
Out-String	Sends objects to the host as strings.
Write-Host	Writes output to screen. Can change colors of text.
Format-Table	Formats the data into a table and displays on screen.
Format-List	Formats the data into a list and displays on screen.
Format-Wide	Formats objects as a wide table that displays only one property of each object.
Export-Csv	Exports objects to a CSV file. Data can't be appended to a file.
Export-CliXML	Exports objects to an XML file.

Examples of using these cmdlets will be seen throughout the book.

It's now time to put everything together and start looking at scripts.

2.5   *Scripts*

Scripts represent a method of saving PowerShell code and reusing it at a future time, either as a scheduled task or as *ad hoc* usage. Chapter 4 covers script development in detail. This section is concerned with converting to PowerShell from other languages.

2.5.1   *PowerShell scripts*

Scripts are text files containing PowerShell commands that are given a .ps1 extension. The same extension is used for scripts in PowerShell v2. Any editor that can output text files can be used to create scripts, ranging from Notepad (still useful to view scripts) to PowerShell-specific editors such as PowerGUI, PowerShellPlus, or the ISE in v2. The PowerShell toolkit, discussed in chapter 4, has more information on these tools.

PowerShell scripts are used by typing the path and name of the script at a Power-Shell prompt. If the script is in the current folder, the path is .\ as in .\myscript.ps1.

One topic that frequently arises is how you can convert existing scripts, written in VBScript or another scripting language, into PowerShell scripts. If you have a large library of VBScripts that are in production use, I'd recommend that you don't rush into converting them. Leave them in use and start developing new scripts in Power-Shell. Convert the existing scripts as they need modification.

In many circumstances you'll need for VBScripts to either be converted into Power-Shell or to interoperate with PowerShell. We'll look at how to do this in the following sections.

2.5.2   *Converting from VBScript*

VBScript has been in use on Windows systems for more than 10 years. A huge body of administration scripts is available, starting with Microsoft's Script Center (see appendix E). Some of the scripts have been converted to PowerShell, but many haven't. So, how do we go about converting a script?

A lot of scripts use WMI, in which case we can use Get-WmiObject, as explained in the next chapter. For other scripts, we start with the VBScript-to-Windows PowerShell Conversion Guide, which is downloadable from Microsoft's Script Center. We'll use this script to try the conversion:

```
Set objFSO = CreateObject("Scripting.FileSystemObject")

If objFSO.FileExists("C:\scripts\librarytime.ps1") Then
    Set objFolder = objFSO.GetFile("C:\scripts\librarytime.ps1")
Else
    Wscript.Echo "File does not exist."
End If
```

It uses the FileExists method of the FileSystemObject to test whether a file exists. If the file exists, a GetFile is performed so that the properties can be accessed. These are VBScript objects that we won't use in the rest of the book where we will concentrate on using .NET when we need to step out of pure PowerShell.

In PowerShell this would become:

```
if (Test-Path -Path "C:\Scripts\LibraryTime.ps1") {
    $file = Get-Item -Path "C:\Scripts\LibraryTime.ps1"
}
else
{
    Write-Host "File does not exist"
}
```

Test-Path returns true or false depending on whether the particular path exists. One advantage of PowerShell is that this same code will work in other providers by just changing the object being tested.

Converting scripts is a big step. It may be better to start small and incorporate VBScript into your early PowerShell scripts.

2.5.3   *VBScript in PowerShell*

VBScript is based on COM, whereas PowerShell is based on .NET. PowerShell can incorporate VBScript objects by using New-Object to create them. This will be covered in chapter 4 in the section on COM.

One way of starting to work with PowerShell from a VBScript base is to incorporate VBScript into your PowerShell scripts so that you're only converting parts of the script. There are a couple of ways to use VBScript functionality in a PowerShell script.

We can start by really incorporating VBScript, as this example demonstrates:

```
$sc = New-Object -ComObject ScriptControl
$sc.Language = "VBScript"
$sc.AddCode('
```

```
Set obj = CreateObject("WScript.Shell")
obj.popup "Popup from PowerShell via VBScript",,"PowerShell in Practice",0
')
$sc.CodeObject
```

VBScript is COM-based, so we need to use the `ComObject` parameter of `New-Object` to define a COM `ScriptControl` object. (This may only be available on 32-bit systems.) There isn't a lot of documentation available on this object, but a good starting point can be found at http://msdn.microsoft.com/en-us/library/aa227633(VS.60).aspx. We then define the language as VBScript (JScript could also be used—in fact it'd be possible to use PowerShell, VBScript, and JScript in a single script). The `AddCode` method is used to define the script. There are some restrictions here, in that it doesn't seem possible to use multiple objects in the same `ScriptControl`. The VBScript is simple, in that it creates a `WScript.Shell` object and displays the `popup`.

This approach has its limitations, but we can move on and use the COM objects directly in PowerShell:

```
$a = New-Object -ComObject WScript.Shell
$a.popup("Popup from PowerShell",$null,"PowerShell in Practice",0)
```

We define the `WScipt.Shell` object directly as a COM object in PowerShell and then call the `popup` method. It's important to note the difference in syntax around using the method. In the first example, we used the VBScript syntax with the arguments listed after the method name and separated by commas. In the second example, we used the .NET syntax with a comma-delimited list of arguments surrounded by parentheses.

Having seen how to use VBScript inside PowerShell, we can now quickly look at using PowerShell inside VBScript for completeness.

2.5.4 *PowerShell in VBScript*

SAPIEN has released a free control that enables us to use PowerShell inside VBScript. This is a valid way to start converting scripts by incorporating PowerShell into existing scripts. The control can be downloaded from http://blog.sapien.com/index.php/2008/06/25/activexposh-is-now-a-free-download/.

The control can be used like this:

```
set ap = CreateObject("SAPIEN.ActiveXPoSH")
ap.OutPutMode = 0
ap.Execute("Get-Service | Where-Object{$_.Status -e 'stopped'}")
```

This is standard VBScript, in that we create the object and then call the `Execute` method to run the PowerShell code.

You'll now have a good understanding of PowerShell and how it works. Congratulations, you're now ready to start building your PowerShell toolkit by looking at how PowerShell works with other technologies to access WMI, Active Directory, and .NET.

2.6   *Summary*

Learning PowerShell is done by using PowerShell. First we need to install and configure it so we can start learning. The PowerShell documentation is a good starting point, and PowerShell supplies four built in learning tools: `Get-Help`, `Get-Command`, `Get-Member`, and `Get-PSDrive`. These are your four best friends as far as learning PowerShell is concerned. Use them to dig into the inbuilt documentation.

PowerShell is a scripting language and command shell. The language has a number of features that need to be mastered, including variables, arrays, loops, branching logic, and functions.

VBScript has been available for a number of years. A guide is available for converting scripts from VBScript into PowerShell. As a first step, it's possible to embed VBScript in PowerShell and vice versa.

This chapter has given you a solid grounding in installing, configuring, and learning PowerShell. You're now ready to start looking beyond PowerShell to the other technologies that need to be mastered in order to successfully administer your Windows systems using PowerShell. In chapter 3, we'll look at using .NET in PowerShell so we have access to a wider range of functionality, WMI so we can access existing Windows management technologies both on local and remote machines; COM so we can access existing applications such as Office, and ADSI so we can work with Active Directory and local security systems.

PowerShell toolkit

This chapter covers

- Using .NET with PowerShell
- Using COM components
- Optimizing use of WMI
- ADSI and PowerShell

PowerShell, like all tools, can't exist in isolation. Up to now, we've concentrated on PowerShell itself. We now turn our attention to other technologies we need in our toolkit to get the most out of PowerShell—.Net, COM, ADSI, and WMI. This may seem like a random collection of letters, but these technologies are essential to getting the most from PowerShell. These tools are the basis of our PowerShell toolkit, and will appear throughout our administrative work. I can't think of an example that doesn't involve at least one of them. Using the PowerShell cmdlets involves using .NET even if it's somewhat removed.

> **.NET** We can make extensive use of .NET with PowerShell. We don't have to become .NET developers to use PowerShell. Most administration tasks can be performed with little or no .NET.

PowerShell is .NET-based and gives us a way to access to nearly the whole of .NET. This may seem to be of more benefit to programmers than administrators. It'd be easy to think that PowerShell is a programming language rather than an administration tool, given some of the PowerShell examples on the internet. Just because you can write Windows Forms applications in PowerShell doesn't mean you should! There's a lot of useful functionality in managed code for the PowerShell administrator, for instance access to SMO to administer SQL Server (see chapter 14) and the interface to IIS 7 (see chapter 13). Microsoft keeps adding functionality into .NET, and administrators should to be aware of the basics. After a quick look at the .NET basics, we'll see how to use .NET code in PowerShell, and look at the issues of using .NET and how to overcome them.

The Component Object Model (COM) is how programs used to be written for Windows systems. It's been replaced by .NET for new systems, but there's still a large amount of COM in use. For a start, ADSI and WMI, the other two technologies that we'll cover, are based on COM. If you look at VBScript, it's COM-based, as is the scripting interface to applications such as Microsoft Office and Internet Explorer (IE). We can't escape knowing about COM just yet, even without thinking about ADSI and WMI. PowerShell has good support for using COM, and we'll learn how to use it later in the chapter.

Active Directory is the foundation of the Windows-based infrastructure in our enterprise. We need to be able to administer Active Directory efficiently, which means automation. This is usually achieved via scripting. ADSI is the interface used by scripts to work with Active Directory. "Didn't we use that in VBScript?" I can hear you asking. Yes we did, and in part we'll be using it in exactly the same way, but—and this is a big but—there's a lot more to working with ADSI in PowerShell, as we'll discover. Chapters 5, 10, and 11 concentrate on administering Active Directory. This section sets the scene for those chapters.

Finally, but definitely not least, is WMI. *Windows Management Instrumentation* is one of the foundation technologies for administering Windows-based systems. Often WMI is the only way you can get to work with a particular aspect of the system. The Microsoft Script Center has many, many examples of using WMI in VBScript. PowerShell has much better support for WMI—in fact it was working on a replacement for wmic, the WMI command-line tool, that started the thought processes that led to PowerShell!

> **WMI**   WMI support is the hidden gold mine for PowerShell adoption. It's so much easier to use WMI that it becomes second nature, rather than "Oh no! It's time to use WMI."

WMI is even more important to the Windows administrator than would seem apparent. It's rare among technologies accessible from Windows-based scripts, as it has built-in support for accessing remote systems. PowerShell v1 doesn't have the capability to access remote machines directly (remote access has been the most requested feature for v2), so we need to learn to work with WMI for this capability. I know of one PowerShell expert who administers more than 400 systems using PowerShell, WMI, and a bit of .NET. WMI support has been radically improved in PowerShell v2, and we'll look at the options this brings.

3.1   *Eureka 2*

When you look at the contents for this chapter, you may think it's just background stuff that you can dip into if and when you need it. I'd advise you to read this before diving into all the scripts in later chapters. I know that's what every author wants, but you'll get more out of the scripts if you understand the background.

I've had a few "wow" moments with PowerShell, and a couple of them involve WMI and ADSI, the tools in this chapter. WMI has been a great tool for Windows administrators to use. The number of examples on the Microsoft Script Center proves that it's one of the main planks of the scripting environment for Windows. If you've used WMI with VBScript, you'll have experienced one of the main frustrations of using VBScript firsthand. It's an absolute pain to format the output, and most VBScripts that use WMI are primarily concerned with formatting the output. How much simpler it is to use (for example):

```
Get-WmiObject -Class Win32_OperatingSystem
```

and let PowerShell do the formatting. Even if we have to change it to:

```
Get-WmiObject -Class Win32_OperatingSystem | Format-List
```

it's still a lot simpler. WMI just got much easier. Look at the example scripts at the beginning of section 3.5 comparing a VBScript example and the same thing in Power-Shell. The VBScript code has 20 lines, versus 2 lines of PowerShell. That's ease of use with a vengeance!

The second Eureka! moment is when I discovered how much easier working with Active Directory became, especially when searching. With VBScript, we had to create an ADO record set by searching via a SQL-like query. The queries could be difficult to create, and having to step through the record set could be awkward. Look at listing 3.4 and compare it with a VBScript equivalent—we have 17 lines of VBScript against 10 lines of PowerShell. It's not such a wide difference as the WMI example, but PowerShell still brings a significant productivity improvement.

> **NOTE**   If we used the Quest AD cmdlets or the Windows Server 2008 R2 AD cmdlets instead of a PowerShell script, we'd be comparing 17 lines of VBScript to one line of PowerShell. That's ease of use.

Bring on PowerShell, where we can create searches using LDAP filters, we can search much faster, and we can access the tombstoned records so potentially we can create our own restore scripts. Things are definitely looking up. Time to start looking at these extra technologies and first on the agenda is .NET.

3.2   *Using .NET*

One point that I made in chapter 1 should be remembered while reading this is: you don't have to become a .NET programmer to use PowerShell. It's necessary to use .NET code to access certain functionality, but most of what you'll be doing is using the PowerShell language. .NET enters the picture because you need to load extra bits and create new objects.

The .NET Framework or just .NET (there are differences but we don't need to worry about them) is the way to create applications in the modern Microsoft environment. Microsoft made .NET available in 2002, and new versions have appeared on a regular basis since then. Each new version of .NET tends to be a superset of the previous version, in that new functionality is added but the old functionality remains more or less intact.

> **.NET VERSIONS** PowerShell v1 needs .NET 2.0. PowerShell v2 needs .NET 2.0 apart from some features that require .NET 3.5 SP1. Unless you need multiple versions of .NET loaded, just load .NET 3.5 SP 1, as it also contains .NET 2.0.

PowerShell is based on .NET, and as we've seen, one of the major features is that PowerShell cmdlets output .NET objects rather than text we're used to in more traditional shells. These .NET objects are passed along the pipeline so they can be used by other cmdlets.

As with any piece of technology, there's a set of terminology we need to master. So we'll start by looking at the terms used when talking about .NET and explain them from an administrator's viewpoint. Application developers may want to skip large parts of this chapter, as I'm covering the subject only enough to help administrators who've never been exposed to this material. This is definitely .NET for administrators rather than a full explanation of .NET.

It's possible to access some .NET functionality, such as the `Math` functions, directly from PowerShell, but as we saw in chapter 2, not everything is immediately available. We'll learn how to load additional .NET functionality, such as SMO or the IIS interface, into PowerShell and how to work with it. Our old friend `Get-Member` will be useful when we start to investigate working with .NET. First, we need to know what we're talking about, so we'll look at .NET terminology.

3.2.1   *Understanding .NET*

.NET is a developer topic, but to get the best out of PowerShell as an administrative tool, we need to dig into the subject a bit. The Microsoft documentation for .NET is available on MSDN.

> **DOCUMENTATION** The documentation available on MSDN is for .NET 3.5, which is the current version at the time of writing. PowerShell is built on .NET and assumes that .NET version 2.0 is in use. Links are avail-able on the MSDN web pages to documentation based on .NET 2.0 where necessary.

The MSDN documentation is written for developers, but an increasing number of PowerShell examples are becoming available on MSDN courtesy of the PowerShell community and especially some of the PowerShell MVPs. It's always worth scrolling to bottom of an MSDN article to see if there's any PowerShell content.

COMMUNITY The PowerShell community is strong and healthy due to a large number of early adopters who believe in sharing. If you have a good example script, please post it on the web for others to share.

Our starting point for this discussion is the .NET framework, which is formally defined on MSDN.

FRAMEWORK

The .NET Framework is best described as the environment and tools required to create, test, and run applications based on the Windows platform. There are two key components to the framework:

- Common Language Runtime (CLR)
- .NET framework class library

The CLR is the runtime mechanism used by .NET applications. It enables applications written in any of the .NET languages, such as C#, to be executed. We don't need to worry about the CLR when using PowerShell.

The class library is our main interest from the framework. If you check http://msdn.microsoft.com/en-us/library/ms229335.aspx, you'll be able to browse the class library. There are literally hundreds of .NET classes available. Luckily we don't need to learn most of these; otherwise we'd never get any administration done! There's also a huge chunk of it we don't need to worry about as administrators—we're not going to be writing Windows forms applications in PowerShell.

It may seem the class library is a huge heap of stuff, but there's some structure to it, namely namespaces and classes.

NAMESPACE

A *namespace* is best thought of as a set of related classes that are grouped together because they deliver a particular set of functionality. In section 3.4, we'll see that the `System.DirectoryServices` namespace contains the classes we use to work with Active Directory. This namespace doesn't deliver all of the functionality required to work with Active Directory. There's also the `System.DirectoryServices.ActiveDirectory`, `System.DirectoryServices.Protocols`, and `System.DirectoryServices.AccountManagement` namespaces to consider.

We'll define a class next, since namespaces contain classes.

CLASS

A *class* is a programming template for creating an object. Objects are what we use in our scripts. The `System.DirectoryServices` namespace mentioned earlier contains two main classes in which we're interested. `System.DirectoryServices.DirectoryEntry` represents an object in Active Directory, such as a user account or a group, whereas `System.DirectoryServices.DirectorySearcher` is used to search Active Directory for objects matching particular criteria. Note that the full class name incorporates the namespace.

In PowerShell v2, we can use the `Add-Type` cmdlet to create our own .NET classes. This is a useful technique, especially where we want to combine properties from a number of objects for our display. The advantage of creating a .NET class is that the type of the properties is checked when values are set—if we have a property that's a string, we can only give it a string value. If we give it an integer, we'll get an error. This approach is reasonably advanced, so I'll cover it in the appendix A.

We're now moving from the abstract to the concrete, in that we've reached something we can work with in the shape of an object.

OBJECT

The word *object* has been used in several different ways already in this book. We've mentioned .NET objects, PowerShell objects, Active Directory objects, and so forth. An object is an instance of a class that we've specifically created within our script. Each object-orientated programming language has its own way of creating objects, and while they all achieve the same end, the syntax is different.

PowerShell has a couple of ways of creating a .NET object. The most obvious way is to use the `New-Object` cmdlet, as shown in listing 3.1.

Listing 3.1   Error message when creating .NET objects

```
PS> $rand = New-Object -TypeName Syste.Random -ArgumentList 42
New-Object : Cannot find type [Syste.Random] :
make sure the assembly containing this type is loaded.
At line:1 char:19
+ $rand = New-Object <<<<  -TypeName Syste.Random -ArgumentList 42
```

This was deliberately typed wrong (honest) to show the error message you get when PowerShell can't work out which .NET class you're trying to access. The message means one of two things:

- There's a mistake, usually a typing mistake, in the class name that's being used.
- The .NET class we're trying to use isn't loaded into PowerShell, in which case we need to load it before we can use it. We'll see how to do that in a while.

Assuming we type everything correctly, we'd have:

```
$rand = New-Object -TypeName System.Random -ArgumentList 42
```

Typename is the .NET class name and *ArgumentList* is the data we need to give the .NET constructor in order for it to create the object. In this case, we're creating an instance of the random number class.

The .NET class documentation normally consists of:

- An overview including what it's used for
- Constructor—the options for how we can create it
- Methods—what actions it can perform
- Properties—what data it contains

There's an alternative way to create an object:

```
$rand2 = [System.Random](42)
```

In this case, we enclose the class in [] and the arguments follow as shown. I tend to use New-Object, as I've found it the simplest to understand. I've had some awkward times with this alternative method when I was first learning PowerShell or when the argument list is complicated.

> **POWERSHELL OBJECTS** One thing to be aware of is that PowerShell doesn't necessarily return a "pure" .NET object. A PowerShell *wrapper* may be placed around the object. The underlying object can be accessed using .psbase, for example $rand.psbase. This approach is needed much less with PowerShell 2.

Having created our object, we now need to see what it can do in terms of methods and properties.

METHODS AND PROPERTIES

A *method* is an action that an object can perform; a *property* is a piece of data belonging to the object. The methods and properties available on an object can be viewed using Get-Member.

> **NOTE** This is a truncated list, so the important points can be seen. If you perform Get-Member on your system, you'll see a lot more methods and properties that I've omitted for brevity and clarity.

```
PS> $f = Get-Item Testfolder_1
PS> $f | Get-Member

   TypeName: System.IO.DirectoryInfo

Name          MemberType      Definition
----          ----------      ----------
Mode          CodeProperty    System.String Mode{get=Mode;}
Create        Method          System.Void Create()
Refresh       Method          System.Void Refresh()
ToString      Method          System.String ToString()

PSChildName   NoteProperty    System.String PSChildName=Testfolder_1

Exists        Property        System.Boolean Exists {get;}
Extension     Property        System.String Extension {get;}
FullName      Property        System.String FullName {get;}

BaseName      ScriptProperty  System.Object BaseName get=$this.Name;}
```

In addition to the methods and properties we were expecting, we've found a few other types of members:

- CodeProperty—accesses a static property of a .NET class (see the following section)
- CodeMethod—not shown but accesses a static method of a .NET class
- NoteProperty—defines a property with a static value
- ScriptProperty—defines a property whose value is the output of a script
- ScriptMethod—defines a method implemented by a PowerShell script

In other words, these are ways to extend the object beyond the basic .NET object. Add-Member can be used to add these additional methods and properties. Chapter 11 of *PowerShell in Action, Second Edition* by Bruce Payette (Manning 2010) has a large section dealing with this.

That closes our look at methods and properties except for the static methods that have been mentioned.

STATIC METHOD

A *static method* (or property) can be accessed directly without creating an instance of the class. This can be readily seen when using the Math class:

```
PS> [System.Math]::Sqrt(16)
4
```

We use a double colon :: to access the method as shown; in this case, taking the square root of 16.

The Math class also has static properties (fields) that can be accessed in a similar way. These can be discovered using [System.math] | get-member -Static.

```
PS> [System.Math]::Pi
3.14159265358979
```

When working with the .NET online documentation, be aware of the S icon indicating static methods and properties, as shown in figure 3.1. In my experience, it's easy to miss these icons and spend a lot of time head scratching and grumbling... I mean troubleshooting.

One item that'll come up fairly frequently is enumerations. They're a simple concept but can be awkward to use if you aren't aware of how they work.

ENUMERATION

Understanding enumerations isn't essential to learning PowerShell but it may help you understand what other people are talking about. An *enumeration* is a closed list.

◆S⬤✕	Sin	Returns the sine of the specified angle.
◆S⬤✕	Sinh	Returns the hyperbolic sine of the specified angle.
◆S⬤✕	Sqrt	Returns the square root of a specified number.
◆S⬤✕	Tan	Returns the tangent of the specified angle.
◆S⬤✕	Tanh	Returns the hyperbolic tangent of the specified angle.
◆S	Truncate	Overloaded. Calculates the integral part of a number.

Top
Fields

	Name	**Description**
◆S⬤✕	E	Represents the natural logarithmic base, specified by the constant, e.
◆S⬤✕	PI	Represents the ratio of the circumference of a circle to its diameter, :

Figure 3.1   Part of online documentation for the System.Math class. Note the S indicating static methods and properties.

The values are defined as part of the .NET framework and can't be changed. As an example, consider what happens when you write to an event log. The entries can only be one of a specified list of types. We can use PowerShell to discover the possible values in a enumeration:

```
PS> [enum]::GetNames([System.Diagnostics.EventLogEntryType])
Error
Warning
Information
SuccessAudit
FailureAudit
```

The .NET documentation will point us to the enumeration we need to use. In this example, it's possible to supply the information as a string that contains one of the values, or we can get the value out of the enumeration:

```
function Write-EventLog
{
param([string]$msg="Default Message", [string]$type="Information")
$log = New-Object System.Diagnostics.EventLog
$log.set_log("Scripts")
$log.set_source("PSscripts")

$log.WriteEntry($msg,$type)
}
```

The example shows a function that's used to write to a specific event log. We'll look at how to create event logs and write to them in more detail in chapter 8. In this function, we pass in two arguments. One is the message and the other is the type of message. We've set `Information` as the default type via a string. The value could have been set by using `$type = [System.Diagnostics.EventLogEntryType]::Information`.

The last area of .NET that we need to look at is the Global Assembly Cache or GAC.

GAC

An *assembly*, in practical terms, is a compiled DLL that contains one of more classes. The *GAC* is a store on the computer that's created when .NET is installed. It is used to store shared assemblies—assemblies stored in the GAC are available to all .NET programs executing on the machine as required.

The contents of the GAC can be browsed, if required, using Windows Explorer, or if the PowerShell Community Extensions are loaded (see chapter 4), a provider for the GAC is available.

You probably feel that you know more about .NET than you ever really wanted to by now, but we'll make all of this worthwhile, by showing you how to use it to perform administrative tasks for which there's no other option.

3.2.2 *Accessing .NET*

Knowing all the theory behind .NET is well and good, but as administrators we want to be able to use this stuff to administer our systems and, hopefully, make our lives easier. We've seen how to find out from MSDN what we need to know in order to use .NET classes, but how are we going to actually use it?

The first thing is to know whether the assembly we need is already loaded, as shown in listing 3.2.

Listing 3.2   .NET assemblies loaded by PowerShell

```
PS> [appdomain]::CurrentDomain.GetAssemblies() |
    Sort-Object -Property Fullname | Format-Table fullname

FullName
--------

System.Data,Version=2.0.0.0,Culture=neutral,PublicKeyToken=b77a5c561934e089
System.DirectoryServices,Version=2.0.0.0,Culture=neutral,
PublicKeyToken=b03f5f7f11d50a3a
System.EnterpriseServices, Version=2.0.0.0,
Culture=neutral, PublicKeyToken=b03f5f7f11d50a3a
System.Management, Version=2.0.0.0,
Culture=neutral, PublicKeyToken=b03f5f7f11d50a3a
System.Management.Automation, Version=1.0.0.0,
Culture=neutral, PublicKeyToken=31bf3856ad364e35
System.Transactions, Version=2.0.0.0,
Culture=neutral, PublicKeyToken=b77a5c561934e089
System.Xml,Version=2.0.0.0, Culture=neutral,
PublicKeyToken=b77a5c561934e089
Update-SDMgp, Version=1.0.2963.20431,
Culture=neutral, PublicKeyToken=null
```

NOTE   This is a truncated list; I've removed the assemblies that are loaded by PowerShell or by snapins.

Once we determine that an assembly isn't available, we need to load it. There are a number of ways of achieving this task. One of the most common is:

```
PS> [system.reflection.assembly]::
loadwithpartialname("Microsoft.Web.Administration")

GAC    Version        Location
---    -------        --------
True v2.0.50727
    C:\Windows\assembly\GAC_MSIL\Microsoft.Web.Administration\
7.0.0.0__31bf3856ad364e35\Microsoft....
```

All we give is the assembly name, rather than the full name we saw in the results of listing 3.2. The load message can be suppressed by using:

```
$null = [system.reflection.assembly]::
loadwithpartialname("Microsoft.Web.Administration")
```

or

```
[void] [system.reflection.assembly]::
loadwithpartialname("Microsoft.Web.Administration")
```

or

```
[system.reflection.assembly]::
loadwithpartialname("Microsoft.Web.Administration") | out-null
```

This method is scheduled for eventual removal from .NET, so although it's used a lot, ideally we should work with the full name. I tend to use one of the cmdlets from the PowerShell Community Extensions (see chapter 4) to derive the full name and use the `load` method:

```
$name = (Resolve-Assembly microsoft.web.administration).Fullname
[system.reflection.assembly]::load($name)
```

Alternatively, `Resolve-Assembly` has an `import` parameter, or in PowerShell v2, there's `Add-Type`, which can be used to load assemblies. A third possibility is to use the method supplied by Lee Holmes of the PowerShell team http://www.leeholmes.com/blog/HowDoIEasilyLoadAssembliesWhenLoadWithPartialNameHasBeenDeprecated.aspx.

However the assembly is loaded, we need to create objects using the classes in the assembly, which we saw how to do in the earlier section on objects. This concludes our brief excursion into .NET. We'll be working with .NET classes when we look at ADSI, and again in the chapters on administering Active Directory and IIS 7.

COM is an older technology, but it's still used in many areas of Windows administration. ADSI and WMI are based on COM, so we need that as background for the discussion of those topics.

3.3   Using COM

COM is to earlier versions of Windows as .NET is to modern Windows. It was the programming methodology of its day. COM is still used in a lot of applications, including Microsoft Office and Internet Explorer. ADSI and WMI are fundamental to a lot of scripting. They're both based on COM. This section will be of benefit when we come to consider them later in the chapter.

COM has superficially similar features to .NET in that classes, objects, methods, and properties are available. They don't necessarily work the same way, at a programming level, as .NET functionality with the same name. But from a Windows administrator's view, we only need to know how to use them. It'll be assumed that you've read the preceding section and understand these terms.

3.3.1   Understanding COM

If you want to see the functionality available through COM, try this:

```
Get-WmiObject -Class Win32_ClassicCOMClass | Select-Object Name
```

Be warned that it's a very long list. Also, accessing the COM classes through WMI doesn't give the full list of objects. This is a major issue with a lot of scripting activity. Writing the script is usually straightforward. The difficulty comes in finding out what you need to use to perform the task.

Internet Explorer (along with Microsoft Office) is known to have a COM interface that we can use. Unfortunately, it doesn't show up in the list generated using WMI. Time for plan B. We should always have a plan B. The Windows Registry has a full record of the COM objects installed on a machine. It can be accessed by:

```
Get-ChildItem -Path "REGISTRY::HKey_Classes_Root\clsid\*\progid" |
 ForEach-Object {
    if ($_.Name -match '\\ProgID$') {
        $_.GetValue("")
    }
} | Where-Object {$_ -like "*Internet*"}
```

We're using the Registry provider to perform a dir on the Classes_Root portion of the registry. In our discussion on providers in chapter 1, I mentioned that HK_Local_Machine and HK_Current_User are exposed as drives. The root of the Registry is available via cd REGISTRY::. For each path that ends in progid, we get the value of the default property, and in this case filter those that contain *internet* in the name.

> **NOTE** This is an adaptation of the script in chapter 18 of *PowerShell in Action, Second Edition* by Bruce Payette. If this is something you'll be doing a lot, consider making it a function and loading it from your profile.

On my machine, the script returns the following list of objects:

- InternetExplorer.Application.1
- InternetManager.SiteConfig.1
- Internet.HHCtrl.1
- Internet.HHCtrl.1
- polmkr.apmGpeInternet.1
- InternetManager.NetConnection.1
- Internet.HHCtrl.1
- InternetShortcut

The naming convention for COM objects is that the first part is the program (Internet Explorer in the first listed object); the second is the component, often the class name; and the third is a version, which we can ignore. Many of the scriptable objects that are related to specific programs will have *Application* as the component name. An internet search for InternetExplorer.Application leads us to part of the Windows 2000 Scripting Guide at http://www.microsoft.com/technet/scriptcenter/guide/sas_ent_qpyo.mspx?mfr=true.

> **RECOMMENDATION** If you haven't read the Microsoft scripting guide, this is a source that will repay the time spent on it. It's concerned with VBScript, but there's a wealth of background knowledge. I recommend adding the guide to your list of favorites. I've produced PowerShell versions of a lot of the scripts on my blog. The address is in listing 3.3

The documentation for COM objects isn't as well organized as that for the .NET framework. This is understandable, as the .NET documentation was produced as part of a concerted effort, whereas the COM documentation grew in an *ad hoc* manner over time. This means that you both have to search for the object you want to use (just tracking down its name can be an interesting activity), then search for the documentation to explain it. Often what you'll find is example scripts rather than full-blown documentation.

Having discovered our interface to Internet Explorer, it's now time to use it.

3.3.2 Accessing COM

Using COM objects is similar to using .NET objects, which we've already covered. As an example, see listing 3.3, in which we'll look at creating a script to access a PowerShell-related web site—in this case one I know well.

> **Listing 3.3 Open a web page from PowerShell**

```
function get-rsblog {
$ie = New-Object -ComObject InternetExplorer.Application
$ie.Navigate("http://richardsiddaway.spaces.live.com/")

while ($ie.busy) { Start-Sleep -seconds 1 }

$ie.Visible = $true
}
```

This is presented as a function, but it could also be used as a script, or if you have several sites you regularly use, you could create a parameter and a `switch` statement to enable the choice. I'll leave that as an exercise for the reader.

In this case, we use `New-Object` to create the `InternetExplorer.Application` object we discovered in the preceding section. The only difference for using it for COM objects is that we use the `-ComObject` parameter rather than `-TypeName`. Once we've created the object, we tell it the site we want to visit using the appropriate URL. Internet Explorer will take a while to open, so we use a `while` loop to check whether IE is busy, and put the script to sleep for a second. Once IE has retrieved the page, we make it visible.

This look at COM has shown us that once we've found and created the object, working with it is similar to working with .NET objects. COM is the basis of many of the Windows-based interfaces, especially WMI, which we'll see later. Active Directory is one of the most important technologies in a Windows corporate environment, and a prime candidate for automation. Active Directory has a COM-based scripting interface known as *ADSI*.

3.4 Using ADSI

"When will Microsoft ship an Active Directory provider (or cmdlets)?" is a frequently asked question. There's no direct support for working with Active Directory in either PowerShell v1 or v2.

> **WINDOWS SERVER 2008 R2** PowerShell cmdlets for Active Directory are available in Windows Server 2008 R2, along with a huge raft of other PowerShell functionality. PowerShell v2 is installed and enabled by default.

Automating Active Directory is one of the major areas of scripting, judging by the number of scripts available and the questions being asked on newsgroups. So we have a declared need to automate Active Directory work and a new shell that doesn't directly support working with Active Directory what are we going to do?

> **NOTE**   The discussion in this section is focused on Active Directory, but the same technologies and interfaces are used to access local user and group accounts, as well as work with *Active Directory Lightweight Directory Services* (*ADLDS*, formerly known as *ADAM*).

The COM-based interface ADSI *has* been used extensively in VBScript to work with Active Directory. As it's COM-based, we can work with it in PowerShell as we've seen. But there's also a .NET wrapper, System.DirectoryServices, that gives .NET access to ADSI. This situation is further complicated in that PowerShell has introduced a type accelerator for System.DirectoryServices called [ADSI] that provides yet another layer of wrapping, as shown in figure 3.2.

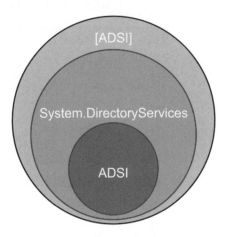

There are third-party tools available for working with Active Directory that will be covered in chapter 4. Detailed background information on ADSI can be found in the SDK (see appendix E).

Figure 3.2   Relationship between the ADSI wrappers in PowerShell

3.4.1   *Understanding ADSI*

The picture so far seems reasonably clear, with a couple of wrappers giving us access to ADSI and then to Active Directory. But there are a number of other .NET namespaces available that complicate the situation. System.DirectoryServices.ActiveDirectory was introduced in .NET 2.0, and System.DirectoryServices.AccountManagement was introduced in .NET 3.5. The relationship between the components is shown in figure 3.3.

Working up from the bottom of the diagram, we have Active Directory and the other data stores, including the local security system and AD LDS. These stores are accessed by the native LDAP APIs built into Windows. These APIs aren't accessible via scripting, or programming, languages. ADSI is the interface we use with scripting languages—originally VBScript, but now PowerShell. The AD APIs are another set of interfaces that bypass LDAP and communicate directly with Active Directory. They weren't available to VBScript.

The introduction of .NET 2.0 brought the System.DirectoryServices (S.DS) namespace into the picture. This is a .NET wrapper for ADSI, but doesn't necessarily

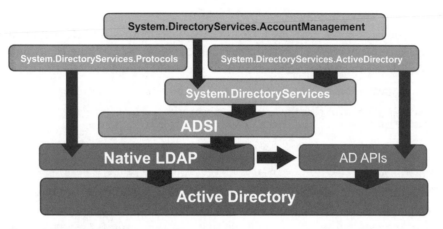

Figure 3.3 Access methods and protocols for working with Active Directory

expose everything that ADSI does, and changes the names of methods. For example, in VBScript we use `SetInfo()` to commit the changes to Active Directory, whereas `System.DirectoryServices` uses `CommitChanges()`. The `System.DirectoryServices.ActiveDirectory` (S.DS.AD) namespace is concerned with Active Directory itself, whereas `System.DirectoryServices` is for working with the data in Active Directory, such as user accounts. S.DS.AD bypasses S.DS and ADSI for some functionality, and accesses the AD APIs directly. `System.DirectoryServices.AccountManagement` was introduced in .NET 3.5 and is for working with security principals such as user and group accounts. It's a wrapper for `System.DirectoryServices`.

   `System.DirectoryServices.Protocols`, introduced with .NET 2.0, sits outside the stack that accesses ADSI. It works directly with the native APIs for Active Directory. It can be fast, but is more complicated to work with compared to the ADSI-based methods.

   Most of the examples we'll use in this and later chapters will use `System.Directory-Services`, though we'll examine `System.DirectoryServices.AccountManagement` when discussing user accounts. We'll avoid the `Protocols` namespace, but will spend some time with the `ActiveDirectory` namespace.

> **ACTIVE DIRECTORY CMDLETS** I've deliberately avoided bringing the Quest or Microsoft Active Directory cmdlets into this discussion. They'll be used in later chapters, but from discussion with users, I know that many organizations don't allow the use of the Quest AD cmdlets. I'll cover working with Active Directory from scripts because of this, and because I believe that if you understand how to perform the task in a script, it aids in the understanding of the cmdlets.

An additional complication is the presence of the accelerators that we discussed earlier in this section.

POWERSHELL ACCELERATORS

PowerShell contains an Active Directory type accelerator [ADSI]. It functions as an accelerator for System.DirectoryServices.DirectoryEntry, the class that we use to work with Active Directory objects such as users and groups:

```
$user = [ADSI]"LDAP://CN=Richard,CN=Users,DC=Manticore,DC=org"
```

```
$user2 = [System.DirectoryServices.DirectoryEntry] `
"LDAP://CN=Richard,CN=Users,DC=Manticore,DC=org"
```

```
$user3 = `
New-Object -TypeName System.DirectoryServices.DirectoryEntry
-ArgumentList "LDAP://CN=Richard,CN=Users,DC=Manticore,DC=org"
```

These three examples all do the same thing. They all generate a PowerShell object that enables us to work with a particular user object. If you perform a Get-Member on any of the created variables, you'll see that that their type is System.DirectorySer- vices.DirectoryEntry. Most people will use the first option because it's less typing, which means it's faster and easier to use, and you're less likely to make a typing error.

PowerShell v2 introduces another accelerator in the form of [ADSISearcher]. This functions as an accelerator for System.DirectoryServices.DirectorySearcher.

We've had a good look at the tools for working with Active Directory. It's now time to take them out of their packaging and put them to use. I don't want to spoil the sur- prises that chapters 5, 10, and 11 will bring, so we'll just get a taste of how we use this part of our toolkit. Before that, we have a bit of a problem to solve.

3.4.2 *Accessing Active Directory*

If we create a user object like this:

```
$user = [ADSI]"LDAP://CN=Richard,CN=Users,DC=Manticore,DC=org"
```

and then put it through Get-Member, we'll get the results shown in figure 3.4.

If you look carefully at the screen shot, you'll see that all that's returned are prop- erties. If you use a tool such as ADSIEdit to check an Active Directory account, you'll see that these are the populated attributes of the user object. All properties and no methods! How can we do anything with this object?

Back in the .NET section earlier in the chapter, I mentioned that PowerShell put a wrapper around the .NET object. This is exactly what's happened here, in that the PowerShell wrapper only returns the populated Active Directory attributes. To get this result, we used:

```
$user | Get-Member
```

To see the methods we need to use psbase to view the actual object:

```
$user.psbase | Get-Member
```

This will give us the information shown in figure 3.5.

In this second screen shot, we can see that the underlying object has a lot of meth- ods and some properties that match the .NET documentation for System.Directory- Services.DirectoryEntry. What does this mean for us in practice?

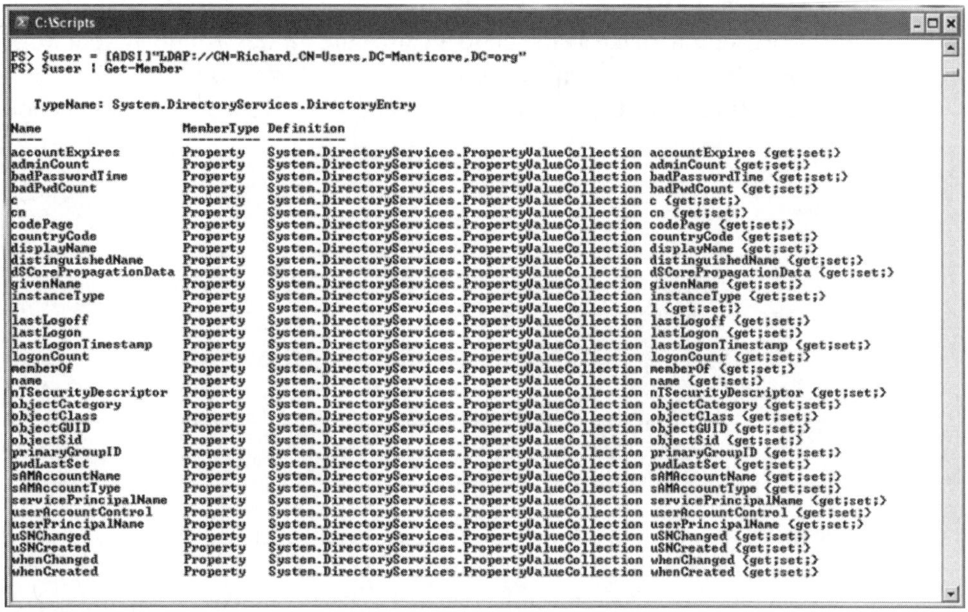

Figure 3.4 Output of `Get-Member` on an Active Directory user object

Figure 3.5 Applying `Get-Member` to the base object of an Active Directory user object

MAKING CHANGES

Assume we want to make a change to an attribute. In this example, we'll work with the l attribute (location), which corresponds to the city field on the Address tab of a user object in Active Directory Users and Computers. We'd use the following code:

```
PS> $user = [ADSI]"LDAP://CN=Richard,CN=Users,DC=Manticore,DC=org"
PS> $user.l
London
PS> $user.l = "Baston"
PS> $user.l
Baston
PS> $user.psbase.CommitChanges()
PS>
```

We create a variable to hold the user object. After examining its value, we change it and then make a call to CommitChanges() to write the result back into the Active Directory database. This can start to get confusing and cumbersome when other methods have to be accessed.

> **NOTE** In PowerShell v2, the need to use psbase has been removed, so that $user.CommitChanges() can be used directly. But when using Get-Member, the methods aren't shown unless psbase is used. Still confusing.

As an alternative approach, PowerShell was changed to incorporate the VBScript approach to working with Active Directory. This resulted in the methods shown in table 3.1 being added to the Active Directory objects. The big drawback to this is that they're hidden. Get-Member doesn't show these methods either on the PowerShell object or using psbase to access the raw object.

Table 3.1   **VBScript-style methods to be used when working with Active Directory objects**

Method	Purpose
Get()	Retrieves the value of a named property. Usually used for single-valued properties.
GetEx()	Retrieves the value of a named property. Usually used for multivalued properties. The values are returned as an array.
Put()	Sets the value of an attribute.
PutEx()	Modifies the values of a multivalued attribute.
SetInfo()	Saves the property values of ADSI object back to the directory store.

This would change our example to:

```
PS> $user = [ADSI]"LDAP://CN=Richard,CN=Users,DC=Manticore,DC=org"
PS> $user.l
London
PS> $user.l = "Baston"
PS> $user.l
Baston
PS> $user.SetInfo()
PS>
```

We can use the Put() method (we'll see an example in chapter 5) or set the attributes as shown.

> **RECOMMENDATION** Use SetInfo() and the associated methods. It's the simplest, and makes transitioning from VBScript examples easier.

When working with Active Directory, we're usually making changes, for example creating or modifying user accounts, or we're searching Active Directory for specific information. Using PowerShell to search Active Directory has a number of advantages when compared to the search capability we had in VBScript.

SEARCHING

We'll see more examples of searching Active Directory in later chapters, but the simple example in listing 3.4 will explain the changes.

Listing 3.4 Searching for a user in Active Directory

```
$struser = "BOSCH Herbert"   <--① Set user

$dom =
[System.DirectoryServices.ActiveDirectory.Domain]::   ② Get current
GetCurrentDomain()                                        domain
$root = $dom.GetDirectoryEntry()

$search = [System.DirectoryServices.DirectorySearcher]$root   <--③ Search root
$search.Filter = "(cn=$struser)"   <--
$result = $search.FindOne()   <--                ④ Search filter
                              ⑤ Find first  <--
if ($result -ne $null)
{                                                ⑥ Show result
  $user = $result.GetDirectoryEntry()
  $user
}
else {Write-Host $struser " Does not exist"}
```

This script will search Active Directory for a specific user. We're testing to see whether a user with this name exists. This could form part of a user creation script, where you want to test that a specific user name isn't already in use. We start by creating a variable to hold the user name ①. I always try to make my Active Directory scripts portable, as I can then reuse them. [System.DirectoryServices.Active-Directory.Domain]::GetCurrentDomain() will return the current domain ②. If we then get a directory entry for the domain, we can use this as the root of our search ③. A search filter is necessary; in this case we use the user name we've defined ④. There shouldn't be more than one user with a given name, so we can use FindOne() ⑤. Incidentally, FindOne() does a FindAll() and takes the first result! The result can then be displayed ⑥—either the user information or a message that we couldn't find that user.

> **NOTE** We didn't have to create an ADO recordset as we do when using VBScript to search Active Directory. This is a major step forward, in that scripts become easier to write and they run more quickly.

Searching Active Directory in PowerShell is much faster than using VBScript. We can also access the tombstoned records in our searches. This means we can think about restoring objects that have been deleted. But that's a treat for a later chapter. For now, we must turn our back on Active Directory and ADSI and start to think about, WMI, the last of our tools.

3.5   Using WMI

WMI is a powerful COM-based technology for obtaining information about your systems, and in some cases making changes to those systems. WMI gives you the keys to the kingdom as far as your system is concerned. In other words, WMI gives you access to everything. It's the ultimate skeleton key for Windows-based machines.

A WMI call can be executed on your local system or on a remote system (assuming that you have the correct level of permissions and that a firewall or some other device doesn't stop you). A mass of WMI-based scripts is available on the Microsoft TechNet Script Center, most of which are concerned with retrieving information from one or more Windows systems. Much of the VBScript-based administration was performed using WMI.

Why then do we need another method of using WMI? The simple answer is ease of use. WMI in PowerShell is so much easier to use. It becomes a familiar tool you want to use rather than a chore. Listing 3.5 is a good representative script for using WMI that I found on the Microsoft Script Center.

Listing 3.5   WMI in VBScript

```
strComputer = "."
Set objWMIService = GetObject("winmgmts:\\" & strComputer & "\root\CIMV2")
Set colCSes = objWMIService.ExecQuery("SELECT * FROM Win32_ComputerSystem")
For Each objCS In colCSes
   WScript.Echo "Computer Name: " & objCS.Name
   WScript.Echo "System Type: " & objCS.SystemType
   WScript.Echo "Number Of Processors: " & objCS.NumberOfProcessors
Next
Set colProcessors = objWMIService.ExecQuery("Select * from Win32_Processor")

For Each objProcessor in colProcessors
   WScript.Echo "Manufacturer: " & objProcessor.Manufacturer
   WScript.Echo "Name: " & objProcessor.Name
   WScript.Echo "Description: " & objProcessor.Description
   WScript.Echo "Processor ID: " & objProcessor.ProcessorID
   WScript.Echo "Address Width: " & objProcessor.AddressWidth
   WScript.Echo "Data Width: " & objProcessor.DataWidth
   WScript.Echo "Family: " & objProcessor.Family
   WScript.Echo "Maximum Clock Speed: " & objProcessor.MaxClockSpeed
Next
```

This isn't easy to use for a number of reasons. First, because it's VBScript, the commands can't be run interactively, which makes testing and debugging more difficult. Second, notice how an object is created that points to the WMI namespace and a WQL query is executed. This is the standard way to retrieve information via WMI in

VBScript. We then have to loop through the returned collection of objects. Finally, note how many lines are required to format the output. It may not be obvious at first glance, but we're interrogating two WMI classes in this script: `Win32_ComputerSystem` and `Win32_Processor`.

Now let's compare this with the PowerShell equivalent. We use `Get-WMIObject` and choose the class we'll read. We then use `Format-List` to select and display the properties. We then repeat for the second class.

The display from PowerShell may be marginally less elegant, but I'll gladly trade that for ease of use. The great advantage of PowerShell is that these commands can be used interactively as well as in a script. Give me ease of use and less typing every time. See listing 3.6.

Listing 3.6   WMI in PowerShell

```
Get-WmiObject -Class Win32_ComputerSystem |
Format-List Name, SystemType, NumberOfProcessors

Get-WmiObject -Class Win32_Processor |
Format-List Manufacturer, Name, Description, `
ProcessorID, AddressWidth, DataWidth, `
Family, MaxClockSpeed
```

3.5.1   *Understanding WMI*

One thing to be aware of with WMI is that it's evolving. New WMI functionality is available in Windows Vista, for instance, that isn't available in earlier versions of Windows. Full information on WMI is available in the WMI SDK (see appendix E). WMI is organized as classes within namespaces. The default namespace is `root\cimv2`. This will be used throughout the book unless stated otherwise; for example chapter 9 makes extensive use of the `root\MicrosoftDNS` namespace. To view the installed namespaces (they'll change depending on the applications and services installed), use PowerGUI or the WMIExplorer.

WMIExplorer looks like a Windows application (to be accurate it's a Windows Forms application). But it's not a compiled .NET executable; it's a PowerShell script. This emphasizes just how much versatility is available through PowerShell. WMIExplorer shows that you can write applications like this in PowerShell. Whether you should do so is a different argument. WMIExplorer was created by Marc van Orsouw (MoW) and can be downloaded from his blog (see appendix E).

> **NOTE**   In the examples in this section, I'll assume you're entering the code in PowerShell yourself as you read about WMI. The resultsets produced by some of these examples are too long to include in the book. These examples are all run on the local machine. Use the `ComputerName` parameter to specify a remote machine.

PowerShell has excellent WMI support via the `Get-WMIObject` cmdlet. In order to see the scope of WMI, try typing the following:

```
Get-WMIObject -list
```

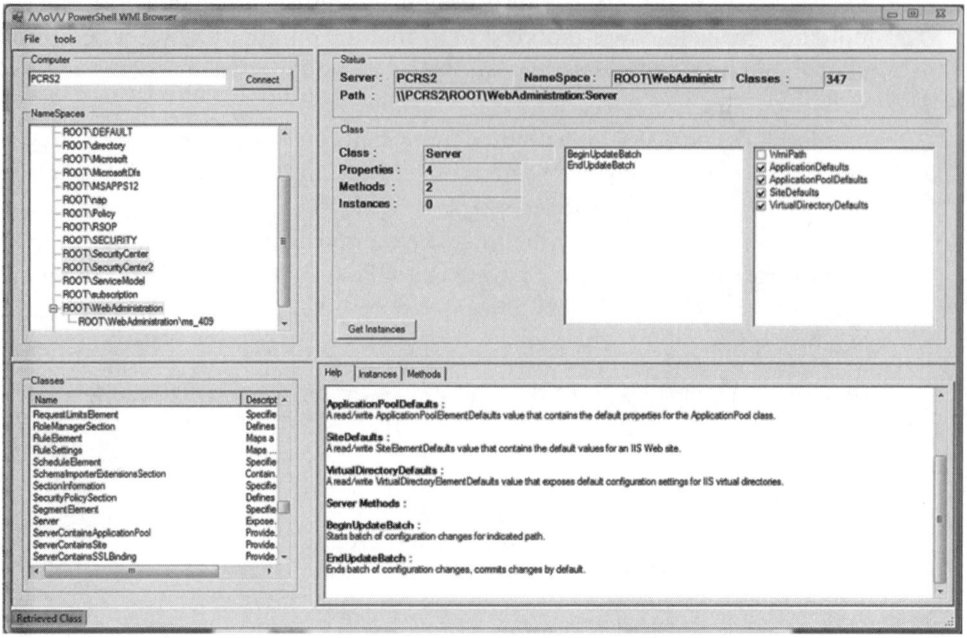

Figure 3.6   WMIExplorer enables you to browse the WMI namespaces and classes on your system, the instances that currently exist, and how to use the WMI methods and properties.

You'll see a long list of WMI classes scrolling by. Many of the class names start Win32_. To make the list more manageable, try:

```
Get-WMIObject -list |
 Where-Object{$_.Name -like "*OperatingSystem*"}
```

This becomes even easier in v2, as we can use:

```
Get-WmiObject -List *OperatingSystem*
```

Either option will return a list of the classes containing *OperatingSystem* in their names. Win32_OperatingSystem looks like it could be interesting:

```
Get-WMIObject -class Win32_OperatingSystem
```

On its own, it doesn't seem to return much. Time to fall back on our old friend, Get-Member:

```
Get-WMIObject -Class Win32_OperatingSystem | Get-Member
```

That's much better. Lots of interesting properties become available now.

> **NOTE**   This is another example of the default formatter restricting the output. When using any PowerShell cmdlet, it's usually a good idea to test it with Get-Member to see if there's any more information to be displayed.

Get-WMIObject has a -Property parameter that lets you select which properties to display. Alternatively, Select could be used. Let's see how much we can do within Get-WMIObject:

```
Get-WMIObject -Class Win32_OperatingSystem `
-property TotalVirtualMemorySize, FreeVirtualmemory, LastBootUpTime
```

The TotalVirtualMemorySize and FreeVirtualmemory properties are returned as kilobytes. The LastBootUpTime is in WMI date format. To convert it to a more readable format, the .NET System.Management.ManagementDateTimeConverter class can be used as shown in Listing 3.7.

Listing 3.7   Retrieving LastBootTime using WMI

```
PS> $t = Get-WMIObject -Class Win32_OperatingSystem |
>> Select LastBootUpTime
>>
PS> $t

LastBootUpTime
--------------
20070406072653.500000+060
```

When converted to a more readable format we get this:

```
PS> Get-WMIObject -Class Win32_OperatingSystem `
-property LastBootUpTime | foreach {
[System.Management.ManagementDateTimeConverter]::
ToDateTime($_.LastBootUpTime) }

06 April 2007 07:26:53
```

The PowerShell Community Extensions contain scripts that can be included in the pipeline for performing this calculation. It'd be a simple matter to include the calculation in a cmdlet that was written to access this information. Alternatively, you could use this:

```
PS> $w1 = Get-WMIObject -Class Win32_OperatingSystem
PS> $w1.ConvertToDateTime($w1.LastBootUpTime)
08 April 2007 10:05:35
```

Very neat. There's an awful lot of functionality in PowerShell and WMI. Every time you think you understand something, you quickly learn there's more to be discovered. WMI contains a wealth of information about your systems. The information returned from WMI is the sort that's easily displayed by PowerGadgets or PowerGUI, as we'll see in chapter 4. In a lot of cases, the only way to access this information is to use WMI. There's no other way to get it, in which case we need the easiest way possible: PowerShell.

The important thing to remember is that PowerShell is .NET-based, as we saw in the first part of this chapter, and underneath the cmdlets and accelerators we're dealing with .NET classes. PowerShell gives us a layer of abstraction that hides some of the more nasty programming stuff. The following examples will use Win32_Process and Notepad, as it's straightforward and definitely something you'll be able to try at home.

3.5.2   *WMI type accelerators*

As we have already seen, `Get-WmiObject` is used to read information about, and in some cases perform actions upon, an existing WMI object. Let's create a WMI object pointing to an existing and open instance of Notepad and use `Get-Member` on it:

```
PS> $g = Get-WmiObject -Class Win32_Process
-Filter "Name = 'notepad.exe'"
PS> $g | Get-Member
   TypeName: System.Management.ManagementObject#root\cimv2\Win32_Process
```

We see that it returns a `System.Management.ManagementObject` of a `Win32_Process` WMI class.

> **NOTE** The output in the example is truncated for brevity. It's also possible to use `$g.GetType() | Format-List`, which returns a lot of information about the .NET object. `GetType` doesn't appear in the list of methods returned in this instance.

If you look at the properties and methods shown by `Get-Member`, there's no method to create an instance.

It's like picking a cup of coffee off a counter where there are many cups of coffee. You can drink it but you can't use it to create another cup. My analogy breaks down slightly, as there's a `clone()` method if we drop into the base object, but that appears to clone the object rather than a new instance of Notepad, so we'll leave that to one side.

[WMICLASS]

If we now look at `[WMIClass]` and use `Get-Member` on it:

```
PS> $c = [WMIClass]'Win32_Process'
PS> $c | Get-Member
   TypeName: System.Management.ManagementClass#ROOT\cimv2\Win32_Process
```

We see that we're using a different .NET class, namely `System.Management.ManagementClass`, which shows us there's a way to create a new instance of the class via the `CreateInstance()` method. `Get-Member` shows us a `Create()` method, and the following:

```
PS> $c.psbase | Get-Member
```

shows us the `CreateInstance()` method that matches the .NET documentation. Either will work. The following:

```
$c.Create("Notepad.exe")
```

is the simplest to use and will create a new process running Notepad.

Using `[WMIClass]` is a shortcut for using `New-Object`:

```
$x = New-Object -TypeName System.Management.ManagementClass
-ArgumentList "Win32_Process"
$x | Get-Member
$x.Create("notepad.exe")
```

To summarize, `Get-WmiObject` is a PowerShell cmdlet to work with the `System.Management.ManagementObject` .NET class, which allows you to read information from and interact with existing instances of WMI classes. `[WMIClass]` is a shortcut (or accelerator) for creating new instances of WMI classes. PowerShell v2 streamlines the process to a degree, in that the `Invoke-WmiMethod` can do it all in one line:

```
Invoke-WmiMethod -Class Win32_Process -Name Create`
-ArgumentList "notepad.exe"
```

Having shown how a new WMI object can be created using `Invoke-WmiMethod`, we need to consider how to remove a WMI object. PowerShell v2 supplies a `Remove-WMI-Object` cmdlet. This takes a WMI path to identify the individual object, or you can use `Get-WMIObject` to identify objects and pipe the result to `Remove-WMIObject`.

WARNING *Make sure you're not using Notepad* when you run the next piece of code:

```
Get-WmiObject -Class Win32_process -Filter "Name='notepad.exe'" |
Remove-WmiObject
```

`Remove-WMIObject` doesn't support the `-whatif` and `-confirm` parameters, so best practice is to use `Get-WmiObject` and the filter capability to identify the correct object before piping to `Remove-WMIObject`.

NOTE `Invoke-WMIMethod` and `Remove-WMIObject` are new cmdlets introduced in PowerShell v2.

[WMISEARCHER]

PowerShell and WMI make a powerful, and in some cases frightening combination. One of the parameters on the `Get-WMIObject` cmdlet is `-filter`. This allows a *WMI Query Language (WQL)* syntax clause to be used to further tighten the search. For example:

```
$s = Get-WmiObject -class Win32_Service
$s
```

returns a list of services, including the `StartMode` and the current state, whether or not it's running.

NOTE `Get-Service` doesn't return the `StartMode`, so we need to use WMI if we want to change how services start.

We saw WQL being used in the VBScript example in listing 3.5. Take a moment to compare how it was used there to what we're doing here.

We can concentrate on a particular service like this:

```
PS> $s = Get-WmiObject -class Win32_Service -filter 'Name = "BITS"'
PS> $s

ExitCode : 0
Name : BITS
ProcessId : 1100
StartMode : Auto
State : Running
Status : OK
```

Note that the `StartMode` is set to auto. Piping $s into get-member, `$s | get-member`, returns a long list of properties and a number of methods, including:

- `PauseService`
- `ResumeService`
- `StartService`
- `StopService`

Looking at the list of cmdlets with `Service` as the noun, you'll no doubt recognize that the methods I just listed are available as cmdlets. This is where WMI becomes frightening:

```
$s.stopservice()
$s = Get-WmiObject -class Win32_Service -filter 'Name = "BITS"'
$s
ExitCode : 0
Name : BITS
ProcessId : 0
StartMode : Auto
State : Stopped
Status : OK
```

Note that we have to refresh the object to see that the service has stopped. If you're running Vista you'll need to start PowerShell with elevated privileges. Using the WMI methods like this, *there are no WHATIF or CONFIRM* options like you get with `Stop-Service`. Be very careful with WMI methods because you don't have a safety net.

> **WARNING**   Using the methods on WMI classes means we're working with the COM object (even if it's in a .NET wrapper). The PowerShell cmdlets were written to explicitly give you a safety net. WMI wasn't.

`[WMISearcher]` is an accelerator for `System.Management.ManagementObjectSearcher`. It searches WMI classes for particular instance(s) based on a WQLquery. WQL is an SQL-like language specifically used to search WMI instances.

```
$query = `
[WMISearcher]`
'Select * from Win32_Process where Name = "notepad.exe"'
$query.Get() | Select Name, Processid | Format-Table -AutoSize
```

Alternatively the following could be used:

```
Get-WmiObject -Class Win32_Process -Filter 'Name = "notepad.exe"' |
Select Name, Processid | Format-Table -AutoSize
```

or the following:

```
Get-WmiObject -Query `
'Select * from Win32_Process where Name = "notepad.exe"' |
Select Name, Processid | Format-Table -AutoSize
```

If you need to search WMI for particular information, you have choices which come down to what sort of object you want to return. If you want to work with the object, use

Get-WMIObject, but if you only want to view information you could use [WMISearcher].

> **NOTE** This is a perfect example of PowerShell delivering information by multiple means. If you look on the internet for using WMI as a search tool, you'll find multiple ways of retrieving the information (they're all on my blog!) as shown here. Which one you should use is determined by what you want to achieve and to a certain degree personal preference. In administrative scripting, the answer is everything. There are no points for style and artistic interpretation!

[WMI]

There's one last WMI accelerator to look at-[WMI]-which is an accelerator for System. Management.ManagementObject. This is the same object type that Get-WMIObject returns. [WMI] gets an object representing an existing WMI object.

We start with using Get-WmiObject to create a variable representing a WMI object.

```
$w1 = Get-WmiObject -Class Win32_Process -Filter "Name = 'notepad.exe'"
$w1 | Get-Member
```

If we try to emulate this with [WMI], we start to run into some issues. The only path that I could get to work was:

```
$w2 = [WMI]'root\cimv2:Win32_Process.Handle="4112"'
$w2 | get-member
```

I tried name, description, and other candidates, but none seemed to work. The reason is because when using [WMI], we can only create an object using a property that's designated as a key for that WMI class. Jeffrey Snover explains how this works on the PowerShell Team blog: http://blogs.msdn.com/powershell/archive/2008/04/15/wmi-object-identifiers-and-keys.aspx. He provides a function to determine the key for a particular WMI class. For a variant of the function, see listing 3.8.

Listing 3.8 Determining the key for a WMI class

```
PS> $t = [WMIClass]"Win32_Process"
PS> $t.psbase.properties |
Select-Object @{Name="PName";Expression={$_.name}} `
-ExpandProperty Qualifiers |
>>Where-Object {$_.Name -eq "key"} |
>>ForEach-Object {$_.Pname}
```

Running the code in the listing will return Handle as the key.

> **NOTE** In PowerShell v2, we don't need to use the psbase qualifier.

We start by creating a new instance of a WMI class, and we need to examine the properties. There are two important points in the way we use Select-Object here. The first is the use of -ExpandProperty, which takes a multivalued property such as an array and enables us to work with the individual values. The second involves

@{Name="PName";Expression={$_.name}}, which is a calculated property. It's created as a hash table (see section 2.4.2) and the name from the expanded list of qualifiers is used as the value in the array. We then filter on key—we're looking for a property that has the value key in its qualifiers.

The following is the full list of information for the Handle property:

```
PS> $t.psbase.properties | Where-Object{$_.Name -eq "Handle"} |
>> Format-List

Name        : Handle
Value       :
Type        : String
IsLocal     : False
IsArray     : False
Origin      : CIM_Process
Qualifiers  : {CIMTYPE, key, MaxLen, read}
```

Alternatively the object could be created like this:

```
$y = [WMI]""
$y
$y.psbase.Path = '\\PCRS2\root\cimv2:Win32_Process.Handle="4112"'
```

Comparing the results of these three techniques, we get:

```
Compare-Object -ReferenceObject $w1 -DifferenceObject $w2
Compare-Object -ReferenceObject $w1 -DifferenceObject $y
```

Both of these comparisons return nothing, which indicates that the objects are the same.

Looking at creating this with .NET:

```
$z = New-Object -TypeName System.Management.ManagementObject `
-ArgumentList '\\.\root\cimv2:Win32_Process.Handle="4112"'
$z | Get-Member
Compare-Object -ReferenceObject $w1 -DifferenceObject $z
```

Again, the same object is created, and again we need to use Handle as the key to creation. The object creation works when we do:

```
$t = Get-WmiObject -Class Win32_process -Filter 'name="notepad.exe"'
```

Because we need to know the path before we can use [WMI], it may be easier to use Get-WmiObject instead. Having discovered what the key is for a particular WMI class, we need to return all current instances and their key values before attempting to create the object. This introduces extra stages into the process.

3.6   *Summary*

PowerShell by itself is a powerful and versatile tool for administering Windows systems. When we start to extend its reach by teaming it up with .NET, ADSI, WMI, and COM, we've suddenly created a toolset that's definitely going to meet our needs for automating the administration of Windows systems.

.NET brings the full power of Microsoft's latest programming frameworks. Power-Shell needs to load some parts of the framework; other parts can be loaded optionally. We may not want to write Windows applications in PowerShell, but the functionality is there for when we need it. We'll return to .NET when we start working with IIS and SQL Server.

COM is an older way of creating programs, but is still in use in many Microsoft applications. It's accessed in a similar way to .NET (ease of use is a big plus for PowerShell) and opens up applications such as Internet Explorer and the Office suite to our scripts.

ADSI is a way to work with Active Directory. PowerShell and Active Directory seem to be a messy combination with too many options. We saw a good way of working with them, and this will be applied in later chapters. Searching Active Directory has become much easier and faster with PowerShell. This will also be explored in further chapters.

WMI is a mainstay of Windows administration. With PowerShell, this is easier to use and much, much easier to output. PowerShell has made WMI a tool that's automatically included in the thought process rather than a tool of last resort. .NET and ADSI will be featured in particular chapters, but we'll repeatedly use WMI through much of the rest of the book.

There's a common theme here. PowerShell has taken the existing administrator's tools and made them easier to use, and in some cases given us access to more powerful alternatives. This toolset forms the foundation of our scripting experience. There are some third-party additions to the toolset; we'll consider them and some best practices next.

Automating administration

PowerShell is fun, and being able to rattle off a script to do something in a fraction of the time we'd take manually is cool, but what benefits do we actually get? In other words, why are we doing this? This point hasn't been emphasized in the previous chapters, but the underlying theme has been that PowerShell is all about automation. Automation brings speed, efficiency, repeatability, and consistency. These are good things in their own right. When added to other things that you can do because of the time you've saved through your automation efforts, the benefits become really worthwhile.

Windows has traditionally been administered through the GUI. PowerShell is all about the command line. We'll look at administration styles and how PowerShell is blurring the boundaries. The introduction of PowerShell into the administration tool-set brings about automation almost as a matter of course.

Automation = scripting?

One school of thought says that we're automating only if the work is being done by a scheduled task. Though that's applicable for a number of tasks such as backup or data loads, should we be performing all administration in this way?

My view is that scripting is automation. We're getting the machine to do the grunt work for us. This frees up time we can spend on other tasks. Do we want to limit ourselves to scheduled tasks? Seems like a restriction we don't need.

I think we have a spectrum of activity from manual performance through scripting to scheduled tasks. Pick where you need to be for a particular task.

Most administrators will view automation as writing scripts. One big question is how do you start writing scripts? PowerShell can be used in exactly the same way interactively as in scripts. That enables us to start developing at the command prompt and to turn our interactive work into scripts that we can reuse and share with others. One name for this is *ad hoc* development.

NOT A DEVELOPMENT METHODOLOGY　Ad hoc development is not a new development methodology. It's simply the way that many administrators work. Define a problem, find a solution, and refine it as needed. Most, if not all, administrators aren't professional developers. They want, and need, enough code to solve their problems. Everything else is usually regarded as overhead.

There's a collective body of knowledge, known as *best practice*, that can be applied to developing and using PowerShell scripts. Most of this is common sense. It's worth reviewing this section, as there may be some ideas that will make your development easier.

　PowerShell doesn't and can't exist in a vacuum. There is a large, and continually expanding, range of tools that can be used with PowerShell. This ranges from editors, to GUI front-ends for PowerShell, to additional cmdlets and providers in the form of snapins or modules. Many of these tools are free downloads that can make administration much easier. We'll be using many of them in future chapters, in addition to seeing how to perform the tasks with scripts using basic Power-Shell functionality.

　Keeping the environment safe is a prime directive for IT administrators. The number of security threats seems to grow every day. PowerShell is more secure than previous scripting environments due to some of the design decisions that were taken. We'll round off this chapter with a general review of PowerShell security, specifically looking at code signing of scripts. Code signing involves certificates, which some administrators view as a scary subject. You don't need to build a full certificate-based infrastructure to enable code signing. We'll take the mystery out of this subject so that it's something you'll be able to do in your environment. We'll start with our original thought: why do we want to do all this?

4.1   Benefits of automation

A long time ago (in a school far, far away), I remember a physics lesson where we were told that simple machines such as levers and pulleys didn't necessarily reduce work, but they did make it easier to perform. The same concept applies to the automation of administration.

Certainly, learning PowerShell and its associated tools takes time and effort. Writing scripts takes time and effort. Why should you bother when you can use the GUI tools to do your job? The answer is that you're saving time and effort over the long term. The payback from learning PowerShell and writing scripts is that you can perform routine tasks more quickly and easily. This enables you to spend more time on other, potentially more interesting things, as well as making your life easier. You can even improve your high score at PowerShell Space Invaders (http://ps1.soapyfrog.com/2007/01/02/space-invaders/).

I have a friend who works in the IT department of a major British university. Every year the University has 7,000+ new students for whom new accounts, mailboxes, and so on need to be created. They have a similar number of accounts that need to be removed due to students leaving at the end of their courses. The PowerShell script would take more than 15 hours to run if it were performed as a single batch. That's a lot of computing effort. Could this work be done manually? It could, but it'd take a lot of manpower and wouldn't be finished in an acceptable time frame. The automated process creates a single user in 8-9 seconds, which is much faster than the task could be performed manually. The effort to create one user, that is, starting the script, is the same as creating 1,000 or more. This is a prime example of where automation is needed to make the task manageable. I wouldn't want to do all that manually! The overall time can also be reduced by processing the data in batches from multiple workstations.

There's also a cost benefit to automating administration. A number of analysts have examined the costs of running an IT infrastructure. The numbers vary, but a good estimate is that at least 70% of the cost of running an IT infrastructure is spent on maintenance and keeping the lights on. Though automating your administration won't necessarily have a huge impact on that figure, it can help to reduce it.

Automation saves us time, effort, and money that we can spend elsewhere. Before we jump into developing scripts, let's review how we actually administer our systems to see where automation can help us and how we go about introducing automation.

4.2   Administration styles

When you think of Windows administration, do you automatically reach for a GUI tool? The common perception of Windows administration is that it's a GUI-based activity. Indeed, UNIX administrators have often pointed out the lack of a good interactive shell on Windows compared to their environment.

Figure 4.1 shows three styles of administration:

Figure 4.1 Administrative styles

- GUI
- Interactive
- Script

GUI is the style that we're used to with Windows. The MMC brings some uniformity, but each version of an application brings changes in the way we use the GUI tools. Features move around the tools, making it sometimes difficult to transition to the new version.

Interactive administration means working at the command prompt(using cmd.exe) using the numerous tools available. Each tool is independent and outputs text, making it difficult to pass information between them. Since Windows 2000, new command-line tools have been added with each new version of Windows. There's no commonality between the syntax of these tools, making learning to use them more difficult.

Scripting for administration has tended to mean VBScript on Windows. This can't be used interactively, which can make development and testing awkward and slow. It hasn't been seen as a mainstream activity for administrators.

PowerShell spans these three styles and makes them a continuum rather than three separate styles. Exchange Server 2007 was the first major product to incorporate PowerShell. It's widely admired in the PowerShell community as the ideal model for building PowerShell support into a product. The Exchange Management Console (GUI) was designed to sit above PowerShell. In fact, the Exchange cmdlets were created first and then the GUI was built to use them. When you perform an action in the GUI, it uses the Exchange PowerShell cmdlets to perform the action. What makes this GUI special is that it then shows you the script it ran.

In Exchange 2007 RTM version, approximately 80% of the administrative tasks can be performed in the GUI. Even though this figure rises with subsequent releases we have to use PowerShell interactively for a significant part of our administration tasks. We can start to learn how to write PowerShell scripts by using the examples the GUI creates for us. We've covered all three of our styles and still remained in PowerShell. One of the real benefits here is that the learning process continues across the three styles. Examining the scripts the GUI creates will help you learn to use PowerShell at the command line.

Unfortunately, not all products have this level of PowerShell support. In order to support other products, we'll have to start writing scripts, which means we need to look at development.

4.3 *Development for administrators*

This section isn't designed to turn you into a developer or introduce a "new development methodology"! IT administrators and developers never seem to talk as much as they should, and they have different outlooks on life. Our goal as administrators is "keep the lights on" and make sure that our systems are running as efficiently as possible. Automation is our way of doing that job easier.

There are a large number of development methodologies in use. Those approaches don't really meet the needs for administrators. What can happen is part of a task is automated because it's easy to do so or a script is found that gives a head start. We then start thinking about how we can extend that script to give us more functionality and do more of the task. As we build up the script, we're extending the reach of automation and making time to automate more of our work.

People come to automation in different ways, but however you arrive at the thought of automating your work, at some stage you'll be developing scripts. The way this thought process happens has been labeled *ad hoc* development.

4.3.1   Ad hoc development

Ad hoc development is a topic that keeps coming up around PowerShell. I first heard it in a talk by Jeffrey Snover, the architect of PowerShell. It has since been picked up and applied to the way administrators develop scripts. It's ad hoc because the development process doesn't necessarily follow a standard development lifecycle.

Administrators will often reach for their scripting tools when there's a task that has to be repeated many times—the "I need 1,000 user accounts created by tonight" type of scenario. Alternatively, the administrator has a routine task that may not take long to perform, but is tedious, so she creates a script to perform the task more efficiently. When using VBScript, our administrator would need to think through everything about the script—design it in effect, write it, test it, and start using it in production. With PowerShell, we can work through a number of stages:

- Working interactively
- Writing a function
- Writing a script
- Make the script production ready
- Possibly create a cmdlet (or an advanced function in PowerShell v2)

This is ad hoc development. We're moving our functionality through an improvement cycle as we need to, rather than to any set plan. As with everything in PowerShell, it all starts interactively at the PowerShell prompt.

INTERACTIVE

One of the great strengths of PowerShell is that the interactive experience is the same as the scripting experience. In other words, if you can do it in a script, you can do it interactively and vice versa. When designing PowerShell, it was assumed that 80% of the users would be working interactively rather than writing scripts, which is one reason why the execution policy defaults to `Restricted`.

All administration scripting begins with a task. For the sake of discussion, we need to know which processes are using the most CPU resources on a machine. Ah! That's easy, you say. We can use `Get-Process`, as in listing 4.1.

Listing 4.1 Get-Process

```
PS> Get-Process

Handles  NPM(K)    PM(K)     WS(K) VM(M)   CPU(s)     Id ProcessName
-------  ------    -----     ----- -----   ------     -- -----------
    166       6     3128      8208    64               592 AcPrfMgrSvc
  29877       9    46200     51176   139              3180 AcSvc
     72       4     2812      6644    56     0.05      4468 ACTray
     74       4     3052      6788    57     0.22      4476 ACWLIcon
     27       1      364      1624    11               580 AEADISRV
    104       3     1284      4184    36              1124 Ati2evxx
    128       3     1932      6320    51              1564 Ati2evxx
    111       4    11240     14012    44              1336 audiodg
     81       3     1288      4044    39     0.12      5120 AwaySch
    853       6     1768      5244    96               600 csrss
```

Listing truncated for brevity

This is good, but we have to scroll up and down the list to work out which processes are causing the most CPU usage. So, let's move this on a stage and sort the results:

```
Get-Process | Sort-Object CPU
```

That doesn't quite do what we want, as the default sort direction is ascending, which puts the interesting results at the bottom of the list. Let's add the -Descending switch, as in listing 4.2.

Listing 4.2 Get-Process with sorted output

```
PS> Get-Process | Sort-Object CPU -Descending

Handles  NPM(K)    PM(K)     WS(K) VM(M)   CPU(s)     Id ProcessName
-------  ------    -----     ----- -----   ------     -- -----------
    385      21    30612     72312   260   458.75     2000 WINWORD
   1049      55    85284     83176   316   247.64     4168 wlmail
    137       6    42608     76796   140   176.17     3280 dwm
    825      37    46348     68388   279    76.08     4120 explorer
    684      86    23944      5776   218    70.47     5188 GROOVE
    772      36    35000     27624   222    46.55     5164 msnmsgr
    144       6     5272      8616    74    45.52     4568 rundll32
    199       8     5904     11472    90    34.26     5152 ipoint
    347      12     7252     11748    90    14.99     4244 MSASCui
    502      13    37716     39304   185     3.31     5420 powershell
    400       9    10136     11260    86     2.81     3728 taskeng
    372      10    11448     17320    98     1.54     5112 cssauth
     64       3     1736      4740    60     1.34     4544 EZEJMNAP
     54       3     1316      7728    62     0.41     3824 notepad
```

Listing truncated for brevity

This is more like it; we can see the processsest we're interested in. The next stage is to reduce the output, as we're only really interested in the top four processes for CPU usage. See listing 4.3.

Listing 4.3   Top four CPU using processes

```
PS> Get-Process | Sort-Object CPU -Descending | Select-Object -First 4

Handles  NPM(K)   PM(K)    WS(K) VM(M)   CPU(s)     Id ProcessName
-------  ------   -----    ----- -----   ------     -- -----------
    366      20   30436    72184   256   465.91   2000 WINWORD
   1049      55   85284    83176   316   247.71   4168 wlmail
    137       6   42608    76796   140   177.72   3280 dwm
    813      36   46084    67776   272    76.08   4120 explorer
```

By now, we have something that starts to deliver value. A simple command-line script delivers the information we need. Or not.

The next problem is that the recipient of this information needs the information in minutes of CPU usage rather than seconds, and only wants to see the process and its CPU usage. Format-Table can be used to display a subset of the data, but we don't have the CPU time in minutes. Format-Table has the capability to use calculated fields.

A *calculated field* is a hash table that contains a Label key to hold the name of the calculated field. This is the name that'll be displayed in the table header. The second key is an expression that's evaluated for each object passed into Format-Table.

SELECT-OBJECT   We can also create calculated fields in Select-Object. Name is used instead of Label. In PowerShell v2 Name can be used in both cases.

In listing 4.4, we take the CPU time and divide it by 60 to give us our CPU usage in minutes. Note that we need to use $_ to represent the object when performing the calculation.

Listing 4.4   CPU usage in minutes

```
PS> Get-Process | Sort-Object CPU -Descending | Select -First 4 |
Format-Table Name, @{Label="CPU(Min)"; Expression={$_.CPU/60}} -AutoSize

Name        CPU(Min)
----        --------
WINWORD  8.04523157166667
wlmail      4.212027
dwm      3.21804062833333
explorer 1.31326841833333
```

This is good, except the formatting on the CPU display is untidy. Let's see if we can straighten it up a bit, as shown in listing 4.5.

Listing 4.5   CPU usage in minutes (tidy)

```
PS> Get-Process | Sort-Object CPU -Descending | Select -First 4 |
 Format-Table Name, @{Label="CPU(Min)";
 Expression={"{0:F3}" -f ($_.CPU/60)}} -AutoSize

Name     CPU(Min)
----     --------
WINWORD  8.142
wlmail   4.213
```

```
dwm       3.238
explorer 1.313
```

Perfect. All we did was change the calculated expression to `"{0:F3}" -f ($_.CPU/60)`. This uses the .NET string formatting functionality via the `-f` operator. In this example, we define a single field in our string `"{0}"`. We populate this field with the value to the right of the `-f` operator, in this case `($_.CPU/60)`. The `F3` part states that we want three decimal places to be displayed.

Instead of dividing the CPU value by 60, we could use the `TotalProcessorTime` property, which is a `TimeSpan` object.

```
PS> (get-process explorer).TotalProcessorTime | get-member
   TypeName: System.TimeSpan

   TypeName: System.TimeSpan

Name               MemberType Definition
----               ---------- ----------
Add                Method     System.TimeSpan Add(TimeSpan ts)
CompareTo          Method     System.Int32 CompareTo(TimeSpan value)
Duration           Method     System.TimeSpan Duration()
Equals             Method     System.Boolean Equals(Object value),
GetHashCode        Method     System.Int32 GetHashCode()
GetType            Method     System.Type GetType()
Negate             Method     System.TimeSpan Negate()
Subtract           Method     System.TimeSpan Subtract(TimeSpan ts)
ToString           Method     System.String ToString()
Days               Property   System.Int32 Days {get;}
Hours              Property   System.Int32 Hours {get;}
Milliseconds       Property   System.Int32 Milliseconds {get;}
Minutes            Property   System.Int32 Minutes {get;}
Seconds            Property   System.Int32 Seconds {get;}
Ticks              Property   System.Int64 Ticks {get;}
TotalDays          Property   System.Double TotalDays {get;}
TotalHours         Property   System.Double TotalHours {get;}
TotalMilliseconds  Property   System.Double TotalMilliseconds {get;}
TotalMinutes       Property   System.Double TotalMinutes {get;}
TotalSeconds       Property   System.Double TotalSeconds {get;}
```

In this case, our code would become:

```
Get-Process | Sort-Object CPU -Descending | Select -First 4 |
 Format-Table Name, @{Label="CPU(Min)";
Expression={"{0:F3}" -f ($_.TotalProcessorTime.TotalMinutes)}}
 -AutoSize
```

At the end of this, we've developed something that matches our requirements even though we hadn't fully defined those requirements to begin with.

> **NOTE** This is still one line of PowerShell, even though we span multiple lines in print! You can see from this where the attraction of the PowerShell "one-liner" comes from.

Even though it's only a single line of code, it's getting cumbersome to type in every time we want to run it. Didn't I tell you the customer has decided that he wants to see this information repeatedly throughout the day. I wouldn't want to keep typing that line of code into PowerShell. Let's turn it into a function, and then we can keep it in memory and rerun it as we require.

FUNCTIONS

We saw in chapter 2 that a function is a named script block that enables us to reuse code. Our PowerShell one-liner doesn't have any input parameters, so it becomes a simple function:

```
function get-topcpu {Get-Process | Sort-Object CPU -Descending |
Select -First 4 |
Format-Table Name,
@{Label="CPU(Min)"; Expression={"{0:F3}" -f
    ($_.TotalProcessorTime.TotalMinutes)}} -Autosize}
```

All we've done is use the `function` keyword, given the function a name, and placed our PowerShell code inside {}. The function is in memory and easily usable. Output is shown in listing 4.6.

Listing 4.6   Using a function to get top four CPU using processes

```
PS> get-topcpu

Name     CPU(Min)
----     --------
wlmail   0.326
explorer 0.249
dwm      0.187
WINWORD  0.177
```

Our function can be seen in the function drive (see section 1.3.4) by using `Get-ChildItem function:get*`. Using the code as a function is easier because tab completion works on the function name—type `get-t` and press the Tab key until `get-topcpu` appears. We could also set an alias for the function:

```
Set-Alias -Name c4 -Value get-topcpu
```

Typing `c4` at the PowerShell prompt now gives us our information. This is even better: we can type `c4` and get the data we need, but the function needs to be loaded into memory every time we start PowerShell. We could load it into our profile so it's automatically loaded when PowerShell starts. Now we have some real benefit. We can run this any time we need and we don't have to retype anything. We start to see some return on the time we invested in creating the function. In PowerShell v2, we could put it into a module (see appendix B). Alternatively we can turn it into a script.

SCRIPTS

The real advantage of scripts is that they store the code on disk between PowerShell sessions. You don't need to retype the code to reuse it, and you don't have to overload your profile. In this case, creating a script is as easy as:

```
PS> 'Get-Process | Sort-Object CPU -Descending | Select -First 4 |
Format-Table Name,
@{Label="CPU(Min)"; Expression={"{0:F3}" -f
    ($_.TotalProcessorTime.TotalMinutes)}}
-AutoSize' > get-topcpu.ps1
```

We take the line of PowerShell, surround it by ' (double quotes would mean we had to escape the quotes we were already using, which would be messy), and pipe it to a file called get-topcpu.ps1. PowerShell scripts always have a .ps1 extension. Our script is then accessed as .\get-topcpu.ps1, or we use *fullpath*\get-topcpu.ps1 if it's not in the current folder. We can share the script with other administrators in our organization, which multiples the benefits, or we could share it with the PowerShell community and spread the benefits across many more people.

PRODUCTION-READY

Our script does what we want, and we can run it as often as we need. At this stage, we have a script that contains only code. If we give the script to another administrator, or don't use it for a number of months, it may not be obvious what our script is doing. We'll have to spend some time working out what it does and how it works. That's wasting the time we spent on developing the script in the first place. We can do a number of things to make the script production-ready:

- Expand any aliases that we've used to make the script more readable
- Add comments and header
- Add error handling

Listing 4.7 shows our script with a header that includes a minimum set of information including author, date, and a brief description of the purpose of the script.

> **Listing 4.7 Production-ready script to retrieve top four CPU using processes**

```
## get-topcpu.ps1
## Richard Siddaway
## 10 August 2008
##
## Uses get-process and returns the top 4 cpu using
##  processes with the time in minutes
Get-Process | Sort-Object CPU -Descending | Select -First 4 |
Format-Table Name, @{Label="CPU(Min)"; Expression={"{0:F3}" -f
    ($_.TotalProcessorTime.TotalMinutes)}} -AutoSize
```

I deliberately didn't use any aliases while developing this to make it easier to follow, so all I've done is add a header section that lists the script name, who wrote it and when, and what it's supposed to do. Other possible actions are covered in section 4.4.

> **CODE EXAMPLES** All of the code examples in the book will show only the working part of the script. The "production-ready stuff" I'll leave to the reader to add so that it meets the requirements of your organization. It also makes the listings shorter and easier to read.

If you have a large script that would benefit from increased performance, you might want to turn it into a cmdlet, or get a friendly developer to do it for you. This would return us to the interactive stage of the cycle, where we can begin our ad hoc development again.

CMDLET
Writing a cmdlet involves using a .NET language, such as C#, to compile a DLL that can be added to your PowerShell environment as a PowerShell snapin for v1 or v2. Alternatively a PowerShell v2 module can be created for that environment. At this stage, you need to either learn how to work with .NET development tools or find a developer to do it for you. In either case, you've moved beyond the scope of this section and this book.

> **ADVANCED FUNCTIONS**   In PowerShell v2, we can create an advanced function. They can be thought of as a cmdlet written in PowerShell. This topic is covered in the appendix B.

In this section, we've looked at how we develop our scripts from simple interactive use of cmdlets to a PowerShell pipeline that gives us exactly the result we require. We then turned that PowerShell line of code into a function or script that we can store and reuse. Developing scripts is an activity that'll save us administrative effort in the future (and don't forget Space Invaders), but is only part of the story. We need to think about how we maintain those scripts.

4.3.2   *Lifecycle*

Everything in IT has a lifecycle. Servers are replaced when they're no longer powerful enough; software is upgraded when new versions are available or the current version is no longer supported. Even our favorite scripts may need to be reworked or replaced as the IT environment changes.

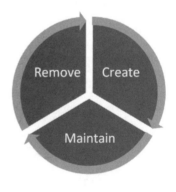

Scripts have a fairly simple lifecycle, as shown in figure 4.2.

We saw script creation in the previous section. Other sources of scripts include script repositories such as the Microsoft Technet Script Center, the PowerGUI site, the PowerShell community site, or individual blogs.

Figure 4.2   Script lifecycle

> **WARNING**   In my experience, any script obtained from the internet—or any other source—should be treated as suspect until proven otherwise. To restate the warning from the beginning of the book: this includes the scripts in this book! I've tested them in my environment, but I don't know and can't guarantee that they're 100% safe for your environment. It's your responsibility to test them.

Script maintenance is one area where we need to apply best practice. How many people and who do you want altering the scripts? How are you going to record changes to the scripts? Most importantly, how are you going the test those changes?

These are questions that can only be answered by you for your organization. As a guide, I'd severely limit the number of people who can modify production scripts (see section 4.6). Change records should be built into the script header as described in section 4.4. Testing should always be done on nonproduction systems. Virtual environments are ideal for this purpose.

One activity that's often overlooked is removing scripts that are no longer required. If you leave them on production systems, they could become a security risk. The scripts may be archived if you think you may need them, but ensure that the archive is protected.

While we're developing our scripts, we need tests to find errors in the script. It's worth keeping test data for big production scripts so that tests can be repeated when the scripts are updated. As an aside, think how much time you spend testing and debugging scripts compared to the original coding. Errors can still occur in scripts despite all this testing, and we need to know how to handle those errors.

4.3.3 *Error handling*

One method of handling errors in PowerShell v1 scripts is to use traps. No, we don't dig a big hole and wait for them to fall in. Well, not quite. PowerShell is an interactive shell as well as a scripting language, so we can type 1/2 at the prompt and get an answer of 0.5. If we type 1/$null, though, we get an error message:

```
Attempted to divide by zero.
At line:1 char:3
+ 1/ <<<< $null
```

This is a .NET exception (error). The way .NET handles errors is to pass them up the chain of routines and programs until they meet something that can handle them, or they reach the top of the stack and cause the program to fail.

If we want to handle errors in our PowerShell scripts, we need to use the trap statement, as shown in listing 4.8.

Listing 4.8 Using a trap

```
## this is a generic trap - that will catch any exception
trap { "Generic Trap"; continue; }

## this catches arithmetic exceptions
trap [ArithmeticException]{"Arithmetic Exception trapped"; continue }

## this is a specific trap for divide by zero
trap [DivideByZeroException]{ "Divide By Zero"; continue; }

$a = 1 / $null;

"Continuing Past the Exception"
```

We have three traps set on this script. The first is a general trap that catches any error not caught by a more specific error. The second catches arithmetic exceptions, and the third catches a specific subset of arithmetic errors—namely divide by zero errors. If we run this script, we'll see output like this:

```
Divide By Zero
Continuing Past the Exception
```

This gives us some better methods to handle the errors. We can make calls to functions or other scripts in the trap statement so we're not limited to printing error messages.

NOTE You won't find any PowerShell about files for trap, as they weren't included in the v1 help system.

The drawback to using traps is that you have to find and understand the .NET exceptions (errors) and code them into PowerShell. This isn't always easy.

PowerShell v2 introduces another method of handling errors—try-catch blocks:

```
Try {some PowerShell statements}
Catch {one or more exceptions}
Finally {some statements you ALWAYS want to be processed}
```

We wrap our PowerShell statements in a try{} script block. If an exception occurs, we execute the error handling code in the catch{} block. The finally{} block is executed regardless of whether there's an error.

PowerShell cmdlets have an -ErrorAction parameter that dictates how they react to errors. We can find some potential errors in our scripts by using the Test-Script cmdlet in version 2 of the PowerShell Community Extensions. Ideally, we want to avoid errors, and one way to do that is to make sure our scripts conform to best practice.

4.4   *Best practice*

Best practice means many things, and getting agreement on what's best practice can be difficult. In this section I'll offer some guidelines. How you apply them depends on how you work and how your organization functions.

4.4.1   *Guidelines*

Scripting can be more forgiving than programming in a .NET language. What we're looking for is a script we can develop in a short time that'll save us as much time and effort as possible in the future. Coding elegance isn't a necessity. There are no points for style and artistic interpretation when scripting!

GOOD SCRIPTS A good script is one that delivers the result you need in a sensible time frame. Good automation is an obvious benefit!

Some of the following guidelines are offered as things that I've found useful. Whether you adopt them is up to you. Other guidelines such as testing should be at the top of everyone's agenda. This isn't an exhaustive list of dos and don'ts, but more of a collection of observations and applied experience.

TESTING

Any script being used in a production environment needs to be tested. Sometimes you'll develop a script and test it as you create it. Other times, it can't be tested until the end of development. Some things to think about:

- Make sure that opening and closing braces match. Every script block in Power-Shell is enclosed in { }. Use an editor that enables you to line them up and visibly show the corresponding closing brace for a given opening brace.
- Check that the conditions on loops are correct, especially the end point.
- Use the –whatif parameter when testing.
- Use an editor with IntelliSense or one that supports tab completion. This prevents you from misspelling variable names.
- Make sure variables are initialized. You don't want to pick up a variable that has a value set somewhere else.

In Microsoft's 2008 Scripting Games, one of the challenges was to debug a script. It's worth looking at as an example of the things that can go wrong. The challenge can be found at http://www.microsoft.com/technet/scriptcenter/funzone/games/solutions08/bpssol07.mspx.

The more experience you get with finding problems in scripts, the easier it becomes and the faster your scripts get into production. That means they start earning their keep sooner and you get the benefits of producing them more quickly.

PowerShell editors such as the ISE in PowerShell v2, the PowerGUI editor, or PowerShell Plus can be used to debug scripts. The more formal debugging process they introduce will get your scripts into production more quickly and easily. It's worth taking the time to learn how to debug scripts using a tool such as these.

KEEP IT SIMPLE

As I said at the beginning of the section, you don't get points for elegance. Keep your coding simple, and if you have to put another line of code in to make it more understandable, do so. Avoid these things in scripts:

- Aliases (more on this later).
- Multiple statements on a line.
- Do loops (while or for are simpler and easier to get the counters right).
- Rewriting VBScript into PowerShell. There are a lot of scripts that literally rewrite VBScript using PowerShell. One of the worst I saw was using ADO recordsets in PowerShell for an Active Directory search.

Simple scripts are easier to understand, explain, and change when needed.

KNOW WHEN TO STOP

Script development can take on a life of its own. Getting everything perfect and polishing that line of code can become compulsive. How can I shave another second of runtime off the script?

Know when to stop.

If it works and runs in sensible time, it's good enough. Get the script into production and automate something else. You can always have another look at the script when you have more experience with PowerShell. In case you're wondering, this is said from personal experience. If I wasn't given deadlines, I'd still be writing this a year from now.

PORTABILITY

Do your scripts need to be portable? By that, I mean will they always be running in the same environment, or are you a consultant taking your scripts from client to client?

If you're always in the same environment, consider hard-coding data such as domain names unless you're working in a multidomain environment. It's one less step you need to code. One less step the script needs to execute. Runtime gains may not be noticeable, but coding may be slightly faster. In a static environment, you can also consider moving functionality into function libraries or modules. They'll always be there and accessible.

If you're constantly moving your scripts, you may want to derive things such as domain names in the script. Nothing is assumed then. Using function libraries may be more difficult.

COMMENTS

Comments can be guaranteed to start an argument! Some people loathe them and do everything they can to not use them. PowerShell treats any line starting with a "#" symbol as a comment. Anything on a line after a "#" symbol is treated as comment. In PowerShell v2 block comments can be used in which everything between <#.. ..#> is treated as a comment. This is useful for temporarily stopping a set of code from running when testing a script.

Comments do make your life simpler when you come back to look at the code. Consider:

- Use comments to describe what action functions perform.
- Document design decisions. Why you're doing something in a particular way can be as important as what's being done.
- Put comments on major blocks of code.
- Remember: comments can start after the code on a line.
- If you have long loops of many nested loops, consider using comments at the start and end of the loops to aid matching

PowerShell is self-documenting (to a large degree) because of the naming conventions for cmdlets, but you'll find comments a big help when you return to a script six months after writing it.

HEADER BLOCKS

In listing 4.7, we used a header block at the start of script. This should be used for all production scripts and should contain:

- Name of script
- Author
- Date of creation
- Purpose
- Change history including date, author of change, and a description of the change

CONFESSION   I won't be putting headers on the scripts you see in the book. This is to save space. In the lines I use for a header on every script, I can supply more scripts. There will be headers on the downloadable version of the scripts!

Using a header block will enhance the maintainability of your scripts. If you use functions in PowerShell v2, you can use the inline help for the same purpose.

VARIABLE NAMES

This one you'll see in all scripting books. Use descriptive variable names:

```
$cn
$compname
```

These two variables both refer to computer names. The second is much more obvious and makes things easier to read. Using $ComputerName is even more obvious, but takes more typing. If you use an editor that includes some kind of IntelliSense for variables, make them as long as you practically need.

There is a range of opinion regarding variable names. The options are to:

- Use camel case
- Use Hungarian notation
- Always capitalize

You'll find advice that supports these viewpoints and other advice that says not to use them. My advice is simple. Decide what you want to use and stick with it. It's better to be consistent than to try and fit somebody else's view of what's right.

Initialize variables in scripts. It does save problems when trying to debug scripts. Guess how I learned that one! It can help to initialize all variables at the beginning of the script, especially if it's a long script.

The other thing with variables is to be careful with the names when using functions, especially if the functions are in another file. You don't want to be in the position where you're inadvertently using the same variable name and causing problems with the value. Also check that you aren't using a PowerShell keyword or reserved word. A list of these can be found with Get-Help about_Reserved_Words.

SIGNING

Signing of scripts gives another level of security to your environment. If you only run scripts signed with an acceptable code-signing certificate, it will be harder for rogue scripts to be executed. This will make your environment more secure

Signing scripts adds another level of complexity to the development environment. Script signing is covered in the last section of this chapter. It's not as bad as you might think.

NO ALIASES

Don't use aliases in scripts. They make the script harder to read and potentially more difficult for someone else to work on. You need to be especially careful if you define your own aliases. How do you know whether another user has those aliases defined? Oops! Your script just broke. Best avoid them.

CODE FORMATTING

Code formatting generates almost as much disagreement as variable names. The important point is to make it readable. I usually indent my script blocks:

```
if ($x -ge 100) {
      Write-Host "$x more than 100"
      $x /= 100
}
else {
      Write-Host "$x less than 100"
      $x *= 100
}
```

This could be written:

```
if ($x -ge 100) {Write-Host "$x more than 100"; $x /= 100}
else { Write-Host "$x less than 100"; $x *= 100 }
```

The first example is more readable, and if there are more lines in the script block then it's even more important to indent it and use the whitespace sensibly. An editor that helps you do this is invaluable.

NAMING CONVENTIONS

This is another area where you'll find lots of dogma. My advice again is to decide what works for you and stick with it. I recommend that you follow the verb-noun naming convention for scripts and functions wherever possible and that you use the standard verbs. The noun should always be singular in PowerShell.

PARAMETERS

When passing parameters into a script or function, I recommend using a param statement rather than $args. When you use param, you have more control in that you can set the type and default value of the parameter.

SCRIPT STORAGE

Where to keep the scripts? In an organization with many people working on the scripts, you may want to use a source control mechanism. If you talk to a friendly developer, he may help you with that. Yes, I'm sure one of them must be friendly.

Keeping a central library of scripts and running them from there will prevent everyone from having a slightly different copy of the same script though PowerShell will treat the scripts as downloaded from the internet and prompt you regarding their use. Alternatively, have a small number of people create the scripts and have everyone use them via PowerGUI.

4.4.2   Functions and libraries

We've seen how functions can be a way to reuse code and make our scripts simpler. They also have the advantage of making script testing easier, as we can test whether a function works before incorporating it into a script. Easier testing means quicker testing, so we get the benefits sooner.

One issue that'll arise is that you'll find that you want to use the same function in a number of scripts. It's possible to have a copy of the function in each script that you create. This is easy to achieve using cut and paste. The advantage of adopting this approach is that the script is totally self-contained and portable. You can move the script to another machine and it'll run. The drawback to this approach is that you have copies of the same function in multiple scripts. If you want to update the function, you have to modify all the scripts. It'd be a bad idea to only update some of the functions. Using the same function name for what would be different functions will lead to mistakes happening.

The alternative is to create a library of functions or even multiple libraries. A library should be given a name such as Library*XXXXX*.ps1 where *XXXXX* describes the library. An example could be LibraryTime.ps1, which contains functions dealing with time and date processing. When the library is required, it can be dot-sourced: `. ./librarytime.ps1` from your script. Alternatively, the functions can be loaded when your profile is executed.

> **NOTE** PowerShell v2 has introduced the concept of modules, which extends the library idea in that some functions in the module can be hidden and only accessed by library functions rather than an external call.

Libraries have the advantage of reducing the maintenance requirements, as we only have a single copy of the function to work with. They do reduce the portability of the code, in that you need to move the library as well as the script that uses it to another machine. Alternatively, consider putting the library in a central location that can be easily accessed. It's only loaded once, so performance shouldn't be adversely affected.

> **RECOMMENDATION** Of the two approaches, the use of libraries should cause the least work and issues over the long run. I recommend the use of libraries (or modules) of functions over copying a function into many scripts.

Best practice can change, and I recommend subscribing to some of the blogs listed in appendix E (especially mine!) where you can keep up to date with current thinking. PowerShell v2 is having an impact on the way we use PowerShell, though the debates still continue.

I've mentioned several times that a number of vendors have produced products incorporating PowerShell or additional cmdlets for PowerShell. We'll quickly look at some of them before learning how to keep our PowerShell environment secure.

4.5 *Automation toolkit*

PowerShell can do a certain amount of automation by itself. In chapter 3, we saw that by using ADSI, WMI, .NET, and COM, we can increase the reach of PowerShell. Ideally we want to administer all of our systems with as much automation as possible. This means having PowerShell support built into the products we use.

Microsoft has made PowerShell part of its Common Engineering Criteria, so expect to see PowerShell support in all major products. Other vendors such as Citrix, IBM, and VMWare are using PowerShell to automate the administration of their products. The creators of administration tools such as Quest, and Special Operations Software are adding PowerShell to their products or even using PowerShell directly.

This section will give an overview of the tools that can be used to extend PowerShell even further. PowerShell is a new technology with a rapidly changing ecosystem. If there's a single point for news regarding PowerShell, it's the team blog at http://blogs.msdn.com/PowerShell/. I also try to keep abreast of the PowerShell news at http://richardsiddaway.spaces.live.com/. This list isn't complete and only includes things that I use on a regular basis. Other tools are available.

DOWNLOAD URLS   The URLs for downloading these tools can be found in appendix E.

A frequent question about PowerShell involves editors. What's wrong with Notepad? As a starter, it'll enable you to create and edit scripts. I still use it for viewing code, as it starts more quickly than other editors. When creating scripts, I tend to use a more sophisticated editor. The scripts in this book were prepared using PowerGUI, PowerShell ISE, or PowerShell Plus.

Microsoft created PowerShell and also has a range of add-ons available.

4.5.1 *Microsoft*

We discussed PowerShell v1 and its prerequisites in chapter 2. PowerShell v2 is also now available. PowerShell support is built into an increasing number of products.

The TechNet Script Center has a number of PowerShell-related features:

- Script repository—instant automation. Don't forget to test!
- Graphical help (v1).
- PowerShell Scriptomatic—creates WMI scripts.
- Cheat sheets and documentation.

PowerShell v2 has a graphical version, shown in figure 4.3. The graphical version of PowerShell will load your profile (note that if you alter the color settings in your profile an error will be reported). It consists of three panes. The upper pane is an editor that supports tab completion and will color-code your text. Graphical PowerShell supports up to eight PowerShell runspaces. You can work on a number of scripts simultaneously using the multitabbed editing space. Scripts, or part of scripts, can be run from within the editor.

The middle pane is an interactive PowerShell prompt (by default it's at the bottom but it can be moved) that supports the same color-coding and tab completion as the editor. Results from running scripts or using the interactive shell are displayed in the lower pane. A graphical help system rounds out the features. This can be accessed separately. I put a shortcut to it on my desktop.

Microsoft product teams are adding PowerShell support as new versions ship, or in some cases as additional downloads. The IIS team provides a PowerShell provider for

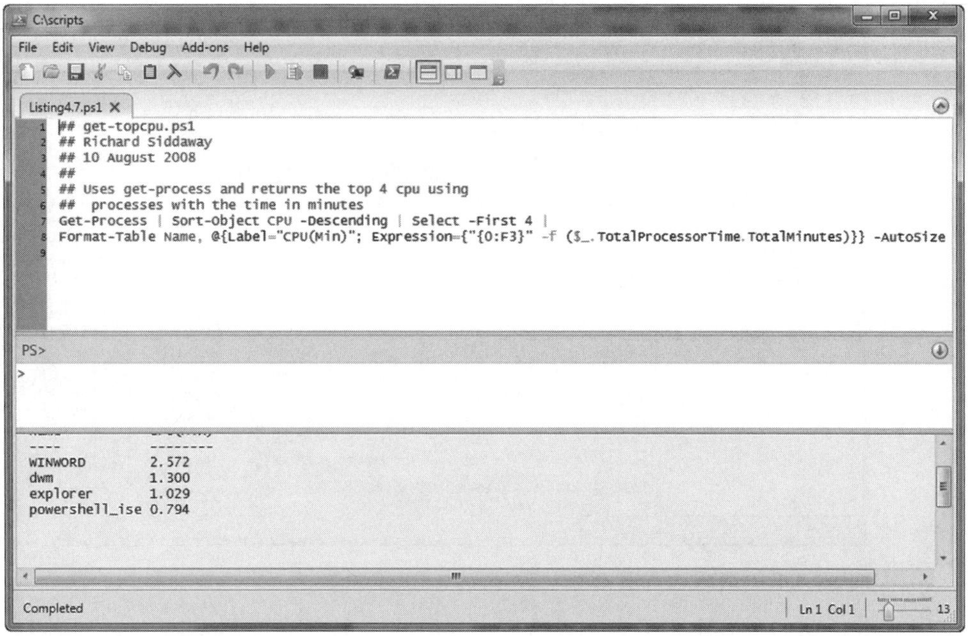

Figure 4.3   PowerShell ISE from PowerShell v2

IIS 7 (Windows 2008 and Windows Vista. It is also included by default in Windows Server 2008 R2). We'll be using the provider in chapter 13.

4.5.2   *Commercial*

Commercial in this section means that it's produced by a tools vendor rather than the PowerShell community. The tool may be free or you may need to buy it. This section is where new tools appear on a frequent basis. Check the URLs I listed earlier for the latest information.

POWERGUI

PowerGUI is a free download. Produced by Quest, it provides a GUI front end to PowerShell. Scripts can be stored and run in PowerGUI, with the results being output into a grid display. Further filtering and sortingcan occur on the displayed data. The script editor also works as a standalone editor, supplying color coding for your scripts and IntelliSense-like completion for PowerShell, .NET, WMI, and variables.

The nodes in the left pane can hold scripts or simple PowerShell commands. The actions at the right side allow further tasks to be performed. PowerGUI is completely customizable, as packs of scripts can be exported for later import into PowerGUI on another machine. A growing library of power packs can be downloaded from the powergui.org site to add to the default network, system, and Active Directory packs. Again, we get instant automation because someone else has done the work. Needs testing though!

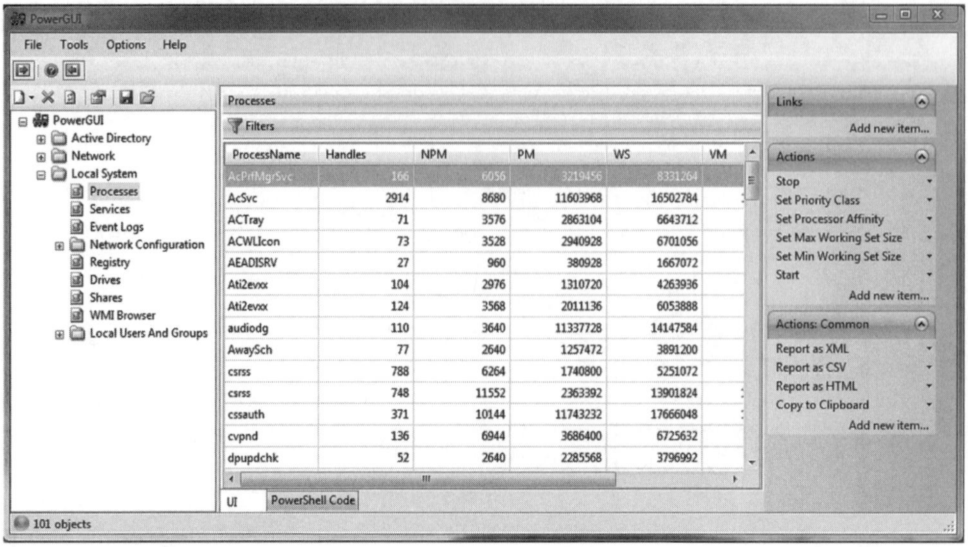

Figure 4.4   PowerGUI console

ACTIVE DIRECTORY CMDLETS

Quest also produces a snapin containing cmdlets for administering Active Directory. The cmdlets are a free download. The cmdlets are all concerned with Active Directory data—users, groups, computers, and so forth. Listing 4.9 shows an example.

Listing 4.9   Deriving nouns list from a snapin

```
PS> Get-Command |
Where-Object {$_.PsSnapin -like "Quest.ActiveRoles.ADManagement"} |
 Sort-Object Noun | Select-Object Noun -Unique

Noun
----
QADAttributeValue
QADComputer
QADGroup
QADGroupMember
QADObject
QADObjectSecurity
QADPasswordSettingsObject
QADPasswordSettingsObjectAppliesTo
QADPermission
QADPSSnapinSettings
QADRootDSE
QADService
QADUser
QARSAccessTemplate
QARSAccessTemplateLink
```

The basic Get-Command is filtered by using Where on the value of the snapin name (you don't want to see how many cmdlets are loaded on this machine!). We then sort on the noun name and select the unique set of nouns. PowerShell really is used to discover things about PowerShell, as we showed in chapter 2.

I'll be using these cmdlets in chapters 5, 10, and 11 when we discuss Active Directory but will be showing how to perform the task in a script as well, because some organizations don't allow the installation of add-ons like this.

One of the big tasks in managing Active Directory is working with Group Policy. We can download some cmdlets for that as well.

GROUP POLICY CMDLETS

SDMSoftware supplies commercial and free cmdlets to work with Group Policy via the GPMC. The free cmdlets can be used to administer Group Policy. The commercial cmdlets allow you to script the actual settings of the policies. Windows Server 2008 R2 also includes cmdlets for administering Group Policies.

POWERSHELL PLUS

PowerShell Plus is a development environment for PowerShell (as well as text, HTML, XML, VB.NET, and C) and provides access to an interactive shell by hosting PowerShell as seen in figure 4.4. IntelliSense-like support is available in the shell and when using the editor.

Scripts can be run from within the editor, with the results displayed in the hosted shell. Windows showing properties and variable values for debugging are visible as in Visual Studio. There's a button to run with elevated privileges, but it opens another

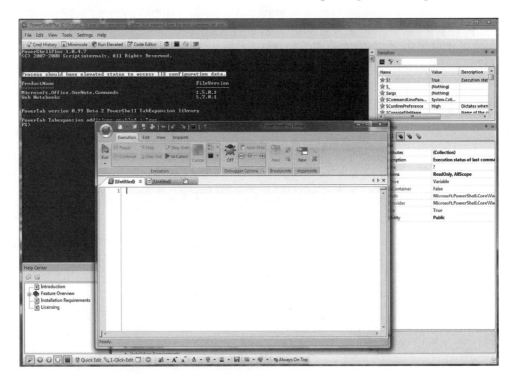

Figure 4.5   PowerShell Plus

instance of PowerShell Plus rather than elevating the current instance. PowerShell Plus is frequently updated.

4.5.3 *Community*

PowerShell has a thriving community with numerous blogs, vendors supplying free versions of cmdlets, community sites, and user groups. There are a lot of PowerShell-based projects on Codeplex.

CODEPLEX

CodePlex is Microsoft's open source hosting site. Yes, you read that correctly. It can be found at http://www.codeplex.com/. There are nearly 50 projects related to Power-Shell. A flavor of the range of projects on offer can be gained from this list:

- PowerShell management library for Hyper-V
- PowerTools for OpenXML-access office documents in OpenXML format
- Windows Automation Snapin for PowerShell
- SharePoint scripts for administration and backup
- PowerShell Remoting
- PowerShell Eventing library
- PowerShell tools for working with Visual Studio

Many of the projects are developer-oriented, but there are a good number of projects for administrators. The most well-known project from Codeplex is probably the PowerShell Community Extensions.

POWERSHELL COMMUNITY EXTENSIONS

The PowerShell Community Extensions (PSCX) add 59 cmdlets (version 2 expands this to 86) to your PowerShell environment, together with a number of useful scripts. Using a script similar to listing 4.8 (the snapin is called pscx), we get the following list of nouns:

ADObject	Assembly	Base64	Bitmap
Byte	BZip2	Clipboard	DhcpServer
DomainController	ExportedType	FileTime	FileVersionInfo
ForegroundWindow	GZip	Hardlink	Hash
Hex	Host	Junction	MacOs9LineEnding
MountPoint	PEHeader	Privilege	Process
PSSnapinHelp	Random	ReparsePoint	Shortcut
ShortPath	SmtpMail	String	Symlink
TabExpansion	Tar	TerminalSession	UnixLineEnding
VolumeLabel	WindowsLineEnding	Xml	Zip

In addition, there's an Active Directory PowerShell provider. Watching a dir through Active Directory seems to go down really well as a demo. We'll meet some of the PSCX cmdlets in later chapters.

Having created our scripts and built our toolkit, we need to think about keeping it out of the hands of the bad guys. Time to think about securing PowerShell.

4.6 Securing PowerShell

Security must be at the top of every administrator's list. Security and usability can pull you in opposite directions. Automation by PowerShell, or any other scripting tool, is a definite move toward ease of use. How can we keep our automation and make sure that we're secure?

PowerShell has a number of security features, as we've already seen, including:

- Can't run a script by double clicking
- Execution policies
- Current folder not on the path

We'll look at some other techniques for keeping our scripts secure and finish off the section, and the chapter, by looking at script signing.

4.6.1 Script security

We need to keep our scripts secure for two reasons. One, we don't want anyone running them who shouldn't. There's no telling what damage could be done by someone running your admin scripts "just to see what happens." Second, we don't want anyone getting access to the scripts and altering them. That could be even nastier!

So how do we keep our scripts secure?

How many people need access to the scripts? Restrict access to only the administrators that need them. Use NTFS permissions to secure the scripts. Put the scripts on an administration machine rather than a file server to which everyone has access.

Severely restrict the number of people who can modify scripts. In many organizations, there's only one person creating or modifying scripts. This is usually because that person is the only one interested or the only one with the skills.

Consider using PowerGUI for running scripts. It can provide a friendly front end, enabling administrators who can't necessarily develop scripts to run scripts.

The maximum security for scripts is created by using the AllSigned execution policy and digitally signing your scripts. When I mention this in talks, a lot of people go pale at the thought. Script signing isn't a scary subject, as we'll see.

4.6.2 Script signing

PowerShell is most secure when used with the AllSigned execution policy. This requires that all scripts be digitally signed using a code-signing certificate from a trusted Certificate Authority. Digitally signing a script identifies the source of the script, or at least who signed it. If your execution policy is set to AllSigned and a signed script is changed, it won't be allowed to be executed until it's signed again.

Code-signing certificates can be supplied by one of the commercial Certificate Authorities for a fee, or a self-signed certificate for which your computer is the Certificate Authority. At this point, you may think that this is too hard. Believe me, it's not.

COMMERCIAL CERTIFICATES If scripts are going to be distributed to other machines either internally or externally to the organization, a commercial code signing certificate must be used. The self-signed certificate is only recognized on the machine on which it was created.

For the rest of this section, we'll use a self-signed certificate for the examples. If you obtain, or already have, a commercial code-signing certificate, you can skip this next section where we look at creating a certificate.

CREATE CERTIFICATE

We can create a self-signed certificate using the makecert.exe utility. The bad news is that it's not part of Windows or PowerShell. You need to download and install the Windows SDK from the Microsoft website. Alternatively, makecert is available if you have Visual Studio installed.

Once makecert is installed, we can create a certificate root and then make the code-signing certificate. We create the root using this syntax:

```
./makecert -n "CN=PowerShell Local CertificateRoot" -a sha1
-eku 1.3.6.1.5.5.7.3.3 -r -sv root.pvk root.cer
-ss Root -sr localMachine
```

It's not quite as bad as it looks, as table 4.1 explains.

Our syntax can be read as making a self-signed certificate root called `PowerShell Local CertificateRoot` using the Sha1 algorithm and an Object Identifier of 1.3.6.1.5.5.7.3.3. The PVK file is called *root* and is stored in the root certificate store on the local machine. Easy.

Full syntax details of makecert can be found by using `makecert /?` for the basic options and `makecert /!` for the advanced options.

Table 4.1 Syntax explanation for creating a certificate root

Parameter	Meaning	Value
-n	Certificate subject name	"CN=PowerShell Local CertificateRoot"
-a	Signature algorithm.	Sha1 (md5 is alternative)
-eku	Object Identifier (OID)	1.3.6.1.5.5.7.3.3
-r	Switch to create a self-signed certificate	
-sv	PVK file (to be created if not present)	root.pvk root.cer
-ss	Certificate store	Root
-sr	Certificate store location	localMachine

The next stage is to run this code:

```
./makecert -pe -n "CN=PowerShell User" -ss MY -a sha1
-eku 1.3.6.1.5.5.7.3.3 -iv root.pvk -ic root.cer
```

This is explained in table 4.2.

Table 4.2 Syntax explanation for creating a certificate

Parameter	Meaning	Value
-n	Certificate subject name	"CN=PowerShell User"
-pe	Private key is exportable	
-a	Signature algorithm.	Sha1 (md5 is alternative)
-eku	OID	1.3.6.1.5.5.7.3.3
-ss	Certificate store	MY
-iv	Issuer's PVK file	root.pvk
-ic	Issuers	Certificate file

Working with PowerShell, we have an advantage. We can look directly into the certificate store. Listing 4.10 will show us the relevant information about the certificate.

Listing 4.10   Viewing the code-signing certificate

```
PS> Get-ChildItem cert:\CurrentUser\My -codesigning | Format-List

Subject      : CN=PowerShell User
Issuer       : CN=PowerShell Local CertificateRoot
Thumbprint   : FC5A497BB74AC542876D4E84B6921B457E04CB10
FriendlyName :
NotBefore    : 16/08/2008 13:08:08
NotAfter     : 31/12/2039 23:59:59
Extensions   :
{System.Security.Cryptography.Oid, System.Security.Cryptography.Oid}
```

Having created our certificate, we should secure it. We don't want the bad guys getting access to it, automatically signing scripts and doing nasty things to your machine, now do we?

SECURE CERTIFICATE

So that the certificate can't be used for automated signing (without your consent), you need to export the private key. This can be performed using IE 5 and above, as shown in figure 4.6.

The procedure to export the private key is straightforward:

1 Open Internet Explorer.   **2** Select Tools.   **3** Select Internet Options.

4 Select Content tab.   **5** Click Certificates.   **6** Select Personal tab.

7 Select the certificate.   **8** Click Export.   **9** Follow the wizard.

10 Importing the private key is achieved using the Import Wizard on the same tab.

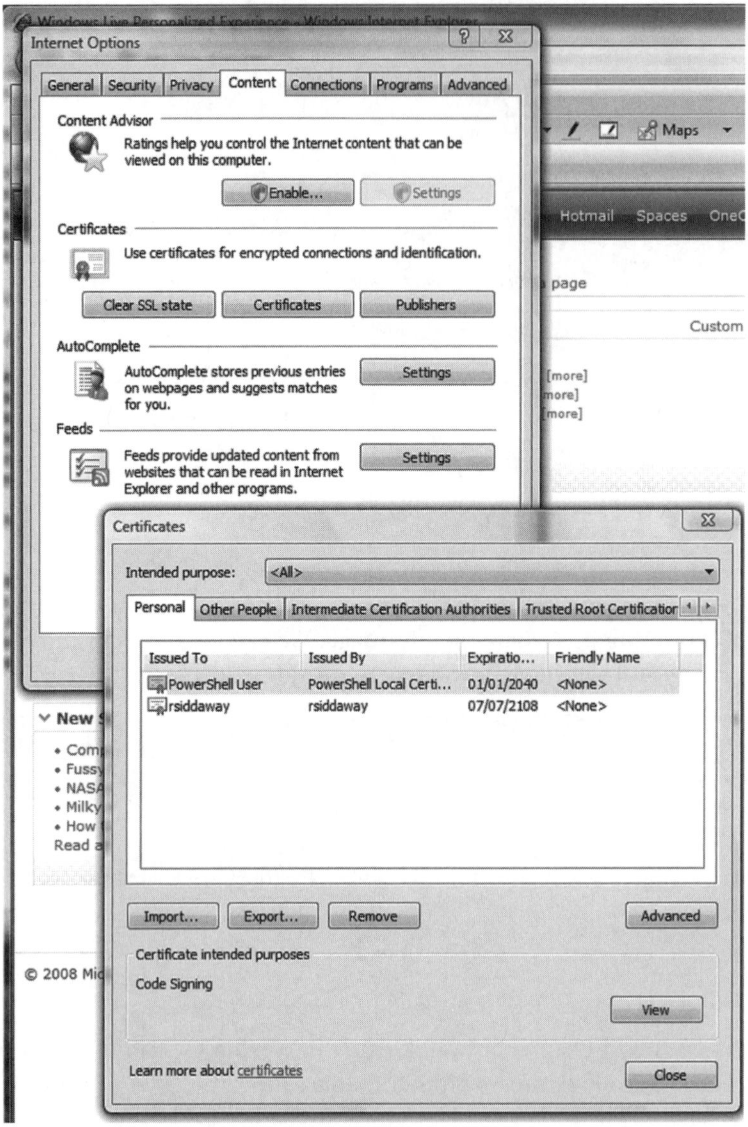

**Figure 4.6
Exporting the
private key using
Internet Explorer**

We have a certificate and we've secured it. Now how do we use it?

SIGN SCRIPTS

We can use Set-AuthenticodeSignature to sign a script. We can experiment on the get-topcpu.ps1 script that we created earlier:

```
$cert = @(Get-ChildItem cert:\CurrentUser\My -codesigning)[0]
Set-AuthenticodeSignature get-topcpu.ps1 $cert
```

Start by creating a variable to represent the code-signing certificate. We then use Set-AuthenticodeSignature to perform the signing. A signed script looks like listing 4.11.

Notice the #SIG labels to delineate the start and end of the signature block. If any changes are made to the script (even adding a space somewhere), the script will have to be signed again.

Listing 4.11   A signed script

```
## get-topcpu.ps1
## Richard Siddaway
## 10 August 2008
##
## Uses get-process and returns the top 4 cpu using
##   processes with the time in minutes
Get-Process | Sort-Object CPU -Descending | Select -First 4 |
Format-Table Name, @{Label="CPU(Min)"; Expression={"{0}" -f
     ($_.TotalProcessorTime.TotalMinutes)}} -AutoSize

# SIG # Begin signature block
# MIIEMAYJKoZIhvcNAQcCoIIEITCCBB0CAQExCzAJBgUrDgMCGgUAMGkGCisGAQQB
# gjcCAQSgWzBZMDQGCisGAQQBgjcCAR4wJgIDAQABBAfzDtgWUsITrck0sYpfvNR
# AgEAAgEAAgEAAgEAAgEAMCEwCQYFKw4DAhoFAAQUnScyXCDkO3/sqNa3xyyjQWKX
# +HKgggI7MIICNzCCAaSgAwIBAgIQYiaQKjtl0JBK3yOcXy34YjAJBgUrDgMCHQUA
# MCsxKTAnBgNVBAMTIFBvd2VyU2hlbGwgTG9jYWwgQ2VydGlmaWNhdGVSb290MB4X
# DTA4MDgxNjEyMDgwOFoXDTM5MTIzMTIzNTk1OVowGjEYMBYGA1UEAxMPUG93ZXJT
# aGVsbCBVc2VyMIGfMA0GCSqGSIb3DQEBAQUAA4GNADCBiQKBgQDRl1fqU4T77reO
# wJ8aw/GBKuynfIGFGxckL6oqCBU4O+yNRQKunOctmydT0lEO/ckiU8fUjk4BZCy5
# BCcZRIkRPv7NukFwLK/vx/fxZS0ykWwO6XRuAzN3H6WDJt46jvP8ApkakLjGe05x
# MyYVEiNFtmeNPTVVxskqg0sPIkeCFQIDAQABo3UwczATBgNVHSUEDDAKBggrBgEF
# BQcDAzBcBgNVHQEEVTBTgBC4i+8s8OP1u+W6T/qMYwj2oS0wKzEpMCcGA1UEAxMg
# UG93ZXJTaGVsbCBMb2NhbCBDZXJ0aWZpY2F0ZVJvb3SCEFjE3UUgk+CmSsbAOmV0
# 02QwCQYFKw4DAh0FAAOBgQAldcu9RzJji6Cv4HX2fBks8tmqzm25CrZfkYSSO6rw
# 7edYCBvc2UXOs52hVYv1fIWKB1q6cPvU11VUjUyUDH6td8JbHjpDX7xjiIpC13pM
# 1DBtoChYzQAkq6bZuK7mKG0LZkwm0zO8BIemZIUIFd9nd0h5Rs3lExAUFS80eYUi
# sDGCAV8wggFbAgEBMD8wKzEpMCcGA1UEAxMgUG93ZXJTaGVsbCBMb2NhbCBDZXJ0
# aWZpY2F0ZVJvb3QCEGImkCo7ZdCQSt8jnF8t+GIwCQYFKw4DAhoFAKB4MBgGCisG
# AQQBgjcCAQwxCjAIoAKAAKECgAAwGQYJKoZIhvcNAQkDMQwGCisGAQQBgjcCAQQw
# HAYKKwYBBAGCNwIBCzEOMAwGCisGAQQBgjcCARUwIwYJKoZIhvcNAQkEMRYEFNWw
# 65/QGdEJyPeY+t1Fg3Kwv6RgMA0GCSqGSIb3DQEBAQUABIGAXekFwJ2yncCT5xNa
# oeB3GxXCGpNjchtUh2D7Fgrq/g5LvLa1VLyeRCiatasZArhw1zttm4t2LUdOS/9S
# ldePSKg2CMDVDagYNjS3Pa6j7JlZco/unc6pMNmUUBZe6WHqmVa82PdlUgROs6ga
# 4nSX/LPheYXtqBY/43J4dsU3+00=
# SIG # End signature block
```

Once we have our certificate, signing subsequent scripts is a matter of using Set-AuthenticodeSignature against the new scripts. We don't have to keep generating new certificates. That's all there is to code signing. Not so scary after all. When a signed script is first run it will generate a one-time prompt to allow it to run.

This brings us to the end of the section of the book dedicated to learning Power-Shell. Well done for sticking with me this far. The fun really ramps up in part 2 when we start to apply everything we've learned to automate user management.

4.7   *Summary*

The main benefit of automating administration is the time and effort that's saved once the script is developed. Remember the creation of those 7,000 user accounts I mentioned at the beginning of the chapter—that could be your task next week! The next chapter is just for you in that case.

Script development can follow an ad hoc methodology by progressing from interactive command line to function to script. This mirrors the administration style, and is helped by products such as Exchange that show the scripts they're using to perform GUI-based actions.

There's a considerable body of best practice around using scripts for automation. Keeping scripts simple and building libraries of functions are good ways to ease the overhead of maintaining your scripts.

PowerShell is supported by an increasing number of vendors and community projects that supply tools to aid your administrative effort. Spanning everything from editors to graphical front end to extra cmdlets, these tools will make your life easier. They're not essential but they do help a great deal.

One important part of PowerShell best practice is security. Keep your scripts safe and only run known scripts. Consider investing in a code-signing certificate and use the AllSigned execution policy for maximum security.

Part 2

Working with people

PowerShell is an automation engine for Windows administration. In part 1, we learned how that engine worked. In parts 2 and 3, we put that engine to work and get the best out of it by using the toolkit we've put together. Part 2, chapters 5-7, covers people-related activities. The servers that we need to administer are covered in part 3.

A lot of administration revolves around people. We need to create and manage their user accounts so they can log on to the systems. They have mailboxes that need to be administered. The desktop systems they use need to be configured and maintained. Chapter 5 will show how to work with user accounts in Active Directory and locally. The time we spent with ADSI and .NET in chapter 3 pays dividends here. Mail access implies Exchange Server 2007 in this case. Chapter 6 is where we dive into administering mailboxes. There's some overlap with user accounts. We'll examine the interactions and provide some best practice guidelines.

Chapter 7 closes part 2 by showing how to work with the user desktop, including configuration settings and applications. WMI and COM will be put to work here. We'll also look at how to work with the latest OpenXML formats in Microsoft Office.

Parts 2 and 3 are built around examples of how to automate particular tasks with PowerShell. It's not possible to cover every variation and possibility in a book this size. You'll gain a thorough understanding of the principles involved, enabling you to build and expand on what you learn.

When working with people, we need to start at the beginning, and that means understanding user accounts and how to automate their administration.

User accounts

"Working with users" is the title of the middle part of this book. Anyone who thought "It would be a nice job but for the users" should be ashamed, very ashamed. Write out 100 times "I mustn't say things like that again." Better still, create a PowerShell script to write it out. There'll be a test.

A large part of administration comes back to users, directly or indirectly. In this chapter, we'll be automating the administration of user accounts. Why do we want to do this? Look back at my example from chapter 4. Do you want to set up 7,000+ users in a few weeks? Automation all the way.

The other reason for automating user account management is consistency. When working as a consultant, I've seen Active Directory implementations where the names are created in every combination you can think of. First name first; surname first; various combinations of commas and spaces between the name parts. Commas should be avoided if possible, as they have to be allowed for in the script;

otherwise the user account won't be found. The rest of the account information is just as inconsistent, with missing or wrong telephone numbers, addresses, and so on. Consistency makes things easier to administer. Be consistent. How do you do that? Automation all the way. Another thing we need to consider is groups. Allocating permissions by groups is best practice in a Windows environment, so we need to know how to create and modify groups.

The chapter will start with a look at the options we have for working with user accounts and groups. In this chapter, most of the scripts will be presented in two variations in order to provide the maximum flexibility. After explaining which options will be used, we'll look at how we work with local users and groups, including creation and modification.

Working with Active Directory users and groups occupies the bulk of the chapter. We start at the logical place by creating a user account. One of the major differences between working locally and working with Active Directory is that with the latter, we're often working with multiple users simultaneously. This will be illustrated by looking at how we can create users in bulk. Not quite on the scale of 7,000 at a time, but we could scale if required. Having created our users, we need to think about modifications to various attributes together with how we move the account to a different Organizational Unit (OU). During the move, the account may need to be disabled. This is a common scenario for dealing with people leaving the organization.

We often need to search Active Directory to find a particular user or possibly to find accounts or passwords that are about to expire. One common need is to discover a user's last logon time. This can be useful for checking who's still active on our directory. I recently checked an AD installation where there were several hundred accounts that hadn't been used for over six months. The disposal of old accounts can, and should, be automated.

The final section of the chapter deals with Active Directory groups. After a group has been created, we'll definitely need to modify its membership and may need to change its scope—the last type of group. We complete the section by answering two questions: "Who's in this particular group?" and "What groups is this user in?" These are questions that can't be easily answered by using the GUI tools.

In order to perform these tasks, we need to use ADSI, which is the primary interface for working with Active Directory, as we saw in chapter 3. There are a few options to consider regarding the exact way we accomplish this before we start creating scripts.

5.1 *Automating user account management*

Before the release of Windows Server 2008 R2, we'd work with user accounts via ADSI, as we saw in chapter 4. This can be performed in a number of ways, including:

- `[ADSI]` type accelerator
- `System.DirectoryServices .NET` classes
- `System.DirectoryServices.AccountManagement .NET` classes
- Quest AD cmdlets (the nouns all start with *QAD*)

Windows Server 2008 R2 introduced a module containing Active Directory cmdlets (see section 5.1.2).

> **POWERSHELL DILEMMA** This illustrates the dilemma that many new Power-Shell users face. "I've found three different ways of performing this task: which one should I use?" The short-term answer, especially if you're new to PowerShell, is whichever one you feel most comfortable with. In the longer term, investigate the possibilities, pick one, and stick with it. One slight problem is that sometimes you need to use multiple methods to cover all eventualities.

ADSI can be used to access AD LDS, previously known as ADAM, via PowerShell in a similar way to Active Directory. The only major change is the way you connect to the directory service. The code to get a directory entry for an Active Directory user is:

```
$user = [ADSI]"LDAP://cn=Richard,cn=Users,dc=Manticore,dc=org"
```

To connect to an AD LDS or ADAM instance, this changes to:

```
$user = [ADSI]
"LDAP://server_name:port/cn=Richard,cn=Users,dc=Manticore,dc=org"
```

If the AD LDS/ADAM instance is on the local machine, this becomes:

```
$user = [ADSI]
"LDAP://localhost:389/cn=Richard,cn=Users,dc=Manticore,dc=org"
```

5.1.1 Microsoft AD cmdlets

When a Windows Server 2008 R2 domain controller is created, a module of Active Directory cmdlets is installed. Modules are covered in more detail in chapter 15 and appendix B. This module can also be installed on Windows Server 2008 R2 servers or Windows 7 machines (using the RSAT download). The module isn't loaded by Power-Shell by default. We use:

```
Import-Module ActiveDirectory
```

The Microsoft AD cmdlets work in a slightly different manner, in that they access a web service running on the domain controller. This performs the actions against Active Directory. The web service is available for installation on Windows Server 2008 or Windows Server 2003 domain controllers, but we'll need a Windows Server 2008 R2 or Windows 7 machine to install and run the cmdlets. The PowerShell v2 remoting capabilities can be used to set up proxy functions for these cmdlets on any machine running PowerShell v2. This technique is described in chapter 13.

A similar approach is taken with Exchange 2010, in that remote access is provided by a web service. These two systems are examples of a "fan-in" administrative model, in that many administrators can connect to the same machine to perform their jobs. Contrast this with the approach we'll see with IIS in chapter 13, where one administrator can work on multiple machines. PowerShell provides many ways to remotely administer our systems. The Active Directory cmdlets interacting with a web service is just one example. The need to install something on the domain controller may be viewed as a negative, in which case the Quest cmdlets could be used, as they only need to be installed on the machine used for administration.

5.1.2 *Recommendations*

When working with Active Directory and PowerShell, we have two main choices: use scripts or use the AD cmdlets from Microsoft or Quest. My preference is to use the cmdlets, but I realize that they aren't available in some tightly controlled environments. I'll concentrate on scripting so that the chapter is applicable to as many people as possible. Even if you use the cmdlets, understanding how to script the task will aid your understanding of the subject.

I don't fully recommend the `System.DirectoryServices.AccountManagement` .NET classes for use with Active Directory for three reasons. First, you need to have installed .NET 3.5, which not everyone can do. Second, the functionality has some gaps; for instance there's no capability to set the `description` attribute (this seems to be a common failing on the .NET classes for working with Active Directory). Finally, the syntax is odd compared to the standard ADSI syntax many people already know. I'll show examples using these classes because there's some useful functionality and because it's new with little documentation.

For local users and groups, the `System.DirectoryServices.AccountManagement` .NET classes are excellent and will be used in the following scripts. Variant scripts using `[ADSI]` will be shown for those users who don't have .NET 3.5 available. For Active Directory-based users, the `[ADSI]` accelerator will mainly be used, with the Microsoft or Quest AD cmdlets used as a variant.

NOTE I won't be providing variant scripts in all the remaining chapters of the book, just where I think there's value in showing two approaches.

First up on the automation express is local users and groups.

5.2 *Local users and groups*

Enterprises use Active Directory to manage users and groups. But they still need to manage local user accounts. This could be because the machine isn't a domain member (for example if it's in a perimeter network).

NOTE If performing this on Windows Vista or Windows Server 2008, Power-Shell needs to be started with elevated privileges—it needs to be started using Run as Administrator. On Windows XP or Windows Server 2003, you must be logged on with an account with Administrator privileges.

As stated earlier, we'll be using the `System.DirectoryServices.AccountManagement` .NET classes in these examples. You must have .NET 3.5 loaded to use this namespace. If it's not possible to use this version of .NET then the scripts shown under the variation headings can be used.

COMPUTER NAMES In the example scripts dealing with local users and groups, the machine name is always `pcrs2`. You'll need to change this in your environment.

Compared to Active Directory, there are a limited number of tasks we'd want to perform against local users. The tasks condense to creation and modification activities against users and groups. We need to create users before we can modify them, so that's where we'll start.

TECHNIQUE 1   User creation

Creating user accounts is the first step in working with users. In this case, we're creating an account on the local machine. Ideally, we're looking for a method that'll work when run locally or against a remote machine. We can achieve this by using the following approach.

PROBLEM
We need to create a local user account on a Windows machine.

SOLUTION
Creating a user account is a common administrative activity and is illustrated in listing 5.1. If it's not possible to use this .NET class, use the variant presented in listing 5.2. Start by loading the `System.DirectoryServices.AccountManagement` assembly as shown in listing 5.1 (see **❶**). PowerShell doesn't automatically load all .NET assemblies, so we need to perform that chore. If an assembly will be used often, put the `load` statement into your profile. Nothing bad happens if you do perform the `load` statement multiple times.

The `[void]` statement is new. All it does is suppress the messages as the assembly loads. If you want to see the messages, remove it. I've used the full name of the assembly (obtained via `Resolve-Assembly` in PowerShell Community Extensions), as some of the other load mechanisms are in the process of being removed. In PowerShell v2 we could use:

```
Add-Type -AssemblyName System.DirectoryServices.AccountManagement
```

as an alternative load mechanism. This avoids the need to use the deprecated .NET method.

Listing 5.1   Creating a local user account

```
[void][reflection.assembly]::Load(                              ❶ Load the
"System.DirectoryServices.AccountManagement, Version=3.5.0.0,      assembly
    Culture=neutral, PublicKeyToken=b77a5c561934e089")          ❷ Create the
                                                                   password
$password = Read-Host "Password" -AsSecureString
$cred = New-Object -TypeName System.Management.Automation.PSCredential
-ArgumentList "userid", $password
                                                                Set the context ❸
$ctype = [System.DirectoryServices.AccountManagement.ContextType]::Machine
$context = New-Object
```

```
-TypeName System.DirectoryServices.AccountManagement.PrincipalContext
-ArgumentList $ctype, "pcrs2"

$usr = New-Object -TypeName                          ◁──④ Create user
System.DirectoryServices.AccountManagement.UserPrincipal
-ArgumentList $context

$usr.SamAccountName = "Newuser1"                     ◁──⑤ Set properties
$usr.SetPassword($cred.GetNetworkCredential().Password)
$usr.DisplayName = "New User"
$usr.Enabled = $true
$usr.ExpirePasswordNow()

$usr.Save()              ◁──⑥ Save
```

The next job after loading the assembly is to generate a password for the new account ②. The method presented here avoids having the password in the script (good security) and doesn't show its value on screen as it is input. Using `Read-Host` with the `-AsSecureString` option means we get prompted for the password, and when we type it, asterisks (*) are echoed back on screen rather than the actual characters. The string we've typed in is encrypted and can't be accessed directly:

```
PS> $password = Read-Host "Password" -AsSecureString
Password: ********
PS> $password
System.Security.SecureString
PS>
```

There's a slight issue with this technique. You can't use the secure string directly as a password in a user account. We resolve this by creating a PowerShell credential as the next step. `Userid` is a placeholder for the account name in the credential. Any string will do.

PowerShell needs to know where to create the account using the `Principal-Context` class ③. This takes a context type, in this case `Machine` (the local SAM store), and the name of the machine. If the name is null then the local machine is assumed.

MACHINE NAME The machine name will need to be changed for your environment.

The `UserPrincipal` class is used to create an empty user account in the data store we set in the context ④. We can then start to set the properties of the user account ⑤ as shown. `SamAccountName` and `DisplayName` should be self explanatory. `$usr.Enabled = $true` means that the account is enabled and ready to use; `$usr.ExpirePassword-Now()` indicates that the user must change the password at first logon.

TRUE OR FALSE The PowerShell automatic variables `$true` and `$false` are used to define Boolean values—true or false. They're of type `System.Boolean`. One thing to explicitly note is that `$true` isn't the same as "true" and `$false` isn't the same as "false." Remember to use the Booleans, not the strings.

Setting the password value is interesting, as it uses the SetPassword method with the password from the credential we created earlier:

```
$usr.SetPassword($cred.GetNetworkCredential().Password)
```

The last action is to write the new user account back to the local data store ❻ using the Save() method.

DISCUSSION

This may seem like a lot of code, especially when compared to the WinNT method presented next, but everything before we create the user object ❹ (in listing 5.1) could be created once and used many times. One property that can't be set using this approach is the description. If you want to use this, consider the WinNT approach presented in listing 5.2. We'll be using ADSI via the [ADSI] accelerator in this example. ADSI can connect to a number of account data stores, including Active Directory using the LDAP provider, which we'll see in later sections, and the WinNT provider for connecting to the local account database. If you've been in IT long enough to remember scripting against Windows NT, you'll remember using WinNT. No prizes for guessing where the name comes from.

> **WINNT AND ACTIVE DIRECTORY** The WinNT provider can be used to connect to LDAP directories such as Active Directory, but it has much reduced capability compared to the LDAP provider.

WinNT and LDAP are case sensitive. Remembering this will make debugging scripts much faster.

Listing 5.2   Creating a local user account using WinNT

```
$computer = "pcrs2"                          ⊲—❶ Computer name
$sam = [ADSI]"WinNT://$computer"             ⊲—❷ Link to SAM
$usr = $sam.Create("User", "Newuser2")       ⊲—❸ Create user
$usr.SetPassword("Passw0rd!")
$usr.SetInfo()

$usr.Fullname = "New User2"                  ⊲—❹ Set fullname
$usr.SetInfo()
$usr.Description = "New user from WinNT"      ⊲—❺ Set Description
$usr.SetInfo()
$usr.PasswordExpired = 1                      ⊲—❻ Force password change
$usr.setInfo()
```

Set a variable to the computer name (change for your environment) ❶. We then need to bind to the local Security Account Manager (SAM) database using the WinNT ADSI provider ❷. Setting the computer name in a variable isn't strictly necessary, but it makes things easier if you want to change the script to accept parameters.

The Create() method is used to create a user object ❸. The first parameter tells the system to create a user, and the second parameter is the account name. Unless you want the account to be disabled, you must set the password at this point.

> **PASSWORD WARNING**   I deliberately wrote this script with the password in the
> script to show how obvious it is. Imagine a scenario where you create a set of new
> accounts. If someone finds the password, you could have a security breach. As
> an alternative, you could leave the account disabled until required.

SetInfo() is used to save the account information back to the database. There are a
few other attributes we want to set. The full name defaults to the account name (login
ID), so changing it to the user's name will make finding the account easier ❹. Using
the .NET method, we couldn't set the description, but it can be done quite easily with
this method ❺. The last setting is to force the users to change their passwords when
they log on for the first time ❻. If PasswordExpired is set to one, the password
change is enforced. A value of 0 for PasswordExpired means that users don't have to
change their passwords.

  It's not strictly necessary to use SetInfo() after every change. The attribute
changes could be rolled up by a single call to SetInfo().

  One way or another, we've created our user. Now we have to think about creating a
group for the user account.

TECHNIQUE 2   **Group creation**

Working with groups is much more efficient than working with individual accounts.
You need to give a set of users access to a resource. Put them in a group and assign the
permissions to the group. Before we can do that, we need to create the group.

PROBLEM

We need to create a local group on a Windows computer.

SOLUTION

Continuing our exploration of System.DirectoryServices.AccountManagement, we
use the GroupPrincipal class to create a group in listing 5.3. After loading the assembly ❶ (in listing 5.3) we set the context to the local machine ❷. This time we're creating a group, so we need to set the group scope to local ❸. This code can be modified
to work at the domain level by changing the context to domain and the group scope
to the appropriate value. Examples of using these .NET classes on Active Directory
accounts will be given later.

Listing 5.3   Create a local group

```
[void] [reflection.assembly] ::Load(
"System.DirectoryServices.AccountManagement,
Version=3.5.0.0, Culture=neutral,
PublicKeyToken=b77a5c561934e089")            ⊲—❶ Load assembly

$ctype =
[System.DirectoryServices.AccountManagement.ContextType]
::Machine

$context = New-Object
-TypeName System.DirectoryServices.
AccountManagement.PrincipalContext
```

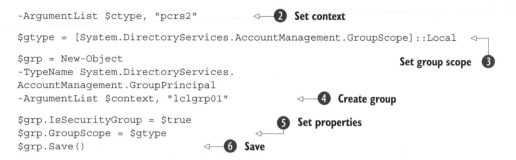

```
-ArgumentList $ctype, "pcrs2"                              ◄── ❷ Set context

$gtype = [System.DirectoryServices.AccountManagement.GroupScope]::Local  ◄──┐

$grp = New-Object                                              Set group scope ❸
-TypeName System.DirectoryServices.
AccountManagement.GroupPrincipal
-ArgumentList $context, "lclgrp01"       ◄── ❹ Create group

$grp.IsSecurityGroup = $true         ❺ Set properties
$grp.GroupScope = $gtype        ◄──┘
$grp.Save()              ◄── ❻ Save
```

The GroupPrincipal class is used to create the group using the context and a group name of lclgrp01 ❹. Set the group scope (type of group) ❺, save the changes ❻, and we're done. We may not need to explicitly set the fact that it's a security group for local groups by using $grp.IsSecurityGroup = $true, but it's useful when working with Active Directory groups.

DISCUSSION

Using ADSI is just as easy, as shown in listing 5.4

Listing 5.4   Create a local group with WinNT

```
$computer = "pcrs2"                              ❶ Connect to machine
$sam = [ADSI]"WinNT://$computer"       ◄──┘
$grp = $sam.Create("Group", "lclgrp02")      ◄── ❷ Create group
$grp.SetInfo()
                                         ❸ Set properties
$grp.description = "New test group"   ◄──┘
$grp.SetInfo()          ◄── ❹ Save
```

After connecting to the local SAM database ❶, we use the Create() method ❷. The parameters indicate that we're creating a group and the group name. This approach allows us to set the description ❸, and we save the new group ❹ to the database.

Note that we also did a SetInfo() immediately after creation. As we'll see when working with Active Directory, saving is needed so we can actually work with the object. Groups need members, so now we'll look at how to add members into a group.

TECHNIQUE 3   **Group membership**

Groups by themselves don't do anything. We need to add members to make them useful. We should remove members from the group when they don't need to be in there anymore. We all clean up group membership—don't we?

PROBLEM

We need to add a new member to a local group.

SOLUTION

The GroupPrincipal class contains methods for modifying the membership of a group. By now, you should see a pattern emerging for how these scripts work. Listing 5.5 demonstrates this pattern. Load the assembly ❶, set the context to the local machine ❷, set the method to find the group ❸, and then find the GroupPrincipal ❹.

Listing 5.5　Modify local group membership

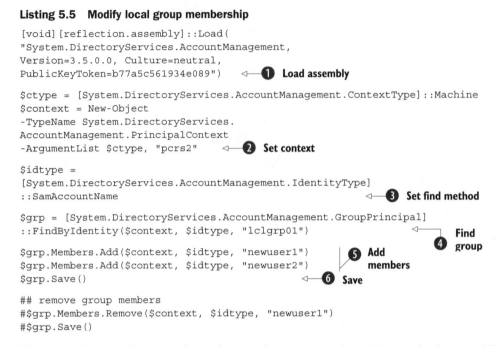

```
[void][reflection.assembly]::Load(
"System.DirectoryServices.AccountManagement,
Version=3.5.0.0, Culture=neutral,
PublicKeyToken=b77a5c561934e089")      ◁━━❶ Load assembly

$ctype = [System.DirectoryServices.AccountManagement.ContextType]::Machine
$context = New-Object
-TypeName System.DirectoryServices.
AccountManagement.PrincipalContext
-ArgumentList $ctype, "pcrs2"     ◁━━❷ Set context

$idtype =
[System.DirectoryServices.AccountManagement.IdentityType]
::SamAccountName                                ◁━━❸ Set find method

$grp = [System.DirectoryServices.AccountManagement.GroupPrincipal]
::FindByIdentity($context, $idtype, "lclgrp01")              ◁━┐ Find
                                                              ❹ group
$grp.Members.Add($context, $idtype, "newuser1")    ❺ Add
$grp.Members.Add($context, $idtype, "newuser2")      members
$grp.Save()                                    ◁━━❻ Save

## remove group members
#$grp.Members.Remove($context, $idtype, "newuser1")
#$grp.Save()
```

The group has a collection of members and we can use the Add() method to modify the membership ❺. Note that we have to give the context and how we're identifying the user as well as the user account to add. A final Save() ❻ and our changes are written back to disk.

To remove group members, we use the Remove() method instead of the Add() method.

DISCUSSION

Using ADSI to modify group membership is equally straightforward, as seen in listing 5.6. We get objects to represent the users and group and use the group's Add() method to add members. Note that we have to give the path to the user, which will be something like WinNT://pcrs2/newuser1. We could input the path directly to Add(). Removing users is equally direct: we use the Remove() method as shown.

Listing 5.6　Modify local group membership with WinNT

```
$grp = [ADSI]"WinNT://pcrs2/lclgrp02"
$user = [ADSI]"WinNT://pcrs2/newuser1"
$grp.Add($user.Path)
$grp.SetInfo()

$user2 = [ADSI]"WinNT://pcrs2/newuser2"
$grp.Add($user2.Path)
$grp.SetInfo()

#$grp.Remove($user2.Path)
#$grp.SetInfo()
```

That's all we're going to look at as far as local users and groups are concerned. Automating local accounts gains us some efficiency improvements, but it's not the whole picture. Enterprises will be using Active Directory to manage the vast majority of their user accounts. With accounts numbering in the hundreds, if not thousands, it's in the automation of Active Directory management that we'll really see some benefit.

5.3   Active Directory users

Active Directory is the foundation of administration in a modern Windows environment. I've given an example of the mass creation of user accounts and the savings that automating that process brought. It's time to start looking at the automation of Active Directory user account management in detail. Though I can't cover all eventualities in a single chapter, the examples here will form a solid start to building automation into your environment.

The majority of the scripts deal with a single object, but in listing 5.11 I show how to create users in bulk. In listing 5.23 where we discuss changing group membership, there's a technique for dealing with all of the users in a particular OU. This technique can be used in the other scripts as appropriate to enable them for bulk processing. In this section, I'll use an ADSI-based script as the primary method, with the Quest and Microsoft AD cmdlets as secondary methods. If it's possible to use these cmdlets in your organization, I recommend you do so.

> **DOMAIN NAMES**   In these scripts I'm working in my test domain. You need to change this for your environment, so you must change the LDAP connectivity strings of the form *LDAP://OU=England,dc=manticore,dc=org* to match your domain.

<hr>

TECHNIQUE 4   **User creation**

<hr>

Any work on user accounts must start with creating that user account

PROBLEM

A user account has to be created in Active Directory.

SOLUTION

Using ADSI, the solution has similarities to that presented in listing 5.2. We start by creating the data, such as the name and user ID that we'll use to create the account ❶ (in listing 5.7). I create the fullname ($struser) from the first and last names, as each will be required later. I've deliberately set the password in the script rather than explain how to use a secure string again. Use the technique shown in listing 5.1 if you want to mask the password. I've included a version of listing 5.7 in the code download file that uses the password-masking technique—look for listing 5.7s.

Listing 5.7   Creating a single user

```
$first = "Joshua"
$last = "TETLEY"        ❶ Define data
$userid = "jtetl"
```

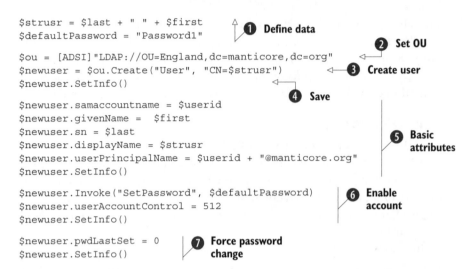

```
$strusr = $last + " " + $first          ① Define data
$defaultPassword = "Password1"
                                                    ② Set OU
$ou = [ADSI]"LDAP://OU=England,dc=manticore,dc=org"
$newuser = $ou.Create("User", "CN=$strusr")         ③ Create user
$newuser.SetInfo()
                                            ④ Save
$newuser.samaccountname = $userid
$newuser.givenName =  $first
$newuser.sn = $last
$newuser.displayName = $strusr                  ⑤ Basic
$newuser.userPrincipalName = $userid + "@manticore.org"    attributes
$newuser.SetInfo()

$newuser.Invoke("SetPassword", $defaultPassword)   ⑥ Enable
$newuser.userAccountControl = 512                     account
$newuser.SetInfo()

$newuser.pwdLastSet = 0        ⑦ Force password
$newuser.SetInfo()                change
```

The next steps are to define the OU where we'll create the user ② then perform the creation ③. The new user account should be immediately saved ④. This ensures that later processing occurs without error.

The attributes concerned with the user's name are set ⑤. Surname is sn and givenName is the first name. The display name is what's shown as the full name in Active Directory Users and Computers (ADUC). The attribute cn is the name shown in AD Users and Computers when the OU is browsed. cn is also used to identify the user when we're creating a directory entry for modification. See listing 5.11.

When first created, an Active Directory account is disabled by default. We need to set a password and set the useraccountcontrol attribute to 512 (normal user) to enable the account ⑥. useraccountcontrol flags are detailed in appendix D. The final process is to set the pwdLastset attribute to zero ⑦. This forces the user to change the password at next logon.

DISCUSSION

That was a fairly lengthy script for creating users. PowerShell cmdlets give a much better experience than scripting, as we'll see in listings 5.8 and 5.8a. There are three separate examples here to illustrate different methods of handling passwords:

- In the first example in listing 5.8 ①, $null password is specified. No password is set and the account is disabled unless it's requested to be enabled. A password has to be supplied before the account can be enabled.
- In the second example ②, no password is specified. No password is set and the account is left in a disabled state. Again, a password is required before the account can be enabled.
- In the final example ③, a user password is specified. The password is set and the account is enabled via the Enable-ADAccount cmdlet.

Note that the Microsoft AD cmdlets all use a prefix on AD for the noun.

Listing 5.8   Creating a single user by Microsoft cmdlets

```
New-ADUser -Name "DARWIN Charles" -SamAccountName "CDarwin" `        ❶
-GivenName "Charles" -Surname "DARWIN" `
-Path 'ou=england,dc=manticore,dc=org' -DisplayName "DARWIN Charles" `
-AccountPassword $null -CannotChangePassword $false `
-ChangePasswordAtLogon $true  -UserPrincipalName "CDarwin@manticore.org"

New-ADUser -Name "NEWTON Isaac" -SamAccountName "INewton" `          ❷
-GivenName "Isaac" -Surname "NEWTON" `
-Path 'ou=england,dc=manticore,dc=org' -DisplayName "NEWTON Isaac" `
-AccountPassword (Read-Host -AsSecureString "AccountPassword") `
-CannotChangePassword $false  -ChangePasswordAtLogon $true `
-UserPrincipalName "INewton@manticore.org"

New-ADUser -Name "SORBY Henry" -SamAccountName "HSorby" `            ❸
-GivenName "Henry" -Surname "SORBY" `
-Path 'ou=england,dc=manticore,dc=org' -DisplayName "SORBY Henry"  `
-AccountPassword (Read-Host -AsSecureString "AccountPassword")`
-CannotChangePassword $false  -ChangePasswordAtLogon $true  `
-UserPrincipalName "HSorby@manticore.org"

 Enable-ADAccount -Identity HSorby          ❸
```

Using the Quest cmdlets is similar. Some of the parameters are slightly different—for example, `Path` and `ParentContainer` respectively for the OU in which the user is created.

Listing 5.8a   Creating a single user with the Quest cmdlets

```
New-QADUser -Name "SMITH Samuel" -FirstName "Samuel" -LastName "SMITH"
-DisplayName "SMITH Samuel" -SamAccountName ssmith
-UserPassword "Password1" -UserPrincipalName "ssmith@manticore.org"
-ParentContainer "ou=England,dc=manticore,dc=org"

Set-QADUser -Identity "manticore\ssmith"
-ObjectAttributes @{useraccountcontrol=512; pwdLastSet=0}
```

The `New-QADUser` cmdlet is used to create user accounts. *New* is used for cmdlets that create objects. Comparing listing 5.8 with listing 5.7: the similarities are obvious. The `-Name` parameter corresponds to cn used to create the user in listing 5.7. Note we need to create the user, then set the `useraccountcontrol` and force the password change by using `Set-QADUser`. These attributes can't be set when creating the account. It just doesn't work.

Creating a single user may be slightly more efficient in PowerShell, especially using the cmdlets. We really gain from automating the bulk creation of user accounts.

TECHNIQUE 5   **User creation (bulk)**

We've seen how to create users one by one. The full benefit of automation is achieved by creating users in bulk. In order to get the most from these techniques, you may want to change your procedures for new joiners to the organization. Get all the new user information in one go and create them using listing 5.9 or 5.10. One or two runs per week and they're all done. It's much more efficient than single-user creation in dribs and drabs.

PROBLEM

We need to create a lot of users at one time.

SOLUTION

Our solution is an adaptation of listing 5.7. Take a moment to compare listing 5.9 with listing 5.7 and you'll see that the content of the foreach loop is a modified version of listing 5.7.

> **FOREACH ALIAS**   Foreach as used here is an alias for Foreach-Object as shown in listing 5.10a.

We start by reading a CSV file called pms.csv and passing the contents into a Foreach_object (in listing 5.9) **1**. The CSV file contains three columns with headers of last, first, and userid. The great advantage of using a CSV file is that we can refer to the column headers in the rest of our script as properties of the pipeline object.

Listing 5.9   Creating users in bulk

1 Read CSV file into loop

```
Import-csv pms.csv | foreach {          ◁──
    $strusr = $_.Last.ToUpper() + " " + $_.First      ◁──2 Create user

    $ou = [ADSI]"LDAP://OU=England,dc=manticore,dc=org"    ◁──
    $newuser = $ou.Create("user","cn=$strusr")            3 Set OU
    $newuser.SetInfo()                        ◁──
                                          4 Save user
    $newuser.samaccountname = $_.userid
    $newuser.givenName =   $_.first
    $newuser.sn = $_.last
    $newuser.displayName = $strusr
    $newuser.userPrincipalName = $_.userid + "@manticore.org"
    $newuser.SetInfo()

    $newuser.Invoke("SetPassword", "Password1")
    $newuser.userAccountControl = 512
    $newuser.SetInfo()

    $newuser.pwdLastSet = 0
    $newuser.SetInfo()                              5 Completion
                                                      message
    Write-Host "Created Account for: "  $newuser.Displayname   ◁──
}
```

We can create the contents of the $struser variable by using $_.last.ToUpper() and $_.first (remember PowerShell isn't case sensitive) **2**. ToUpper() is a string-handling method that converts all characters to uppercase. $_ refers to the object coming down the pipeline. In this case, the object is a line from the CSV file. The column headers are properties, so $_.first means the contents of the column named first in the current row. This is real processing power.

I've hard coded an OU for this batch of users **3**. In a typical organization, you may be creating users in a number of OUs, so this could become another column in the

CSV file. After we create the user ❹, we proceed to complete the attributes as before. The only difference is that we're reading them from the pipeline object rather than coding them into the script. The last line of the script ❺ writes out a message to state that creation is complete.

By adding a couple of commands and changing the way we get the data, we've turned a script to create a single user into one that can create many. The time and effort to go from listing 5.7 to 5.9 is minimal. The administrative effort that will be saved is huge and will easily pay back the investment.

DISCUSSION

In listing 5.8, we had a script to create a single user with the AD cmdlets. This is can also be turned into a bulk creation script, as in listing 5.10.

Listing 5.10   Creating users in bulk with Microsoft cmdlets

```
Import-Csv -Path users2.csv | foreach {
New-ADUser -Name "$($_.Given) $($_.Surname)" `
-SamAccountName $_.Id -GivenName $_.Given `
-Surname $_.Surname `-Path 'ou=england,dc=manticore,dc=org' `

 -DisplayName "$($_.Given) $($_.Surname)" `
 -AccountPassword $null -CannotChangePassword $false `
 -ChangePasswordAtLogon $true     `
 -UserPrincipalName "$($_.Id)@manticore.org"
 }
```

In this case, I've used the parameters as subexpressions for variety. It's not usually necessary to do this, but is worth demonstrating. We have seen how to create a user account with the Microsoft cmdlets. Listing 5.10a shows how we can perform the same action with the Quest cmdlets.

Listing 5.10a   Creating users in bulk with Quest cmdlets

```
Import-Csv pres.csv | ForEach-Object {
$name = $_.last.ToUpper() + " " + $_.first
$upn = $_.userid + "@manticore.org"
New-QADUser -Name $name -FirstName $_.first -LastName $_.last.ToUpper()
 -DisplayName $name -SamAccountName $_.userid -UserPassword "Password1"
 -UserPrincipalName $upn  -ParentContainer "ou=USA,dc=manticore,dc=org"

Set-QADUser -Identity $upn
-ObjectAttributes @{useraccountcontrol=512; pwdLastSet=0}
 }
```

These examples follow the same format as listing 5.9. We take a CSV file and pass it into a `foreach` loop. The data for the parameters is read from the pipeline as before. After looking at listing 5.10, there are no real differences in this one as to how we handle the data apart from the fact that I create a variable for the UPN. This is so that it can be used in both cmdlets. It's more efficient to only create it once. I haven't specifically written out a message, because the two cmdlets automatically create messages.

The names in the CSV files are those of English scientists, British prime ministers, and US presidents respectively, in case you were wondering. Unfortunately, things never remain the same in IT, so we have to tear ourselves away from PowerShell Space Invaders and modify some users. An admin's work is never done.

TECHNIQUE 6   User modification

After creating a user account, it's more than probable that we'll need to make modifications. People move departments; telephone numbers change; even names can change. We may want to increase security by restricting most users to being able to log on only during business hours.

Active Directory can hold a lot of information about your organization. If you keep the information up to date and accessible then you can leverage the investment in Active Directory and you don't need a separate phone book system, for instance.

PROBLEM

We have to make modifications to one or more user accounts in Active Directory.

SOLUTION

Using ADSI, we retrieve a directory entry for the user account we need to modify and set the appropriate properties. This is one of the longest scripts we'll see, but as we break it down, you'll see that it's not as bad as it looks. I've organized the script to match the tabs on the user properties in ADUC.

> **SCRIPT USAGE**   I don't expect this script to be used in its entirety. In normal use, I'd expect a few attributes to be changed rather than a bulk change like this. It's more efficient to present all the changes in one script. Then you can choose which attributes you need to modify.

In listing 5.11, we start by getting a directory entry for the user ❶. This is the part that will change in your organization. If you're making the same change to lots of users, put them into a CSV file and use a foreach loop in a similar manner to listing 5.9.

Listing 5.11   Modifying user attributes

```
$user = [ADSI]                                                    ❶ Get user
"LDAP://CN=CHURCHILL Winston,OU=England,DC=Manticore,DC=org"
$user.Initials = "S"                                             ❷ Start of General tab
$user.Description = "British PM"
$user.physicalDeliveryOfficeName = "10 Downing Street"
$user.TelephoneNumber = "01207101010"                           ❸ Office
$user.mail = "wsc@manticore.org"                              ❹ Email
$user.wwwHomePage = "http://www.number10.com"
$user.SetInfo()
                                                              ❺ Start of
$user.streetAddress = "10 Downing Street"                        Address
$user.postOfficeBox = "P.O. 10"                          ❻ PO Box
$user.l = "London"                          ❼ City
$user.St = "England"
                               ❽ State/province
```

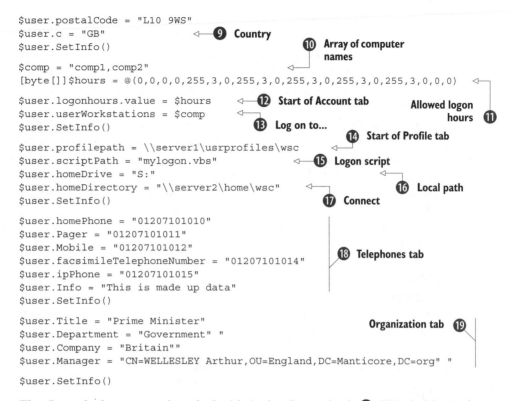

```
$user.postalCode = "L10 9WS"
$user.c = "GB"                          Country
$user.SetInfo()
                                                        Array of computer
$comp = "comp1,comp2"                                   names
[byte[]]$hours = @(0,0,0,0,255,3,0,255,3,0,255,3,0,255,3,0,255,3,0,0,0)

$user.logonhours.value = $hours         Start of Account tab
$user.userWorkstations = $comp                          Allowed logon
$user.SetInfo()                         Log on to...            hours

$user.profilepath = \\server1\usrprofiles\wsc      Start of Profile tab
$user.scriptPath = "mylogon.vbs"        Logon script
$user.homeDrive = "S:"
$user.homeDirectory = "\\server2\home\wsc"         Local path
$user.SetInfo()                         Connect

$user.homePhone = "01207101010"
$user.Pager = "01207101011"
$user.Mobile = "01207101012"
$user.facsimileTelephoneNumber = "01207101014"     Telephones tab
$user.ipPhone = "01207101015"
$user.Info = "This is made up data"
$user.SetInfo()

$user.Title = "Prime Minister"                 Organization tab
$user.Department = "Government" "
$user.Company = "Britain""
$user.Manager = "CN=WELLESLEY Arthur,OU=England,DC=Manticore,DC=org" "

$user.SetInfo()
```

The first tab that we need to deal with is the General tab ❷. This holds the name information, which can be modified as shown. Usually the attributes we use in ADSI match those shown in ADUC. I've annotated those that are different such as office ❸ and email address ❹. I've used SetInfo() after each tab's worth of changes to ensure that they're written back. If you cut and paste the script, it's less likely the SetInfo() will be forgotten.

Moving on to the Address tab ❺, we find simple data such as the PO Box ❻ as well as number of catches. The City field on ADUC we have to treat as l (for location) ❼, and state\province becomes st ❽. Setting the country requires the use of the two-character ISO code in the c attribute ❾. In this case, GB is the ISO code for the United Kingdom, even though Great Britain is only part of the UK!

TIP If you can't remember the ISO code for a particular country or aren't sure what to use, use ADUC to set the country by name on one user and ADSIEdit to check what code has been entered. With Windows Server 2008 ADUC, use the Attribute tab to view the data.

On the Account tab ⑫, we can also set the workstations a user can log on to ⑬ as well as the hours of the day he can log on. We need to create an array of workstation names ⑩ and use this to set the attribute. The logon hours attribute is more complicated, in that we have to create an array of bytes as shown ⑪. Three bytes represent a day (starting at Sunday) and each bit represents a one-hour time span. All zeros means the user isn't allowed to log on, and if all values are set to 255 (default) the user can log on 24x7. In the case shown, the user is restricted to logon times of Monday to Friday 8 a.m. to 6 p.m. If you want to use this, I recommend setting up one user in ADUC and copying the resultant values. This is definitely the quickest way to get it right.

The Profile tab **14** is for setting logon scripts and home drives as shown. The only difficulty here is the attribute names, as I've annotated, especially the scriptpath **15** which supplies the logon script to be run for the user. The local path **16** refers to the drive to be mapped to a user's home area and the connect attribute **17** supplies the UNC path to the user's home area. When you're setting telephone numbers on the Telephones tab **18**, remember that the numbers are input as strings rather than numbers.

The final tab I'll deal with is the Organization tab **19**. The attribute names match the ADUC fields as shown. Note that the Manger entry must be given the AD distinguished name as its input. The Direct Reports field is automatically backfilled from the Manager settings on other users. You can't set it directly.

DISCUSSION

I haven't given a full alternative using the cmdlets in this section. We can use the Microsoft cmdlets like this:

```
Get-ADUser -Identity hsorby | Set-ADUser -Department Geology
Get-ADUser -Identity hsorby -Properties Department

Get-ADUser -Identity hsorby -Properties *
```

The most efficient way to perform bulk changes is to use `Get-ADuser` to return the users in which we're interested and then pipe them into `Set-AdUser`. This way we can easily test which users are affected. The change can be examined with `Get-ADUser`. When we use `Get-ADUser`, we normally only get a small subset of properties returned. We can generate more data by explicitly stating which properties we want returned.

With the Quest cmdlets, we'd use the `Set-QADUser` cmdlet and use either one of the predefined parameters or the `-ObjectAttributes` parameter as shown in listing 5.10a.

TECHNIQUE 7   **Finding users**

We've seen how to create and modify user accounts in Active Directory. One of the other tasks we need to perform frequently is searching for particular users. No, not under the desk, but in Active Directory. In this section, we'll look at searching for an individual user, disabled accounts, and accounts that are locked out. You'll see other searches that look at logon times and account expiration later in the chapter.

Searching Active Directory requires the use of LDAP filters. They're explained in appendix D.

> **DELETED USER ACCOUNTS**   Searching for deleted user accounts will be covered in chapter 10

We'll start with searching for a single user.

PROBLEM

We need to search Active Directory for specific users or accounts that are disabled or locked out.

SOLUTION

We can use the `System.DirectoryServices.DirectorySearcher` class to perform our search. In PowerShell v2, this can be shortened slightly by using `[ADSISEARCHER]`. Using `System.DirectoryServices.DirectorySearcher` makes searching faster and simpler compared to previous scripting options. We need to start by creating a variable with the name of the user to search for ❶ (in listing 5.12). We can search on other attributes, as we'll see later. We want to search the whole Active Directory, because we can't remember where we put this user. We can use `GetDomain()` to determine the current domain ❷. Using this method makes our script portable across domains. We then get a directory entry ❸ for the domain.

Listing 5.12 Searching for a user account

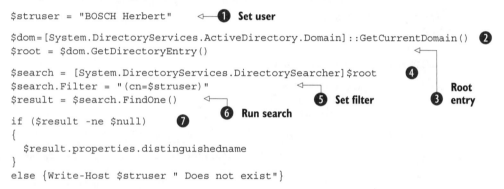

```
$struser = "BOSCH Herbert"        ◁──❶ Set user

$dom=[System.DirectoryServices.ActiveDirectory.Domain]::GetCurrentDomain()  ❷
$root = $dom.GetDirectoryEntry()                                      ◁

$search = [System.DirectoryServices.DirectorySearcher]$root      ❹
$search.Filter = "(cn=$struser)"              ◁                        Root
$result = $search.FindOne()      ◁                    ❺ Set filter   ❸ entry
                                         ❻ Run search
if ($result -ne $null)      ❼
{
  $result.properties.distinguishedname
}
else {Write-Host $struser " Does not exist"}
```

Creating a search as shown ❹ will set the domain as the root of the search—we search the whole domain. We're looking for a particular user, so we need to set an LDAP filter for that user ❺. The `cn` attribute holds the name of the user account in Active Directory. It's possible to search on most attributes.

> **PAGE SIZE AND TIMEOUT** There's a limit on the number of results that will be returned from an LDAP search. The default limit is 1,000. If your results will exceed this number, add the line `$search.PageSize = 1000` after the filter. This will cause the results to be returned in batches (pages) of 1,000. When using the cmdlets, use the `PageSize` and `SizeLimit` parameters to control the return of data.
>
> There's a timeout of 120 seconds on the server side, at which point the server will return only the results found up to that point. The default client-side timeout is infinite.

When we run this search, we only expect a single result, so we use `FindOne()` ❻. As we'll see later, if we expect multiple results to be returned, we use `FindAll()`. Interestingly, `FindOne()` does a `FindAll()` and returns only the first result. If you've performed

Active Directory searches using VBScript in the past, note that we don't need to use an ADO recordset.

We perform a final check to see if we actually have a result ❼ and then we can display the distinguished name of the user. This will tell us where the user is hiding.

DISCUSSION

Using the cmdlets is even simpler. The Microsoft cmdlets give us:

```
Get-ADUser -Identity hsorby
```

And the Quest cmdlets produce:

```
$struser = "BOSCH Herbert"
Get-QADUser -ldapFilter "(cn=$struser)"
```

We could make this one line by putting the name into the -Identity parameter. The cmdlet automatically produces output, including the distinguished name, which minimizes the amount of code we need.

Our search script can be easily modified so that we can search for different things. Two examples are searching for disabled accounts and locked-out accounts, as shown in listing 5.13.

Listing 5.13   Disabled user accounts

```
$dom = [System.DirectoryServices.ActiveDirectory.Domain]
::GetCurrentDomain()
$root = $dom.GetDirectoryEntry()

$search = [System.DirectoryServices.DirectorySearcher]$root

$search.Filter =  "(&(objectclass=user)(objectcategory=user)      ❶ Search filter
(useraccountcontrol:1.2.840.113556.1.4.803:=2))"
$result = $search.FindAll()                             Find all disabled
                                                      ❷ accounts
foreach ($user in $result)
{
  $user.properties.distinguishedname
}
```

We create the search so that we're searching the whole domain again. The main difference in this script is the search filter ❶. Our LDAP filter will find user accounts. We need the objectclass and the objectcategory, as computer accounts also use the user class! The last part of the filter is where we look at the useraccountcontrol attribute and perform a bitwise AND on it with the value 2 (account disabled). The syntax looks bad, but just think of it as a long-winded way of saying "bitwise". The only part we need to think about changing is the final value, which is what we're searching for. The possible values for useraccountcontrol are listed in appendix D.

In case there's more than one disabled account, we use FindAll() to return multiple results ❷, which we can then display.

I'm almost embarrassed to present the cmdlet equivalents as they are so short. We'll start with the Microsoft cmdlet:

```
Search-ADAccount -AccountDisabled -UsersOnly |
select Name, distinguishedName
```

The Quest version is even shorter:

```
Get-QADUser -Disabled
```

It doesn't get any easier than that! The cmdlet also displays the results. What more can you ask for? Well, it doesn't make the tea for one...

Moving on, users and passwords don't mix. Users seem to take great delight in forgetting passwords and locking themselves out of Active Directory, usually on a Monday morning when they've just got back from vacation. Eventually, they may get around to ringing the help desk and you can check to see if they're locked out. Alternatively, you can use listing 5.14 to find the locked-out accounts.

Listing 5.14 Locked user accounts

```
Add-Type -AssemblyName System.DirectoryServices.AccountManagement       ❶

$ctype =
[System.DirectoryServices.AccountManagement.ContextType]::Domain
$context = New-Object -TypeName
    System.DirectoryServices.AccountManagement.PrincipalContext
-ArgumentList $ctype, "manticore.org", "DC=Manticore,DC=org"            ❷

$date = (Get-Date).AddDays(-1)        ❸

$mtype =
[System.DirectoryServices.AccountManagement.MatchType]
::GreaterThan                                                           ❹

$results =
[System.DirectoryServices.AccountManagement.UserPrincipal]
::FindByLockoutTime($context, $date, $mtype)                           ❺
if($results -ne $null){
  foreach ($result in $results){$result.distinguishedname}
}
else{Write-Host "No users locked out"}
```

System.DirectoryServices.AccountManagement from .NET 3.5 has a nice method, FindByLockoutTime(), which we can use to find locked accounts. In addition, we can see how to use these classes in a domain environment. As usual, we start by loading the .NET assembly ❶. In this case, I've used Add-Type from PowerShell v2. In PowerShell v1 you can use the load command from listing 5.1. The context in this case is a domain rather than a single machine. ContextType is set to Domain as shown, and the PrincipalContext is set to the name of the domain ❷. The arguments are the context type we created in ❶; the name of the domain and container we're working with, respectively. The container defined by the LDAP distinguished name of the domain.

The lockout time on the user accounts will be compared to a value we create ❸. We use Get-Date to retrieve the current date and use the AddDays() method to set the date back, in this case by one day. We're adding a negative number. There isn't a method to subtract days, so we fall back on this slightly inelegant approach. We'll be searching for accounts locked out in the last 24 hours. By varying this value, we can control how far back we look for locked-out accounts.

The comparison operator for our search is provided by the MatchType ❹. In this case we're looking for values greater than the reference value—lockouts that have occurred since the reference time. The search is performed by the FindByLockout-Time() method with the context, reference date, and operator as parameters ❺. The usual check on the results and displaying the distinguished names completes the script. This is the easiest method to script for searching for locked-out accounts that I've found.

If you want a super easy way of finding locked-out accounts, it doesn't get much easier than using the AD cmdlets. The Microsoft cmdlet syntax is:

```
Search-ADAccount -LockedOut
```

and the syntax for the Quest cmdlet is very similar:

```
Get-QADUser -Locked
```

These will retrieve all locked-out accounts in the domain.

We've looked at searching for disabled accounts; we should now look at how to enable or disable them.

TECHNIQUE 8   Enabling and disabling accounts

Listing 5.4 showed how to disable or enable a local user account. This script shows how to perform the same action on an Active Directory account.

PROBLEM

We need to disable or enable an Active Directory account.

SOLUTION

An Active Directory user account can be disabled by modifying the useraccountcontrol attribute, as shown in listing 5.15. This is the domain equivalent of listing 5.1 in that it toggles between enabled/disabled—it'll enable a disabled account and vice versa. We use ADSI to connect to the relevant account, retrieve the useraccountcontrol attribute, perform a bitwise exclusive OR on it, and write it back. The bitwise exclusive OR will toggle the disabled bit to the opposite value; that is it will disable the account if enabled and enable if disabled.

Listing 5.15   Disabling Active Directory user accounts

```
$user = [ADSI]"LDAP://CN=BOSCH Herbert,OU=Austria,DC=Manticore,DC=org"
$oldflag = $user.useraccountcontrol.value
$newflag = $oldflag -bxor 2
$user.useraccountcontrol = $newflag
$user.SetInfo()
```

DISCUSSION

The AD cmdlets provide specific commands to disable and enable user accounts:

```
Disable-ADAccount -Identity HSorby
Enable-ADAccount -Identity HSorby
```

```
Disable-QADUser -Identity "CN=BOSCH Herbert,OU=Austria,DC=Manticore,DC=org"
Enable-QADUser -Identity "CN=BOSCH Herbert,OU=Austria,DC=Manticore,DC=org"
```

All we need is to pass the identity of the user to the cmdlet and it does the rest. I can type this faster than opening the GUI tools, especially if I know the user ID so I can use domain\userid as the identity with the Quest cmdlets. (See appendix D for an explanation of the differences between the two sets of cmdlets when handling identities.)

One problem that you may find is disabling an account and moving it to a holding OU pending deletion. We've seen how to disable it, and we'll now turn to the move.

TECHNIQUE 9   **Moving accounts**

One method of organizing users in Active Directory is to have OUs based on department or location. This can enable us to apply specific group policies to those users. If the users move to a different location or department, we need to move the account to the correct OU so they receive the correct settings. When people leave the organization, their user accounts should be deleted. Many organizations will have an OU specifically for accounts that are to be deleted, so the accounts have to be moved into the correct OU.

PROBLEM

A user account has to be moved to another OU.

SOLUTION

The [ADSI] accelerator gives us access to a MoveTo method, but we have to remember that it's on the base object, so we need to include .psbase in PowerShell v1. In v2, this isn't an issue, as it has been made visible. Listing 5.16 demonstrates how we use the MoveTo() method to move a user account into a new OU.

Listing 5.16   Moving Active Directory user accounts

```
$newou = [ADSI]"LDAP://OU=ToBeDeleted,DC=Manticore,DC=org"
$user = [ADSI]"LDAP://CN=SMITH Samuel,OU=England,DC=Manticore,DC=org"

$user.psbase.MoveTo($newou)
```

Using the [ADSI] type accelerator, we set variables to the user and target OU. If you were to perform $user | get-member, you wouldn't see any methods on the object apart from two conversion methods. But by using $user.psbase | get-member, we drop into the underlying object as discussed in chapter 2. There we can see a MoveTo() method that will do just what we want. We call the method with the target OU as a parameter and the user is whisked off to his new home. If we have to move a number of accounts from an OU, we can modify the script to read the OU contents and then perform a move on the selected accounts.

> **WITHIN A DOMAIN ONLY** The techniques in this section only work within a domain; they can't be used for cross-domain moves.

DISCUSSION

The AD cmdlets don't provide a cmdlet to explicitly move users between OUs, but we can use the generic cmdlets for moving AD objects. All we need to provide is the identity of the user and target OU. Using the Microsoft cmdlet we can perform a move like this:

```
Move-ADObject
-Identity "CN=HUXLEY Thomas,ou=starking,dc=manticore,dc=org"
-TargetPath "ou=england,dc=manticore,dc=org"
```

The Quest cmdlet is similar, but notice the parameter is called `NewParentContainer` rather than `TargetPath`. There are just enough differences like this to get confusing if you use both sets of cmdlets on a regular basis:

```
Move-QADObject
-Identity "CN=SMITH Samuel,OU=England,DC=Manticore,DC=org"
-NewParentContainer "OU=ToBeDeleted,DC=Manticore,DC=org"
```

These cmdlets also work with groups and computer accounts. When we're not creating, moving, or modifying user accounts, someone is bound to ask for information such as the last time Richard logged on to the domain.

TECHNIQUE 10   **Last logon time**

Finding the last logon time for a user isn't straightforward. When Active Directory was introduced with Windows 2000, an attribute called `lastlogon` was made available. This is stored on a domain controller by domain controller basis. Each domain controller stores the date and time it last authenticated that user. The attribute isn't replicated.

Windows 2003 introduced another attribute called `lastlogontimestamp`. It does replicate between domain controllers, but it's only updated if the user hasn't logged on to that domain controller for more than a week. The value can easily become more than a week out of date. This attribute is really of use for determining if a user hasn't logged on for a significant period, for example finding all of the users who haven't logged on for a month or more.

PROBLEM

Determine the last time a user logged on to the domain.

SOLUTION

As discussed, in listing 5.17 we'll use the `lastlogon` and `lastlogontimestamp` attributes to find when a user last logged on to the domain. By using `System.Directory-Services.ActiveDirectory.Domain` we can retrieve information about the current domain ❶. This includes a list of the domain controllers ❷ in the domain. By looping through this list, we can check each domain controller in turn for the last logon information. This wouldn't be practical in a domain with many domain controllers, so the list of domain controllers to check could be manually created.

Listing 5.17 Last logon times

```
$dom = [System.DirectoryServices.ActiveDirectory.Domain]
::GetCurrentDomain()                                           ❶

foreach ($dc in $dom.domaincontrollers) {    ←—❷ Iterate through domain controllers

$ldapstr = "LDAP://" + $dc.Name + "/cn=richard,cn=users,dc=manticore,dc=org"    ❸
```

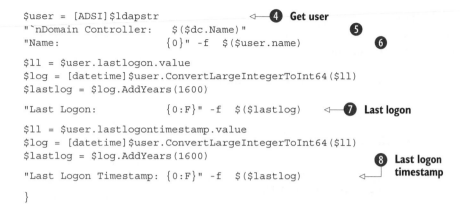

```
$user = [ADSI]$ldapstr                    ←──④ Get user
"`nDomain Controller:    $($dc.Name)"         ⑤
"Name:                  {0}" -f  $($user.name)   ⑥

$ll = $user.lastlogon.value
$log = [datetime]$user.ConvertLargeIntegerToInt64($ll)
$lastlog = $log.AddYears(1600)

"Last Logon:            {0:F}" -f  $($lastlog)    ←──⑦ Last logon

$ll = $user.lastlogontimestamp.value
$log = [datetime]$user.ConvertLargeIntegerToInt64($ll)
$lastlog = $log.AddYears(1600)                   ⑧ Last logon
                                                    timestamp
"Last Logon Timestamp: {0:F}" -f  $($lastlog)    ←─┘
}
```

The LDAP string we use to connect is slightly modified to include the fully qualified domain name of the domain controller ❸. Note the use of the + symbol for string concatenation. Previously we've performed a serverless binding and not worried about which domain controller we connected to. Using the LDAP string, we connect to the designated domain controller and access the user account ❹ stored on that machine.

We can now print the required information starting with the domain controller ❺ name. We're substituting into the string, but need to use the $() to ensure the name is evaluated before substitution; otherwise the name of the object would be output! The `n before the domain controller is a special character that forces a new line. Special characters are detailed in appendix A.

The name ❻, lastlogon ❼, and lastlogontimestamp ❽ are displayed using the string formatting operator -f. The fields within the string are enclosed in {} and substituted by the variables to the right of the -f operator in turn. The two logon times are stored in ticks (10,000th of a second, counting from January 1, 1600). We need to convert the number that's stored in Active Directory into a 64-bit integer and then into a date.

When we use $log = [datetime]$user.ConvertLargeIntegerToInt64($ll) to create the date it starts counting from 0 AD so the date is 1,600 years too low. We need to add 1,600 years to the resultant date to make it match the calendar.

In listing 5.18 we use the FromFileTime() method of the datetime class which automatically performs this addition. A simple example illustrates how it works.

```
PS> $d = Get-Date
PS> $d

25 March 2010 21:36:47

PS> $d.Ticks
634051498076096000
PS> [datetime]::FromFileTime($d.Ticks)

25 March 3610 21:36:47
```

We get the date and save it to a variable. The date and number of ticks can be viewed. When we convert the number of ticks back to a date the 1600 years is automatically added.

DISCUSSION

Using the cmdlets is a little simpler, but we still need to query multiple domain controllers, as shown in listing 5.18.

Listing 5.18   Last logon times using Microsoft cmdlets

```
Get-ADDomainController -Filter *| foreach {
    $server = $_.Name
    $user = Get-ADUser -Identity Richard `
      -Properties lastlogon, lastlogondate, lastlogontimestamp `
      -Server $($server)

  $t1 = [Int64]::Parse($($user.lastLogon))
  $d1 = [DateTime]::FromFileTime($t1)

  $t2 = [Int64]::Parse($($user.lastLogontimestamp))
  $d2 = [DateTime]::FromFileTime(t2)

  Add-Member -InputObject $($user) -MemberType Noteproperty `
   -Name "DCName" -Value $($server) -PassThru -Force |
   Format-Table DCName, `
   @{Name="LastLogonTime"; Expression={$($d1)}},`
   lastlogondate, `
   @{Name="LastLogonTimeStamp"; Expression={$d2}
}}
```

Get-ADDomainController will only return a single domain controller by choice. This can be overridden by specifying * in the filter parameter. Each domain controller is queried for the last logon time information. Note that lastlogondate is new in Windows Server 2008 R2. I'm using Add-Member to add the domain controller name as a new property on the user object. This enables us to see to which domain controller the information relates. Note how we have to work to retrieve the date from the Int64 that's held in Active Directory.

The Quest solution is similar to listing 5.18 in that we connect to the domain ❶ (in listing 5.19) and loop through the domain controllers ❷ as before. We print the domain controller name ❸ and then connect to the domain controller of interest ❹. $null is used to suppress the informational messages regarding the connection. The user information is retrieved and displayed ❺. The date creation is handled automatically ❻. We then disconnect from the domain controller.

Listing 5.19   Last logon times using Quest cmdlets

```
$dom = [System.DirectoryServices.ActiveDirectory.Domain]
::GetCurrentDomain()                                          ❶
foreach ($dc in $dom.domaincontrollers) {                     ⤎
                                                                 Iterate through
"`nDomain Controller:    $($dc.Name)"        ❸              ❷ domain controllers

$null = Connect-QADService -Service $dc.Name      ❹

Get-QADUser -Identity 'manticore\Richard' |                   ❺ Get
Select-Object name, lastlogon, lastlogontimestamp | Format-List  ⤎   user

Disconnect-QADService    ⤎❻ Disconnect
}
```

These solutions aren't satisfactory because we have to query a number of domain controllers to get an exact time. But if we only need an approximate last logon time, using the lastlogontimestamp is a simpler option.

In addition to knowing when users last logged on, we may need to know when their passwords or, in the case of temporary staff, their accounts are going to expire.

TECHNIQUE 11   Password expiration

The default maximum password age is 42 days and is controlled by domain-level group policy. This is often altered to meet an organization's particular needs. Users will often forget that passwords need changing, especially mobile users who're rarely in the office. It can often save administrative effort to remind them that their passwords will need changing ahead of time. It's usually possible to change a password when connected by VPN, but not if the password has already expired. Prompting users to change passwords ahead of time can solve the problem before it arrives.

PROBLEM

We need to find the users whose passwords will expire within a given time frame.

SOLUTION

This involves searching the domain, so we return to our search script and modify the LDAP filter to check the pwdlastset attribute. The expiration date for the password isn't stored directly. The date the password was last set is stored in the pwdlastset attribute. Unfortunately, this isn't directly accessible because it's a COM large integer, like the logon times we saw in the previous example. We need to convert some dates into the correct format and use them in our search filter, as in listing 5.20.

Listing 5.20 Password expiration check

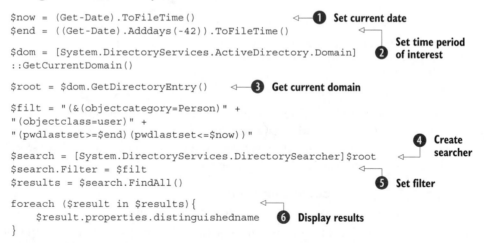

```
$now = (Get-Date).ToFileTime()                    ← ❶ Set current date
$end = ((Get-Date).Adddays(-42)).ToFileTime()     ←
                                                     ❷ Set time period
$dom = [System.DirectoryServices.ActiveDirectory.Domain]    of interest
::GetCurrentDomain()

$root = $dom.GetDirectoryEntry()    ← ❸ Get current domain

$filt = "(&(objectcategory=Person) " +
"(objectclass=user) " +
"(pwdlastset>=$end)(pwdlastset<=$now))"
                                                   ❹ Create
$search = [System.DirectoryServices.DirectorySearcher]$root  ← searcher
$search.Filter = $filt                            ←
$results = $search.FindAll()                       ❺ Set filter

foreach ($result in $results){                    ←
    $result.properties.distinguishedname    ❻ Display results
}
```

Start by using the current date (Get-Date) and convert it into the correct format using the ToFileTime() method ❶. If we assume that we have a 42-day maximum password age then all passwords should've been reset at least 42 days ago. We need to decide how many days ago we want to check for password reset. If you're looking at passwords that will expire in the next 10 days, we're interested in those set 32 days ago, and so forth. As I'm using a test domain, I had to force some of this, so my example shows a date of 42 days in the past—in other words, all password changes ❷. You'll need to set this value depending on your password policy and how far ahead you want look.

We get the current domain root ❸ and create a directory searcher ❹, as we've seen previously. The filter ❺ is interesting in that we need the `objectcategory` and `objectclass` to restrict the search to users. Leave off the `objectcategory` and you'll get computer accounts as well.

> **COMPUTER PASSWORDS** Computer passwords set themselves—don't try to change them manually.

We check the `pwdlastset` attribute for accounts that fall between our chosen dates using `FindAll()` and display the results ❻. We're using a `DirectorySearcher` object so you don't have access to the full property list. We can use the distinguished name to access a `DirectoryEntry` object and list full names, and so on. We could even send the user an email (PowerShell v2 has a `Send-MailMessage` cmdlet or we can script it).

DISCUSSION

A similar result can be achieved using the cmdlets:

```
$now = (Get-Date).ToFileTime()
$end = ((Get-Date).AddDays(-42)).ToFileTime()

$filt = "(&(objectcategory=Person)" +
"(objectclass=user)(pwdlastset>=$end)" +
"(pwdlastset<=$now))"

Get-ADUser -LDAPFilter $filt

$now = (Get-Date).ToFileTime()
$end = ((Get-Date).Adddays(-42)).ToFileTime()

$filt = "(&(objectcategory=Person)" +
"(objectclass=user)(pwdlastset>=$end)" +
"(pwdlastset<=$now))"

Get-QADUser -ldapFilter $filt
```

We set the start and end dates of our search and use the same LDAP filter as earlier. We get the same result, but with less code.

Temporary workers are often given accounts with an expiration date. Searching for these is similar to searching for expiring passwords.

TECHNIQUE 12   Account expiration

This is another search scenario, except this time we'll be using the `accountexpires` attribute. One big plus of creating search scripts in this way is that the only real change is the LDAP filter. The body of the script remains the same.

PROBLEM

We need to know which accounts will expire within a given time frame.

SOLUTION

Modifying our LDAP filter to use the accountexpires attribute enables us to find accounts that will expire within a certain number of days, as shown in listing 5.21. This is a variation on the password expiration script we saw previously. Set the start and end dates of our search ❶. In this case, we're interested in accounts that will expire in the next 60 days. Get the current domain root and create a searcher ❷. The search filter is simpler in that we're looking at the user object class and we want to find accounts where the accountexpires attribute falls between our two given dates ❸. We use Find-All() because we expect multiple results and we display the results ❹ as previously.

Listing 5.21   Account expiration check

```
$now = (Get-Date).ToFileTime()
$end = ((Get-Date).Adddays(60)).ToFileTime()      <--❶ Set dates

$dom = [System.DirectoryServices.ActiveDirectory.Domain]
::GetCurrentDomain()

$root = $dom.GetDirectoryEntry()                                    ❷ Create
                                                                      searcher
$search = [System.DirectoryServices.DirectorySearcher]$root    <--┘
$filt = "(&(objectclass=user)" +
"(accountexpires<=$end)" +
"(accountexpires>=$now))"

$search.Filter = $filt     <--❸ Search filter

foreach ($result in $results){
    $result.properties.distinguishedname     <--❹ Display results
}
```

DISCUSSION

Using the cmdlets is easy. All we need to do is define the end date of our search. Using the Microsoft cmdlet, we have this syntax:

```
Search-ADAccount -AccountExpiring `
-TimeSpan 60.00:00:00 -UsersOnly |
Format-Table Name, Distinguishedname
```

The Quest cmdlet has a simpler syntax:

```
Get-QADUser -AccountExpiresBefore $((Get-Date).AddDays(60))
```

With the Microsoft cmdlets, we use a TimeSpan to look 60 days ahead. We use the -UsersOnly parameter to only give us user accounts. The Quest cmdlet only has to be given the date that's 60 days ahead.

This completes our look at user accounts in Active Directory. You've seen a lot of material in this section that should cover most of your needs for automating the administration of user accounts. The scripts are easily modifiable, especially the search and modification scripts. They can all easily be adapted to accept parameters or to read from a file using the examples already given. I'm going to round off the chapter with a look at Active Directory groups.

5.4   *Active Directory groups*

Active Directory groups are manipulated in a similar manner to the local groups we've already seen. We have the alternative of using cmdlets in this case. We'll look at creating and modifying groups, and finish the section by discovering how to display nested group memberships from the perspective of a group and a user-something you definitely can't do in the GUI.

TECHNIQUE 13   **Group creation**

Group creation is similar to creating local groups.

PROBLEM

We need to create an Active Directory group.

SOLUTION

The group can be created using ADSI in a similar manner to creating a user in Active Directory, as shown in listing 5.22. There are a number of group types available in Active Directory. We start by creating constants that define the available types and scopes of groups ❶ (in listing 5.22). We bind to the OU where we'll create the group ❷. The group type and scope are combined at the bit level using a binary or operation ❸. I deliberately made this a universal group so that it's obvious that this works. The default group is a global security group. The group is created ❹ and immediately saved.

Listing 5.22   Creating Active Directory group

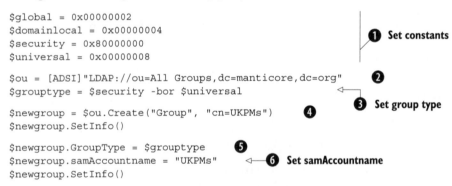

```
$global = 0x00000002
$domainlocal = 0x00000004                         ❶ Set constants
$security = 0x80000000
$universal = 0x00000008

$ou = [ADSI]"LDAP://ou=All Groups,dc=manticore,dc=org"    ❷
$grouptype = $security -bor $universal
                                                  ❸ Set group type
$newgroup = $ou.Create("Group", "cn=UKPMs")    ❹
$newgroup.SetInfo()

$newgroup.GroupType = $grouptype    ❺
$newgroup.samAccountname = "UKPMs"    ❻ Set samAccountname
$newgroup.SetInfo()
```

Processing is completed by setting the group type ❺ and a samaccountname ❻. We need samaccountname or a random one is generated. A final SetInfo() writes everything back to the database.

DISCUSSION

If we use the cmdlets, we need to supply the information shown. The code matches the script, but each cmdlet is only one line of code. We start with the Microsoft cmdlet, New-ADGroup, and then look at the Quest cmdlet. New-QADGroup:

```
New-ADGroup -Name "English Scientists" -SamAccountName EngSci `
 -GroupCategory Security -GroupScope Global `
-DisplayName "English Scientists" `
 -Path "OU=England,dc=manticore,dc=org" `
```

```
-Description "Members of this group are English Scientists"

New-QADGroup -Name "USPres" -SamAccountName "USPres" `
-GroupType "Security" -GroupScope "Universal" `
-ParentContainer "ou=All Groups,dc=manticore,dc=org"
```

After creating our group, we need to populate it with members.

<hr>

TECHNIQUE 14   ## Changing membership

Managing group membership will be a mixture of manual and automated procedures. I hate to say it, but not everything can be automated. If you can use the cmdlets, they're ideal for adding single users to a group. If you're creating a group with a
number of users that can be identified to an LDAP search, then use the following
script as a guide. It could just as easily be searching on a department or location. If the
users are scattered across your Active Directory, then collect their names into a CSV
file and modify the script to read the file and add the users to a group.

Group membership can also be set as the user account is created.

PROBLEM

All of the users in an OU need to be put into a group.

SOLUTION

An LDAP search filter is used to find all of the user accounts in a given OU, and we can
use that information to add the users to the group, as in listing 5.23. We start by creating a directory entry ❶ (in listing 5.23) for the group. A directorysearcher ❷ is created to find all of the users in the OU. Note that we set the root of the search to the
OU. There's no need to search the whole directory when we know the users are in a
single OU.

Listing 5.23   Changing Active Directory group membership

```
$group = [ADSI]"LDAP://cn=UKPMs,ou=All Groups,dc=manticore,dc=org"   ⬸❶ Group
$root = [ADSI]"LDAP://ou=England,dc=manticore,dc=org"
$search = [System.DirectoryServices.DirectorySearcher]$root            ❷ Search
$search.Filter = "(&(objectclass=user)(objectcategory=user))"             for users
$result = $search.FindAll()

foreach ($user in $result)    ⬸❸ Loop through results
{                                                              ❹ Add user
  $group.Add("LDAP://" + $user.properties.distinguishedname)   ⬸
  $group.SetInfo()                                             ⬸
                                                        ❺ Save
$message = $user.properties.distinguishedname +
  " added to group " + $group.cn
Write-Host $message              ⬸❻ Message
}
```

We loop through our results ❸ and use the Add() method of the group to add ❹ the
user into the group. We're constructing the AD path for the user, which is the input
parameter the method expects. $user.properties.distinguishedname is used to
access the distinguished name property because we're dealing with a directorysearcher resultset rather than a user object.

As usual, we use `SetInfo()` to write ❺ the information back to disk. The script finishes by writing a message ❻ to say the user has been created. If we wanted to remove users from a group, we could use the `Remove()` method instead of `Add()`.

DISCUSSION

We can use the cmdlets in a number of ways to solve this problem. One solution is to search on an attribute and pipe the results into the cmdlet we use to add a group member:

```
Get-ADUser -Filter {Title -eq "Scientist"} `
-SearchBase "OU=England,dc=manticore,dc=org" | foreach {
  Add-ADGroupMember -Identity EngSci -Members $($_.DistinguishedName) }
```

Quest has analagous cmdlets:

```
Get-QADUser -SearchRoot "ou=USA,dc=manticore,dc=org" |
ForEach-Object {Add-QADGroupMember
-Identity "CN=USPres,OU=All Groups,DC=Manticore,DC=org"
-Member $_.distinguishedname }
```

Use `Get-QADUser` (equivalent to a directory searcher) pointed at the OU with the users. Pipe the results into a `foreach` where we use `Add-QADGroupMember` to add the user to the group. The `-Identity` parameter refers to the group, and `-Member` to the user. The cmdlets automatically print the results on screen as shown in figure 5.1.

After creating our groups and populating them with users, we may need to change the scope of the group.

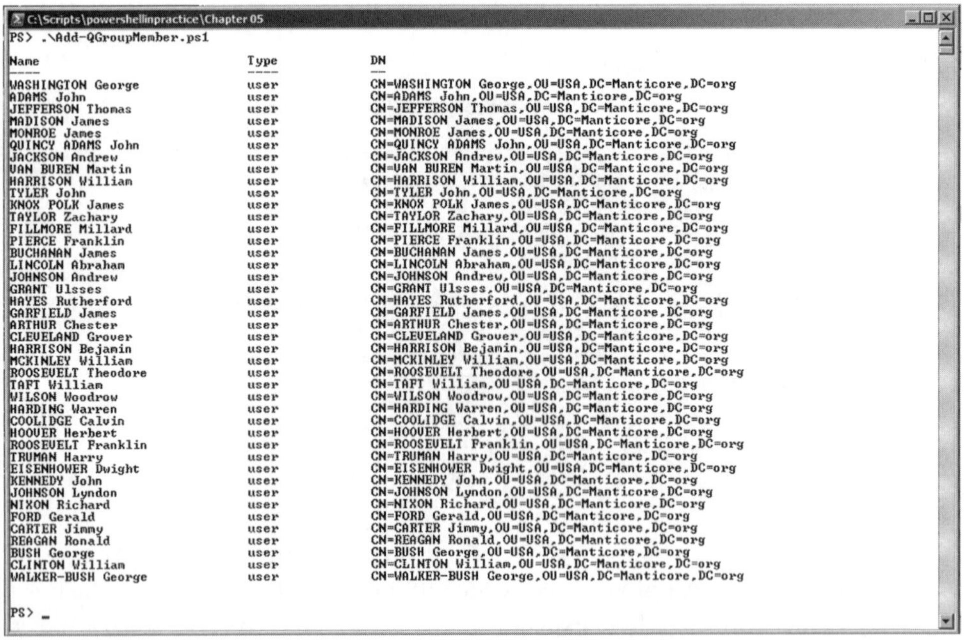

Figure 5.1   Output when using Add-QADGroupMember

TECHNIQUE 15 **Changing scope**

Groups can be changed from distribution lists to security groups (going the other way, you'll lose the permissions the group has) and the group scope can be changed within the limits given next. Distribution groups don't have their own constant, so just leave out the security group value.

Only some group scope changes are supported:

- Universal to global
- Global to universal
- Domain local to universal
- Universal to domain local

In all cases, the group membership has to support the new scope; for instance a global group can't be changed to a universal group if it's a member of other global groups.

PROBLEM

Our universal group must be changed to a global group.

SOLUTION

The group scope is changed by modifying the grouptype attribute, as shown in listing 5.24. The script starts by defining the constants ❶ that we use to create the group. Comparison with listing 5.22 will show them to be the same as used in that script. We have to get a directory entry for the group ❷, and create ❸ and set the new group type ❹. The script finishes by saving the change to disk ❺. The creation of the group type is a binary bit operation as in listing 5.22.

Listing 5.24 Changing Active Directory group scope

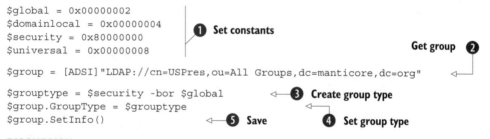

```
$global = 0x00000002
$domainlocal = 0x00000004        ❶ Set constants
$security = 0x80000000
$universal = 0x00000008
                                                        Get group ❷
$group = [ADSI]"LDAP://cn=USPres,ou=All Groups,dc=manticore,dc=org"

$grouptype = $security -bor $global      ❸ Create group type
$group.GroupType = $grouptype
$group.SetInfo()                    ❺ Save        ❹ Set group type
```

DISCUSSION

The change can be accomplished by using cmdlets. We define the group together with the new type and scope:

```
# Microsoft
Get-ADGroup -Identity EngSci
Set-ADGroup -Identity EngSci  -GroupScope Universal
Get-ADGroup -Identity EngSci

# Quest
Set-QADGroup -Identity "cn=UKPMs,ou=All Groups,dc=manticore,dc=org"
-GroupScope "Global" -GroupType "Security"
```

We need to consider two final tasks regarding groups to complete our work with Active Directory. One question that will arise is "Which groups is this user a member of?" But before we consider that, we need to be able to find all of the members of a group.

TECHNIQUE 16   **Finding group members**

Discovering the members of a group can be thought of as two separate problems. We have a problem—the direct group membership—that can be resolved easily. This is the list of members you'd see on the Members tab of the Properties dialog in Active Directory Users and Computers.

The second problem is more complex, in that we want to find all of the members, including those users that are members of a group—members of the group in which we're interested. The group nesting may occur to any number of levels.

PROBLEM

We need to find all the members of a group.

SOLUTION

We solve this problem by creating a function that will list the group members, as shown in listing 5.25. If a member is itself a group, we get the function to call itself using the name of that group. This is known as *recursion*. The primary goal of this section is to resolve the nested group membership. But before we review that script, we'll look at reading the direct membership of a group:

```
$group = [ADSI]"LDAP://cn=UKPMs,ou=All Groups,dc=manticore,dc=org"
$group.member | Sort-Object
```

After retrieving a directory entry object for the group, we can display the members using $group.member. Piping this into a sort makes the output more readable.

Listing 5.25   Get nested group membership

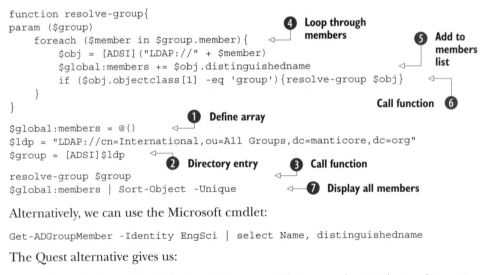

```
function resolve-group{
param ($group)
    foreach ($member in $group.member){        ← ❹ Loop through members    ❺ Add to members list
        $obj = [ADSI]("LDAP://" + $member)
        $global:members += $obj.distinguishedname        ←
        if ($obj.objectclass[1] -eq 'group'){resolve-group $obj}        ←
    }
}                                               ❻ Call function
$global:members = @()        ← ❶ Define array
$ldp = "LDAP://cn=International,ou=All Groups,dc=manticore,dc=org"
$group = [ADSI]$ldp        ←
                            ❷ Directory entry      ❸ Call function
resolve-group $group        ←
$global:members | Sort-Object -Unique        ← ❼ Display all members
```

Alternatively, we can use the Microsoft cmdlet:

```
Get-ADGroupMember -Identity EngSci | select Name, distinguishedname
```

The Quest alternative gives us:

```
Get-QADGroupMember -Identity "cn=USPres,ou=All Groups,dc=manticore,dc=org"
```

Discovering the nested group membership is more complicated than retrieving the membership of a single group, as listing 5.25 shows. The script consists of two parts: a function, `resolve-group`, that reads the group membership, and the main part of the script that gets the group and displays the membership. We start the script by creating an empty array (developers will refer to this as *declaring* an array) **❶**. The point to note here is the way the variable is defined: `$global:members`. The addition of `global:` to the variable makes it a variable of global scope, meaning that we can access the same variable in the main part of the script and in the function. This will be important.

ADSI is used to get a directory entry **❷** for the group. We then call the `resolve-group` function **❸**, passing in the group as a parameter. The `$group` within the function is in a different scope than the `$group` outside the function.

A `foreach` loop is used to read the group membership **❹** from the member property. A directory entry is created for each member **❺** and added to our globally available array. We test the group member, and if it's a group **❻**, we call the `resolve-group` function using the member as a parameter.

DISCUSSION

Congratulations! You now understand recursion, as the function will keep calling itself as many times as necessary. As the array we created to hold the membership is global in scope, it can be accessed through the various levels of recursion.

Once the function has finished processing the direct and nested membership, we return to the main part of the script. The contents of the array are sorted and the unique values **❼** are displayed. Using the `-Unique` parameter prevents duplicate entries from being displayed, and means that we don't have to write code to deal with them. This makes the script easier to write and understand.

There's a simpler way to get this information using the Microsoft cmdlet `Get-ADGroupMember`. The `-Recursive` parameter displays nested group membership:

```
Get-ADGroupMember -Identity international -Recursive |
select Name, DistinguishedName
```

The Quest alternative is to use the `-Indirect` parameter:

```
Get-QADGroupMember -Identity 'manticore\international' -Indirect
```

Having mastered recursion in the previous example, we'll use it again to determine all of the groups of which a particular user is a member.

TECHNIQUE 17 **Finding a user's group membership**

One last Active Directory script and then we're done.

PROBLEM

We need to find all of the groups of which the user is a member.

SOLUTION

The `memberof` attribute holds the groups of which the user is a member. We can recursively check those groups for other groups to determine the full list of groups where the user is a member, as shown in listing 5.26. The processing starts by getting a directory entry for the user ❶. We use the memberof property to find the groups of which the user is a direct member ❷. The group is passed into the function resolve-membership, where the distinguished name is written ❸ to screen.

For each of the groups, we get a directory entry ❹ and test to see if it's a member of any groups. If it is, we call the function with the name of each group. ❺ Recursion keeps this script compact. It is a topic that many find difficult but the examples in the book should make it easier to use. Once you have worked through a few scripts of your own you'll be proficient.

Listing 5.26   Get user's group membership

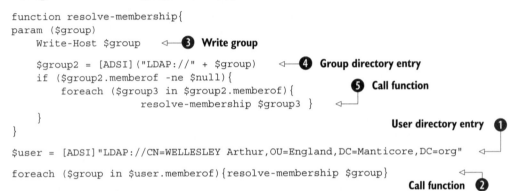

```
function resolve-membership{
param ($group)
    Write-Host $group      ◁——❸ Write group

    $group2 = [ADSI]("LDAP://" + $group)    ◁——❹ Group directory entry
    if ($group2.memberof -ne $null){
                                             ❺ Call function
        foreach ($group3 in $group2.memberof){
                    resolve-membership $group3 }    ◁
    }
}                                               User directory entry ❶

$user = [ADSI]"LDAP://CN=WELLESLEY Arthur,OU=England,DC=Manticore,DC=org"   ◁

foreach ($group in $user.memberof){resolve-membership $group}   ◁
                                            Call function ❷
```

DISCUSSION

I haven't produced a version using the cmdlets, as there isn't a built-in way to produce this information, and we just replace the [ADSI] lines ❹ and ❶ in listing 5.26 with Get-ADGroup/Get-QADGroup and Get-ADUser/Get-QADUser respectively.

5.5   *Summary*

Automating Active Directory administration involves working with users and groups or performing searches. We can perform these tasks by scripting based on ADSI or by using the AD cmdlets from either Microsoft or Quest .

Creation and modification scripts follow a pattern of getting a directory object, making changes (or creating a child object), and saving back to the database. Searching has its own pattern of defining the root of the search, defining the search filter, performing the search, and displaying the results.

There's useful functionality in the System.DirectoryServices.Accountmanagement classes, though a few holes also exist.

After creating and modifying our user account, it's time to turn our attention to our email system. Email has become a business critical tool, and by combining our mailbox and user account administration techniques, we can automate and streamline our processes.

Mailboxes

6

This chapter covers

- Managing mailboxes and mail enabled objects
- Managing distribution lists
- Managing mail protocols and quotas
- Reporting on mailbox statistics

Email is the number one business tool today, and one of the items guaranteed to get users upset if it doesn't work properly. We, as administrators, need to keep email working. In a Microsoft environment, email means Exchange. In this chapter, we'll be looking at email from the user's perspective—her mailbox—and how we can automate its administration throughout the mailbox lifecycle of creation, modification, and destruction. In chapter 12, we'll look at administering Exchange servers.

> **EXCHANGE TERMINOLOGY** It's assumed that the reader is familiar with Exchange terminology and administration.

This is a book about PowerShell, so I'll be concentrating on Exchange Server 2007, which is dependent on PowerShell for administration. It's possible to administer Exchange 2003 through PowerShell. A good example of this can be found in Jonathan Medd's power pack for PowerGUI, which can be downloaded from the PowerGUI site (see appendix E). Exchange 2010 builds on the foundation of

Exchange 2007, so all the concepts in this chapter can be ported directly to Exchange 2010 when it comes into production.

Exchange Server 2007 provides two management tools. There's a GUI tool called the *Exchange Management Console* and there's PowerShell, known as the *Exchange Management Shell*. Exchange Server 2007 has been held up by the PowerShell community as a poster child of PowerShell implementation. The PowerShell cmdlets were created first, then the GUI was layered over the top of the cmdlets. In fact, there are some tasks (approximately 20%) that can only be performed in PowerShell: there's no functionality available in the GUI to perform these tasks.

Any action performed in the GUI actually runs a PowerShell cmdlet in the background. There's an option to display the PowerShell command that's being executed; this can be copied and used as the basis of a future script. An example is shown in figure 6.1. This is a great way to learn to use PowerShell.

EXCHANGE SERVER 2007 Exchange Server 2007 for production use is 64-bit only, which can make life difficult for experimenting. There's also a 32-bit evaluation version that can be used in desktop virtualization products. It's time limited, but in my experience it still works after the time expiry. It does remind you it has expired, though! Running an expired version in the demo of a talk always seems to get a laugh for some reason.

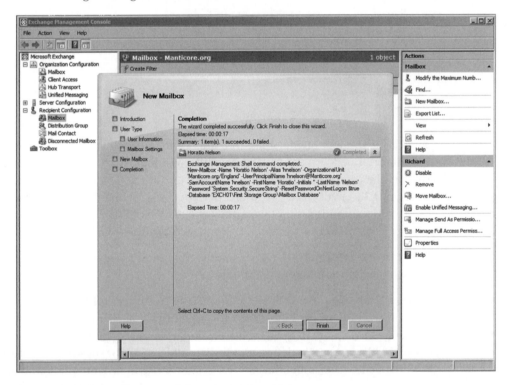

Figure 6.1 **Exchange Management Console showing script**

When Exchange Server 2007 is installed, it requires PowerShell v1 to be available and installed. The Exchange cmdlets (approximately 400 in number) are installed via a snapin as we'd expect, but the snapin isn't added directly to PowerShell. A console file, as discussed in chapter 2, is used to create a separate Exchange Command Shell. The snapins can be easily added to standard PowerShell if required by putting the following lines in your profile:

```
Add-PSSnapin Microsoft.Exchange.Management.PowerShell.Admin
Add-PSSnapin Microsoft.Exchange.Management.Powershell.Support
```

> **MANAGEMENT TOOLS** If you want to install the Exchange Server 2007 management tools on Windows Vista, you need to use the SP1 version of Exchange Server 2007.

6.1   *Automating mailbox management*

Before we get around to using PowerShell, we need to spend a little time thinking about how we'll administer Exchange 2007. One of the changes that have been introduced is that the Exchange attributes aren't visible in ADUC. If you use ADSIEdit or the Object tab in Windows 2008 ADUC, you can view and work with the attributes as required, but that's like using a sledgehammer to crack a nut.

The nature of PowerShell lends itself to easy usage and increased productivity, meaning that many tasks can be performed interactively. But one issue must be addressed before we start solving our administration problems: who will perform the administration? In many organizations, especially large ones, different teams are responsible for administering Active Directory and Exchange. The same team may be responsible for both in smaller organizations. During the lifecycle of a mailbox, there are a number of times when work has to be performed in both Active Directory and Exchange, particularly during the creation and deletion of mailboxes. Either the same individuals perform both tasks or the process must encompass both teams to ensure the work is completed.

Exchange introduces a number of cmdlets that can be used to work with Active Directory. These cmdlets aren't fully featured as far as Active Directory is concerned. They only supply the functionality required to complete the Exchange-related tasks. Using the Quest AD cmdlets and the Exchange cmdlets together enables some tasks to be performed that neither can perform alone. Exchange 2007 needs SP3 (available in mid-2010) to run on Windows Server 2008 R2, so using the Exchange cmdlets and the Microsoft AD cmdlets together requires a more restrictive environment. This also applies to installing the administration tools on Windows 7. Exchange 2010 uses a web service-type remoting configuration similar in concept to the Microsoft AD cmdlets. Using the AD cmdlets and Exchange 2010 together is a simpler proposition that can be installed immediately.

Exchange has three classes of objects we need to be concerned with when considering the user aspects of email:

- Mailbox-enabled
- Mail-enabled
- Contact

A *mailbox-enabled* user is an Active Directory user that has a mailbox hosted on the Exchange server. A *mail-enabled* user has an account in Active Directory, but uses a mailbox on an external server. Only the email address is stored in Active Directory. A *contact* is an external person whose email address we want to be available to many people via the address book. We'll start our examination of administering the user aspects of email by learning how to create mailboxes.

TECHNIQUE 18   **Create a mailbox**

Creating a mailbox for a user can occur at the time a user account is created, or a mailbox can be created for an existing user (see section 6.3.1). The example shown here uses the Exchange New-Mailbox cmdlet to create the user account and simultaneously creates the mailbox. If the two actions need to be separated, consider using the scripts presented in chapter 5 to create the user account and use the command in listing 6.3 to create the mailbox.

PROBLEM

We need to create a user account and mailbox for a new user in our organization.

SOLUTION

The New-Mailbox cmdlet provides the functionality to perform both tasks, assuming that we're using an account that has the required permissions for Active Directory and Exchange. This script, like many in this chapter, was derived by running the Create Mailbox Wizard and utilizing the subsequent script. It's referred to as a script, but in reality it's a single line of PowerShell!

Listing 6.1   Creating a user account and mailbox

```
New-Mailbox -Name 'NELSON Horatio' -Alias 'hnelson'          ❶
-OrganizationalUnit 'Manticore.org/England'                  ⟵ ❷ OU naming
-UserPrincipalName 'hnelson@Manticore.org'
-SamAccountName 'hnelson' -FirstName 'Horatio' -Initials ''
-LastName 'NELSON'
-Password 'Password1'          ❸        ❹ Force password
-ResetPasswordOnNextLogon $true    ⟵           reset
-Database 'EXCH01\First Storage Group\Mailbox Database'      ❺
```

If we're creating the user account and the mailbox, we need to provide the required information for Active Directory and Exchange. The -Alias parameter ❶ supplies the email alias that'll be used by the user. Note that by default, it's the same as the SamAccountName. The way the organizational unit name is presented ❷ may be unfamiliar. It's in effect presented as a path—*domain name\OU hierarchy*. This should be compared to the way distinguished names are used in the AD cmdlets to supply the same information.

In this case, I've hard-coded the password into the script ❸. If you want to add an additional layer of security to your scripts, consider using the technique that utilizes Read-Host to obtain the password as a secure string that was presented in chapter 5.

EXCHANGE GUI SCRIPTS   If the Create Mailbox Wizard is used and the resultant script copied for subsequent use, the value entered for the password is *not* copied into the script. Instead, the script reads as -Password 'System. Security.SecureString'. In other words, the .NET object type is shown rather than the value. This will occur in a number of places within Exchange when copying a script from the wizard. Double-check any scripts created using the wizard for this occurrence.

The -ResetPasswordOnNextLogon parameter ❹ is set to $true to force the user to change her password when she logs on for the first time. Our final piece of required information is the Exchange database ❺ where we'll be creating the mailbox. This is presented as *server\storage group\database*.

USER ACCOUNT ENABLED   The user account is automatically created in the enabled state.

DISCUSSION
By using the techniques utilized in listing 5.10, we can adapt our script to enable the creation of users and mailboxes in bulk. The adapted version is shown in listing 6.2.

Listing 6.2   Creating user accounts and mailboxes in bulk

```
Import-Csv pres.csv | ForEach-Object {      ◁──❶ Read CSV
$name = $_.last.ToUpper() + " " + $_.first
$upn = $_.userid + "@manticore.org"                    ❷ Create
                                                         variables

New-Mailbox -Name $name -Alias $_.userid    ◁──┐ Create account
-OrganizationalUnit 'Manticore.org/England'    ❸ and mailbox
-UserPrincipalName $upn
-SamAccountName $_.userid -FirstName $_.first -Initials ''
-LastName $_.last.ToUpper()
-Password 'Password1'
-ResetPasswordOnNextLogon $true
-Database 'EXCH01\First Storage Group\Mailbox Database'     }
```

Comparing the previous two listings shows that the only real changes are putting the original script inside a foreach-object loop and reading the required data from a CSV file. Ideally the CSV file would be created by the HR department as part of the process used when new people join the organization. This was also discussed in section 5.3.2.

We start by reading the CSV file ❶ and passing its contents onto the pipeline. Remember that with PowerShell, the header row in a CSV file provides the field names that we can use to refer to data on the pipeline.

Within the foreach loop, we combine the first and last names to create the full name ❷. The user principal name ($upn) is created at the same time. We then use the variables we've created or the data on the pipeline (for example, $_.first for first name) to supply the values for creating users and mailboxes in New-Mailbox ❸.

Moving to this type of process, we create a CSV file with the first and last names of the user and a user ID. This is then used to create the user account and mailbox. For large numbers of users, this will be a significant time saving over performing these actions manually.

MULTIPLE ADMIN TEAMS   If the organization has separated user creation and mailbox creation into separate groups of administrators, the same CSV file can be used by both. Use it with listing 5.10 to create the users. It can then be used with a modified version of the following script to create the mailbox.

Creating new users and mailboxes may form the majority of our creation activity, but we may have a requirement to create a mailbox for an existing user account or create a mail contact.

6.2   *Enabling mail*

Creating mailboxes as we create the user accounts is one aspect, but we also need to consider the situation where we have existing accounts and need to give access to email. There are three variations:

- Create a mailbox for an existing account.
- Enable an existing account to receive email on an external email address.
- Create a contact for a person external to the organization.

GLOBAL ADDRESS LIST   All of these objects will be automatically included in the Global Address List unless they're specifically excluded.

We'll start with creating a mailbox for an existing user. I've used this technique where Active Directory accounts already exist and the organization is migrating to Exchange from another email system. It's the quickest and most efficient way to perform this task, though I recommend that you do it one OU at a time. It's always fun to challenge a GUI user to a race!

TECHNIQUE 19   **Mailboxes**

In Exchange terms, a *mailbox* resides on an Exchange server within the organization. The user associated with that mailbox has an account in Active Directory that he uses to authenticate to the network. His Active Directory account is also used to facilitate the authorization (or denial) of access to network resources.

PROBLEM

An existing user account in Active Directory needs to have a mailbox created.

SOLUTION

The `Enable-Mailbox` cmdlet can be used to create the mailbox, as shown in listing 6.3. The cmdlet provides the functionality to create a mailbox for an existing user. We need to provide the identity of the user together with the email alias and the mail database in which we'll create the mailbox. The format of the identity should be noted. In this case, it has the form *domain/OU/user*. The mailbox database is specified as *server\storage group\database*.

Listing 6.3   Creating a mailbox for an existing user

```
Enable-Mailbox -Identity 'Manticore.org/England/HORNBLOWER Horatio'
-Alias 'hhorblow' -Database 'EXCH01\First Storage Group\Mailbox Database'
```

DISCUSSION

If there are many users who require a mailbox, the bulk approach to creating user accounts and mailboxes shown previously can be utilized. We can also use:

```
Get-User -OrganizationalUnit "England" |
Enable-Mailbox `
-Database 'EXCH01\First Storage Group\Mailbox Database'
```

This is a purely Exchange solution to the problem. `Get-User` will also fetch the user accounts in all child OUs of the given OU. We may want to spread our mailboxes over a number of databases, as in listing 6.3a.

Listing 6.3a   Creating a mailbox for many existing users

```
$maxdb = 4
Get-User -OrganizationalUnit "Austria" | foreach `
 -begin {$db = 1} `
 -process {
    switch ($db){
    1 {$maildb = "Exch01\SG1\MailDb1"}
    2 {$maildb = "Exch01\SG2\MailDb2"}
    3 {$maildb = "Exch01\SG3\MailDb3"}
    4 {$maildb = "Exch01\SG4\MailDb4"}
    }
    Enable-Mailbox -Identity $_.DistinguishedName -Database $maildb `
       -Alias $_.samaccountname -Displayname $_.Name ##-WhatIf
    if ($db -eq $maxdb){$db=1} else {$db++}
}
```

We start by creating a variable to hold the maximum number of databases. We can use `Get-User` to fetch the user accounts from Active Directory. The accounts are piped into `foreach`, where we use the `$db` variable to decide in which database we'll create the mailbox. Note that the `-begin` script block is used to set the initial value to 1. `Enable-Mailbox` creates the mailbox in the appropriate database. We then increment the database number (reset to 1 if required) to start the cycle for the next mailbox. This gives us a rough distribution of new mailboxes. An alternative, though slower, method would be to find the smallest database each time and use that as the target.

There may be some cases where a user in Active Directory isn't entitled to a mailbox, but there's also a requirement for this individual to be emailed from within the organization.

TECHNIQUE 20   Mail-enabled

In Exchange terminology, a *mail-enabled* account is an Active Directory account that uses an external email system rather than having a mailbox on the internal email system. This scenario may fit a contractor or member of staff from a partner organization who must be able to authenticate in Active Directory, but whose mail will be directed to her external account.

PROBLEM

We need mail to be sent to a user with an external email address. The user must also appear in the internal address lists.

SOLUTION

We'll mail-enable the user account. Creating a mail-enabled account is similar to creating a mailbox-enabled user, as shown in listing 6.4. We need to supply the identifying information such as name, and the `samaccountname`. A password needs to created, and the account enabled. If we compare this to the script to create a new mailbox discussed earlier in the chapter, we can see that the only real difference is that we're supplying an external email address in place of specifying the database in which to create the mailbox.

Listing 6.4 Creating mail-enabled account

```
New-MailUser -Name 'NIMITZ Chester' -Alias 'cnimitz'
-OrganizationalUnit 'Manticore.org/USA'
-UserPrincipalName 'cnimitz@Manticore.org'
-SamAccountName 'cnimitz' -FirstName 'Chester' -Initials ''
-LastName 'NIMITZ' -Password 'Password1'
-ResetPasswordOnNextLogon $true
-ExternalEmailAddress 'SMTP:cnimitz@navy.com'
```

DISCUSSION

In the case of an existing account, we can use `Enable-MailUser` instead, as in listing 6.5.

Listing 6.5 Mail-enabling an existing account

```
Enable-MailUser -Identity 'Manticore.org/USA/PATTON George'
-Alias 'gpatton' -ExternalEmailAddress 'SMTP:gpatton@army.com'
```

Our final type of mail object is a contact.

TECHNIQUE 21   ## Contact

A *contact* is an object that provides a link to an external email address. There will be people external to your organization whom you need to email on a frequent basis. That's not just your mum! On an individual basis, it's possible to create your own contact list in Outlook. If a number of your users need to email these people, it's more efficient to create a single contact that everyone can use.

PROBLEM

We need to provide the email addresses of external people such as business partners, customers, and suppliers in the address list so that they can be accessed by the whole organization.

SOLUTION

We'll create a contact for these people, as shown in listing 6.6. The information required is similar to that for a normal user account. We supply the naming information together with the OU in which we want to create the contact. The final piece of information is the external email address associated with the contact.

Listing 6.6 Creating a contact

```
New-MailContact -ExternalEmailAddress 'SMTP:jmarlbor@army.com'
-Name 'MARLBOROUGH John' -Alias 'jmarlbor'
-OrganizationalUnit 'Manticore.org/Contacts'
-FirstName 'John' -Initials '' -LastName 'MARLBOROUGH'
```

DISCUSSION

Last Christmas, I was asked if I could set up email contacts for several hundred customers so that we could email a Christmas greeting. After specifying the information I required in terms of names and email addresses, I piped the contents of a CSV file into the `New-MailContact` cmdlet. I used the techniques shown earlier for bulk creation. A job that would've taken literally hours, assuming terminal boredom didn't set in, was completed in minutes.

We've seen how to create our mailbox and mail-enable users. The next stage in the lifecycle is starting to modify these mailboxes.

6.3 Modifying mailboxes

There are a number of settings that administrators can modify on mailboxes. These include control of the mailbox size, which protocols can be used to access the mailbox, moving mailboxes between databases, and disabling mail.

These actions can be performed in the GUI, but in many cases it's more efficient to use PowerShell. Some of these actions will be used more frequently than others. I suspect the settings that are most often used are those to do with the mailbox size limits.

TECHNIQUE 22   **Mailbox size limits**

Mailbox size limits can be set in a number of places, including the server, the database, and the individual mailbox. Exchange defines three limits; in ascending order, these are:

- Issue Warning Quota
- Prohibit Send Quota
- Prohibit Send and Receive Quota

The limits apply to when the user is warned that the mailbox is filling up, when no more messages can be sent, and finally when no more messages can be sent or received. At this point, you have to start cleaning out the mailbox—unless you can convince your friendly Exchange administrator to increase the size of the mailbox. Strangely, I can't remember ever seeing a request to have a mailbox reduced in size!

> **NOT FOR USERS' EYES!**   Don't let users read this section. If they discover how easy this is, they'll all want a bigger mailbox.

The `*-Mailbox` cmdlets will come to our aid here. Remember that `get` and `set` are the verbs that correspond to reading and writing information in PowerShell.

PROBLEM

A user is continually filling his mailbox. It's been decided that because of the nature of his role that his mailbox will be configured with larger quota limits.

SOLUTION

Changing the quota limits on a mailbox is accomplished with the `Set-Mailbox` cmdlet, as shown in listing 6.7. The task requires little typing, if tab completion is used, so it's ideal as an interactive task. The first step is to check the current limits ❶. `Get-Mailbox` will return a large set of information about the mailbox, including the quota limits. We want to reduce the output, so we use a select to restrict our output to the name and the quotas.

WILDCARDS The use of a wildcard in the property names makes this even easier. It's seemingly the little things like this that show how much thought has gone into PowerShell.

The quota properties show a setting of unlimited, which means that the server or database default has been applied to the mailbox. In order to change the setting on the mailbox, we need to use the Set-Mailbox cmdlet ❷. We identify the mailbox using the samaccountname in this instance.

Listing 6.7 Changing mailbox quota limits

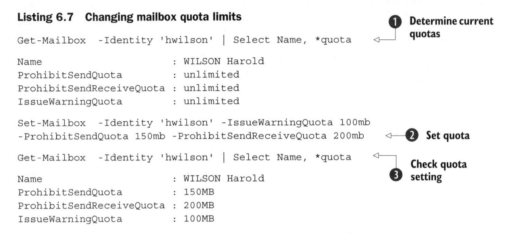

```
Get-Mailbox  -Identity 'hwilson' | Select Name, *quota     ⟵──┘  ❶ Determine current
                                                                   quotas
Name                       : WILSON Harold
ProhibitSendQuota          : unlimited
ProhibitSendReceiveQuota   : unlimited
IssueWarningQuota          : unlimited

Set-Mailbox  -Identity 'hwilson' -IssueWarningQuota 100mb
 -ProhibitSendQuota 150mb -ProhibitSendReceiveQuota 200mb   ⟵── ❷ Set quota

Get-Mailbox  -Identity 'hwilson' | Select Name, *quota     ⟵──┐
                                                              │ Check quota
Name                       : WILSON Harold                  ❸ setting
ProhibitSendQuota          : 150MB
ProhibitSendReceiveQuota   : 200MB
IssueWarningQuota          : 100MB
```

DISCUSSION
The quota settings need to be set individually. This is where tab completion becomes so useful. Type the hyphen and the first part of parameter name, or even the first letter, and keep pressing Tab until the desired parameter is shown. The second point to note is that we can give the quota limits in megabytes, or even gigabytes, as shown. When we're working in the GUI, we have to work in kilobytes, which isn't nearly as convenient. A final check of the mailbox settings ❸ shows that the new quota limits have been applied.

If users are accessing their mailboxes using Outlook, there's no need to configure other protocols. But there may be users who need to use other protocols such as IMAP, POP, or OWA (Outlook Web Access). These settings are handled slightly differently.

TECHNIQUE 23   Enabling IMAP

There are three protocols that can be used to access mailboxes, apart from using Outlook: POP, IMAP, and OWA. Exchange Server 2007 has a concept of *server roles*. In this concept, there's a separation between the server managing the mailboxes, the *mailbox server,* and the server managing access through these additional protocols, the *client access server.*

SERVICES   The appropriate service needs to be running on the client access server for these additional protocols to work.

We need to use a different cmdlet to work with these settings—the `Get-` and `Set-CAS-Mailbox` cmdlets, where *CAS* stands for *client access server.*

PROBLEM

One of our users can only access her mailbox by using IMAP. Your task, should you choose to accept it, is to enable IMAP on the mailbox.

SOLUTION

If these settings are enabled via the GUI, it's simply a case of checking a box. When using PowerShell, we use a Boolean value to represent whether the protocol is enabled. The property value is set to true or false to indicate enabled or disabled, as shown in listing 6.8.

Listing 6.8   Enable IMAP on a mailbox

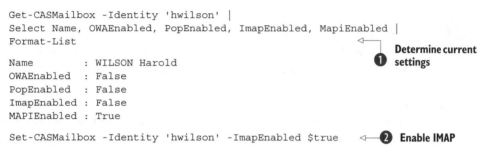

```
Get-CASMailbox -Identity 'hwilson' |
Select Name, OWAEnabled, PopEnabled, ImapEnabled, MapiEnabled |
Format-List
                                                          Determine current
                                                        ❶ settings
Name        : WILSON Harold
OWAEnabled  : False
PopEnabled  : False
ImapEnabled : False
MAPIEnabled : True

Set-CASMailbox -Identity 'hwilson' -ImapEnabled $true   ❷ Enable IMAP
```

DISCUSSION

It's always wise to determine the current settings before we start making changes. We may even find that the settings have already been enabled. In this case, we use `Get-CASMailbox` ❶ and supply the relevant identity. A `Select` is used to reduce the number of properties we'll be examining. Note that the properties are all the names of the protocol concatenated with the word *enabled.* These properties take a Boolean, true or false, value. This particular user can only use MAPI to access the mailbox.

NOTE   This isn't the default state. I deliberately configured the user this way before starting the example.

We can use the `Set-CASMailbox` cmdlet to enable the protocol ❷. Note that apart from the identity, we only have to give the `-IMAPEnabled` parameter the value `$true`. `$true` is one of the PowerShell automatic variables.

POP is enabled in a similar manner.

TECHNIQUE 24   **Enablin**

As discussed in the previous example, POP can be enabled or disabled by setting the value of the appropriate property to true or false respectively.

PROBLEM

We have to be able to modify the POP settings on the mailbox.

SOLUTION

The *CASMailbox cmdlets can also work for us in this scenario. If we want to enable the protocol ❶, we use Set-CASMailbox and set the -PopEnabled parameter to $true—we turn it on. Conversely, we can turn the protocol off ❷ by setting the parameter to false. See listing 6.9.

Listing 6.9   Modifying the -PopEnabled settings

```
Set-CASMailbox -Identity 'hwilson' -PopEnabled $true     ◁─❶ Enable POP protocol

Set-CASMailbox -Identity 'hwilson' -PopEnabled $false    ◁─❷ Disable POP protocol
```

DISCUSSION

Modifying the protocols that users can use is one way that we can allow access to mailboxes but we need to accommodate other types of user as well. Mobile users, who are rarely in the office, need to access their mailboxes across the Internet. One method of achieving this is to use OWA.

TECHNIQUE 25   Enabling OWA

There are a number of configuration steps to enable OWA access across the enterprise. The server configuration is beyond the scope of this book, but we can look at configuring the mailboxes to enable this method of access.

PROBLEM

How can we determine which users don't have OWA enabled? Once we've determined this, we also need to be able to enable OWA for those users in the most efficient manner.

SOLUTION

We first find out who doesn't have OWA access and then we enable those users. We can discover which users don't have OWA enabled by first performing a Get-CASMailbox on the user population. A filter can be applied by using Where-Object (where) to check the OWAEnabled property on each object (user) coming down the pipeline ❶. $_.OWAEnabled refers to the OWAEnabled property on the current object on the pipeline. The ! means *not*—we're checking for users where the property isn't enabled, as shown in listing 6.10.

Listing 6.10   Enabling OWA

```
Get-CASMailbox | Where{!$_.OWAEnabled}        ❶

Get-CASMailbox | Where{!$_.OWAEnabled} | Set-CASMailbox -OWAEnabled $true   ❷
```

The next step is to enable OWA access ❷. We can use our previous line of code, and rather than displaying the results, we can pipe them into the Set-CASMailbox cmdlet and give the -OWAEnabled parameter a value of true. Straightforward but very powerful.

DISCUSSION

I've been asked to perform this task in the past against a 12,000-seat Active Directory. I didn't really like the idea of checking each account manually, so I wrote a script. In those days, I was limited to using VBScript. It took 86 lines of code. PowerShell does it in one!

TECHNIQUE 26 Adding an email address

When we create a mailbox, an email address is created according to the policies that are in force within the Exchange organization. There are situations where the user requires another email address, for instance due to a name change, but needs to keep the old name as well. These email addresses work for incoming mail. Outgoing mail will be labeled as coming from the primary SMTP address.

PROBLEM

A user asks if it's possible to add another email address to her mailbox for incoming mail.

SOLUTION

We know that `Set-Mailbox` can be used to make changes to the mailbox settings. After looking at the help file (remember our four friends from chapter 2: `Get-Help`, `Get-Command`, `Get-Member`, and `Get-PSDrive`), we discover an `EmailAddresses` parameter we can use. Before we start adding email addresses, it might be a good idea to view the currently defined addresses ❶ (in listing 6.11). `Get-Mailbox` retrieves the information and we use a `select` to restrict the display to the data points of interest in this situation.

> **TIP** When I'm working with mailboxes like this, I'll often use `Get-Mailbox` to establish that I'm using the correct mailbox. Use the up arrow key to display the previous command and change `Get` to `Set`. This saves some typing and helps avoid mistakes.

`Set` is the verb we need when making changes ❷. Note that I haven't explicitly used the `-Identity` parameter in listing 6.11. If you look at the help file, you'll see that this is a positional parameter. PowerShell will assume that the first values you input will be assigned to the `-Identity` parameter.

Listing 6.11 Add an email address to a mailbox

❶ Check current addresses

```
Get-Mailbox "WELLESLEY Arthur" | Select Name, EmailAddresses

Set-Mailbox "WELLESLEY Arthur" -EmailAddresses `
  ((Get-Mailbox "WELLESLEY Arthur").EmailAddresses +
"ironduke@manticore.org")
```

❷ Add address

The `-EmailAddresses` parameter is used to set the new address. We need to be careful to ensure that we add an email address rather than overwriting the existing addresses. We create a list of current addresses by using the `Get-Mailbox` cmdlet, and then we add the new address to the list. Note the use of parentheses to wrap the new list of addresses and to work with the object returned from `Get-Mailbox`.

DISCUSSION

One of the useful things about Exchange from the user's perspective is the address list. It makes it easy to find the email addresses of people within the organization to whom you want to send an email. These address lists are maintained automatically by Exchange. But occasionally there may be a reason for a particular user not to be included in the address list.

TECHNIQUE 27   Hiding an address from the address list

The default for Exchange is that all users are shown in the address list. Occasionally we may need to hide a user from the address list.

PROBLEM

There are a number of possible scenarios regarding being visible to the address list. A user may need to be hidden from the address list. We may need to determine which users are hidden from the address list. Finally, we may need to make all hidden users visible again.

SOLUTION

We can perform this action by using the `Set-Mailbox` cmdlet, as in listing 6.12. Hiding the user from the address book is another tick box in the GUI. In PowerShell, it's another Boolean value. We use `Set-Mailbox` ❶ and the `-HiddenFromAddressListsEnabled` parameter is given a value of true.

Listing 6.12   Hide a mailbox from the address list

```
Set-Mailbox  -Identity 'hwilson' -HiddenFromAddressListsEnabled $true        ❶

Get-Mailbox | Where {$_.HiddenFromAddressListsEnabled}        ❷

Get-Mailbox | Where {$_.HiddenFromAddressListsEnabled} |
Set-Mailbox -HiddenFromAddressListsEnabled $false            ❸
```

DISCUSSION

Finding users who are hidden from the address lists ❷ is a matter of piping the output of `Get-Mailbox` into the `Where-Object` cmdlet and filtering on the `Hiddenfrom-AddressListsEnabled` (remember that we use $_to refer to the current object on the pipeline) property as shown.

The two commands can be combined ❸ to find all users hidden from the address list and reveal them by setting `-HiddenfromAddressListsEnabled` to false. In other words, it's not hidden. You can hide, but we'll find you!

TECHNIQUE 28   Moving a mailbox

A mailbox is created in a particular database on a particular server. At some time during a mailbox's lifecycle, we may need to move it to another database or even to another server. This could be for a number of reasons including:

- Balancing the database or server load.
- The current server is being decommissioned.
- There's a problem with the database.

It's possible to move mailboxes from servers running earlier versions of Exchange into an Exchange Server 2007 database.

PROBLEM

The workload on the mail databases has become uneven and we need to move the mailbox to another database.

SOLUTION

PowerShell uses verb-noun syntax for cmdlets. We're working with mailboxes, which gives us the noun, and we want to perform a move. Move-Mailbox is the answer, as shown in listing 6.13. As a reference point, we want to check the current database hosting the mailbox ❶. We only need to view the name and the database, so a select is used to restrict the returned data. The Get-Mailbox portion of the previous line can be used to return the mailbox. This can then be piped into the Move-Mailbox cmdlet ❷. We only need to define a couple of parameters. The first is the BadItemLimit. This defines how many bad items we're allowed to skip before canceling the move. In this case, we're not allowing any. The second parameter is the new database given as *server\storage group\database*.

Listing 6.13   Move a mailbox to another database

```
Get-Mailbox "PERCEVAL Spencer" | Select Name, Database        ❶

Get-Mailbox "PERCEVAL Spencer" | Move-Mailbox -BadItemLimit '0'
-TargetDatabase 'EXCH01\Second Storage group\MaiboxDatabase 2'    ❷

Get-Mailbox "PERCEVAL Spencer" | Select Name, Database        ❸
```

When the cmdlet is started, you'll be asked to confirm the action, as shown in figure 6.2. This confirmation action is automatic and shouldn't be overridden.

DISCUSSION

Additionally, a progress bar is displayed at the top of the PowerShell window. This is particularly useful when moving multiple or very large mailboxes. Our final action is to perform another Get-Mailbox ❸ to check that the move succeeded.

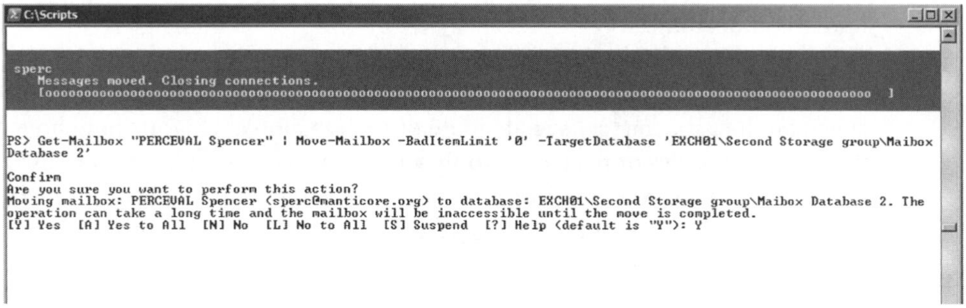

Figure 6.2   Move-Mailbox confirmation and progress bar.

The final parts of this section deal with disconnecting and reconnecting mailboxes.

TECHNIQUE 29   Disabling mail

Disabling a mailbox or any of the other mail-related user objects does more than stop access to the mailbox. It removes the Exchange information from the user object and puts the mailbox into disconnected mode. This is equivalent to the tombstone state in Active Directory, and eventually the mailbox will be permanently deleted from the system. The default time period before it's deleted is 30 days.

Rather than disabling the mailbox in this way, it's possible to use the script from chapter 5 to deny the user the ability to log in on a 24x7 basis—he can't logon at all. This is discussed in a post by Jonathan Noble at http://jonoble.spaces.live.com/blog/cns!CC73D8744F0894A5!643.entry.

> **WARNING-NO SCRIPT**   When you disable a mailbox in the Exchange Management Console, you don't see the script! This is one of the few places where the GUI fails to show the correct PowerShell command.

When you disable a mailbox via the GUI or the command line, it happens immediately.

PROBLEM

You need to disable a mailbox for a user because he no longer needs to use email.

SOLUTION

Once we know which user to disable, a single line of PowerShell will accomplish the task, as in listing 6.14. This could be run in the time it would take to open the GUI! The act of disabling the mailbox is simple ❶. Put the appropriate identity into `Disable-Mailbox` and it happens.

Listing 6.14   Disable a mailbox

```
Disable-Mailbox -Identity "FITZROY Angus"        ❶ Disable
                                                    mailbox
                                                             ❷ Show disabled
                                                                mailboxes
Get-MailboxStatistics | Where {$_.DisconnectDate}
```

DISCUSSION

It's possible that an error could be made and the wrong user could have her mailbox disabled. We need to be able to see the mailboxes that are disabled. The Exchange terminology refers to them as being disconnected, and they're available in the GUI under that heading.

If you want to do this from the command line, it needs a little thought ❷. Use `Get-MailboxStatistics` (which we'll see more of later) and use a `where` cmdlet to check on the `DisconnectDate` attribute of each mailbox. This attribute holds the date the mailbox was disconnected. It's only set on mailboxes that have been disconnected. On normal mailboxes, the attribute is empty (null). We're performing an implicit comparison, and only those mailboxes which have the attribute set will return true and therefore be passed.

> **WARNING**   If you're doing a number of these actions, consider using the `-whatif` and/or the `-confirm` parameters as a safety net before making the final deletion.

Similar cmdlets, `Disable Mail-User` and `Disable-MailContact`, can be used to remove the email functionality from mail-enabled users and contacts, respectively. Having learned how to disable a mailbox and discover the disconnected mailboxes in our system, it would be appropriate to learn how to reconnect them.

TECHNIQUE 30   Reconnecting a mailbox

We may need to reconnect a mailbox to a user account for a number of reasons, including:

- Giving an existing mailbox to a new employee where the emails of the previous role holder need to be available to the new employee.
- The mailbox has been imported from a .PST file during a migration activity.
- Recovery from an error.

Whatever the reason, we need to identify the mailbox and the user account, and connect the mailbox to the user account. This sets the permissions on the mailbox and populates the appropriate Active Directory attributes.

PROBLEM

We need to reconnect a user to his mailbox.

SOLUTION

This is another case where we need to match the identities of the mailbox and the user account to ensure the correct user gets access to the mailbox. We're led to the `Connect-Mailbox` cmdlet by applying our knowledge of the PowerShell naming conventions. We're working with a mailbox (noun) and we want to connect it to a user (verb). The information supplied to the cmdlet consists of the identity of the mailbox. In this case, we're using the name that you'd see in the Exchange Management Console. We also need to supply the database information. The format is *server\storage group\database*. Note that the fully qualified domain name has been used for the server in listing 6.15.

Listing 6.15   Connect a mailbox to a user account

```
Connect-Mailbox -Identity "FITZROY Angus"
-Database 'Exch01.Manticore.org\First Storage Group\Mailbox Database'
-User 'Manticore\afitz' -Alias 'afitz'
```

After identifying the mailbox, we need to identify the user to whom we're going to connect it. The user is identified as *domain\samaccountname*. The samaccountname is also used for the email alias.

If we perform this action in the Exchange Management Console, the script that's produced looks like this:

```
Connect-Mailbox -Identity '2026f71f-f55f-4385-b40d-bdf7bf01077f'
-Database 'Exch01.Manticore.org\First Storage Group\Mailbox Database'
-User 'Manticore\afitz' -Alias 'afitz'
```

Note that we use a GUID to identify the mailbox rather than the name we used earlier. When working interactively at a PowerShell prompt or when performing this action in a script, I'd recommend using the name to identify the mailbox if at all possible. GUIDs are more difficult to type (and get right) compared to a name.

DISCUSSION

That concludes our look at modifying mailboxes. Though we haven't looked at every possibility, the concepts you've learned in this section can be applied across a whole range of scenarios when working with mailboxes. One useful idea is to check the help file for the cmdlets we've been using. Learning the parameters that are available and looking at examples will give you lots of ideas for how they can be used to automate more processes. The other major administration area we need to consider is distribution groups. These are useful in saving everyone a lot of typing when they want to send an email to multiple people.

6.4   *Distribution groups*

Distribution groups (or *distribution lists*) are a good way to organize your recipients. Put a set of linked users into a distribution group, and you can send an email to the group rather than emailing each individual member separately. This saves a lot of time and effort from the user's viewpoint, as well as ensuring that it's possible to send a notification to all interested people. The group will appear in the Exchange address lists.

You may want to create a distribution group for various groups of users, including:

- All members of a department or team
- All members of a project
- All users with a particular role
- All users in a particular location

If you've created groups in Active Directory, you'll have noticed that they are split into security groups and distribution lists. The difference is that a security group can be used to grant permissions to access files and other resources, whereas a distribution group doesn't support this option.

As a slight complication (IT complicated? Never!), it's possible to mail-enable a security group, but it has to be an Active Directory universal group (one that's available across domains in the AD forest). At this point, keeping track of distribution group membership can be difficult if you start nesting groups within groups.

UNIVERSAL ONLY Exchange Server 2007 distribution groups can only be Universal groups. This means that the forest and domain functional levels must be at least Windows 2000-native. Universal groups are used so that members from across the forest can be located in the same group.

In chapter 5 when we were creating groups, we had to define a group type for security groups (see listing 5.22). If we use a similar script to create a distribution group, we just leave the group type at the default setting.

Exchange Server 2007 introduces a number of cmdlets for working with distribution groups. If we just want to know the distribution groups that are available in our Exchange organization, we can use:

```
Get-DistributionGroup
```

This will display the distribution lists currently defined within Active Directory. If you're not sure about the cmdlets that are available to work with distribution groups, or any other aspect of Exchange or PowerShell itself, remember that we can fall back on Get-Command. In this case, we could use:

```
Get-Command *distributiongroup
```

This would display a list of the appropriate cmdlets. If you're not quite sure of the name, try altering the search criteria, for example:

```
Get-Command *distribution*
```

Now that we know how to find the distribution groups, we need to go back to the beginning and discover how to create the things in the first place.

TECHNIQUE 31 Creating a distribution group

Creating a distribution group can be performed in one of two ways. Either create the group and mail-enable it simultaneously, or create a group and then mail-enable it. The first option would be used when the same people administer Active Directory and Exchange. If there's significant separation between the Active Directory and Exchange administrators, then use the second option.

PROBLEM

We need to create a distribution group. In this instance, we can administer Active Directory and Exchange so we'll create the distribution group directly.

SOLUTION

Exchange Server 2007 provides a number of DistributionGroup cmdlets. If we want to create a distribution group, we can use the New-DistributionGroup cmdlet. If you compare the script in listing 6.16 to the earlier scripts we used to create a mailbox-enabled user, you'll notice a number of similarities. We supply a number of pieces of information, including the name of the group, the fact that it's a distribution group, where we want the group to be placed in Active Directory, the email alias, and the samaccountname. The last parameter is essential; otherwise a random name will be assigned by Active Directory. In order to keep administration simple, it's always best to explicitly define the samaccountname for groups-security or distribution.

Listing 6.16 Creating a distribution group

```
New-DistributionGroup -Name 'Navy' -Type 'Distribution'
-OrganizationalUnit 'Manticore.org/England' -SamAccountName 'Navy'
-Alias 'Navy'
```

DISCUSSION

If we need to create a number of distribution groups, consider adapting the script we used in chapter 5 when performing a bulk creation of Active Directory. The only changes we make are to wrap a foreach-object script block around the previous script and substitute $_.*attributename* for the data used with the parameters. An Import-Csv cmdlet is used to read the data and put it on to the pipeline, as shown in listing 6.17.

Listing 6.17 Bulk creation of distribution groups

```
Import-Csv groups.csv | ForEach {
    New-DistributionGroup -Name $_.name -Type 'Distribution'
    -OrganizationalUnit $_.ou -SamAccountName $_.name
    -Alias $_.name
}
```

This is a good example of the type of script development that's often performed by administrators. We start with a script that's produced by the GUI, in this case Exchange Management Console. The script is used to create distribution groups one at a time by changing the data passed to the parameters. A further change gives us a script that we can use to perform bulk creation of groups. All we're changing is the data, rather than the script itself.

There's no set schedule on this type of development. It's often driven by necessity. "Oh, I need to create a number of groups. I know! I'll make that change to the creation script so I can read a CSV file." That's why it's referred to as ad hoc development, as we discussed in chapter 4.

These scripts cover the situation where we control everything. What do we do if the Active Directory people won't let us create groups?

TECHNIQUE 32   ## Mail-enabling a group

In larger organizations, there may well be a division between the Active Directory administrators and those working with Exchange. In this case, we have to be able to mail-enable an existing group.

> **PERMISSION DELEGATION**   One possible way around this situation is to ask for permissions to be delegated for you to create and manage groups in a specific OU. This way, the Exchange administrators can create the distribution groups and manage their membership rather than needing to call on the Active Directory administrators for the creation aspects. I've worked in this way on a large Exchange rollout, and it was very effective.

PROBLEM

Our colleagues in the Active Directory team have created a group and asked us to mail-enable the group.

SOLUTION

PowerShell is consistent in its use of verbs. We used `Enable-MailUser` when we wanted to add a mailbox to an existing user account. We still want the verb `Enable`, but this time we add it to the noun `DistributionGroup`. The `Enable-DistributionGroup` cmdlet can be used to solve this problem. This is a straightforward operation, as all we have to do is supply the identity of the group and the email alias we want to use, as shown in listing 6.18. All of the other information we had to provide when we were creating a new group in the previous section already exists.

Listing 6.18 Mail-enabling a group

```
Enable-DistributionGroup -Identity 'Manticore.org/USA/Army' -Alias 'Army'
```

DISCUSSION

In PowerShell, the opposite of `Enable` is `Disable`, assuming the cmdlet writers follow the guidelines on the standard PowerShell verbs. So if we needed to remove the mail capability from the group for any reason, we'd use:

```
Disable-DistributionGroup -Identity 'Manticore.org/USA/Army'
```

The distribution groups we've been working with so far have been static groups. The group membership is defined, and only changes when an administrator performs an action on the group using PowerShell or the Exchange Management Console (which actually uses PowerShell in the background). There's another type of group whose membership is dynamic and is determined as required.

TECHNIQUE 33   *Dynamic distribution group*

Dynamic distribution groups may also be referred to as *query-based distribution groups*. The idea behind these groups is that the membership isn't statically defined as with most groups, but that it's dynamically determined, as required. The membership at a point in time is determined by an LDAP query performed against Active Directory. The results of the query define the group membership at that time.

As far as the user is concerned, the group functions the same as any other group, in that it appears in the address list and is accessed in the same way as any other group.

> **PERFORMANCE WARNING**   At some stage in the proceedings, the LDAP query to determine group membership has to be performed. If the query is complicated or there are a large number of users or other objects in the Active Directory, the query could take a significant length of time to complete. This could delay the transmission of the email as well as put extra overhead on the Global Catalog server that's used to resolve the query.

If you're creating the dynamic distribution group in the Exchange Management Console, there's a restricted choice in terms of how the query can be defined, as shown in figure 6.3.

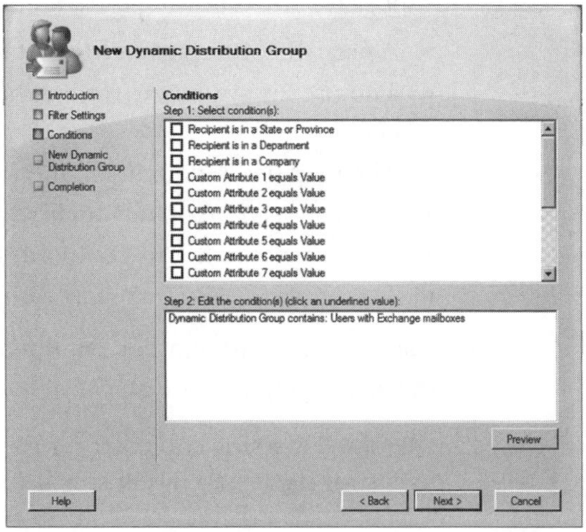

PROBLEM

We need to create a distribution group that can have a rapidly changing membership list.

SOLUTION

We could create a normal distribution group and accept the extra administrative overhead to update the group on a frequent basis. But we've embraced the spirit of

Figure 6.3   Creating a dynamic distribution group

automation and have determined that a dynamic distribution group would meet our needs. In this case, the dynamic distribution group has been created in the Exchange Management console and we've copied the script, which is shown in listing 6.19. All good administrators copy scripts whenever they can.

Listing 6.19   Creating a dynamic distribution group

```
New-DynamicDistributionGroup -Name 'Prime Ministers'
-IncludedRecipients 'MailboxUsers' -ConditionalDepartment 'Downing Street'
-OrganizationalUnit 'Manticore.org/England' -Alias 'PrimeMinisters'
-RecipientContainer 'Manticore.org/England'
```

DISCUSSION

We can use the `New-DynamicDistributionGroup` cmdlet to create the group. Any related cmdlets with the same noun can be viewed by using:

```
Get-Command *dynamicdistributiongroup
```

We need to supply a name, parent OU, and email alias for the group as we did for the static distribution group. One of the options is the type of recipients (`-Included-Recipients`) included in the group. In this case, we're only including mailbox users. We could include mail-enabled users or even contacts. The OU in which to find these mailbox-enabled users is defined using `-RecipientContainer`. The query that will generate the group membership is defined by `-ConditionalDepartment`. In other words, in this case we're looking for mailbox-enabled users in a particular OU who are members of a particular department. This translates to the following LDAP query:

```
(&(department=Downing Street)(objectClass=user)
(objectCategory=person)(mailNickname=*)
(msExchHomeServerName=*)
(!(name=SystemMailbox*))(!(name=CAS_*)))
```

This looks for the following criteria:

- A user whose department is set to Downing Street.
- The user is a person (rather than a computer, which is also based on the user class).
- The user has a mail nickname (alias).
- The user can be on any mailbox server.
- The username doesn't contain the string `SystemMailBox`.
- The username doesn't start with `CAS_`.

It's easier to use the cmdlet parameters or even the wizard to generate the query, rather than trying to code an LDAP query like this.

> **WARNING**   A script copied from the internet should always be viewed as suspect until it's tested, especially if it's heavily aliased, which can make it difficult to read. I'd like to claim my scripts should be an exception, but they should be tested as well, as there may be something in your environment that doesn't work with the scripts.

One question we may get asked is who's included in this distribution group. This could be significant for distribution lists that handle confidential information.

TECHNIQUE 34   View distribution group membership

Distribution groups are Active Directory groups, so we can use Active Directory Users and Computers to view the membership. We can also use the Exchange Management Console, but it's quicker to use PowerShell.

PROBLEM

We need to review the membership of a distribution group to determine if it still meets our needs. The other variation on this question is if I send this email to this group, who'll actually get the email (and possibly confidential attachment)?

SOLUTION

We could use the GUI-based tools to perform this task, but using PowerShell will be more efficient (and more fun). When retrieving information, we always use the verb `Get`, and as we want to view distribution group membership, we use the cmdlet in listing 6.20.

Listing 6.20   View members of a distribution group

```
Get-DistributionGroupMember -Identity 'Manticore\Navy'
```

DISCUSSION

When dealing with a static distribution group, we can find the membership list by using `Get-DistributionGroupMember` as shown. The only information required is the identity of the distribution group. In this case it is identified in *domain\name* format.

In the case of a dynamic distribution group, we can't see the members directly because they aren't stored anywhere. The membership list is derived when a message is sent. We need to be a bit creative in how we solve this variant of the problem, as listing 6.21 demonstrates.

Listing 6.21   View members of a dynamic distribution group

```
$filter = (Get-DynamicDistributionGroup `
-Identity 'Prime Ministers').ldaprecipientfilter      ◁—❶ Get filter

Get-QADuser -ldapfilter $filter    ◁— Get users matching filter
```

We can find the group membership by combing functionality from Exchange and the Quest AD cmdlets. This extensibility is one of the real strengths of PowerShell. By creating a PowerShell instance that has the AD cmdlets snapin and the Exchange snapin loaded, we can access the power of both. If you're not allowed to add software to your environment, you can always use the filter in an Active Directory search using the searching scripts in chapter 5 as a starting point.

> **REMEMBER**   We use the `Add-Snapin` cmdlet in our profile to load the snapins automatically when PowerShell starts.

The first thing we have to do is retrieve the LDAP filter ❶. A variable `$filter` is created and its value is set equal to the LDAP filter. If we use a `Get-DynamicDistributionGroup` cmdlet and enclose it in parentheses, as shown, PowerShell will treat it as an object, in which case we can access the `ldaprecipientfilter` property in the same way that we'd access a property on any other object.

The filter is then used in `Get-QADUser` to fetch the list of users that currently match that filter. Depending on the rate of change of group membership, we may well get different answers when we run this script at different times. The Exchange `Get-User` cmdlet has a `-Filter` parameter, but it doesn't accept an LDAP filter. We'd need to rewrite the filter, which may not be possible given the syntax required for the parameter.

The next step on the road for administering distribution lists is to modify their membership.

TECHNIQUE 35   Modify distribution group membership

We can only modify the membership of static distribution groups directly. The membership of dynamic distribution groups is only determined by the LDAP filter when the group is used. If the membership of the dynamic group doesn't meet our needs, we'll need to modify the LDAP filter.

PROBLEM
We've been asked to add another member to a distribution group.

SOLUTION
In PowerShell, the verb `Add` is used when we want to add more information into a container. In this case, we want to add another member to the collection members belonging to the distribution group. With the `Add-DistributionGroupMember` cmdlet, we only need to specify the identity of the group and the identity of the member we want to add to the group, as in listing 6.22.

Listing 6.22   Modifying distribution group membership

```
Add-DistributionGroupMember -Identity 'Manticore\Navy' `
-Member "CHURCHILL Winston"
```

DISCUSSION
If we need to remove a member from a group, we'd use `Remove-DistributionGroup-Member`.

This concludes our excursion into the world of distribution groups. With the scripts presented in this section, you'll be more than capable of automating this aspect of Exchange administration. The next topic we need to consider is the type of information we can obtain when looking to generate reports on the mailboxes in our environment.

6.5   *Mailbox statistics*

We've already seen how to find the mailboxes that have been disconnected from their user accounts. `Get-Mailboxstatistics` can give a lot of useful information about the mailboxes. There doesn't seem to be an equivalent for getting the same information about databases, but we'll discover a way to overcome that when we reach chapter 12. For now, we'll concentrate on retrieving information regarding mailboxes.

TECHNIQUE 36   **Determining the largest mailboxes**

There are two questions to ponder when considering mailbox size:

- Do you know which users have the five largest mailboxes in your organization?
- How do you measure mailbox size?

We'll answer the first question in a while, but first we need to think about mailbox size. The obvious way to measure size is by the total amount of space occupied by the messages in the mailbox. But a user could have a small number of relatively large emails, because those emails have large attachments, in which case the mailbox will be easy to use. On the other hand, a mailbox with a very large number of small messages may be difficult to use due to the sheer number of messages. In either case, the user may need prompting, or help, in removing or archiving messages.

PROBLEM

We've been asked to determine the users with the largest mailboxes by size and by the total number of items in the mailbox.

SOLUTION

In both cases—size of mailbox and number of items—we can answer the question using Get-MailboxStatistics. The variation, and fun, comes with what we do with the data further along the pipeline. Get-MailboxStatistics displays itemcount rather than itemsize by default. To find the five mailboxes with the largest number of messages, we start with Get-MailboxStatistics ❶ as in listing 6.23. The next step is filter out the system mailboxes using a where command. Note the use of -notlike as the comparison operator and that we can use wildcards with the like family of operators.

Listing 6.23   Determine largest mailboxes

```
Get-MailboxStatistics |Where {$_.Displayname -notlike "SystemMail*"} |
sort itemcount -desc | select -first 5                    ◁—❶ By item count

Get-MailboxStatistics |Where {$_.Displayname -notlike "SystemMail*"} |
sort TotalItemsize -desc | select -first 5 |
Select DisplayName, TotalItemSize, StorageLimitStatus     ◁—❷ By size
```

Once the system mailboxes have been filtered out, we can sort the mailboxes on itemcount. We want to see the mailboxes with the largest number of items, so we sort in a descending manner. In the script, we used -desc instead of the full parameter name -descending. PowerShell will happily take a partial parameter name as long as it can be resolved unambiguously. An error will be generated if PowerShell can't successfully resolve the abbreviated parameter name. The final action on the pipeline is to select the first five objects and pass them to the default display.

> **TIP**   Be sure to remember the difference between using the like family of operators and the match family. Like operates on strings and can use wildcards as shown. Match works with regular expressions. From the names, you might think they did the same thing, but they're used in different ways. The operator help files can supply more information. Use Get-Help about*operator* to see the list of the available help files.

DISCUSSION

The alternative is to find the largest five mailboxes as measured by size ❷. This is similar to the previous script, except we sort on totalitemsize and we specify in the select that we want to use the mailbox display name, total item size, and the storage limit status.

TECHNIQUE 37   **Reporting on mailbox sizes**

Another possibility is that you may want to report on all of the mailboxes by size or item count.

> **WARNING**   In a large organization, this may generate very large reports. This can be tackled either by producing the report by database, or by restricting the report to the first 20, 30, 50, or whatever by putting select -first n after the sort.

Perhaps you want to move mailboxes between databases depending on their size. A possible scenario could involve establishing a database specifically for the largest mailboxes. The mailbox quota limits could be established at the database level rather than configuring individual mailboxes.

PROBLEM

We want to understand the distribution of mailbox sizes within our organization.

SOLUTION

As before, Get-MailboxStatistics is the tool for this job. The scripts are almost identical. The difference arises because of the different property used for sorting, as you can see in listing 6.24. The results of running the scripts are shown in figure 6.4. As in the previous listing, we start with Get-MailboxStatistics, pipe into the same where, followed by a sort on itemcount ❶. We then use Format-Table to produce our report. We can effectively perform a select at the same time due to the property selection. The interesting part of this is the use of the calculated field in the Format-Table cmdlet. By default, the totalitemsize property is displayed in bytes with a B at the end. In this example, I've converted the value to a string, removed the B, and then divided by 1MB.

Listing 6.24   Report mailbox sizes

```
Get-MailboxStatistics |Where {$_.Displayname -notlike "SystemMail*"} |
sort itemcount -desc |
format-table DisplayName, ItemCount, @{Label="Approx Size (MB)";
Expression={
[int](($_.totalitemsize.ToString().Replace("B", ""))/1mb)}},      ❶ By item
StorageLimitStatus -autosize                                          count

Get-MailboxStatistics |Where {$_.Displayname -notlike "SystemMail*"} |
sort totalitemsize -desc |
format-table DisplayName, ItemCount, @{Label="Approx Size (MB)";
Expression={
[int](($_.totalitemsize.ToString().Replace("B", ""))/1mb)}},
StorageLimitStatus -autosize                                       ❷ By size
```

This result is converted to an integer to remove the decimal parts. The calculation could be replaced by these alternatives:

- `$_.TotalItemSize.Value.ToGB()`
- `$_.TotalItemSize.Value.ToMB()`

DISCUSSION

If we want to view the information based on mailbox size, we replace the sort property with totalitemsize ❷. The rest of the script is the same. The results are worth comparing, as a user with the mailbox occupying the most space doesn't necessarily have the most items in the mailbox, as shown in figure 6.4.

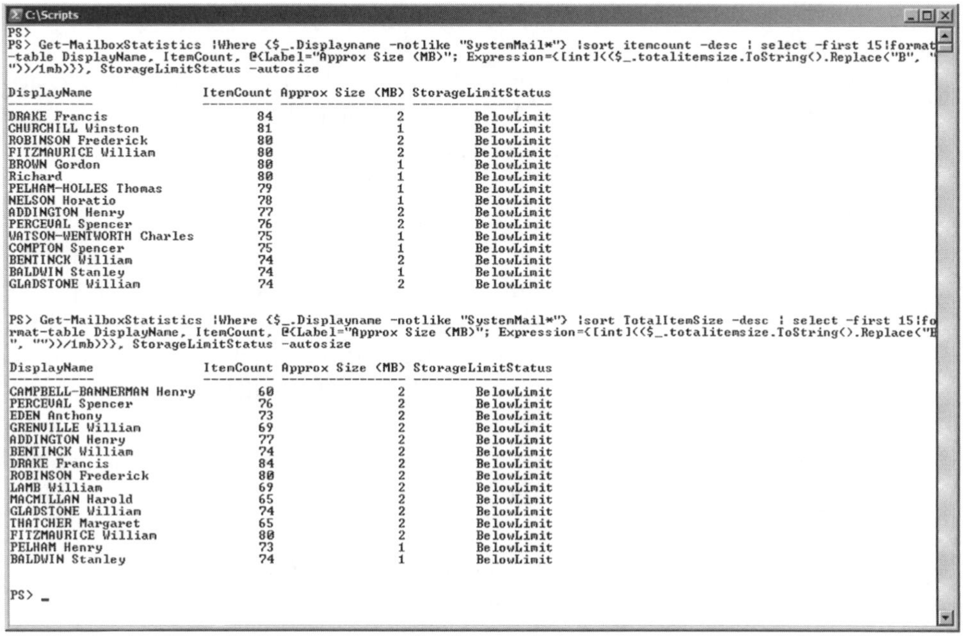

Figure 6.4 Mailbox size scripts

> **REPORT RESTRICTION** In the figure, the scripts have been modified to only select the first 15 mailboxes, so that the comparison between the two approaches could be seen.

The final stage in the lifecycle is deleting the mailbox from the server.

6.6 *Deleting mailboxes*

We saw earlier that disabling a mailbox causes the Exchange information to be removed from a user account, and the mailbox to be disconnected. In time it'll be deleted from the server. The situation may arise where we need to force the deletion of a mailbox and possibly of the user account as well. Be careful deleting mailboxes. If it's the wrong one you could end up in this situation:

```
Remove-Mailbox -wrongone | Revise-CV
```
In other words, you need to revise your CV (résumé) because you have to look for another job!

TECHNIQUE 38   Deleting a mailbox

When we disable a mailbox, the user account is left in Active Directory. There are scenarios where we may want to delete the account and either disconnect the mailbox so that it'll be deleted during the regular cleanup operations or delete it immediately.

If the administration of Active Directory and Exchange is performed by the same people, the solution presented here could be used. Otherwise, disabling the mailbox and then using the procedure in the following section will be necessary. The Active Directory team will need to delete the user.

PROBLEM

A user has left the organization and it's been determined that the user account and mailbox should be deleted. This approach may also be useful if test accounts have been created and now need removing.

SOLUTION

We have two alternatives. First, we can delete the user account and let the Exchange cleanup operation eventually remove the mailbox. Alternatively, we can delete the user account and force the immediate removal of the mailbox. The Remove-Mailbox cmdlet meets our needs perfectly, as shown in listing 6.25. If we use it with just the identity parameter ❶ we'll delete the user from the Active Directory. The user object is tombstoned and will remain in that state for 60 or 180 days, depending on the version of Windows used to create the Active Directory, before final removal. The mailbox will be disconnected and remain in that state for 30 days, by default, before permanent deletion.

Listing 6.25   Delete a mailbox

```
Remove-Mailbox -Identity "FITZROY Angus"        ❶

Remove-Mailbox -Identity "FITZROY Angus" -Permanent $true        ❷
```

DISCUSSION

If required the -permanent parameter can be used ❷. This will cause the user object to be tombstoned as previously, but will immediately remove the mailbox from the Exchange database. The disconnect stage is completely bypassed.

> **WARNING**   Use the -permanent option with care, as the only way to retrieve the mailbox is to perform a restore.

In the case of the first option presented here, or if we've already disconnected the mailbox, we may need to consider permanently removing a disconnected mailbox from the database.

TECHNIQUE 39   Purging a mailbox

As we've seen, mailboxes aren't usually deleted but left in a disconnected state for a period of time. We need to be able to purge disconnected mailboxes from the server

PROBLEM

We have one or more disconnected mailboxes we need to remove from the server.

SOLUTION

`Remove-Mailbox` is the answer to this question. This time, though, we need to be able to identify the disconnected mailbox to remove. We've seen previously that `GetMailboxStatistics` can be used to access disconnected mailboxes. We can use that command to find the mailbox GUID, which will uniquely identify it, as shown in listing 6.26. The database containing the disconnected mailbox is also required.

Listing 6.26 Purge a mailbox from the server

```
Remove-Mailbox -Database 'Exch01\Mailbox Database'
-StoreMailboxIdentity (Get-MailboxStatistics |
    Where {$_.DisplayName -eq "FITZROY Angus"}).MailboxGuid
```

DISCUSSION

Remember that this is a permanent removal, with a restore being the only way to reverse the action.

6.7 Summary

In this chapter, we've seen the lifecycle of mailboxes from creation through modification and to the final act of destruction. The various mail objects can be simply and efficiently created with PowerShell. In some instances, it may be necessary to split the work among multiple administration teams.

Modifying mailboxes can include changing size limits as well as enabling or disabling functionality. Moving mailboxes between databases can be performed interactively if required.

Distribution groups are used to group recipients who all need to get the same messages on a regular basis. They save a lot of effort from a user perspective. Creating a group and changing its membership are similar to actions performed when creating Active Directory security groups. Dynamic distribution groups are a special case, in that the membership is derived when the group is accessed. The current membership can be viewed by combining the functionality of Exchange and AD cmdlets.

The final stage in the lifecycle is removal. This can either be staged or immediate depending on the requirements.

After considering user accounts and mailboxes, we must turn our attention to the user's desktop, which is the next and final chapter in this part. We'll see how PowerShell and WMI give us a powerful method of interrogating the desktop machine for configuration and status information. We'll explore methods to change the configuration as well as investigate how to work with the Office applications. Much of the information in chapter 7 will be useful when working with servers as well as desktops.

Desktop

This chapter closes out the part of the book dealing with users and leads into chapter 8, which opens the server administration section.

> **HOW TO USE THE SCRIPTS** Many of the scripts presented in this chapter could be run interactively from the PowerShell prompt rather than as a script. If anything is run frequently, consider creating a function with the computer name as a parameter. Alternatively, PowerGUI could be utilized (see section 4.5.2).

Group Policy is used to configure and manage desktops in many corporate environments. Group Policy is a great technology that's underutilized in many cases. Group Policy objects (GPOs) are great for configuring the computer, but they don't report back the actual configuration. There will still be a need to investigate desktop (or server) issues even with an extensive utilization of GPO-based technologies.

This chapter shows how to investigate those issues by discovering information about the computer, and how to configure aspects of the computer that can't be reached by other means. In this chapter, we'll make extensive use of the WMI and COM capabilities of the Windows environment. Using these technologies in Power-Shell was covered in chapter 3. If you jumped straight into the sections of the book covering the scripts, it might be worth looking at chapter 3 as a refresher before delving too far into this chapter.

7.1 Automating desktop configuration

In most organizations, there are a lot more desktops (that does include laptops for this discussion) than servers. This means that there will be a lot more administrative effort spent on the desktop estate. Anything that can reduce that overhead will have a beneficial impact on the company. This is where automation comes into the picture. If I can make changes remotely or remotely discover information that will help me resolve the user's problems, I can be more productive. How can I be more productive? The answer in the Windows environment of today is to use PowerShell.

When we want to investigate an issue with a user's computer (or a server), we need to know how it's configured. The first part of this chapter uses PowerShell and WMI to discover configuration information. A number of scripts are presented that show how to go about discovering this information. Rather than running these scripts individually, we may decide to create a standard script that returns the common information we'll want to know. The second stage is to then run individual scripts to dig further into the issues. A good example of how to do this has been created by Alan Renouf (http://teckinfo.blogspot.com/2008/10/powershell-audit-script_15.html). The output from the WMI scripts is presented in an HTML page that can be viewed in a browser, as shown in figure 7.1

After discovering our information, we may need to make changes to the configuration. The machine configuration section finishes with some examples. Setting IP addresses is delayed until chapter 9.

It's also possible to work with what the user sees on the machine—his desktop experience. We can discover information about the desktop and other folders that are special to the user, including examining the contents of the Recycle Bin.

The final section of the chapter deals with applications. The Office applications Word and Excel have been chosen as examples because they can be found in most Windows environments. You can combine the discovery scripts presented in the first section with the information regarding Office applications to create a system to document and report on the machines in your environment. But before we can do that, we need to learn how to discover that information.

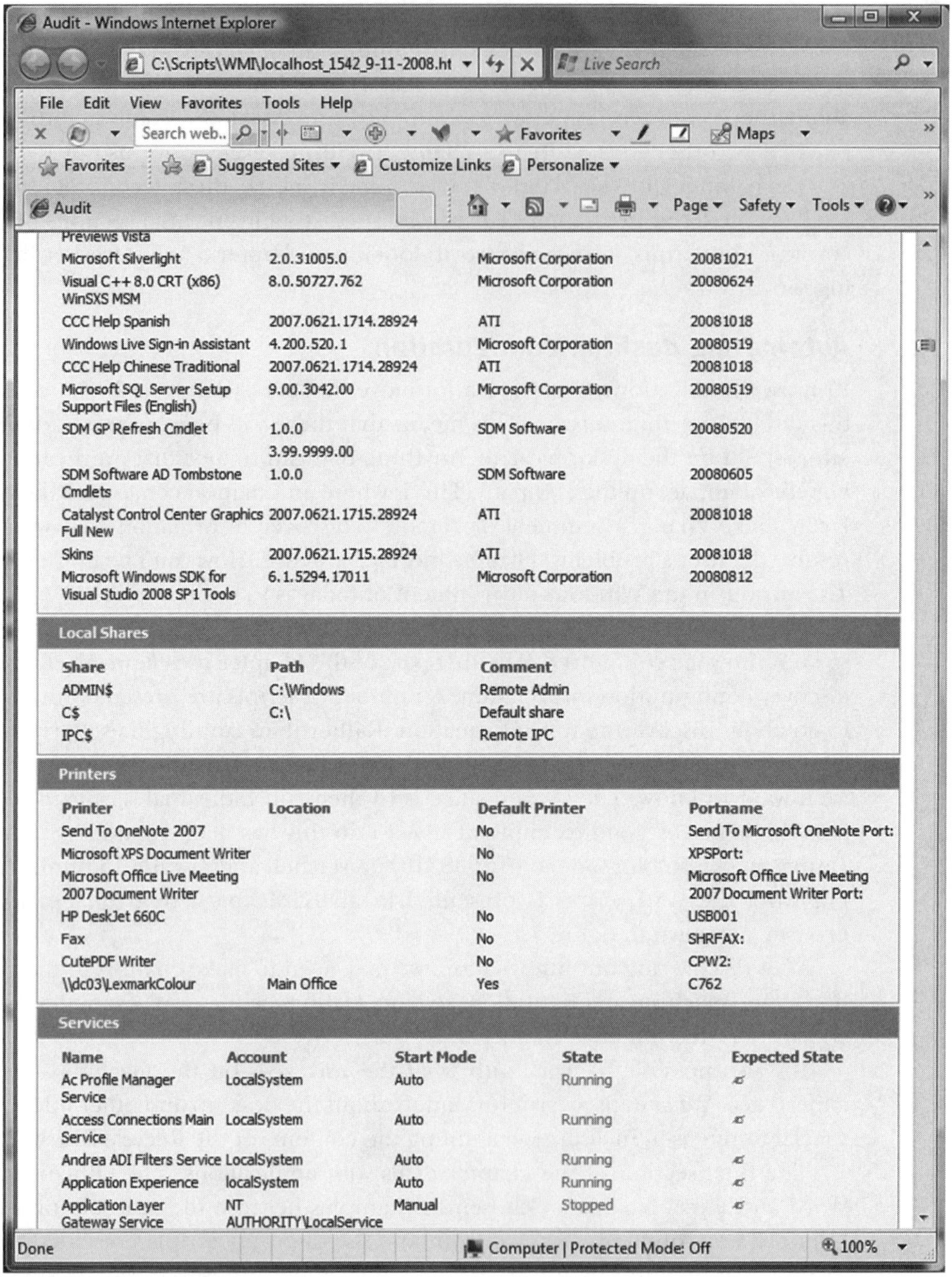

Figure 7.1 Presenting configuration information via HTML

7.2 *Machine configuration*

Machine configuration can be split into a number of areas. A lot of the time, when we need to work with a machine's configuration, we really just want to report on that configuration. How many organizations have a database of their machine configurations? I suspect that the answer is not many. It would be relatively straightforward to take these scripts and push the results into a set of SQL Server tables to create such a database. We'll see an example in chapter 14.

> **REMOTE RUNNING**   All of the scripts in this section are shown running against the local machine. They can be run equally well against a remote machine by using the -ComputerName parameter and supplying the NETBIOS name, IP address, or fully qualified domain name of the relevant computer. This doesn't require the remoting capabilities of PowerShell v2.

Examples of where we're only reporting include retrieving the OS or BIOS information. In some cases, we actually need to modify the machine configuration, for example altering the IP address or default gateway. This may be more likely on servers than workstations.

> **NOTE**   Many of the scripts in this chapter use Windows Management Instrumentation (WMI) . WMI is blocked by default by the Windows firewall that's present in the latest versions of the Windows OS. Ensure that the firewall is configured to allow WMI access. WMI can take a long time to time out in certain instances. Ensure that firewalls aren't blocking WMI to avoid the wait.

WMI can supply a huge amount of information about your system. It's a constantly evolving technology, as each new version of Windows introduces new classes to the default namespace (root\cimv2) and also brings completely new namespaces. Most of the system information and machine configuration classes are contained in root\cimv2, as explained in the WMI section in chapter 3. You did read that section, didn't you? If you skipped that section, it would be worth reading to refresh yourself on how WMI works with PowerShell. One thing to remember with WMI is that you can use PowerShell itself to help you discover what classes are available by using the following:

```
Get-WmiObject -Namespace 'root\cimv2' -List
```

This will give you a list of the classes belonging to the namespace. Remember that the default namespace contains literally hundreds of classes. In order to reduce the wait, try limiting the number of classes returned by trying:

```
Get-WmiObject -Namespace 'root\cimv2' -List -Class *network*
```

Any suitable item can be used as the basis of the search. Wildcards are accepted as shown.

The logical place to start with the machine configuration is by obtaining some standard and fairly basic information about the machine. This is the sort of information that we're likely to need in many troubleshooting situations.

TECHNIQUE 40   **System configuration**

A system administrator, or help desk operative, needs to have access to system configuration information. Ideally this will be available to them through a configuration database as described previously. If a configuration database isn't available then we can fall back on WMI to supply the information.

DATA SUBSET This is only a small subset of the information that can be obtained. Examining the classes shown here or investigating other classes will enable a more detailed report to be generated.

The solution shown here is displayed onscreen. If a permanent record is required, Out-File could be used instead of Format-List. Remember to use the -Append parameter on all but the first section of the script; otherwise you'll experience one of those "Oops! I wish I hadn't done that" moments when you realize you've overwritten all of the data.

PROBLEM

The basic system configuration must be discovered. We want to know the OS and service pack, computer model and manufacturer, basic processor information, and the BIOS version.

SOLUTION

There isn't a single WMI class that we can use to retrieve all of the information we require. This means that a number of individual commands needs to be used, as shown in listing 7.1. The advantage of this approach is that it's easy to extend the script by introducing additional items such as physical disks or reporting on additional properties from the existing classes.

Listing 7.1   Basic system configuration information

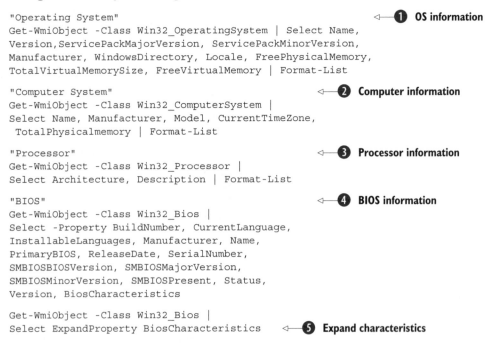

```
"Operating System"                                          ◁───❶ OS information
Get-WmiObject -Class Win32_OperatingSystem | Select Name,
Version,ServicePackMajorVersion, ServicePackMinorVersion,
Manufacturer, WindowsDirectory, Locale, FreePhysicalMemory,
TotalVirtualMemorySize, FreeVirtualMemory | Format-List

"Computer System"                                           ◁───❷ Computer information
Get-WmiObject -Class Win32_ComputerSystem |
Select Name, Manufacturer, Model, CurrentTimeZone,
 TotalPhysicalmemory | Format-List

"Processor"                                                 ◁───❸ Processor information
Get-WmiObject -Class Win32_Processor |
Select Architecture, Description | Format-List

"BIOS"                                                      ◁───❹ BIOS information
Get-WmiObject -Class Win32_Bios |
Select -Property BuildNumber, CurrentLanguage,
InstallableLanguages, Manufacturer, Name,
PrimaryBIOS, ReleaseDate, SerialNumber,
SMBIOSBIOSVersion, SMBIOSMajorVersion,
SMBIOSMinorVersion, SMBIOSPresent, Status,
Version, BiosCharacteristics

Get-WmiObject -Class Win32_Bios |
Select ExpandProperty BiosCharacteristics     ◁───❺ Expand characteristics
```

WMI can supply a varied and rich set of information. In this example, we're drawing on four different WMI classes to supply the information. In all cases, the default namespace is being used (root\cimv2). In fact, it's used in all of the scripts in this section. The script is an ideal candidate for running against multiple computers.

We start by looking at the operating system ❶. As you might guess, we use the Win32_OperatingSystem class. Many classes in WMI are quite sensibly named, and so relatively easy to find. In this case, we select a number of properties, including the version, service pack, locale, and some information on the memory available in the machine. A Format-List is used at the end of the pipeline to ensure a consistent display.

> **NOTE** In all parts of the script, I could've dropped Format-List from the end of the pipeline and substituted it for the select command. That would be acceptable if I only wanted to display to the screen. The way I've written the script, I think it's easier to modify if you want to output the data to a file instead of to the screen. All you have to do is substitute Out-File and the name of the file in place of Format-List. Don't forget the -append.

Win32_OperatingSystem and the other classes used in this chapter have more properties than we're using in these examples. When we use Get-WmiObject, there's a default formatter that controls which properties are returned. The default formatters are investigated in appendix A. If you want to see the names of all of the properties and methods available to the particular WMI object we're working with, then use

```
Get-WmiObject -Class Win32_OperatingSystem | Get-Member
```

If you want to quickly see the values of the properties, use:

```
Get-WmiObject -Class Win32_OperatingSystem | Select *
```

The other point to note about this listing is that there's a label before each use of Get-WmiObject. In each case, we have a single string on the line. One convenient piece of functionality in PowerShell is that if we place a string by itself on a line, it's automatically treated as output to be directed to the standard output device—in this case the screen. This is good technique for listing progress through a script, as well as helping to comment the script. Two birds with one stone !

After the OS, the next area that will interest us is the machine itself ❷. This follows the same format as the previous line, except we're using the Win32_ ComputerSystem class. Information such as manufacturer, model, and the physical memory can be discovered. Troubleshooting a user's problem can often be easier and quicker when we know some basics about the machine. If we know that a particular model has had an issue with a piece of software, it could help narrow our search for a solution.

The final two sections of the script find basic information about the processor ❸ and the BIOS ❹.

SYSTEM DOCUMENTATION　The possibility of using these scripts to populate a configuration database has been mentioned. The other possibility is to combine the scripts and output the results to a file. Any time there was a change to the machine, the script could be rerun. If required, the information could be written into a Word document using the scripts in the last section of this chapter as a guide.

WMI will sometimes return a collection of values as a single property. This happens with `Win32_Bios` in the `BiosCharacteristics` property **❺**. We can use the `-Expand-Property` parameter of `select` to list the members of the property collection.

DISCUSSION

In many cases, as here, the information in the property collection is stored as digits, each with a special meaning. Using the `-ExpandProperty` parameter doesn't add meaning; it just lists them. If you want to see what the numbers mean, the best way to find the information is to search on the Microsoft website for the documentation of the WMI class.

　If it becomes necessary to add meaning to the numbers, pass the expanded characteristics into a `foreach` command that contains a `switch` statement. The meaning of each characteristic can be then be written out. I haven't included this, in the interest of space, but it's included in the downloadable scripts.

TECHNIQUE 41　　**Discovering the operating system**

The operating system is fundamental to the correct operation of the machine and the installed software. As administrators, we need to know that the correct version is installed on our machines and that it's configured correctly.

PROBLEM

We need to be able to discover information about the version of the operating system and its configuration.

SOLUTION

WMI provides another class—`Win32_OperatingSystem`—to provide this information, as shown in listing 7.2. WMI has so much information available to us that we could almost start thinking "WMI is the answer; now what was my problem?"

Listing 7.2　Operating system information

```
Get-WmiObject -Class Win32_OperatingSystem |
Select BootDevice, BuildNumber,BuildType, Caption,
Codeset, CountryCode, Debug, InstallDate,
NumberofLicensedUsers, Organization, OSLanguage,
OSProductSuite, OSType, Primary, RegisteredUser,
SerialNumber, Version
```

DISCUSSION

The `Win32_OperatingSystem` class returns more than 70 properties. It's worth experimenting by using the following line of code in order to see the amount of information that can be retrieved:

```
Get-WmiObject -Class Win32_OperatingSystem | Select *
```

Several of these properties, such as CountryCode and Codeset, will be numbers. If required, their meanings can be discovered in the WMI documentation. It's usually enough to know what should be configured and then to look for the anomalies. After all, you'd expect all of the machines in the same location to use the same country code and OS language!

One issue that costs administrators a good deal of time and effort is patching. Knowing which service pack and hotfixes are installed on a machine is essential to keeping them secure.

TECHNIQUE 42 Discovering service packs on the OS

Service packs are issued at irregular intervals during the lifecycle of a version of Windows. A service pack will usually contain all of the previously released hotfixes and service packs in one package. Ideally, service packs should be installed as soon as they've been tested for your environment. Unless this is an automated procedure, it's easy for machines to be missed.

There are tools can tell us which service packs and hotfixes have been and still need to be installed on every system in our environment. When we're troubleshooting a problem, it's not always possible to access that information. Being able to generate a report showing the latest service pack installed on your machines could be very useful.

PROBLEM

We need to be able to discover the service pack applied to the operating system on a set of machines within our infrastructure.

SOLUTION

We can read a file to get the computer names and then discover the service pack level by using WMI. In previous examples, we've used Import-Csv to read a CSV file with the data we'll be using in the script. There's another cmdlet, Get-Content ❶, that we can use to read text files. As we're only reading a single column of names, either method will work.

> **SAMPLE FILE** A sample computers.txt file is supplied with the script downloads. It shows three different ways to call the local machine! Add other computer names or IP addresses as required.

It can be useful to read the contents of a file into an array, especially if you'll be using it multiple times in your script. Performing the read once will improve the performance and efficiency of your script. As an example, consider combining the scripts in listing 7.2 and listing 7.3. We're using the same data in both, so why read it twice?

Listing 7.3 Service pack information

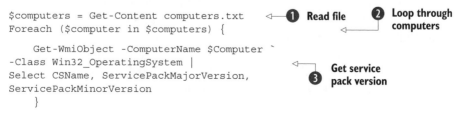

```
$computers = Get-Content computers.txt          Read file    Loop through
Foreach ($computer in $computers) {                          computers

    Get-WmiObject -ComputerName $Computer `
-Class Win32_OperatingSystem |                              Get service
Select CSName, ServicePackMajorVersion,                     pack version
ServicePackMinorVersion
    }
```

Our data is in an array at this point, so we won't use the Foreach-Object cmdlet we've used in other scripts. We turn to the foreach loop command as shown ❷. Within the foreach loop, we use Get-WmiObject to access the Win32_OperatingSystem class ❸ to read the service pack version. One important change from using Import-Csv is that our foreach isn't on the pipeline. We can't use $_ to represent the computer name in this instance. We use $computer instead, which is the foreach variable. Note that we're outputting the major and minor version numbers of the service pack. The minor version number will normally be zero.

Putting all of this together, the script can be read as:

1 Read a list of computer names.
2 For each computer name in the list.
3 Use WMI to get the service pack version.

A similar structure can be used to discover the hotfixes installed on a machine.

TECHNIQUE 43   **Hotfixes**

Hotfixes, or *patches*, are usually produced in response to a bug. They can be applied to a machine manually or by automatic means. It's possible that the method of application doesn't keep a centralized record of the patches that have been installed. Without this information, you, as an administrator, can't determine whether your machines are vulnerable to a new exploit that the patch will stop.

PROBLEM

We need to determine the hotfixes that are installed on a machine, and whether a particular hotfix is installed on the machine.

SOLUTION

We use a different WMI class this time. If this script is compared to the one in listing 7.4, we can see that they're very similar. We start, again, by reading the file of computer names ❶ and loop ❷ through that list. The output will consist of a list of the applied patches.

Listing 7.4 Hotfix information

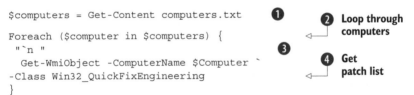

```
$computers = Get-Content computers.txt      ❶      ❷ Loop through
                                                       computers
Foreach ($computer in $computers) {
 "`n "                                       ❸
  Get-WmiObject -ComputerName $Computer `           ❹ Get
-Class Win32_QuickFixEngineering                       patch list
}
```

This could be quite long, so we put a blank line between the outputs of the different computers ❸. This is accomplished using the `n special character, which denotes a new line. Special characters are explained in appendix A.

We need to use a different WMI class to find the installed patches. We use Win32_QuickFixEngineering ❹. The default format has the information we need, so we don't need to use the select or format cmdlets.

POWERSHELL JOBS   PowerShell v2 introduces the ability to run PowerShell commands as background jobs. This functionality enables us to perform tasks asynchronously. If we had a large number of computers in our list, it could take quite a while before all of the results were returned and we were given back control of the PowerShell prompt. This makes this type of task ideal for running as a job. When we run the command as a job, we get the prompt back immediately, so we can continue working while the job runs in the background. Once it has finished, we can investigate the results at our convenience.

DISCUSSION

In PowerShell v2, we could use a new cmdlet—Get-Hotfix—instead:

```
$computers = Get-Content computers.txt
Foreach ($computer in $computers) {
    "`n $computer"
    Get-HotFix -ComputerName $computer
}
```

As it stands, the script will display all of the hotfixes installed on the system. Much of the time, we may want to check whether a particular hotfix is applied on the machines, as in listing 7.5.

Listing 7.5   Check for specific hotfix

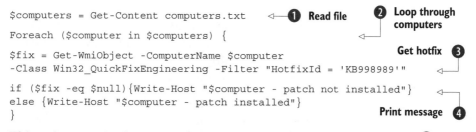

```
$computers = Get-Content computers.txt        ←  ❶ Read file        ❷ Loop through
                                                                        computers
Foreach ($computer in $computers) {           ←

                                                                    Get hotfix ❸
$fix = Get-WmiObject -ComputerName $computer
-Class Win32_QuickFixEngineering -Filter "HotfixId = 'KB998989'"   ←

if ($fix -eq $null){Write-Host "$computer - patch not installed"}  ←
else {Write-Host "$computer - patch installed"}
}                                                              Print message ❹
```

This script starts in the same way, by reading the file of computer names ❶ and looping through them ❷. In this case, we put the results ❸ of the Get-WmiObject cmdlet into a variable. The -Filter parameter is used to restrict Get-WmiObject to only look for the specified hotfix. This will give a significant boost to the script's performance. The way PowerShell works is that it will return nothing if it can't find the specified patch on the machine. We can exploit that fact to determine the patch's existence.

If the patch doesn't exist the variable is null (nothing has been returned). We can use an if statement ❹ to test whether the variable is null, and if it is, we get a message to tell us the patch isn't installed. If the variable isn't null it means that WMI found the patch and we can write out the appropriate message.

Get-Hotfix can also be used in this situation:

```
$computers = Get-Content computers.txt
Foreach ($computer in $computers) {
    "`n $computer"
    Get-HotFix -Id KB972636 -ComputerName $computer
}
```

In addition to the installed hotfixes, we'll also be interested in the installed software.

TECHNIQUE 44   ## Listing installed software

Many organizations will have policies to determine what software is allowed to be loaded on desktop machines. If a software asset management system isn't in place, it can be difficult to know what software has been installed. Also, when troubleshooting, it can be useful to know what software has been installed, and especially what versions of the software.

PROBLEM
We need to create a report listing the software loaded on our machines.

SOLUTION
The `Win32_Product` WMI class is available on all recent versions of Windows, up to and including Windows Server 2008, Windows Vista, and Windows 7. We use the `Win32_product` class to read the list of software installed under the control of the Windows installer, as shown in listing 7.6.

Listing 7.6 Installed software

```
Get-WmiObject -Class Win32_product | Select Name, Caption,
IdentifyingNumber, InstallLocation, Vendor, Version |
 Export-Csv software.txt -NoTypeInformation
```

DISCUSSION
Within the PowerShell community, a lot is made of the "PowerShell one liner." The way the pipeline works in PowerShell enables us to put a lot of functionality into a single line of code. This script, though fairly simple, achieves a lot. It's also expandable, while remaining (technically) within the one-line constraint.

> **IMPORTANT NOTE**   Only software installed through the Windows installer will be discovered by this script. This will include most modern software, but there's always the possibility that some software has been installed by other means.

The script returns a lot of information, as with most WMI classes. A select (`Select-Object` cmdlet) is used to restrict the data passed along the pipeline. Our problem statement was that we needed to create a report listing the installed software.

 One of the easiest ways to do this is to create a CSV file containing the information. We can use the `Export-Csv` cmdlet to create and write to the CSV file. By default, `Export-Csv` will write the .NET type information into the first row of the CSV file. This can cause problems when we try to read the CSV file outside of PowerShell. The `-NoTypeInformation` parameter will prevent the type information being written to the file.

 The example only creates a report for the local machine. We can extend the script to work with remote machines. Create a file with the computer names. This can be a CSV file or a text file. Read the file and pipe it into a `foreach` loop. Use the `-Computername` parameter in `Get-WmiObject` to read the information from the appropriate computer. The information can then be exported to a file. In these cases, we usually want to create one file per computer, so create a filename in the loop and incorporate the computer name and the date.

Our investigation of the machine configuration has encompassed the hardware, the OS, and the installed software. This gives us the basic building blocks, but one area we haven't looked at yet is the disks.

TECHNIQUE 45   **Monitoring free disk space**

As you'd expect, there are a number of classes that deal with disks:

- `Win32_DiskDrive`
- `Win32_DiskDrivePhysicalMedia`
- `Win32_DiskDriveToDiskPartition`
- `Win32_DiskPartition`
- `Win32_DiskQuota`
- `Win32_LogicalDisk`
- `Win32_LogicalDiskRootDirectory`
- `Win32_LogicalDiskToPartition`
- `Win32_LogonSessionMappedDisk`
- `Win32_MappedLogicalDisk`

Physical disks are investigated using `Win32_DiskDrive`. `Win32_DiskDriveToDisk-Partition` is especially useful, as it enables us to discover which partitions are on which physical disk. In this instance, we're concerned with disk space.

PROBLEM

Monitoring available disk space is a common task for administrators. We may also need to quickly discover how much free space is available on a given disk when we need to move data around or install software.

SOLUTION

If we use the `Win32_LogicalDisk` class and a calculated field, we can even get the answer in GB rather than bytes, as in listing 7.7.

Listing 7.7   Free disk space

```
$HardDisk = 3
Get-WmiObject -Class Win32_LogicalDisk `
-Filter "DriveType = $HardDisk" |
Format-Table DeviceId, @{Label="Freespace(GB)";
Expression={($_.FreeSpace/1GB).ToString("F04")}} -auto
```

There are a number of interesting points in this script. In the first line of the script, I've defined a variable called `$HardDisk` with a value of 3. This is then used in the `-Filter` parameter of `Get-WmiObject`. A filter is in effect a WMI Query Language (WQL) query, but we only need to give the part of the query after the `WHERE` statement. The full query would be:

```
"SELECT * FROM Win32_LogicalDisk WHERE DriveType = '$HardDisk'"
```

The WHERE clause is acting as a filter, and so is the part we use in our filter parameter as shown in the script. In listing 7.7, we've defined the query to only look at disks where the drive type equals the value of the variable.

The query will only return information on local hard disks—type 3 disks. There's a clue in the name of the variable. I could've just hard-coded the disk type into the script, but this allows us to change the disk type easily, as it's at the top of the script. It also demonstrates how we can substitute into strings. If a variable is placed inside a double-quoted string as in this example, its value will be substituted into the string when the script executes.

> **QUOTES** The way that PowerShell allows us to put variables inside strings and then substitute the value of the variable is a useful technique. It greatly simplifies a number of tasks, especially building commands in this way and creating output messages. It only works with strings bounded by double quotes.

DISCUSSION

The second interesting—and again useful—feature is the calculated field in the For-mat-Table cmdlet. It reads:

```
@{Label="Freespace(GB)"; Expression={($_.FreeSpace/1GB).ToString("F04")}}
```

This isn't as complicated as it would seem, as we can see by breaking this down. Start at the outside with @{}, which denotes this is a hash table. We know that hash tables consist of key-value pairs. In this case, we have two keys—Label and Expression. The Label is a string that defines the name of the field, as shown in figure 7.2.

The Expression is where all the hard work is done, as we take the value of the Freespace property (which is in bytes) and convert it to gigabytes by dividing by 1GB. Remember that PowerShell recognizes KB, MB, and GB as values. This calculation leaves a large number of decimal places, so we'll format the output by converting the number to a string using "F04" as the format string. This will restrict the display to four decimal places. What we've done is take a value in bytes and convert it into a more meaningful form given the size of the hard disks in use today.

Calculated fields can be used in a select statement, except that Label is changed to Name:

```
C:\Scripts
PS> $HardDisk = 3
PS> Get-WmiObject -Class Win32_LogicalDisk -Filter "DriveType = $HardDisk" | Format-Table DeviceId, @{Label="Freespace(G
B)"; Expression={($_.FreeSpace/1GB).ToString("F04")}} -auto

DeviceId Freespace(GB)
-------- -------------
C:       36.4808


PS>
```

Figure 7.2   Using a calculated field

```
$HardDisk = 3
Get-WmiObject -Class Win32_LogicalDisk `
-Filter "DriveType = $HardDisk" |
Select DeviceId, @{Name="Freespace(GB)";
Expression={($_.FreeSpace/1GB).ToString("F04")}}
```

When we create a calculated field using select, it becomes part of the object and can be used later on the pipeline exactly like any other property. The member type for these properties created as calculated fields is NoteProperty.

> **GET-PSDRIVE** In PowerShell v2, Get-PSDrive has been amended to give used and free space for filesystem drives.

One configuration item that can have a major impact is the IP address. We'll look at that in chapter 9.

TECHNIQUE 46   Renaming a computer

When a Windows machine is built, it'll be assigned a randomly created name. This name will need to be changed to fit our naming conventions. We may also need to change the name of a machine if it changes role or location.

PROBLEM
How can we change the name of a Windows machine?

SOLUTION
Another aspect of the Win32_ComputerSystem class comes into play, as in listing 7.8.

Listing 7.8   Change computer name

```
$computer = Get-WmiObject -Class Win32_ComputerSystem
$computer.Rename("newname",$null,$null)
```

Set a variable to Win32_ComputerSystem. The Rename() method is used to change the name. We need to give the new computer name as the first parameter. The other parameters are the administrator ID and password, which aren't necessary if you're working on the local machine and are logged in as the administrator.

DISCUSSION
There are a couple of points worth remembering about computer renaming. Using this technique on a machine does *not* change the name in Active Directory. If the machine is a domain member, perform the name change through the system configuration to ensure AD is updated.

In the PowerShell v2 beta process, a Rename-Computer cmdlet was introduced. This was removed in the final version. Any mention of using this cmdlet you find in documentation or examples should be ignored.

Changing the name of the computer will force a reboot. There are also times when we need to manually reboot or shut down the system.

TECHNIQUE 47   Restarting a computer

There are many situations when we need to restart or even shut down a system. The ability to restart a system remotely is useful. If we have a remote desktop connection, we can log on and perform the reboot. It's more efficient to run the first option in this script.

There are many applications that use a number of different servers. These systems must be shut down in the right order; for example if we have a SharePoint environment, we must shut down the SharePoint servers before we shut down the SQL Server back end. If we perform the shutdowns by a script, we'll always get them in the right order. This is important if we're working late and need to get it right!

PROBLEM
What's the most efficient way to remotely restart or shut down a system?

SOLUTION
The OS controls the machine, so we need to look at the `Win32_OperatingSystem` class.

> **WHATIF WARNING** There's no warning, `whatif`, or confirmation when using these WMI methods. If we use the PowerShell 2.0 `Restart-Computer` cmdlet, we can use the `-whatif` parameter. Use `Stop-Computer` for a complete shutdown.

In listing 7.9, we start by creating a variable to represent the computer's `Win32_OperatingSystem` class. We can then call the `Reboot()` method ❶ to cause a restart, or we can make the machine shut down by using `Win32Shutdown()` ❷. In this example, a computer name is given, so it's acting on a remote machine.

Listing 7.9   Restarting the system

```
$computer = Get-WmiObject -CompterName pcrs2 -Class Win32_OperatingSystem
$computer.ReBoot()       ⟵❶ Reboot

$computer = Get-WmiObject -CompterName pcrs2 -Class Win32_OperatingSystem
$computer.Win32Shutdown(5)        ⟵
                                  ❷ Shutdown
```

DISCUSSION

The numeric value we pass as a parameter to `Win32Shutdown()` defines how the machine closes down. Table 7.1 shows that the values are paired with a difference of four between the members of a pair. The second value in the pair causes the activity to happen immediately and force the closure of any open applications.

We've seen in this section that we can discover a lot of extremely valuable information about the configuration of our systems using PowerShell and WMI. We can also configure the machines remotely using the same tools. These activities affect the machine, but what can we do for the user? This aspect of the desktop will be examined next.

Value	Meaning
0	Log off
4	Forced logoff
1	Shutdown
5	Forced shutdown
2	Reboot
6	Forced reboot
8	Power off
12	Forced power off

Table 7.1
`Win32Shutdown` **values**

7.3 User features

In an Active Directory-based environment, a lot of the configuration work that directly affects the user will be performed by Group Policy. PowerShell isn't directly usable from Group Policy. There's a certain amount of configuration work we may need to perform, especially concerning the folders such as the desktop that are known as *special folders*. Printers and the recycle bin are parts of the desktop environment that we may need to work with when administering the user's desktop.

See appendix D for a list of special folders.

As an introduction to special folders, we'll work with the desktop folder.

TECHNIQUE 48 **Minimizing windows**

When working on a Windows machine, we often find ourselves in the position of having multiple windows open. Many years ago when I spent my time directly supporting users, I remember being called over by a user who was having difficulty opening a particular spreadsheet. After a bit of digging, we realized he already had the file open but couldn't see it because it was hidden behind a number of other windows. A function to minimize all of the open windows would've been useful.

PROBLEM

I have too many windows open on my desktop and have lost track of what's open. I don't want to close the applications, as I have work in progress using the applications.

SOLUTION

We can use the Shell object to help us in this situation, as in listing 7.10.

Listing 7.10 Minimizing desktop windows

```
$a = New-Object -ComObject Shell.Application
$a.MinimizeAll()
```

The shell is the interface we work with in Windows OSs. The Shell COM object gives us the ability to access and work with that shell. We can create an object representing the shell by using New-Object. We need to use -ComObject, as this is COM-based. If we don't put in this parameter, PowerShell will assume that we're trying to work with a .NET object that it won't be able to find. This will cause it to object (sorry) by throwing an error.

DISCUSSION

There are a number of useful methods on the Shell object, which we can find by using:

```
$a | Get-Member
```

We can stop and start services, set the machine time, shut down Windows, and search for files and printers, for example. Using the MinimizeAll() method, as shown in the listing Get-Member produces, causes all of the windows to minimize. It's possible to use UndoMinimizeAll() to reverse this.

Now we've minimized all of the windows we can see the desktop. Users seem to fall into two groups—those who have hardly any icons on their desktops and those whose desktop is completely covered in icons. There's a problem with this last situation.

TECHNIQUE 49   Desktop contents

The problem with having a lot of icons on the desktop is that only a few characters of the file or application name are displayed. This can lead to a lot of wasted time as we search through the icons on the desktop looking for that elusive file.

PROBLEM
I have too many files and icons on my desktop. How can I see what's really there?

SOLUTION
Using the Shell object, we can drill down into the desktop contents, as in listing 7.11.

Listing 7.11 Viewing the desktop contents

```
$a = New-Object -ComObject Shell.Application
$desktop = 0x0
Get-ChildItem $a.Namespace($desktop).Self.Path
```

DISCUSSION
We start as before, by creating an instance of the Shell object. We need to set a variable to represent the desktop. This is in hexadecimal format, as shown by the 0x prefix. Appendix B lists the special folders and their representative values. A lot of the scripts that you see on the web will have the values for the special folders shown as hexadecimal.

Get-ChildItem will return a list of the files in the desktop folder. We specify the path to the desktop folder as shown.

Hexadecimal conversions
We can use the following function to convert a decimal number to hexadecimal:

```
Function tohex{
param ([int]$i =0)
[convert]::ToString($i,16)
}
```

This function accepts an integer as input and uses the System.Convert class to convert the integer to a string represent a hexadecimal (base 16) number. This method can also be used to convert to binary (base 2) and octal (base 8). If you need to convert a hexadecimal number back to a decimal number, use this conversion: [convert]::ToString(0xF,10). The number to be converted has to be presented in hexadecimal format.

TECHNIQUE 50　Adding a file to the desktop

I store a number of small files on my desktop. Usually they're pieces of information that I know I'll require on a frequent basis, such as the IP addressing scheme for my virtualized environment (don't ask) or important information such as the deadline for my next chapter that I have to keep handy. Opening Notepad, typing the information, and saving the file to the desktop is tedious. There's an easier way to do it.

PROBLEM

We want to preserve the current process information in a file on the desktop so that we can refer to it at a later time.

SOLUTION

This problem can be solved by modifying listing 7.11. We create the COM object representing the shell. We can then use the `desktop` namespace to create a file path, as in listing 7.12.

Listing 7.12　Create a file on the desktop

```
$a = New-Object -ComObject Shell.Application
$file = $a.Namespace(0x0).Self.Path + "\process.csv"
Get-Process | Export-Csv -Path $file-NoTypeInformation
```

`Get-Process` can be piped into an `Export-Csv` that writes the data into our file. `-NoTypeInformation` prevents the .NET type information being written to the first line of the CSV file

DISCUSSION

We could create a string holding some data and pass that to `Out-File` to create a TXT file on the desktop instead. If we need to access the file, we can create the file path as shown.

TECHNIQUE 51　Listing cookies

Many internet sites will create a cookie to hold information relevant to your visit to the site. The problem with cookies is that you don't necessarily know that they've been created. In the past, I've had problems with particular sites that changed in various aspects. The cookies I had for the site wouldn't work with the new version, so I had to delete the cookies. Internet Explorer is an all-or-nothing proposition. It'd be better to be able to find which cookies were causing the problem and delete only those, rather than all cookies.

PROBLEM

What cookies have been saved on your machine? You don't know?

SOLUTION

We can access the cookie folder (don't you wish they'd been called jars rather than folders?) and determine which cookies are present, as in listing 7.13.

Listing 7.13 Discovering cookies

```
$a = New-Object -ComObject Shell.Application
Get-ChildItem $a.Namespace(0x21).Self.Path   |
Sort LastWriteTime -Descending
```

The shell object is created and the `Get-ChildItem` cmdlet is used to list the contents of the cookie folder. We can sort the information using the PowerShell pipeline to pass the objects into `Sort` based on `LastWriteTime`.

DISCUSSION

This means we can easily see the most recent cookies. It would be a simple matter to replace `Sort LastWriteTime -Descending` with

```
Where {$_.LastWriteTime -le (Get-Date).AddDays(-90)} | Remove-Item
```

This would enable us to delete old cookies. Set the number of days to compare against to a value that suits your system.

Another special folder we need to consider is the recycle bin.

TECHNIQUE 52   **Viewing recycle bin contents**

When we delete a local file from our machines, it doesn't immediately vanish. It's moved into the recycle bin for possible restoration. We need to empty the recycle bin to finally remove the file.

> **ACKNOWLEDGMENT** This script and the following one are adapted from a blog post by Thomas Lee: http://tfl09.blogspot.com/2007/01/manipulating-recycle-bin-in-powershell.html. These scripts don't work on Windows Vista/ Windows Server 2008 and above, but alternatives are provided.

PROBLEM

It looks like an important file we need has been deleted. How can we check the recycle bin to see if it's there?

SOLUTION

The recycle bin is a special folder and can be accessed in the same way as the others, as in listing 7.14.

Listing 7.14 Opening the recycle bin

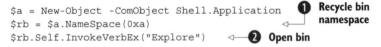

```
$a = New-Object -ComObject Shell.Application    ❶ Recycle bin
$rb = $a.NameSpace(0xa)                             namespace
$rb.Self.InvokeVerbEx("Explore")    ❷ Open bin
```

We create the shell object as before, but this time we create a variable representing the recycle bin namespace ❶. `Self` represents the recycle bin folder. We use the `Invoke-Verb()` method to explore (open) the recycle bin window ❷. This would make a useful function that could be invoked with a single command.

DISCUSSION

The recycle bin folder can be investigated using our trusty `Get-Member` cmdlet:

```
$rb.Self | gm
```

`Get-Member` has `gm` as an alias.

ALIASES   I find I spend more time writing scripts than working interactively. I only use aliases at the command prompt, and even then only the most common ones, as this ensures my scripts are understandable and portable. I recommend that custom aliases never be used in scripts. They may not be present on other machines.

If we dig a little further, we find a `verbs()` method:

```
$rb.self.verbs()
```

The verbs in the list match the context menu you get when you right-click a desktop object. We could use this method to open a file or application on the desktop. If you're using Windows Vista/Windows Server 2008 or above, this script may not work. In that case, we can use plan B and access the recycle bin contents like this:

```
$a = New-Object -ComObject Shell.Application
$a.NameSpace(0xa).Items() | Format-Table Name, Path -AutoSize
```

The recycle bin has a verb that we can use to empty it, as we'll see next.

TECHNIQUE 53   **Emptying the recycle bin**

The contents of the recycle bin can take up valuable disk space. We can reclaim this space by emptying the recycle bin.

WARNING   Once a file has been deleted from the recycle bin, there's no native way to restore that file. It means turning to our backup system. You do perform backups, right?

PROBLEM
It would be useful to empty the recycle bin on a periodic basis as part of our housekeeping routines for a machine. Can we do that from a script?

SOLUTION
The recycle bin has an entry on its context menu to empty it. We gain access to the recycle bin as before. We then use `InvokeVerb()` to trigger the action, as in listing 7.15. A confirmation dialog box will pop up asking if you want to perform the action.

Listing 7.15   Emptying the recycle bin

```
$a = New-Object -ComObject Shell.Application
$rb = $a.NameSpace(0xa).Self
$rb.InvokeVerb("Empty Recycle &Bin")
```

DISCUSSION
This technique works on Windows XP/2003 but not on Windows Vista/2008 or later. An alternative for Vista, and above, would be to use this to pipe the items in the recycle bin into `Remove-Item`:

```
$a =  New-Object -Com Shell.Application
$a.NameSpace(0xA).Items() | Remove-Item -Recurse
```

TECHNIQUE 54   **Sending a printer test page**

One thing that sticks in my mind from my time directly supporting users is that a lot of reported problems revolved around printing. My colleagues working in this area assure me that this still is the case. I dedicate the next couple of scripts to every administrator who has had to troubleshoot a printing issue with the hope they may be of some help.

PROBLEM

One step that's often needed when we start investigating printing issues is to attempt to print a test page. This will quickly show whether we can communicate with the printer. Usually we do this through the GUI controls, or we ask the user to do it on a remote machine. Can we perform this action remotely?

SOLUTION

We've seen that WMI has the capability to access remote machines. There's a WMI class specifically meant for working with printers, as shown in listing 7.16.

Listing 7.16 Print a test page

```
Get-WmiObject -Class Win32_Printer | Select Name        ❶
$printer = Get-WmiObject -Class Win32_Printer        ❷
-Filter "Name = 'HP DeskJet 660C'"
$printer.PrintTestPage()        ❸
```

We need to start by checking the printers installed on the machine ❶. This enables us to ensure that we're working with the correct printer. The -computername parameter can be used to specify a remote machine to access. Once we know the name of the printer we need, we can use that in a filter ❷ to create an object for the printer. A call to the PrintTestPage() method produces the test page ❸.

> **PRIVILEGES** When using Windows Vista/2008, we need to start PowerShell with elevated privileges. We right-click the PowerShell icon and select Run As Administrator.

DISCUSSION

We could test all printers on a machine using a foreach-object cmdlet and combining the lines of code. Alternatively listing 7.16 could be used to test a printer on a number of machines. The return code would have to be checked to confirm the test page was successfully printed.

The other aspect of printers that we need to consider is the printer drivers that are installed on the machine.

TECHNIQUE 55   **Printer drivers**

Printer drivers can cause issues. I've seen drivers for printers from the same manufacturer causing problems because they used different versions of the same file. We need to be able to determine information about our printer drivers.

PROBLEM

We have a number of printers installed on the machine; how can we check that the correct drivers are installed?

SOLUTION

WMI can provide this information—specifically the Win32_PrinterDriver class. A Select statement will reduce the amount of data returned to us, as in listing 7.17. Use Get-Member to determine other useful information that's available.

Listing 7.17   View printer drivers

```
Get-WmiObject -Class Win32_PrinterDriver |
Select Name, ConFigFile, DependentFiles, Driverpath |
Format-List
```

DISCUSSION

We've examined the machine configuration and how we can work with features of interest to the user such as the desktop and their printers. The last section in this chapter will cover working with the standard Office applications Word and Excel.

7.4   Office applications

It's a fair assumption to say that the Microsoft Office applications will be found on almost every desktop machine in work environments. It's possible to work with most of the Office applications using PowerShell. There are COM objects representing most of the them. In this section, we'll concentrate on using Word and Excel, as these are the two applications we're most likely to use as administrators. We'll start with Excel by looking at how we can create a spreadsheet and then put data into it. Spreadsheets seem much more useful when they have data. In the same way, we'll look at creating a Word document and how to push text into the document.

> **NOTE**   In this section, we'll just look at using the COM methods to work with Excel and Word. If the Office 2007 applications are in use, it's possible to use the OpenXML format for the documents. This involves delving into the depths of XML, which may not appeal to all administrators. An example of using OpenXML will be given at the end of this section.

The Microsoft Technet script center has a lot of VBScript examples of using Excel that can be converted to PowerShell. The first thing we need to do is to create an Excel spreadsheet.

TECHNIQUE 56   Creating an Excel spreadsheet

Creating an Excel spreadsheet should be a simple act, in theory. But there's a slight problem in the shape of a bug in Excel versions up to Excel 2007 that can prevent this from working if you don't happen to be in the U.S. After reading this, it won't matter where you live. If you're using Excel 2010, then the first version in listing 7.18 can be used wherever you live and work.

PROBLEM

We need to create an Excel spreadsheet from within a PowerShell script.

SOLUTION

The `Excel.application` COM object can be used to create a spreadsheet.

Listing 7.18   Create Excel spreadsheet

```
$xl = New-Object -ComObject "Excel.Application"   ←──❶ U.S. version
$xl.visible = $true
$xlbooks =$xl.workbooks.Add()
```

```
$xl = New-Object -ComObject "Excel.Application"
$xl.visible = $true
$xlbooks =$xl.workbooks
$newci = [System.Globalization.CultureInfo]"en-US"
$xlbooks.PSBase.GetType().InvokeMember("Add",
[Reflection.BindingFlags]::
InvokeMethod, $null, $xlbooks, $null, $newci)
```
◁─**②** **International version**

DISCUSSION

If you live in the U.S. or are using a machine that's configured to the U.S. locale—see the Control Panel -> Regional and Language settings (figure 7.3). Then you can use the first option in listing 7.18.

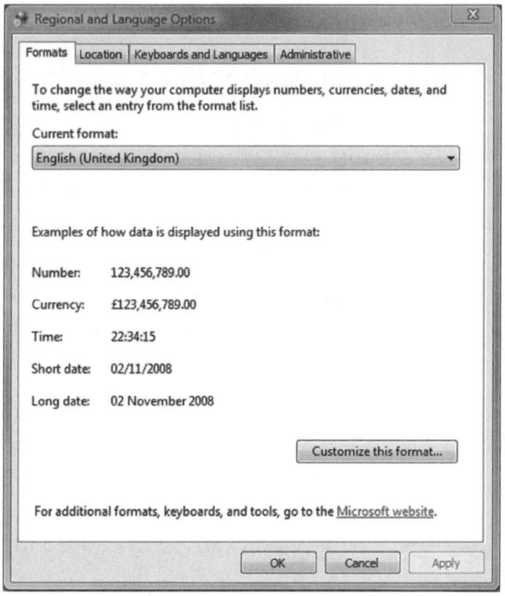

Otherwise, you have to use the second, international option. If you want to remain with PowerShell rather than succumbing to the GUI, you can check the culture by typing $psculture (in PowerShell v2). If en-US isn't returned then you need to use the second option in listing 7.18.

The simple way to create a spreadsheet **①** starts by creating the COM object using New-Object. We make it visible. Administrators are clever people, but working on an invisible spreadsheet may be a step too far,

Figure 7.3   Regional settings

especially on a Monday morning. At this point, we have only the Excel application open. We need to add a workbook to enable us to use the spreadsheet.

If the machine isn't using the U.S. culture—I live in England so $psculture returns en-GB—we have two options. The first option is to change the culture on the machine to en-US, which isn't convenient. Otherwise, we have to use the second option given in the listing.

We start in the same way by creating the COM object and making the spreadsheet visible. A variable $xlbooks is created that represents the workbooks in the spreadsheet. A second variable $newci is created that represents the culture. Note that we're forcing the culture used to create the workbook to be U.S. English. The last line is a bit complicated, but we're dropping down into the base workbook object and invoking the add method using the U.S. English culture. If you don't want to see the long list of data onscreen when this last line is run, then add | Out-Null to the end of the line. This is awkward, but it does get us past the bug. The good news is that once we've created our workbook, we can add data into it.

Adding data to a spreadsheet

A spreadsheet without data isn't much use to us, so we need to investigate how we can add data into the spreadsheet and perform calculations on that data.

PROBLEM

We need to populate our spreadsheet with some data.

SOLUTION

Expanding on the previous script, we can create a worksheet to hold the data. The starting point is to remove any previous versions of the spreadsheet ❶, as shown in listing 7.19. We use Test-Path to determine whether the file exists and Remove-Item to delete it. The -confirm parameter could be used with Remove-Item as an additional check if required. This is useful if working with important data.

Listing 7.19 Add data to Excel spreadsheet

```
$sfile = "C:\test\test.xlsx"                               ❶ Delete
if(Test-Path $sfile){Remove-Item $sfile}                     previous files

$xl = New-Object -comobject "Excel.Application"
$xl.visible = $true
$xlbooks =$xl.workbooks
$newci = [System.Globalization.CultureInfo]"en-US"
$wkbk = $xlbooks.PSBase.GetType().InvokeMember("Add",
[Reflection.BindingFlags]
::InvokeMethod, $null, $xlbooks, $null, $newci)             ❷ Create
$sheet = $wkbk.WorkSheets.Item(1)                              spreadsheet

$sheet.Cells.Item(1,1).FormulaLocal = "Value"
$sheet.Cells.Item(1,2).FormulaLocal = "Square"
$sheet.Cells.Item(1,3).FormulaLocal = "Cube"               ❸ Set headers
$sheet.Cells.Item(1,4).FormulaLocal = "Delta"

$row = 2                                                    ❹ Row counter

for ($i=1;$i -lt 25; $i++){                     ❺ Create data

    $f = $i*$i

    $sheet.Cells.Item($row,1).FormulaLocal = $i
    $sheet.Cells.Item($row,2).FormulaLocal = $f
    $sheet.Cells.Item($row,3).FormulaLocal = $f*$i
    $sheet.Cells.Item($row,4).FormulaR1C1Local = "=RC[-1]-RC[-2]"

    $row++
}
 [void]$wkbk.PSBase.GetType().InvokeMember("SaveAs",
[Reflection.BindingFlags]
::InvokeMethod, $null, $wkbk, $sfile, $newci)               ❻ Save

[void]$wkbk.PSBase.GetType().InvokeMember("Close",
[Reflection.BindingFlags]                                  ❼ Close
::InvokeMethod, $null, $wkbk, 0, $newci)
$xl.Quit()                                                 ❽ Quit
```

The next step is to create the spreadsheet. In this case, I've used the international method. Once the workbook is created, we can create a worksheet ❷. Worksheet cells are referred to by the row and column as shown ❸ by creating the column headers.

A counter is created ❹ for the rows. A `for` loop ❺ is used to calculate the square and the cube of the loop index. This is a simple example to illustrate the point. In reality, the data could be something like the number of rows exported compared to the number of rows imported for each table involved in a database migration. Note that the difference between the square and the cube is calculated by counting back from the current column.

We save the spreadsheet when all of the data has been written to it ❻ and close the workbook ❼. Note that we have to use a similar construction to adding a workbook, in Excel 2007 and earlier, to get around the culture issue. If we were using the en-US culture, those lines would become:

```
$wkbk.SaveAs("$file")
$wkbk.Close()
```

The last action is to quit the application ❽.

DISCUSSION

There are numerous reasons why you would want to record data into a spreadsheet but the performance implications must be understood. Working with Excel in this manner can be slow.

> **RECOMMENDATION** Adding data into an Excel spreadsheet in this manner can be extremely slow. In fact, painfully slow if a lot of data needs to be written into the spreadsheet. I strongly recommend creating a CSV file with the data and manually importing it into Excel instead of working directly with the spreadsheet.

This technique could be used to create reports, for instance from some of the WMI-based scripts we saw earlier. The machine name and relevant information could be written into the spreadsheet. Alternatively, we can write the data to a CSV file and then open it in Excel.

TECHNIQUE 58 **Opening a CSV file in Excel**

We have seen how writing data directly into a spreadsheet is slow. Slow tends to get frustrating, so we need another way to get the data into a spreadsheet. If we can write the data to a CSV file, we can open that file in Excel. It's much faster and more satisfying.

PROBLEM

Having decided that we need to speed up creating our spreadsheet, we need to open a CSV file in Excel.

SOLUTION

The `Open` method will perform this action, as in listing 7.20.

Listing 7.20   Open a CSV file

```
$xl = New-Object -comobject "excel.application"
$xl.WorkBooks.Open("C:\Scripts\Office\data.csv")
$xl.visible = $true
```

DISCUSSION

As with previous examples, we start by creating an object to represent the Excel application. We can then use the Open method of the workbooks to open the CSV file. The only parameter required is the path to the file. The full path has to be given. We then make the spreadsheet visible so we can work with it.

Alternatively we could use:

```
Invoke-Item data.csv
```

This depends on the default action in the file associations being to open the file in Excel. Hal Rottenberg graciously reminded me of this one.

The other major Office application is Word, which we'll look at next.

TECHNIQUE 59   Creating and writing to a Word document

Creating a Word document is straightforward compared to creating an Excel spreadsheet. There's only a single method regardless of location. The ability to add text into a Word document from within our script enables us to automate our processes and create the reports detailing our activities all in one pass. This is efficiency.

PROBLEM

We need to create a report from within our script.

SOLUTION

We adapt the script from listing 7.18 to create the report. The New-Object cmdlet ❶ is used to create an instance of the Word.Application object, as shown in listing 7.21. Note that we need to tell PowerShell we're dealing with a COM object. If this is forgotten, the error message will say that it can't find the type word.application and tell you to check that the assembly is loaded.

Listing 7.21   Add text to a Word document

```
$word = New-Object -ComObject "Word.application"    ◁──┐  ❶ Create Word
$word.visible = $true                                       document
$doc = $word.Documents.Add()
$doc.Activate()

$word.Selection.Font.Name = "Cambria"
$word.Selection.Font.Size = "20"
$word.Selection.TypeText("PowerShell")
$word.Selection.TypeParagraph()         ◁──❷ Add header

$word.Selection.Font.Name = "Calibri"
$word.Selection.Font.Size = "12"
$word.Selection.TypeText("The best scripting language in the world!")
$word.Selection.TypeParagraph()         ◁──
                                          ❸ Add text
$file = "c:\scripts\office\test.doc"
$doc.SaveAs([REF]$file)                 ◁──❹ Save document
$Word.Quit()                  ◁──❺ Quit Word
```

The Word application is made visible so that we can work with it. Finally, we add a document to the application. At this point, we have a blank document to start typing into, exactly as if we'd double-clicked on the Word icon. We can take this a stage further by writing text into the document from our script.

A header can be added ❷ by defining a font name, a font size, and the text to be added. The `TypeParagraph()` method is used to denote a new paragraph. These actions are repeated ❸ to add text to the document. The script closes by defining the filename to be used by the file; we save the file ❹ using the REF to reference the filename in the variable and then quit Word ❺.

DISCUSSION

This approach could be used to document machine information. The information is produced by utilizing the WMI scripts described in the first part of the document. It's written into a Word document by a variation of this script.

TECHNIQUE 60   Creating a configuration report

This is the fun part of the chapter where we combine everything we've learned previously to produce a Word document from a PowerShell script that will document our system. The document will be produced using the COM approach we've used so far, and as a bonus we'll look at using the OpenXML format for Word documents that was introduced with Office 2007.

The OpenXML document format is in effect a set of XML files within a zip file. The files can be examined by changing the extension (DOCX) of a Word 2007 document to ZIP. Opening the zip file allows the individual files to be read. We need to use XPath functionality to work with these files. XPath is a technology not usually associated with administrators! A tutorial on XPath can be found at http://www.w3schools.com/XPath/default.asp.

Before we can work with OpenXML documents, we need to load the OpenXML Power Tools. The binaries can be downloaded from the links in appendix E. First off, we'll work with the Word COM object.

PROBLEM

A configuration report must be produced for a system. The report must be created in a Word document for distribution.

SOLUTION

The configuration information can be obtained by using the WMI scripts from the first section of the chapter. This script brings together a number concepts starting with a function ❶. The function takes three parameters that contain the font name, the font size, and the text to be written into the document, as shown in listing 7.22. Within the body of the function, the font name and size are set. The text is written and the paragraph is closed.

Listing 7.22   Create a configuration report

```
function add-data {          ◄── ❶ Write data
param ($font, $size, $text)
$word.Selection.Font.Name = $font
$word.Selection.Font.Size = $size
$word.Selection.TypeText("$text")
$word.Selection.TypeParagraph()
}
```

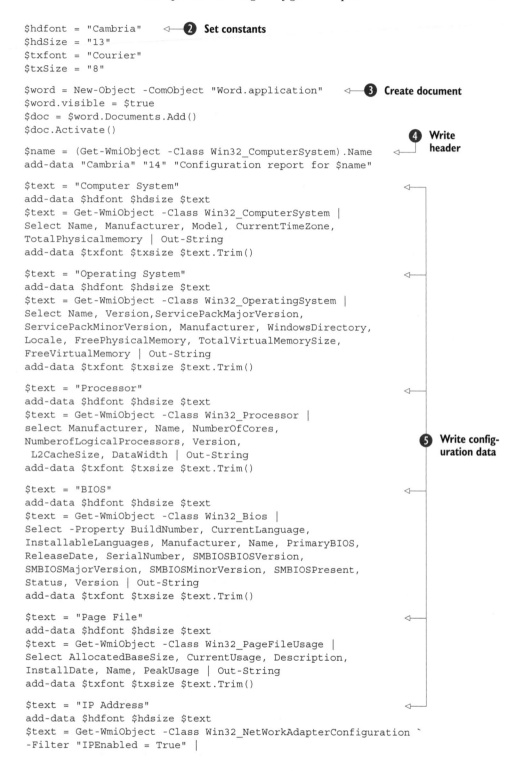

```
$hdfont = "Cambria"        <--2  Set constants
$hdSize = "13"
$txfont = "Courier"
$txSize = "8"

$word = New-Object -ComObject "Word.application"   <--3  Create document
$word.visible = $true
$doc = $word.Documents.Add()
$doc.Activate()
                                                        4  Write
                                                           header
$name = (Get-WmiObject -Class Win32_ComputerSystem).Name   <--
add-data "Cambria" "14" "Configuration report for $name"

$text = "Computer System"                                    <--
add-data $hdfont $hdsize $text
$text = Get-WmiObject -Class Win32_ComputerSystem |
Select Name, Manufacturer, Model, CurrentTimeZone,
TotalPhysicalmemory | Out-String
add-data $txfont $txsize $text.Trim()

$text = "Operating System"                                   <--
add-data $hdfont $hdsize $text
$text = Get-WmiObject -Class Win32_OperatingSystem |
Select Name, Version,ServicePackMajorVersion,
ServicePackMinorVersion, Manufacturer, WindowsDirectory,
Locale, FreePhysicalMemory, TotalVirtualMemorySize,
FreeVirtualMemory | Out-String
add-data $txfont $txsize $text.Trim()

$text = "Processor"                                          <--
add-data $hdfont $hdsize $text
$text = Get-WmiObject -Class Win32_Processor |
select Manufacturer, Name, NumberOfCores,
NumberofLogicalProcessors, Version,                          5  Write config-
 L2CacheSize, DataWidth | Out-String                            uration data
add-data $txfont $txsize $text.Trim()

$text = "BIOS"                                               <--
add-data $hdfont $hdsize $text
$text = Get-WmiObject -Class Win32_Bios |
Select -Property BuildNumber, CurrentLanguage,
InstallableLanguages, Manufacturer, Name, PrimaryBIOS,
ReleaseDate, SerialNumber, SMBIOSBIOSVersion,
SMBIOSMajorVersion, SMBIOSMinorVersion, SMBIOSPresent,
Status, Version | Out-String
add-data $txfont $txsize $text.Trim()

$text = "Page File"                                          <--
add-data $hdfont $hdsize $text
$text = Get-WmiObject -Class Win32_PageFileUsage |
Select AllocatedBaseSize, CurrentUsage, Description,
InstallDate, Name, PeakUsage | Out-String
add-data $txfont $txsize $text.Trim()

$text = "IP Address"                                         <--
add-data $hdfont $hdsize $text
$text = Get-WmiObject -Class Win32_NetWorkAdapterConfiguration `
-Filter "IPEnabled = True" |
```

```
Select DNSHostName, Caption, MACaddress, IPAddress,
IPSubNet, DefaultIPGateway, DHCPEnabled, DHCPServer,
DHCPLeaseObtained, DHCPLeaseExpires, DNSServerSearchOrder,
DNSDomainSuffixSearchOrder, WINSPrimaryServer,
 WINSSecondaryServer | Out-String
add-data $txfont $txsize $text.Trim()

$file = "c:\scripts\office\$name config report .doc"    ←─❻ Save and close
$doc.SaveAs([REF]$file)
$Word.Quit()
```

The body of the script starts by defining some constants ❷ for font names and sizes. Note that the sizes are defined as strings rather than integers. A Word document is created ❸ using the technique from the previous script.

At this point, we can start adding our configuration information into the document. The computer name is retrieved using the `Win32_ComputerSystem` class ❹ and substituted into a string that's passed into the function we defined at the beginning of the script.

> **FUNCTION DEFINITIONS** Functions must be defined before they're used. Best practice is to do it at the beginning of the script.

The configuration data can now be added to the document. I've chosen to use the WMI scripts from earlier in this chapter. Other WMI classes are available. The script is modular, so it's easy add or change the WMI classes used to derive the configuration information. For each set of configurations ❺, we define a title such as `"Computer System"` that we write using the header font and size we defined in the constants ❷. Using `Get-WmiObject` with our chosen class, we select the properties we want to record. The information is piped into `Out-String` so that a string is available to write into the Word document, rather than trying to write the object! The `add-data` function is used to write the data as previously, but we use the `Trim` method to remove the whitespace from before and after the data. This isn't essential, but it does make the report look better.

The Courier font is used for the data to ensure that spacing and formatting is preserved. Courier is a fixed-space font, so each character takes up the same amount of space. If a proportional spaced font such as Calibri (default in Word 2007) is used, the formatting will be lost.

When all of the configuration data has been written into the file, we need to create a filename that incorporates the machine name ❻ and then save and close the file. The configuration reports can be kept in a common folder. As WMI can be used to access remote machines, the computer name can be used in the `Get-WmiObject` cmdlet. The computer name can be passed into the script as a parameter.

DISCUSSION

As an alternative to using the COM object, we can create a Word document using the OpenXML format, as in listing 7.23. This may seem more complicated than using the more traditional COM object (and it is), but by adopting a standard approach using functions, we can make it straightforward. By comparing the two methods in this way, we can use a method we understand to help us understand the new method.

Listing 7.23   Using OpenXML

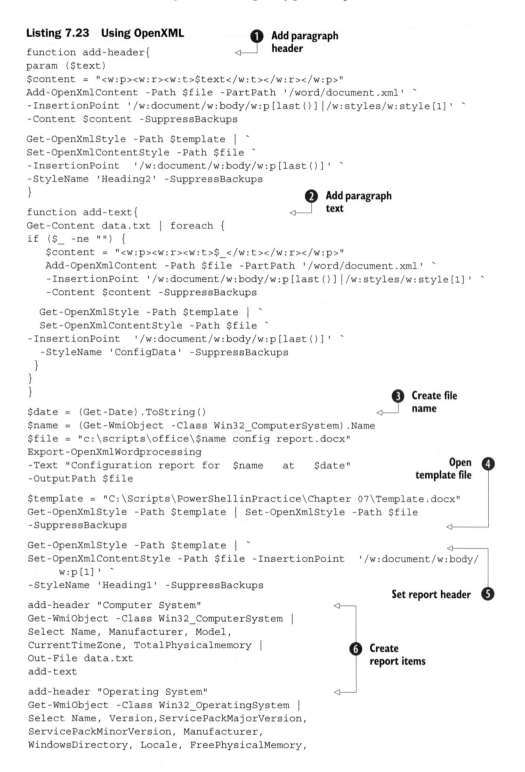

① Add paragraph header

② Add paragraph text

③ Create file name

④ Open template file

⑤ Set report header

⑥ Create report items

```
function add-header{
param ($text)
$content = "<w:p><w:r><w:t>$text</w:t></w:r></w:p>"
Add-OpenXmlContent -Path $file -PartPath '/word/document.xml' `
-InsertionPoint '/w:document/w:body/w:p[last()]|/w:styles/w:style[1]' `
-Content $content -SuppressBackups

Get-OpenXmlStyle -Path $template | `
Set-OpenXmlContentStyle -Path $file `
-InsertionPoint  '/w:document/w:body/w:p[last()]' `
-StyleName 'Heading2' -SuppressBackups
}
function add-text{
Get-Content data.txt | foreach {
if ($_ -ne "") {
  $content = "<w:p><w:r><w:t>$_</w:t></w:r></w:p>"
  Add-OpenXmlContent -Path $file -PartPath '/word/document.xml' `
  -InsertionPoint '/w:document/w:body/w:p[last()]|/w:styles/w:style[1]' `
  -Content $content -SuppressBackups

 Get-OpenXmlStyle -Path $template | `
 Set-OpenXmlContentStyle -Path $file `
-InsertionPoint  '/w:document/w:body/w:p[last()]' `
  -StyleName 'ConfigData' -SuppressBackups
 }
}
}
$date = (Get-Date).ToString()
$name = (Get-WmiObject -Class Win32_ComputerSystem).Name
$file = "c:\scripts\office\$name config report.docx"
Export-OpenXmlWordprocessing
-Text "Configuration report for  $name    at    $date"
-OutputPath $file

$template = "C:\Scripts\PowerShellinPractice\Chapter 07\Template.docx"
Get-OpenXmlStyle -Path $template | Set-OpenXmlStyle -Path $file
-SuppressBackups

Get-OpenXmlStyle -Path $template | `
Set-OpenXmlContentStyle -Path $file -InsertionPoint  '/w:document/w:body/
    w:p[1]' `
-StyleName 'Heading1' -SuppressBackups

add-header "Computer System"
Get-WmiObject -Class Win32_ComputerSystem |
Select Name, Manufacturer, Model,
CurrentTimeZone, TotalPhysicalmemory |
Out-File data.txt
add-text

add-header "Operating System"
Get-WmiObject -Class Win32_OperatingSystem |
Select Name, Version,ServicePackMajorVersion,
ServicePackMinorVersion, Manufacturer,
WindowsDirectory, Locale, FreePhysicalMemory,
```

```
TotalVirtualMemorySize, FreeVirtualMemory |
Out-File data.txt
add-text

add-header "Processor"
Get-WmiObject -Class Win32_Processor |
select Manufacturer, Name, NumberOfCores,
NumberofLogicalProcessors, Version, L2CacheSize,
DataWidth | Out-File data.txt
add-text

add-header "BIOS"
Get-WmiObject -Class Win32_Bios |
Select -Property BuildNumber, CurrentLanguage,
InstallableLanguages, Manufacturer, Name,
PrimaryBIOS, ReleaseDate, SerialNumber,
SMBIOSBIOSVersion, SMBIOSMajorVersion,
SMBIOSMinorVersion, SMBIOSPresent, Status,
 Version | Out-File data.txt
add-text

add-header "Page File"
Get-WmiObject -Class Win32_PageFileUsage |
Select AllocatedBaseSize, CurrentUsage, Description,
InstallDate, Name, PeakUsage | Out-File data.txt
add-text

add-header "IP Address"
Get-WmiObject
-Class Win32_NetWorkAdapterConfiguration
-Filter "IPEnabled = True" |
Select DNSHostName, Caption, MACaddress, IPAddress,
IPSubNet, DefaultIPGateway, DHCPEnabled, DHCPServer,
DHCPLeaseObtained, DHCPLeaseExpires, DNSServerSearchOrder,
DNSDomainSuffixSearchOrder, WINSPrimaryServer,
WINSSecondaryServer | Out-File data.txt
add-text
```

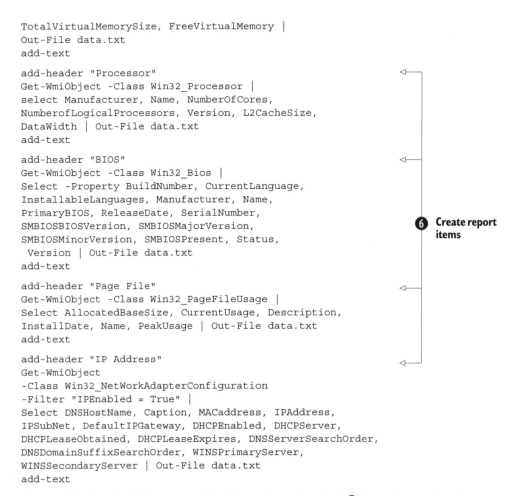

6 Create report items

The script starts by defining two functions. One function ❶ is used to write the paragraph headers in the report; the second ❷ is used to add the body of the text in the paragraph. The functions will be explained later in the context of creating the report.

The body of the script opens by using Get-Date ❸ to retrieve the current date. A filename is constructed after we've retrieved the computer name. The Export-Open-XMLWordProcessing cmdlet is used to create the document. We need to give the cmdlet some text to put into the document and the filename.

When using the COM model in the previous script, we set the style of the text, the font and size, before we wrote the text. In the OpenXML format, we set the style after the text has been written. We have to define a template file ❹ from which we can use the styles defined in it.

TEMPLATE FILE The template file I used in this example is available in the scripts download for this chapter.

We get the styles from the template file and put them into the report file we're creating. Note the use of the -SuppressBackups parameter ❺. This prevents a backup of the file being generated. I recommend using this parameter to stop your disk filling with lots of copies of your file. The default setting is that a backup is produced at every change.

Having defined the template document, we can use `Get-OpenXmlStyle` and `Set-OpenXmlContentStyle` to set the font and size of the text. The `-InsertionPoint` parameter takes an XPath definition, which reads as the first paragraph in the body of the document.

After this point, the report creation consists of defining the paragraph header ❻ and passing it to the `add-header` function, followed by the use of a WMI class to generate the report text. In this case, we have to write the text to a file and then call the `add-text` function.

`add-header` takes the text as a parameter and puts it into the correct XML tags to define its position in the paragraph. `Add-OpenXmlContent` writes the XML into the file. Remember that a DOCX file is a compressed set of XML files. The actual text is stored in the document.xml file in the Word folder. An insertion point of the last paragraph is used to ensure that the data doesn't get overwritten. Backups are suppressed. The second part of the function sets the style of this text as discussed earlier.

The `add-text` function is similar, except it reads the contents of the file and for each record checks whether the string is empty. If it's not empty, the string is written into the document and the font set to Courier by using the `ConfigData` style.

In some ways, the OpenXML format is easier to use, and in others it's harder. It's the format that will be most used in the future. Wise administrators will ensure that they have at least an understanding of how to work with it.

7.5   Summary

Administering the desktop estate in our environments can consume a large proportion of our time and effort. Much of the effort is spent discovering basic information about the systems showing problems. We can automate the discovery process using PowerShell and WMI. This can consist of a standard script returning a basic set of information and scripts that enable us to dig deeper to resolve particular issues. The issue can then be resolved using WMI and PowerShell, providing us with a powerful discovery and resolution method.

The user's desktop can be investigated using COM functionality to access the special folders. We can discover how things are configured, and then manipulate and change them as required.

The Office applications are extremely widespread in the Windows environment. We can create and access documents using these applications in PowerShell. This enables us to produce a reporting and documentation system for our machines based on using PowerShell with WMI and COM.

There are other aspects of a machine configuration and well-being, such as processes, services, event logs, and the registry that need to be included in this framework. These will be covered in the next chapter, which has sections that could also be applied to the desktop. Likewise, a large part of the material in this chapter could be applied to servers as well as desktops.

Part 3

Working with servers

In the previous two parts of the book, we learned how to use PowerShell. We've taken that knowledge and applied it to performing administration tasks that directly impact the user community. In part 3, we'll turn our attention to working with Windows servers and the applications that run on our servers.

Desktop administration tends to be about performing the same acts on many machines. Server administration is about performing a wider range of actions on a smaller number of machines. The other major difference is that an individual desktop machine having problems doesn't impact the business (unless it belongs to a senior manager, of course). A server that's having problems could stop a business-critical application and have a major impact on the business. Server administration has a bigger impact on the user community than desktop administration, as it affects the whole user community rather than an individual.

Server administration should be taken to mean remote administration. The servers are usually in a data center that may be at the other end of the building or the other end of town. In some cases, the data center may be in a different part of the country or even a different country. We shouldn't assume that we can gain physical access to the servers. Work remotely and embrace automation. It leaves more time for the fun things such as investigating what we can administer with PowerShell and how we can perform those actions remotely.

We'll start our look at servers in chapter 8 by understanding how to administer the basic aspects of a Windows server, including the filesystem, services, processes, the Registry and the event logs. While reading this chapter, keep in mind that parts of the material we covered in chapter 7 can be applied to servers also.

DNS, AD structure, AD topology, Exchange 2007, IIS 7, and SQL Server are covered in chapters 9 to 14. In each chapter, we'll look at how to administer the individual application from an "on-server" and remote viewpoint. In many cases, the same tools allow both. Some applications, such as IIS 7 and SQL Server, supply multiple methods of administration by PowerShell. We'll examine the options and make recommendations as to the best tools to use in particular circumstances. Chapter 15 brings together some of the innovations in the PowerShell world and how these can be applied.

Windows servers

8

This chapter covers

- Services and Processes
- Administering the filesystem
- Working with the Registry
- Managing Event Logs

This chapter opens the third and major part of the book, where we look at how we can administer our Windows servers, and the applications they host, by using PowerShell.

> **REMEMBER** Many of the scripts and tasks that were covered in chapter 7 also need to be performed on servers. Likewise, some of the material in this chapter can be applied to desktop machines. The two chapters form a bridge between the desktop and server aspects of administrator's activities.

In the introduction to this part, I made the point that server administration should be viewed as an activity to be performed remotely. PowerShell has a number of ways of supplying the capability to perform remote administration:

- Some cmdlets have a remote capability.
- Scripts can use WMI or .NET to access remote systems.
- PowerShell v2 brings a remoting capability based on the *Windows Remote Management* service.
- Some PowerShell providers, for example the one in SQL Server 2008, provide access to remote machines.

The techniques that apply in a given situation will be highlighted, as will any known issues with the remote capability. In all cases, firewalls can block access via these remoting technologies. Make sure that the firewall on the remote computer doesn't block the required protocols.

In this chapter we'll start by looking at how we'll administer our Windows server. This will create the foundation for later chapters, when we look at the applications hosted on the servers.

8.1 *Automating server administration*

One of my main areas of work is as an IT architect. I spend my time designing and implementing systems to solve business problems. One of the first things I have to do when presented with a new problem is to determine the customer's requirements. The same concept applies to server administration. What are our requirements? We can't decide how we'll automate our administration until we know what we'll administer.

When we think about administering the server itself rather than the applications hosted on it, we tend to arrive at the following suspects:

- Services
- Processes
- Filesystem
- Registry
- Event logs

The system configuration section from chapter 7 is also applicable to servers. Many of the scripts presented in that section are WMI-based and are therefore directly applicable to remote administration. Anything to save you from running around so much.

Services and processes define what's running on the server. These, in many cases, are the applications we'll be dealing with in subsequent chapters. At this stage we're concerned with the basics; are they running and how do we manage them?

The filesystem is an essential part of any server. We need to be able to work with files and the folder hierarchy irrespective of the applications in use. The registry is a repository of configuration information that we have to be able to access. We'll see the registry provider in action. Now you can do a `dir` through the registry. Awesome!

Event logs are where we find the diagnostic information we need when things go wrong. Reading the data in the event logs is good, but we also need to be able to write to the event logs and even create our own logs.

We need to consider one more thing before we dive into all the fun stuff with PowerShell. There's a new kid on the block in the Windows world: Windows Server Core.

8.1.1 Server Core

Server Core is an install option for Windows Server 2008 (and R2). It's a stripped down version without a GUI, which may seem an odd option for a Windows system. The command prompt is the only way to locally manage a Server Core machine, though GUI tools can be used from a remote machine. Once chosen, the only way to revert to a GUI-based version of Windows is to reinstall. Likewise, a GUI-based version of Windows can't be converted to a Server Core version without reinstalling.

One of the real benefits of running Server Core is the reduced number of services, leading to a reduced patching requirement. Anything that reduces patching is a benefit to an administrator.

There are a number of roles for which Server Core is ideal, including domain controllers, DNS servers, or file and print servers. One thing that's missing in the original Windows Server 2008 release is the .NET framework. This means that ASP.NET can't be used, and also PowerShell can't be installed in the normal way. (Dmitry Sotnikov has shown how it's possible to install PowerShell v2 on a Server Core machine: http://dmitrysotnikov.wordpress.com/2008/05/15/powershell-on-server-core/.)

> **NOTE** Sotnikov's method for installing PowerShell on Server Core isn't a supported or recommended approach for production machines. It should be viewed as a proof of concept. Many aspects of a Server Core installation can be managed remotely via WMI.

In Windows Server 2008 R2, a subset of the .NET framework can be installed on Server Core, meaning that PowerShell is available as an optional feature. If you're using Server Core in your environment consider upgrading to R2 if at all possible.

The first things we need to look at are services and processes. In other words, what's running on our systems and how can we manage them.

8.2 Services and processes

Services and processes together make up the applications running on our systems. Some services such as Exchange or SQL Server provide applications; others provide the background functionality we need for a healthy, working system. Knowing what's running, and possibly more importantly, what should be running, gives us a powerful administrative handle on our systems.

Some of the processes we have running are from applications we've explicitly started. PowerShell can be used to manage the processes we have running, including the creation of new processes. There's a mesh of dependencies between services on a Windows system. We could use the GUI tool to trace these, but it's easier with PowerShell as we'll see. We can even display the information graphically, which can make the dependencies more obvious.

TECHNIQUE 61   **Service health check**

One common troubleshooting scenario is that a service has stopped for some reason. It's not necessarily the primary service that's causing the problem, but a service on which that service is dependent that's having problems. Big fleas have little fleas upon their back to bite 'em and little fleas have...

PROBLEM

We need to view the services installed on the system to determine which services are running and if any of their dependent services haven't started.

SOLUTION

PowerShell provides a `Get-Service` cmdlet that we can use to investigate the status of our services. In PowerShell v1, this script can only be run against the local system. If we want to work with remote systems, we need to use WMI. PowerShell v2 adds a `computername` parameter so we could modify the script to incorporate the dealing with services on remote computers.

> **NOTE** PowerShell v2 also adds `DependentServices` and `RequiredServices` parameters. These will only show the status of the dependent or required service. The status of the parent service isn't shown. The script could be modified to work with these parameters if required.

The script in listing 8.1 starts by using `Get-Service` in its default mode to generate a list of services installed on the local machine ❶. The list is sorted by the display name of the service. This is the name that's shown in the Services administration tool. The display name isn't necessarily the same as the service name, as can be seen by running `Get-Service`, or by looking at the examples in table 8.1.

Name	Display name
Afd	Ancilliary Function Driver for Winsock
Tdx	NetIO Legacy TDI Support Driver
NSI	Network Store Interface Service

Table 8.1
Sample service names and display names.

The services are piped into a `foreach` cmdlet that performs the bulk of the work in the script. An initial check on the status of the service is used to determine how the information is displayed. A service that's stopped ❷ will be displayed with red text on a white background, whereas a running service ❸ will be displayed in the normal colors normally used by PowerShell. Note how `n is used to force the display to be on a new line in the `Write-Host`.

> **NOTE** The colors can be easily changed depending on the colors used on your machine. The list of allowable colors can be seen in the help file for `Write-Host`.

After displaying the status of the service, we perform a `Get-Service` on the individual services and expand the property that holds the services that are depended on **4**. Another `foreach` is used to display whether these services are stopped **5** or running **6**.

Listing 8.1 Service health check

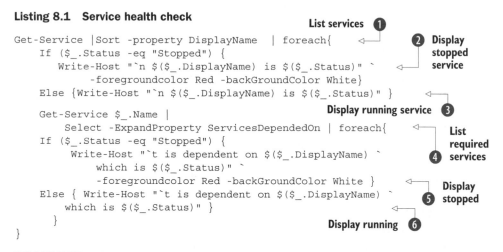

```
Get-Service |Sort -property DisplayName  | foreach{          List services  1
    If ($_.Status -eq "Stopped") {                                        2  Display
        Write-Host "`n $($_.DisplayName) is $($_.Status)" `                 stopped
                -foregroundcolor Red -backGroundColor White}               service
    Else {Write-Host "`n $($_.DisplayName) is $($_.Status)" }

    Get-Service $_.Name |                        Display running service  3
        Select -ExpandProperty ServicesDependedOn | foreach{         List
    If ($_.Status -eq "Stopped") {                                   required
        Write-Host "`t is dependent on $($_.DisplayName) `          4  services
                which is $($_.Status)" `
                -foregroundcolor Red -backGroundColor White }      Display
    Else { Write-Host "`t is dependent on $($_.DisplayName) `       5 stopped
        which is $($_.Status)" }
    }                                           Display running  6
}
```

DISCUSSION

Exchange Server 2007 has a cmdlet that produces similar output for the Exchange services. Variants could be written that just tested the SQL Server services, for instance.

One interesting variation is to display the results graphically. Netmap is a tool that can be used to create and view network graphs. PowerShell scripts to work with it can be downloaded from http://dougfinke.com/blog/?p=465. As an example, we could look at the DHCP client service. The services that the DHCP client is dependent on are listed in table 8.1. But as figure 8.1 shows, there's a further layer of dependencies in that the Tdx and NSI services both have dependent services. This diagram could be extended to include all services, but the level of detail wouldn't lend itself to being easily reproduced.

Now that we know what services are on our systems, how do we go about managing them?

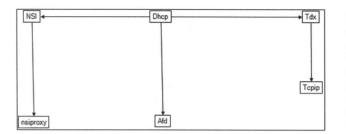

Figure 8.1 Hierarchy of services on which the DHCP client service is dependent. There are three primary dependencies, two of which have a further dependent service. All of the services in the hierarchy must be working for DHCP to work.

TECHNIQUE 62   **Managing services**

There are a number of cmdlets available to manage services:

- `Get-Service`
- `Restart-Service`
- `Set-Service`
- `Stop-Service`
- `New-Service`
- `Resume-Service`
- `Start-Service`
- `Suspend-Service`

The cmdlet names are self-describing in terms of functionality. In PowerShell v1, the service cmdlets are restricted to the local machine. This is extended in version 2, in that `Get-Service` and `Set-Service` have a `-computername` parameter added so we can work with remote systems. It's not possible to use the `ReStart-`, `Resume-`, `Start-`, `Stop-`, or `Suspend-Service` cmdlets against a remote machine. We can perform these actions using WMI or the `Set-Service` cmdlet. `Set-Service` can work with the service startup type, but `Get-Service` can't display the startup type because the .NET object doesn't incorporate the startup type.

PROBLEM

Many of our major applications run as services, for example SQL Server and Exchange. How can we quickly, and easily, determine which services are running if the users report problems accessing the systems?

SOLUTION

PowerShell and WMI, where necessary, enable us to view and manage the services on our systems. The first thing we usually want to know is whether our services are running. In PowerShell, whenever we have to retrieve information, the verb to use is *Get*. We're dealing with services, so our command in listing 8.2 becomes `Get-Service` ❶. The standard output is shown in the truncated listing and consists of the service name, display name, and its status in terms of whether it's running. With PowerShell vv2, we can interrogate the services on remote machines by using a `-ComputerName` parameter. Alternatively, we can use the `Win32_Service` WMI class. The cmdlets that have a `-ComputerName` parameter use the local credentials and don't allow them to be changed. `Get-WmiObject` does allow the use of alternate credentials.

The PowerShell pipeline enables us to take the results of our discovery ❷. In this case, we want all of the services whose name starts with the letter S and we can use `Where-Object` to limit our output to those services that are actually running. We could take this a step further and pipe these results in to a `Stop-Service` cmdlet. We find all of the running services whose names start with S and stop them.

> **NOT ME**   I often include this in PowerShell introductory sessions. Strangely enough, none of the people who encourage me to try this in the demonstration are willing to perform the same action on their machines.

This leads to a reminder about one of PowerShell's failsafe mechanisms—the `-whatif` parameter ❸. We can see what the results of our actions would be if we actually performed them by using -whatif, as in listing 8.2. It's a good idea to test these types of actions using -whatif.

Listing 8.2 Managing services

```
PS> Get-Service                                    ◄──❶ Get-Service

Status    Name                DisplayName
------    ----                -----------
Running   AEADIFilters        Andrea ADI Filters Service
Running   AeLookupSvc         Application Experience
Stopped   ALG                 Application Layer Gateway Service
Running   AppHostSvc          Application Host Helper Service
Running   Appinfo             Application Information
Stopped   AppMgmt             Application Management

Listing truncated to save space           ❷ Filter Get-
                                              Service
Get-Service s* | where {$_.Status -eq "Running"}   ◄──┘

Get-Service s* | where {$_.Status -eq "Running"} | ❸ Stop-Service
Stop-Service -whatif                               ◄──┘

$s1 = Get-WmiObject -class Win32_Service -Filter "Name='W32Time'"
$s1.stopservice()                                  ◄──┐ WMI and
                                                   ❹  services
```

DISCUSSION

WMI can also be used to manage services. But be aware that the *-Service cmdlets don't use WMI to perform their functions. We can use WMI directly to manage services ❹. Using the Win32_Service class will return information about all services. The -Filter parameter can be used to restrict the action to a single service as shown. Get-Member can be used to view the list of properties and methods available when using this WMI class:

```
$s1 | Get-Member
```

There's a method that will stop the service. A -whatif parameter isn't available when using the StopService() method in WMI. The service will be stopped immediately. WMI gives us the ability to administer services on remote machines. In PowerShell v2, some of this functionality is available through the Set-Service cmdlet.

TECHNIQUE 63   **Managing processes**

Processes are the other major area we have to look at in this section. We're often dealing with applications such as Microsoft Word when we think of processes. All processes consume resources, usually thought of as CPU cycles and memory (physical and virtual). As administrators, we need to be aware of the resources that applications are consuming. It could be that an application is taking more resources than it should, which is having an adverse effect on other processes.

PROBLEM

One common scenario for an administrator is that the phone rings and an irate voice tells you that the system is running slow, which is stopping everyone from working properly. There are numerous possible reasons that could cause this slowdown. One area that has to be investigated is how the processes are using CPU and memory.

SOLUTION

Get-Process is at the heart of any understanding of resource usage by processes. We can use it to view the CPU and memory usage by process. Get-Process is the cmdlet that we need when we want to investigate processes. In PowerShell v2, it gets a -ComputerName parameter so that we can look at the processes on remote machines. In PowerShell v1, we can use the Win32_Process WMI class to achieve the same goal as Get-WMIObject can access remote machines. The default output of Get-Process in listing 8.3 **1** shows a number of useful pieces of information, including:

- CPU usage
- Physical memory usage-both paged and nonpaged
- Virtual memory usage
- Working set size
- Number of handles

We can restrict the data by only asking for particular processes, either filtering by name or by property, as in listing 8.3. Get-Process returns a large number of properties. They can be viewed by using Get-Member **2**. The default display is to show the processes sorted by name.

Listing 8.3 Managing processes

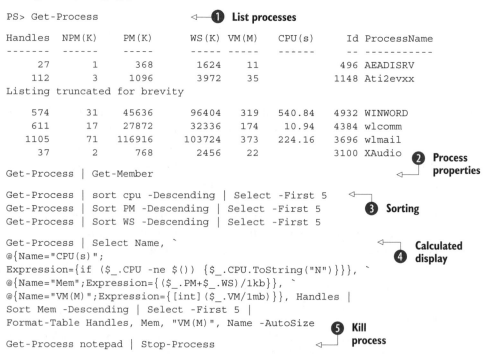

```
PS> Get-Process                          ◄──1  List processes

Handles  NPM(K)    PM(K)     WS(K) VM(M)    CPU(s)     Id ProcessName
-------  ------    -----     ----- -----    ------     -- -----------
     27       1      368      1624    11               496 AEADISRV
    112       3     1096      3972    35              1148 Ati2evxx
Listing truncated for brevity
    574      31    45636     96404   319    540.84    4932 WINWORD
    611      17    27872     32336   174     10.94    4384 wlcomm
   1105      71   116916    103724   373    224.16    3696 wlmail
     37       2      768      2456    22              3100 XAudio    2  Process
                                                                        properties
Get-Process | Get-Member                                          ◄──┘

Get-Process | sort cpu -Descending | Select -First 5     ◄──┐
Get-Process | Sort PM -Descending | Select -First 5          3  Sorting
Get-Process | Sort WS -Descending | Select -First 5

Get-Process | Select Name, `                          ◄──┐
@{Name="CPU(s)";                                          4  Calculated
Expression={if ($_.CPU -ne $()) {$_.CPU.ToString("N")}}}, `  display
@{Name="Mem";Expression={($_.PM+$_.WS)/1kb}}, `
@{Name="VM(M)";Expression={[int]($_.VM/1mb)}}, Handles |
Sort Mem -Descending | Select -First 5 |
Format-Table Handles, Mem, "VM(M)", Name -AutoSize    5  Kill
                                                         process
Get-Process notepad | Stop-Process                   ◄──┘
```

DISCUSSION

In many cases, we're more interested in the processes that are consuming most of a particular resource, usually CPU or memory. PowerShell has a `Sort-Object` cmdlet. We can sort by various properties and select the top five, or whatever seems suitable, and just display those processes ❸. This is a useful technique, but the results shown by sorting by Paged Memory (PM) and Working Set (WS) for instance will be slightly different. What we really need is a combined measure that will show those processes that take the most memory overall.

We can't do this directly. But by starting with `Get-Process` ❹ we can calculate what we need. The bulk of the work is performed in the `Select-Object` cmdlet. In addition to selecting the process name and handles, we calculate three fields. The CPU(s) field gives a neater display in that CPU usage is rounded to two decimal places. Note how the `if` statement is used in the `Expression` script block. The Mem field simply adds the WS and the PM, with the result returned as kilobytes. As a contrast, the virtual memory is returned as an integer number of megabytes.

We can sort on calculated fields. In this case the combined memory calculation. The first five results are selected and `Format-Table` is used to control the order of display.

ONE LINE In listing 8.3 ❹ is a single line of PowerShell code! It's split for clarity of display purposes.

The thought process that has brought us to this long line of code is typical of the way that we as administrators produce scripts. We start with the output of the cmdlets, then start sorting and selecting specific properties to refine our results. If we can't achieve the results we need, we have to get more complicated and start calculating fields. This approach was described in more detail in chapter 4.

If we find a process that's taking too big a share of the resources, we may need to stop it. We can use `Stop-Process` and ensure we identify the process correctly. There's a big opportunity for mistakes here. A better solution is to make sure we get the correct process and pipe the results into `Stop-Process` ❺. This reduces the chances of a mistake being made.

TECHNIQUE 64 Launching processes

The final activity involving processes we need to consider is how we can create them. Processes are created by the OS, applications, and services. We may need to start our own processes either because we need to start an application or as part of the activity involved in solving a problem.

PROBLEM

We need to start an application on a local or remote system. This application may need to start at a specific time (use Windows scheduler to run PowerShell) or could be used for diagnostic purposes.

SOLUTION

WMI provides two methods we can exploit to solve this problem. The first is usable in PowerShell v1 or v2, but the second method is only applicable to version 2. We also have a direct method using `Start-Process`, which is only available in version 2 and only works on the local computer, as shown in listing 8.4.

Listing 8.4   Creating processes

```
$c = [WMIClass]"Win32_Process"                          ◄── ❶ Version 1 or 2
$c.Create("notepad.exe")

Invoke-WmiMethod -Class Win32_process -Name Create      ◄── ❷ Version 2
-ArgumentList notepad.exe

Start-Process notepad                                   ◄── ❸ Version 2, local only
```

DISCUSSION

The object of the exercise in this example is to start a process that allows us to start an instance of Notepad. Notepad is a good test bed when experimenting with processes. It won't damage your system, unless you start hundreds of instances. It's possible to make a mistake, such that you create an infinite loop that continually spawns processes. You'll only do this once and become very paranoid about loops afterward. Yes, this is experience talking but it was a long, long time ago. Honest!

Our first example uses the `[WMIClass]` accelerator ❶ we discussed in chapter 3. This enables us to create an instance on a WMI class, in this case the `Win32_Process` class. Unfortunately, this is a two-step process, as we then have to use the `Create()` method to actually create the process. We need to give the application that'll run in the process as a parameter. If the application path isn't known to Windows, we need to give the full path. This approach can be used on remote computers. We amend the first line to include the computer name and use the full WMI path to the class.

```
$c = [WMIClass]"\\computer1\root\cimv2:Win32_Process"
```

The `Create()` method is used in exactly the same way.

PowerShell v2 brings a slightly easier to use option in the form of the `Invoke-WmiMethod` cmdlet ❷. We need to supply the WMI class, the method, and the arguments as shown. This cmdlet has a `-ComputerName` parameter so that we can work with remote machines:

```
Invoke-WmiMethod -Computername computer1 -Class Win32_process
-Name Create -ArgumentList notepad.exe
```

`Start-Process` ❸ can be used on the local machine to create a process for an application.

In addition to starting processes, we need to think about terminating processes. We can use WMI, though `Remove-WMIObject` is only available in PowerShell v2:

```
Get-WmiObject -Class win32_process -Filter "Name='calc.exe'" |
Remove-WmiObject
```

Other alternatives include using the `Stop-Process` cmdlet on the local machine or using the `kill` method on the process object:

```
Stop-Process -Name notepad
Get-Process notepad | Stop-Process

$p = Get-Process notepad
$p.Kill()
```

The Kill() method is the one I'd recommend least. Ideally, you should use Power-Shell v2 and the Stop-Process cmdlet so that the -whatif and -confirm parameters are available.

The combination of PowerShell and WMI is the recommended method for working with remote processes. The remoting capabilities in PowerShell v2 could be used if available. This concludes our work with services and processes. The next major activity we need to consider is administering the filesystem.

8.3   *Filesystem*

Administrators always seem to be tinkering around in the filesystem. It's where most of us probably started as administrators. Even if we're working with server-based applications such as Exchange or SQL Server, we still need to interact with the filesystem. PowerShell gives us a number of tools for working with the filesystem. We don't have the space to cover all of the possible scenarios in this section. We could probably fill another book with examples of just working with the filesystem. The examples in this section will provide a starting point for further experimentation, and will cover the most common administrative tasks regarding the filesystem.

PowerShell has the concept of *providers* for working with data stores. The filesystem provides the model for providers. Though PowerShell treats the filesystem as just another provider, in reality the other providers often don't supply the same level of functionality as the filesystem provider. Table 8.2 lists the cmdlets that can be used to work with files.

Table 8.2   Cmdlets for working with files

Cmdlet	Synopsis
Clear-Item	Deletes the contents of an item, but doesn't delete the item.
Copy-Item	Copies an item from one location to another.
Get-ChildItem	Gets the items and child items in one or more specified locations.
Get-Item	Gets the item at the specified location.
Invoke-Item	Performs the default action on the specified item.
Move-Item	Moves an item from one location to another.
New-Item	Creates a new item.
Remove-Item	Deletes the specified items.
Rename-Item	Renames an item.
Set-Item	Changes the value of an item to the value specified in the command.

In the filesystem provider, a file or folder is regarded as an item, and it's the provider's task to provide the interface to the `*-Item` and `*-ItemProperty` cmdlets. These cmdlets together with a number of others are known as the *core commands* and theoretically should be available in all providers. The full list of core commands can be found by typing:

```
Get-Help about_Core_Commands
```

In addition to being able to work with the files themselves, we need to be able to access the contents of the files, which we can using the cmdlets in table 8.3.

Table 8.3   Cmdlets for working with file content

Cmdlet	Synopsis
Add-Content	Adds content to the specified items, such as adding words to a file.
Clear-Content	Deletes the contents of a item, such as deleting the text from a file, but doesn't delete the item.
Get-Content	Gets the content of the item at the specified location.
Set-Content	Writes or replaces the content in an item with new content.

In addition to the cmdlets listed in the table, we have other ways to work with text type files including:

- `Export-Csv`
- `Import-Csv`
- `Out-File`

XML files have been deliberately left until chapter 13. We'll see these cmdlets in action in the rest of this section. The starting point for the filesystem though has to be folders.

TECHNIQUE 65   **Creating folders**

In the Windows filesystem, folders are used as a method of grouping and organizing files into a treelike structure. Before we can work with files, we need to consider how we'll organize our files and how we'll create the folders we'll need. Examples of creating folders and files are also given in section 2.4.4 dealing with `for`, `do`, and `while` loops, and section 2.4.5 dealing with functions.

PROBLEM

We need a method of creating one or more folders.

SOLUTION

The cmdlet we need to perform this task can be discovered by remembering the verb-noun syntax of PowerShell. If we want to create something, the verb to use is New. In this case, we want to create a folder in the filesystem and folders are counted as items in a provider. This means we need the `New-Item` cmdlet, shown in listing 8.5.

Listing 8.5   Creating folders

```
New-Item -Name TestFolder -Path c:\scripts -ItemType Directory
```

DISCUSSION

New-Item only requires three pieces of information in order to create a folder. The name of the folder, the path to the folder (remember the standard limits on path length in Windows), and the fact that we're creating a folder. In the filesystem provider, the -ItemType parameter can only accept values of Directory or File. Power-Shell will prompt for a type if you don't supply one.

> **NOTE** There are two aliases available when creating folders—md and mkdir. They're used in the same way as the cmd.exe commands.

Having created our folder, we now need something to put in it.

TECHNIQUE 66 Creating files

The files on our systems tend to fall into one of two categories. One possibility is that they're application-specific, such as a file created by Word or a SQL Server database file. On the other hand, they may be a text file that we can work with directly in our PowerShell scripts. This assumes that we have the permissions required to work with the particular files in question!

PROBLEM

Our computer systems are never static. This is where some of the challenge and fun comes into being an administrator. Applications take more resources over time. Disks fill up. New applications are introduced. These activities all involve changes to the system.

One thing we need to be aware of is change over time. This can only be recognized if we have a record of previous states. We can view the current state of our processes and services, but to save the previous state, we need to write the data into a file that we can access at a later date. How can we save this information using PowerShell?

SOLUTION

PowerShell provides several ways to create and write to a file, as shown in listing 8.6. The best one to use depends on circumstances. One of the great strengths of Power-Shell is that there are multiple ways to achieve a goal. This can also be perceived as a weakness, especially by someone setting out to learn PowerShell. The best advice I can give is to look at the alternatives and settle on which works best in your particular circumstances. This may well involve experimentation. Never be afraid to experiment—that's why you can use the same commands from the prompt as in your scripts!

Listing 8.6 Creating files

```
New-Item -Name testfile.txt -Path c:\scripts\testfolder -ItemType File
-Value "This is a one line file"                                          ❶

Get-Service | Out-File -FilePath c:\scripts\testfolder\sp.txt             ❷
Get-Process | Out-File -FilePath c:\scripts\testfolder\sp.txt -Append

Get-Process |
Export-Csv -Path c:\scripts\testfolder\testprc.csv -NoTypeInformation     ❸
```

We can use New-Item to create a file ❶. We follow the same pattern as when creating a folder, and supply the name, the path, and the type of item we're creating. We also have the option to add content to the file at the time of creation by using the -value parameter. If this is omitted, an empty file is created, as in the examples in chapter 2. The Set-Content cmdlet can be used to put content into the empty file. If it's used against a file that already has content, that content will be overwritten. This option is good if we need to create an empty file or we have content available to write to the file as one piece.

Our second option involves using Out-File ❷. In the first part of the script, we pipe the results from using Get-Service into our file. The second part appends the results of Get-Process. Note the use of the -Append parameter. This forces the data to be appended to the end of the file rather than overwriting the file contents, which is the default behavior. One of the best uses of Out-File is where we need to keep appending data to a file. Add-Content can also be used to append data to a file.

The final option is to use Export-Csv ❸. A text file was produced in the previous two cases. In this example, we're creating a delimited file where the fields are separated by commas. We need to give the path to the file pipe in the data we wish to write into the file. The -NoTypeInformation parameter prevents the .NET type information from being written into the first row of the file. We don't usually need this information, so it's best to use this parameter as a matter of routine.

NOTE   Export-Csv doesn't have the capability to append data to a file.

DISCUSSION

In addition to being able to create and write to files, we need to be able to delete them at the appropriate time. The script in listing 8.7 is used to clean up the contents of my Temp folder on a periodic basis (when I remember to do it).

Listing 8.7   Removing files

```
Remove-Item C:\temp\*.tmp -Recurse
Remove-Item C:\temp\low\*.tmp -Recurse
Remove-Item C:\temp\*.log -Recurse
Remove-Item C:\temp\*.txt -Recurse
Remove-Item C:\temp\*.cvr -Recurse
Remove-Item C:\temp\*.od  -Recurse
Remove-Item C:\temp\*.exe -Recurse
Remove-Item C:\temp\*.dll -Recurse
Remove-Item C:\temp\*.xml -Recurse
Remove-Item C:\temp\*.Hxc -Recurse
```

Note the use of the -Recurse parameter. This will recursively follow the subfolder tree within the Temp folder to delete all of the files with the given extension. My scripts of this sort tend to be built up over time, so I end up with repeated calls like this (quick and dirty scripting). If we want to make the script more concise, we can always do this:

```
"tmp", "log", "txt", "cvr", "od", "exe", "dll", "xml", "Hxc" |
foreach {Remove-Item "$env:temp\*.$_" -Recurse}
```

Simply pipe the list of extensions into a `foreach` cmdlet that calls `Remove-Item`. This also showcases the use of an environmental variable `temp`, which gives the path to the temporary folder. We access environmental variables via the `$env` variable, which represents the environment drive in PowerShell.

Once we've written our data into a file, we'll need to read the data in the file.

TECHNIQUE 67   **Reading files**

Being able to write data into our files is a good thing. It's even better if we can access the data in those files. At this point, we can start to save data for reuse in our scripts, or even for other purposes.

PROBLEM

The data in files, of various formats, has to be read so that we can use it in our scripts.

SOLUTION

In a similar manner to the situation with writing data, PowerShell provides a number of ways to read the data in a file, as shown in listing 8.8. The simplest way to read the data is to use `Invoke-Item` ❶. `Invoke-Item` performs the default action on a file. This will open the file in the application associated with the file type, assuming the file associations have been created in the normal manner. In this case, we're opening an Excel spreadsheet using the Excel application. `Invoke-Item` will open .txt files in Notepad and .csv files in Excel. We can open the file in its default application and manually read the data, or work with it within the application, but we can't work with the data using a PowerShell script using this approach.

Listing 8.8   Reading files

```
Invoke-Item F:\Blog\blogstats.xlsx        ❶

if (Test-Path c:\scripts\testfolder\testfile.txt){
Get-Content -Path c:\scripts\testfolder\testfile.txt}        ❷

Import-Csv -Path c:\scripts\testfolder\testprc.csv |        ❸
Select Name, PeakPagedMemorySize, PeakWorkingSet,
PeakVirtualMemorySize | Format-Table -AutoSize
```

DISCUSSION

`Get-Content` can be used to read the contents of a file ❷. One source of error in our scripts is that the file we're trying to use isn't actually present. We can avoid this by using `Test-Path` as shown. This cmdlet returns `$true` if it finds the file and `$false` if it doesn't. Performing this test allows us to avoid the error.

The best way to read a .csv file is to use `Import-Csv` ❸. The great thing about this approach is that the field names in the header row in the file can be used in the script after the file has been read. This can either be in a `select` statement as here or referred to as `$_.fieldname` when appropriate; for example in a `foreach` cmdlet. Examples of this will appear throughout the book.

When using `Get-Content` or `Import-Csv`, it's often desirable to read the contents of the file into a variable. Script ❸ would become:

```
$data = Import-Csv -Path c:\scripts\testfolder\testprc.csv
$data | Select Name, PeakPagedMemorySize,
PeakWorkingSet, PeakVirtualMemorySize |
Format-Table -AutoSize
```

We could use the same variable in a number of subsequent statements. This approach is worth adopting if you'll be performing a number of actions on the data. It saves the overhead of rereading the file.

These examples show how we can use pieces of PowerShell functionality to read the contents of a file. One other scenario we need to think about is how we search a set of files to find the one that contains the data in which we're interested.

TECHNIQUE 68   Searching files

There are two basic approaches to searching the contents of files. One approach is to explicitly read each file and loop through each record, testing to determine whether it has the content we need. The second is to wrap all of that functionality into a single command. This is the approach we'll take using the `Select-String` cmdlet.

PROBLEM

We need to find a particular piece of text in one or more files from a given set of files.

SOLUTION

`Select-String` provides a search facility similar to that found in the UNIX `grep` command or Windows `findstr`, but it doesn't have a `recurse` parameter to search subfolders. We again get multiple ways to address this problem, which boil down to using regular expressions or a simple text search, as in listing 8.9.

Listing 8.9   Searching files

```
Select-String -Path $pshome\*.ps1xml -Pattern "EventType" -SimpleMatch     ❶

Select-String -Path "c:\scripts\testfolder\*.txt"     ❷
-Pattern "\s{4}Windows\s" -CaseSensitive
```

DISCUSSION

In the first example, we're using a simple text-matching approach One of the cmdlets introduced in PowerShell v2 is `Get-ComputerRestorePoint`, which returns a list of the available restore points on the system. One of the properties returned is `EventType`, which provides information on the event that triggered the creation of the restore point. While experimenting with the cmdlet, I discovered that though just running the cmdlet provides a text description of the `EntryType`, if I used a `select` or `Format-List` with the cmdlet I got an integer returned as the `EntryType`. With a bit more digging, I discovered that this cmdlet is returning WMI objects and that the change in data being returned is a formatting issue. How could I match the integers with the text?

I knew that the formatting data was held in the PowerShell folder in XML files with an extension of .ps1xml. `Select-String` can be used to search those files for all occurrences of `EntryType` ❶. The data returned includes the file name, the line number within the file, and the contents of the line. In this case I'm using a simple string-matching approach.

NOTE $pshome is a built-in PowerShell variable that contains the path to the PowerShell installation folder. On a 32-bit machine, it'll be c:\windows\ system32\windowspowershell\v1.0. On a 64-bit machine, the answers will be different depending whether the 64- or 32-bit version of PowerShell is used.

The second approach is to use a regular expression as the pattern we're searching against ②. I must confess that I don't like using regular expressions. They seem to be one of those arcane pieces of technology that I've never had the time to sit down and master. They're incredibly powerful and if you haven't spent time learning how to use them, I'd definitely recommend it as time well spent.

The path to the files is supplied as is the pattern we want to use for searching. The example shows I'm searching for four spaces—\s is a space and {4} indicates I want four in a row. After that, we're looking for the word *Windows*, followed by another space. The capitalization in Windows is preserved by using the -CaseSensitive parameter.

NOTE   More on regular expressions can be found in appendix A.

One of the advantages of using Select-String for these searches is that we can search text files and XML files. Before we can perform the search, we need to know where our files are located.

TECHNIQUE 69   **Searching for files**

Most systems will contain thousands of files. How many times have you thought, "I know I put that information in a file, but where's the file?"

PROBLEM

We need to be able to find a file, or set of files, given the name of the file.

SOLUTION

There's a WMI class, CIM_DataFile, that's ideal for solving this problem. Get-WMIObject is our way to access this data, as in listing 8.10. We can perform our search based on a number of criteria. In the first example we're using the file name. Note that this doesn't include the extension. Our second example uses the extension as the filter criteria. When using the extension, we don't include the dot—we only use the text part of the extension.

These two examples search the whole machine. We can restrict our search to a particular folder, as shown in the third example. The use of \\ as the delimiter on the path is deliberate and necessary when passing paths into WMI cmdlets. It's possible to combine these filters as required using the WQL syntax.

Listing 8.10   Searching for files

```
Get-WmiObject -Class CIM_DataFile -Filter "FileName='sp'"

Get-WmiObject -Class CIM_DataFile -Filter "Extension='txt'" |
Select Name

Get-WmiObject -Class CIM_DataFile `
-Filter "Path='\\scripts\\testfolder\\'" |
 Select Name
```

DISCUSSION

Alternatively we could use `Get-ChildItem`:

```
Get-ChildItem -Path c:\ -Filter "sp*" -Recurse
Get-ChildItem -Path c:\ -Filter "*.txt" -Recurse
Get-ChildItem -Path c:\scripts | select Name
```

Which should we use? It depends! Compare the output of these two commands:

```
Get-WmiObject -Class CIM_DataFile
-Filter "Path='\\scripts\\strings\\'"  | Get-Member

Get-ChildItem -Path c:\scripts\strings | Get-Member
```

The objects that are returned carry different information. It would be worthwhile to explore the differences to determine which will best meet your needs.

This concludes our look at the filesystem. The examples in this section will provide a firm basis for extending your knowledge of how to administer the filesystem using PowerShell. It's time for us to turn our attention the part of Windows administration that many people would prefer to leave alone. The registry has definitely had bad press. Though it's possible to completely wreck your system by being careless when working with the registry, those administrators who take the time to learn how to do it properly end up with a powerful tool at their disposal.

8.4   *Registry*

The registry is the fundamental store for configuration information on a Windows system. Many applications follow the .NET approach and utilize XML configuration files, but the registry is still heavily used. A lot of the information in the registry would be useful if we could access it. Traditionally, we've used Regedit.exe to work with the registry. PowerShell provides an alternative in the shape of a registry provider.

> **BE VERY, VERY CAREFUL** This is when I should point out that altering the registry can damage your computer setup, which will necessitate a rebuild. I'm assuming that you won't trash your registry just for giggles, but accidents do happen. So, unless you like rebuilding Windows systems, "Let's be careful in there."

We discussed the concept of providers in the early chapters. A provider is a method of exposing a data store as if it were the filesystem. PowerShell supplies a number of providers that expose various data stores as additional PowerShell drives. A truncated list is shown here:

```
PS> Get-PSDrive

Name          Provider         Root
----          --------         ----
Alias         Alias
C             FileSystem       C:\
D             FileSystem       D:\
Env           Environment
```

Function	Function	
HKCU	Registry	HKEY_CURRENT_USER
HKLM	Registry	HKEY_LOCAL_MACHINE

This shows that two drives, HKCU: and HKLM:, are created by PowerShell. We can access these two parts of the Registry as if they were the filesystem, including the use of standard navigation and manipulation commands. These two parts of the registry are the parts we're most likely to need to access, but there are other parts these drives can't reach. In all, there are six sections to the registry:

- HKEY_CURRENT_USER
- HKEY_LOCAL_MACHINE
- HKEY_CLASSES_ROOT
- HKEY_CURRENT_CONFIG
- HKEY_USERS
- HKEY_PERFORMANCE_DATA

Our first task is to find a method of accessing the whole of the registry.

TECHNIQUE 70 Accessing the registry

Before we jump into the registry itself, it's worth spending a bit of time thinking about location. When all we had to think about was our local disks and a few network drives, life was fairly simple. We knew which drive we were on and where our stuff should be. With PowerShell's ability to create drives pointing to other data stores, things are more complicated, as I found out the hard way.

One of the early meetings of the PowerShell User Group involved me giving a demonstration of PowerShell being used to administer Active Directory. I finished the demonstration with the Active Directory provider from PowerShell Community Extensions (PSCX). Even after a couple of years, doing a `dir` through AD is still a cool demonstration and this was the first time I'd shown it. The demonstration was scripted and worked perfectly.

The night before the User Group meeting, Quest released a beta of its Active Directory cmdlets. Now this was beyond cool. There was no way I could leave them out. I created another demonstration script for the cmdlets and tested it until it worked perfectly. By this time, it was late and without thinking it through, or testing, I joined the two demonstration scripts together.

The talk went well. The first part of the demonstration went well. It reached the join and collapsed. The second part completely failed because I'd left my location in the AD provider and forgotten to swap back to the filesystem to pick up the scripts for the second part. The moral of the story is this: always know where you are and don't change the demo.

We can combine a couple of problems here. How can we keep track of where we are and how can we access the registry?

PROBLEM

We know that we can use `cd HKLM:` or `cd HKCU:` to access parts of the registry, but we need to be able to access the whole registry. While we're doing this, it would be a good idea if we could return to our starting point in terms of location.

SOLUTION

We can access the whole registry and keep track of our location in, and among, the various providers by using the `*-Location` cmdlets, as in listing 8.11. The `Set-Location` cmdlet ❶ can be used to change the current location in a provider, such as the filesystem, and between providers or the drives they expose. The `Path` parameter gives the location we want to move to. PowerShell can create aliases of commands to reduce the amount of typing. The alias of `Set-Location` is `cd`, as shown. The use of commands from DOS and Unix shells is one of the things that makes PowerShell easier to learn.

Listing 8.11   Accessing the registry

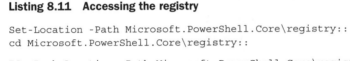

Move into Registry

```
Set-Location -Path Microsoft.PowerShell.Core\registry::
cd Microsoft.PowerShell.Core\registry::
```

❷ Save current location

```
PS> Push-Location -Path Microsoft.PowerShell.Core\registry::
PS> Get-ChildItem
```

❸ Perform listing

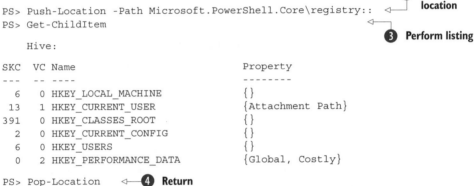

```
    Hive:

SKC  VC Name                          Property
---  -- ----                          --------
  6   0 HKEY_LOCAL_MACHINE            {}
 13   1 HKEY_CURRENT_USER             {Attachment Path}
391   0 HKEY_CLASSES_ROOT             {}
  2   0 HKEY_CURRENT_CONFIG           {}
  6   0 HKEY_USERS                    {}
  0   2 HKEY_PERFORMANCE_DATA         {Global, Costly}

PS> Pop-Location      ❹ Return
```

The one odd thing is the path we've constructed to enter the Registry. It's composed of two elements: PSSnapin name and the provider name, followed by two colons, for example `PSSnapin\Provider::`. We can discover the PSSnapin and provider names by using:

```
Get-PSProvider | select Name, PSSnapin
```

PowerShell really can be used to discover how to make PowerShell work.

As I related earlier, not keeping track of location can lead to problems. In the example it wasn't too bad, but a similar lack of awareness once led a colleague to type `del *.*` in the root of the C: drive. Time to rebuild!

PowerShell provides `Push-Location` ❷ to save the current location. The location is pushed onto a stack.

> **NOTE** A *stack* is a store in memory. It's exactly analogous to a stack of plates. We can add a plate to the top of the stack or we can take a plate off the top of the stack. We can't access a plate, or piece of data, that isn't on the top of the stack.

We can use the default stack or we can use the `-StackName` parameter to create, or use, a new stack. `Push-Location` does two jobs, in that we can also use the `-Path` parameter to provide a location to move to (as `Set-Location`) at the same time as putting the current location on the stack.

DISCUSSION

Once we've moved to the desired location, we can perform our tasks, in this case a Get-ChildItem to display the registry. ❸ We can return to our starting location by using Pop-Location to take the top location off the stack ❹ and set that to be the current location. Pop-Location can be used with the default stack or a named stack in the same way as Push-Location.

> **RECOMMENDATION** If you're going to be working in other providers extensively, I strongly recommend that you use Push-Location and Pop-Location in your scripts. This ensures that you always start from a known point and that you can easily return to that point.

Now that we know how to access the registry, it's time to look at reading the data that we find there.

TECHNIQUE 71 Reading registry data

The registry consists of a tree structure of *keys* and *key values*. The PowerShell registry provider treats registry keys in the same way that the filesystem provider treats files—as items. Registry key values are treated as item properties. We need to be aware of this difference and use the appropriate tools.

PROBLEM

The registry provider enables us to access the data stored in the registry as if it were the filesystem. How can we view registry data?

SOLUTION

There is a set of standard cmdlets that work with providers, as shown in listing 8.12. They can be viewed using Get-Help about_providers. We start by using Push-Location to store our current location and to move to the registry entry we want to view ❶. This task could also have been achieved using Set-Location either in one pass or by stepping through the structure of the registry. If a step-by-step approach is used, we can use Get-ChildItem at each step to examine the entries. Beware: this can lead to distractions if you spot something interesting!

Listing 8.12   Reading registry data

```
PS> Push-Location `                                                       ❶ Move
-Path HKLM:\software\microsoft\powershell\1\shellids                        to key
PS> Get-ChildItem                                          ◁———❷ Display key


    Hive: HKEY_LOCAL_MACHINE\software\microsoft\powershell\1\shellids

SKC  VC Name                                Property
---  -- ----                                --------
  0   2 Microsoft.PowerShell               {ExecutionPolicy, Path}

PS> Get-ItemProperty Microsoft.PowerShell   ◁———❸ Display key values

PSPath : Microsoft.PowerShell.Core\Registry::
HKEY_LOCAL_MACHINE\software\microsoft\
powershell\1\shellids\Microsoft.PowerShell
```

```
PSParentPath     : Microsoft.PowerShell.Core\Registry::
HKEY_LOCAL_MACHINE\software\microsoft\powershell\1\shellids

PSChildName      : Microsoft.PowerShell
PSDrive          : HKLM
PSProvider       : Microsoft.PowerShell.Core\Registry
ExecutionPolicy  : RemoteSigned
Path             : C:\Windows\system32\WindowsPowerShell\v1.0\powershell.exe

PS> Pop-Location      ◁──❹  Return
```

Get-ChildItem is used to view the available entries ❷. Note that the key values are returned as properties. In addition to the *-Item cmdlets we've discussed, there's a set of *-ItemProperty cmdlets we can use to work with properties:

- Clear-ItemProperty
- Get-ItemProperty
- New-ItemProperty
- Rename-ItemProperty
- Copy-ItemProperty
- Move-ItemProperty
- Remove-ItemProperty
- Set-ItemProperty

DISCUSSION

PowerShell's consistent verb naming conventions means that we need the Get-Item-Property cmdlet to read the key values ❸. Be aware that some other information will be displayed as well as the values in which we're interested. The data is shown in the listing. We could modify the execution policy by accessing through the registry in this manner. It's more efficient to use the *-ExecutionPolicy cmdlets. Finally, we use Pop-Location ❹ to return to our known starting point.

It's possible to short-circuit this procedure by a single call to Get-ItemProperty:

```
Get-ItemProperty `
-Path HKLM:\software\microsoft\powershell\1\ `
shellids\Microsoft.PowerShell
```

We can examine portions of the registry, in the same way we can dir through a folder hierarchy, for example:

```
Get-ChildItem -Path HKLM:\software\microsoft\powershell -Recurse
```

The next item on the agenda is learning how to create entries in the registry. This is fun.

TECHNIQUE 72   **Creating registry entries**

This section deals with performing modifications to the registry. This activity should always be treated with care. Now that we have the obligatory warning out of the way, we can learn how to use our PowerShell knowledge to create registry entries.

PROBLEM

The registry is used to store configuration data as we have seen. There's a periodic need to store configuration data in the registry, perhaps to enable a particular application to work or to prevent an attack on our systems. We need to be able to create and write to registry entries. Please note that this should be a safe example to try, as it doesn't modify live data.

SOLUTION

The `*-Item` and `*-ItemProperty` cmdlets solve this problem for us. We'll create a counter for the number of entries in the software key of the local machine hive for the purposes of this exercise. A key and a key value will have to be created. In this example, we don't move into the registry. All of these tasks can be performed by using the registry drives that are created by the provider, as shown in listing 8.13.

The first task is to examine the Registry key HKLM:\software ❶. This shows a number of keys usually related to software vendors; for example, on my machine there are more than 180 entries in the Microsoft key.

Listing 8.13   Creating registry entries

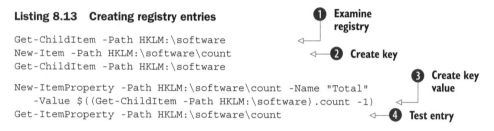

```
Get-ChildItem -Path HKLM:\software                          ❶ Examine
                                                               registry
New-Item -Path HKLM:\software\count                         ❷ Create key
Get-ChildItem -Path HKLM:\software

New-ItemProperty -Path HKLM:\software\count -Name "Total"   ❸ Create key
   -Value $((Get-ChildItem -Path HKLM:\software).count -1)     value
Get-ItemProperty -Path HKLM:\software\count                 ❹ Test entry
```

`New-Item` is used to create the key ❷. We have to provide the path to the item we're creating. As we can only create keys in the registry, we don't have to provide a type for the item. The new key can be seen when we use `Get-ChildItem` as shown.

> **ALIASES** `Get-ChildItem` is aliased to `dir` and `ls`. In PowerShell v2, use `Get-Alias -Definition Get-ChildItem` to see the aliases. I tend to use `ls` at the PowerShell prompt, as it's less typing! In scripts I use the full cmdlet name.

DISCUSSION

After creating the key, we need to create a value. Key values are manipulated using the `*-ItemProperty` cmdlets. In this case, `New-ItemProperty` is used for creation. The command has to be supplied with the path to the key, a name for the item, and a value ❸. We're using the count of items in the software key minus one to account for the count key itself as the value.

`Get-ItemProperty` is used to examine the value ❹ as we've previously seen. The last activity we need to consider is how to change registry values and how to delete registry keys.

TECHNIQUE 73   **Managing registry data**

Managing data is often described by using the acronym *CRUD* (not a reflection on the quality of the data) which stands for *Create, Read, Update, and Delete*. It would be possible to do this manually using Regedit.exe, but scripting the solution using PowerShell is a better alternative.

PROBLEM

All data follows a lifecycle and registry keys are no exception. Once the keys been created, we need to be able to manage them in a safe manner.

SOLUTION

We've seen how create and read the data; now we need to discover how perform the update and deletion. We will be using the *-ItemProperty and *-Item cmdlets, as shown in listing 8.14. The verb *Set* is used to perform changes, and *Remove* when we need to delete.

Listing 8.14   Managing registry data

```
Set-ItemProperty `
-Path HKLM:\software\count -Name "Total" -Value 67        ❶
Get-ItemProperty -Path HKLM:\software\count               ❷        ❸ Delete
                                                                      value
Remove-ItemProperty -Path HKLM:\software\count -Name "Total"
Remove-Item -Path HKLM:\software\count                    ❹ Delete key
Get-ChildItem -Path HKLM:\software        ❺
```

Changing a registry key value is achieved by using Set-ItemProperty ❶. In the same way as when we created the key value, we supply the path (key) the name and the actual value. The change can be verified using Get-ItemProperty ❷.

The functionality to wrap registry changes inside transactions was introduced in PowerShell v2. This will provide another level of protection to Registry data.

DISCUSSION

Deleting data from the registry follows a reverse path to creation. The key value is deleted first using Remove-ItemProperty ❸. This cmdlet needs to know the path to the key and the name of the value to remove.

> **EVENT LOGS**   One thing to think about is creating an event log to record when scripts are run and what changes are performed by the script. This creates an audit trail for your administration, which allows you to prove what you've done, and possibly prove your script didn't do something wrong. Creating and writing to event logs is covered in the next section.

The key itself is removed using Remove-Item ❹. A final check can be performed to verify that the key has been removed ❺. These commands can be executed at the PowerShell prompt or within a script.

Working with the filesystem, services, processes, and the registry are all necessary skills for the administrator. At some stage, we need to start investigating what's happening on our systems. The event logs are used to record this information. The next, and last, section in this chapter shows how PowerShell can be used to interrogate and administer the event logs.

8.5   *Event logs*

Event logs are used by Windows and applications for recording events that occur on the system. The information that's recorded may be of several forms:

- Error   ■ Warning

- Information   ■ SuccessAudit

- FailureAudit

There are a number of standard event logs, with more being created as applications are installed or additional functionality is installed. Event logs are the first port of call for an administrator when troubleshooting problems. I've lost track of the number of times looking at the event logs has enabled me to solve a problem. This includes issues from Active Directory replication not working to cluster nodes refusing to failover. If I were to give a new administrator one tip, it would be learn how to discover information in the event logs: "Learn PowerShell" wouldn't be a tip...it would be an order!

We can use the event viewer to read the logs. It's possible to filter the view. Using PowerShell, we can interrogate and search the logs based on any of the information in the logs. PowerShell v1 only allowed us to read the event logs. If we wanted to do anything else, we had to write scripts as in listings 8.16 through 8.19. PowerShell v2 introduces a number of new cmdlets to work with event logs:

```
PS> Get-Command *eventlog

CommandType     Name
-----------     ----
Cmdlet          Clear-EventLog
Cmdlet          Get-EventLog
Cmdlet          Limit-EventLog
Cmdlet          New-EventLog
Cmdlet          Remove-EventLog
Cmdlet          Show-EventLog
Cmdlet          Write-EventLog
```

We'll see examples of using these as alternatives to the scripts. We can export the information in the logs, possibly for importing into a database. A further possibility is to create our own logs, for instance to record the use of our production scripts. The user running the script could be recorded as well as the actual script used.

PowerShell can be used to configure the event logs. WMI or the *-EventLog cmdlets in PowerShell v2 can be used to manage the event logs of remote servers. There may be a performance issue if attempting to manage a large number of servers in a single script.

Before we do any of this, we have to learn to read the logs.

TECHNIQUE 74 Reading event logs

Before we can read the logs, we need to discover what logs are available on the system. PowerShell supplies a cmdlet Get-Eventlog to read the logs. This can also be used to discover the event logs on the system:

```
Get-Eventlog -List
```

This will return a lot of useful information, as shown in figure 8.2.

```
C:\Scripts
PS> Get-EventLog -List

Max(K) Retain OverflowAction       Entries Name
------ ------ --------------       ------- ----
25,600      0 OverwriteAsNeeded      3,999 Application
15,168      0 OverwriteAsNeeded          0 DFS Replication
20,480      0 OverwriteAsNeeded          0 HardwareEvents
   512      7 OverwriteOlder             0 Internet Explorer
20,480      0 OverwriteAsNeeded          0 Key Management Service
16,384      0 OverwriteAsNeeded          0 ODiag
16,384      0 OverwriteAsNeeded        512 OSession
   512      7 OverwriteOlder             0 Scripts
20,480      0 OverwriteAsNeeded      6,041 Security
20,480      0 OverwriteAsNeeded     21,097 System
15,360      0 OverwriteAsNeeded      1,510 Windows PowerShell
```

**Figure 8.2
Discovering the event
logs. The maximum size
in kilobytes and the
number of entries supply
information regarding
log usage. The retention
days and overflow action
determine what happens
if the log becomes full.**

The default information includes the number of entries in the log, the maximum size
of the logs, and what the logs are configured to do when they become full. This data
was taken from the laptop I normally use. These events had built up in less than a
month of normal usage. Note how many entries there are in the system log.

> **NOTE** Get-EventLog can't read the new style event logs introduced with Win-
> dows Vista and Windows Server 2008. We'll see how to work with these logs at
> the end of this section.

Having found the logs, we can now discover how to read them.

PROBLEM

There's information in the event logs that we need to retrieve. How can we do achieve
this?

SOLUTION

We've already seen that we can use Get-EventLog to discover the logs on the system.
We can also use it to read the data in the event logs, as in listing 8.15. We can retrieve
the contents of a particular log ❶ by using its name with the -LogName parameter. It
has to be the name of the log rather than the display name. Wildcards aren't permitted. This will display all of the entries in the particular log. In the case of the system
log, this could be many thousands of entries. This will take a long time to scroll up the
screen. We can restrict the number of entries returned by using the -newest parameter, or the –after and –before parameters in version 2 to restrict the returned entries
by date. An integer value is supplied to the parameter and the cmdlet will only return
that number of entries, starting with the most recent. Using this parameter can be useful if you want to check that an event has just happened.

> **REQUIRED PARAMETER** The logname parameter is required. This means that if
> you don't supply it, PowerShell will prompt you for the value. Many cmdlets
> have required parameters. The help file for a cmdlet will indicate which
> parameters are required.

If we're only interested in a particular event, we can filter on EventId ❷. This immediately restricts the amount of data that's returned to more manageable proportions.

One problem with using the `EventId` as a filter parameter is that we have to know what the event IDs mean. Many event IDs are documented on the Microsoft and other web sites.

Listing 8.15   Reading event logs

```
Get-EventLog -LogName System                                      ◁─❶ Read all

Get-EventLog -LogName System | Where {$_.EventId -eq 7036}   ◁─❷ Filtering data

Get-EventLog -LogName System |
Where {$_.Timewritten -gt ((Get-Date).Adddays(-2))}      ◁─❸ Filtering by time

Get-Eventlog security |
where {$_.TimeWritten -gt (get-date).AddDays(-7)
-and $_.TimeWritten -lt (get-date) ).AddDays(-2)  }
| Sort EventId | Group EventId                                 ◁─❹ Grouping events
```

The date and time when an event occurs (`TimeGenerated`) are written to the log. The time the entry was written is also recorded. On a busy system, there may be more than a slight difference between the two. We can filter on time ❶. Looking at the system log again, we compare the `TimeWritten` property against a date. In this case, we take the current date and subtract two days. Note that we have to use `AddDays()` but supply a negative number. It would've been simpler if we had methods to perform a subtraction. Don't try to define a date that you'll then subtract from the current date. You'll end up with a `TimeSpan` object, which won't work in this context.

It may sometimes be useful to group the events so we can see how many events of a particular type are happening. In particular, we may want to do this against the security log. For instance, if we see a large number of failed logins or failed attempts to access a particular file, it may be a warning that an attack is being mounted against the system. In this case, we read the security log ❹. We perform a filter to restrict the data to a particular time period. The example shows us reading data between seven and two days old. The entries are sorted on event ID and then the data is grouped (`group` is an alias for `Group-Object`).

DISCUSSION

PowerShell must be started with elevated privileges to access the security logs. In Windows Vista/2008 and above when UAC is turned on, this means using Run as Administrator, and logging on using an account with administrator privileges on XP/2003.

Having discovered that we can read the logs, is there a way that we can copy the data to another file for further analysis?

TECHNIQUE 75   **Exporting logs**

There's often a requirement to preserve the information in event logs. Files can be created to store the data. These files can either be the final home of the data, or they could be used as an intermediary stage to loading the data into a database.

PROBLEM

The data in the event logs has to be exported to CSV files. The file names have to include the date so that we can easily ascertain the period covered by the events in the file.

SOLUTION

We've seen that the Get-EventLog cmdlet can be used to read the contents of the event log. This can be combined with the Export-Csv cmdlet to produce the required file, as in listing 8.16.

Listing 8.16   Copy event logs

```
$date = get-date                                    ◄──❶ Current date

if ($date.Month -le 9) {
    $fname = $date.Year.ToString() + "0" +
$date.Month.ToString() + $date.Day.ToString() +
"_security.txt"
    }
                                                    ◄──❷ Create file name
else {
    $fname = $date.Year.ToString() + $date.Month.ToString() +
$date.Day.ToString() + "_security.txt"
    }                                                     ❸ Export
                                                            security
get-eventlog security | export-csv $fname  -noTypeInformation  ◄─┘ log

$fname = $fname -replace "security", "application"       Export  ❹
get-eventlog application |                           application log
export-csv $fname    -NoTypeInformation  . . . . . . . . . .  ◄─┘

$fname = $fname -replace "application", "system"
get-eventlog system | export-csv $fname  -noTypeInformation  ◄─❺ Export system log
```

DISCUSSION

This script can be used to create a copy of the data in the three main event logs—application, security, and system. Remember that PowerShell will have to be running with elevated privileges to access the security log.

The script starts by retrieving the current date ❶. Any time you want to manipulate the date information, it's easier to create a variable that can hold the date. We can use the date information to create the file name ❷. The year, month, and day are concatenated, in that order, with the name of the log and a file extension. There are two variations on the way the file name is produced, depending on the number of digits in the month. A leading zero is added for months with only a single digit—January to September. The file names can be sorted on the date part when created in this style.

We could use the -f operator to format the filename for us:

```
$fname = "{0}{1:00}{2:00}_security.txt" -f `
$date.Year, $date.Month, $date.Day
```

The first part, {0}{1:00}{2:00}_security.txt, defines three fields that will be filled by the data on the right side of the -f operator, plus the static part of the file name. The first field takes the year, which will be four digits, whereas the month and day are substituted into the second and third fields respectively. These two fields are defined as being two digits wide, so a leading zero is automatically appended for a day or month value of 9 or less. These formatted strings look a bit scary, but it's worth getting to know how to use them, as they can save a lot of effort.

The only thing left to do is to get the data from the event log ❸ and write it out to the file. We use the `-noTypeInformation` parameter on `Export-Csv` to avoid writing the .NET type information into the first line of the file. This technique can be applied to other logs, including the application ❹ and system logs ❺ as shown. The `-replace` operator can be used to modify the file name to reflect the correct log. The file name is a string, so we could use `$file.Replace()` instead.

Having explored how we can read from the event log, it's now time to look at writing to an event log. Before we can write to a log, we need to be able to create a log.

TECHNIQUE 76   Creating an event log

Windows supplies a number of event logs by default and will create others depending on the applications and functionality installed on the system. The generic system and application logs would seem ideal to use for recording events from our scripts. If a specialized log is created just for scripting events that we create, we can have much greater control of the data. The data will be easier to search, as it's restricted to scripting events.

PROBLEM

We've decided to create an event log specifically for events from our scripts.

SOLUTION

This problem requires using some, but not a lot, of .NET code. Just one little line. This problem can be solved using a static method of the `System.Diagnostics.EventLog` class. Static methods were explained in chapter 3; to recap they're methods that can be used without creating an object. The `CreateEventSource` method is given two parameters, as shown in listing 8.17.

Listing 8.17   Create an event log

```
[System.Diagnostics.EventLog]::CreateEventSource("PSscripts","Scripts")
```

The first parameter is the event source. Sources are registered against a particular event log. They're in effect a handle for the particular log. Figure 8.3 shows the central part of the event viewer console. Our Scripts log is the selected log and it contains a single event. The log name and source can be seen in the lower part of the panel.

The second parameter is the name of the log. `CreateEventSource` can be used to create a source for an existing event log, or as in this case, it'll create the event log if it doesn't already exist. .NET code will rarely get any simpler.

DISCUSSION

The PowerShell v2 version of this is just as simple:

```
New-EventLog -LogName Scripts -Source PSscripts
```

It has parameters for the log name and source as seen previously. Having created an event log, we need to learn how to populate it. This means we have to use a bit more .NET code, but it's straightforward, as we shall see.

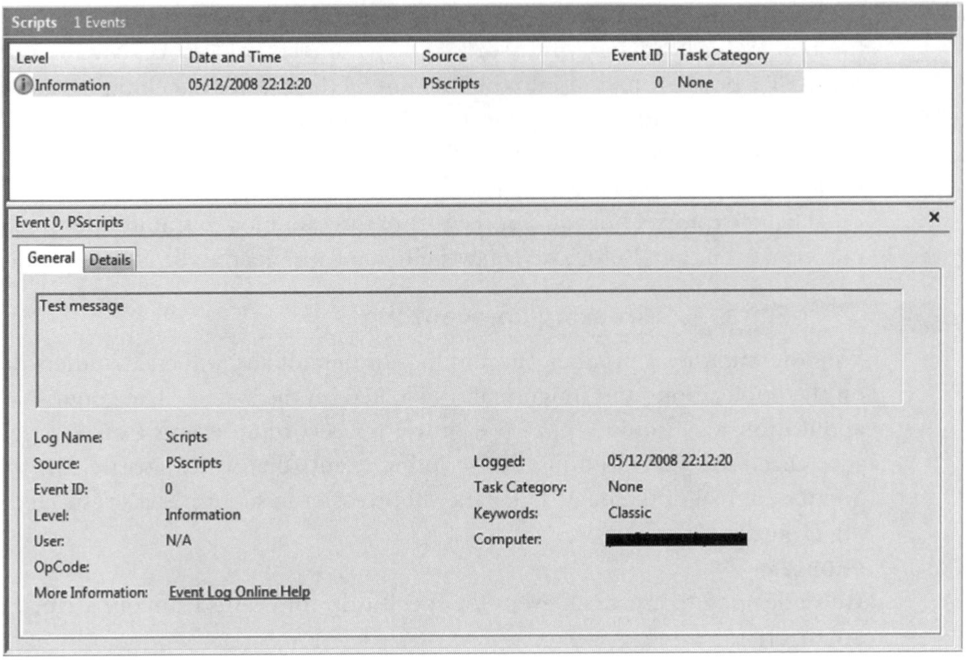

Figure 8.3   Event log example with source. The computer name is blacked out to obscure the internal domain for security reasons.

TECHNIQUE 77   Creating events

Having seen how to create an event log, we now need to think about writing events into the log. An empty log isn't going to do us much good. Ideally, this should be done in a way that allows the functionality to be used from any of our scripts without having to copy the code into every script.

PROBLEM

In order to keep track of which scripts are run when, we want to be able to write an entry into the event log as the script is executing. So that we get the most out of the time we spend developing the functionality, we also want to be able to call at any time during the execution of the script. There are much more interesting things to do than write variations on the same code. Write once, run many times.

SOLUTION

We can solve this by creating a function using the System.Diagnostics.EventLog class we saw in the previous example. Our problem statement said that we needed to be able to use this from multiple scripts without putting the code into every script. The best way to achieve this is to create a function that we load into memory when we start PowerShell. How do we do this? We either put the function into our profile or use a dot-sourced call to a script containing the function into the profile, as in listing 8.18. In both cases we have it loaded and ready to use. Now all we've got to do is write it!

Listing 8.18   Write to an event log

```
function Write-EventLog
{
param([string]$msg = "Default Message", [string]$type="Information")
$log = New-Object System.Diagnostics.EventLog
$log.set_log("Scripts")
$log.set_source("PSscripts")

$log.WriteEntry($msg,$type)
}
```

The function takes two parameters—a message and the event type. Event types can one of several types, including information, warning, and error. If we want to see the available types, we can use:

```
[enum]::GetNames([System.Diagnostics.EventLogEntryType])
```

This is explained in chapter 3. As a quick recap, [enum] is a shorthand for the `Sys-tem.Enum` class. The `Enum` class is the base class for enumerations, which are closed lists. Enums are often used for parameters where there's a discrete set of possibilities. The contents of a particular enumeration can be found in the .NET documentation.

The bulk of the function is taken up by creating an object using the `System.Diag-nosticsEventLog` class. We then set the log and the source we want to use. The final action is to write the event message and the event type to the log.

We can use our function from the PowerShell prompt or from within a script by a simple call to the function:

```
Write-EventLog "Testing Function use" "Information"
```

The first parameter is the message and the second is the event type.

DISCUSSION

We can test that the event has been written to the log by using:

```
Get-EventLog -LogName Scripts
```

This will show the log entries including the messages. The PowerShell v2 version is:

```
Write-EventLog -LogName Scripts -Source PSscripts `
-EntryType "Information" `
-Message "Testing the event log" -EventId  1
```

We have to provide an `EventId` when using this cmdlet. It'd be worthwhile document-ing the IDs to be used with the event log when it's created. After learning how to cre-ate and write to event logs, it's now time to learn how to manage them.

TECHNIQUE 78   Managing event logs

Administering computer systems involves a number of activities, including configur-ing the system components and creating backups. In this section, we'll look at both of these activities in relation to the event logs on our systems.

> **NOTE** If you want to work with the Security event log, you'll need to be work-ing with elevated privileges.

The scripts in this section are WMI-based and written to work against the local machine. Using the `-computername` parameter, we can manage event logs on remote systems.

PROBLEM

We need to be able to configure the event log and be able to back it up.

SOLUTION

The WMI class `Win32_NTEventLogFile` is available to us for performing these actions. There are two main parameters we think about configuring for an event log file:

- The maximum file size (`MaxFileSize`)
- Action to take when the log is full (`OverWritePolicy`)

Event log configuration can be achieved with the `Win32_NTEventLogFile` WMI class, as in listing 8.19. We start by creating a WMI object for the log ❶. In this case, we're configuring the Application log. The file size is set using the `MaxFileSize` parameter. We have to use the `psbase` construction to get to the underlying object so we can call the `Put()` method. This saves the configuration change. `Win32_NTEventLogFile` can only be used against the "old-style" event logs in Windows 2003 and earlier. It won't work against the new-style logs in Vista/Windows 2008.

Listing 8.19   Managing event logs

```
$applog = Get-WmiObject -Class Win32_NTEventLogFile      ◁──❶ Set max size
-Filter "LogFileName = 'Application'"
$applog.MaxFileSize = 26214400
$applog.psbase.Put()

$log = Get-WmiObject -Class Win32_NTEventLogFile      ◁──❷ Backup event log
-Filter  "LogFileName = 'Application'"
$ret = $log.BackupEventLog("c:\test\applog.evt")
if ($ret.returnvalue -eq 0){$log.ClearEventLog()}
else {Write-Host "could not back up log file"}
                                                      ❸ Size triggered
Get-WmiObject -Class Win32_NTEventLogFile |      ◁─┘   backup
Where {$_.FileSize -gt 10MB} | Foreach {
    $file = "c:\test\" + $_.LogFileName + ".evt"
    $_.BackupEventLog($file)
    $_.ClearEventLog()
}
                                                      ❹ Records triggered
$date = Get-Date                                 ◁─┘   backup
Get-WmiObject -Class Win32_NTEventLogFile |
Where {$_.NumberofRecords -gt 5} | Foreach {
    $file = "c:\test\" + $_.LogFileName + "_{0}_{1}_{2}.evt" -f
            $date.Year, $date.Month, $date.Day
    $_.BackupEventLog($file)
    $_.ClearEventLog()
}
```

`Win32_NTEventLogFile` can also be used to back up the event logs. If we want to back up a single log, we can apply a filter to restrict ourselves to the particular log ❷. We can use the `BackupEventLog()` method to perform the backup. The backup file is the only parameter. If the return code is zero, we can then clear the event log.

It may be desirable to back up and clear the event log depending on a trigger. This could be when the log reaches a particular size ❸ or when it has more than a preset number of records ❹. All of the logs are retrieved via WMI. The test is applied, and for each log that passes the test, a backup file is created and then the logs are cleared.

DISCUSSION

PowerShell v2 cmdlets allow us to configure the event logs and clear the event logs:

```
Limit-EventLog -LogName scripts -MaximumSize 25MB
Clear-EventLog -LogName scripts
```

We don't get a cmdlet to perform the backup.

> ### Windows 2008 and Vista logs
>
> A new type of event log was introduced in Windows Server 2008 and Windows Vista. At the moment, all we can do is retrieve records from these logs using `Get-WinEvent` in PowerShell v2. This is used in a similar manner to `Get-EventLog`, which we have already seen in detail.
>
> This completes our look at event logs. We've covered most if not all of the tasks that administrators need to perform on them. You should be well placed to administer your event logs using PowerShell after reading this section.

8.6   *Summary*

We've looked at a number of facets of server administration in this chapter. The services and applications need to be managed. This can involve discovering their status as well as creating or terminating processes. These techniques will be useful when considering specific applications in later chapters. Think about the situation where you can write a script that tests the status of the required services running on a remote machine and then starts them if they aren't running.

The filesystem involves us in a number of activities. Some activities are simple such as creating files and folders. Other activities are much more involved, in that we have to read or write the contents of the files. At some stage, we'll need to be able to search the contents of files for particular pieces of text or possibly search through the filesystem for a particular file. How many times have you had a user come along and say "I can't find my file. It's called xyz.txt. Can you find it for me?" Now you can.

The registry holds configuration data that we need to be able to read and possibly change. Accessing and modifying the registry can be regarded as a dangerous occupation but the tools in PowerShell enable us to perform these tasks in a safe and controlled manner.

The activities we've been performing when administering the servers are recorded in the event logs. We looked at reading the contents of the event logs so we can diagnose issues. Event logs are also objects that we need to administer. We can change the settings of an existing log and create new logs. Backing up the event logs gives us a way to keep the records for future use.

A book this size can't exhaustively cover every variation involved in administering the server. The examples in this chapter form a firm foundation for undertaking the core administrative tasks on a Windows server. Now that we know how to do that, we can start looking at the applications running on the server, starting with DNS.

DNS 9

DNS is at the heart of the modern Windows environment. It's the telephone directory of our network. If it's missing, or working incorrectly, our systems can't talk to each other, we can't logon because we can't find a domain controller, and our applications may not work properly.

BAD HAIR DAY All things considered, if DNS isn't working properly, we're definitely in the realm of "admins running around with their hair on fire" as one famous PowerShell speaker so vividly describes it.

The object of this chapter is to show you how to use PowerShell to administer and check your DNS systems to ensure that you don't find yourself in such an exciting predicament. In administration terms, excitement is bad—very bad. We want calm. Lots and lots of calm.

DNS is one of those systems that we expect to set up and it'll just keep on working. But mistakes happen. One large IT vendor lost access to its website because of an error that had been made during a change to the DNS configuration.

> **ASSUMPTION** This chapter won't explicitly explain the workings of DNS. It's assumed to be understood. It's further assumed that Windows Server 2008 DNS is being used. The scripts were created and tested using Windows Server 2008. They should work with Windows Server 2003 and Windows Server 2008 R2.

Administrators need to be able to check the configuration of their DNS system, including servers, zones, and where applicable, individual records. We also need to be able to configure IP settings and check those settings when troubleshooting. In this chapter, you'll learn how to do all of this from PowerShell.

The chapter is split into five main sections. We'll look at automating DNS administration and the tools that we have available. The next section will cover DNS servers and how we can discover, report, and when necessary, change the configuration. DNS zones are our third topic, where we discover how to manage their lifecycle from within PowerShell.

DNS records are the low-level building blocks. A large proportion of our records may be created automatically, but we still need to create records from time to time. We'll find techniques for managing the major records types we're likely to need, together with templates that we can apply when creating other records.

> **TEACH A MAN TO...** There's a famous proverb about teaching a man to fish. We could adapt that for our PowerShell experiences. Give an admin a PowerShell script and you enable him to solve a problem. Give an admin a set of templates for creating scripts and he can solve anything.

The hierarchy of these DNS objects is shown in figure 9.1.

The chapter concludes by looking at the IP configuration of systems. How we can test it and how we can configure it? We'll also look at test IP connectivity. We have to start at the beginning, though, by considering what tools we have available for working with DNS and IP configurations.

9.1   *Automating DNS administration*

Having looked at all of the good things we can do to (and with) DNS, how are we going to achieve all of this?

PowerShell doesn't have any native tools for working with DNS or IP configurations. PowerShell v2 introduces a `Test-Connection` cmdlet that's a PowerShell version of the classic `ping` utility. By this stage in your discovery of PowerShell, you should automatically think that if PowerShell can't do it natively, we can probably do it in WMI.

Windows Server 2008 installs a WMI provider for DNS when the DNS service is installed. Documentation for the provider can be found at http://msdn.microsoft.com/en-us/library/ms682125(VS.85).aspx. This provider can also be found in

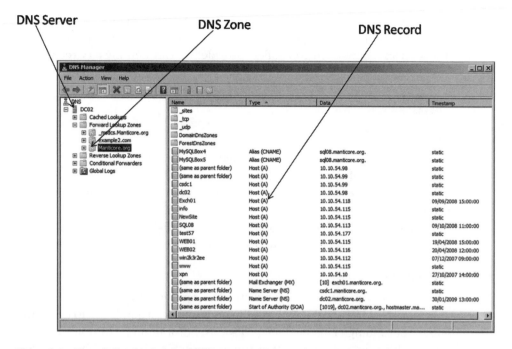

Figure 9.1 The relationship between DNS servers, zones, and records is illustrated using the DNS Manager console.

Windows Server 2003 when DNS is installed. The `Get-WmiObject` cmdlet allows us to work with remote machines so we don't have to have PowerShell installed on the DNS server.

PERMISSIONS You must start PowerShell with administrative privileges to be able to use the DNS WMI provider when using Windows Server 2008. This requirement has been relaxed in Windows Server 2008 R2, and the DNS WMI classes are available from a standard nonelevated console.

The WMI provider for DNS installs another WMI namespace. The DNS functionality is stored in the `MicrosoftDNS` namespace. The classes available within the namespace can be viewed by using `Get-WmiObject`'s `-List` parameter, as follows:

```
Get-WmiObject -List -Namespace 'root\MicrosoftDNS' |
  Sort name | Select name
```

The sort and select make the results more presentable and easier to read. Before working with WMI and DNS, I strongly recommend running this example and examining the output. It may be worthwhile to print off the list of classes for future reference. This is the sort of information I have pinned up around my desk.

OBJECT MODEL The WMI objects that the WMI provider supplies aren't arranged in a hierarchical fashion. Each WMI class is self-contained.

If you've taken any Microsoft exam involving infrastructure, you'll know that one thing that keeps popping up is that DNS stores SRV (Service) records, which define the services that domain controllers provide. We can view the SRV records on a particular domain controller using this code:

```
Get-WmiObject  -ComputerName dc02 -Namespace 'root\MicrosoftDNS'
-Class MicrosoftDNS_SRVType |
Select DnsServerName, OwnerName, TextRepresentation |
Sort OwnerName
```

This is a quick and easy check that's much simpler than opening up the DNS management console and checking each of the many nodes where SRV records can be found. With this code, we can quickly check whether a particular domain controller has registered its SRV records.

When we think of DNS, we tend to start by thinking about DNS servers, and this is where we start using PowerShell to administer DNS.

9.2   *DNS server*

One quick check can determine if the DNS service is running on the server in question when troubleshooting DNS problems. It's always a good idea to check whether the service is running. This may seem obvious, but a number of times I've seen people spend a long time checking other things before checking the obvious. Create a troubleshooting checklist for likely scenarios and build PowerShell scripts to perform the tests. The following can be used as a start for DNS tests:

```
Get-WmiObject -Class Win32_Service -Filter "Name like '%DNS%'"
-ComputerName DC02
```

The -Class and the -ComputerName parameters define what we're testing and the computer respectively. If you need to test a number of machines, put the names in a CSV file and use Import-Csv to read it, then put the test in foreach cmdlet.

The filter parameter is interesting because we want to restrict our test to the DNS server. As written, the filter will return the DNS server service and DNS client service. The example shows how to use the LIKE operator in a WQL-based WMI filer. The % symbol is a wildcard character equivalent to the * symbol in PowerShell strings.

There's an alternative that can be used in PowerShell v2:

```
Get-Service *dns* -ComputerName DC02
```

This is simpler to code and easier to understand. All we need to do is define the services we're interested in and supply the computer name. The command can be made part of a loop if multiple computers have to be tested:

```
Import-Csv machines.csv |
Foreach{ Get-Service *dns* -ComputerName $_.Computername}
```

It'd be possible to make this more generic and have the service to test in the file as well, or possibly as a parameter if this is turned into a function.

TECHNIQUE 79   Enable remote administration

An administrator's job can be split into two parts. There are those tasks that are repetitive and mundane, and then there are the more interesting challenges such as integrating new technologies into our environment.

We want to be concentrating on the latter and automating the former. This keeps life interesting and allows us to use PowerShell to its maximum potential. We want to get it to do as much of the heavy lifting as possible for us. One slight roadblock we need to deal with is the Windows firewall. This isn't just an issue on DNS servers. This has to be applied to all servers we need to administer remotely, especially if we want to use WMI.

PROBLEM

The Windows firewall is designed to prevent access from external protocols and commands that haven't been authorized. This is preventing us from performing administration remotely. We need to configure the firewall to allow remote administration.

SOLUTION

There isn't a PowerShell solution to this problem. We have to revert to using another solution such as the `netsh` command, as shown in listing 9.1. This task has to be performed on full install and server core installs on Windows Server 2008 machines.

Listing 9.1   Enable remote administration

```
Netsh firewall set service RemoteAdmin

Netsh advfirewall set currentprofile settings remotemanagement enable
```

DISCUSSION

We need to run two commands. The first will enable remote WMI access. The second will enable remote administration. These commands remain in force until the configuration is deliberately changed.

Now that we can access our DNS servers, we can examine the configuration.

TECHNIQUE 80   View server configuration

DNS is one of those services that we install and tend to leave alone. It sits there, minding its own business, and responds to the requests for IP addresses that we keep sending. This makes it a well-behaved citizen on our corporate network. Until things decide to take a turn for the worse. When DNS has problems, it means the whole network has problems.

One of the standard questions when troubleshooting is "What has changed?" The first response you get will always be "Nothing" but a little perseverance often reveals that something has changed, together with the comment "But it couldn't possibly be that..."

In an ideal world, we'd maintain a configuration database that stored all of the configuration information from all of our systems. This database would be kept up to date in an automated manner (using PowerShell of course) and would be available to answer these questions. Most organizations aren't in a position to follow this practice, so we need an alternative.

What we can accomplish easily is to record the configuration information to a series of files. WMI would be used to gather the information, and we can store the information in Word documents as we saw in section 7.4.5. If we're feeling ambitious, we could decide to write the data to a database. This option will be covered in chapter 14.

PROBLEM

We need to view and record the configuration of our DNS servers so that we can determine whether any changes have occurred that could contribute to our situation. This moves the problem back a stage. How can we create a report of the server configuration?

SOLUTION

Many of the scripts discussed in chapter 7 can be used to create configuration reports for our servers. We also need to document the DNS settings. We could take screen shots of the DNS Manager Administration console (see figure 9.2), but a preferable solution is to generate the report using WMI. The `MicrosoftDNS` namespace can be of assistance, as shown in listing 9.2.

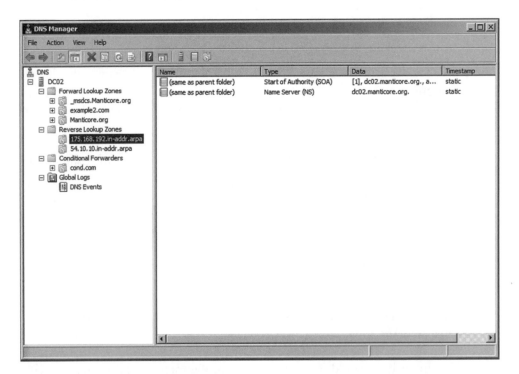

Figure 9.2   DNS Manager Administration console showing the zones present on a server. The properties on each of the nodes would have to be recorded (often multitabbed dialogs) in order to fully document the DNS environment.

Listing 9.2 View server configuration

```
Get-WmiObject -Namespace "root\microsoftdns"  -Class MicrosoftDNS_Server
-ComputerName DC02
```

The first stage in tackling this problem is to look at the MicrosoftDNS WMI namespace. As we saw in section 9.1, we can use Get-WmiObject's -List parameter to display a list of the WMI classes in the namespace. Examining the list of classes shows a Microsoft_DNS class that might meet our needs.

When we use a WMI namespace other than the default, which is root\cimv2, we need to supply the namespace to Get-WmiObject. We also need to supply the WMI class.

The -ComputerName parameter allows us to run this script against remote systems. In this way, we can document all of our DNS servers from one machine instead of logging on to each in turn. That saves us a lot of time.

DISCUSSION

In its current form, the script will output the information to the screen. This is acceptable when we want to view the present configuration and possibly compare it to a stored version. We can generate the stored version using the techniques in section 7.4.5 to create a Word document. Alternatively we could use the options in listing 8.6 to create a text or CSV file. A final option would be use Export-CliXML to persist the PowerShell object created by Get-WmiObject as an XML file. One thing with PowerShell is that we always have choices. The right choice for your environment will depend on what you need to achieve.

> **AUTOMATE FILE COMPARISON** If we create a file of our starting configuration and another containing our current configuration, we can use Compare-Object to test for differences between the files as shown in listing 1.4.

Now that we can view and store the DNS server configuration, how can we make changes to that configuration?

TECHNIQUE 81 Configuring round robin

In this section we'll concentrate on a couple of changes that are useful examples of server administration. These can serve as examples and templates. The MSDN documentation on the MicrosoftDNS WMI namespace includes details of the other methods and properties available to us.

There are a number of situations where we need to load-balance an activity across multiple machines. This can be accomplished in a number of ways using functionality built into the Windows OS, third-party hardware devices, or by using the round robin capability in DNS. Round robin DNS isn't always a suitable answer, but it's readily available and easy to configure.

PROBLEM

Round robin is controlled at the server level. We need to be able to turn it on or off as we require.

SOLUTION

We saw in the previous example how it's possible to view the DNS server configuration using WMI. We'll build on that knowledge to control the settings on the server, including round robin, in listing 9.3. The solution starts by retrieving the server configuration information using WMI ❶. This is performed in exactly the same manner as in listing 9.2. Reuse is a wonderful thing! I've used a different computer this time. Leaving out the -ComputerName parameter causes the command to be executed against the local system. Instead of displaying the information to the screen, we'll save it to a variable so that we can work with it.

Listing 9.3 Configure RoundRobin

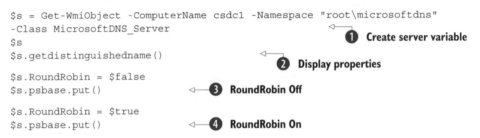

```
$s = Get-WmiObject -ComputerName csdc1 -Namespace "root\microsoftdns"
-Class MicrosoftDNS_Server
$s                                              ◁────❶ Create server variable
$s.getdistinguishedname()
                                                ◁────❷ Display properties
$s.RoundRobin = $false
$s.psbase.put()                        ◁────❸ RoundRobin Off

$s.RoundRobin = $true
$s.psbase.put()                        ◁────❹ RoundRobin On
```

Once we've stored the configuration information in the variable, we can use that data. The variable is a .NET object holding the properties and methods available to that particular class. We can display all configuration properties by using the variable name ❷ or we can display a single property.

The property for the round robin setting is Boolean. It can only be configured as true or false, which causes it to turn on or off respectively. Setting the RoundRobin property to $false turns it off ❸. We need to save the configuration, so we need to use the Put() method.

DISCUSSION

This method isn't exposed on the object we get returned from Get-WmiObject (try using Get-Member on it to see the results). We need to drop into the underlying object using the .psbase suffix to see, and use, the Put() methods

> **PSBASE** Always check the underlying object using .psbase if you can't see the methods or properties that you think should be available.

The change can be reversed by setting the property to $true ❹ and calling Put(). One thing that you must do after making a change like this is make sure that you record the change!

TECHNIQUE 82 **Configuring conditional forwarding**

DNS is used to look up an IP address so that our machine can communicate with another machine. When we're dealing with machines on our internal network, we should have a complete set of DNS records for the machines on the network. Our DNS servers won't have information for machines in other DNS zones, belonging to other organizations.

DNS servers surmount this problem by forwarding the requests to other DNS servers. The forwarding process will eventually lead to a server that has the information we need.

PROBLEM

Forwarding in this manner will resolve external internet addresses, but it won't do anything for a separate DNS domain that we may host internally. During a merger, we may be able to communicate across the internal network with the other organization, but we may not have integrated the DNS infrastructure of the two organizations.

We may also want to create a shortcut. If we know the IP addresses of the DNS servers for a particular domain, we can configure conditional forwarding. This will immediately cause the DNS servers to forward requests for IP addresses in the given domain to a specific set of servers. The question is how do we configure this?

SOLUTION

Figure 9.2 shows the Conditional Forwarders node in DNS. We could perform this task through the GUI. That wouldn't be any fun, though. A much better idea is to use PowerShell and the DNS WMI provider.

The way that we configure conditional forwarding is closely related to how we create a DNS zone. Compare listing 9.4 with listing 9.6 where we investigate how to create a DNS zone. Examining the conditional forwarders in the DNS manager console shows that they're specialized zones that only contain the IP addresses of DNS servers authorative for that zone.

Listing 9.4   Configure conditional forwarding

```
$ip = "192.168.40.1", "192.168.40.2"
$z = [WMIClass]"\\dc02\root\MicrosoftDNS:MicrosoftDNS_Zone"
$z.CreateZone("cond.com", 3, $false, $null, $ip)
```

Listing 9.4 starts by defining an array of IP addresses. The addresses have to be given as strings. We then use `[WMIClass]` to create an instance of a DNS zone on the server we're targeting—in this case `dc02`.

The `CreateZone` method is used to create the zone. A number of parameters have to be supplied, starting with the name of the DNS zone that will be conditionally forwarded. The next parameter, value `3`, indicates a zone forwarder as explained in table 9.1.

`$false` indicates that the zone isn't Active Directory-integrated. This means that if we want to configure multiple servers with this conditional forwarder, we have to do each separately. That's why we script it. Write once, run many. The `$null` parameter is a placeholder that's used for other purposes. Our final parameter is the list of IP addresses we created at the beginning.

After learning how to configure our DNS server, we need to look at one more activity at the server level before we start investigating DNS zones.

TECHNIQUE 83   **Clearing the server cache**

When a DNS server supplies an address to satisfy a client request, the data is stored in the server's DNS cache. The cached information is then used if the same address is requested. This increases the speed of response, especially for addresses that are frequently requested. The data in the cache is of limited life defined by the *time to live (TTL)* property, which is set when the record is created.

PROBLEM

If we change the IP address of one of our servers, the DNS server will continue to supply the old address while that record is in its cache. We need to be able to remove that old, stale information from the DNS server's cache.

SOLUTION

The cache is an all-or-nothing proposition, so there isn't a way to remove a single, stale record, but we can clear the whole cache using the technique in listing 9.5. This causes the cache to repopulate so that the correct addresses are supplied to DNS clients.

Listing 9.5 Clear server cache

```
$cache = Get-WmiObject -ComputerName DC02 -Namespace 'root\MicrosoftDNS'
-Class MicrosoftDNS_Cache
$cache.ClearCache()
```

There's a WMI class that represents the cache. We use `Get-WmiObject` to create a variable for the cache object. The `MicrosoftDNS_Cache` WMI class in the `MicrosoftDNS` namespace is used to access the cache.

DISCUSSION

We can control which DNS server we're working with. This is one parameter to double check. It would be embarrassing to clear the wrong cache! Once we have our variable, we can use the `ClearCache()` method to perform the task.

This concludes our look at the DNS server. In the next section, we move down a level and consider DNS zones.

9.3   *DNS zones*

A *DNS zone* is used to store DNS records. The zone may match our Active Directory name if the zone is internal. It may match the company name if external-facing, such as Microsoft.com. Zones may be Active Directory-integrated or exist in separate files with a separate replication topology. The examples in this section assume that Active Directory-integrated DNS is being used.

Most of our day-to-day activity with DNS occurs within a zone. We're usually concerned with the records or the zone configuration. But before we can attempt to perform any of those tasks, we need to create a DNS zone on our server.

TECHNIQUE 84   **Creating a DNS zone**

DNS zones are the containers for DNS records and can be divided into two distinct types. *Forward DNS zones* are used to supply an IP address when the name of the machine is supplied. *Reverse DNS zones* supply the name of a machine when an IP address is supplied.

Creating DNS zones isn't an everyday task. One area where the ability to regenerate the DNS infrastructure quickly will pay off is in a disaster recovery situation. Script the creation of your DNS zones and you know that part of the rebuild will occur properly and rapidly. The creation of test environments that mimic the production environment should also be scripted for speed and accuracy.

There are a number of zone types that can be created by this method. The possible zone types are listed in table 9.1.

We'll concentrate on creating a primary zone, as this is the most likely scenario in an Active Directory environment.

Value	Zone type
0	Primary zone
1	Secondary zone
2	Stub zone
3	Zone forwarder

Table 9.1   DNS zone types

PROBLEM

We're required to create forward and reverse DNS zones to accommodate a new suite of functionality in the organization.

SOLUTION

The creation of DNS zones involves using the `MicrosoftDNS` WMI namespace so we can perform this task remotely as well as on the local machine, as shown in listing 9.6. We've seen `[WMIClass]` being used in a number of examples in earlier chapters. One of the great things with PowerShell is that the same techniques are applicable over and over again. This consistency is one of the great strengths of the tool and is something that we should aim to emulate. Once you've discovered a way to perform a task, stick with it. You know the method will work and this will make you more productive.

Listing 9.6   Create DNS zone

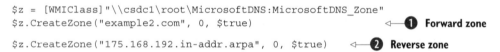

```
$z = [WMIClass]"\\csdc1\root\MicrosoftDNS:MicrosoftDNS_Zone"
$z.CreateZone("example2.com", 0, $true)                    ←—❶ Forward zone

$z.CreateZone("175.168.192.in-addr.arpa", 0, $true)    ←—❷ Reverse zone
```

Creating a zone involves using the `[WMIClass]` type accelerator to create a WMI object for the zone. We can then call the `CreateZone()` method ❶. The structure of the path to the WMI class is *\\computer_name\namespace:class*. This is consistent across WMI. If you're working locally or using PowerShell remoting, the computer name isn't necessary.

The parameters represent the zone name and the zone type, described in the previous table. The Boolean value `$true` indicates that the zone is Active Directory-integrated. This example creates a forward lookup zone

We need to create a primary zone. Active Directory forward zones are always considered as primary because they're writable due to their multimaster nature. One of the good features of using Active Directory-integrated DNS is that we only need to create the zones on a single DNS server. Active Directory will replicate the information to the other appropriate DNS servers.

DISCUSSION

A reverse lookup zone is created in a similar manner ❷. Note the format of the zone name. Having created our zone, we need to be able to discover the other zones on the DNS server and examine their configuration.

| TECHNIQUE 85 | **Viewing zone configuration** |

A DNS server can contain one, several, or many zones. When the DNS service is started, the zone data is loaded by DNS either from Active Directory or from a file.

PROBLEM

Windows machines quickly stop communicating if DNS can't resolve the names correctly. We can't even log on without it. This could occur if the zones aren't loaded or are misconfigured so that they haven't replicated correctly. When troubleshooting DNS, we need to be able to determine which zones are available on our server and how those zones are configured.

SOLUTION

We have gotten to know the `MicrosoftDNS_Zone` class quite well by now. It's going to prove its worth by solving this problem for us as well, as shown in listing 9.7.

Listing 9.7   View zone configuration

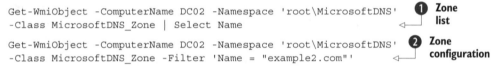

```
Get-WmiObject -ComputerName DC02 -Namespace 'root\MicrosoftDNS'      ❶ Zone
-Class MicrosoftDNS_Zone | Select Name                                  list

Get-WmiObject -ComputerName DC02 -Namespace 'root\MicrosoftDNS'      ❷ Zone
-Class MicrosoftDNS_Zone -Filter 'Name = "example2.com"'               configuration
```

There are two aspects to this problem:

- What zones are present?
- How is a zone configured?

We can answer the first part of the question by determining the names of the zones that are loaded ❶. We use `Get-WmiObject` and supply a computer name. The WMI namespace has to be supplied, as it's not the default root space. The WMI class also has to be supplied. Normally this command would display information about all of the instances of this class—all zones—but in this instance we've restricted ourselves to returning just the name. This is an important test, as there are DNS zones that have to present for Active Directory logon to work correctly. If the zones aren't present, this is one possible test to determine the problem.

DISCUSSION

A filter can be used to restrict the returned information to a single zone ❷. We use the same computer name, WMI namespace, and class as before, but this time we add a filter based on the names of the zone.

Now that we know the names of the zones on the server, we can think about examining the contents of the zone.

| TECHNIQUE 86 | **Viewing zone contents** |

DNS zones contain DNS records. We've seen how to view the configuration properties of a zone. Now it's time to view the records contained within the zone. This is useful for a number of reasons, including checking that individual records are contained in the zone. This technique could also be used to compare the contents of a zone on two different systems to ensure that replication has occurred correctly.

PROBLEM

Disaster recovery involves a lot of planning for the worst and finding ways to mitigate those risks. DNS is one of the foundations of a modern Windows infrastructure. In the event of a disaster, we'd need to ensure that we could recreate our DNS zone contents. One possible way of achieving this would be to create a permanent record of the contents as part of the DR documentation. We need to be able to view the zone contents before we write it to a disk file.

SOLUTION

WMI provides the means to solve this problem. We need to get some information out of WMI so we need to use `Get-WmiObject`. `Get-WmiObject` is the core of this solution. PowerShell has superb WMI support that gets even better in version 2. What isn't widely known is that some of the early work that became PowerShell involved a new version of a command-line WMI utility. Expect WMI to be at the core of PowerShell for a long time.

The `MicrosoftDNS` namespace is used together with the `MicrosoftDNS_AType` class. This combination will retrieve the entire list of A records on the server that we define in the `-ComputerName` parameter. We don't want this, so we need to employ a filter to restrict the output, as shown in listing 9.8.

Listing 9.8   View zone contents

```
Get-WmiObject -Namespace 'root\MicrosoftDNS'
 -Class MicrosoftDNS_AType  -ComputerName DC02 `
-Filter "ContainerName ='example2.com'" |
 Select OwnerName, IPAddress
```

DISCUSSION

It's always better to restrict the output with a WMI filter than to put a where statement further down the pipeline. This is because the filtering is applied as the data is retrieved, rather than after it's returned. The net effect is to reduce the amount of data returned and to reduce network utilization. Overall, the command will run more quickly.

The filter in this case is set to only accept records where the `ContainerName` matches a specific value. `ContainerName` is the property that holds the zone name. The net effect is that the A records contained in the particular zone will be retrieved. We can then limit the display to the machine name (`OwnerName`) and the IP address. A further refinement would be to use the `-Property` parameter to restrict the returned data to only the properties we need. I tend not to use this option. I like to keep my scripts generic, as I often find myself having to modify scripts for new troubleshooting scenarios.

A RECORDS ONLY   Only DNS A records will be displayed. We'd need to repeat with other record types if we required a complete view of the contents. The different types of records discussed in section 9.4 could be substituted in the script.

In technique 92, we look at how we can query a DNS server for an individual record. We could achieve this using by modifying the filter to include an IP address or using a `where` statement. If the record type is known, this may be a better solution, but if all of the records associated with a given machine name or IP address are required, use technique 92. This script could be easily modified to create a file containing the information. We could pipe the data into `Out-File` or `Export-Csv` as shown in technique 66, where we discuss creating files.

We've discussed the data lifecycle a number of times, and DNS zones follow this lifecycle. The final act we have to perform on our zone is to delete it when it's no longer required.

TECHNIQUE 87   Deleting a DNS zone

When a DNS zone is no longer required, we should ensure that it's deleted. This ensures that the DNS server's resources are concentrated on properly serving the production environment and that the information isn't available to potential attackers. When we delete an Active Directory-integrated zone, the replication system will ensure that the zone will be also be deleted on the other DNS servers.

> **BACKUP** It's a good idea to create a backup of the zone before deleting. You never know when you might need it.

Zone deletion is something that we could perform in the GUI, but we wouldn't have a record of the activity. If we use a PowerShell script, we can delete the zone and create a record in the event log (see section 8.5 for scripts to create and write to event logs) so that the activity can be tracked.

PROBLEM

We need to delete a DNS zone in such a way that we can record the activity.

SOLUTION

Section 8.5 showed how to record the event. We can use the WMI DNS provider to perform the actual deletion. The zone is deleted by creating a variable for the zone we need to delete. It's strongly recommended that you use `Get-WmiObject` by itself to determine the correct zone before you wrap the rest of the script around the call. Deleting the wrong zone would be generally considered a bad thing to do.

Once we've determined that we have the correct zone, we call the `Delete()` method on the zone to perform the deletion. The PowerShell object doesn't expose this method, so we have to use .psbase to access the underlying object, as shown in listing 9.9. This is a slightly messy way of working, but things get much better in Power-Shell v2.

Listing 9.9   Delete a DNS zone

```
$zone = Get-WmiObject -ComputerName DC02 -Namespace 'root\MicrosoftDNS'
-Class MicrosoftDNS_Zone -Filter 'Name = "example2.com"
$zone.psbase.Delete()
```

DISCUSSION

One of the WMI improvements in PowerShell v2 is a `Remove-WmiObject` cmdlet. We can use this to modify the script to a single line of PowerShell:

```
Get-WmiObject -ComputerName DC02 -Namespace 'root\MicrosoftDNS'
-Class MicrosoftDNS_Zone -Filter 'Name = "example2.com"' |
Remove-WmiObject
```

Use `Get-WmiObject` to identify the correct zone as previously demonstrated. We can then pipe the object that `Get-WmiObject` produces into `Remove-WmiObject`. This has the benefit that we can use the `Get` cmdlet to ensure that we have the correct zone, then add the `Remove` cmdlet to the pipeline.

DNS zones exist for the purpose of containing DNS records. We need to discover how to manage DNS records using PowerShell.

9.4 DNS records

The DNS records are the working end of the DNS system. Are the correct records in place? Do we need to create any records for specific purposes? Modern Windows OSs will register their own records in DNS, or DHCP can be configured to provide this service. These records are the standard forward lookup (A) and reverse lookup (PRT) records. But there are still occasions, for instance if we create a new web server or mail server, where we need to register a specific record.

We'll look at how we can create a number of different record types. These are the records that we're most likely to have to create. The records have different formats, so it's a useful exercise to examine how to create multiple record types. Forward lookup (A) records and reverse lookup (PTR) records are the building blocks of DNS. We also need to consider IPv6 records (AAAA), mail server (MX), and alias (CNAME) records. This will cover the most common scenarios we're likely to meet and give us a foundation for any other type of record that we may come across.

One theme that keeps coming through with PowerShell is that we have multiple ways to achieve a given outcome. This is true with creating DNS records. We can either use the `MicrosoftDNS_ResourceRecord` class or we can use a specific class for each different type of record. Examples of both are supplied in the following listings.

We'll need to supply a text representation of a record if we use the `MicrosoftDNS_ResourceRecord` class. This will look something like:

```
test57.Manticore.org IN A 10.10.54.177
```

or:

```
177.54.10.10.in-addr.arpa IN PTR test57.manticore.org
```

We can view the text representations of the records by using this script. We use the WMI provider to retrieve the records and select the data we require:

```
Get-WmiObject -ComputerName DC02 -Namespace 'root\MicrosoftDNS'
-Class MicrosoftDNS_ResourceRecord | Select TextRepresentation
```

The `MicrosoftDNS_ResourceRecord` class is a generic class for working with DNS records. There are also classes for dealing with specific record types; for instance, the `MicrosoftDNS_AType` or the `MicrosoftDNS_PTRType` class as we'll see in the examples in this section. Figure 9.3 shows the previous script being modified to discover PTR and MX records. This would be a suitable use for PowerGUI, as the individual requests can be stored and used as required.

This becomes useful when we want to examine *SRV records*. These are used by clients to discover the services that domain controllers offer, including logon to the domain. If the SRV records for a domain controller aren't available, the users won't be able to log on. SRV records can be viewed as follows:

```
Get-WmiObject -ComputerName DC02 -Namespace 'root\MicrosoftDNS'
-Class MicrosoftDNS_SRVType | Select TextRepresentation
```

This will display all the SRV records on the DNS server. We usually want to be more selective, as there could be a lot of records in a big Active Directory environment. Often we're interested in the records relating to a particular domain controller, so we modify the script by using a filter in the `Get-WmiObject` cmdlet:

```
Get-WmiObject -ComputerName DC02 -Namespace 'root\MicrosoftDNS'
-Class MicrosoftDNS_SRVType
-Filter "SRVDomainName = 'csdc1.manticore.org.'" |
Select TextRepresentation
```

This will return the SRV records stored in the DNS server for a given domain controller. If the correct records aren't present, logon or another service from the domain controller will fail. I wouldn't recommend creating SRV records using PowerShell or

```
C:\Scripts
PS> Get-WmiObject -ComputerName DC02 -Namespace 'root\MicrosoftDNS' -Class MicrosoftDNS_PTRType | Select TextRepresentat
ion

TextRepresentation
------------------
20.175.168.192.in-addr.arpa IN PTR test2.example2.com.
20.175.168.192.in-addr.arpa IN PTR test.
77.175.168.192.in-addr.arpa IN PTR test77.example2.com.
78.175.168.192.in-addr.arpa IN PTR test78.example2.com.
10.54.10.10.in-addr.arpa IN PTR xpn.manticore.org.
100.54.10.10.in-addr.arpa IN PTR win2k3r2ee.manticore.org.
112.54.10.10.in-addr.arpa IN PTR win2k3r2ee.manticore.org.
113.54.10.10.in-addr.arpa IN PTR sql08.manticore.org.
115.54.10.10.in-addr.arpa IN PTR web01.manticore.org.
116.54.10.10.in-addr.arpa IN PTR web02.manticore.org.
118.54.10.10.in-addr.arpa IN PTR exch01.manticore.org.
177.54.10.10.in-addr.arpa IN PTR test57.manticore.org.
98.54.10.10.in-addr.arpa IN PTR dc02.manticore.org.


PS> Get-WmiObject -ComputerName DC02 -Namespace 'root\MicrosoftDNS' -Class MicrosoftDNS_MXType | Select TextRepresentati
on

TextRepresentation
------------------
Manticore.org IN MX  10 exch01.manticore.org.


PS>
```

Figure 9.3 Using the Microsoft DNS WMI provider to display the text representation of DNS records. This can be used to determine the format of the information needed to create new DNS records.

any other means. In the event that the domain controller hasn't registered the records, it's usually because of an underlying problem that should be investigated and rectified so that the domain controller can register the records itself.

Other types of DNS records may need to be created as we discussed earlier. The most common type of record is the A, also known as *glue record*, which links a machine name to an IP address.

TECHNIQUE 88   Creating DNS A records

DNS A records are where the relationship between a machine name and an IP address are recorded. We may create an MX record so that we can find our email servers, or a CNAME record to provide an alias for a machine (or possibly a website), but we need to have an A record to go with these other records. The A record provides the glue that binds these other type of records to an IP address.

In many cases, Windows will create these records for us. We need to know how to create them to cover the case where we need to guarantee the contents of the DNS zone, for example if we're adding multiple IP addresses to a network interface.

PROBLEM

DNS records often have to be created during the commissioning process of new servers and services. The records can be created manually using the GUI tools, but this doesn't leave an audit trail. Audit records are available if we create the records in a script, especially if we use the techniques from section 8.5 to write the information into an event log.

SOLUTION

We're using a WMI class to solve this problem for us, as shown in listing 9.10. We've seen this pattern a few times already. We first create an instance of the class. We then set variables to represent the data we need to create the particular object. The final step is to use a create method (not always called Create()) to perform the actual creation. We'll see variations on this theme used in solving many of the problems in this section. It's one of the fundamental PowerShell techniques. We'll also see it used in subsequent chapters, particularly chapter 13 on IIS.

> **NOTE**   This solution is used to create an IPv4 record. We need to use the solution in the next section if we want to create an IPv6 record.

We want to create a DNS A record, so we use the MicrosoftDNS_AType class ❶. The starting point is to create a variable to represent our WMI class. We use [WMIClass] to define the path to the WMI class in the form *computer_name\wmi_namespace:wmi_class*.

Listing 9.10   Create DNS A record

```
$rec =
    [WmiClass]"\\DC02\root\MicrosoftDNS:MicrosoftDNS_AType"        ⬅──┐ Create
                                                                   ❶ instance
$server = "dc02.manticore.org"
$zone = "example2.com"              ❷ Define parameters
$name = "Test2.example2.com"
```

```
$class = 1
$ttl = 3600                                    ❷ Define parameters
$address = "192.168.172.20"

$rec.CreateInstanceFromPropertydata(
        $server, $zone, $name, $class, $ttl, $address)    ◁——❸ Create records
```

The second step is to create the data we'll feed into the actual creation process ❷:

- The DNS server on which the record will be created.
- The zone that will store the record.
- The fully qualified domain name (FQDN) of the computer.
- The class of record. A value of 1 means that it's a standard IN internet record.
- The TTL value for the record in seconds.
- The IP address to be associated with the machine name.

The `CreateInstanceFromPropertyData()` method ❸ is used to perform the record creation. This must be one of the longer method names we'll use in this book: It's not something I want to type that often. The data we discussed is used as arguments for the method as shown.

> **PARAMETER ORDER** The parameters have to be presented to the method in the order shown.

DISCUSSION
One thing we can do with this is extend the script to deal with creating multiple records. We'll assume that we have a CSV file containing two fields, namely machine name and IP address. The script is modified to become listing 9.11.

Listing 9.11 Create multiple DNS A records

```
                                          ❶ Read file
Import-Csv iprec.csv | Foreach -Begin {      ◁——┘
        $rec = [WmiClass]"\\DC02\root\MicrosoftDNS:MicrosoftDNS_AType"
        $server = "dc02.manticore.org"    ◁——
        $zone = "example2.com"              ❷ Set constants
        $class = 1
        $ttl = 3600
    } `                      ❸ Process data
    -Process {          ◁——┘
        $name = $_.FQDN
        $address = $_.IPAddress

        $rec.CreateInstanceFromPropertydata(
            $server, $zone, $name, $class, $ttl, $address)
    }
```

The script starts by reading a CSV file ❶. The data is passed into a `foreach` statement. We use a `-Begin` script block to define the constant data ❷ such as the server and zone names. A `-Process` script block ❸ is used to take the machine name (FQDN) and the IP address and use the `CreateInstanceFromPropertyData()` method to create the record.

This is a useful example of how we can take a script that performs a function once and turn it into a script that does the same thing many times. The `-Begin`, `-Process`, and `-End` parameters are well worth remembering when working with a `foreach` cmdlet. It's possible to save processing time this way.

IPv4 records like this have been the standard for many years. IPv6 is coming into use, as it's introduced in Windows Vista, Windows 7 and Windows Server 2008. We need to adapt our script to manage IPv6 records.

TECHNIQUE 89   ## Creating DNS AAAA records

TCP/IP is the standard networking protocol suite. One issue is that the number of possible addresses is finite and forecast to run out in the near future. An enhancement in the form of IPv6 radically increases the number of addresses that are available. Yes, your fridge can have its own IP address!

At present, IPv6 isn't widely adopted, but both Windows Vista and Windows Server 2008 have a new TCP/IP stack that facilitates using IPv6. In order to future-proof our administration skills, we need to know how to create a DNS record for an IPv6 address.

PROBLEM

We learned how to create an IPv4 address record in the previous section. How can we create an IPv6 IP address record?

SOLUTION

We adapt listing 9.12 to use a different WMI class that allows us to work directly with IPv6 addresses. Comparing listing 9.12 to listing 9.11, we start by creating a WMI object for the IPv6 address ❶. Note that we're using the `MicrosoftDNS_AAAAType` class. An IPv6 AAAA record is analogous to an IPv4 A record.

Listing 9.12 Create an IPv6 AAAA record

```
$rec = [WmiClass]"\\DC02\root\MicrosoftDNS:MicrosoftDNS_AAAAType"    ⟵

$server = "dc02.manticore.org"                  Create WMI object ❶
$zone = "example2.com"
$name = "Testip6.example2.com"
$class = 1
$ttl = 3600
$address = "fe80::f564:22dd:b7d9:4eb"           ⟵ ❷ IPv6 address

$rec.CreateInstanceFromPropertydata(
     $server, $zone, $name, $class, $ttl, $address)
```

Most of the parameters we've seen before. The server, zone, class, and TTL all match the previous listing. The name is obviously different, but the real difference is in the address. IPv4 addresses are 32 bits long and are normally represented in a dotted-decimal format such as 192.168.172.20. IPv6 addresses are 128 bits long (that's why there are so many of them) and are represented in a hexadecimal format such as fe80::f564:22dd:b7d9:4eb ❷.

DISCUSSION

The double colon is used to represent parts of the address that are composed of consecutive zeroes, so it expands to fe80:0000:0000:0000:f564:22dd:b7d9:4eb.

This isn't the place for a full tutorial on Ipv6, so after learning how to create the records, we'll move on to the records we need to keep our email flowing.

TECHNIQUE 90   Creating DNS MX records

Email is the primary communication mechanism for many companies. A Windows-based email server will register its own A records by default. But the outside world needs to be able to find the email server. This is enabled by the creation of *MX (Mail Exchange) records* in DNS. These aren't required internally, but are required in the external internet-facing DNS.

Organizations often have multiple systems accepting email. In this situation, multiple MX records are created to enable redundancy through round robin DNS. Creating multiple records takes more effort to do manually, but is relatively easy for a PowerShell script.

PROBLEM

We need to quickly create MX records in our internet-facing DNS. It may be necessary to configure multiple records to facilitate availability of service.

SOLUTION

We'll continue to use the DNS WMI provider, but this time we'll look at the `MicrosoftDNS_MXType` class. Creating an MX record is slightly different. In previous records, we've been mapping a machine name to an IP address. In this case, we're mapping a mail domain to a machine name.

We start by creating our WMI object, as in listing 9.13. This time we'll use the `MicrosoftDNS_MXType` class ❶. We could also use the `MicrosoftDNS_ResourceRecord` class and give the required information in the form of a text representation, as shown in figure 9.3. Once we've created the object, we need to define the data we'll feed into the creation process.

Listing 9.13   Create an MX record

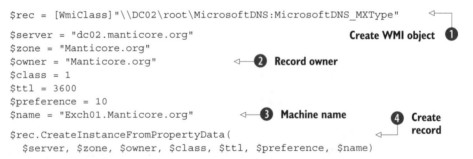

```
$rec = [WmiClass]"\\DC02\root\MicrosoftDNS:MicrosoftDNS_MXType"

$server = "dc02.manticore.org"                          Create WMI object ❶
$zone = "Manticore.org"
$owner = "Manticore.org"          ❷ Record owner
$class = 1
$ttl = 3600
$preference = 10
$name = "Exch01.Manticore.org"    ❸ Machine name           ❹ Create
                                                              record
$rec.CreateInstanceFromPropertyData(
  $server, $zone, $owner, $class, $ttl, $preference, $name)
```

Much of the information will be familiar from the previous examples. Instead of defining a machine name as the record owner, we use the mail domain ❷. The owner is usually the domain for MX records.

A piece of information that we haven't seen before is the *preference*. This is used to set a preference for which mail server is actually used. The mail servers that have MX records with lower preference values will be given priority over servers with higher values. Configuring multiple mail servers with the same preference value will initiate load balancing for incoming mail.

The final piece of data is the FQDN of the mail server that can accept mail for the mail domain ❸. A call to the `CreateInstanceFromPropertyData()` method ❹ creates the record.

DISCUSSION

We may need to create multiple MX records where we have several mail servers and we need to control which mail servers will be used.

> **DNS RECORDS FOR MAIL**   A DNS A record needs to be created for the mail server as well. The MX record points to the A record, which supplies the IP address.

The MX record is effectively a pointer to another record. MX records are specific to email servers, but we may need to create pointers for other purposes.

TECHNIQUE 91 Creating DNS CNAME records

A CNAME or alias record is a pointer to another record. We define a name and then provide a pointer to an A record that will give us the IP address.

PROBLEM

We need to be able to define another name for our database server. The application is expecting a particular name, but we can't change the server name because of the other applications that access it. How can we resolve the new name to the correct server?

SOLUTION

We create a pointer from our alias to the correct server using a CNAME record, as in listing 9.14. There's a class in the DNS WMI namespace that we can use. I mentioned earlier in the chapter that many of the scripts we create for administration follow established patterns. There's a distinct pattern to creating DNS records, such that it'd be easy to combine these scripts into a function that used a `switch` statement to decide which record type to create, and then input the rest of the information as arguments to the function.

Listing 9.14 Create a CNAME record

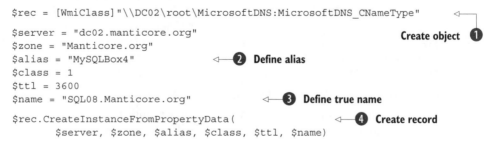

```
$rec = [WmiClass]"\\DC02\root\MicrosoftDNS:MicrosoftDNS_CNameType"          ⟵┐
                                                              Create object ❶
$server = "dc02.manticore.org"
$zone = "Manticore.org"
$alias = "MySQLBox4"            ⟵❷  Define alias
$class = 1
$ttl = 3600
$name = "SQL08.Manticore.org"            ⟵❸  Define true name

$rec.CreateInstanceFromPropertyData(            ⟵❹  Create record
       $server, $zone, $alias, $class, $ttl, $name)
```

Following our pattern, we create a WMI object for the CNAME record ❶. We set the usual data. This time we need to set the alias ❷ and the real name ❸. We can then create the record ❹.

DISCUSSION

It's worth comparing the data required for creating an alias with that required for an MX record as presented in listing 9.13.

> **ERROR REPORT**   I've seen this script report errors, but it still continues and generates the correct record. If you see an error message, double-check that the record was created successfully. Using a FQDN for the alias rather than just the server name may resolve the issue.

So far, we've looked at records that are used for a forward lookup where we want to end up with an IP address. The final record type we'll look at creating performs the reverse function and gives use a machine name when we have an IP address.

TECHNIQUE 92   **Creating DNS PTR records**

PTR records aren't always created by machines in a Windows infrastructure. It depends on the way the DNS settings have been configured on the client. DHCP can be configured to create PTR records for its clients. If we create an A record manually or through a script, we need to create the corresponding PTR record.

PROBLEM

We need to create PTR records for machines that don't have them created automatically.

SOLUTION

We can use a variation of our established pattern to create them using WMI. This time, we'll use the `MicrosoftDNS_ResourceRecord` class to create the PTR record in listing 9.15. This class can be used to create any type of DNS record by varying the text that's used. There are two reasons for using this class here. (1) It hasn't already been used and it needs to be covered. (2) I couldn't get the `MicrosoftDNS_PTRType` WMI class to work correctly in my testing. It may have been the combination of PowerShell v2 beta and Windows Server 2008 that caused this. This class definitely works with PowerShell v2 on Windows Server 2008 R2. I know this method works and like all good admins I'll stick with what I know works.

Listing 9.15   Create PTR record

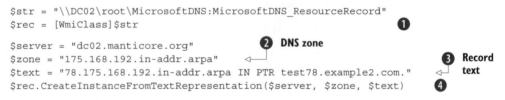

```
$str = "\\DC02\root\MicrosoftDNS:MicrosoftDNS_ResourceRecord"
$rec = [WmiClass]$str                                                    ❶

$server = "dc02.manticore.org"              ❷  DNS zone
$zone = "175.168.192.in-addr.arpa"    ◁──┘                        ❸ Record
$text = "78.175.168.192.in-addr.arpa IN PTR test78.example2.com."  ◁┘   text
$rec.CreateInstanceFromTextRepresentation($server, $zone, $text)       ❹
```

We start by creating the object ❶. There are only three pieces of data that we present using this technique: the server name, the zone ❷, and the record text ❸. The zone is a reverse lookup zone, so its name includes the subnet reversed. The text gives the reversed IP address of the system and the machine name. The `CreateInstanceFrom-TextRepresentation()` ❹ method is used to perform the creation.

DISCUSSION

If we're going to create multiple records in one pass we should use string substitution to create the text for the record. We've configured our server and created zones and records, so it's now time to discover how to find those records when we need to check on our systems.

TECHNIQUE 93   **Querying DNS records**

DNS is used for name resolution in a Windows environment. The records that are stored in DNS come from a number of sources. They can be created by our systems when they start up, they can be created by DHCP, they can be created by scripts as we've seen previously, or we could even create them manually using the DNS administration console. Some of these methods may be error-prone to a greater or lesser degree.

DNS records need to be maintained and will eventually have to be deleted. Clients will be given the wrong DNS information if old, stale records aren't removed, leading to problems on our network.

PROBLEM

Testing network connectivity is a standard troubleshooting technique. One of the steps in the troubleshooting progression is to check the data held in DNS. Machines won't be able to communicate if this information is out of date or wrong. In order to complete our testing, we need to be able to query the data held in DNS either by computer name or by IP address.

SOLUTION

We need to see all of the records held in DNS for a particular computer. We can use the `MicrosoftDNS_ResourceRecord` WMI class to return this information, as shown in listing 9.16.

Listing 9.16   Querying a DNS record

```
Get-WmiObject -ComputerName DC02 -Namespace 'root\MicrosoftDNS'     ◄─┐
 -Class MicrosoftDNS_ResourceRecord
-Filter "OwnerName = 'csdc1.manticore.org'"              Query by name  ❶

Get-WmiObject -ComputerName DC02 -Namespace 'root\MicrosoftDNS'     ◄─┐
-Class MicrosoftDNS_ResourceRecord
-Filter "RecordData = '10.10.54.99'"                    Query by address  ❷
```

The solution is presented in two parts to simplify the discussion. In the first instance, we want to search for DNS records using the name of the machine ❶. Using our trusty `Get-WmiObject` again, we give it the name of the DNS server in the `-ComputerName` parameter. The DNS namespace is used, but this time we use `MicrosoftDNS_ResourceRecord` for the class. This will ensure that we retrieve all of the required records.

A filter is used to restrict the data returned to that pertaining to the computer in which we're interested. Note that we're using the FQDN rather than just the NetBIOS name. This will return all records that have the `OwnerName` property set to the particular computer name.

Assuming that we haven't worn out `Get-WmiObject`, we'll use it again to test the IP address ❷. This version is identical to our previous example, except that we're comparing the `RecordData` property to the IP address. We have to present the IP address as a string.

DISCUSSION

As an enhancement, we could combine the filters into a single statement. Alternatively we could create a function that combined both scripts and accepted a computer name and IP address as arguments.

Now that we know how to create and find records, it's time to consider how we can delete them.

TECHNIQUE 94 Deleting DNS records

We need our DNS records to be always available so that communications across our networks proceed in a smooth manner. DNS records, like all data, will eventually become out-of-date and will have to be removed. DNS has a self-cleaning mechanism known as *scavenging*. Old, stale DNS records are removed from the server when this mechanism is activated. But there is a delay before the scavenging will pick up a stale record. In certain circumstances, this is unacceptable.

PROBLEM

One of our servers has failed. We need to remove the records pertaining to this server from DNS to ensure that other machines don't attempt to communicate with the failed machine. This situation is a potential problem if we're using round robin DNS, for instance, and need to remove the DNS record for a particular machine that has failed so that we drop it out of the load-balancing configuration.

SOLUTION

Our WMI classes have a method we can use to delete the records. Alternatively, PowerShell v2 introduces a cmdlet that'll do the job for us, as shown in listing 9.17. Consideration of the code shows that in both cases we're using WMI to create an object representing the record and we then perform a delete action.

Listing 9.17 Delete a DNS record

```
$rec = Get-WmiObject -ComputerName DC02 -Namespace 'root\MicrosoftDNS'
-Class MicrosoftDNS_AType  -Filter "IPAddress = '192.168.172.20'"

$rec.psbase.Delete()                                       PowerShell vl ❶

Get-WmiObject -ComputerName DC02 -Namespace 'root\MicrosoftDNS'
-Class MicrosoftDNS_AType  -Filter "IPAddress = '192.168.172.17'" |
Remove-WmiObject
                                                           PowerShell v2 ❷
```

In the first example ❶, we create a variable `$rec` for the DNS record. We use the DNS namespace and the class representing the type of record we want to remove. A filter containing the IP address is used to confine our attentions to the record we actually want.

DOUBLE CHECK At this stage of the proceedings, it's worth double-checking that we actually have the correct record to delete. Simply display the contents of $rec.

We need a method to delete the record. Now that we have a variable to work with, we can use Get-Member to discover the methods:

```
$rec | Get-Member
```

This doesn't show any methods that could be used to perform a deletion, though. We came across a similar problem in section 3.4.2 when discussing Active Directory objects. We can find what we need by using psbase to access the underlying .NET object rather than the PowerShell wrapper:

```
$rec.psbase | Get-Member
```

We delete the DNS record by using the methods on the underlying object as follows:

```
$rec.psbase.Delete().
```

Alternative

If you don't have access to a DNS server to test using psbase, you can see a similar result by using the Win32_Process class on the local machine. Create an object for a new process and use Get-Member. You won't see a delete method. Accessing the underlying object using psbase reveals a delete method:

```
$p = [WMIClass]"Win32_Process"
$p | Get-Member
$p.psbase | Get-Member
```

DISCUSSION

Our second option only works in PowerShell v2. We use Get-WmiObject to retrieve the record we need to delete ❷. We then pipe the results into Remove-WmiObject, which will perform the deletion. I prefer this approach because using Get-WmiObject directly enables us to view the results. We can then refine the query, if necessary, so that we're targeting the correct record. Once we've determined that we have the correct record, we simply pipe it into Remove-WmiObject. A good demonstration of interactive PowerShell. It's also a good way to avoid deleting the wrong record, which would be embarrassing.

We've looked at the DNS server, the DNS zones, and records in this chapter. The last section will complete the picture by showing us how to work with the settings on client machines.

9.5   Client settings

DNS and IP configuration needs to be correct for network connectivity to function correctly between Windows machines. We've examined the DNS server side of the puzzle in previous sections of this chapter. In this section we'll learn how to check the IP configuration of a machine and to test its connectivity.

Administrators will instinctively reach for the ipconfig and ping utilities to perform these tasks. (If only I had a dollar for every time I've used ping or ipconfig!) These utilities can be used directly in PowerShell but still only return text.

There are PowerShell alternatives that we can use that have the advantage of allowing us to work with objects. After we've tested the configuration and the connectivity, we may need to make changes. This can also be accomplished with PowerShell.

TECHNIQUE 95   IP address configuration

One of the first tools that an administrator learns to use is ipconfig. It enables us to discover how our IP addresses and related information is configured. If a networking-related issue is suspected, one of the first things we'll need to do is to check the IP address, subnet mask, and other data.

PROBLEM

Administrators often use ipconfig to determine the IP configuration of a system. How can we retrieve the same information in PowerShell?

SOLUTION

It would be possible to use ipconfig and expend a lot of effort extracting the required data and formatting as required. A preferred solution would be to generate the information in PowerShell, using WMI, as in listing 9.18.

Listing 9.18   IP address configuration

```
Get-WmiObject -Class Win32_NetWorkAdapterConfiguration `
 -Filter "IPEnabled = True" |
Select DNSHostName, Caption, MACaddress, IPAddress,
IPSubNet, DefaultIPGateway, DHCPEnabled, DHCPServer,
DHCPLeaseObtained, DHCPLeaseExpires, DNSServerSearchOrder,
DNSDomainSuffixSearchOrder, WINSPrimaryServer,
WINSSecondaryServer
```

It may not look it, but technically this is one line of PowerShell! If we're working at the command line, we can reduce the typing by using IP*, DHCP*, DNS*, and WINS* to select multiple properties with minimal effort. I wouldn't recommend using this style in scripts, though.

We can use the NetworkAdapterConfiguration class to discover this information. The network adapters that we're interested in will be those that are enabled to communicate over TCP/IP. This is indicated by the IPEnabled property being set to true.

DISCUSSION

In much earlier incarnations of Windows, we may have expected to find other protocols such as Novell's SPX in use. Today, TCP/IP will form the great majority of network connections on your Windows systems.

Once we've identified the adapters we're interested in via the -Filter parameter, we can select the particular properties in which we're interested. It would be beneficial to compare the output from this line of PowerShell with that obtained from ipconfig.exe. The other advantage to the script is that we can run it against remote machines by specifying the -ComputerName property.

It's one thing to be able to discover the IP address and other TCP/IP-related information, but how can we set this information?

TECHNIQUE 96   Setting an IP address

When Windows is first installed, it tells the network card to obtain an address via DHCP. This is fine for workstation machines, as we more than likely want to manage their IP information by DHCP. Servers for the most part should have static IP addresses. We could go into the properties of each network card and configure the TCP/IP information, but that might involve walking to the computer room. Ideally we need to be able to do this remotely.

PROBLEM

We have one or more remote machines where we need to set the IP address and other TCP/IP properties.

SOLUTION

Having previously discarded the idea of walking to the computer room, we'll have to use WMI and the NetWorkingAdapterConfiguration class to solve this problem. This script is the equivalent of opening the properties of a network connection and manually setting the TCP/IP properties.

> **WARNING**   This could severely damage your computer's ability to communicate on the network if used incorrectly. Make sure the values being used are correct.

There will be a number of network adapters in a server machine. I've worked on systems with 10 extra network cards that were combined for load-balancing and failover. This made a dozen cards before we started looking at the other connections that are counted as network connections. We need some way to identify the particular card we want to configure, as in listing 9.19. The easiest way is to look at the descriptions ❶. Once we've identified the card, we can use the description of the card in a WMI filter to create an object representing the card ❷. Note the use of single and double quotes around the filter string.

Listing 9.19   Setting the IP address configuration

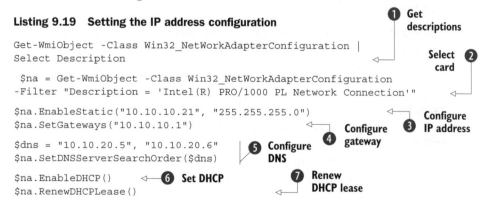

```
Get-WmiObject -Class Win32_NetWorkAdapterConfiguration |
Select Description

 $na = Get-WmiObject -Class Win32_NetWorkAdapterConfiguration
-Filter "Description = 'Intel(R) PRO/1000 PL Network Connection'"

$na.EnableStatic("10.10.10.21", "255.255.255.0")
$na.SetGateways("10.10.10.1")

$dns = "10.10.20.5", "10.10.20.6"
$na.SetDNSServerSearchOrder($dns)

$na.EnableDHCP()
$na.RenewDHCPLease()
```

❶ Get descriptions

❷ Select card

❸ Configure IP address

❹ Configure gateway

❺ Configure DNS

❻ Set DHCP

❼ Renew DHCP lease

The IP address and subnet mask are configured using the `EnableStatic()` method ❸. This will remove the setting to use DHCP and set the values. The addresses have to be presented as a string, as shown.

Other information needed with a static address includes the default gateway ❹ and the DNS servers ❺. Normally two DNS servers are defined, so put both addresses in the string as shown.

> **PRIVILEGES**   You need to Run as Administrator (Vista/2008) or be logged in with Administrator credentials (XP/2003) to run the code in listing 9.19. This restriction has been relaxed on Windows Server 2008 R2.

DISCUSSION

If it becomes necessary to revert to using DHCP, the `EnableDHCP()` method ❻ will do this. Using this method will remove the static IP address and the subnet mask, but it won't remove any other information such as the default gateway or DNS servers we've defined either manually or via a script. Having reverted to DHCP, it may be necessary to force a renewal of the DHCP lease by using `RenewDHCPLease()` ❼. There are a number of other methods available to use via this WMI class:

- `DisableIPSec`
- `EnableIPSec`
- `ReleaseDHCPLease`
- `SetDNSDomain`
- `SetDynamicDNSRegistration`
- `SetIPConnectionMetric`
- `SetTcpipNetbios`

- `EnableDHCP`
- `EnableStatic`
- `RenewDHCPLease`
- `SetDNSServerSearchOrder`
- `SetGateways`
- `SetIPXFrameTypeNetworkPairs`
- `SetWINSServer`

This one WMI class enables us to configure the networking connectivity of our systems. This can be used remotely making it even more efficient.

TECHNIQUE 97   **Testing IP connectivity**

Testing the IP connectivity from a machine or between two machines is a basic troubleshooting activity. One of the first things you learn as an administrator is to use the `ping` utility.

> **FIREWALL**   The Windows firewall prevents `ping`-type activities by default. The use of ICMP needs to be enabled so that we can perform these tests.

`Ping` can be used in PowerShell, but because it returns text, it's not easy to work with the output.

PROBLEM

We need to test network connectivity from within PowerShell.

SOLUTION

There's a WMI class we can use to test IP connectivity. PowerShell version 2 makes it easier to use by wrapping the functionality within a cmdlet, as in listing 9.20.

Listing 9.20 Testing IP connectivity

```
Get-WmiObject -Class Win32_PingStatus -Filter "Address = '127.0.0.1'"

Test-Connection -Destination 127.0.0.1       ❷ Cmdlet              WMI  ❶
Test-Connection -Destination Computer01
Test-Connection -Destination 192.168.37.56
Test-Connection -Destination fe80::f564:22dd:b7d9:4ea
Test-Connection -Destination 127.0.0.1, 192.168.37.56
"127.0.0.1","192.168.37.56" | foreach {Test-Connection -Destination $_}
```

The WMI class used to perform this test is Win32_PingStatus ❶. We use a filter to define the address we want to test. One interesting difference is that on Windows Vista and Windows Server 2008, using this WMI class returns the IPv4 and IPv6 addresses associated with the machine.

In PowerShell v2, we have the same functionality supplied in a cmdlet—Test-Connection ❷. We can supply one or more destinations, either as IP addresses or as names, and they'll be tested in turn. IPv4 and IPv6 addresses can be used. The addresses to be tested can also be supplied along the pipeline.

NOTE Test-Connection 127.0.0.1 | select IPV4Address -First 1 is a quick way to get the local IP address using PowerShell.

DISCUSSION

One common troubleshooting scenario is to ping the localhost, then the local machine address, followed by the default gateway, and finally a remote machine on another subnet. This could be achieved in one line of PowerShell by simply listing the addresses as shown and piping into Test-Connection. Alternatively, the addresses could be supplied in a CSV file if required.

In the event that there are a large number of addresses to test, the -AsJob parameter runs the tests as a PowerShell background job.

9.6 Summary

PowerShell doesn't have native tools to work with DNS. The DNS WMI provider can be used in PowerShell so that we can administer local and remote DNS servers. This is automatically installed when we install DNS.

WMI gives us access to the server configuration, DNS zones, and DNS records. We can manage the full lifecycle for these objects from PowerShell. We can also compare and contrast settings and data across servers. This means we can ensure the correct settings are applied uniformly across the environment and that the data is consistent.

There are a number of DNS record types that we may need to create. These can all be created using PowerShell and WMI. The ability to interrogate DNS and check the records means that we can troubleshoot issues such as the nonregistration of SRV records quickly and efficiently.

Client machines and servers have IP configurations. We can use PowerShell and WMI to check the configuration and make changes as appropriate. The connectivity between machines can be checked using WMI or new functionality in PowerShell v2.

In this chapter, we've seen several instances where Active Directory is dependent on DNS. We've already looked at configuring Active Directory user accounts in chapter 5. In the next chapter, we'll build on this chapter and the work we've done with user accounts by examining how we can administer the Active Directory structure with PowerShell.

Active Directory structure

This chapter covers

- Working with Organizational Units
- Administering Group Policies
- Protecting objects from accidental deletion
- Restoring deleted Active Directory objects

In chapter 5, we looked at user accounts and groups in Active Directory. This is the most volatile data in Active Directory, but it has the least impact on our Active Directory as a whole. Figure 10.1 shows a three-layer view of Active Directory. At the bottom we find data that changes slowly such as sites, site links, and domain controllers. Though these items don't change often, they can have a huge impact on Active Directory, and the user population, if things go wrong. We'll be looking at how to administer this layer in chapter 11.

The middle layer comprises our OU structure, the GPOs that we link to the OUs, and how we protect Active Directory. This layer changes more rapidly than the bottom layer and usually has a lower impact. But I've seen GPO errors have a devastating effect on Active Directory. Watching servers drop out of use as the GPO replicates isn't a pretty sight. This is the topic for this chapter, where we'll look at the Active Directory schema, organizational units, GPOs, and how we can add further security to our AD objects.

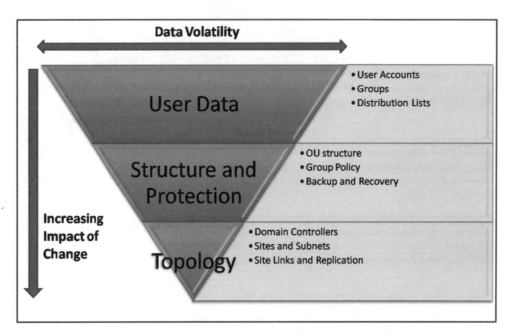

Figure 10.1 Frequency of change to Active Directory objects. The topology changes slowly, but changes can have a large impact. The structure changes more rapidly but tends to have less of an impact. User data changes most frequently, but has the least impact on the directory as a whole.

We normally don't touch the AD schema apart from updating it for new versions of Active Directory or AD-aware applications such as Exchange. It has a lot of useful information. We'll look at accessing the schema to discover its version and change the display defaults we use in Active Directory Users & Computers. Code to discover the forest and domain levels will also be examined.

OUs are the containers we use to give structure to our domains. They contain the user and computer accounts we work with on a day-to-day basis. The full lifecycle of OUs will be examined with scripts to perform all common administrative actions that occur during this lifecycle. This will include how to discover the objects contained within an OU.

GPOs are used to control all aspects of our managed environment. We won't look at scripting the contents of the GPO, but we'll examine how create and link them to our OUs. A common question is "What GPOs are linked where in my domain?" Power-Shell can be used to discover this information for us.

The final section of the chapter shows how to stop Active Directory objects from being accidentally deleted. It also explains how to restore a deleted object, and what you need to do to repopulate the attributes on the object.

10.1 *Automating Active Directory administration*

When we start to work with the objects considered in this chapter, we have two choices regarding our approach. We can use the .NET classes in PowerShell and script our solutions in this style. Alternatively, we can assemble a toolkit of cmdlets to perform these tasks. Most of the solutions in this chapter will be presented in both styles.

A number of the scripts in this chapter will help you with "the guy who set it up has left" scenario. In other words, no one knows exactly how the Active Directory is configured. You can use the scripts to discover what's happening as well as document the configuration.

10.1.1 *.NET*

In this chapter, we'll be mainly using classes in the `System.DirectoryServices.ActiveDirectory` and `System.DirectoryServices` namespaces. They build from the way we used them in chapter 5. These scripts can be used on any Active Directory version as long as we have a machine running PowerShell in the domain.

10.1.2 *Cmdlets*

Cmdlets are available from a number of sources. In this chapter we'll see examples of working with:

- The AD and GPO cmdlets that ship with Windows Server 2008 R2. These cmdlets are supplied as modules—`ActiveDirectory` and `GroupPolicy` respectively. They're loaded using `Import-Module`. The AD cmdlets work against a web service on the domain controller rather than a direct ADSI call. The web service is available for download to install on Windows Server 2008 and Windows Server 2003 domain controllers. It'll be necessary to have a Windows 7 or Windows Server 2008 R2 machine in the domain to host the cmdlets.
- The Quest cmdlets, which can be used from an administration workstation or server without installation on a domain controller. We'll make extensive use of the `*-QADObject` cmdlets in this chapter. The Quest cmdlets all have a *QAD* prefix attached to the noun in order to distinguish them.
- SDM Software, which provides cmdlets for working with GPOs and tombstone objects. SDM provides a number of snapins to download and install rather than the single snapin we see with Quest.

One question I'm often asked is which set of cmdlets I use. I use all three sets wherever possible. There are cases where one has functionality that the other doesn't, or one has easier syntax. If I had to choose, I'd probably use the Microsoft cmdlets on Windows Server 2008 R2 and the Quest/SDM cmdlets on Windows Server 2008 and 2003.

Now that we know the outlines of what we're looking at and the tools we're using, it's time to dive into the details, starting with the Active Directory schema.

10.2 *Schema*

The schema defines the types of objects that can be created in our Active Directory as well as the attributes those objects may possess. It's created when Active Directory is installed, and in the vast majority of organizations it's subsequently ignored until it's time for an upgrade. Changes to the schema are rare events and should be under tight change control.

SCHEMA CHANGES Schema updates are one-way: you can't remove classes or attributes that have been added. In the later versions of Windows, you can disable these new classes or attributes under certain circumstances.

When Active Directory was first introduced, it was thought that companies would be adding classes and attributes to Active Directory to support their applications. This hasn't happened for the most part. Most schema upgrades seem to be either when Active Directory is upgraded or when a new version of Exchange is introduced.

Many administrators don't like touching the schema because it's seen as risky. Sound planning and preparation will contain the risk. There aren't a lot of tasks we really need to do to the schema, but being able to find your way around it can be useful.

TECHNIQUE 98   Schema version

One thing that consultants seem to spend a lot of time doing is digging into the current state of a system to find how it's configured and set up. The documentation never seems to cover the information we need.

Microsoft has introduced new functionality with each new version of Active Directory. That functionality is linked to the forest and domain levels, which we'll examine in the next section. The schema version is important so we know what updates have been applied and what functionality is available. It's also possible for schema updates to occur if beta or release candidate versions of Windows have been applied. This leaves the schema in a state that may not be supportable.

PROBLEM
A standard issue with the "guy who set it up has left" scenario is the schema version. Did he apply any updates? We need to determine the version of the schema so that we know what functionality should be available and that the schema is in a supportable state.

SOLUTION
The `System.DirectoryServices.ActiveDirectory` namespace supplies an `Active-DirectorySchema` class that we can use to discover this information, as in listing 10.1. We saw in chapter 5 how we could access and manipulate objects in Active Directory. Unfortunately, accessing the schema is slightly different. The starting point is creating an object for the schema ❶. We can do this by using the `System.Directory-Services.ActiveDirectory.ActiveDirectorySchema` class as shown. That name is a mouthful—not something I'd want to try saying quickly five times. This class has a static method `GetCurrentSchema()` that we use. Remember, we need `::` to access static methods.

SCHEMA CLASSES The `System.DirectoryServices.ActiveDirectory.Active-DirectorySchema` class has methods that enable us to view the classes and attributes in the schema. It has faster access than `ADSIEdit`.

After we have our schema object, we can get a directory entry for it ❷. This gives us access to the information on the schema. The particular attribute we use to see the schema version is called `ObjectVersion` ❸. This can take one of a discrete set of values. The most efficient way to test the value is to use a `switch` statement. See listing 2.6 for another example.

Listing 10.1 Schema version

```
$sch = [System.DirectoryServices.ActiveDirectory.ActiveDirectorySchema]::
GetCurrentSchema()                  ❶
$de = $sch.GetDirectoryEntry()      ◄──❷ Create directory entry
switch ($de.ObjectVersion)          ❸
{
    13{"{0,25} " -f "Schema Version 13 = Windows 2000"; break}
    30{"{0,25} " -f "Schema Version 30 = Windows 2003"; break}
    31{"{0,25} " -f "Schema Version 31 = Windows 2003 R2"; break}
    44{"{0,25} " -f "Schema Version 44 = Windows 2008"; break}
    47{"{0,25} " -f "Schema Version 47 = Windows 2008 R2"; break}
    default{"{0,25} {1,2} " -f `
      "Unknown Schema Version", $de.ObjectVersion; break}
}
```

DISCUSSION

It would be possible to use a number of `if` statements to produce the same result, but a `switch` statement is more efficient. Each line consists of a condition to test—for instance, is the `ObjectVersion` value equal to 13 as shown on the first line? If the `ObjectVersion` value matches the test value, the script block is executed. In this case, we output a string giving the version number and the associated version of Windows. The `break` statement causes processing to jump out of the `switch` statement. If we didn't use `break`, the other tests would be performed, and we want to stop processing at the first match.

> **FORMATTING** I've deliberately used the string-formatting capabilities in this script and the next because they're part of an Active Directory reporting script. The output is designed to be written to text files for further use.

The default value catches anything that doesn't match one of the test values. If we get to this point, it means that either we have an odd value for the schema version which needs further investigation, or our script needs updating to allow for a new version of Windows!

The script becomes much easier to maintain using a `switch` statement. A new line containing the value to test and the associated text needs to be added into the statement. One thing to keep in mind is how the script will be maintained. At some stage, we'll need to perform maintenance or updates on our scripts, and writing with that in mind will save a lot of muttering in the future.

This script can't be shortened by using cmdlets. If desired, lines 1 and 2 of the script could be replaced by a single line using the Microsoft cmdlet:

```
$de = Get-ADObject
-Identity "CN=Schema,CN=Configuration,DC=Manticore,DC=org"
-Property ObjectVersion
```

A similar syntax is available with the Quest cmdlet

TECHNIQUE 99 **Forest and domain level**

An Active Directory *forest* is a collection of one or more domains that share common information such as the schema and the global catalog. The domain level, and in Windows Server 2003 or later the forest level, controls the functionality available within Active Directory. Changing the domain or forest level is a one-way process. We may still need to report on the levels, either when investigating an Active Directory that's new to us or to prepare a report documenting our AD.

PROBLEM

The forest and domain levels need to be determined for all of the domains in our Active Directory forest. We need to derive the information in a form that can be incorporated into a report. The task should be accomplished with the least amount of administrative effort. Sounds like an MCP exam question.

SOLUTION

We can determine the forest and domain levels by using the GUI tools. But this information would then need to be typed into our report and would also require more administrative effort in a forest with a significant number of domains. We'll use the System.DirectoryServices.ActiveDirectory namespace again to solve this problem.

The script in listing 10.2 starts by creating an object for the forest ❶. We can use the GetCurrentForest() static method of the System.DirectoryServices.ActiveDirectory.Forest class for this. The information we need is stored as properties of this object ❷. I've used a formatted string in this example, as I wanted to be able to pipe the output directly into a text file. If the data is only required onscreen, we could use a simple piece of code:

```
$for | Select Name, ForestMode, RootDomain
```

This displays the forest name, root domain, and the forest level. The forest level is stored in the ForestMode property. The Domains collection of the forest object stores the information we need. A foreach loop can be used to iterate through the domains in the collection ❸. Within the loop, the domain name, parent domain, and domain level (domainmode) are displayed ❹. The parent domain is useful, as it enables us to picture the structure of the domain trees. The netmap technique discussed in section 8.2.1 could be used to create a visual display of the forest structure.

Listing 10.2 Forest and domain levels

```
$for =
[System.DirectoryServices.ActiveDirectory.Forest]::
GetCurrentForest()                                    ⬅—❶ Get forest object

"{0,15}  {1,2} " -f "Name:", $for.Name                   ❷ Forest
"{0,15}  {1,2} " -f "Forest Mode:", $for.ForestMode        data
"{0,15}  {1,2} " -f "Root Domain:", $for.RootDomain

foreach ($domain in $for.Domains){    ⬅—❸ Domains
```

```
"{0,8} {1,2} " -f "Name:", $domain.Name
"{0,25} {1,2} " -f "Parent Domain:", $domain.Parent
"{0,25} {1,2} " -f "Domain Mode:", $domain.DomainMode
}
```

4 **Domain data**

DISCUSSION

The following could be used to display the domain data onscreen if there's no requirement to save to a file:

```
$for.Domains | Select Name, Parent, DomainMode
```

The Microsoft AD cmdlets supply `Get-ADForest` and `Get-ADDomain` cmdlets that simplify this code:

```
$for = Get-ADForest
$for | Format-List Name, ForestMode, RootDomain
foreach ($domain in $for.Domains){
    Get-ADDomain $domain | Format-List Name, Parent, DomainMode}
```

I stated earlier that modifying the schema is a rare occurrence. It certainly fits into the lowest part of our triangle in figure 10.1. One thing we may want to think about doing though is modifying the way display names are created when using the GUI tools.

TECHNIQUE 100   Default display name

When we use PowerShell to create our user accounts, we can control the format of the display names, as we saw in chapter 5. But the GUI tools default to displaying the

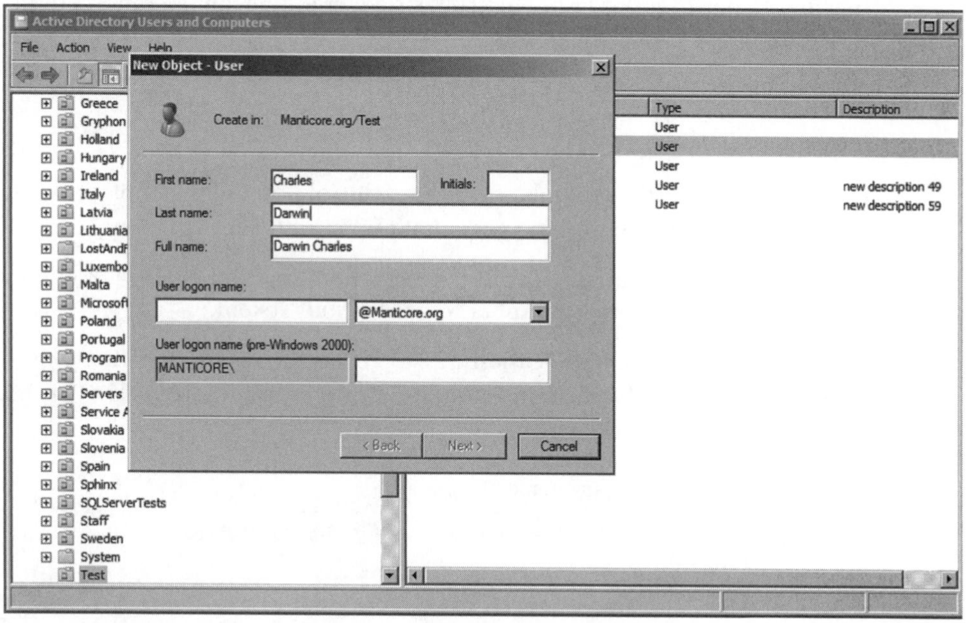

Figure 10.2   Creating a user in ADUC automatically creates the display name. We want to ensure that this is automatically created as last name followed by first name to give us consistency between our scripts and the GUI tools.

names as first name followed by last name. This makes browsing more difficult, as first names tend not to be as selective as last names.

Some organizations and admins advocate creating names as last name followed by a comma followed by first name. This is a bad idea.

> **AVOID THE COMMA**   Adding a comma into the name causes difficulties when we create LDAP strings and we have to escape the comma. Don't use it. If you find your user accounts are structured like this, then try and get a change approved to modify the process and rename the accounts. It'll make automation much easier.

Figure 10.2 shows a user being created, where the display name is automatically created as last name followed by first name. This ensures consistency and helps prevent those that haven't yet adopted PowerShell for performing their administration from feeling neglected.

PROBLEM

Many organizations attempt to handle this using procedures, but someone forgets or nobody tells the new guy and odd names get produced. What we want to be able to do is apply the same rules in the GUI as we do in our scripts. Our task is to modify the way display names are created when we use the GUI tools. We need to change the default behavior to that shown in figure 10.2.

SOLUTION

There are a number of display specifiers in Active Directory. We set the appropriate specifier to perform this task. This isn't, strictly speaking, an operation on the schema, but it fits logically into this section.

We need to access the display specifier we need which can be found at:

```
cn=User-Display,cn=409,cn=DisplaySpecifiers,
CN=Configuration,DC=Manticore,DC=org
```

in my test domain. These display specifiers control how the GUI tools present information. The 409 refers to the code page that's used in the environment.

> **CODE PAGE**   This will vary if you're using a non-English language. You'll need to determine the correct number to use for your system.

As shown in listing 10.3, the easiest way to access the display specifiers without hard-coding the name of the domain into the script is to use RootDSE **1**. This binds us to the root of our Active Directory.

Listing 10.3   Default display name

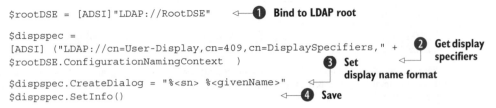

```
$rootDSE = [ADSI]"LDAP://RootDSE"        <--1  Bind to LDAP root

$dispspec =
[ADSI] ("LDAP://cn=User-Display,cn=409,cn=DisplaySpecifiers," +    2  Get display
$rootDSE.ConfigurationNamingContext  )             3  Set          specifiers
                                                       display name format
$dispspec.CreateDialog = "%<sn> %<givenName>"    <--
$dispspec.SetInfo()                         <--4  Save
```

The script is also made more portable by creating it in this manner. We then need to create a directory entry for the User-Display specifier ❷. If we wanted to view the set of display specifiers, we could use the following:

```
$disp =
[ADSI]("LDAP://,cn=409,cn=DisplaySpecifiers," +
$rootDSE.ConfigurationNamingContext )
$disp.children
```

After accessing the user-display specifier, we change the CreateDialog property ❸. The value used translates as *last name first name* separated by a space. sn and given-name are names used in Active Directory for these attributes. The full range of attributes and characters that can be used in the CreateDialog value can be viewed by accessing KB250455 on the Microsoft website.

> **TEST** As with all of the scripts in this book that may potentially perform changes to your environment, you should test this one thoroughly to ensure it performs as you expect.

The final act of the script is to save the changes back into Active Directory ❹. The next time a user is created using ADUC, the dialog will work as shown in figure 10.2.

DISCUSSION

We can display and modify the specifier using Get-ADObject and Set-ADObject (Set-QADObject could also be used). Using the RootDSE to get the configuration naming context keeps it portable. The CreateDialog property isn't part of the default property set, and so has to be explicitly defined when we want to view it:

```
Get-ADObject       `
-Identity "cn=User-Display,cn=409,cn=DisplaySpecifiers, `
$((Get-ADRootDSE).configurationNamingContext)" `
-Properties CreateDialog |
Format-List *

Set-ADObject `
-Identity "cn=User-Display,cn=409,cn=DisplaySpecifiers,`
$((Get-ADRootDSE).configurationNamingContext)"    `
-Replace @{CreateDialog = "%<sn> %<givenName>"}
```

This chapter is about the structure of Active Directory. The primary object concerned with the logical structure within a domain is the OU. OUs are used for the delegation of administration and to provide a structure for linking GPOs, as we'll see in the following sections.

10.3   *Organizational units*

OUs are the subcontainers within an Active Directory domain that we use to bring structure and order to our environment. OUs are designed so that the domain structure is flexible and (relatively) easily modified. We saw how to move users between OUs in chapter 5. Later in this section, we'll see how to move whole OUs and the complete set of their child objects.

The rate of change on OUs is much less than that of the user population, but higher than the physical topology of our Active Directory. Changing an OU in some way will impact only a portion of our Active Directory. This puts the OU changes in the middle of the frequency and impact diagram, as can be seen in figure 10.1. The diminished impact level doesn't mean we can perform changes without a proper change control mechanism.

Active Directory creates a number of containers and OUs when it's installed. We need to learn how to create our own OUs before we can go much further with them.

TECHNIQUE 101   **Creating an OU**

Creating an OU is similar to creating a user object. The script presented in this section should be compared with that in listing 5.7. In this section, we look at creating a single OU. In the next section we'll examine how to create a number of nested OUs.

PROBLEM

We have to create an OU structure for the users and computers we'll be creating in Active Directory. We can't put them in the default containers because we can't apply GPOs to them. Our starting point is to create one or more OUs in the root of the domain.

SOLUTION

The script presented in listing 5.7 will be modified to perform this task; the modified version is shown in listing 10.4. OUs are much simpler objects than users, which means we don't need to set as many attributes. Whenever we're creating objects in Active Directory, we need to start by getting a directory entry for the parent object ❶. This syntax is the long version of:

```
$parent = [ADSI]$ldap
```

In this case, the domain is the parent object. This listing hard-codes the domain name into the script. If the script is required to be portable, the first two lines of the next listing can be substituted for the first two lines of this script.

Once we have the directory entry for the parent, we can then find the collection of children belonging to the parent ❷. The Add() method is used to perform the creation ❸. The OU name is given in the first parameter and the type of object (organizationalUnit) given in the second parameter. We must remember to save the newly created object back to Active Directory using SetInfo(); otherwise our new OU will disappear.

Listing 10.4 Create OU

```
$ldap = "LDAP://dc=Manticore,dc=org"                                        ❶ Parent
$parent = New-Object DirectoryServices.DirectoryEntry $ldap                    directory
$OUs = $parent.get_children()                              ❷ Child objects     entry

$newOU = $OUs.add("OU=PwrShlPractce1", "organizationalUnit")  ❸ Create OU
$newOU.SetInfo()

$newOU.Description = "Powershell in Practice OU 1"    ❹ Set description
$newOU.SetInfo()

Write-host "Created OU: PwrShlPractce1"    ❺ Confirm
```

It's a good idea to set a description for the OU (or any other object). It helps us remember why we created it in the first place. After setting the description ❹, we need to use `SetInfo()` again to save the change. The script finishes by outputting a message to say we've created the OU ❺. We could also write a message to the event logs if required.

DISCUSSION

The script in listing 10.5 shows how to create an OU using the Quest cmdlets. There isn't a set of cmdlets for working with OUs, so we have to use the generic `*-QADObject` cmdlets.

Listing 10.5 Create OU by cmdlet

```
$dom =
[System.DirectoryServices.ActiveDirectory.Domain]::
GetCurrentDomain()
$root = $dom.GetDirectoryEntry()

New-QADObject -Name PwrShlPractce2
-ParentContainer $root.DistinguishedName.ToString()
-Type 'OrganizationalUnit' -NamingProperty 'ou'
-Description "Powershell in Practice OU 2"
```

This is actually a three-line script. The first two lines create a directory entry object for the root of the domain. Using the `GetCurrentDomain()` static method of the `System.DirectoryServices.ActiveDirectory.Domain` class, we create a .NET object for the domain. `GetDirectoryEntry()` creates the directory entry that enables us to get the distinguished name to use as the parent container. This approach has the advantage of not having the domain hard-coded, so it is portable between domains.

The `New-QADObject` cmdlet is used to create the OU. We give the new OU a name and define the previously derived distinguished name of the domain as the parent. The `-Type` and `-NamingProperty` parameters are used to set the fact that we're creating an OU as opposed to another type of object. We can set the description in the same cmdlet. There's no need for a message to confirm the creation because the cmdlet outputs one automatically.

This becomes even simpler with the Microsoft cmdlets:

```
New-ADOrganizationalUnit -Name "PwrShlPractce3"
-Description "Test OU Number 3"
```

A new OU is created in the root of the domain. In Windows Server 2008 R2, by default the OU is protected from accidental deletion (see technique 112 in section 10.5). If we don't want it protected, we need to use `-ProtectedFromAccidentalDeletion $false`. A child OU is created by defining the path to the parent OU:

```
New-ADOrganizationalUnit -Name "Child1"
-Description "Child of Test OU Number 3"
-Path "OU=PwrShlPractce3,DC=Manticore,DC=org"
```

We've seen how to create on OU. This is useful, but we often need to create multiple nested OUs. That's the next step in our exploration of OUs.

TECHNIQUE 102   Bulk creation and nesting

There are numerous ways to organize the OU structure of an Active Directory domain. Three AD experts will give you at least four good answers and a lot of entertainment listening to the debate. One good way is to base the OU structure on geography—the different locations your organization occupies. This should be the least changeable possibility in theory.

This means that we usually end up repeating the OU structure beneath our geography-based OUs. An example is shown in figure 10.3, though it's not based on geography—at least I don't know of anywhere called Pwrshpractce3.

This becomes a tedious chore to perform in the GUI if we have a large number of locations. I became interested in scripting OU creation when I had to set up the OU structure for a 90+ site Active Directory!

PROBLEM

We've defined our problem as how to create an OU structure that consists of a number of nested OUs. The process must be repeatable for when we add new locations into our Active Directory environment.

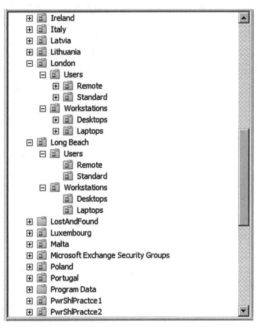

Figure 10.3   Repeating OU structure within a geographic-based OU structure

SOLUTION

The script presented in the previous section can be used as the basis of solving this problem. We can make the script generic by using variables rather than hard-coding the data, as in listing 10.6. The technique of importing the data from a CSV file can be used again here. This gives us the situation where we just change the input data to make the script reusable across any domain and across numerous situations, including initial domain creation and addition of locations to the AD.

Listing 10.6   OU bulk creation

```
clear-host
Import-Csv ou.csv | Foreach {              ❶
    $ldap = "LDAP://" + $_.ParentOU                              ❷ Set parent
    $parent = new-Object DirectoryServices.DirectoryEntry $ldap   ⤶  container
    $OUs = $parent.get_children()                              ❸

    $newOU = $OUs.add("OU=" + $($_.Name), "organizationalUnit")   ⟵─❹ Create OU
    $newOU.SetInfo()                           ❺
```

```
$newOU.Description = $_.Description        ◁──6  Set description
$newOU.SetInfo()                            7
Write-host "Created OU: " $_.Name          8
}
```

If you spend a lot of time working with PowerShell, you'll end up with a fairly busy display with the results of previous scripts and command-line activity on display. One thing I've found useful is clearing the screen before running a script that will do a significant amount of work. It seems easier to keep track of what's going on if you start with a clear PowerShell console. I use a `clear-host` command at the top of my scripts achieve this. You could just use `cls`, but I don't like using aliases in scripts.

> **ASSUME** I won't necessarily show a `clear-host` command at the top of all scripts, but assume that it could be used unless there's a specific reason not to use it.

The first working line of the script reads the contents of a CSV file ❶. This CSV file has the following columns:

- ParentOU
- Name
- Description

The CSV file contents are piped into a `foreach` cmdlet that'll operate on each record passing along the pipeline. CSV files are the best way to handle this, because the column headers become the variable names that are used in the `foreach` processing block. The `parentOU` value (remember that `$_` represents the object coming along the pipeline) is used to get a directory entry for that OU ❷. It's used as the parent container for the new OU.

Our parent container will have children ❸. We then add the new OU into the children of the parent OU ❹ and save the new OU back into AD ❺. This is exactly the way we created an OU in the previous section, except we're supplying the data via the pipeline.

A description is set ❻ and saved ❼ before we write out our message confirming the creation of the OU ❽. The script will then loop back to process the next record on the pipeline. This process happens much faster than you're reading this section and far, far faster than me writing about it.

DISCUSSION

We can use the `New-QADObject` cmdlet in exactly the same way, as shown in listing 10.7.

Listing 10.7 OU bulk creation

```
clear-host
Import-Csv qou.csv | Foreach {
    New-QADObject -Name $_.Name -ParentContainer $_.ParentOU
    -Type 'OrganizationalUnit' -NamingProperty 'ou'
    -Description $_.Description
}
```

This script could be presented as one line of PowerShell if we put a semicolon after the clear-host so that it reads:

```
Clear-host; Import-Csv qou.csv | Foreach {New-QADObject. . . . . }
```

We can put a huge amount of functionality into a small script with PowerShell. This is where our productivity gains will come from. It doesn't take long to write and test something like this that can then be used repeatedly. I haven't given an example using the Microsoft cmdlets, but it's straightforward to adapt listing 10.7 using the syntax given in the previous section.

Our example starts by clearing the screen. It's probably more important to do this when using the cmdlets, as they tend to output a good deal of information. We then import our CSV file and pipe it into the foreach cmdlet. The CSV file has the same format as used in listing 10.7. Within the foreach cmdlet, we use the New-QADObject to create the OUs as previously discussed. This time we use variables to represent the data coming along the pipeline rather than hard-coding the data.

One thing that's guaranteed in an administrator's life is that someone will ask for a report on whatever you're working on. At some stage, we'll be asked to produce a report detailing our OU structure.

TECHNIQUE 103   Listing OUs in a domain

OUs simplify our management of Active Directory, as they allow us to use the structure they create to restrict the number of objects we're working with at any one time. But in a large or complicated Active Directory domain, we may not be able to visualize the whole structure. We need to be able to produce a report detailing our OU structure.

PROBLEM

How can we create a report that lists all of the OUs in our domain? Ideally, we'd want the listing to be available onscreen or to be written into a file. The report should be formatted to enable the relationship between the OUs to be clearly seen. Figure 10.4 shows an example of the requirements.

SOLUTION

We know that we can use the [ADSI] type accelerator to get a directory entry for the domain; we also know we can access the children of the domain. This gives us the top-level OUs in the root of the domain. We then need to look in each OU and get any child OUs, and then look in those OUs for their child OUs, and so on. This could be solved in a brute-force approach, but a neater solution is to use recursion so that the function we use to get the children calls itself for each child OU, as in listing 10.8. This isn't as complicated as it sounds. Honest.

Listing 10.8   List OUs in a domain

```
Function DisplayOU{
param($strLDAP)                                    4  LDAP
                                                      string

    $item = [ADSI]"$strLDAP"                        5  Distinguished
    $disp =  $item.distinguishedName.ToString()        name
```

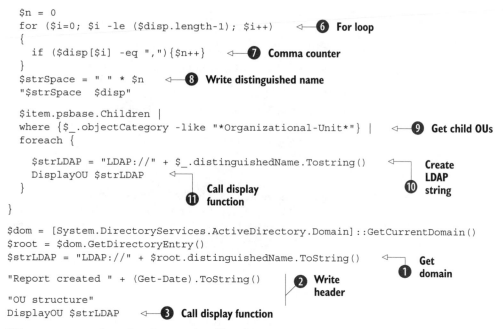

```
$n = 0
for ($i=0; $i -le ($disp.length-1); $i++)      ←  6  For loop
{
   if ($disp[$i] -eq ","){$n++}      ←  7  Comma counter
}
$strSpace = " " * $n      ←  8  Write distinguished name
"$strSpace   $disp"

$item.psbase.Children |
where {$_.objectCategory -like "*Organizational-Unit*"} |      ←  9  Get child OUs
foreach {

   $strLDAP = "LDAP://" + $_.distinguishedName.Tostring()   ←┐  Create
   DisplayOU $strLDAP   ←                                      │  LDAP
}                                  Call display                │ 10 string
}                               11  function

$dom = [System.DirectoryServices.ActiveDirectory.Domain]::GetCurrentDomain()
$root = $dom.GetDirectoryEntry()
$strLDAP = "LDAP://" + $root.distinguishedName.ToString()   ←┐  Get
                                                              1  domain
"Report created " + (Get-Date).ToString()   │ 2  Write
                                             │    header
"OU structure"                               │
DisplayOU $strLDAP   ←  3  Call display function
```

When we use a function in a script like this, we have to declare the function at the beginning of the script. It has to be this way; otherwise the following commands won't know what we're talking about when we make a call to the function. This is why the order of the annotation in the listing may seem odd, as I've started the annotation and discussion from the point at which the script starts processing.

The bulk of the script is taken up with the DisplayOU function. The script actually starts by using the GetCurrentDomain() static method of the .NET class System.DirectoryServices.ActiveDirectory.Domain. A directory entry is derived from this domain object and an LDAP string containing the distinguished name of the domain is created **1**. We can create a dated report by using Get-Date to retrieve the current date. The result is converted to a string **2** so that it can be written directly with the report header. A subheader of "OU Structure" is written out. PowerShell has the wonderful facility of treating a line with just a string as output that will be displayed to the console.

The LDAP string that we created earlier is now used as a parameter to our DisplayOU function **3**. The function starts by defining the incoming parameter **4**. This is used to create a directory entry and get the distinguished name **5**. One of the requirements was that we structured the report so that the relationship between the OUs was obvious. We achieve this by indenting child OUs with respect their parents, as shown in figure 10.4.

The indentation is controlled by the depth of the OU structure, which we measure by the number of commas in the distinguished name. A for loop **6** is used to look at each character in the distinguished name. A counter $n is incremented **7** if the character is a comma. The indentation spacing is created by creating a string of spaces

Hello World

One of the first examples that you'll see in many programming language books is a program to type out "Hello World." In PowerShell we can write such a program as follows:

```
'"Hello World"' > hw.ps1
```

The quoting is a little special for this. We have double quotes around the words *Hello World* and single quotes around the whole structure. This ensures that the double quotes are passed through into the script:

```
PS> cat .\hw.ps1
"Hello World"
```

This means that the text is treated as a string by PowerShell. If we didn't have the quotes, PowerShell would try to interpret *Hello* and *World* as PowerShell commands. This would cause a failure. Note that the quotes aren't echoed back to the command line:

```
PS> ./hw.ps1
Hello World
```

whose length matches the counter. This is then written out as a prefix to the distinguished name ❽.

The directory object that we created at the beginning of the function is then used to find the children of this OU ❾. Note how we use a `where` statement to restrict ourselves to organizational units. For each child OU, we create an LDAP string from the distinguished name ❿ and call our `DisplayOU` function with that string as a parameter ⓫. In this way, we'll iterate through the OU structure of the domain and produce an output like that in figure 10.4.

The way we use `GetCurrentDomain` to derive the domain name makes our script portable between domains. If we want to use the script to create the report as output that we can use later in a Word document, we could pipe the output into a text file:

```
./get-allou.ps1 | set-content reports\ou.txt
```

The script could also be enhanced to write the information directly into a Word document using the techniques we discovered in section 7.4.

DISCUSSION

Not to be outdone by scripting, the cmdlets can also be used to produce a similar result, as shown in listing 10.9.

Listing 10.9   List OUs in a domain using cmdlets

```
Get-QADObject -Type 'OrganizationalUnit' | Format-Table Name, DN -AutoSize
```

We can use `Get-QADObject` to return a list of the OUs in the domain. We need to use the `-Type` parameter to restrict the returned data to organizational units; otherwise we may get back a bit more data than we bargained for. The output of this cmdlet is

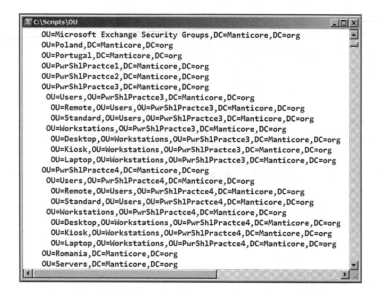

Figure 10.4   The output of all of the OUs in a domain produced as an indented list. The level of indenting is controlled by the depth of the OU structure so that the parent-child relationships are displayed correctly.

piped into `Format-Table` so that the name and the distinguished name (DN) can be displayed. It's slightly more work (but not impossible) to create an indented list similar to the previous listing. I'll leave that with you as tonight's homework assignment. With Windows Server 2008 R2, we could also use:

```
Get-ADOrganizationalUnit -Filter * | select DistinguishedName
```

An OU can contain various types of objects such as user accounts, computers, other OUs, groups, or email contacts. One common task we'll be faced with is discovering just what's in a particular OU.

TECHNIQUE 104   ## Discovering child objects

A number of years ago, I was involved in a migration from Novell Netware to Active Directory. The new user accounts had all been created in a holding OU; as the users actually moved across to be based in the AD environment (new workstations, home data migrated, and so forth), the accounts were moved into specific OUs. I was tasked with keeping track of the total numbers migrated—moved into the proper OUs—and was asked to produce a report. The report had to be run multiple times to make sure the project managers had the correct information, especially when it was time to bill the customer.

Rather than counting by hand, I wrote a script to perform this task. Unfortunately it was in the days before PowerShell. In a similar situation, I'd use the same approach, only this time I'd want to use PowerShell.

PROBLEM

We need to generate a report listing the objects in a particular OU. We also need to generate a count of the objects.

SOLUTION

This task could be performed by using ADUC, but using PowerShell is a more efficient process. We can adapt the scripts in the previous section to enumerate and count the objects in an OU, as in listing 10.10. The starting point for most administration scripts in Active Directory is creating a directory entry object ❶. In this script we're using `New-Object` and giving `DirectoryServices.DirectoryEntry` as the type of object we're creating. The LDAP string is accepted as the argument list to pass to the object constructor. We could've used `[ADSI]` instead of `New-Object`; it's a shortcut or accelerator for this process.

After creating the directory entry, we need to get the children of the object ❷. A `foreach` loop is used to iterate through the child objects ❸. We'll display the name and distinguished name of the object as we process each child object. A counter is also incremented.

At the end of the script, we display the number of objects in the OU ❹.

Listing 10.10   List OU contents

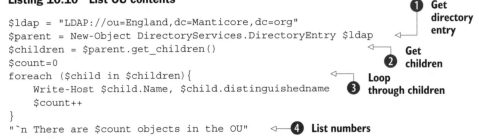

```
$ldap = "LDAP://ou=England,dc=Manticore,dc=org"
$parent = New-Object DirectoryServices.DirectoryEntry $ldap          ◄── ❶ Get
$children = $parent.get_children()              ◄── ❷ Get                directory
$count=0                                             children             entry
foreach ($child in $children){                  ◄── Loop
    Write-Host $child.Name, $child.distinguishedname  ❸ through children
        $count++
}
"`n There are $count objects in the OU"         ◄── ❹ List numbers
```

DISCUSSION

A similar result can be obtained by using the cmdlets, as in listing 10.11.

Listing 10.11   List OU contents using cmdlets

```
Get-QADObject -SearchRoot "ou=England,dc=manticore,dc=org"

(Get-QADObject -SearchRoot "ou=England,dc=manticore,dc=org").count
```

We're assuming that we don't know what types of objects are in the particular OU, so we use the `Get-QADObject` cmdlet rather than a specific user or computer cmdlet. The only parameter we need to supply is the OU of interest. The cmdlet displays name, type, and DN by default.

Alternatively we can use:

```
Get-ADObject -Filter * -SearchBase "ou=England,dc=manticore,dc=org"
| Format-Table Name, distinguishedname -AutoSize
```

Note the similarities and differences between the syntax. Tab expansion is useful to avoid tripping over these differences.

A count of the number of objects can be obtained by wrapping the previous line in parentheses. This treats the PowerShell commands inside as an object. We can then use the `count` property of the collection to tell us how many objects are in the OU.

MISMATCH The two methods shown in this section don't give identical results. When using the cmdlets, the count shows one more object than is present. This is because the cmdlet displays and counts the parent OU as part of the total.

A possible refinement to the scripts in this section would be to use the `Group-Object` cmdlet to produce a count of the number of each type of object in the OU.

TECHNIQUE 105   Moving an OU

Organizational units are designed to give us structure within our domains. This structure is flexible. We saw how to move user accounts between OUs in chapter 5 (technique 9).

PROBLEM

Can we extend the flexibility of OUs to move a whole OU, its contents, and the contents of any child OUs to a new parent?

SOLUTION

The wrapper that PowerShell puts round Active Directory objects hides the methods of these objects. But by using the .psbase qualifier, we can drill down into the base object. When we do this, we discover a `MoveTo()` method we can use to solve this problem.

The script in listing 10.12 starts by generating a directory object for the OU to which we're moving our target OU. We then generate a directory entry for the OU that we're moving. If you've run the examples under technique 103, you'll know that there are a number of child OUs under this OU.

We then use the `MoveTo()` method on the base object of our directory object to perform the move. The new parent OU is given as a parameter. The final line of the script writes a message informing us that the move has happened.

Listing 10.12   Move an OU

```
$newhome = [ADSI]"LDAP://OU=PwrShlPractce2,DC=Manticore,DC=org"
$ou = [ADSI]"LDAP://OU=Workstations,OU=PwrShlPractce3,DC=Manticore,DC=org"
$ou.psbase.MoveTo($newhome)
Write-Host "Moved OU"
```

DISCUSSION

The Quest cmdlets don't have a specific cmdlet for working with OUs, so we use the `Move-QADObject` cmdlet in listing 10.13. The `-Identity` parameter supplies the OU that'll be moved and the `-NewParentContainer` supplies the place to which it'll be moved. If it's possible to use an Active Directory provider in the environment, for example that from the PowerShell Community Extensions, we can use `Move-Item` to perform the move.

Listing 10.13   Move an OU with cmdlets

```
Move-QADObject -Identity "ou=users,ou=PwrShlPractce3,dc=manticore,dc=org"
-NewParentContainer "ou=PwrShlPractce1,dc=manticore,dc=org"
```

In Windows Server 2008 R2, we need to deal with the `ProtectedFromAccidental-Deletion` setting:

```
Set-ADOrganizationalUnit -ProtectedFromAccidentalDeletion $false
-Identity "OU=Child1,OU=PwrShlPractce3,DC=Manticore,DC=org"

Move-ADObject -Identity "OU=Child1,OU=PwrShlPractce3,DC=Manticore,DC=org"
-TargetPath "OU=PwrShlPractce1,DC=Manticore,DC=org"

Set-ADOrganizationalUnit -ProtectedFromAccidentalDeletion $true
-Identity "OU=Child1,OU=PwrShlPractce1,DC=Manticore,DC=org"
```

A move can be thought of as copying and deleting the original. We need to remove the protection from the source, perform the move, and put the protection back onto the OU in its target location.

The last act in the lifecycle of an OU is its deletion. This is also the last task we'll consider in this section of the chapter.

TECHNIQUE 106   Deleting an OU

Over the lifetime of an Active Directory installation, OUs will come and go as the needs of the organization cause reorganizations within the domain. When an OU is empty and will remain empty for the foreseeable future, it's time to remove it from the directory. Simple housekeeping of this sort can go a long way to making our Active Directory installations easier to manage.

PROBLEM

We no longer require a particular OU. How can we delete the object and any child objects (including other OUs)?

SOLUTION

Our directory entry object has a method we can use to perform this task. We start by creating a directory entry object for the OU in question using the [ADSI] type accelerator. As we've seen previously, using Get-Member on these objects doesn't show any methods, but if we use .psbase we can see a DeleteTree() method. A quick check of the documentation shows this will do exactly what we want.

> **WARNING**   At this point, we need to stop and double-check that we're deleting the correct OU. Wiping out an OU with lots of active users isn't recommended. It doesn't take long to realize the magnitude of such as mistake. This is one place where a strong change control system can really help you.

The DeleteTree() method is used to remove the OU and all child objects, as in listing 10.14. In PowerShell v2, you don't need the psbase. You can access the method directly even though it still doesn't show when Get-Member is performed on the object.

Listing 10.14   Delete an OU

```
$ou = [ADSI]"LDAP://OU=PwrShlPractce4,DC=Manticore,DC=org"
$ou.psbase.DeleteTree()
```

DISCUSSION

We can also use the AD cmdlets to perform the activity, as in listing 10.15.

Listing 10.15 Delete an OU using cmdlets

```
Remove-QADObject `
-Identity "OU=PwrShlPractce3,DC=Manticore,DC=org" `
-DeleteTree

Warning!
Are you sure you want to delete this object and its children:
    OU=PwrShlPractce3,DC=Manticore,DC=org?
[Y] Yes  [A] Yes to All  [N] No
[L] No to All  [S] Suspend  [?] Help
(default is "Y"):
```

In this case, we do get a warning and we're asked to confirm the action, which is a useful bonus. Windows Server 2008 has a way of helping relieve some of the risk around this activity, which we'll see in section 10.5. This has to be removed before we can delete the OU. We also are asked to confirm the deletion:

```
Set-ADOrganizationalUnit -ProtectedFromAccidentalDeletion $false
-Identity "OU=PwrShlPractce3,DC=Manticore,DC=org"

Remove-ADOrganizationalUnit -Identity "OU=PwrShlPractce3,DC=Manticore,DC=org"
```

This has completed our journey around the OU lifecycle. It's time to move on to looking at GPOs and how we can use PowerShell to help administer this powerful aspect of our Active Directory.

10.4 Group Policies

Administrators view Group Policies as the way that they configure, control, and manage the machines in an Active Directory environment. Parts of the user population may view them more as a "Big Brother" that stops them from doing what they want. GPOs (Group Policy Objects) are an essential part of managing a Windows infrastructure.

There are literally thousands of settings that are available for configuration through Group Policy. Don't worry; I'm not going to list them here. This section is more about how we can use PowerShell to help us manage out Group Policies. Before we can use PowerShell with our Group Policies, we need to install extras into PowerShell.

SDM Software produces a number of free snapins for working with Group Policies. These products are available from http://www.sdmsoftware.com/freeware.php. The basic Group Policy snapins needs Group Policy Management Console (GPMC) to be loaded, as it works with the APIs made available by the GPMC. After the installation routine has run, the snapins can be added to PowerShell with:

```
Add-PSsnapin SDMSoftware.PowerShell.GPMC
```

Other cmdlets are available for testing group health and invoking Group Policy updates. The GPMC cmdlets don't give us the facility to script the contents of our Group Policies, though that feature is available in a commercial offering.

Windows Server 2008 R2 introduces a set of cmdlets from Microsoft for working with Group Policy. They're available as a module so need to be loaded:

```
Import-Module GroupPolicy
Get-Command -Module GroupPolicy
```

These R2 cmdlets match the SDM cmdlets for functionality, more or less. Similar recommendations apply as with the AD cmdlets: use the R2 cmdlets with Windows Server 2008 R2 and the SDM cmdlets with other platforms.

The first step in working with Group Policies is creating a new policy.

TECHNIQUE 107   Creating a GPO

Getting a GPO into use so that we can use it to manage our systems is a three-stage process:

1 Create the GPO.
2 Configure the settings to achieve our goal.
3 Link the GPO to one or more OUs.

The free GPO cmdlets can't help us with the second stage, but they can help with the first and third stages. We'll look at linking GPOs in the next section, but first, how can we create them?

PROBLEM
We want to quickly create a new GPO so that we can get started on configuring the new policy. Ideally we want to be able to make use of the starter GPO functionality in Windows Server 2008.

SOLUTION
The SDM GPMC cmdlets provide a way to achieve this goal quickly, as in listing 10.16.

Listing 10.16   Create a GPO

```
New-SDMgpo -Name "PowershellinPractice"
```

DISCUSSION
The New-SDMgpo cmdlet is used to create a new GPO. The verb *New* is used any time we need to create something. The only parameter we need is the name of the new GPO. We can create our GPO from scratch, or in Windows Server 2008 we can give the name of a starter GPO and use that as a template.

In Windows Server 2008 R2 we have a similar syntax:

```
New-GPO -Name "PowerShellinPractice" -Comment "Test GPO creation"
```

Once we've created our GPO, we can modify the settings and then we need to link it to an OU.

TECHNIQUE 108   Linking a GPO

A GPO can be linked to a number of Active Directory containers—domain, site, and OU. Usual practice is link to an OU. The settings are then applied to all child OUs unless deliberately blocked. Blocking can be overridden, but then we get into the realms of MCSE exam questions with messy diagrams so we won't go there. It's possible to link a GPO to many OUs and have many GPOs linked to a single OU.

PROBLEM

Linking a GPO to a single OU is straightforward if we do it in the GUI just after creating the settings. If we want to link it to a number of OUs, can we find a more efficient way of performing this task?

SOLUTION

We can simply link a cmdlet by using the `Add-SDMgplink` cmdlet as shown in listing 10.17. The name of the GPO is required (otherwise we don't know what we're linking). The `-Scope` parameter indicated the OU to which we'll link the GPO.

It gets confusing when we consider the `-Location` parameter, as it sounds as if it means the same as the scope—where we're applying the GPO. The location actually refers to the GPO's order in the list of GPOs to be applied to that particular OU, where 1 is the top of the list and -1 is the bottom.

Listing 10.17 Link a GPO

```
Add-SDMgplink -Name "PowershellinPractice"
-Scope "OU=PwrShlPractce1,DC=Manticore,DC=org" -Location 1
```

DISCUSSION

The script as presented will apply a single GPO to a single OU. The 2008 R2 equivalent is:

```
New-GPLink -Name PowerShellinPractice
-Target "OU=PwrShlPractce1,DC=Manticore,DC=org" -LinkEnabled Yes
```

If we want to apply the same GPO to multiple OUs we can create a CSV file with the list of OUs (remember cut and paste) and read it using `Import-Csv`. The data can be passed into a `foreach` cmdlet that calls `Add-SDMgplink`. We've seen this technique in a number of places, and it's one we'll keep returning to, as it's very useful.

At some stage we'll be asked to unlink the GPO, as in listing 10.18. This doesn't delete the GPO, but only stops it acting on the particular part of our directory.

Listing 10.18 Unlink a GPO

```
Remove-SDMgplink -Name "PowershellinPractice" `
-Scope "OU=PwrShlPractce1,DC=Manticore,DC=org"
```

We use `Remove-SDMgplink` and supply the name of the GPO and the OU from which we want to remove the link. Our R2 alternative is:

```
Remove-GPLink -Name PowerShellinPractice
-Target "OU=PwrShlPractce1,DC=Manticore,DC=org"
```

If we want to delete the GPO, we can use `Remove-SDMgpo` as shown in listing 10.19, which will delete the GPO. This has the effect of unlinking as well.

Listing 10.19 Delete a GPO

```
Remove-SDMgpo -Name "PowershellinPractice"
```

This cmdlet will ask for confirmation of the action. The two cmdlets have similar names, so be careful if using Tab completion! We have a similar alternative in R2:

```
Remove-GPO -Name PowerShellinPractice
```

Now that we've seen how to create and link GPOs, we need to consider how we can report on the GPOs being applied in our directory.

TECHNIQUE 109   ## Listing GPOs

A list of the GPOs that exist in the domain can be produced by running one of these commands (*SDM* first followed by the Microsoft cmdlet):

```
Get-SDMgpo -Name *
Get-GPO -All | Select DisplayName
```

A slightly more useful report can be produced by examining the list of GPOs linked to a particular OU:

```
Get-SDMgplink -Scope "OU=Finland,DC=Manticore,DC=org"
```

> **NOT RSOP** These reports don't give you a Resultant Set of Policy report. That needs to be generated explicitly. There are cmdlets in the toolkit to perform this task.

This would have to be repeated for every single OU in the domain to get the full picture of GPO deployment.

PROBLEM

Our task is to display the GPOs that are linked to the domain OUs. The output should reflect the OU structure.

SOLUTION

We can modify the script we saw in technique 103 to produce listing 10.20, which will list the OUs in the domain and the linked GPOs.

Listing 10.20   List GPO links by OU

```
#Requires -Version 2.0
Function DisplayOU{
param($strLDAP)
    $item = [ADSI]"$strLDAP"
    $disp =  $item.distinguishedName.ToString()        ⬅  ❻ Get distinguished
                                                            name
    $n = 0
    for ($i=0; $i -le ($disp.length-1); $i++)
    {
        if ($disp[$i] -eq ",") {$n++}
    }
    $strSpace = " " * ($n+1)          ❼ Display              Get linked  ❽
    "$strSpace    $disp"          ⬅    OU name                GPOs

    $linked = $item.gpLink.ToString() -split "[",0,"simplematch"    ⬅

    foreach ($link in $linked){
        if ($link.length -gt 1 ) {
        $gpopath = $link -split ";"
```

```
        $gponame = $gpos[$gpopath[0].Replace("LDAP://","")]

        $gpocount[$gponame] ++

        "$strSpace    $gponame"          <-- 9 Display GPO names
    }
}

$item.psbase.Children |
where {$_.objectCategory -like "*Organizational-Unit*"} | foreach {

  $strLDAP = "LDAP://" + $_.distinguishedName.Tostring()
  DisplayOU $strLDAP                          <-- 10 Recursive call
}
}

$gpos = @{}                           <-- 1 Create hash tables
$gpocount = @{}
Get-SDMgpo * | Foreach {              <-- 2 Get GPO list
  $gpos += @{$_.Path = $_.Name}
  $gpocount += @{$_.Name = 0}
}

$dom =
[System.DirectoryServices.ActiveDirectory.Domain]::
GetCurrentDomain()
$root = $dom.GetDirectoryEntry()                  <-- 3 Get domain

$strLDAP = "LDAP://" + $root.distinguishedName.ToString()     <-- 4 Create LDAP string

"Report created " + (Get-Date).ToString()
"GPO Links"
DisplayOU $strLDAP        <-- 5 Call display function

""
"GPO linkage table"                               <-- 11 Display the GPO links
"The following GPOs are NOT linked if the value is zero"
$gpocount
```

This script builds on listing 10.8, so we'll concentrate on the additions to produce the GPO listing. We start by creating a couple of hash tables ❶. They'll hold the list of GPO names ❷ together with their paths and the number of times they're applied, respectively. The reason for these objects will become apparent in a while. After getting a directory entry for the domain ❸, we create the LDAP string for the domain name ❹, write out some header information, and call our display function ❺. This immediately gets the distinguished name of the object ❻ and produces an indented listing of the OU names ❼ as we've seen previously.

> **ANNOTATION** The annotation order may appear odd in listing 10.20 due to the necessity of the function being declared before the main body of the script. The annotation follows the way the script works when it's run.

We now start on the GPOs. The OU directory entry object has a property called `gplink` that holds the GPOs linked to this OU. We can create a collection of the GPOs by using the `split` operator ❽. The `simplematch` parameter has to be used to prevent a regular expression match.

POWERSHELL VERSION 2   This script is written with PowerShell v2 so that the `-split` operator could be used. If you're using v1 then use the `split()` method on the string. The `#Requires -Version 2.0` statement will ensure that the script doesn't run on a v1 installation. This line must be removed if you're modifying the script for PowerShell v1.

A `foreach` is used to iterate through the list of linked GPOs. After testing that there's data in the link string, we perform another split on the GPO path and remove the front part of the path (`LDAP://`). The counter is incremented (++ means increase by one) and we display the GPO name ❾. The script progresses by getting the child OUs and calling the `displayOU` ❿ function for each of them.

The final part of the script displays the number of times each GPO is linked ⓫. The bonus part of the script is that we can easily see any GPOs that aren't linked so that they can be removed, or we can investigate why they aren't linked. An admin's work is never done.

DISCUSSION

If we were using the 2008 R2 Group Policy cmdlets, we could replace `Get-SDMGPO *` with `Get-GPO -All` in listing 10.20.

We can't perform exactly the same operation just using cmdlets, but we can come close. The code is shown in listing 10.21. It uses the SDM Software cmdlets

Listing 10.21   List GPO links by OU using cmdlets

```
Clear-Host
"Domain links"
Get-SDMgplink -Scope "dc=manticore,dc=org" |        ◁━❶ Domain links
   Format-Table Name, Enforced, Enabled -AutoSize

Get-QADObject -Type 'OrganizationalUnit' | Foreach {   ◁━❷ OU links
    "`nOU - $_"
    Get-SDMgplink -Scope $_.DN |
      Format-Table Name, Enforced, Enabled -AutoSize
}
```

The `Get-SDMgplink` cmdlet will show us the GPOs linked to a single OU as we've already seen. We deliberately clear the screen and write out a header before retrieving a list of the GPOs linked to the domain ❶. We can display additional information showing whether the GPO is enabled and/or configured to override a block.

The domain OUs are found using `Get-QADObject` with the type set to organizational unit. The `Foreach` statement ❷ will use the distinguished name of the OU to define the scope for displaying the GPOs.

Our alternative code uses the R2 cmdlets:

```
Get-GPInheritance -Target "ou=Greece,dc=manticore,dc=org"   |
Format-Table Path, GpoLinks, InheritedGpoLinks -Wrap

Get-ADOrganizationalUnit -Filter * | foreach {
    "`n OU $_.DistinguishedName "
    Get-GPInheritance -Target $_.DistinguishedName |
    Format-Table Path, GpoLinks, InheritedGpoLinks -Wrap
}
```

When considering GPOs, the last point we may need to think about is discovering where a particular GPO is linked. Listing 10.22 gets the list of GPOs, and for each of them, discovers where that GPO is linked.

Listing 10.22   List GPO links by GPO

```
Get-SDMgpo * | foreach {
    "`nGPO: $($_.Name) is linked to:"
    Get-SDMgplink -Name $_.Name |
     Format-Table Path, GPOInheritanceBlocked -AutoSize
}
```

Surprisingly, it doesn't seem possible to perform this action using the R2 cmdlets. The only way I can think to get that information is to run the reports in the next section, but produce an XML output, then extract the information from the XML. Messy!

We've seen how we can use PowerShell to discover how our GPOs are linked in the domain. The next step to understanding the environment is discovering what those GPOs are actually doing.

TECHNIQUE 110   **Listing GPO contents**

The easiest way to view the settings applied by a particular GPO is to run a report. It's not feasible to trawl through the thousands of settings checking each one, especially when we only need to know the configured settings. Reports can be created using the GPMC. Opening the GPMC and running a report for every GPO can be tedious, though.

PROBLEM

How can we create a report for every GPO in our domain that shows the configured settings? Ideally we'd like the solution to be adaptable so that the settings for only a single GPO are reported.

SOLUTION

We already know how to get a list of the GPOs in the domain. The cmdlets work with the GPMC, and there's a cmdlet that creates a settings report. Our script starts by using Get-Location to determine the path to the current folder. If required, a specific path could be entered instead.

We use Get-SDMgpo to return the list of GPOs, as shown in listing 10.23. For each GPO, we create a filename to hold the report and use Out-SDMgpSettingsReport to create the report. The ReportHTML parameter causes the report to be rendered as HTML. If this parameter isn't used, the report will be produced in XML.

Listing 10.23   List GPO contents

```
$here = (get-location).path
Get-SDMgpo -Name * | foreach {
    $file = $here + "\" + $_.Name.Tostring() +".htm"
    Out-SDMgpsettingsreport -Name $_.Name -FileName $file -ReportHTML
}
```

DISCUSSION

A sample report is shown in figure 10.5.

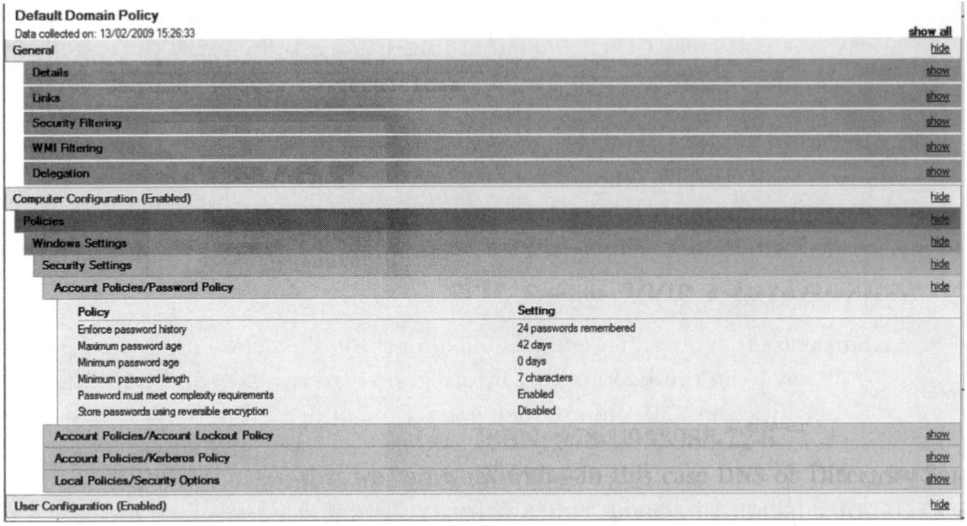

Figure 10.5 A report on the contents of the Default Domain Policy rendered in HTML.

The same report can be produced in Windows Server 2008 R2 using:

```
Get-GPO -All | foreach {
    $file = "d:\scripts\gpo\$($_.Displayname).htm"
    Get-GPOReport -Name $_.Displayname -ReportType HTML -Path $file
}
```

The SDM and Microsoft cmdlets and their parameters have slightly different names, but they're similar enough to work out what's happening. The results are the same in either case.

This is a simple way to produce a record of the settings of your GPOs. The script could easily be run on a periodic basis to preserve a record of any changes. This script is an ideal companion to the next script, in that a backup of the GPO at a point in time and a record of the settings could be produced together.

TECHNIQUE 111 **GPO backup**

GPOs will be backed up as part of the Active Directory backup regime. But there may be cause to create a backup for a specific purpose such as preserving a record of changes or for transferring the GPO settings to a test environment for further development work.

Mergers and acquisitions are a major source of changes to Active Directory configurations. It's possible that such activity will involve the transfer of GPOs between domains.

PROBLEM

We need to generate a backup of our GPO settings so that they can be applied in another domain for testing purposes.

SOLUTION

We start by generating a list of GPOs as shown in listing 10.24. Get-SDMgpo expects the name of a GPO. If we want all GPOs, we need to use * as a wildcard. The GPOs are piped into Export-SDMgpo, which will create a backup in the given folder.

Listing 10.24   Backup GPOs

```
Get-SDMgpo * | Export-SDMgpo -Location "C:\gpobackup"
```

DISCUSSION

When you look at the backup folder, you'll see a subfolder for each GPO. It'll be named using the GUID of the GPO, which isn't very user friendly. The backups in the folder can be viewed by using:

```
Get-SDMgpo * | Get-SDMgpoBackups -Location "c:\gpobackup"
```

which will retrieve the available backups for each GPO. We can use Import-SDMgpo to restore one or more GPOs.

Windows Server 2008 R2 provides similar functionality:

```
Backup-GPO -All -Path d:\scripts\gpo
```

Restore-GPO can be used to restore the settings. Now that we know how to protect our GPOs, we should look at protecting the rest of the Active Directory data and look at how we can restore objects that get deleted.

10.5   *Protection and recovery*

Our backup regime should be the primary protection and recovery mechanism for Active Directory. This includes standard backup tools as well as third-party Active Directory tools that enable recovery without performing an authoritative restore.

There two things we can do to protect our Active Directory data or make it easier for us to recover individual objects that get deleted. Protection from accidental deletion is a technique that reduces the risk of the wrong object being deleted, and the ability to access AD tombstone records means we can restore objects that have been deleted without having to perform an authoritative restore.

TECHNIQUE 112   **Protection from accidental deletion**

In technique 106, we looked at how we can delete an OU and its contents. In chapter 5, we learned how to delete individual user accounts and groups.

One definition of *automation* is that it's the mechanism by which we make mistakes at a faster rate. We need to ensure that we don't fall into that situation. Thinking back to technique 106, we don't want to be in the situation where we hit Enter to run our script and then think "Oops, didn't mean to delete PwrShlPractce4" or words to that effect. Even the best of admins make mistakes, and a mistake of this sort means we have to perform an authoritative restore with all of the pain involved in that activity—unless we know how to protect ourselves from this scenario.

Windows Server 2008 introduced a feature into Active Directory known as *Protection from Accidental Deletion*. It should be known as the AD admin's best friend. There's a tick box on the object tab in an AD object's properties that allows this to be set (Advanced features must be selected from the View menu). Don't go searching for the property related to this because there isn't one. As an aside, that would make a good interview question...

Selecting the tick box causes the security settings on the object to be changed so that the Delete permission is denied to the Everyone group. This is great, but—and it's a big but from the administrator's view point—the settings are only made on that object. They don't flow to any child objects. This leaves us with a lot of clicking to do in ADUC.

PROBLEM

How can we set Protection from Accidental Deletion on all of the objects in an OU?

SOLUTION

We need to modify the security settings on the individual objects so that they're protected from accidental deletion, as shown in listing 10.25. This may look complicated, but when we break it down, it's quite logical. The starting point is the parent OU. We need the directory entry object for it, so we use the [ADSI] type accelerator to create it for us. The security information is held in the `ObjectSecurity` property, which we get next ❶. We know that we need to deny the `delete` and `DeleteTree` permissions to solve this problem. The `System.Security.AccessControl.AccessControlType` and the `System.DirectoryServices.ActiveDirectoryRights` enumerations hold the relevant values. Variables are created ❷ to hold these values, which will make the rest of the script easier to read.

Listing 10.25   Protect from accidental deletion

```
$ou = [ADSI]"LDAP://ou=Thunderbirds,dc=manticore,dc=org"    ❶ Get OU security
$sec = $ou.psbase.ObjectSecurity                              settings

$act = [System.Security.AccessControl.AccessControlType]::Deny
$adrights = [System.DirectoryServices.ActiveDirectoryRights]::Delete
$adrights2 = [System.DirectoryServices.ActiveDirectoryRights]::DeleteTree

$who = New-Object -TypeName System.Security.Principal.NTAccount
-ArgumentList "", "Everyone"

$newrule1 = New-Object -TypeName `                       Who does
System.DirectoryServices.ActiveDirectoryAccessRule `    this apply to ❸
-ArgumentList $who, $adrights, $act

$sec.AddAccessRule($newrule1)                            Set rights and
$ou.psbase.CommitChanges()       ❹ Stop delete          control type ❷

$newrule2 = New-Object -TypeName `
System.DirectoryServices.ActiveDirectoryAccessRule `
-ArgumentList $who, $adrights2, $act

$sec.AddAccessRule($newrule2)
$ou.psbase.CommitChanges()       ❺ Stop deletetree
```

```
$ou = [ADSI]"LDAP://ou=Thunderbirds,dc=manticore,dc=org"
foreach ($child in $ou.psbase.children)
{
  $user = [ADSI]$child
  $sec = $user.psbase.ObjectSecurity

  $sec.AddAccessRule($newrule1)
  $user.psbase.CommitChanges()

  $sec.AddAccessRule($newrule2)
  $user.psbase.CommitChanges()
}
```

Refresh
6 OU object

7 Apply to
child objects

Having decided that we'll deny the `delete` and `deletetree` permissions, the next step is to decide who'll be denied this permission **3**. We create a new object of type `System.Security.Principal.NTAccount` to define to whom these permissions will be assigned. The target is the Active Directory group Everyone.

> **EVERYONE** Using the group Everyone really does mean that these permissions are applied to everyone. You'll be told you don't have permissions to perform the deletion even if you explicitly log on with Domain Admin credentials.

The permissions are applied as Active Directory access rules using the `System.DirectoryServices.ActiveDirectoryAccessRule` class **4**. The arguments represent who it'll be applied to (Everyone), the rights (Delete), and action (Deny). The changes are then saved using `CommitChanges()`. Permissions are applied singly, so we have to repeat for the `DeleteTree` permission **5**. Note that we're adding the rules to the `ObjectSecurity` property.

DISCUSSION

Protection from Accidental Deletion is now set on the OU, and if you open ADUC and look at the object tab, you should see that the protection box is ticked.

> **DISCOVERY** I worked out how to do this by starting at the end point. I knew I needed to apply an access rule and found the .NET class to perform that action. Looking at the information it needed, I worked backward to understand how to create each piece of data. The .NET documentation explains the type of each piece of data, which is a good starting point for working out how to use it and leads you to the relevant .NET class.

We've protected the OU, but we haven't protected the objects in the OU. We'll start by refreshing the OU object **6**, just in case someone has sneaked a few new users in while we were concentrating on the OU. The child objects of the OU are held in the `children` collection. We can use a `foreach` loop to iterate through these objects, get the `ObjectSecurity` collection for each, and add the rules **7**. We've already created the rules in the previous part of the script, so it's a simple matter of reusing the objects.

> **WARNING** Using Protection from Accidental Deletion won't stop a rogue administrator from manually unsetting the protection and deleting something.

One thing I've noticed is that sometimes when this script is run, it appears not to have worked. The protection tick box on the object tab isn't set. If you go into any object in the OU and manually set the tick box, all of the other objects will have it set. Likewise, if you run the script in an OU where one or more objects already have this set, the tick box is set properly.

`Set-ADObject` in Windows Server 2008 R2 has a `-ProtectedFromAccidental-Deletion` parameter that can be used to protect objects:

```
Get-ADObject -SearchBase "OU=Thunderbirds,DC=Manticore,DC=org"
-Filter {ObjectClass -eq "user"} | foreach {
    Set-ADObject -ProtectedFromAccidentalDeletion $true
      -Identity $_.DistinguishedName
}
```

We can easily test whether the object is protected:

```
Get-ADObject -SearchBase "OU=Thunderbirds,DC=Manticore,DC=org"
-Filter {ObjectClass -eq "user"}
-properties ProtectedFromAccidentalDeletion |
Format-Table Name, ProtectedFromAccidentalDeletion -AutoSize
```

Note that we have to explicitly include the `ProtectedFromAccidentalDeletion` property. In my opinion, the ease of invoking this protection makes a strong case for upgrading to be able to use these cmdlets. The next section only reinforces this thought as we think about restoring deleted objects.

TECHNIQUE 113   Object recovery

Active Directory doesn't make an object immediately disappear when we delete it. The object hangs around for a while in a sort of limbo state known as a *tombstone*—morbid but I didn't choose it. This tombstone object can be restored (or reanimated) if the tombstone period hasn't expired. This gives us 60 or 180 days depending on the version of Windows used to first install Active Directory. Once the tombstone period has expired, the tombstoned object is purged from Active Directory.

> **ACTIVE DIRECTORY RECYCLE BIN**   Windows Server 2008 R2 introduces the recycle bin to Active Directory. The bin holds deleted objects for a period equal to the tombstone period before actually performing the tombstone actions. During their time in the recycle bin, objects can be restored, with all their attributes, using native PowerShell cmdlets.

Why should we bother restoring a deleted object? Why not just create a new object with the same name? The problem is that Windows doesn't necessarily work on the name of the object. It's more likely to work with the SID. This is especially true when dealing with access permissions.

PROBLEM

Our problem is how to reanimate a tombstoned object in Active Directory.

SOLUTION

The solution problem is to use the tombstone cmdlets from SDM Software, as shown in listing 10.26.

Listing 10.26 Restore a tombstoned object

```
Get-SDMADTombstone | Where {$_.cn -like "*pig*"} | Restore-SDMADTombstone
```

DISCUSSION

Compared to some of the scripts we've seen in this chapter, this probably seems an anticlimax, but it's a powerful and useful tool for the AD administrator.

> **RECOMMENDATION** It's possible to perform this task using the System. DirectoryServices.Protocols classes directly in PowerShell. These classes aren't well documented and work differently than the .NET classes we've seen in the book. I really recommend using these cmdlets to perform this task.

There are two cmdlets in the SDMSoftware.PowerShell.AD.Tombstones snapins:

- Get-SDMADTombstone
- Restore-SDMADTombstone

For our experiment in using the tombstone cmdlets, we'll call on the assistance of Mr. Guinea Pigge. His account resides in OU=Test,DC=Manticore,DC=org and the object name is CN=PIGGE Guinea.

If we use Get-SDMADTombstone without any filters, we'll get back more data than we want to deal with. Think how many accounts, groups, computers and so on were deleted from your AD over the last two or six months! The simplest filter to apply is based on the common name as shown. When an object is tombstoned, the common name changes so we use -like to allow partial matches. If more than one object is returned, the filter can be refined using additional filters in the where script block. A comparison on when it was deleted is a good option.

Once we've narrowed the search to a single object, we can pipe it into Restore-SDMADTombstone. This will restore the object to the container it was deleted from, which is stored in the tombstoned object's LastKnownParent property. If that container has been deleted as well then we need to restore the container before restoring the object.

One issue is that the tombstoned object has most of its properties stripped away. This means that when we restore it, we need to recreate this data. The options are recreating manually based on knowledge of the object, or if we're in a Windows Server 2008 Active Directory, mounting a snapshot backup and copying the data onto the restored object.

The latest version of the Quest AD cmdlets also include the capability of restoring a tombstoned object using Restore-QADDeletedObject. In a Windows Server 2008 R2 environment with the AD recycle bin enabled, it'll restore from the recycle bin.

The Microsoft R2 cmdlets also can restore from the recycle bin:

```
Get-ADObject -Filter {(isdeleted -eq $true) -and (Name -like "*pigge*")}
-IncludeDeletedObjects -Properties * | Restore-ADObject
```

With this cmdlet, remember to use -Properties *; otherwise only the skeleton of the object will be restored and the attributes will have to be populated another way.

10.6   *Summary*

Our Active Directory structure has a medium volatility but a medium-to-high impact on the directory as a whole. The two main areas we deal with in this chapter are organizational units and GPOs. OUs are fundamental to the structure of our domain. Managing their lifecycle through PowerShell gives us the ability to quickly and easily add a new standard subunit to our domain. Extending our knowledge from chapter 5 enables us to view and work with the child objects of an OU. This includes traversing the entire OU structure if necessary.

GPOs are a main part of our ability to control our environment. Using the GPMC cmdlets, we can control their lifecycle using PowerShell. The huge number of settings available to us makes an efficient reporting mechanism vital. The HTML reports we produce can be easily viewed outside PowerShell, making them ideal for distribution.

The schema holds very useful information. We can make modifications that make our GUI tools easier to use.

One scenario we need to avoid is accidentally deleting data from Active Directory. We can use the security permissions on Active Directory objects to prevent this occurrence. Windows Server 2008 gives this option via the GUI, whereas the techniques we've seen enable us to apply it to Windows Server 2003-based Active Directory as well. We can also recover tombstoned objects through PowerShell.

In chapter 11, we'll continue our examination of how we can administer Active Directory by looking at the lowest layer of our triangle. We'll look at the Active Directory topology with sites, subnets, and site links all under the microscope. Domain controllers are a crucial aspect of Active Directory and will also be examined.

Active Directory topology

11

This chapter covers
- Discovering and managing domain controllers and global catalogs
- Working with Active Directory sites and subnets
- Administering Active Directory site links and replication schedules

This chapter discusses how we can automate the administration of our Active Directory topology. The topology is composed of the physical aspects of Active Directory:

- Domain controllers
- Sites
- Subnets
- Site links

These are the aspects that control the Active Directory service, as opposed to the Active Directory data we looked at in chapters 5 and 10. In terms of figure 10.1, this chapter is all about those objects at the bottom of the diagram—low volatility but potentially a huge impact if mistakes are made.

PRODUCTION FOREST   Don't experiment with these techniques in a production forest. This is the ideal scenario for utilizing your favorite virtualization technology such as VMware, Hyper-V, or Xen.

Replication latency must be taken into account when working at this level in Active Directory. The changes must have time to replicate to the required domain controllers before they become effective and usable. If the wait for replication becomes too long, we can always force it to happen. This is explained in technique 119. It's all right if you want to peek before we get there.

The scripts in this chapter will use the .NET classes we discussed in section 3.4. The available AD cmdlets are more suited to working with the data within Active Directory, as we saw in chapters 5 and 10.

PERMISSIONS   Many of the scripts in this chapter work at the forest level. In order for them to run successfully, you'll need to start PowerShell with an account that has Enterprise Admin privileges or Domain Admin privileges in a few cases.

What's involved in automating the administration of our Active Directory topology?

11.1   *Automating AD topology administration*

This chapter uses a number of concepts involving the Active Directory topology. *Domain controllers* are the servers that host and control Active Directory. *Sites* are used to control replication between domain controllers, as well as which domain controllers a user will use for authentication.

Active Directory *subnets* define the range of IP addresses available within a site. They're used by clients to determine site membership. The final elements in the topology are *site links*, which are used to control replication between domain controllers in different sites.

The .NET classes we'll be using are part of the `System.DirectoryServices.` `ActiveDirectory` namespace. These classes are specifically created for administering Active Directory. PowerShell automatically loads these classes for you as part of the `System.DirectoryServices` assembly. The assemblies loaded by PowerShell can be viewed by using:

```
[appdomain]::currentdomain.getassemblies() |
 sort -property fullname | format-table fullname
```

The scripts follow a few similar patterns. We get the current forest, or domain, and work with the data. Alternatively, we need to derive a forest (or domain) context and use that to create objects for our sites, subnets, or site links.

We'll use fewer of the AD cmdlets in this chapter compared to chapters 5 and 10. The cmdlets are geared to working with Active Directory data such as users, computers, and groups rather than the topology.

Administrators work with Active Directory via domain controllers. Users need domain controllers to authenticate. This makes domain controllers crucial to our

Active Directory, so they're the best place to start learning how to use PowerShell with this part of Active Directory.

11.2 Domain controllers

Domain controllers are the servers that host Active Directory. They have to be available, and discoverable, for users to log on to the network and access their resources. We'll use PowerShell to work with, and configure, domain controllers.

> **DOMAIN CONTROLLER PROMOTION**   One task we won't try to perform using PowerShell is promoting a member server to be a domain controller. That task is still reserved for the `dcpromo` utility, though the scripts presented in the book can be utilized to configure the server prior to promotion.

The first thing we need to do with our Active Directory is to find the domain controllers.

TECHNIQUE 114   Discovering domain controllers

This is an essential task in its own right, but is also the foundation for a number of subsequent tasks.

> **Number of domain controllers**
>
> One question that comes with depressing regularity on the forums is, "My only domain controller has failed and I don't have any backups. What can I do?"
>
> The kindest answer is usually along the lines of "Make sure your résumé is up to date."
>
> All production domains should have a minimum of two DCs. This can be ignored for a test domain if you can afford to lose it!

Now that we know what we should have, we need to see if this is the case.

PROBLEM

We need to be able to find the domain controllers in our Active Directory domain so that we can work with them in our scripts.

SOLUTION

Domain controllers belong to a domain. If we create an object for the domain, we'll be able to discover our domain controllers. The `System.DirectoryServices.Active-Directory.Domain` class has a static method that enables us to create an object for the current domain, as in listing 11.1.

Listing 11.1   Discover domain controllers

```
$dom =
[System.DirectoryServices.ActiveDirectory.Domain]::
GetCurrentDomain()
$dom.FindAllDomainControllers() |
 select Name, SiteName, IPAddress | Format-Table
```

We can then use the `FindAllDomainControllers()` method to discover the domain controllers. A `select` and `Format-Table` are used to create a tabular display. The `Format-Table` cmdlet is used to force a tabular display. It can be left off, or alternatively don't use the `select` and move the properties to the `Format-Table` and use an `-AutoSize` parameter. Many of the scripts in this chapter are modified from a set I use for AD audit and discovery. They usually terminate with a `Select-Object` as I output the data to a file. I've added `Format-Table` to force a tabular display.

> **IP ADDRESSES** If you run the scripts in listing 11.1 or 11.2 on a Windows Server 2008 domain controller, you may get an IPv6 address returned for the machine you're using. Domain controllers running earlier versions of Windows will return IPv4 addresses.

DISCUSSION

It's worth spending some time investigating the information available in the domain and domain controller objects:

```
$dom | Get-Member
$dcs = $dom.FindAllDomainControllers()
$dcs | Get-Member
```

The global catalog is hosted on some, but not necessarily all, domain controllers. Discovering the global catalog servers is the next part of understanding our domain controller configuration.

TECHNIQUE 115   **Discovering global catalog servers**

The *global catalog* is a subset of the attributes of all objects in our Active Directory forest. It's especially important in a multidomain forest. Some applications such as Exchange 2007 require access to a global catalog server. Global catalogs are maintained at the forest level because they can maintain data from all domains in the forest. The global catalog is hosted on one or more domain controllers.

PROBLEM

The global catalog servers in our forest have to be found. We can then determine that all users and applications requiring direct access to a global catalog server can find one in their home site.

SOLUTION

We can adopt a similar solution to the previous script, except we'll be working at the forest rather than domain level. The `System.DirectoryServices.ActiveDirectory.Forest` class has a static method to retrieve the current forest. We can then use the `FindAllGlobalCatalogs()` method to retrieve the list of global catalog servers.

Listing 11.2 Discover global catalog servers

```
$for =
[System.DirectoryServices.ActiveDirectory.Forest]::
GetCurrentForest()
($gc = $for.FindAllGlobalCatalogs()) |
 select Name, IPAddress | Format-table
```

DISCUSSION

In this example we created a variable to hold the collection of global catalog servers. If the script in listing 11.2 is dot-sourced, we'll have the variables available in memory for further investigation, as we discussed in listing 11.1.

Once we've discovered our global catalogs, we can decide whether we need to promote any further domain controllers to be global catalogs.

TECHNIQUE 116 ## Promoting to a global catalog server

The first domain controller in our forest will be a global catalog. No other domain controllers will be global catalogs by default.

PROBLEM

We need to promote one or more domain controllers to be global catalogs.

SOLUTION

The .NET domain controller (DC) class, `System.DirectoryServices.ActiveDirectory.DomainController`, can be used to promote a domain controller to be a global catalog. Using this class is convoluted, as we'll see in listing 11.3.

The script starts by defining the FQDN ❶ of the domain controller we'll be turning into a global catalog. A context type has to be defined for the object with which we'll be working ❷. We used contexts in chapter 5 when we looked at managing AD accounts using `System.DirectoryServices.AccountManagement`. `S.DS.AD.DirectoryContextType` is an enumeration, which is a closed list as discussed in section 3.2.1. The list of values in the enumeration can be discovered by using:

```
[enum]::GetNames([System.DirectoryServices.ActiveDirectory.
    DirectoryContextType])
```

The third step is to create a `DirectoryContext` ❸. This uses the context type and the name of the domain controller as arguments. Putting all of this together, we use the context as the argument to the `GetDomainController()` static method ❹. Phew! Now that we have our domain controller, we can call the `EnableGlobalCatalog()` method ❺ to perform the promotion.

Listing 11.3 Enable a global catalog server

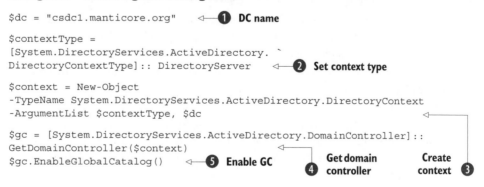

```
$dc = "csdc1.manticore.org"        ◁── ❶ DC name

$contextType =
[System.DirectoryServices.ActiveDirectory. `
DirectoryContextType]:: DirectoryServer    ◁── ❷ Set context type

$context = New-Object
-TypeName System.DirectoryServices.ActiveDirectory.DirectoryContext
-ArgumentList $contextType, $dc                                      ◁──

$gc = [System.DirectoryServices.ActiveDirectory.DomainController]::
GetDomainController($context)            ◁──
$gc.EnableGlobalCatalog()   ◁── ❺ Enable GC      ❹ Get domain      Create
                                                     controller       context ❸
```

DISCUSSION

It'll take some time for replication to occur to the newly promoted global catalog server.

An organization's Active Directory isn't set in stone and will change. It may be necessary to stop a domain controller from being a global catalog server, possibly as part of a decommissioning process. The script in listing 11.4 can be used to remove the global catalog.

Listing 11.4   Disable a global catalog server

```
$dc = "csdc1.manticore.org"
$contextType =
[System.DirectoryServices.ActiveDirectory. `
DirectoryContextType]:: DirectoryServer
$context = New-Object
-TypeName System.DirectoryServices.ActiveDirectory.DirectoryContext
-ArgumentList $contextType, $dc

$gc = [System.DirectoryServices.ActiveDirectory.GlobalCatalog]::
GetGlobalCatalog($context)
$gc.DisableGlobalCatalog()
```

The script is similar to the one we used to enable the global catalog. The difference occurs at the end, where we use the context to get a global catalog rather than a domain controller. We can then use the `DisableGlobalCatalog()` method.

> **FRUSTRATION AVOIDANCE**   The `GlobalCatalog` class also contains a method called `EnableGlobalCatalog()`. Don't try to use it because it won't work. The correct way to create a global catalog is to use the `DomainController` class as shown.

Active Directory was a big step forward when it was introduced because the domain controllers are multimaster, so that we can perform updates at any DC and the changes will replicate. But this doesn't mean that all domain controllers are equal. We need to consider the FSMO roles to understand this.

TECHNIQUE 117   **Discovering FSMO roles**

In theory, all domain controllers are equal, but it turns out some are more equal than others. There are a number of roles that can only be held by one domain controller at a time. These roles can be moved between domain controllers.

We'll see how to discover which domain controllers hold these roles and then how to transfer the role to another domain controller.

PROBLEM

We need to discover the FSMO role holders. Some of the roles such as the RID Master and the PDC Emulator can become critical if the DC holding the role is unavailable. Once we know the role holders, we can ensure our monitoring includes those machines.

FSMO roles

FSMO stands for *Flexible Single Master Operations.*. The following FSMO roles are defined:

Forest level (one each per forest):

- Schema Master—only DC on which schema updates can be performed.
- Domain Naming Master—controls changes to forest structure, such as adding or removing domains.

Domain level (one each per domain):

- PDC Emulator—emulates PDC if NT domain controllers exist. Also controls time synchronization and has password changes immediately replicated.
- RID Master—issues RIDs to other domain controllers to ensure that unique SIDs are issued to new objects.
- Infrastructure Master—maintains references to objects in other domains in a multidomain forest.

SOLUTION

We need to look at the forest and domain objects to discover all of the FSMO role holders, as shown in listing 11.5. Our starting point is to clear the screen (not 100% necessary, but it makes the display neater) and create an empty hash table ❶. Hash tables were covered in section 2.4.2 if you need a refresher. The two role holders at the forest level are found by creating an object for the current forest ❷. We then use the SchemaRoleOwner and NamingRoleOwner properties to get the names of the domain controllers. Note how we create an entry in the hash table by referring to the new key and supplying the associated value.

The pattern is repeated for the domain ❸. This time, the role holders are the PdcRoleOwner, RidRoleOwner, and InfrastructureRoleOwner. Once we have all of the roles, we list the information ❹. The hash table will display the key-value pairs that correspond to the role and the holder, respectively. The output can be seen in figure 11.1.

Listing 11.5 Discover FSMO role holders

```
clear-host
$roles = @{}      ⟵❶ Create hash table

$for =
[System.DirectoryServices.ActiveDirectory.Forest]:
:GetCurrentForest()                          ⟵❷ Get forest

$roles["SchemaMaster"] = $for.SchemaRoleOwner
$roles["DomainNamingMaster"] = $for.NamingRoleOwner

$dom =
```

```
[System.DirectoryServices.ActiveDirectory.Domain]::
GetCurrentDomain()                                    ⊲──❸ Get domain
$roles["PDCEmulator"] = $dom.PdcRoleOwner
$roles["RIDMaster"] = $dom.RidRoleOwner
$roles["InfrastructureMaster"] = $dom.InfrastructureRoleOwner

$roles    ⊲──❹ List roles
```

DISCUSSION

This script assumes that we only want to display the role holders for the current domain and the forest. If we have a multidomain forest, we may want to display all role holders across all domains. This can be achieved by altering the script. Use the domains collection on the forest object and iterate through them using `foreach`. For each domain, get a domain object and list the role holders. It'll be necessary to add the domain name into the data; otherwise we won't know which domain controllers correspond to which domain.

If a domain controller holding a role becomes unavailable for an extended period of time, we may need to transfer the role to another domain controller.

TECHNIQUE 118   Transferring FSMO roles

Moving FSMO roles between domain controllers is straightforward. It doesn't happen automatically, though. I've transferred these roles between servers situated in southeast England and the midwest of the U.S. in past projects. The transfer happened flawlessly, though it was interesting watching the faces of people who'd never done this before.

> **TRANSFER, NOT SEIZE** A transfer is a graceful transition where both servers are available. If the current role holder is unavailable the role must be seized using `ntdsutil`, in which case you should ensure that the original role holder doesn't come back online.

The roles can be transferred using the GUI, but it involves three different tools. We'll make this more efficient by using a single script.

PROBLEM

The FSMO roles don't automatically transfer between domain controllers. The roles have to be transferred to another domain controller if the role holder will be offline for any great length of time.

SOLUTION

We can get access to the `rootDSE` on the domain controller, which will become the role holder and set the relevant properties so that it's the acknowledged role holder. This is shown in listing 11.6.

All objects in Active Directory have a unique *security identifier (SID)*. This includes the domain itself. We need to use the SID to transfer one of the roles, so the first task is to find it. We can access the current domain ❶ and use the `objectSID` property to give us the SID ❷ which is stored in the variable as an array. The `rootDSE` on the domain controller ❸ that'll become the role holder is accessed.

There are a number of ways of looping through the list of roles. I think the easiest is to create an array of the roles ❹ and use foreach to iterate over the collection. Note the format of the property—become*XXXXX* where *XXXXX* is the role.

Listing 11.6 Transfer all FSMO roles

```
$dom =
[System.DirectoryServices.ActiveDirectory.Domain]::     ❶ Get domain
GetCurrentDomain()

$sid = ($dom.GetDirectoryEntry()).objectSid     ◁—❷ Get SID
$dc = [ADSI]"LDAP://csdc1/rootDSE"
                                                ❸ Connect to DC
$fsmo = "becomeSchemaMaster", "becomeDomainMaster", `
"becomeRidMaster", "becomeInfraStructureMaster",
"becomePDC"                                     ◁—❹ Set roles

foreach ($role in $fsmo){
    if ($role -eq "becomePDC"){ $dc.Put($role, $sid[0])}   ◁—❺ Transfer role
    else {$dc.Put($role, 1) }
    $dc.SetInfo()              ◁—❻ Save
}
```

We need to check whether the role being transferred is the PDC emulator ❺. If it is, then we use the Put() method to set the property. The value is the SID of the domain. Note that we're treating the SID as an array and only taking the first element. For any other role, a value of 1 is used to indicate that the role is being transferred. The last act of the loop is to save the change back to Active Directory ❻.

DISCUSSION

There will be latency due to replication before all of the domain controllers are aware of the change.

> **.NET DOMAIN CONTROLLER CLASS** The System.DirectoryServices.Active-Directory.DomainController class has a TransferRoleOwnership method for moving FSMO roles. It doesn't fully work with Windows Server 2008. I recommend that it not be used.

The previous script works fine for an organization that has all of the FSMO roles on the same domain controller. If we want to spread the roles across multiple servers, we need to modify our script to accommodate moving a given role to a specific server.

Listing 11.7 Transfer a single FSMO role

```
param([string]$server, [string]$fsmo)     ◁—❶ Parameters
$dom =
[System.DirectoryServices.ActiveDirectory.Domain]::
GetCurrentDomain()
                                          ❷ Domain SID
$sid = ($dom.GetDirectoryEntry()).objectSid     ◁—
$dc = [ADSI]"LDAP://$server/rootDSE"
                                          ❸ Connect to DC
switch ($fsmo.ToLower()){
    "schema" {$role = "becomeSchemaMaster"; break}    ❹ Set roles
```

```
      "domain" {$role = "becomeDomainMaster"; break}
      "rid"    {$role = "becomeRidMaster"; break}
      "infra"  {$role = "becomeInfraStructureMaster"; break}
      "pdc"    {$role = "becomePDC"; break}
      default {
         Write-Host "Role must be one of schema," + `
           domain, rid, infra, pdc"
         return
            }

}

if ($role -eq "becomePDC"){ $dc.Put($role, $sid[0])}    ⬅—❺ Transfer role
else {$dc.Put($role, 1) }
$dc.SetInfo()              ⬅—❻ Save
```

In section 4.4.2, we discussed functions and how to use parameters. They can be used with scripts in the same way. This script takes two parameters ❶—the server name and the role to be transferred. Figure 11.1 shows the script being used. The domain SID ❷ is obtained and the connection to rootDSE on the domain controller is made ❸. It's not necessary to always obtain the SID, but it leaves the script directly comparable to the previous example. The purist may want to move these lines into the if statement so that they only run when required.

A switch statement is use to set the role property based on the input parameter ❹. In theory, the case we use for the input parameter shouldn't matter, but we'll play it safe and force it to lowercase. A default statement is used to catch an error where the role isn't entered correctly. This can be seen working in the next figure

The last lines of the script set the role ❺ and save the change ❻ as we've seen previously. We can use this script by supplying the domain controller that'll hold the role and the role we want to transfer; for example:

```
.\move-afsmo.ps1 "dc02" "pdc"
```

Examples for all of the FSMO roles are shown in figure 11.1.

```
⅀ C:\Scripts\DomainControllers                                    _ □ X
PS> .\move-afsmo.ps1 "schema" "dc02"
Role must be one of schema, domain, rid, infra, pdc
PS> .\move-afsmo.ps1 "dc02" "schema"
PS> .\move-afsmo.ps1 "dc02" "domain"
PS> .\move-afsmo.ps1 "dc02" "rid"
PS> .\move-afsmo.ps1 "dc02" "infra"
PS> .\move-afsmo.ps1 "dc02" "pdc"
PS>
PS> .\get-fsmo.ps1

Name                          Value
----                          -----
InfrastructureMaster          DC02.Manticore.org
RIDMaster                     DC02.Manticore.org
DomainNamingMaster            DC02.Manticore.org
PDCEmulator                   DC02.Manticore.org
SchemaMaster                  DC02.Manticore.org

PS>
```

Figure 11.1 Using the script to transfer a single FSMO role. Note the error message if the correct parameters aren't supplied. The figure also shows the result of running the script to discover the FSMO roles.

We've seen how to find our domain controllers, how we can modify them, and how we can move the FSMO roles. We'll close this section on domain controllers by considering replication.

Monitor replication

Active Directory can accept changes, such as a new user, on any domain controller. That data is then replicated to all domain controllers in the domain, and possibly the forest. Replication can be adversely affected by networking issues or hardware problems such as a hard disk that becomes corrupted or a network card failing. If replication isn't working correctly, problems such as users not being able to log on will manifest themselves.

It's surprising how many people install Active Directory and just leave it. They don't check the event logs on domain controllers or check that replication is working correctly. We saw how to access the event logs in chapter 8, and you're about to learn how to check on replication. Put these techniques together to create a script that examines the health of your Active Directory on a regular basis. It's much better for you to find problems than for your users to find them.

PROBLEM
The help desk has received a number of calls about users having problems logging on to the network. We need to determine whether our domain controllers are replicating information correctly.

SOLUTION
Determining whether replication is working isn't as straightforward as some of the problems we've solved. We'll look at replication from the viewpoint of a single domain controller and then look at comparing the replication state between domain controllers.

The script in listing 11.8 uses techniques we've seen earlier, when we were looking at enabling or disabling the global catalog. A domain controller name **1** and a context type **2** are used to create a directory context **3**. The directory context is then used to create a domain controller object **4**. We can use the GetAllReplication-Neighbors() method to find the information we need about this domain controller's replication state **5** and display it.

Listing 11.8   Examine replication synchronization

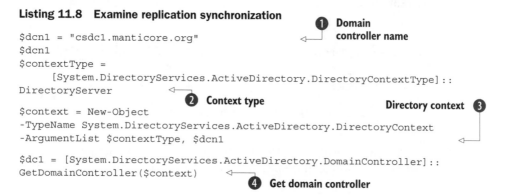

```
$dcn1 = "csdc1.manticore.org"                          ← Domain
                                                         controller name
$dcn1
$contextType =
     [System.DirectoryServices.ActiveDirectory.DirectoryContextType]::
DirectoryServer        ←
                          ❷ Context type                    Directory context ❸
$context = New-Object
-TypeName System.DirectoryServices.ActiveDirectory.DirectoryContext
-ArgumentList $contextType, $dcn1                                    ←

$dc1 = [System.DirectoryServices.ActiveDirectory.DomainController]::
GetDomainController($context)        ←
                                        ❹ Get domain controller
```

```
$dc1.GetAllReplicationNeighbors() |
  select PartitionName, SourceServer,
UsnLastObjectChangeSynced, LastSuccessfulSync,
LastAttemptedSync, LastSyncMessage,
ConsecutiveFailureCount
```
⑤ View replication data

DISCUSSION

Here's part of the output from this script:

```
csdc1.manticore.org

PartitionName            : DC=Manticore,DC=org
SourceServer             : DC02.Manticore.org
UsnLastObjectChangeSynced : 787396
LastSuccessfulSync       : 07/03/2009 20:40:59
LastAttemptedSync        : 07/03/2009 20:40:59
LastSyncMessage          : The operation completed successfully.

ConsecutiveFailureCount  : 0
```

This script will show all of the domain controllers that are directly replicating with this domain controller and the state of replication for each Active Directory partition.

Active Directory is distributed across a number of partitions which replicate independently. Our output shows the partition representing the Active Directory data (users, groups, and so on). The source server is the domain controller with which our server is replicating.

Every time an object is changed in Active Directory, the *USN (update sequence number)* is incremented. The USN of the last object to be replicated is shown, as are the date and time of the last attempt at replication and the last successful replication. If they don't match, you immediately know you have problems.

Likewise, if the LastSyncMessage shows anything but "The operation completed successfully." it's time for deeper investigations. The ConsecutiveFailureCount should be zero if everything is working correctly.

So far we've seen how to test replication on a single domain controller, but like Oliver we want more. Listing 11.9 shows how can we ensure that a partition is replicating correctly across all domain controllers.

Listing 11.9 Show up-to-dateness vector

```
$d = [ADSI]""              ◄── ① Get domain root
$dom =
[System.DirectoryServices.ActiveDirectory.Domain]::   ② Get domain
GetCurrentDomain()                                        object

$dom.FindAllDomainControllers() | foreach {  ◄── ③ Get DCs
    $_.Name                                           ④ Get replication
    $_.GetReplicationCursors($d.distinguishedName)      data
}
```

We can test the replication between domain controllers by comparing the UptoDateness USN (also known as the *up-to-dateness vector*) on the source server with the same attribute stored on the target server for that domain controller, which produces output like this:

```
CSDC1.Manticore.org

PartitionName          : DC=Manticore,DC=org
SourceInvocationId     : 3242a94a-7538-47bd-9aa3-be4d3b56d813
UpToDatenessUsn        : 787396
SourceServer           : DC02.Manticore.org
LastSuccessfulSyncTime : 07/03/2009 20:36:13

PartitionName          : DC=Manticore,DC=org
SourceInvocationId     : b2f36313-5342-4324-8336-ffb554fb28ee
UpToDatenessUsn        : 403995
SourceServer           : CSDC1.Manticore.org
LastSuccessfulSyncTime : 07/03/2009 20:38:40
```

The script gets the domain **❶** and creates a domain object **❷**. We use the `FindAllDo-mainControllers()` **❸** method and use `foreach` to execute the `GetReplicationCursors()` method on each domain controller **❹**. This method expects a partition as the input parameter. In this case, we're examining the default partition.

For each domain controller, we'll get output showing the partition, source server, and `UpToDatenessUSN`, among other information. The `UpToDatenessUSN` shown by csdc1 for the data coming from dc02 should match the `UpToDatenessUSN` recorded by dco2 for itself.

It's necessary to repeat this for all partitions to get a complete picture of the replication state. In a large domain with many domain controllers, it'd be wise to modify the script so that smaller groups of domain controllers were processed at a time.

If we find a discrepancy between the data stored on replication partners, we may need to trigger replication to bring the domain controllers back into synchronization.

TECHNIQUE 120   Triggering replication

In Active Directory, replication happens without our intervention. We set up the domain controllers and they work out how to replicate among themselves. They keep replicating data until something changes. That change may be a network (or machine) problem that prevents replication. We need to be able to manually force domain controllers to replicate.

PROBLEM

We're taking a domain controller offline for an extended period of time, so we have to force replication to be certain that all changes have been replicated out to Active Directory instances on other domain controllers.

SOLUTION

Active Directory works out how the domain controllers should replicate among themselves. Each domain controller has one or more neighbors with which it replicates. We can use that to trigger replication throughout the domain if required, as in listing 11.10.

Listing 11.10   Trigger replication

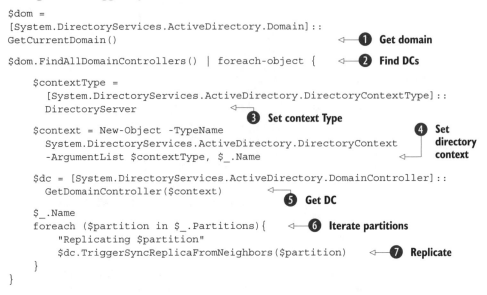

```
$dom =
[System.DirectoryServices.ActiveDirectory.Domain]::
GetCurrentDomain()                                        ←① Get domain

$dom.FindAllDomainControllers() | foreach-object {        ←② Find DCs

    $contextType =
      [System.DirectoryServices.ActiveDirectory.DirectoryContextType]::
      DirectoryServer
                                    ←③ Set context Type

    $context = New-Object -TypeName                              ④ Set
      System.DirectoryServices.ActiveDirectory.DirectoryContext    directory
      -ArgumentList $contextType, $_.Name                 ←        context

    $dc = [System.DirectoryServices.ActiveDirectory.DomainController]::
      GetDomainController($context)              ←
                                              ⑤ Get DC
    $_.Name
    foreach ($partition in $_.Partitions){    ←⑥ Iterate partitions
        "Replicating $partition"
        $dc.TriggerSyncReplicaFromNeighbors($partition)    ←⑦ Replicate
    }
}
```

The early part of the script we've seen before. The more we automate our activities, the more we'll see the same patterns of code being used. We get the current domain ❶ and find all of the domain controllers in the domain ❷. We pipe the domain controllers collection into a `Foreach-Object` cmdlet where we create a context type ❸ and a directory context with the context type and the domain controller name ❹, then get the domain controller object ❺ we use as our trigger point.

The domain controller name is printed and we loop through the partitions hosted on that domain controller ❻. It's possible that not all partitions will be on all domain controllers; for example DNS can be targeted to a specific set of domain controllers. The `TriggerSyncReplicaFromNeighbors()` method is used to force the replication ❼. It requires a partition name as a parameter.

DISCUSSION

Don't try this in a domain with a large number of domain controllers. There could be an enormous spike in the network traffic, plus the script could take a long time to run. If there are a large number of DCs, split them up and either work with them singly or feed a number of names into the script at a time.

This concludes our examination of domain controllers. These scripts will enable us to perform the daily administration tasks involving domain controllers. It's time to step up a level in scale and look at Active Directory sites.

11.3   *Sites*

Active Directory sites define locations. They're the physical manifestation of our Active Directory being used to control replication as well as being used to find domain controllers and other services. A well-designed and healthy site topology is a basic requirement for a well-behaved Active Directory. It's also essential for Exchange 2007, as we'll see in the next chapter.

The first thing we need to be able to do is find out what sites are defined and just what information is available.

TECHNIQUE 121   Listing sites

There's a lot of useful information lurking in our sites. The GUI tool doesn't give us this information in an easy-to-access manner.

PROBLEM
How can we discover the sites that are defined in our AD and simultaneously discover the related data we need to properly understand our Active Directory topology?

SOLUTION
The site information can be found on the forest object we've used previously. Sites are defined at the forest level. We can use the GetCurrentForest() static method of the System.DirectoryServices.ActiveDirectory.Forest class to create an object for the forest, as in listing 11.11. One of the properties on this object is a collection of site objects. We can display the information by simply accessing the property. The quantity of information forces us to display it as a list rather than a table.

Listing 11.11   List sites

```
$for =
[System.DirectoryServices.ActiveDirectory.Forest]::
GetCurrentForest()
$for.sites
```

DISCUSSION
The information for one site is shown in figure 11.2. Some of the information is missing because I only have a single site in my Active Directory at this point.

The site information includes the name and the domains in the site. Sites can span domains. It means there's a domain controller for that domain located in the particular site. The Servers property refers to domain controllers only. It doesn't list other servers such as Exchange or SQL Server.

```
C:\Scripts                                                                      _ □ ×
Name                            : Site1
Domains                         : {Manticore.org}
Subnets                         : {10.10.54.0/24}
Servers                         : {CSDC1.Manticore.org, DC02.Manticore.org}
AdjacentSites                   : {Default-First-Site-Name}
SiteLinks                       : {DEFAULTIPSITELINK}
InterSiteTopologyGenerator      : DC02.Manticore.org
Options                         : None
Location                        :
BridgeheadServers               : {}
PreferredSmtpBridgeheadServers  : {}
PreferredRpcBridgeheadServers   : {}
IntraSiteReplicationSchedule    :
```

Figure 11.2   Display of the information available for a site when accessed through PowerShell and .NET

AdjacentSites refers to those sites that are directly linked to our site through site links. The bridgehead servers are the domain controllers that are used to replicate with other sites.

Now that we know how to list the sites, it's time to discover how to create them.

TECHNIQUE 122   **Creating a site**

Site creation is a task that tends to happen in bursts. There's a big burst of activity when Active Directory is first installed. After that, sites are only created when changes to the organization's locations occur. This is most often seen in merger and acquisition activity.

PROBLEM

Your company has acquired another company. The acquired company's Active Directory will be merged into your AD. You need to create the necessary sites in your Active Directory to accommodate this change.

SOLUTION

.NET comes galloping to the rescue. There's a .NET class we can use to solve this problem, as shown in listing 11.12. We start by finding the current forest ❶. A context type of Forest is created ❷. In this script, we've used the type directly rather than going through the enumeration as we have in previous examples. Either will work, though I prefer using the enumeration as I think it's a better aid to understanding what's happening.

We use the forest and context types to create a context ❸ and create the site using the ActiveDirectorySite class ❹. The change must be saved to Active Directory ❺ to make it usable.

Listing 11.12 Create sites

```
$for =
[System.DirectoryServices.ActiveDirectory.Forest]::
GetCurrentForest()                                      ⟵─❶ Get forest

$fortyp = [System.DirectoryServices.ActiveDirectory.`
DirectoryContextType]"Forest"                           ⟵─❷ Context type

$forcntxt = New-Object -TypeName `
System.DirectoryServices.ActiveDirectory.DirectoryContext
-ArgumentList $fortyp, $for                             ⟵─❸ Context

$site = New-Object -TypeName
     `System.DirectoryServices.ActiveDirectory.ActiveDirectorySite
-ArgumentList $forcntxt, "MyNewSite1"         ⟵┐
$site.Save()                          ⟵─❺ Save    ❹ Create site
```

DISCUSSION

One drawback to using the .NET class is that it's not possible to set the Description property on the site object. An alternative for the creation process would be to combine the two scripts so that the description was set at creation time. An example of how to use the GetDirectoryEntry() method is presented in section 11.5.2; in the mean time, we'll see how to modify a site after it has been created.

TECHNIQUE 123   Modifying a site

The major modifications to a site would be changing the metadata, such as the description, or changing the subnets associated with a site. We'll look at moving subnets between sites later.

PROBLEM

Changes within the organization can create a need for the metadata held about a site to be changed. We need to be able to change the description of our sites to accommodate these changes.

SOLUTION

We know this isn't possible with .NET, so we need to use ADSI, as shown in listing 11.13.

Listing 11.13   Modify site properties

```
$root = [ADSI]"LDAP://RootDSE"              ◄── ❶ Get RootDSE
$site = [ADSI]"LDAP://CN=MyNewSite3,CN=Sites,`
$($root.configurationNamingContext)"        ◄── ❷ Get site

$site.location = "Building Z"                    ┐ ❸ Modify
$site.description = "Site for New Building Z"     │
$site.SetInfo()                             ◄── ❹ Save
```

DISCUSSION

Site information is held in the *configuration context.* The easiest way to access this context is to start by creating an object pointing to rootDSE ❶. The *configuration naming context* is a property of rootDSE that we can use to create an ADSI object for our site ❷. The metadata is stored as properties whose values can be changed ❸. The changed data is saved ❹ to Active Directory.

An important part of Active Directory maintenance is removing objects that are no longer required. This applies equally well to sites.

TECHNIQUE 124   Deleting a site

Deleting a site from Active Directory will probably be a rare activity. If a site is to be deleted, ensure that any users who relied on domain controllers in that site for authentication can find another domain controller so that they can still access the domain.

PROBLEM

As business needs change, we may need to delete a site from Active Directory.

SOLUTION

The simplest way to accomplish this is to use ADSI, as in listing 11.14.

Listing 11.14   Delete a site

```
$root = [ADSI]"LDAP://RootDSE"
$site = [ADSI]"LDAP://CN=MyNewSite3,CN=Sites, `
$($root.configurationNamingContext)"

$site.DeleteTree()
```

DISCUSSION

We use `rootDSE` and the configuration naming context in the same way as the previous example. This makes our script more portable, as we aren't hard-coding the forest name. The `DeleteTree()` method is called to perform the deletion.

This concludes our examination of Active Directory sites. Subnets are closely associated with sites, and we'll turn our attention to them in the next section.

11.4 Subnets

This section is about creating subnets in Active Directory, not about the subnetting of networks. A subnet is linked to an Active Directory site and defines the range of IP addresses Active Directory expects to see in that site. They're used to enable newly promoted domain controllers to determine in which site they belong.

Correctly defined subnets are essential for machines to determine their site membership. This will reduce network traffic by ensuring that services, such as domain controllers, are accessed from the site in which they're situated. A subnet can only be linked to a single site, but a site can have many subnets associated with it.

Our first step with subnets is discovering which ones have been defined in our Active Directory. This will enable us to determine whether we need to create further subnets.

TECHNIQUE 125   **Listing subnets**

The list of subnets defined in Active Directory can be seen using Active Directory Sites and Services, but using PowerShell gives us more flexibility in how we look at the data.

PROBLEM

We need to determine which subnets have been defined in Active Directory, and which sites are linked to those subnets. The data should be output in a format that can easily be formatted into a tabular display.

SOLUTION

There are a number of ways to retrieve this information. I prefer to read the individual subnet objects and create an object containing the data I want to display, as shown in listing 11.15. This gives me more flexibility for future work.

Let's start by creating an empty array ❶. This will be used to hold our data. The second task is to find our `subnets` container ❷. Subnets are stored at the forest level rather than the domain (there's no difference for a single-domain forest), so I've hard-coded the forest name. It's possible to change this to bind to the root of Active Directory using `RootDSE` if you want to make this portable (see later examples).

We'll use `foreach` to examine each subnet (the children of the `subnets` container) in turn ❸. The loop starts by getting a directory object for the subnet ❹. An empty object is then created ❺. If you pipe `$data` into `Get-Member`, the returned type is a `Selected.System.String` with `NoteProperties` added for each property in the `select` statement. It would be possible to create a PowerShell object using `New-Object` and then add each property with `Add-Member`. I first saw this way of creating objects in a post on Jonathan Noble's blog (search for "Noble musings").

Listing 11.15   List subnets

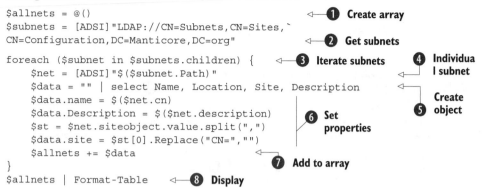

```
$allnets = @()                                            ← 1  Create array
$subnets = [ADSI]"LDAP://CN=Subnets,CN=Sites,`
CN=Configuration,DC=Manticore,DC=org"                     ← 2  Get subnets

foreach ($subnet in $subnets.children) {     ← 3  Iterate subnets       4  Individual subnet
    $net = [ADSI]"$($subnet.Path)"                                       ←
    $data = "" | select Name, Location, Site, Description    ←
    $data.name = $($net.cn)                                      Create object  5
    $data.Description = $($net.description)    6  Set
    $st = $net.siteobject.value.split(",")       properties
    $data.site = $st[0].Replace("CN=","")
    $allnets += $data                         ←
}                                                  7  Add to array
$allnets | Format-Table    ←  8  Display
```

DISCUSSION

Now that we have an object, we need to add some properties **6**. The subnet location and description are found in the relevant properties. The site that the subnet is associated with is found using the `siteobject` property. But this is a distinguished name, so we split the string into an array using the `Split()` operator. The name of the site is in the first element of the array. The `Replace()` method can be used to remove the `CN=` from the beginning of the distinguished name. The name of the site is the final property we need.

> **PROPERTY VALUE COLLECTION** The data is handled as `$data.name = $($net.cn)` and so on using subexpessions because ADSI returns the properties as `PropertyValueCollections`, from which we need to pick the data.

Our object is added to the array **7** and we loop for the next subnet. The data is displayed using `Format-Table` **8**. Alternatively, it could be exported to a CSV file for future use or further processing could be performed. Notice that the description property isn't set. We'll learn how to perform that task shortly.

Now that we know what subnets we have, the next task is to look at creating new subnets.

TECHNIQUE 126   Creating a subnet

Subnets are closely associated with sites in Active Directory. When we create the subnet, we have to know with which site the subnet will be associated.

PROBLEM

A subnet has to be created in Active Directory to facilitate the incorporation of a new location.

SOLUTION

The .NET `ActiveDirectorySubnet` class solves this problem for us, as shown in listing 11.16. The first three lines of the script get the forest **1**, and use a forest context type **2** to create a forest context **3**. We then set the data we'll use to create the subnet **4**. The site name and subnet name must be given; the location is optional.

Listing 11.16   Create a subnet

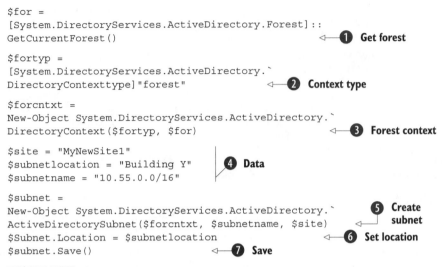

```
$for =
[System.DirectoryServices.ActiveDirectory.Forest]::
GetCurrentForest()                                    ◄─① Get forest

$fortyp =
[System.DirectoryServices.ActiveDirectory.`
DirectoryContexttype]"forest"                         ◄─② Context type

$forcntxt =
New-Object System.DirectoryServices.ActiveDirectory.`
DirectoryContext($fortyp, $for)                       ◄─③ Forest context

$site = "MyNewSite1"
$subnetlocation = "Building Y"          ④ Data
$subnetname = "10.55.0.0/16"

$subnet =
New-Object System.DirectoryServices.ActiveDirectory.`  ⑤ Create
ActiveDirectorySubnet($forcntxt, $subnetname, $site)  ◄─   subnet
$Subnet.Location = $subnetlocation                    ◄─⑥ Set location
$subnet.Save()                          ◄─⑦ Save
```

DISCUSSION

It's good practice to complete the location and description fields, as it can save time and effort in the future trying to discover where a subnet or site is actually situated.

After creating the subnet ⑤, we can set the location ⑥ and save our changes ⑦. Once we've created our subnets, we may need to modify them at some time.

TECHNIQUE 127   **Modifying a subnet**

There isn't much to modify with subnets, except which site it's in. This has an impact on Active Directory joined computers, as they use the subnet information to determine site membership, which controls which domain controllers will be used for authentication.

PROBLEM

The reorganization of the company and its locations means that we have to change the Active Directory site with which a subnet is affiliated.

SOLUTION

This task can't be performed using .NET, so we need to look at using ADSI, as in listing 11.7. Start by connecting to rootDSE ①. We can then access the subnet we need to change ②. The structure of the LDAP string may look odd. That's because the / character is reserved in ADSI, which means that the subnet name 10.56.0.0/24 wouldn't be interpreted correctly when we try to access it. We need to make sure the / is read as part of the name so we put a \ in front of it as an *escape character*. An escape character forces the next character to be read literally rather than being interpreted as a reserved character.

> **CHILD OF SITES**   The subnets container is a child of the sites container. This is one of things that can easily get forgotten when you're building a script from scratch. I can confirm from experience that forgetting this causes a lot of frustration in debugging the script.

The properties we need to change are set ❸ and saved ❹. When we change the site association, we need to set the `siteobject` property ❻ with the distinguished name of the new site ❺ and make sure we save the change ❼.

Listing 11.17   Modify a subnet

```
$root = [ADSI]"LDAP://RootDSE"                                      ◁──❶ Get AD root
$subnet = [ADSI]"LDAP://CN=10.56.0.0\/24,CN=Subnets,CN=Sites,
$($root.configurationNamingContext)"                               ◁──❷ Get subnet

$subnet.location = "Building Z"                                    ❸ Set
$subnet.description = "Subnet for New Building Z"                     properties
$subnet.SetInfo()                                                 ◁
                                                                  ❹ Save
$newsite =
[ADSI]"LDAP://CN=MyNewSite3,CN=Sites, `
$($root.configurationNamingContext)"     ◁──❺ Get new site        ❻ Change
                                                                     subnet's site
$subnet.siteObject = $newsite.distinguishedName                   ◁
$subnet.SetInfo()                                     ◁──❼ Save
```

DISCUSSION

It's strange how we keep forgetting the final change when doing this interactively.

Next we'll look at how to remove subnets from Active Directory. One thing I've noticed over the years is that people seem not to want to remove objects from AD. I've seen user accounts where the user left the company two or three years ago. Use Power-Shell to find these unused objects and remove them. Put AD on a diet and it'll be easier to manage.

TECHNIQUE 128   **Deleting a subnet**

Deleting a subnet can be a simple tidying up exercise, as AD will use the most granular subnet available. For example, if we designate 10.10.0.0/16 to a site, it also covers 10.10.54.0/16, so we wouldn't explicitly have to define the child subnets. Whatever the reason, we remove subnets in a similar manner to sites.

PROBLEM

A subnet is no longer required and has to be deleted from Active Directory.

SOLUTION

Listing 11.18 shows a solution similar to that presented in section 11.3.4. Simply get the ADSI object for the subnet and call the `DeleteTree()` method as shown.

Listing 11.18   Delete a subnet

```
$root = [ADSI]"LDAP://RootDSE"
$subnet = [ADSI]"LDAP://CN=10.56.0.0\/24,CN=Subnets,CN=Sites,
$($root.configurationNamingContext)"
$subnet.DeleteTree()
```

DISCUSSION

One drawback to the deletion scripts is that there's no easy way to have a check before deletion (remember the `-confirm` and `-whatif` parameters on `Remove-Item`). This would be a compelling reason to move to using Microsoft's AD provider if you upgrade to Windows Server 2008 R2, as it means you can use `Remove-Item` and its extra safety features. AD administration with a safety net! I can sense a lot of relieved admins as this gets adopted. Microsoft's AD provider is also available if you install the AD web service on your Windows Server 2003 or Windows Server 2008 domain controllers and use the AD cmdlets from a Windows 7 or Windows Server 2008 R2 administration machine.

So far in our look at the Active Directory topology, we've learned how to work with domain controllers, sites, and subnets. The last component we need to consider is the links between sites that we use to control replication.

11.5   Site links

Site links are in effect containers for two or more Active Directory sites. The link has some properties of its own, the most important of which are the cost (an arbitrary number) and a replication schedule. It's important that the site links are defined and created correctly so that Active Directory replication isn't hindered.

Consider figure 10.1: site links definitely belong in the bottom part of the diagram. They don't change frequently but they can have a big impact on the organization if they're misconfigured and cause Active Directory replication problems.

The first exercise we need to consider is discovering the site links that exist in our Active Directory.

TECHNIQUE 129   Listing site links

Site link documentation is essential to understanding the Active Directory topology.

PROBLEM

The documentation has vanished, as has the guy who created the links. We need to understand our Active Directory topology, especially the site links used to control replication.

SOLUTION

Figure 11.2 shows that the output from listing the Active Directory sites includes the site links. The information is better presented by showing which sites are part of a particular site link rather than which links are associated with a site, as in listing 11.19.

The first part of the script we've seen several times in this chapter. We create a forest context ❸ by using the current forest ❶ and the context type of forest ❷. The next step is to use `rootDSE` ❹ as a shortcut to the configuration naming context so that we can find the `sites` container ❺ to use as the root of our search. We're using the `sites` container as our starting point because it's the parent container for site links. There are two possible types of site link (RPC and SMTP) and starting at this level ensures we find all links.

An ADSI searcher is created ❻ using .NET. If we have access to PowerShell v2, we can simplify this line slightly:

```
$search = [ADSISearcher]$root
```

Listing 11.19 List site links

```
$for =
[System.DirectoryServices.ActiveDirectory.Forest]::
GetCurrentForest()                                          ◄——❶ Get forest

$fortyp =
[System.DirectoryServices.ActiveDirectory.`      ❷ Context
DirectoryContexttype]"forest"               ◄——┘   type                Get ❺
                                                              configuration
$forcntxt = New-Object                                            context
System.DirectoryServices.ActiveDirectory.`      ❸ Forest
DirectoryContext($fortyp, $for)             ◄——┘   context
                                                ❹ Get
$dse = [ADSI]"LDAP://RootDSE"              ◄——   rootDSE
$root = [ADSI]"LDAP://cn=Sites,$($dse.configurationNamingContext)"   ◄——

$search = [System.DirectoryServices.DirectorySearcher]$root          ◄——
$search.Filter = "(objectclass=sitelink)"         ◄——┐           Filter on
$results = $search.FindAll()             ◄——        ❼ site links
                                         Find all
if ($results -ne $null){   ◄——┐      ❽ links
  foreach ($result in $results){ ❾ Test for           Create
    $link =                    results              searcher ❻
        [System.DirectoryServices.ActiveDirectory. `
        ActiveDirectorySiteLink]::
        FindByName($forcntxt, $result.Properties.name)  ◄——❿ Get link
    $link                                          ◄——┐
  }                                              ⓫ Display data
}
else {Write-Host "No Site-Links exist"}   ◄——⓬ Error message
```

DISCUSSION

We want to restrict the objects that are returned so that we get only site links ❼. The LDAP filter will return all objects whose object class is sitelink.

> **ADSIEDIT** When I was researching this script, I wasn't sure how to create the correct filter so that I only returned site links. How did I find this out? I cheated and used ADSIEdit to look at the attributes of an existing site link. It showed that a simple filter on objectclass would do the trick. ADSIEdit is a great tool for drilling down into Active Directory objects—think of it as the Get-Member for AD.

We use FindAll() ❽ to return all of the site links. If no site links exist in our forest, the $results variable will be empty-null (equal to $null). You can save processing time and prevent script errors by testing the results variable against $null ❾. If there are no links, a message is displayed ⓬.

Assuming that we've found some site links (a single Site Active Directory may not have any if the default site has been deleted), we can loop though them. The site link name can be obtained from our results, and together with the forest context we created earlier, can be used to create an object for the link ❿. The properties of the link can be displayed ⓫ including the constituent sites and the cost. The information for the replication schedule is discussed in section 11.5.4.

The script in listing 11.19 looks at site links that include sites as a property. If we want to look at the sites in our forest and see which links are connected to a particular script, it's a much simpler task. We use the sites collection of the current forest object and select the name and the links, as shown in listing 11.20.

Listing 11.20   Site links by site

```
$for =
[System.DirectoryServices.ActiveDirectory.Forest]::
GetCurrentForest()

$for.sites | Format-Table Name, SiteLinks
```

One idea for extending this work would be to use the mapping technique we saw in chapter 8 when looking at services. This would produce a graphical view of the links between sites.

Now that we know what links exist, how can new ones be created to fill in the gaps?

TECHNIQUE 130   Creating a site link

The organizational changes we discussed earlier that cause Active Directory sites to be created also mean we need to create new site links.

PROBLEM

We've used the script in section 11.3.2 to create two new sites. We now need to create a site link to control the replication between the sites.

SOLUTION

The `ActiveDirectorySiteLink` can be used for this task, as shown in listing 11.21. Working at the forest level, we start by creating a forest context ❶ in the usual way. The `ActiveDirectorySiteLink` class is used to create a new link object ❷ giving the name of the new link as one of the parameters.

> **LINK NAMES**   I tend to create link names using the sites that form part of the link in the name. I find this helps when working with the links, as it's immediately obvious which sites are involved in the link. Other naming conventions are available.

The `ActiveDirectorySite` class can be used to find the sites ❸ that will be added to the link. A link always contains a minimum of two sites. Best practice is to have only two sites in a link. The sites are added to the link ❹. This has to be done one site at a time. There doesn't appear to be a way to perform a bulk addition of sites to the link.

The link cost ❺ and the replication interval ❻ properties are set. The interval is given as *hh:mm:ss*—hours, minutes, and seconds, respectively. I haven't set a replication schedule in this script but have implicitly accepted the default 24 x 7 schedule. If a different schedule is required, the script presented in technique 133 can be used to control the schedule.

> **REPLICATION INTERVAL**   The replication interval can't be lower than 15 minutes. The default is 3 hours (180 minutes in the GUI).

The new link is saved ❼ and a directory entry created so that we can set the link description ❽. A final save ❾ ensures that everything is written back to Active Directory.

Listing 11.21 Create site link

```
$for =
[System.DirectoryServices.ActiveDirectory.Forest]::
GetCurrentForest()

$fortyp =
[System.DirectoryServices.ActiveDirectory.`
DirectoryContexttype]"forest"

$forcntxt = New-Object
System.DirectoryServices.ActiveDirectory.`
DirectoryContext($fortyp, $for)                    ⟵──❶ Forest context

$link = New-Object -TypeName
    System.DirectoryServices.ActiveDirectory.ActiveDirectorySiteLink
-ArgumentList $forcntxt, "MyNewSite3-MyNewSite4"    ⟵
                                                     ❷ New link
$site1 =
[System.DirectoryServices.ActiveDirectory.ActiveDirectorySite]::
FindByName($forcntxt, "MyNewSite3")                         ⟵

                                                     Find sites ❸
$site2 =
[System.DirectoryServices.ActiveDirectory.ActiveDirectorySite]::
FindByName($forcntxt, "MyNewSite4")                        ⟵

$link.Sites.Add($site1)      ❹ Add sites
$link.Sites.Add($site2)         to link                  ❻ Set
                                                            replication
$link.Cost = 150                        ⟵─❺ Set cost       interval
$link.ReplicationInterval = "01:00:00"              ⟵
$link.Save()                                   ⟵              Set ❽
                                       ❼ Save           description
$linkde = $link.GetDirectoryEntry()
$linkde.Description = "Links sites MyNewSite3 and MyNew Site4"  ⟵
$linkde.SetInfo()                                      ⟵─❾ Save
```

DISCUSSION

I'm not going to present a script to explicitly modify the properties of a site link. The script in technique 133 can be easily modified to change the cost, replication interval, or even the member sites if required. To remove a site use the following syntax:

```
$link.Sites.Remove($site_name)
```

Before we turn our attention to manipulating replication schedules, let's discover how we can delete a site link.

TECHNIQUE 131 **Deleting a site link**

Any organizational change that modifies the Active Directory sites that are in use will also alter the set of site links we need to use.

PROBLEM

A number of sites have been removed from our Active Directory topology. We need to remove the corresponding links to ensure that the replication topology is kept at maximum efficiency.

SOLUTION

The `ActiveDirectorySiteLink` class has a `delete` method we can use for this task, as shown in listing 11.22.

Listing 11.22 Delete site link

```
$for =
[System.DirectoryServices.ActiveDirectory.Forest]::
GetCurrentForest()

$fortyp =
[System.DirectoryServices.ActiveDirectory.`
DirectoryContexttype]"forest"

$forcntxt = New-Object
System.DirectoryServices.ActiveDirectory.`
DirectoryContext($fortyp, $for)                     ◁─❶ Forest context

$link =
[System.DirectoryServices.ActiveDirectory.`
ActiveDirectorySiteLink]::
FindByName($forcntxt, "TestLink")                   ◁─❷ Get link

$link.Delete()                   ◁─❸ Delete
```

DISCUSSION

The forest context ❶ is retrieved and used with the link name to create ❷ the `Active-DirectorySiteLink` object. The `Delete()` method ❸ is then used to remove it.

As part of our work with Active Directory, we need to be able to discover the schedules controlling replication.

TECHNIQUE 132 **Determining replication schedules**

When a site link is created, a replication interval (default 180 minutes) and schedule (default 24 x 7) are created.

> **SCHEDULE** The schedule controls when replication can start, *not* when replication can happen. If the schedule is only set for 1-2 a.m. then replication can start during that period, but once started, it'll continue until finished even if that goes beyond 2 a.m.

Accessing the schedule in the GUI is awkward in that AD Sites and Services has to be opened, then we have to drill down into the transport mechanisms to find the site link, open its properties, and finally click on the Schedule button. This will show the schedule on an hourly basis for each day of the week. Additionally, we can't just use the `InterSiteReplicationSchedule` property, because if a schedule is set as 24 x 7 then nothing shows when you list the `InterSiteReplicationSchedule` property. If it's set to anything else, then we get `System.DirectoryServices.ActiveDirectory.ActiveDirectorySchedule` returned instead of the actual schedule. Let's write a script that will sort this out for us.

PROBLEM

We want an easy way to see the replication schedules of our site link. Ideally we want the display to show more detail than the GUI tools.

SOLUTION

What we want is a display like figure 11.3. We need to unravel the way AD stores the schedule information to get to that display. The script to do so is shown in listing 11.23.

Listing 11.23   Display replication schedule

```
$sched = @()                                         ◄─┐
$days = "Sunday", "Monday", "Tuesday",                 ❶
"Wednesday", "Thursday", "Friday", "Saturday"    ◄─┘
hours = " "*11

for ($j=0; $j -le 23; $j++){$hours += "{0,-4}" -f $j}
$sched += $hours                                        ❷

$for =
[System.DirectoryServices.ActiveDirectory.Forest]::
GetCurrentForest()                                                    ◄─┐

$fortyp =
[System.DirectoryServices.ActiveDirectory.`
DirectoryContexttype]"forest"                              ◄─❸

$forcntxt = New-Object
System.DirectoryServices.ActiveDirectory.`
DirectoryContext($fortyp, $for)                           ◄─┘

$link =
[System.DirectoryServices.ActiveDirectory.`
ActiveDirectorySiteLink]::
FindByName($forcntxt, "MyNewSite3-MyNewSite4")      ❹

for ($i=0; $i -le 6; $i++) {    #days       ❺
    $out = ""
    $out += $days[$i].PadRight(11)
    for ($j=0; $j -le 23; $j++) { #hours               ❻
        for ($k=0; $k -le 3; $k++) { #15 minutes       ❼
            if ($link.InterSiteReplicationSchedule.    ❽
                    RawSchedule.psbase.GetValue($i,$j,$k)){$out += "Y"}
            else {$out += "n"}      ❾
        }
    }
    $sched += $out       ❿
}
$sched     ⓫
```

DISCUSSION

I like this script because it gives me more information than the GUI and makes that information easier to access. The display in figure 11.3 shows the replication schedule for 15-minute intervals through the whole week. The numbers across the top row are the hours of the day (24-hour clock). I chose to show when replication is allowed with a capital *Y* and when it isn't with a lowercase *n*. This makes the replication schedule easier to understand.

It's time to see how we get to this display. We start by creating a couple of arrays ❶. The first is empty and will hold the schedule data, whereas the second holds the days

```
C:\Scripts\Sites                                                                                    _ □ ×
             0   1   2   3   4   5   6   7   8   9  10  11  12  13  14  15  16  17  18  19  20  21  22  23
Sunday     nnnnnnnnnnnnnnnnnnnnnnnnnnnnnnnnnnnnnnnnnnnnnnnnnnYYYYYYYnnnnnnnnnnnnnnnnnYYYYYYYYYYYYYYYYYYYYYYYY
Monday     nnnnnnnnnnnnnnnnnnnnnnnnnnnnnnnnnnnnnnnnnnnnnnnnnnYYYYYYYnnnnnnnnnnnnnnnnnYYYYYYYYYYYYYYYYYYYYYYYY
Tuesday    nnnnnnnnnnnnnnnnnnnnnnnnnnnnnnnnnnnnnnnnnnnnnnnnnnYYYYYYYnnnnnnnnnnnnnnnnnYYYYYYYYYYYYYYYYYYYYYYYY
Wednesday  nnnnnnnnnnnnnnnnnnnnnnnnnnnnnnnnnnnnnnnnnnnnnnnnnnYYYYYYYnnnnnnnnnnnnnnnnnYYYYYYYYYYYYYYYYYYYYYYYY
Thursday   nnnnnnnnnnnnnnnnnnnnnnnnnnnnnnnnnnnnnnnnnnnnnnnnnnYYYYYYYnnnnnnnnnnnnnnnnnYYYYYYYYYYYYYYYYYYYYYYYY
Friday     nnnnnnnnnnnnnnnnnnnnnnnnnnnnnnnnnnnnnnnnnnnnnnnnnnYYYYYYYnnnnnnnnnnnnnnnnnYYYYYYYYYYYYYYYYYYYYYYYY
Saturday   nnnnnnnnnnnnnnnnnnnnnnnnnnnnnnnnnnnnnnnnnnnnnnnnnnYYYYYYYnnnnnnnnnnnnnnnnnYYYYYYYYYYYYYYYYYYYYYYYY
```

Figure 11.3   Display of the replication schedule for a site link. *Y* **means replication is enabled and** *n* **means it isn't. Each character represents a 15-minute block of time.**

of the week. If you don't want to type the days of the week into a script like this, you can generate them this way:

```
$days = 0..6 | foreach{([System.DayofWeek]$_).ToString()}
```

Use the range operator to pipe the numbers 0 through 6 into foreach. The System. DayofWeek enumeration is used to generate the name of the weekday.

The next job is to create the top row of the table that holds the hours. Our starting point is a variable $hours that has 11 spaces. This is padding to allow for the column of day names in the table. The values are simply numbers, so we can use a loop to put each integer value into a four-character field using the -f operator and the .NET string formatting functionality. It's then appended to the $hours variable. Once completed, the hours variable is appended to the array holding the schedule ❷. We then need to generate a forest context ❸, going through the usual steps to create it.

The ActiveDirectorySiteLink class has a FindByName() method that uses the forest context and the name of the link ❹ A site link has an InterSite-ReplicationSchedule.RawSchedule property consisting of 672 Boolean entries in a three-dimensional array. Each value represents a period of 15 minutes counted sequentially from 00:00 on Sunday. We can use a set of nested loops to unravel these entries.

The outer loop ❺ counts through the seven days of the week. The processing for each day initializes an empty string as an output variable and adds the day of the week name to it. We pad the name to 11 characters to make everything line up. It's much easier to read that way. The middle loop counts through the hours of the day ❻ and the inner loop counts the 15-minute blocks of each hour ❼. The correct value is retrieved from the schedule using the loop counters as indices ❽. If set to True, the output variable has a Y appended and if it's false, an n is appended ❾. At the end of the loop representing the days, the output variable is appended to our schedule array ❿.

When all 672 values have been processed, we can display the schedule ⓫ to produce the display seen in figure 11.3.

Now that we know how to display the schedule, let's look at changing it. That will give us another excuse to run our display script to check the results.

TECHNIQUE 133   **Setting replication schedules**

The ability to set replication schedules at an hourly level may seem to give us enough granularity, but there are circumstances where we need more. Imagine the situation where a busy WAN link can only be used for replication in the evening and at lunchtime. Even worse, we have to ensure that we don't start replicating after 13:45., as the users will be ramping up their use of the bandwidth by 14:00.

Now take that problem and extend it across a number of links. We need to be able to automate these changes.

PROBLEM

We've been told that replication is only allowed during limited time periods—in this case 12:00-13:45 and 18:00 to 23:59. We need to manipulate our replication schedule with a finer degree of control than allowed by the GUI tool.

SOLUTION

The schedule values can't be set directly. We need to create a schedule object and use it to set the schedule on the site link. In the GUI, we can set or clear individual blocks of time to control replication. Using the `ActiveDirectorySchedule` class, we find two methods. The first is `SetDailySchedule()`, which will create a schedule for everyday of the week for the given times. The second method, `SetSchedule()`, can be used to set the schedule for individual days. The results are cumulative when the two methods are used in combination, as we'll see shortly.

Site links are among the group of objects that sit at the forest level. This group also includes sites and subnets, which we discussed in earlier sections. This means we have to start our script in listing 11.24 by creating a forest context. We can do this by getting the current forest ❶ and creating a context type of forest ❷. These are used to create the forest context ❸. An object can be created for the site link ❹ using the forest context and the name of the link.

Our next task is to create the schedule we'll apply ❺. The `ResetSchedule()` method can be used to completely clear the schedule ❻. If this is then applied to the site link, replication won't be possible.

Part of our task was to enable replication between 18:00 and midnight. We want this to apply every day of the week, so we use the `SetDailySchedule()` method ❼. The four parameters give the start and end times for the period of replication. The times are read as pairs, where the first member of the pair is the hour (based on a 24-hour clock) and the second is the hour quarters.

Listing 11.24   Set replication schedule

```
$for =
[System.DirectoryServices.ActiveDirectory.Forest]::
GetCurrentForest()                                        ◁──❶ Get forest

$fortyp =
[System.DirectoryServices.ActiveDirectory.`
DirectoryContexttype] "forest"                  ◁──❷ Context type
```

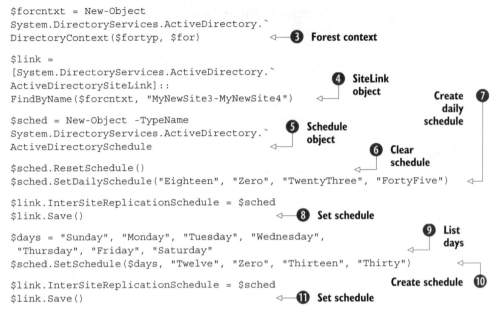

```
$forcntxt = New-Object
System.DirectoryServices.ActiveDirectory.`
DirectoryContext($fortyp, $for)
```
❸ **Forest context**

```
$link =
[System.DirectoryServices.ActiveDirectory.`
ActiveDirectorySiteLink]::
FindByName($forcntxt, "MyNewSite3-MyNewSite4")
```
❹ **SiteLink object**

❼ **Create daily schedule**

```
$sched = New-Object -TypeName
System.DirectoryServices.ActiveDirectory.`
ActiveDirectorySchedule
```
❺ **Schedule object**

❻ **Clear schedule**

```
$sched.ResetSchedule()
$sched.SetDailySchedule("Eighteen", "Zero", "TwentyThree", "FortyFive")
```

```
$link.InterSiteReplicationSchedule = $sched
$link.Save()
```
❽ **Set schedule**

❾ **List days**

```
$days = "Sunday", "Monday", "Tuesday", "Wednesday",
 "Thursday", "Friday", "Saturday"
$sched.SetSchedule($days, "Twelve", "Zero", "Thirteen", "Thirty")
```

❿ **Create schedule**

```
$link.InterSiteReplicationSchedule = $sched
$link.Save()
```
⓫ **Set schedule**

DISCUSSION

We can determine the correct values to use by examining the contents of two enumerations. The hours can be seen by using:

```
[enum]::GetNames([System.DirectoryServices.ActiveDirectory.HourOfday])
```

This will display the names of the hours from Zero to TwentyThree.

The quarter hour divisions can be seen using:

```
[enum]::GetNames([System.DirectoryServices.ActiveDirectory.MinuteOfHour])
```

which will display the values Zero, Fifteen, Thirty, and FortyFive, representing the four 15-minute periods we can use. The name of the enumeration is misleading, as it only has the quarter-hour values.

Once we've determined the schedule to use, we set the InterSiteReplication-Schedule property to the schedule ❽ and save it.

The other method we can use to set the schedule is more granular. We need to give SetSchedule() an array containing the days we want it to apply ❾ and the beginning and end times ❿. This schedule is then set ⓫ and saved.

The days of the week can be obtained from an enumeration, but it's a generic .NET enumeration:

```
[enum]::GetNames([System.DayofWeek])
```

rather than a specific one for Active Directory.

This completes our look at site links and the Active Directory topology.

11.6 *Summary*

The Active Directory topology consists of domain controllers, sites, subnets, and site links. We've seen how to find the domain controllers and global catalog servers in our AD. Domain controllers are tasked with replicating Active Directory information between themselves. The scripts in this chapter will enable us to test whether replication is working and force it to happen if required.

Active Directory sites and subnets are used to define the physical topology. We've seen how to apply PowerShell to the lifecycle of these objects.

Active Directory replication is controlled by AD site links. The lifecycle of these links can be controlled by PowerShell. We've seen how to work with the replication schedule to extract more information than is available in the GUI. In addition, we can create replication schedules with a finer degree of control than we can when we use the GUI tools.

This chapter concludes our direct work with Active Directory. We'll turn our attention back to Exchange 2007 in the next chapter. We'll build on chapter 6, but this time we'll concentrate on the Exchange servers rather than the mailboxes.

Exchange Server
2007 and 2010

This chapter covers

- Working with storage groups and databases
- Managing Exchange policies
- PowerShell in Exchange 2010

We saw in chapter 6 how Exchange Server 2007 was designed with PowerShell at the heart of the administration toolset. While reading this chapter, the information in chapters 5, 6, and 11 should be kept in mind. Exchange 2007 has methods for working with Active Directory users (chapter 5) and AD sites (chapter 11) that give useful variations on the examples in those chapters. Chapter 6 covers individual mailboxes; this chapter concentrates on the administration of the servers that host those mailboxes.

POWERSHELL V2 Exchange 2007 doesn't install on Windows Server 2008 R2 as of the time of writing. This capability should be available later in 2010 when SP 3 is delivered. I wouldn't recommend upgrading PowerShell v1 to v2 on a system that's already in production. In theory, everything should work okay, but email is a business-critical system. Installing Exchange 2007 SP2 on Windows Server 2008 with PowerShell v2 is supported.

Exchange 2010 administration builds on the foundation laid by the 2007 version. This chapter and chapter 6 can be applied to both versions. In chapter 6, I stated that a user will be upset if his mailbox isn't available. Think of the level of upset if all the mailboxes in a database aren't available, or even worse, none of the mailboxes in any of the databases on a server can be accessed. We need to adopt a common-sense approach to administering our Exchange servers that incorporates recognized best practice.

> **SCRIPTS**   A number of the examples in this chapter will be short compared to previous chapters. This is due to the Exchange team producing a superb set of cmdlets that really fit with the administrative tasks we need to perform. If an example of how to implement PowerShell to administer an application is ever needed, this is the one to choose.

If you don't work with Exchange on regular basis, I recommend rereading the introductory part of chapter 6 as a refresher on how PowerShell is integrated into Exchange 2007 and the relationship between the GUI tools and the cmdlets.

Exchange 2007 exposes a lot of functionality through PowerShell. This chapter will concentrate on the server-based tasks associated with mailboxes. We start by looking at the range of functionality that's available via PowerShell in Exchange 2007. After a quick look at the Active Directory functionality that's available and the administration scripts that are provided, we discover how to test the health of our Exchange systems.

The administration of the Exchange organization and our servers is discussed before we look at storage groups and databases. Exchange allows us to create a wide range of policies to simplify and automate administration. We can work with these policies through PowerShell. Certificate administration as it affects Exchange will be discussed, followed by a look at resource mailboxes. We'll close the chapter with a brief look at the functionality introduced with Exchange 2010 that allows us to work remotely through PowerShell.

Our first task is discover what we can do with PowerShell on an Exchange server.

12.1 *Automating Exchange Server 2007 administration*

There are a large number of cmdlets for Exchange 2007. The breadth they cover can be examined by using:

```
Get-Command `
-PSSnapin Microsoft.Exchange.Management.PowerShell.Admin |
Group Noun | Sort Name
```

With 394 Exchange cmdlets spread across 139 nouns, we're not going to cover all of them in a single chapter. It'll take the most conscientious admin quite a while to get all of those cmdlets fixed in her mind. This is where we flip back to chapter 2 and remember that we can use PowerShell as our discovery tool. For instance, if we need to work with the Exchange databases, we can use:

```
Get-Command *database*
```

This will generate a list of the cmdlets dealing with databases. The scripts provided by the Exchange team (see section 12.1.2) will also be listed. If we only want cmdlets, we can change the command to be:

```
Get-Command *database* -CommandType cmdlet
```

We can discover cmdlets by the action they perform. If we need to think about the tests we can run on our Exchange system, then we'd use:

```
Get-Command -Verb test
```

> **USE THE SNAPIN** The examples presented here will also include the standard PowerShell cmdlets as well as the Exchange cmdlets. If we need to filter out the standard cmdlets, we can use the PSSnapin parameter to restrict our search to the Exchange cmdlets, as shown in the first example in this section.

We'll take a brief aside to look at the cmdlets Exchange provides for working with Active Directory before looking directly at the Exchange functionality.

12.1.1 *Exchange AD cmdlets*

There are a number of Exchange cmdlets for working with Active Directory. We've seen that we can use the New-Mailbox cmdlet for creating user accounts. The cmdlets for working with distribution groups also work directly with AD.

We can, assuming we have the permissions, work with Active Directory users and groups. There are pairs of *Get/Set-* cmdlets for the nouns *User* and *Group*. These cmdlets will enable us to work with the main user attributes. Get-User is especially useful when Exchange and AD administration are divided and the Exchange administrators need to access the user accounts to create or modify mail settings.

Active Directory permissions can be manipulated using the *-ADPermission cmdlets. Add-ADPermission could be used to configure Protection from Accidental Deletion on an object by denying the Delete permission to the Everyone group.

Exchange 2007 uses the Active Directory site topology for internally routing messages. There are two cmdlets for working with sites. Get-ADSite, by default, returns a list of the sites in the AD topology and whether they're a hub site for Exchange. The other information available through this cmdlet is the standard AD information a site object would show in the GUI.

Set-ADSite can be used to configure an Active Directory site as an Exchange hub site, which will then override the default message routing.

> **AD ADMINISTRATORS** If AD and Exchange administration are separated in the organization, it'd be worth talking to the AD admins about the *-ADSite and *-ADSiteLink cmdlets and what they do. They'll get upset if they think you're modifying their AD topology.

Get-ADSiteLink can be use to view the site link information, including the cost. The cost is the important parameter for Exchange, as it's used to determine message routing paths. Set-ADSiteLink can be used to assign an Exchange cost to a link that overrides the AD cost *for Exchange only*. It doesn't modify the AD cost.

These are the only cmdlets available for working directly with the AD topology. Windows 2008 R2 doesn't include any, either. The Quest AD cmdlets and the Microsoft cmdlets in Windows Server 2008 R2 are completely compatible, and complementary, to the Exchange cmdlets.

Next on the agenda is a look at the scripts packaged with Exchange 2007.

12.1.2 Exchange scripts

The Exchange team has supplied a number of scripts to aid the administration of our Exchange organization. These scripts are installed during the creation of the Exchange server. They can be found in the Exchange installation directory.

Scripts are supplied to perform a number of tasks:

- Spam statistics, including top blocked domains and IP addresses
- Configuring AD LDS on Edge servers
- Enabling cross-forest connectors
- Moving the Transport database
- Configuring and resetting the search index

These scripts are a good set of examples. They appear to be written in a number of different styles, but are readily understandable.

An important part of administering any system such as Exchange is proving that our system is healthy.

TECHNIQUE 134   **Exchange Server health**

If we sit and wait for problems to find us, we'll always be reactive. Often, users will be the first to discover a problem with the email server. This situation puts us into a defensive position. It's much better to be aware of any potential problems and deal with them before they become apparent.

With Exchange, we have a significant number of Windows services we need to check. All of these services need to be running for us to have a healthy server. There's also a significant body of best practice knowledge available for Exchange Server 2007. Incorporating this into our testing would be useful for confirming that our Exchange servers are configured correctly.

PROBLEM

We've been tasked with discovering whether all of the requisite services are available on our Exchange servers. As part of our investigation, we also want to a test to determine whether our servers are configured according to current best practice.

SOLUTION

There are two Exchange cmdlets we can use for these tests, as shown in listing 12.1. When we use Test-ServiceHealth, we obtain the data shown in figure 12.1. The display shows the Exchange roles (I only had Mailbox, Client Access, and Hub Transport available on the my test machine). There's an entry for each role to show whether the required services are running. This gives us a rapid view of the state of the server.

Listing 12.1 Testing the health of Exchange

```
Test-ServiceHealth
```

```
Test-SystemHealth
```

The final two columns show whether individual services are running. This part of the display includes Exchange-specific services as well as dependent services such as the IIS Administration service.

> **CONCEPT REUSE** This idea of testing whether the required and dependent services are running is useful. In chapter 14, we'll look at developing something similar for SQL Server.

Our second cmdlet was `Test-SystemHealth`. This cmdlet will examine our Exchange system and report back on items that don't meet best practice. The results will change

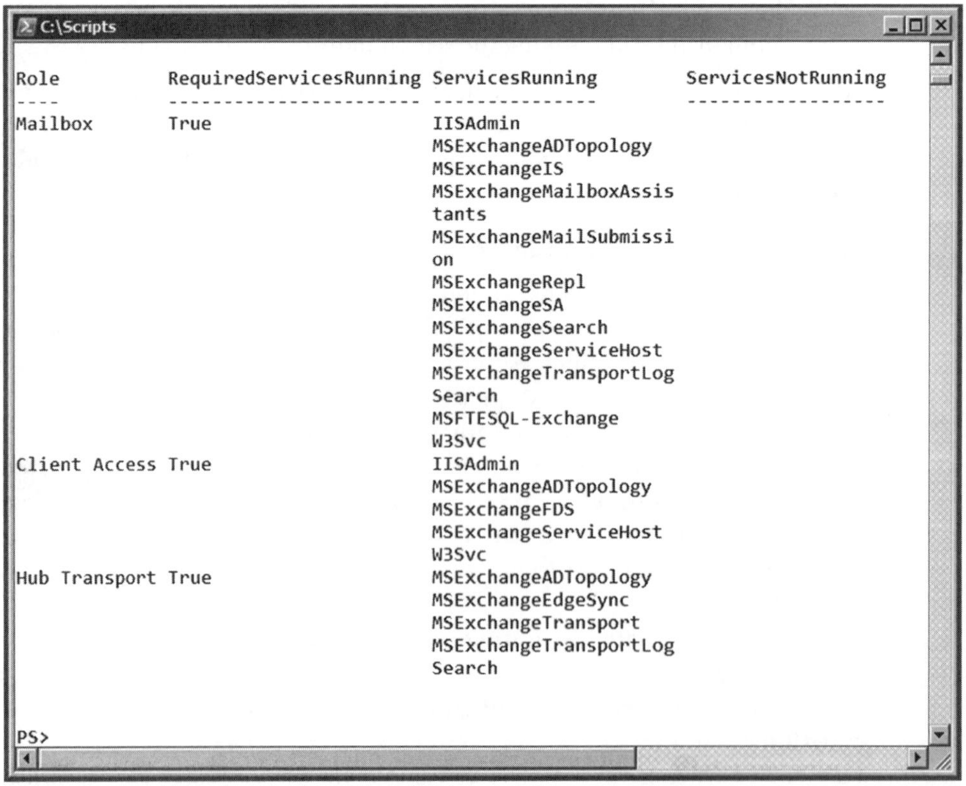

Figure 12.1 The results of running the `Test-ServiceHealth` cmdlet. The services required by each Exchange role are displayed. The display is broken down into services that are running and services that aren't running.

between systems and as best practice evolves. A configuration file containing the latest best practice data is downloaded as part of the exercise.

DISCUSSION

When I ran listing 12.1 on my system, I was told that I was running a trial version of Exchange and that the grace period had expired. Some of the information that's more useful in a production environment includes checks on the last time the data stores were backed up.

There are also cmdlets to test connectivity over various protocols such as MAPI or POP. Replication can be tested as can the flow of mail.

The mailbox server is at the heart of our Exchange infrastructure. Mailbox data stores are covered next.

TECHNIQUE 135   Exchange organization

The Exchange *organization* is at the top of the pyramid of Exchange objects. When you look at the Exchange Management Console, it contains additional nodes for Mailbox, Client Access, Hub Transport, and Unified Messaging. Modifications to the organizational level configuration won't be very common.

PROBLEM

We need to be able to view and modify the configuration of the Exchange organization.

SOLUTION

The `*-OrganizationConfiguration` cmdlets can be used, as in listing 12.2. `Get-OrganizationConfig` will show obvious information such as the name of the Exchange organization and whether it's mixed-mode. More useful information includes:

- Mime types that are enabled within the organization
- The spam confidence level junk threshold-controls the volume of messages that are redirected to the users Junk Mail folder
- The state of the email address policy
- The GUID of the organization
- When the Exchange organization object was created, and more importantly when it was last changed

The organization level configuration can be modified using `Set-OrganizationConfig`. For instance, the SCL junk threshold can be changed like so:

```
Set-OrganizationConfig -SCLJunkThreshold 7
```

This modifies the junk threshold downward from the default of 8. More messages will be directed to the junk folder, and less spam will get through to the user's inbox.

Listing 12.2   Working with the Exchange organization

```
Get-OrganizationConfig

Set-OrganizationConfig
```

DISCUSSION

Other cmdlets exist to modify settings at the organizational level:

- `*-TransportConfig` can be used to read or change the way messages are transported, including dumpster size for storage groups, maximum message size, and the maximum number of recipients.
- `*-ResourceConfig` for working with resources such as room sizes and equipment available.
- `*-AvailabilityConfig` controls the access levels for free/busy information.

TECHNIQUE 136   Exchange Servers

We've already seen how to test the health of our servers. In this section, we'll look at discovering the configuration of those servers and how we can modify that configuration.

One slight drawback to Exchange 2007 is that we have a number of server roles. This granularity has to be reflected in how we administer our servers. The different roles mandate configuration differences that we need to understand.

PROBLEM

We need to be able to view and modify the configuration of the Exchange servers in our organization.

SOLUTION

The `*-*Server` cmdlets can be used to read the configuration information for servers, as in listing 12.2. We can start with `Get-ExchangeServer`, which will return information on every Exchange server within Active Directory including the AD site, the installed server roles, Exchange Edition, and the domain controllers that the server is configured to use.

Listing 12.3   Discovering servers

```
Get-ExchangeServer

Get-MailboxServer
Get-ClientAccessServer
Get-TransportServer

Get-UMServer
```

DISCUSSION

We can modify, via `Set-ExchangeServer`, the domain controllers and global catalogs that the Exchange server will use for accessing Active Directory. This is a good idea if we have a big, fast 64-bit global catalog server with enough memory to hold the AD database. Speedy! `Set-ExchangeServer` also can be used to enable error reporting.

    EDGE SERVERS   Edge Servers exist in the perimeter network and don't participate in AD. We'll ignore them for the purposes of this discussion.

Each of the other cmdlets deals with a specific server role. There's a corresponding `Set-` cmdlet for modifying the server configuration. The `Set-TransportServer` cmdlet is probably of most interest, as it's used to set the transport options on Hub Transport servers (and Edge servers). There's a long list of options including:

- Internal and external DNS configuration
- External postmaster address
- Connection limits
- Maximum delivery and submission threads to throttle the flow of mail
- Message-tracking configuration
- Notification time-outs and retry intervals

Where multiple instances of a server role exist in an organization, these cmdlets can be used to record the configuration and to modify the configuration to ensure uniformity where required.

Mailbox servers are of the most interest to our users, because that's where their mailboxes are hosted. The data stores on those servers are the subject of our next topic.

12.2   Data stores

In Exchange 2007, the rules on the number of databases have been changed. In previous versions, we could have up to 5 databases in each of 4 storage groups, for a maximum of 20 databases. Now we can have up to 50 databases in the Enterprise version of Exchange 2007. There can be a maximum of 50 storage groups, but the 50-database limit still applies regardless of the number of storage groups.

The storage group is the unit of backup, because the databases within the storage group share a common set of log files. In Exchange 2010, storage groups disappear and we work directly with the databases. Exchange 2007 will be around for long enough to make this topic worth covering.

Exchange 2007 introduced a couple of new high availability options in the form of local continuous replication (LCR) and cluster continuous replication (CCR). Exchange 2007 SP1 introduced standby continuous replication (SCR). These three configurations require that there only be a single database per storage group. Microsoft best practice is that storage groups be configured with one database.

Putting this together, we need to be able to create a number of storage groups and databases in an efficient manner.

TECHNIQUE 137   Creating storage groups

Before we jump into creating our storage groups, we should take a quick look to see what groups are already available. This can be done using a single cmdlet:

```
Get-StorageGroup
```

As with all cmdlets, it's worth taking the time to use Get-Member to discover what other data we can access besides the default display.

PROBLEM

Our organization is expanding, so we need to create another database on the Exchange server. Before we can do that, we must create a new storage group.

SOLUTION

When Exchange is installed, it creates the initial databases on the C: drive by default. This isn't a good place to keep our databases, as this drive is usually quite small (by Exchange standards) and performance will be impacted.

> **BEST PRACTICE** We should put our logs and databases on different drives as best practice. I'm deliberately ignoring that to set up a later example.

We can create a storage group using the `New-StorageGroup` cmdlet, as in listing 12.4.

Listing 12.4   Creating a storage group

```
New-StorageGroup -Server 'EXCH01' -Name 'SG4'
-LogFolderPath 'C:\ExchangeData\sg4\logs'
 -SystemFolderPath 'C:\ExchangeData\sg4\data'
```

DISCUSSION

The required parameters include the server on which the storage group will reside, the name of the group, and the folders to store the logs and the database, respectively.

> **FOLDERS** If the default locations aren't being accepted when creating storage groups, the folder structure must be created before running this script. If the folders haven't already been created, the script will throw an error and stop. Oops!

In case you're thinking this would be easier in the GUI, think of the case of CCR or SCR where you need identical storage group and database configuration on two, or possibly more, Exchange servers. Using PowerShell improves setup speed and accuracy.

Now that we have a storage group, we should create something for it to store.

TECHNIQUE 138   Creating databases

Storage groups aren't much use without databases. The two objects are created separately because we can have multiple databases in a storage group.

PROBLEM

We need to create a database to store the mailboxes of new users and make it available for use.

SOLUTION

The `New-MailboxDatabase` cmdlet is our tool in this example, as shown in listing 12.5. This needs a few parameters. The name of the new database and the storage group in which it'll reside are required. The location of the log files is controlled by the storage group. We then tell the cmdlet where to create the database. Note the parameter name. The path we use was established when we created the storage group. We're adding the name of the database to that path.

Listing 12.5 Creating a database

```
New-MailboxDatabase -Name 'MailDb4'
-StorageGroup 'SG4'
-EdbFilePath 'C:\ExchangeData\sg4\data\MailDb4.edb'

Mount-Database -Identity "Exch01\SG4\MailDb4"
```

DISCUSSION

Newly created databases aren't mounted by default. We need to issue the command to mount the database so it can be used. Notice the server\storage group\database structure for the identity of the database. This structure can be used in any cmdlet working with databases when we need to identify the database.

> **MOUNT COMMANDS** The `Mount-` and `Dismount-Database` cmdlets apply to public folder databases as well as mailbox databases.

We can combine this example and the preceding example for a script that can create our storage groups and databases in one operation.

One perennial problem for the Exchange administrator is monitoring the distribution of mailboxes across the databases.

TECHNIQUE 139   Mailbox distribution

Some years ago, I was involved in a large Exchange migration. I was moving more than 7,000 mailboxes onto three Exchange servers, each of which had 16 databases. One of the issues I had was ensuring an even distribution of mailboxes across the databases. I wrote a script (VBScript because this was several years *BP—Before Power-Shell*) to discover the information, but it wasn't as easy to do compared to PowerShell.

PROBLEM

An even distribution of mailboxes across our databases balances the load on the various components of our Exchange mailbox server. How can we determine whether the databases are equally loaded?

SOLUTION

We can use `Get-MailboxStatistics` to find the size of each mailbox. Combining them at the database level produces our desired result, as shown in listing 12.6.

This may look complicated, but it breaks down into two nested loops using the `Foreach-Object` cmdlet. As usual I've used the alias `Foreach` to save space. We start by creating an empty array to hold our results ❶. Our goal is to find the number of mailboxes and the size of the databases. This makes our next task ❷ finding the mailbox databases. The databases are piped into `foreach`, which has a `-process` and an `-end` script block. The `-process` block commences by creating a new object ❸ and defining a number of properties for the object ❹. Note that we have to give initial values for the properties. An error will be generated if the value isn't supplied. The properties are:

- Database name
- Number of mailboxes
- Number of mail items
- Total size of the mailboxes

At this point, we're creating one object per database to hold this information.

In order to populate these properties, we use Get-MailboxStatistics with a filter based on the database name ❺. The second -process block of the second foreach increments the count and adds the number of items and the size of the mailbox to the running total ❻. When all of the mailboxes for that particular database have been processed, the -end block appends our object ❼ to the array.

After all of the databases have been processed, the array is piped to a Format-Table cmdlet to display the data ❽. We'll get one line per database, listing the name, number of mailboxes, number of mail items, and cumulative size of the database.

Listing 12.6   Mailbox distribution

```
$sizes = @()                                        ◄——❶ Create array
Get-MailboxDatabase | Foreach `                     ◄——
-Process {                                              ❷ Get databases        ❸ Create
    $data = New-Object -TypeName System.Object      ◄──┘                         object
    Add-Member -InputObject $data -MemberType NoteProperty
      -Name Database -Value $_.Name                                   ◄┐
    Add-Member -InputObject $data -MemberType NoteProperty
      -Name Count -Value 0                                            ◄│
                                                                       │  ❹ Create
    Add-Member -InputObject $data -MemberType NoteProperty            ◄│     properties
      -Name Item -Value 0                                            ◄│
    Add-Member -InputObject $data -MemberType NoteProperty
      -Name Size -Value 0                                            ◄┘

    Get-MailboxStatistics -Database $_.Name | Foreach `           ◄─────┐
    -Process {
        $data.Count ++
        $data.Item += $_.ItemCount                         ❻ Populate
        $data.Size += $_.TotalItemSize.Value.ToKB()           properties
    }`
    -End {$sizes += $data}      ◄——❼ Add to array          Get mailbox
}`                                                          statistics ❺
-End {
    $sizes | Format-Table -auto     ◄——❽ Display results
}
```

DISCUSSION

The array of objects could be exported to a CSV file for further processing if required.

DELETED ITEMS   The size figures don't include the deleted items or any other of the standard mailbox database overhead. We're concentrating purely on live mail items. These figures will give a reasonable approximation to the total size of the databases.

There will be times when we don't need the full set of information. The number of mailboxes per database will be sufficient for our needs. A simple count of mailboxes per database can be found using:

```
Get-Mailbox | group database
```

The `Get-Mailbox` cmdlet returns all mailboxes. `Group` is an alias for `Group-Object` that we saw in chapter 1 (see listing 1.5). It'll group the mailboxes on the given property—in this case, the database name. The display from this "script" is shown in figure 12.2.

```
C:\Scripts                                                                    _ □ X
PS> Get-Mailbox | group database

Count Name                        Group
----- ----                        -----
   58 EXCH01\First Storage G...    {BALFOUR Arthur, BONAR LAW Andrew, DOUGLAS-HOME Alec, EDEN Anthony...}
    5 EXCH01\SG3\MailDb3           {SCHIERHUBER Agnes, ETTL Harald, MARTIN Hans-Peter, RACK Reinhard...}
    4 EXCH01\SG4\MailDb4           {MOLZER Andreas, RESETARITS Karin, KARAS Othmar, SEEBER Richard}
    4 EXCH01\SG2\MailDb2           {PRETS Christa, LICHTENBERGER Eva, VOGGENHUBER Johannes, SCHEELE Karin}
    5 EXCH01\SG1\MailDb1           {SWOBODA Hannes, PIRKER Hubert, LEICHTFRIED JOrg, BERGER Maria...}

PS>
```

Figure 12.2 Using `Group-Object` to count the number of mailboxes per database.

The display could be made neater by changing the command:

```
Get-Mailbox | group database | Format-Table Count, Name
```

This will drop the group property with its long list of mailboxes. If the results are to be persisted, use `select` instead of `Format-Table` and pipe to a file.

   If our databases show a wide range of sizes, we can use `Move-Mailbox` to redistribute the mailboxes between the databases. Ideally, we want to distribute new mailboxes across our databases to prevent this situation from arising.

TECHNIQUE 140   Distributing mailboxes

An ounce of prevention is worth a pound of cure. If we distribute mailboxes across our databases as we create them, we can keep the database loading in balance. This will reduce the amount of monitoring and remedial work the databases require.

> **ASSUMPTION** In the examples in this section, I'm assuming that the user accounts are already created. These scripts could be combined with those presented in chapters 5 and 6 to create a user and mailbox creation mechanism that fits your organizations process and distributes the mailboxes across the databases.

If we have multiple servers in our environment, this approach can be expanded to balance across servers and databases.

PROBLEM

How can we distribute mailboxes across multiple databases on a relatively even basis? This should occur as we create the databases.

SOLUTION

There are several possible solutions to this problem. The two examples presented here select each database in turn to receive the next mailbox or distribute the mailboxes using a scheme based on the alphabet.

One thing to note in listing 12.7 is that I'm using Get-User in both of the scripts in this section. The Quest cmdlets, a script, or Windows 2008 R2 AD cmdlet could be substituted if required, as we saw in chapter 5.

In my test environment I have four databases. We start by fixing this number as a constant ❶. The users who are getting mailboxes are selected ❷ by OU in this case. The -begin script block sets the starting database ❸. If we wanted this to be random we could change the line to read:

```
$db = Get-Random -Minimum 1 -Maximum 5
```

where we derive a random number between one and four. Get-Random is found in PowerShell v2. A switch statement ❹ is used to choose the database based on the value of the $db variable. The mailbox is then created ❺. If desired, the script can be tested by uncommenting the -whatif parameter. The value of the $db variable is then incremented, or reset ❻, ready for the next mailbox.

Listing 12.7   Distributing mailboxes

```
$maxdb = 4
Get-User -OrganizationalUnit "United Kingdom" | foreach `
  -begin {$db = 1} `
  -process {
    switch ($db){
    1 {$maildb = "Exch01\SG1\MailDb1"}
    2 {$maildb = "Exch01\SG2\MailDb2"}
    3 {$maildb = "Exch01\SG3\MailDb3"}
    4 {$maildb = "Exch01\SG4\MailDb4"}
    }
    Enable-Mailbox -Identity $_.DistinguishedName -Database $maildb
     -Alias $_.samaccountname -Displayname $_.Name ##-WhatIf
    if ($db -eq $maxdb){$db=1} else {$db++}
}
```

❶ Number of databases
❷ Get user accounts
❸ Initial database
❹ Choose database
❺ Create mailbox
❻ Next database

DISCUSSION

Many organizations will use a distribution scheme based on an alphabetic distribution, as in listing 12.8.

Listing 12.8   Distributing mailboxes by name

```
Get-User -OrganizationalUnit "Sweden" | foreach {
    switch -regex ($_.Name.ToString().SubString(0,1)){
    "[A-G]" {$maildb = "Exch01\SG1\MailDb1"}
    "[H-M]" {$maildb = "Exch01\SG2\MailDb2"}
```

❶ Get user accounts
❷ Choose database

```
"[N-S]" {$maildb = "Exch01\SG3\MailDb3"}
"[T-Z]" {$maildb = "Exch01\SG4\MailDb4"}
}
Enable-Mailbox -Identity $_.DistinguishedName -Database $maildb
  -Alias $_.samaccountname -Displayname $_.Name ##-WhatIf
}
```

Create **3**
mailbox

In this case, the four databases will contain mailboxes such that those names starting with the letters A-G are in database 1, H-M are in database 2, and so on. The users are selected as in the previous example ❶. The variable used in the `switch` statement is the first character of the user name ❷. In this script, we've introduced the `-regex` parameter into the `switch` statement. This instructs `switch` to match the cases based on regular expressions rather than simple string matching. The switch will match the variable against `"[A-G]"` for instance, which means match against all letters between A and G. The script then creates the mailbox ❸ as before.

Alternatively, we may decide to move the whole database to a new disk volume.

TECHNIQUE 141 Moving a database

When Exchange is first installed, it creates the databases on the C: drive in the Program Files folder. This isn't a good place for them to be. We need to move the databases to another location. Databases may also become too large for the disk on which they're situated.

PROBLEM

A growth in user numbers means our database has outgrown the disk space. We need to move the database to a larger disk volume.

SOLUTION

We need to move the storage group and the database to complete this task, as shown in listing 12.9.

Listing 12.9 Moving a mailbox database

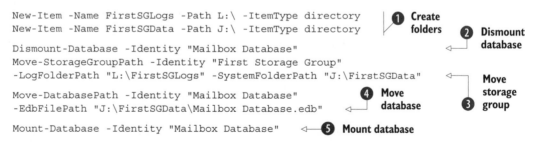

```
New-Item -Name FirstSGLogs -Path L:\ -ItemType directory
New-Item -Name FirstSGData -Path J:\ -ItemType directory

Dismount-Database -Identity "Mailbox Database"
Move-StorageGroupPath -Identity "First Storage Group"
-LogFolderPath "L:\FirstSGLogs" -SystemFolderPath "J:\FirstSGData"

Move-DatabasePath -Identity "Mailbox Database"
-EdbFilePath "J:\FirstSGData\Mailbox Database.edb"

Mount-Database -Identity "Mailbox Database"
```

❶ Create folders
❷ Dismount database
Move storage group ❸
❹ Move database
❺ Mount database

DISCUSSION

This script should be compared with those presented in techniques 137 and 138, where we created a storage group and database respectively. Our first task is to create the folders for the logs and the database files ❶. These are on separate drives to conform to best practice.

The mailbox database must be dismounted ❷ before any of the moves can occur. The `Move-*` cmdlets will implicitly dismount the database if it's mounted. It's better to dismount it explicitly, because this helps us to remember to mount it again after the move. The database won't be much use to us until we do that. We'll be asked to confirm when dismounting the database, moving the storage group, and moving the database. Progress bars will be displayed as the log files and database files are moved.

> **DRIVES**   In this example, we're conforming to best practice and separating the database and log files on to different disk volumes.

The storage group is moved by supplying a new path for the log files and the system folder ❸. The current log files will be moved into the new path. The database file can then be moved ❹. The full path to the database file must be supplied. A common error is to leave the database file name off the path. This will cause an error. At the end of the script, the database can be mounted ❺, ready for the users to access their mailboxes. We need to manually delete the old folder structure.

The last example in this section deals with end-of-life databases and how we can remove them from our environment.

TECHNIQUE 142   Removing a database

All good things must come to an end, and this holds true for mailbox databases. Occasionally we'll need to remove a database and its associated storage group. The important thing is to ensure we safely move the mailboxes to another database before we remove the database.

PROBLEM

A business relocation has left fewer users on a particular Exchanger server. We've decided to consolidate the mailboxes into a single database.

SOLUTION

The PowerShell cmdlet naming conventions make this script almost completely self-describing. It should be possible for you to read and immediately understand what listing 12.10 is doing if you've read the rest of the book. If not, I'll assume you're looking for the answer to an immediate problem and provide a discussion of the script.

Listing 12.10   Removing a mailbox database

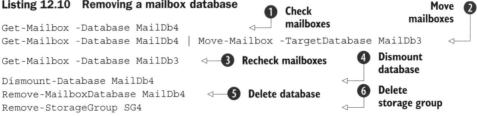

DISCUSSION

In an exercise like this, the first thing we should do is get a list of the mailboxes held in the database ❶. MailDb4 is the database we'll remove. This list can be used as a check that we've completed the move of the mailboxes later on.

The mailboxes can be moved by using `Get-Mailbox` and piping the results into a `Move-Mailbox` cmdlet ❷. The number of mailboxes moved simultaneously can be controlled by using the -MaxThreads parameter. We could use the techniques in technique 140 to distribute mailboxes between multiple databases instead of targeting a single database.

> **SAME SERVER**   The script in listing 12.10 assumes that we're moving the mailboxes to another database on the same server. We can use the server\storage group\database syntax to define a target database on another server.

We can issue a Get-Mailbox against the target database ❸ to check that all of the expected mailboxes have been migrated. The remaining steps dismount the database ❹, delete the database ❺, and finally delete the storage group ❻. We'll be asked for confirmation at each of these steps. In addition, we'll receive a warning about manually deleting the database file and log files to complete the removal process. We won't be able to create a storage group or database with the same name while these files exist.

We've learned to manage the mailbox databases and the mailboxes (chapter 5). Now it's time to look at the way we can simplify and automate the administration by applying polices to various aspects of our Exchange infrastructure.

12.3   *Policies*

In listing 6.7, we looked at applying mailbox size quotas. This is one type of policy. Ideally we want to apply our policies at the Exchange organizational level and allow them to cascade down to our servers, data stores, and mailboxes.

Exchange 2007 enables us to create a number of different policy types. We'll examine some of them in this section, starting with address policies.

TECHNIQUE 143   **Email address**

Email addresses are usually of the form *name@company.xx. XX* can be com, co.uk, or any other recognized domain. A default email policy is created when Exchange is installed that will create a default address. Organizations may require some users to have more than one email address, or even groups of users may have totally different email addresses (merger and acquisition scenarios). The groups of users may overlap, requiring differing email addresses to be created for each user. This should be automated using email address policies. The extant email policies can be viewed using Get-EmailAddressPolicy.

This can display all policies, or a specific policy can be displayed by supplying the identity of the policy. The GUID can be used, but it's a lot less frustrating to use the name!

Before we can view the policies, we need to think about creating one or more policies.

PROBLEM

A specific group of users needs to have their email addresses set to a specific email domain.

SOLUTION

The policy is created using `New-EmailAddressPolicy`. PowerShell's verb-noun naming context makes writing and reading scripts much easier. It does make writing about them an exercise in stating the obvious sometimes, though.

We're creating a new policy, so we need to give it a name and decide which types of recipients will be included in the policy. We can include all types, as in listing 12.11, or restrict ourselves to one or more types such as mailbox users, mail users, contacts, and so forth.

A filter of some sort is usually applied to ensure that the email address policy is applied to the correct group of people. This can be applied by creating conditions based on the users' department, state or province, company attributes, or the value of one of the custom attributes. Alternatively, an LDAP type filter can be used in the `-RecipientFilter` parameter.

Listing 12.11   Creating an email address policy

```
New-EmailAddressPolicy -Name 'Downing Street'
-IncludedRecipients 'AllRecipients'
-ConditionalDepartment 'Downing Street' -Priority 'Lowest'
-EnabledEmailAddressTemplates 'SMTP:%s%1g@downingstreet.org'

Update-EmailAddressPolicy -Identity 'Downing Street'
```

The policy has to be given a priority so that the application order of multiple policies can be established. The final parameter defines the email address template that'll be applied to the user. It consists of the email domain preceded by rules that define the style in which the addressee's name will be defined. In this example, it's surname (`%s`) followed by the first letter of the given name (`%1g`). Similar rules can be written to match the common styles of email addresses—for example, given-name.surname (`%g.%s`) or first letter of given name followed by surname (`%1g%s`).

DISCUSSION

Creating an email policy doesn't actually apply the policy. We need to run `Update-EmailAddressPolicy` to make the changes to the user's email addresses. Once a policy is in place, any users that match its criteria will automatically be assigned the correct email addresses.

If policies need to be modified, we can use `Set-EmailAddressPolicy`. A policy that's no longer required can be deleted using `Remove-EmailAddressPolicy`.

Emails are concerned with transporting information around our organization and between organizations. We can use transport rules to control this flow of information.

TECHNIQUE 144   **Transport rules**

We use *transport rules* to control how emails flow around the organization. We can control many aspects of mail flow, for instance:

- We can control who can send emails to whom within the organization.
- We can stop groups of people from sending emails outside of the organization.

- We can control the information that can be contained in an email—for example we can prevent emails that contain specific words, phrases, or patterns (regular expressions) from being sent.
- We can control the size and type of attachments that can be emailed.

Transport rules can be a big help in meeting our compliance obligations.

PROBLEM

A group within our organization is working on a confidential project. We don't want them to be able to send emails to anyone who's not working on that project.

SOLUTION

Transport rules tend to consist of a condition (a user is a member of a particular group), an action (delete the message), and possibly an exception (don't apply the rule in the case of a particular user).

Two cmdlets are extremely useful for discovering the possible criteria, as shown in listing 12.12. Get-TransportRulePredicate will display a list of the possible rule predicates—the criteria that can be applied in the action and exception parts of the rule. Get-TransportRuleAction will display a list of the possible actions that can be performed.

Listing 12.12   Transport rule to restrict sending capability

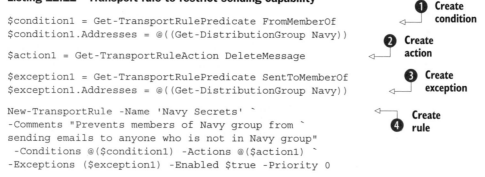

```
$condition1 = Get-TransportRulePredicate FromMemberOf
$condition1.Addresses = @((Get-DistributionGroup Navy))

$action1 = Get-TransportRuleAction DeleteMessage

$exception1 = Get-TransportRulePredicate SentToMemberOf
$exception1.Addresses = @((Get-DistributionGroup Navy))

New-TransportRule -Name 'Navy Secrets' `
-Comments "Prevents members of Navy group from `
sending emails to anyone who is not in Navy group"
 -Conditions @($condition1) -Actions @($action1) `
-Exceptions ($exception1) -Enabled $true -Priority 0
```

❶ Create condition

❷ Create action

❸ Create exception

❹ Create rule

Our rule creation script commences by creating a condition ❶. In this case, it's that all emails sent from a group will be affected by the rule. We have to define the condition type, then add the address as a second step. An array is used as the mechanism to allow multiple addresses to be affected by the policy.

An action ❷ that we'll apply to the message is defined. In this case, the message will be deleted. At this stage, the users can't send emails to anyone. This may make our lives as admins easier, but will upset the users, so we'd better define an exception ❸. The exception allows this group to send emails to other members of the group.

The final statement in the script brings the condition, action, and exception together in the New-TransportRule cmdlet. We complete the cmdlet by providing a name and description, and by enabling the policy ❹.

DISCUSSION

We have a full suite of cmdlets for working with transport rules so we can enable/disable rules, change (set) rules, view (get) rules, and remove rules.

CAN'T COPY FROM EMC   The creation of transport rules is one of the few places where it's not possible to simply copy and reuse the PowerShell script created by the Exchange Management Console. If we try, we get a result similar to that in listing 12.13.

Listing 12.13   Incorrect script produced by EMC

```
New-TransportRule -Name 'Size Limit' -Comments ''
-Conditions `
'Microsoft.Exchange.MessagingPolicies.`
Rules.Tasks.FromPredicate',`
'Microsoft.Exchange.MessagingPolicies.`
Rules.Tasks.AttachmentSizeOverPredicate'

-Actions `
'Microsoft.Exchange.MessagingPolicies.`
Rules.Tasks.DeleteMessageAction'

-Exceptions `
'Microsoft.Exchange.MessagingPolicies`
.Rules.Tasks.SentToPredicate'

-Enabled $true -Priority '0'
```

Careful examination of the script shows that the conditions, actions, and exceptions aren't properly defined. The display shows the .NET object types we're using rather than the values. We have to do all the hard work ourselves to create the full suite of conditions, actions, and exceptions. The next example shows how this can be modified to give us a working script.

TECHNIQUE 145   **Attachments**

Users can attach a file to an email message and send it to other users who may be internal or external to the organization. It's possible for large attachments to cause problems at mail gateways and with network bandwidth if sent to many recipients. A policy that restricts the size of attachments can be used to counter this problem.

We may also want to create attachment policies to restrict the types of file that can be attached or even prevent some users from sending email messages with attachments. In our previous example, we prevented a group of users from sending emails to anyone who wasn't in their group. We could also prevent them from sending attachments.

PROBLEM

One user has been flooding the network with large attachments. We need to restrict the size of files that can be attached to email messages sent by that user.

SOLUTION

Our first action in listing 12.14 is to create a transport rule condition ❶ that states who the rule applies to. Alternatively, this condition could be applied to a group, as we've seen. The second condition sets the maximum size of attachments that are allowed ❷. In this case, we've been harsh and said we'll apply a limit of 20KB.

KB, MB PowerShell recognizes the labels KB, MB, and GB (v2 adds TB and PB) and uses them in the same way we do as admins.

If you want to see the actual values, try this:

```
1kb,1mb,1gb,1tb,1pb | foreach{"$_".PadLeft(16)}
```

Once we've created our conditions, we can create the action we'll perform on the message ❸. We've decided that we'll delete the message. All rules have an exception, and our exception ❹ is that messages sent to a particular user are exempt from the policy.

Listing 12.14 Creating an attachment policy

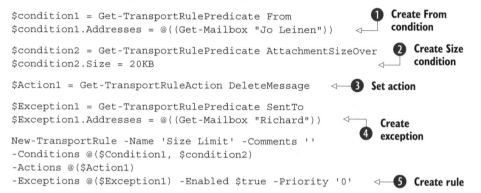

```
$condition1 = Get-TransportRulePredicate From                    ❶ Create From
$condition1.Addresses = @((Get-Mailbox "Jo Leinen"))                condition

$condition2 = Get-TransportRulePredicate AttachmentSizeOver      ❷ Create Size
$condition2.Size = 20KB                                             condition

$Action1 = Get-TransportRuleAction DeleteMessage      ❸ Set action

$Exception1 = Get-TransportRulePredicate SentTo
$Exception1.Addresses = @((Get-Mailbox "Richard"))          Create
                                                       ❹ exception
New-TransportRule -Name 'Size Limit' -Comments ''
-Conditions @($Condition1, $condition2)
-Actions @($Action1)
-Exceptions @($Exception1) -Enabled $true -Priority '0'   ❺ Create rule
```

Our final task ❺ is to bring the conditions, actions, and exceptions together to create the rule. We can also enable the rule at the same time.

We need to look at one other type of rule to complete our understanding of this topic: the journal rule.

TECHNIQUE 146 Journal rules

There are many reasons, commercial as well as regulatory, why organizations need to archive emails. In some sectors, information such as this has to be kept for a number of years. Backup isn't suitable for performing this task, as emails could be sent and deleted between backups. We need a mechanism that can capture emails in flight and automatically make a copy.

PROBLEM

We have to be able to make a copy of all emails sent by or sent to a particular set of recipients in our organization.

SOLUTION

The first step, before we look at listing 12.15, is to create a mailbox to act as the recipient for journaled emails. We can use the script from listing 6.1 to perform this act.

The `New-JournalRule` cmdlet is our method of creating the rule. We start by providing a name for the rule and the email address of the journal mailbox. The email address can be supplied by pointing to the user account associated with the mailbox, as shown. The format is `domain\OU\user`.

Listing 12.15 Creating a journal rule

```
New-JournalRule -Name 'Navy Journal rule'
-JournalEmailAddress 'manticore.org/users/NavyJournal'
-Scope 'Global' -Enabled $true -Recipient 'navy@manticore.org'
```

DISCUSSION

The rule has to be given a scope, which tells it which messages the rule applies to. The global scope will apply the rule to all messages. There are three possible scopes, as detailed in table 12.1.

Table 12.1   Journal rule scopes

Scope	Definition
Global	Global rules process all email messages that pass through a Hub Transport server. This includes email messages that were already processed by the external and internal rules. The default value is Global.
Internal	Internal rules process email messages that are sent and received by recipients in the Exchange Server 2007 organization.
External	External rules process email messages that are sent to recipients or from senders outside the Exchange Server 2007 organization.

The final steps in creating the rule are to enable it and to determine which recipients are affected by the rule. If possible, apply the rule to groups and distribution lists rather than individuals. It's possible to create a rule and not enable it. The rule could then be enabled at a later date using `Enable-JournalRule`.

This concludes our look at Exchange polices. The overview presented here should give you sufficient information to extrapolate to other scenarios. Our next topic concerns certificates and how they relate to Exchange operations.

12.4 *Certificates*

Email carries a lot of confidential information for an organization. We must ensure that access to email is secure and, where appropriate, email traffic is encrypted. Certificates are used to provide this security.

> **RUN AS ADMINISTRATOR** When working with Exchange certificates—especially if making changes—PowerShell must be started with elevated privileges.

Administering Exchange certificates is only possible through PowerShell. Don't use the Certificate console to administer Exchange certificates.

Our first task is to discover which certificates Exchange is using.

TECHNIQUE 147   **Viewing certificates**

Windows has a storage area specifically for certificates. PowerShell exposes this store as PowerShell drive. `Get-ChildItem` allows us to explore this drive.

```
PS> Get-ChildItem cert:

Location    : CurrentUser
StoreNames  : {SmartCardRoot, UserDS, AuthRoot, CA...}

Location    : LocalMachine
StoreNames  : {SmartCardRoot, AuthRoot, CA, Trust...}
```

We can drill down further. `Get-ChildItem cert:\currentuser` shows a number of substores:

- `SmartCardRoot`
- `UserDS`
- `AuthRoot`
- `CA`
- `AddressBook`
- `Trust`
- `Disallowed`
- `My`
- `Root`
- `TrustedPeople`
- `TrustedPublisher`

One more level and we start to see the certificates:

```
Get-ChildItem cert:\currentuser\root
```

This is fine for most certificates, but we need a more direct method for finding the certificates that are specific to Exchange.

PROBLEM

The Exchange certificates must be examined to determine expiry dates and their purpose.

SOLUTION

In listing 12.16, the cmdlet `Get-ExchangeCertificate` ❶ will display any and all certificates that explicitly relate to the Exchange server. The default display ❷ shows the certificate thumbprint, the services it applies to, and the server.

Listing 12.16 Viewing the Exchange certificate

```
Get-ExchangeCertificate                              ◄──  ❶ View certificate

Thumbprint                                Services   Subject    ◄──┘ ❷ Certificate details
----------                                --------   -------
095E4E55442E2C5E35FC1957F7AAA8BD12A00C53  IP.WS      CN=Exch01

Get-ExchangeCertificate | select *   ◄──❸ View all properties    ❹ View certificate store
Get-ChildItem cert: -Recurse |
where{$_.Thumbprint -eq ((get-exchangecertificate).Thumbprint)}  ◄──┘
```

DISCUSSION

There are times when this isn't enough and we need to examine the certificate in more detail. Selecting all of the certificate's properties ❸ enables us to view the details, including expiry date.

Administrators of a curious nature can discover where the certificates are actually stored by searching the certificate store ❹. The `-Recurse` parameter ensures that we search all subfolders. The thumbprint of our Exchange certificate is used as the filter criterion. Alternatively, if the thumbprint is pasted into the where clause, it's a string so it must be in quotes.

Certificates don't last forever; we need to renew them periodically.

Self-signed certificates

Exchange 2007 installs with a self-signed certificate that's valid for one year. Self-signed certificates are generated by the Exchange server. This will work for some functionality such as autodiscovery and OWA, but not for Outlook Anywhere. The self-signed certificate will need renewing to ensure continued access to Exchange.

PROBLEM
The self-signed Exchange certificate is approaching its renewal date. We must ensure that it's renewed before it expires.

SOLUTION
As shown in listing 12.17, a new self-signed certificate can be generated ❶ by using New-ExchangeCertificate. The cmdlet doesn't require any parameters. Remember that PowerShell will soon prompt us if it needs parameters.

A confirmation message ❷ is automatically generated (looks like I was working late when the old one was generated). The thumbprints of the current and new certificates are presented. This is useful, as it saves typing the thumbprint string.

Listing 12.17   Renewing the self-signed certificate

```
New-ExchangeCertificate                           ❶ Create
                                                    certificate

Confirm                                           ❷ Confirmation
Overwrite existing default SMTP certificate,         dialog
'095E4E55442E2C5E35FC1957F7AAA8BD12A00C53'
(expires 09/09/2009 23:59:03), with certificate
'3825E95A627D724EEAD1469224EB62A342D0E37B'
(expires 18/04/2010 21:23:40)?

[Y] Yes  [A] Yes to All  [N] No  [L] No to All
[S] Suspend  [?] Help (default is "Y"): Y         ❸ New
                                                     certificate
Thumbprint                       Services  Subject   details
----------                       --------  -------

3825E95A627D724EEAD1469224EB62A342D0E37B  .....   CN=Exch01
                                                  ❹ Enable
Enable-ExchangeCertificate -Thumbprint               certificate
"3825E95A627D724EEAD1469224EB62A342D0E37B" -Services "IIS"

Get-ExchangeCertificate | select Thumbprint, Services  ❺ Check services

Remove-ExchangeCertificate -Thumbprint            ❻ Remove old
"095E4E55442E2C5E35FC1957F7AAA8BD12A00C53"           certificate
```

DISCUSSION
When we confirm the action, the new certificate will be created and the details ❸ will be displayed. At this point, the certificate hasn't been enabled for any services. This is achieved using Enable-ExchangeCertificate ❹. The certificate has to be identified

by its thumbprint (a great reason to bless the inventor of cut and paste) and the services it'll apply to are identified as a comma-separated list.

Our old friend `Get-ExchangeCertificate` ❺ can be used to view the certificate and the associated services (if required). The old certificate can be removed ❻ once it's no longer required.

Self-signed certificates are useful in certain circumstances, but if we want to use the full range of Exchange functionality, we need to invest in a certificate from a commercial certificate authority (CA).

TECHNIQUE 149   Third-party certificates

We need to use a third-party certificate if we want to exploit the full functionality of Exchange 2007. This task builds on the previous task.

Obtaining and using a certificate from a commercial authority is a multistep process:

- Generate certificate request and send to authority (with payment)
- Obtain certificate file
- Install certificate
- Enable certificate

The first part is where life gets interesting.

PROBLEM

A certificate request file has to be generated to be sent to a commercial CA.

SOLUTION

We use the `New-ExchangeCertificate` cmdlet as in the previous example. This time, we have to supply a lot more information. Listing 12.18 shows the script; figure 12.3 shows an annotated view. It should help the explanation, as we can't put the normal annotation markers onto a single line of PowerShell.

The first parameter is a switch to tell the cmdlet that we want to generate a certificate request. A path to the request file is needed. This can be located anywhere on your disk that's convenient. The file can be given any arbitrary name. We want the private key to be exportable for backup and the certificate should have a friendly name.

Listing 12.18   Requesting a certificate

```
New-ExchangeCertificate -GenerateRequest -Path c:\request.txt
-PrivateKeyExportable $true
-FriendlyName "My SAN certificate"
-DomainName autodiscover.manticore.org, exch01.manticore.org,
owa.manticore.org
-SubjectName "cn=exch01.manticore.org"
```

DISCUSSION

The *SAN* in the friendly name stands for *subject alternate name*. Obtaining a certificate of this sort means that we can use a single certificate for a number of purposes. This is where some of the confusion regarding Exchange certificates arises. It comes down to giving the certificate request a list of the FQDNs of the services we want to deliver. The domain name parameter is used to do this. In the example, we're supplying the FQDN for the autodiscovery service, OWA, and the Exchange server itself.

The final parameter is the name of the server.

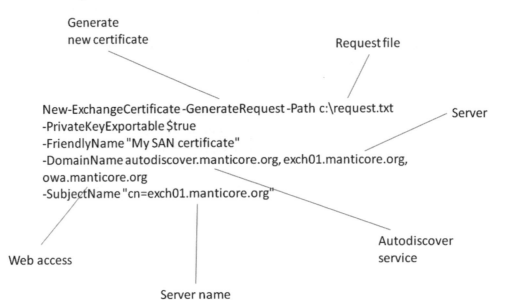

Figure 12.3   Generating a certificate request. The `New-ExchangeCertificate` **cmdlet is used to generate the request.**

Once we're sure of the parameters we want to input into `New-ExchangeCertificate`, we can run it and generate the request file. The file isn't in a readable format, as can be seen from the following example:

```
PS> cat c:\request.txt
-----BEGIN NEW CERTIFICATE REQUEST-----
MIID5DCCAswCAQAwHzEdMBsGA1UEAwwUZXhjaDAxLm1hbnRpY29yZS5vcmcwggEi
MA0GCSqGSIb3DQEBAQUAA4IBDwAwggEKAoIBAQCHnpx97sjsSfC24smKecU6jE7q
fT/eIHg45Wej6Ei6vkwXmucwK5HlL0EPe3YuTFWd5KtuCmvH+lRi/2xsfYbUrPgi
YVxEOJmeUO5kiPlBzuIbB3wFbpaNDBnIknTq3iYqNsxJc/rBHwyTzz2Eawl9N8f4
jSMmix56BwE4rTM5MdGLHCHnyDqtlYEE+jHF2WsoTKqVjh0IiKl5W5AI1hLFQsOE
hkV2PTfEFbtAeW2jtFaG4rwHWQc8hMacKSqoUxyvC9uLL7LDFk+8leRnpkl+cnma
lzS8z9EEeasYp9Z+1/XGJg8Das7jhTHDTAVndp2rsvMjYp7rzZHBvrbt9H2lAgMB
AAGgggF+MBoGCisGAQQBgjcNAgMxDBYKNi4wLjYwMDEuMjBLBgkrBgEAAYI3FRQx
PjA8AgEFDBRFeGNoMDEuTWFudGljb3JlLm9yZwwRTUFOVElDT1JFXFpY2hhcmQM
DnBvd2Vyc2hlbGwuZXhlMHIGCisGAQQBgjcNAgIxZDBiAgEBHloATQBpAGMAcgBv
AHMAbwBmAHQAIABSAFMAQQAgAFMAQwBoAGEAbgBuAGUAbAAgAEMAcgB5AHAAdABv
AGcAcgBhAHAAaABpAGMAIABQAHIAbwB2AGkAZAB1AHIADAQAwgZ4GCSqGSIb3DQEJ
DjGBkDCBjTAOBgNVHQ8BAf8EBAMCBaAwTgYDVR0RBEcwRYIaYXV0b2Rpc2NvdmVy
Lm1hbnRpY29yZS5vcmeCFGV4Y2gwMS5tYW50aWNvcmUub3JnghFvd2EubWFudGlj
b3JlLm9yZzAMBgNVHRMBAf8EAjAAMB0GA1UdDgQWBBRwAYI8NnDigTnvZqiWgMl6
+R1gvTANBgkqhkiG9w0BAQUFAAOCAQEAgk7vsQFqX46Wj5jNn8ZBiulWpUWj7glf
pxNCrOZg8HLQHC8S7s6gfQXFCFrcfa8cjR6NrNblke9EaLXBuRoXkxpo+OL9qq/8
UHo0wo5288sVJy9A4DkJXK2LxkIGy+iVtgzgpDmkvfosLkOmiI1Fn9NMbUR+pfyn
```

7ypJ6lyQpgPHtV09+7jf3XSSpuG9LbmM++qt7aCEtZFJzBAfOAd60+BKoqYpVEiU
Q6fQWr/Al5nD2gnr9PdZ/IdM473HhiOzClH2sp3/2SVux0t49HZMzoxrJogC2PbC
U5UCNTGoqYjdVu50OeT6zsqqUfMD2B2tmfchTnIkSaPwanUnd2wJlg==

```
-----END NEW CERTIFICATE REQUEST-----
```
Cat is an alias for Get-Content.

When the certificate is sent back to us, we need to import it into Exchange and enable the services as we've seen previously, and as shown in listing 12.19.

Listing 12.19   Installing an Exchange certificate

```
Import-ExchangeCertificate -path c:\certname  |
Enable-ExchangeCertificate -Services IIS, POP, IMAP
```

If required, old or expired certificates can be removed.

This completes our look at certificates. Our next topic expands on the work we did in chapter 6 by looking at resource mailboxes.

12.5 Resource mailboxes

In chapter 6 we looked at working with users' mailboxes. These aren't the only type of mailbox we can create in Exchange 2007. We can create mailboxes for meeting rooms and equipment such as projectors. Now we can directly invite the meeting room to our meeting.

Before we can start to use these meeting rooms, we have to create the mailboxes for them.

TECHNIQUE 150   Creating a resource mailbox

One perennial problem in many organizations seems to be finding a meeting room. The systems of booking a meeting room and scheduling a meeting don't necessarily match up so that we either struggle to find a room after the meeting is booked or we book a room and struggle to get everyone into it at the same time.

PROBLEM

We've been asked to provide mailboxes for meeting rooms so that they can be booked as part of the meeting request.

SOLUTION

We can use the New-Mailbox cmdlet to perform this task, as shown in listing 12.20.

Listing 12.20   Creating a resource mailbox

```
New-Mailbox -Name 'Room 02' -Alias 'room02'
-OrganizationalUnit 'Manticore.org/Meeting Rooms'
-UserPrincipalName 'room02@Manticore.org' -SamAccountName 'room02'
-FirstName '' -Initials '' -LastName '' -Database 'EXCH01\SG4\MailDb4'
-Room
```

DISCUSSION

If we compare this to creating a normal mailbox, there are a few differences. We don't find many meeting rooms that have a first name, initials, or a last name, so we can input those as empty strings, as shown.

Empty versus null

An empty string isn't the same thing as a null string. This isn't always intuitive and can cause problems if the wrong option is chosen.

Try this:

```
PS> $str1 = "a"
PS> $str2 = "a"
PS> $str1 -eq $str2
True
PS> $str1 = ""
PS> $str2 = $null
PS> $str1 -eq $str2
False
```

Create two strings each equal to a. This could also be achieved by using $str1 = $str2 = "a", which is a useful technique if we need to initialize a number of variables to the same value. If we compare these strings, we find they're equal as we'd expect.

$str1 is now set to be empty and $str2 is set to be equal to null. A comparison shows that they aren't equal.

The -Room parameter indicates that we're creating a mailbox for a meeting room. Another option is to use -Equipment if we want a calendar for some piece of equipment such as a projector or flip chart. Using either of these options causes the associated Active Directory account to be disabled.

An organizational unit was created specifically for meeting rooms. This helps keep them organized, and if they're all together, it may stop some helpful soul from inadvertently activating the accounts.

After creating the accounts, the next item is to be able to view our resource mailboxes.

TECHNIQUE 151   Viewing resource mailboxes

The *I* in IT stands for information and one thing we can be sure of is someone will come knocking on our door asking for information. In this case, they want to know about resource mailboxes.

PROBLEM

A report is required detailing the mailboxes associated with meeting rooms and potentially other resources.

SOLUTION

We've seen that Get-Mailbox can be used to view information about user mailboxes. It can also be used for viewing resource mailboxes, as in listing 12.21.

Listing 12.21   Viewing resource mailboxes

```
Get-Mailbox -RecipientTypeDetails "RoomMailbox"
```

DISCUSSION

If we want to view all of the meeting room mailboxes, we use the command as given. We can use a `select` statement to extract specific information that doesn't show in the default view. Alternatively `Get-Mailbox` can be used and an individual resource mailbox can be specified.

The Exchange 2007 SP1 help information for `Get-Mailbox` states that the recipient type is `ConferenceRoomMailbox`. This is incorrect. If you run with this value, an error will be thrown and a list of options will be presented. This isn't the full list of options. The following options can be used:

- `None`
- `SharedMailbox`
- `EquipmentMailbox`
- `MailUniversalDistributionGroup`
- `DynamicDistributionGroup`
- `SystemMailbox`
- `Contact`

- `NonUniversalGroup`
- `AllUniqueRecipientTypes`

- `UserMailbox`
- `LegacyMailbox`
- `MailContact`
- `MailNonUniversalGroup`

- `PublicFolder`

- `MailForestContact`
- `UniversalDistributionGroup`

- `DisabledUser`

- `LinkedMailbox`
- `RoomMailbox`
- `MailUser`
- `MailUniversalSecurityGroup`
- `SystemAttendantMailbox`

- `User`
- `UniversalSecurityGroup`

- `MicrosoftExchange`

If we don't specify a recipient type, we'll get user mailboxes.

The final configuration item to cover in this section is who can control the calendar of the meeting room.

TECHNIQUE 152   **Calendar settings**

The whole point of giving a meeting room a mailbox is that it gets a calendar. You weren't expecting the meeting room to send an email detailing when it was free were you?

The room's calendar can be accessed through the free/busy service and the room can be scheduled into the meeting just like any other attendee. But we still need someone to manage that calendar, for instance so that conflicts can be resolved.

PROBLEM

We have to define the users who have control of the meeting room calendars.

SOLUTION

The mailbox calendar settings need to be modified, so we use the `Set-MailboxCalendarSettings` cmdlet, as in listing 12.22. We start by examining the properties of the calendar of our meeting room. The default formatting is overridden by using `select *` to return all properties. The resource delegates are the people who can manage that particular calendar.

Listing 12.22   Modifying calendar settings

```
Get-MailboxCalendarSettings -Identity room02 | select *

$users = @("Hornblower Horatio", "Drake Francis")
Set-MailboxCalendarSettings -Identity room02 -ResourceDelegates $users

Get-MailboxCalendarSettings -Identity room02 | select ResourceDelegates
```

DISCUSSION

It's normal practice to allocate this task to more than one person. This is accomplished by creating an array of the names of the users who are being delegated the right to manage the calendar. We use the Active Directory name (cn property) for each user.

The delegation is set with `Set-MailboxCalendarSettings`. The final line of the script shows how to check that delegates for the calendar.

NOTE   This technique can also be used to delegate access to user mailboxes.

We've finished our examination of using PowerShell to administer Exchange 2007. As a taste of what's to come, we'll conclude the chapter with a quick look at its successor, Exchange Server 2010.

12.6   *Exchange Server 2010*

Exchange Server 2010 was released during the writing of this book. Exchange 2010 has PowerShell v2 as a prerequisite rather than v1 as in Exchange 2007. This opens Exchange to the remoting capabilities of PowerShell. We'll be looking at remoting in detail in the next chapter; a quick look at the Exchange 2010 capabilities is worthwhile as there are differences.

There are two PowerShell icons available in Exchange 2010. One is labeled *local* and provides access to PowerShell on the local server. The other icon is, interestingly, just labeled *PowerShell* and gives access to the remote capabilities.

TECHNIQUE 153   Remote capabilities

A machine running PowerShell v2 can create a remote session to PowerShell on the Exchange server. Certificates are used by default to authenticate the connection, though this check can be bypassed as shown in listing 12.23. The ability to access Exchange 2010 enables us to access remote functionality without installing the administration tools on the local machine.

PROBLEM

How can we administer our Exchange server from a remote machine?

SOLUTION

A PowerShell session is created to form the connection to the remote Exchange server.

Listing 12.23   Remote connection to Exchange 2010

Create option

```
$SkipCertificate =
New-WSManSessionOption -SkipCACheck -SkipCNCheck -SkipRevocationCheck

$Session =
```

```
New-PSSession -ConfigurationName Microsoft.Exchange
 -ConnectionUri https://Exch01/PowerShell/
-Authentication NegotiateWithImplicitCredential          ❷ Create
-SessionOption $SkipCertificate                          ◄──┘ session

Import-PSSession $Session    ◄──❸ Import functionality
```

DISCUSSION

PowerShell remoting uses the WS-Management protocol to communicate with the remote machine. The default option is to use the Exchange certificate to secure the connection. This will involve a number of checks being performed on the certificate. If the certificate is a commercial certificate, this will work without further configuration. In the case of a self-signed certificate, we can either import the self-signed certificate into our local machine or bypass the certificate checking.

The checks on the certificate can be bypassed by configuring a number of options on the WS-Management session ❶. The parameters used cause a number of the normal checks to be skipped. These parameters, defined in table 12.2, should only be used on internal, trusted and secure networks.

Table 12.2   Parameters for skipping certificate checks

Parameter	Meaning
-SkipCACheck	The check that the certificate is signed by a trusted CA isn't performed.
-SkipCNCheck	The check that the common name on the certificate matches the server name isn't performed.
-SkipRevocationCheck	The revocation lists aren't checked to determine whether the certificate has been revoked.

Our next action is to create a PowerShell session to the remote machine ❷. A session is a persistent connection that gives us a speedier response, as the communication lines between the two machines remain open until we explicitly close them.

> **SESSION VARIABLE**   When using sessions, it's best practice to use a variable to represent the session as shown here. This makes it much easier to refer to the session in other commands.

The -ConfigurationName parameter ensures that the remote session is pointing to the Exchange configuration for PowerShell rather than the default PowerShell configuration. In other words, we're connecting to the Exchange Management Shell, which has the Exchange snapin preloaded. The -ConnectionUri defines the connection endpoint on the Exchange server. This SSL connection is secured by the Exchange certificate—hence the reason for skipping the checks when using a self-signed certificate.

We can authenticate ourselves to the session by using the -Authentication parameter. The value we supply tells the remoting system to authenticate using the credentials we used to log on to our local machine. Our final parameter supplies the options for the session that we created earlier in the listing.

Once our session is created, we can then work with the session to administer the remote instance of Exchange 2010. We can use the `Invoke-Command` cmdlet to send individual commands to the remote machine. Alternatively, we can import the Exchange functionality into our local PowerShell ❸. As shown, all of the Exchange cmdlets will be imported into the local session. It's possible to restrict which cmdlets are imported, for example if we only work with mail boxes then we only need to import the mailbox cmdlets we would modify the import statement to be:

```
Import-PSSession $Session -CommandName *Mailbox
```

> **POWERSHELL PROFILE** These commands could be part of our PowerShell profile if we're often going to be working with Exchange through remote PowerShell.

A function is created on our local machine to represent the cmdlet on the remote machine. The `Export-PSSession` cmdlet can be used to export the functions to a module that we can import into future sessions, again through the PowerShell profile if required. In either case, we have the Exchange functionality on our local machine so we can perform remote administration of the Exchange server.

This brief look to the future shows that we still have a lot more to gain, as administrators, as PowerShell itself evolves and it's built into more products.

12.7   *Summary*

Exchange 2007 is probably the most complex application we'll put into our organization. We've seen how we can administer the servers comprising that Exchange organization. Mailbox servers have a lifecycle for the mail databases that we can administer using our PowerShell knowledge.

Exchange 2007 becomes simpler to administer when we use policies to control items such as email addresses and message attachment sizes. We can also use policies to control who can send messages to whom. The use of certificates in an Exchange environment requires management using PowerShell. We can use mailboxes to represent meeting rooms and equipment, though it does seem odd inviting a projector to my meeting.

Exchange 2010 builds on the use of PowerShell we've seen with Exchange 2007 and adds more flexibility to our administration through the use of PowerShell remoting.

Exchange 2007 and 2010 use IIS in a number of ways. The installation of IIS is one of the prerequisites for installing Exchange. IIS is also used in its own right. We'll be discovering how to administer IIS with PowerShell in the next chapter.

IIS 7 and XML

This chapter covers

- Comparing PowerShell techniques for working with IIS
- Administering web sites and application pools
- Managing web applications and virtual directories
- Working with XML and configuration files

Internet Information Server (IIS) has been part of Windows since the days of the NT. The primary use of IIS is to host web-based applications by delivering web pages. It's also one of the supporting technologies for a number of other applications including Exchange, SharePoint, and SQL Server (in the form of Reporting Services). IIS appears in so many places that knowledge of how to administer it is a "must-have" skill for many administrators.

In this chapter we'll concentrate on IIS itself, though the skills and techniques acquired here will be usable wherever IIS is encountered. The chapter concentrates on IIS 7 and 7.5 on Windows Server 2008 and Windows Server 2008 R2, respectively. It may be possible to take some of the techniques and work with IIS 6 (Windows Server 2003), especially the use of WMI, though it should be noted that the WMI providers in IIS 6 and IIS 7 are different.

IIS servers are often deployed in web farms—a number of identically configured machines all providing the same application (or applications). This scenario is perfect for automation, in that we need to perform exactly the same actions on a number of servers and we can save wear and tear on our legs by not having to walk round the server farm.

> **BACKUP** It's strongly recommended that you make a backup of the IIS configuration before making any of the changes in this chapter. How to do this with PowerShell is covered in technique 167.

The chapter starts by looking at the tools available for automating IIS administration. We'll examine each of the PowerShell tools by using it to create a website. The creation and administration of these websites will form a loose theme throughout the chapter. I have a preferred toolset for working with IIS, which I'll explain at the end of the section. But feel free to convert the other examples into one of the other toolsets if they fit better with the way you prefer to use PowerShell. Variety is the spice of life, after all.

This section of the chapter will also cover PowerShell remoting. IIS administration provides excellent opportunities for using the remoting capabilities of PowerShell v2. The topic is explained with practical examples of administering IIS.

Websites are further explored, together with their associated application pools. We'll also consider web application and virtual directories. The full lifecycle of these objects will be shown to provide the complete administration toolset.

IIS uses XML for storing configuration information. We need to understand how to work with XML files before we can look at the IIS configuration files.

> **EXPERIMENTING** Remember that if you want to experiment with the techniques in this chapter, Windows Vista and Windows 7 have IIS as an optional feature that can be installed. The WMI provider and .NET classes become available when IIS is installed on these platforms in just the same way they do on servers. The IIS provider also works on these platforms, as we'll see later.

It's now time to jump in and start looking at the PowerShell toolset for IIS.

13.1   *Automating IIS 7 administration*

This section covers two main themes. First we'll examine the tools that are available within PowerShell for working with IIS. This may seem like overkill, but some organizations won't allow additional software to be installed, so administrators in that situation need to know what alternatives are available. The last part covers how we can use PowerShell remoting to help us administer IIS.

IIS, of all the applications we'll examine in this book, probably has the richest toolset available for working with PowerShell. It's time to investigate those tools.

13.1.1 *IIS administration tools*

PowerShell provides a number of ways to administer our IIS systems:

- Through a .NET managed code provider
- Through WMI
- Wrapping WMI in .NET code to make remote access easier
- Through IIS cmdlets
- Through an IIS provider
- Through wrapping appcmd.exe, the IIS command-line tool, in a PowerShell script, but I view that as a last resort, as it's a more complex way to perform the tasks.

These tools can be used on the local machine, accessed through RDP, or we can combine with PowerShell remoting for the ultimate PowerShell experience. The toolset will work with IIS 7 on Windows Vista, Windows 7, and Windows Server 2008 including R2.

This diversity can be viewed as one of the strengths of PowerShell or as a weakness. My view is that it shows PowerShell's strength because we have the flexibility to choose the way we want to work.

Even though we have a wide range of techniques for working with IIS, we're limited when it comes to accessing IIS remotely, as table 13.1 indicates.

Method	Works remotely?
.NET	No
WMI	Partial
WMI with .NET	Yes
IIS cmdlets	No
IIS provider	No

Table 13.1 Methods of accessing IIS through PowerShell

This slows us down only slightly, as we'll see.

In this section I'll demonstrate each approach, but for the bulk of the chapter I'll use the IIS provider and cmdlets. We'll start with the .NET managed code, though before we dive into that, we need to create a few folders we can use in our examples throughout the chapter, as shown in listing 13.1.

Listing 13.1 Create test folders

```
New-Item -ItemType Directory -Path c:\inetpub -Name testnet
New-Item -ItemType Directory -Path c:\inetpub -Name testwmi
New-Item -ItemType Directory -Path c:\inetpub -Name testnw
New-Item -ItemType Directory -Path c:\inetpub -Name testcdlt
New-Item -ItemType Directory -Path c:\inetpub -Name testprov
```

Repeated calls to New-Item enable us to create the required folders. It's not elegant, but it works! When time is short, sometimes a brute-force approach is the best solution. There are no points for style and artistic interpretation in this game. Okay, I give up-here's the elegant version:

```
"testnet", "testwmi", "testnw", "testcdlt", "testprov" |
foreach {New-Item -ItemType Directory -Path c:\test -Name $_}
```

13.1.2 .NET

When we install IIS 7, we also get access to a DLL containing the .NET namespace for working with IIS. This assembly isn't loaded into PowerShell automatically, so the first thing we need to do is load the assembly, as shown in listing 13.2.

Listing 13.2   Create a site with .NET

```
[system.reflection.assembly]::
loadfrom("c:\windows\system32\inetsrv\`                                    2  Create
microsoft.web.administration.dll")     <--1 Load assembly                     server
                                                                              object
$server = New-Object microsoft.web.administration.servermanager     <--

$server.Sites.Add(
"TestNet", "http", "*:80:testnet.manticore.org", "c:\inetpub\testnet")    <--

$server.CommitChanges()     <--4 Save                              Add site 3
```

The assembly is loaded ❶ using the loadfrom() method. We know where to find the DLL, which makes this the easiest and simplest method to perform the load. Alternatively, we could use Add-Type if using PowerShell v2. Once the assembly is loaded, we can create an object for the IIS server ❷. When working with the Microsoft. Web.Administration classes, we always have to start with the ServerManager object.

Websites are treated as part of the properties of the server. We use the Add() method of the sites collection ❸ to create our site. The parameters give the site name, the protocol, the binding (IP address, port, and DNS name [host header]), and the physical path for the site. We'll see this information used in the other methods of creating sites. The site name works for my environment. Change the domain name to reflect yours.

We must remember to save our changes ❹. One thing we'll find with this method is that we'll need to refresh the server object after making changes. We'll need to perform the second line of our code again before performing any other actions.

This technique is only usable on the local machine. It's not possible to access IIS remotely in this manner.

The way that PowerShell makes WMI easier to use has been a major theme throughout the book. We'll continue exploring this theme as we look at creating a website using the WMI provider.

13.1.3 WMI

Installing IIS also creates a new WMI namespace for us. The namespace is a direct child of the root namespace, called webadministration. The extent of the namespace can be discovered by using:

```
Get-WmiObject -Namespace 'root\webadministration' -List
```

This will supply a list of the classes available to us. Examining the list reveals that we have WMI functionality for administering all of the major elements of IIS. We'll need to use two of these classes to create a new website, as in listing 13.3.

Listing 13.3   Create a site with WMI

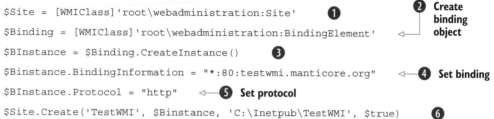

```
$Site = [WMIClass]'root\webadministration:Site'              1
$Binding = [WMIClass]'root\webadministration:BindingElement'
$BInstance = $Binding.CreateInstance()                        3
$Binstance.BindingInformation = "*:80:testwmi.manticore.org"
$BInstance.Protocol = "http"
$Site.Create('TestWMI', $Binstance, 'C:\Inetpub\TestWMI', $true)
```

In section 3.5 we looked at the WMI type accelerators. We'll use the [WMIClass] type accelerator to create the WMI objects we need. The starting point is to create a WMI object for the new website ❶ and the binding ❷. A specific instance of the binding element has to be created ❸. We can then supply the binding information ❹ and the protocol used to access the site ❺. The binding contains the same port as the previous example, but has a different host name, which removes any possible conflicts.

   The site can then be created ❻. We need to provide the site name, the binding information, and the physical path for the site as before. The final Boolean value instructs the server to automatically start the site if set to $true.

> **NO MESSAGES**   No messages of completion or indication of success are returned when using this approach.

The IIS WMI provider requires Packet Privacy authentication, which prevents us from using the [WMIClass] type accelerator remotely. But we can wrap the WMI calls in .NET code to create a site on a remote machine, as shown in listing 13.4.

Listing 13.4   Create a site with WMI and .NET

```
$conopt = New-Object System.Management.ConnectionOptions
$conopt.Authentication =
    [System.Management.AuthenticationLevel]::PacketPrivacy

$scope = New-Object System.Management.ManagementScope
$scope.Path = "\\.\root\WebAdministration"
$scope.Options = $conopt

$path = New-Object System.Management.ManagementPath
$path.ClassName = "Site"
$site =
New-Object System.Management.ManagementClass($scope, $path, $null)

$path2 = New-Object System.Management.ManagementPath
$path2.ClassName = "BindingElement"

$bind =
New-Object System.Management.ManagementClass($scope, $path2, $null)
$BInstance = $bind.psbase.CreateInstance()

$Binstance.BindingInformation = "*:80:testnw.manticore.org"
$BInstance.Protocol = "http"

$site.Create('testnw', $Binstance, 'C:\Inetpub\testnw', $true)
```

This example may look more complicated than our previous examples, but it's really an expanded version of the WMI listing, as we'll see. Our example starts by creating a connection and setting the options on that connection. In this case, we have to use Packet Privacy for the authentication level **❶**.

> **PACKET PRIVACY**   PowerShell v1 can't utilize Packet Privacy or other forms of WMI authentication, but the WMI objects in version 2 can. We can use `Get-WmiObject` against the IIS WMI provider by using the `-Authentication` parameter and giving it a value of 6.

The WMI namespace is set next **❷**. The path is set as *server\root\namespace*. In this instance, I'm using . for the server, meaning the local host. We can use a server name to work remotely. The connection options need to be provided to the scope to ensure the connection succeeds.

The WMI class we need to use, `Site`, is defined **❸** and then we can create an object representing our new site **❹**. The arguments represent the namespace, the class, and any options we want to define. At this point, we don't want to supply any options, so we use the `$null` value to show this. A value must be supplied, even if it's just saying that we don't have any options today.

A similar exercise is performed for the binding elements **❺**, after which we create an instance of the binding element **❻**. The last part of the script sets the binding information and the access protocol **❼**. The final line creates the script supplying name **❽**, binding information, physical path, and the command to automatically start the site, as we saw previously.

13.1.4   *IIS cmdlets and provider*

When the release of PowerShell v1 was announced at IT Forum (Barcelona, November 2006), it was demonstrated as part of the conference keynote speech. One part of the demonstration showed administering IIS with PowerShell cmdlets. The demonstration received a good response but it turned out those cmdlets were just a proof of concept for the demonstration. There were lots of disappointed PowerShell users!

But once Windows 2008 was released, a PowerShell provider for IIS soon followed. The original technology preview concentrated on the provider. The PowerShell community kept asking for more cmdlets, and by the time it was released, it had a good supply of cmdlets and a well-behaved provider. The IIS 7 PowerShell provider is available as a 32- or 64-bit download from http://www.iis.net (a Microsoft site maintained by the IIS team) for Windows 2008.

> **WARNING**   There are a number of good examples for the provider and cmdlets on the IIS.net site. Be aware that some of the examples haven't been updated as the technology has progressed and are out of date. The concepts are correct but sometimes the syntax is wrong.

The provider and cmdlets are automatically installed when IIS is enabled on Windows 2008 R2.

ELEVATED PRIVILEGES Elevated privileges are required to access the provider in both versions of Windows 2008.

The provider installation routine creates an IIS PowerShell Management Console icon, which loads the snapin via a PowerShell console file and sets the location to IIS:\. It can be loaded into any other PowerShell session by using:

```
Add-PsSnapin Webadministration
```

In Windows 7/2008 R2, it's a module! Modules are covered in appendix B. The listings in the chapter are applicable however the code is loaded. Now that we have our cmdlets installed, let's create a website using the code in listing 13.5.

Listing 13.5   Listing 13.5 Create a site with the IIS cmdlet

```
New-WebSite -Name testcdlt -Port 80 -HostHeader "testcdlt.manticore.org"
-PhysicalPath "c:\inetpub\testcdlt"
```

PowerShell enables us to discover how to use PowerShell so it is easy to find the cmdlets dealing with websites:

```
Get-Command *site
```

This will return a number of cmdlets with the noun *WebSite* and the verbs *Get-*, *New-*, *Remove-*, *Start-*, and *Stop-*. We need the `New-WebSite` cmdlet for creation. We can give a name, the port, and the physical path as parameters with this cmdlet. The `HostHeader` parameter is important—without it the binding defaults to `*:80:`, meaning all IP addresses on port 80 with no specific name. Unfortunately, this matches the binding for the default website, which means our poor new website won't start. If we try to start the site, we'll get an error:

```
Start-Website : Cannot create a file when that file already exists.
```

This isn't the most intuitive error message! What it means is that we need to change the binding information, for which we can use `Set-WebBinding`. Our code would become:

```
New-WebSite -Name testcdlt -Port 80 -PhysicalPath "c:\inetpub\testcdlt"
Set-WebBinding -Name testcdlt -BindingInformation "*:80:"
-PropertyName HostHeader -Value testcdlt.manticore.org

Get-WebBinding -Name testcdlt

Start-Sleep -Seconds 5
Start-Website -Name testcdlt
```

We need to supply the name of the website and the current binding information to the relevant parameters. We then change the `HostHeader` value to our preferred option. If we are performing this at the command line, we don't need the `Start-Sleep`, but in a script I've found that it's required to give IIS a chance to catch up with the script. It's much better to get it right first time and supply all of the information.

Our final script in this section, shown in listing 13.6, looks at using the IIS provider. A provider exposes a data store to PowerShell as if it were the filesystem. This means that we should be able to use the same commands to navigate the provider that we use in the filesystem. We should also be able to use the cmdlets we use in the filesystem to work with the data in the provider.

Listing 13.6   Create a site with the IIS provider

```
cd IIS:\sites

New-Item testprov
-bindings @{protocol="http";bindingInformation=":80:testprov.manticore.org"}
-physicalPath c:\inetpub\testprov

cd \
cd c:
```

A provider is exposed as a drive in PowerShell. We can view the drives using Get-PSDrive and navigate into the root of the IIS drive using cd IIS:\. Performing a dir at this point reveals three subfolders, as shown in figure 13.1

We can use the navigation commands to jump into the sites container. The New-Item cmdlet is used to create the site. The provider understands that at this location, the item to create is a website. Compare this command with the use of New-Item earlier in this section, when we were creating folders in the filesystem. We had to tell it to create a folder, as files and folders can be created in the filesystem.

The parameters we're using with New-Item may not be familiar—especially when compared to the filesystem usage. This is because the IIS provider modifies the cmdlets by adding additional parameters. We can see the changes by using:

```
Get-Command new-item -syntax
```

If we try this in the C: drive and IIS: drive, the results show the additions.

Using New-Item, we supply the site name, the binding information, and the physical path as we'd expect. The bindings are supplied as a hash table containing the protocol and actual binding information. This information is in a similar format to our other examples.

When using the provider in a script, it's always a good idea to return to a known point. In this case, we end the script by navigating to the root of the IIS: drive and then back to the C: drive.

> **NO ALIASES**   One thing to note is that the IIS provider doesn't create any default aliases for the cmdlets. If you want to create aliases for cmdlets that you'll be using from the command line, it'll save typing. Don't use them in scripts you want to use across multiple machines!

Figure 13.1   The three subfolders available at the root of the IIS: drive when using the IIS PowerShell provider.

In these examples, we've looked at creating a website using techniques that are available to us. In addition to demonstrating the techniques, it also gives us a good number of sites to play with in the rest of the chapter. Did I say *play with?* Sorry, I meant *experiment.*

The examples we've seen have all been run on the local machine. We don't want to keep going into the machine room to perform these tasks or spend our time using Remote Desktop to connect to multiple machines to perform the same task. The solution to this problem is PowerShell remoting.

TECHNIQUE 154   PowerShell remoting

We briefly looked at PowerShell remoting in the previous chapter. That was in a specific context for Exchange 2010. In this section, we'll look at the more general case of using PowerShell to access remote machines. This functionality is especially useful in the case of web farms, where we may want to perform the same action on a number of servers.

PowerShell v1 enabled some cmdlets such as `Get-WmiObject` to work with remote machines. This capability has been extended to many more cmdlets including the `*Service`, `*Process`, and `*Eventlog` cmdlets. We can discover the cmdlets that can work directly with remote machines by finding which ones have a `-ComputerName` parameter

```
Get-Help * -Parameter computername
```

As an example, we can discover the hotfixes installed on a remote machine:

```
Get-HotFix -ComputerName RSLaptop01
```

The advantage of using cmdlets in this way is that syntax is easy to use and we don't need to do anything except add an extra parameter when using the cmdlet. The disadvantage of using cmdlets in this way is that the cmdlet has to create a connection to the remote machine, run our command, then tear down the connection. This is a processing overhead if we need to perform multiple actions on the same machine.

PROBLEM
How can we make our remote sessions more efficient by reducing the processing overhead?

SOLUTION
This example shows how to use PowerShell-based remoting. It's a good example of a "fan-out" approach: one workstation administers many servers. Compare listing 13.7 to the Exchange 2010 example we saw at the end of the last chapter, which is a good example of the "fan-in" approach. Expect to see more of both as PowerShell adoption expands.

PowerShell v2 needs to be installed on the local and remote machines, the `winrm` service (display name is *Windows Remote Management [WS-Management]*) needs to be running on both machines, and `Enable-PSRemoting` needs to be run on both machines to perform the required configuration. The starting point of the example is the creation of a PowerShell session ❶. This just takes the computer name as a parameter. Using a variable to represent the session makes using it much easier in later statements.

Listing 13.7 Working remotely with PowerShell and IIS

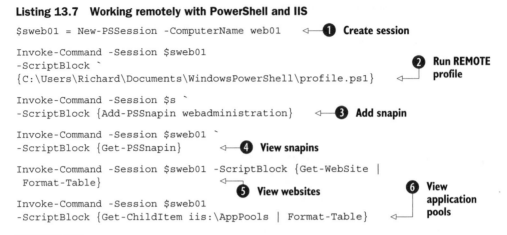

```
$sweb01 = New-PSSession -ComputerName web01        ←──① Create session

Invoke-Command -Session $sweb01
-ScriptBlock `                                              ② Run REMOTE
{C:\Users\Richard\Documents\WindowsPowerShell\profile.ps1}  ←─┘  profile

Invoke-Command -Session $s `
-ScriptBlock {Add-PSSnapin webadministration}      ←──③ Add snapin

Invoke-Command -Session $sweb01 `
-ScriptBlock {Get-PSSnapin}            ←──④ View snapins

Invoke-Command -Session $sweb01 -ScriptBlock {Get-WebSite |
 Format-Table}                     ←─┐
                                      ⑤ View websites            ⑥ View
Invoke-Command -Session $sweb01                                     application
-ScriptBlock {Get-ChildItem iis:\AppPools | Format-Table}  ←─┘      pools
```

DISCUSSION

As an aside in the early CTPs of PowerShell v2, what's now called a *PowerShell session* was referred to as a *runspace*. Expect to see this term used in blog posts and other discussions from this period. Simply replace PSSession for RunSpace and the listings should be reusable. (Yes it's confusing and caused some interesting discussion during testing.) Once we've created the session, we could enter it (Enter-PSSession) or import the functionality (Import-PSSession). In this case, we want to run some commands interactively through the session. When we create a session in this way, the PowerShell profile(s) on the remote machine aren't executed. We need to run the profile ❷ or perform individual configuration actions such as adding snapins ❸. We'll see Invoke-Command a lot when using remoting. It's possible to have multiple remote sessions open, so we need to supply the session and use the -ScriptBlock parameter to supply the command we want to execute.

When our session is configured, we can then execute commands through the session such as viewing the available snapins ❹, using a cmdlet to view websites ❺, or using the provider to view application pools ❻. Sometimes the formatting doesn't get preserved when the data is returned to the local machine. This can be solved by adding a Format-Table command to the scriptblock as shown.

> **RECOMMENDATION** My recommendation is to adopt PowerShell v2 as soon as possible. Install it and the IIS PowerShell provider on your IIS systems. This will give you the best, richest experience as well as making the administration of extensive web farms much simpler. Do more with less!

Before we finish with remoting, we need to look at running scripts through remote sessions. So far we've been running individual commands through Invoke-Command, which will get tedious if we need to perform a large set of linked tasks. It's also awkward if we need to use a large loop or functions. The answer is the same as when we're running PowerShell on the local machine—use a script.

We have two options:

```
Invoke-Command -Session $sweb01 -ScriptBlock {c:\script\scrpt1.ps1}

Invoke-Command -Session $sweb01 -FilePath {c:\script\scrpt1.ps1}
```

Option 1 uses the `-ScriptBlock` parameter we've already seen. It runs a script that's situated on the remote machine. This is good for running a profile or script that's already on the remote machine. The drawback to this approach is that the script on the remote machine has to be maintained. That's straightforward if we're talking about one machine, but by the time we get to 10, 20, or more, it doesn't become feasible unless we can use an automated delivery mechanism.

Option 2 is similar, but it uses the `-FilePath` parameter instead of `ScriptBlock`. This will look for the script on the local machine and run it against the remote machine. We only maintain a single copy of the script in an easily accessible place. It's ideal for running against multiple remote machines. When using this technique, it's difficult to perform actions such as `Import-Csv` into the script, as the location of the file is unclear to PowerShell. It doesn't seem possible for PowerShell to "reach" back to the local machine to access a file through the remoting mechanism. Even using a UNC path doesn't work.

The answer is to think about what we need to do and to use the technique that's most efficient for performing the task. We can use PowerShell to copy scripts to remote machines if required.

> **LOCAL VERSUS REMOTE** In the rest of the chapter, I'll present the use of the IIS provider and cmdlets as if we were using them locally. These commands could be run remotely using the techniques from this section. I won't refer to this repeatedly, though it should be kept in mind. I'll also assume that the provider is loaded when discussing its use and that of the accompanying cmdlets.

Having learned how to use PowerShell-based tools for administering IIS both locally and remotely, we'll turn our attention to administering the objects within IIS. We'll continue our examination of websites and dive into the related topic of application pools as well.

13.2 *Websites and application pools*

We saw a number of ways to create websites in the previous section. In this section we'll turn our attention to administering those sites. *Application pools* enable us to separate the processing of individual websites. We'll also see how we can work with these objects.

TECHNIQUE 155   **Viewing websites**

Many web servers host a number of websites. This maximizes the use of server resources. But it creates a problem for us as administrators, because we need to be able to find out what's happening on our web servers. If we have a single web server, we can always use the IIS Manager console to attach to the remote server. That isn't practical when you have a number of servers.

PROBLEM

The users are on the phone complaining that the website isn't available! We need to check quickly whether it's still running.

SOLUTION

We can use the IIS cmdlets to view the sites or WMI to view the websites on a server hosting IIS, as in listing 13.8. The easiest way to view the basic information about our websites is to use the Get-WebSite cmdlet ❶. The output is shown in figure 13.2. We get a tabulated display showing the website name, the ID, the state, physical path, and bindings. Glancing at the bindings for the default website shows how multiple bindings are displayed. In some ways, the state is the most important, as it provides a quick check that the website is up.

An identical display is returned if we use the provider ❷. Any bets on how the cmdlet works? I've used the alias ls for Get-ChildItem in this example. Despite what might be thought from reading my blog. I do use aliases at the command line. They still should be avoided in scripts.

The final option presented here is to use WMI ❸. We've seen Get-WmiObject many times. The two major differences are that we're using the webadministration namespace and the authentication requirements.

Listing 13.8   Viewing website status

```
Get-WebSite                    ⟵❶ Cmdlet

ls iis:\sites                              ⟵❷ Provider

#Requires -version 2.0
Get-WmiObject -ComputerName 'Web01' -Namespace "root\webadministration"
-Class Site -Authentication 6   ⟵❸ WMI
```

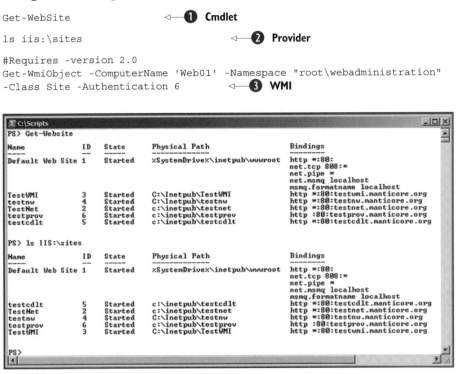

Figure 13.2   Viewing websites using the cmdlets and the provider.

DISCUSSION

We discovered earlier that the IIS WMI provider requires Packet Privacy (authentication and packet encryption) when accessing a remote machine. The value 6 assigned to the `-Authentication` parameter is how we specify Packet Privacy. The meaning of other values can be found in the help file. The authentication parameter is only available in PowerShell v2, which is why we use `#Requires -version 2.0` to ensure that the script can't be run on PowerShell v1. This command can also be used to stop scripts running if certain snapins or versions of snapins aren't available. See `Get-Help about_Requires` for full details.

> **GADGETS**   We could use PowerGadgets with these scripts to create a simple warning system if our websites stopped working. The gadget could be hosted on the Windows Vista sidebar or as a Windows 7 desktop gadget.

We now know how to create websites and how to view their status. Let's see how we can control the status with PowerShell.

TECHNIQUE 156   **Controlling websites**

If we examine the IIS Manager console, we'll see prominent controls for stopping, starting, and restarting websites. These tasks may need to be performed on a relatively frequent basis.

PROBLEM

Our website has stopped. How can we restart it?

SOLUTION

We have cmdlets for controlling website status, as shown in listing 13.9. We usually want our websites to be automatically started when the IIS server starts. The techniques we have for creating websites either default to this state or allow us to set the website to this configuration. Our first task then is to stop a website ❶. An individual website can be stopped by using `Stop-WebSite` and providing the name of the site. Using `Get-WebSite` before and after the stop allows us to determine whether the task worked. It also allows us to check the name of the website.

In a similar manner, we can use `Start-WebSite` to start a website ❷. In the example we use `Get-WebSite` with a `where` statement to filter the sites that are in a state of being stopped. We can pipe the results into `Start-WebSite`, which will start all of the stopped sites. We can, of course, just start an individual site by supplying its name in the same way that we used `Stop-WebSite`.

Listing 13.9   Controlling websites

```
Get-Website
Stop-Website -Name testwmi        ◁——❶ Stop site
Get-Website

Get-Website | where{$_.state -eq "Stopped"}
Get-Website | where{$_.state -eq "Stopped"} | Start-Website   ◁——❷ Start site
Get-Website

Restart-WebItem -PSPath iis:\sites\TestNet
Get-ChildItem iis:\sites | Restart-WebItem    ◁——❸ Restart site
```

DISCUSSION

Sometimes we'll have one or more websites that are running but that need to be recycled, possibly because of a configuration or file change.

> **RESTART-WEBSITE**   You may see reference to a `Restart-WebSite` cmdlet. This cmdlet doesn't actually exist. Use `Restart-WebItem` as shown, or `Stop-WebSite` and `Start-WebSite` run sequentially.

We can restart (recycle) websites by using the `Restart-WebItem` cmdlet ❸. The first technical preview of the IIS provider had many fewer cmdlets, and those tended to be generic such as `*-WebItem`. The `WebItem` cmdlets work with IIS paths rather than object names. We can provide the path to a single site as shown, but if we want to recycle all of the websites, we need to be slightly more creative.

We can use `Get-ChildItem` to return all of the site information, as we saw in the previous listing. That information can then be piped into `Restart-WebItem` as shown. The IIS path is automatically picked up by `Restart-WebItem` and the object is recycled. The wonders of the pipeline! After using PowerShell for a few years, we do get to expect this sort of power. If a reminder is needed of how much we gain from the pipeline, try reverting to VBScript for a task or two.

Application pools are used to separate the processes used in IIS websites and applications so that an issue with one site doesn't affect all sites. We need to consider these objects next.

TECHNIQUE 157   ## Creating an application pool

When it's first installed, IIS creates a single application pool. All subsequent websites and web applications use the default application pool unless a specific one is created for that site or application. It's possible to specify the application pool to use during the creation of a site.

PROBLEM

We have a number of websites running on our server, all using the same application pool. Additional application pools need to be created so that we can separate the processes of each site.

SOLUTION

We can solve this problem using a cmdlet or the provider. These two methods are essentially similar, as shown in listing 13.10. It often becomes a matter of preference as to which one is used. We'll start by using the `New-WebAppPool` cmdlet ❶. The only parameter we need to supply is a name.

Our alternative method is to use the provider and the `New-Item` cmdlet ❷. When creating objects using the provider, I've found it easier to navigate to the part of the provider dealing with that object type. Then we don't need to worry about specifying the type of object to create—the provider does that for us.

Listing 13.10 Create application pool

```
New-WebAppPool -Name wmipool      ◁──❶  Cmdlet

cd IIS:\AppPools
ls
New-Item netpool     ◁──❷  Provider
cd \
cd c:
```

DISCUSSION

We start by navigating into the application pools. A directory listing is obtained to check the names of the application pools that currently exist. I don't use the `ls` alias because I'm from a UNIX background (honest)—I use it because it's only two characters long and saves a fair amount of typing over `dir` considering how often I use it. The letters are also in a more accessible combination on the keyboard.

> **GET-WEBAPPPOOL** There isn't a `Get-WebAppPool` cmdlet, so we need to use the provider. The inconsistency in cmdlet provisions is one of the charms of the IIS provider. It also shows that the provider came first and the cmdlets were developed later.

`New-Item` is used to create the application pool, and we navigate back to our standard location to finish the task. This example was copied directly from command-line input. The same commands could be run from a script (better still, expand the aliases).

After creating some application pools we had better learn how to control them.

TECHNIQUE 158   **Controlling an application pool**

In section 13.2.2 we learned how to control websites. The ability to control application pools may be even more important. Our website may contain a number of applications, each using its own application. We gain more granular control of our web server if we can control the individual application pools.

PROBLEM

We need the ability to control individual application pools to ensure that we maintain a fine degree of control over our IIS server.

SOLUTION

The `*-WebAppPool` cmdlets will enable us to meet this challenge, as shown in listing 13.11. We can start this exercise by viewing the current state of the application pools ❶. This includes whether the application pool is running.

An individual application pool can be stopped by using `Stop-WeAppPool` with the name of the application pool ❷. Alternatively, we could use `Stop-WebItem` and supply the path to the particular pool we want to stop. Viewing the state of the application pools after performing the stop confirms our actions.

When we want to start the application pool ❸, we can use `Start-WebItem` with the path to the pool or `Start-WebAppPool` with the name of the application pool.

Listing 13.11   Control an application pool

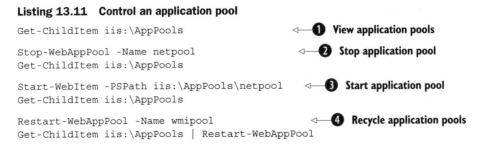

```
Get-ChildItem iis:\AppPools
```
① View application pools

```
Stop-WebAppPool -Name netpool
Get-ChildItem iis:\AppPools
```
② Stop application pool

```
Start-WebItem -PSPath iis:\AppPools\netpool
Get-ChildItem iis:\AppPools
```
③ Start application pool

```
Restart-WebAppPool -Name wmipool
Get-ChildItem iis:\AppPools | Restart-WebAppPool
```
④ Recycle application pools

DISCUSSION

We do get a `Restart-WebAppPool` cmdlet, so we can use that to restart (recycle) individual application pools by name ④. The whole collection of application pools can be restarted by using `Get-ChildItem` to pipe the pools in to the `restart` command. It's possible to use `Restart-WebItem` as we saw in the section on controlling websites.

We've looked at creating and controlling websites and application pools. It's time to consider how we can put the two objects together.

TECHNIQUE 159   Modifying website configuration

When we create a website, we have the opportunity to assign an application pool to the site. If this opportunity isn't taken, the default application pool is utilized. A badly configured IIS server may have all of its websites and applications running on a single application pool.

PROBLEM

We need to correct an incorrectly configured IIS server by assigning separate application pools to the websites.

SOLUTION

We need to work within the IIS provider to perform this reconfiguration task, as in listing 13.12.

Listing 13.12   Modify a site configuration

```
Get-ChildItem iis:\AppPools

Set-ItemProperty -Path iis:\Sites\testwmi
-Name ApplicationPool -Value wmipool

Get-ChildItem iis:\AppPools
```

DISCUSSION

PowerShell has a number of cmdlets that should work within all providers:

- `*-ChildItem`
- `*-Content`
- `*-Item`
- `*-ItemProperty`
- `*-Location`
- `*-Path`

These are known as the *core commands*. More details can be found in the help file `Get-Help about_Core_Commands`. We've already used the `*-Item` cmdlets in this chapter to work with the item as a whole; now it's time for the `*-ItemProperty` cmdlets. We use the `ItemProperty` cmdlets to administer individual properties on objects.

In the present case, we need to modify the `ApplicationPool` property of a website. The verb *Set-* is used when we want to change something. `Set-ItemProperty` needs to be given the path to the site we must reconfigure. The `-Name` parameter controls which property is changed, whereas the `-Value` parameter supplies the name of the new application pool.

The new application pool must exist for the change to work. If this was a change that had to happen before other changes could be implemented, we could create the application pool in the script and use `Test-Path` to confirm its existence before performing the subsequent actions.

The creation of websites and application pools has been considered, as has their modification. We can now consider how we'll remove these objects when they're no longer required.

TECHNIQUE 160   **Removing a website and application pool**

One thing that I've discovered over the years is that while projects can always find time to implement new features, it's often another matter when it comes time to tidy up and remove parts of the infrastructure that are no longer required. This can leave our infrastructure vulnerable, as the attack surface is larger. It can also cause server resources to be consumed supporting the no-longer-required elements that would be better employed supporting current business processes.

PROBLEM

We've inherited a web server farm that has a number of sites and application pools. How can we easily remove them?

SOLUTION

The verb *Remove* is used when we wish to delete an object. We can pair it with the appropriate noun or use *Item* to work with the provider, as in listing 13.13. If we're removing a website and the associated application pool, we have to remove the website before we can remove the application pool. An application pool can't be deleted while it remains linked to a website or a web application.

An application pool or website can be deleted by using the `Remove-WebAppPool` or `Remove-WebSite` cmdlet respectively ❶. We need to pass the name of the object to be deleted as a parameter.

Listing 13.13 Remove website

```
Remove-WebSite -Name testnet
Remove-WebAppPool -Name netpool

Remove-Item iis:\Sites\testwmi
Remove-Item iis:\AppPools\wmipool
```

❶ Remove by cmdlet

❷ Remove by provider

DISCUSSION

The Remove-Item cmdlet can be used to delete objects via the provider ❷. The path to the object is the only parameter needed. The before and after state could be viewed using the techniques we've seen earlier in the chapter.

We'll complete this section by applying what we've discovered to simultaneously configuring multiple machines.

TECHNIQUE 161   **Configuring a new website on multiple machines**

IIS is often deployed in web farms with multiple identically configured machines. Adding a new application to a web farm can be a tedious and repetitive task. It cries out for automation.

PROBLEM

We have to deploy a new application to the 10 servers in our web farm.

SOLUTION

We solve this by writing a script that combines what we've seen previously regarding PowerShell remote administration and IIS administration. The script is shown in listing 13.14.

Listing 13.14   Creating a website on multiple machines

```
$source = "c:\Scripts\IIS\NewSite"      ◁──❶ Set source folder
Import-Csv servers.csv | foreach {      ◁──
    $dest = '\\' + $_.Server + '\C$\Inetpub'    ❷ Read CSV file

    Write-Host "Copying Files to $dest"
    Copy-Item -Path $source `
    -Destination $dest -Recurse
    -Force -Verbose                  ◁──❸ Copy website files

    $web = New-PSSession -ComputerName $_.Server    ◁──❹ Create session

    Invoke-Command -Session $web
    -ScriptBlock {Add-PSSnapin WebAdministration}    ◁──❺ Add snapin

    Invoke-Command -Session $web
    -ScriptBlock {New-WebAppPool -Name NewSite}    ◁──❻ Create
                                                       application pool
    Invoke-Command -Session $web
    -ScriptBlock {New-WebSite -Name NewSite -Port 80
        -PhysicalPath "c:\inetpub\NewSite" -ApplicationPool NewSite}    ◁──

    Invoke-Command -Session $web                              Create site ❼
    -ScriptBlock {Set-WebBinding
    -Name NewSite -BindingInformation "*:80:" -PropertyName HostHeader
        -Value NewSite.manticore.org}          ◁──
                                               ❽ Set binding
    Invoke-Command -Session $web
    -ScriptBlock {Get-WebBinding -Name NewSite}    ◁──❾ Check binding

    Invoke-Command -Session $web -ScriptBlock {Start-Sleep -Seconds 5}

    Invoke-Command -Session $web
     -ScriptBlock {Start-Website -Name NewSite}    ◁──❿ Start website

    Remove-PSSession -Session $web    ◁──⓫ Close session
}
```

The outcome of this script is that we copy a folder to the web server and create a website to use that folder. This is repeated for a number of servers. We start by setting the source of the folder we copy to the remote machine ❶. The CSV file containing the list of servers is read and contents piped into a foreach ❷. The folder containing the files used in the website is copied to the remote server ❸. We use -Recurse to ensure that subfolders and their contents are copied. The -Verbose parameter gives better feedback on the progress of the copy.

A remote session is created to the server ❹. Then the IIS snapin is loaded ❺, and a web application pool ❻ and a website ❼ are created using the code we saw earlier. Creating the application pool first enables us to reference it when we create the site and save a processing step. The site bindings are created ❽ and checked ❾. After a pause to allow the server to catch up, the website is started ❿. The session is closed ⓫ and we loop back for the next server to process.

DISCUSSION

In this script, we used Invoke-Command for each step. An alternative would be to put steps 6-10 into a separate script and call them like this:

```
Invoke-Command -Session $web -FilePath {c:\scripts\iis\new-application.ps1}
```

We don't need to wrap the individual statements with Invoke-Command if we use this technique. It's neater coding but more difficult to describe. In Windows 2008 R2, we can also create an NLB cluster or add a node to an existing cluster in the same script. If you've worked with NLB, this will be a great step forward.

This concludes our examination of websites. We'll look next at web applications.

13.3 *Web applications and virtual directories*

The alternative to creating multiple websites on our server is to create a web application. This is similar to creating a website, in that we need to define where the files used in the site will reside. We don't need to worry about things such as the site bindings, because our web application lives inside a website.

We can have multiple web applications inside our website—a good example is Exchange and the multiple applications such as OWA.

TECHNIQUE 162   **Creating a web application**

Our starting point with these objects is creating them. This is a cmdlet-only operation. The provider deals directly with sites and application pools, but treats applications as properties of sites. It's probably possible to use New-ItemProperty, but the investment in time and effort in learning how to do it isn't worth the gain when we have a perfectly good cmdlet waiting to go to work for us.

PROBLEM

We need to create a new web application on our server.

SOLUTION

Our cmdlet is New-WebApplication, as shown in listing 13.15. We've already seen that using application pools to isolate the processes of different websites and applications is generally seen to be "a good thing." As good administrators, we'll follow best practice and start by creating a new application pool ❶. The previous section discusses application pools in detail.

Listing 13.15   Creating a web application

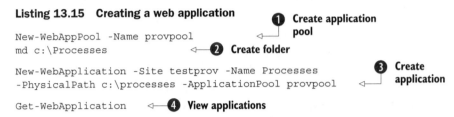

```
New-WebAppPool -Name provpool
md c:\Processes
New-WebApplication -Site testprov -Name Processes
-PhysicalPath c:\processes -ApplicationPool provpool
Get-WebApplication
```

❶ Create application pool
❷ Create folder
❸ Create application
❹ View applications

A folder to hold the files associated with our application would be nice, so we create that next ❷. The most important step is to create the actual application. We use the `New-WebApplication` cmdlet ❸. The parameters define the website used to host the application. Testprov is a site we created earlier. The application has to have a name; otherwise we won't be able to talk about it or use it. Our folder from the previous step tells the application where to look for its files, and the final parameter links the application to the application pool from the first step.

The web applications hosted on our server can be investigated using `Get-WebApplication` ❹. Many applications require multiple folders. These are referred to as *virtual directories*.

<hr>

TECHNIQUE 163   Add a virtual directory

Containers are used in a number of areas of computing. We have OUs in our Active Directory, we have folders in the filesystem, and we have hives in the registry. In a similar manner, we can use virtual directories to subdivide the files we need in our web application.

PROBLEM

We've created a web application to display process information. We now need to extend the application to cover data relating to services.

SOLUTION

The most efficient way to solve this problem is to use the `New-WebVirtualDirectory` cmdlet, as in listing 13.16. The whole idea of this is to give some structure to our web application, so we'll create a separate folder for the new files ❶. This doesn't have to be a separate folder on the same volume. It could be a subfolder in an existing file path, or it could even be on a different server if we wanted a number of machines to access the same files. If a different server is used, make sure the network connections are fast!

Listing 13.16   Creating a virtual directory

```
md c:\services
New-WebVirtualDirectory -Site testprov -Application Processes
-Name Services -PhysicalPath c:\services
Get-WebVirtualDirectory
```

❶ Create folder
❷ Create virtual directory
❸ View virtual directories

DISCUSSION

The virtual directory can then be created ❷. Its position in the hierarchy of objects on our IIS server is defined by supplying the website and application that'll be hosting the new directory. A name is supplied together with the physical path to the folder.

Our application now has a new virtual directory. We can view the fruits of our labor by using `Get-WebVirtualDirectory` ❸ to investigate the virtual directories on the server.

We won't do much in the way of modifying our applications and virtual directories, but we do need to think about removing them.

TECHNIQUE 164   **Removing virtual directories and web applications**

Administrators seem to spend more time installing new applications and features compared to removing those applications and features that are no longer required. Finding the time to perform house-cleaning operations can be difficult, but will save time in the long run. Using PowerShell to automate the cleanup will save us time and effort, but remember that automation can be viewed as a way to make mistakes faster, so double-check and always remember the `-Whatif` parameter.

PROBLEM

We're changing the servers that support our web applications and need to remove the application from the old web server.

SOLUTION

The verb *Remove* is used whenever we need to delete something. We need to remove the virtual directory first. The directory is identified by supplying the website, application, and name of the directory, as shown in listing 13.17. Then the application can be removed. We only need to supply the website and application.

Listing 13.17   Remove a web application

```
Remove-WebVirtualDirectory -Site testprov -Application processes
-Name services

Remove-WebApplication -Site testprov -Name processes
```

DISCUSSION

This process removes the application and virtual directory from the web server configuration. It doesn't remove the physical files and folders from the web server's filesystem. We can use `Remove-Item` with the appropriate path to perform that part of the task.

Our examination of the objects we can administer on the IIS server is complete. We'll conclude this chapter with a look at the IIS configuration files and how to work with XML.

13.4   *XML and configuration files*

XML is everywhere. It's a common standard for exchanging information between systems or for presenting information that's machine-readable as well as human-readable (sometimes). PowerShell uses XML in a number of places:

- Help files
- Type files
- For persisting objects

XML is of special relevance to this chapter because in IIS 7, the configuration information is stored in XML files rather than the binary metabase used in previous versions of IIS. This provides the ability to directly configure the web server by accessing the XML configuration files. The configuration files used by ASP.NET applications are also XML files, meaning we can configure the application and the server using the same tools and techniques.

> **NOTE** I made a conscious decision to keep all of the XML-related material together, as I think this aids understanding compared to scattering it throughout the book.

The IIS provider supplies a number of cmdlets for working with IIS configuration files:

- `Add-WebConfiguration`
- `Backup-WebConfiguration`
- `Clear-WebConfiguration`
- `Get-WebConfiguration`
- `Restore-WebConfiguration`
- `Select-WebConfiguration`
- `Set-WebConfiguration`

There are also a number of cmdlets for manipulating the individual properties within the configuration files:

- `Add-WebConfigurationProperty`
- `Get-WebConfigurationProperty`
- `Remove-WebConfigurationProperty`
- `Set-WebConfigurationProperty`

These cmdlets can be thought of as being analogous to the `*-Item` and `*-ItemProperty` cmdlets we've used on the filesystem and the registry. But they use XPath to describe the path to the data rather than the file paths we're accustomed to using. We'll consider working with generic XML files and then look at the IIS configuration files, but before that, we'll look at the tools that PowerShell provides for working with XML files.

TECHNIQUE 165   Persisting objects

One of the fundamental pillars of PowerShell is that it works with .NET objects. Usually these objects disappear when our script finishes (it's called *garbage collection* if you want to impress the developers) or the PowerShell session is closed. This is usually the behavior that we need, but sometimes we need to keep these objects so that we can reuse them. We want them to persist in the environment.

PROBLEM

How can we save objects from our PowerShell session for future access?

SOLUTION

We've saved data into files previously. This time, we'll save the whole object into an XML file. PowerShell provides a pair of cmdlets for solving this problem. Export-Clixml can be used to create an XML file representing the object. We can then recreate that object using Import-Clixml, as in listing 13.18.

Listing 13.18 Persisting PowerShell objects

```
Get-Process | Export-Clixml -Path proc.xml          ◄──❶ Create object

$p = Import-Clixml -Path proc.xml                    ◄──❷ Recreate object
$p

$p | where {$_.Handles -gt 500}                      ◄──❸ Use object
```

DISCUSSION

Get-Process is a good place to start experimenting with the *-Clixml cmdlets, as we can guarantee its availability. The output from Get-Process is piped into Export-Clixml ❶. We have to supply a path for the file. If a file with the same name exists, it'll be overwritten.

It's possible to export an object directly, so this would also work:

```
$proc = Get-Process
Export-Clixml -InputObject $proc -Path proc.xml
```

The original is preferred, as it's more efficient and better PowerShell to use the pipeline. Regardless of how the file is produced, it provides a good example of the verbosity of XML, as the file is nearly 5.5MB in size! A smaller file can be created using:

```
Get-Process powershell | Export-Clixml -Path pp.xml
Get-Content pp.xml
```

A single process creates a file of 278KB.

When we need to access this data again, we can use Import-Clixml to perform the re-creation of the object ❷. Typing the variable name will give us a display identical to that we would've received if we'd run Get-Process to screen instead of performing the export. We can use the object created from the XML file in exactly the same way as an object created to hold the output of Get-Process ❸. For instance, we can use the object to find the processes that have more than 500 handles open.

One word of warning about using this technique is required. The original object and the recreated object contain the same properties but they're different type. If we test the type of the objects produced by Get-Process:

```
PS> Get-Process | get-member
   TypeName: System.Diagnostics.Process
```

We can see that we are dealing with System.Diagnostics.Process objects (full details on MSDN). But if we repeat the exercise using the recreated object:

```
PS> $p | Get-Member
   TypeName: Deserialized.System.Diagnostics.Process
```

We find that the object type has changed. This will only be of importance if the type of the object is referenced and used in the script; otherwise it's an "under the hood" change that doesn't affect how we use the object.

PowerShell v2 also brings the `ConvertTo-XML` cmdlet to the party. This functions in a similar manner to `Export-Clixml` but creates the XML in memory rather than as a file:

```
PS> $x = Get-Date | ConvertTo-Xml
PS> $x | Get-Member
    TypeName: System.Xml.XmlDocument
```

This creates an XML document that we can read using the standard techniques. Other options include creating the XML as a string (`-as String`) or as an array of strings (`-as Stream`). Try:

```
Get-Process powershell | ConvertTo-Xml -As String
```

The XML will be displayed onscreen and we can merrily scroll up and down reading the data. The amount of detail is reduced compared to using `Export-Clixml`.

XML files are a common occurrence in modern IT environments. It's time for us to turn our attention to reading these files using PowerShell.

TECHNIQUE 166　　**Reading XML**

In a while, we'll see how to read IIS configuration files, but we also need to understand how to read XML files with PowerShell.

> **EXAMPLE FILE**　I've tried to ensure that the examples I've used throughout the book have been directly relevant to administrators. I'm going to break that rule with this example, as the XML files I know will be available (the PowerShell format and type files) are too big and complicated. I've created an XML file detailing some PowerShell books and blogs that we'll use instead. The file is included in the script download.

A bit of caution: the majority of examples in this section use PowerShell v2.

PROBLEM

How can we read the data in an XML file?

SOLUTION

PowerShell provides a number of different ways of tackling this problem using both generic file access cmdlets and XML-specific cmdlets, as shown in listing 13.19.

Listing 13.19　Reading XML

```
Get-Content powershell.xml           ◁──❶ Read whole file

Select-String -Path powershell.xml -Pattern "url" -SimpleMatch        ❷ Select
Select-String -Path powershell.xml -Pattern "Siddaway" -SimpleMatch   lines

Select-Xml -Path powershell.xml -XPath "/PowerShell/blogs/blog"   ◁──❸ Attempt read
Select-Xml -Path powershell.xml -XPath "/PowerShell/blogs/blog" |
select -ExpandProperty Node                                       ◁──❹ Find blogs
```

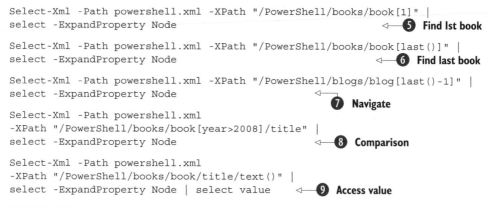

```
Select-Xml -Path powershell.xml -XPath "/PowerShell/books/book[1]" |
select -ExpandProperty Node                          ⑤ Find lst book
```

```
Select-Xml -Path powershell.xml -XPath "/PowerShell/books/book[last()]" |
select -ExpandProperty Node                          ⑥ Find last book
```

```
Select-Xml -Path powershell.xml -XPath "/PowerShell/blogs/blog[last()-1]" |
select -ExpandProperty Node
                                                     ⑦ Navigate
Select-Xml -Path powershell.xml
-XPath "/PowerShell/books/book[year>2008]/title" |
select -ExpandProperty Node                          ⑧ Comparison
```

```
Select-Xml -Path powershell.xml
-XPath "/PowerShell/books/book/title/text()" |
select -ExpandProperty Node | select value      ⑨ Access value
```

DISCUSSION

Let's start by viewing the whole file ❶. We know that XML is a text-based format and we know that Get-Content can be used to read and display the contents of files. Reviewing the file content, we can see that we have three PowerShell-related blogs and two books. I strongly recommend the three blogs as good sources of information on PowerShell.

> **OPEN FILE** It may be useful to keep a PowerShell window open to view the file while working through the rest of the examples. It should make the explanations easier to follow.

This technique is good if we want to view the whole file. But if the file is large or we need to extract individual pieces of data, we need to be able drill into the file. Power-Shell v1 doesn't have any cmdlets for dealing directly with XML, but we can use Select-String, as we're dealing with text-based files ❷. One advantage of using Select-String is that we can access the XML node structure as well as the data values. In the first example, we're looking for the text "url", which is a node name. This will return the three lines containing the URL nodes. In a similar manner, searching for a name will return all of the lines that contain that name, whichever type of node it may be. The results of these commands are shown in figure 13.3.

If we want to use more precision in reading the XML file, we have to turn to the Select-XML cmdlet in PowerShell v2. This uses XPath to read the file. Now before everybody runs shrieking from the room, XPath is quite logical and straightforward to use. We can only provide an overview here, but there are XPath tutorials on MSDN or http://w3schools.com.

Select-XML expects the path to the XML file and an XPath search query to retrieve the XML nodes in which we're interested ❸. The easiest way to understand the query is to follow it down through the XML file. /PowerShell/blogs/blog means that we start at the root of the XML <PowerShell>, then follow through <blogs> and select all of the nodes labeled <blog>. The output is shown in figure 13.3.

Unfortunately, we don't get quite what we wanted, as the display shows. Select-XML returns XML node objects rather than the information in those nodes. We need

```
C:\scripts                                                                    _ □ X
Windows PowerShell
Copyright (C) 2009 Microsoft Corporation. All rights reserved.

PS> Select-String -Path powershell.xml -Pattern "url" -SimpleMatch

powershell.xml:5:        <url>http://richardsiddaway.spaces.live.com</url>
powershell.xml:9:        <url>http://dmitrysotnikov.wordpress.com</url>
powershell.xml:13:       <url>http://blogs.technet.com/jamesone</url>


PS> Select-String -Path powershell.xml -Pattern "Siddaway" -SimpleMatch

powershell.xml:5:        <url>http://richardsiddaway.spaces.live.com</url>
powershell.xml:6:        <author>Richard Siddaway</author>
powershell.xml:20:       <author>Richard Siddaway</author>


PS> Select-Xml -Path powershell.xml -XPath "/PowerShell/blogs/blog"

Node                      Path                            Pattern
----                      ----                            -------
blog                      C:\scripts\powershell.xml       /PowerShell/blogs/blog
blog                      C:\scripts\powershell.xml       /PowerShell/blogs/blog
blog                      C:\scripts\powershell.xml       /PowerShell/blogs/blog


PS> Select-Xml -Path powershell.xml -XPath "/PowerShell/blogs/blog" | select -ExpandProperty Node

url                                       author
---                                       ------
http://richardsiddaway.spaces.live.com    Richard Siddaway
http://dmitrysotnikov.wordpress.com       Dmitry Sotnikov
http://blogs.technet.com/jamesone         James O'Neill


PS>
```

Figure 13.3   The output of using `Select-String` and `Select-Xml` on our example XML file.

an extra step to get the actual data ❹. Using a `Select-Object` and expanding the node property, we can now see the information we wanted, as displayed in figure 13.3.

We can be more precise in how we retrieve data, as the remaining examples illustrate. `/PowerShell/books/book[1]` ❺ will return the first book node, whereas `/PowerShell/books/book[last()]` ❻ will return the last. We can also navigate through the XML `/PowerShell/blogs/blog[last()-1]` ❼, which will return the second-to-last blog.

It's also possible to perform comparisons ❽. `/PowerShell/books/book[year>2008]` `/title` will return the title of any book whose year (of publishing) is greater than 2008.

We can also select the text (data) in the XML node ❾. For example, `/PowerShell/books/book/title/text()` will select the text from the title node. If we stop at just expanding the node, we get a lot of information returned that masks the data. We use a second `select` to restrict our output to the textural data (value) that we require. Comparing the results with and without the final `select` is a worthwhile exercise.

PSCX   PowerShell Community Extensions also have a cmdlet called `Select-Xml`.

This section has supplied the basics of working with XPath via `Select-XML`. The tutorials and further experimentation are strongly recommended.

TECHNIQUE 167	**Backing up the IIS configuration**

At the beginning of the chapter, I suggested that backing up the IIS configuration was a good idea. The first law of admins: "He who backs up lives to restore another day." We've seen that the configuration files are XML-based. XML is effectively text, so we could just copy the files. But that means tracking down their hiding place. There's a better way.

PROBLEM

We're about to make a change to the configuration of our IIS server and need to back up the configuration so we can perform a rollback on the change if problems arise.

SOLUTION

The IIS provider supplies a cmdlet we can use to perform the backup. Our backup mechanism isn't hugely sophisticated, but it does give us a quick and easy way to create a configuration backup. The normal backup systems can then back up our backup files to tape, and so forth.

> **DATA BACKUPS** This technique performs a backup on the configuration; it doesn't back up the files in our websites and web applications.

We don't have a lot of control over the location of the backup files. They have to be in a subfolder of "$($env:windir)\system32\inetsrv\backup". This means that we need to ensure we have a way of distinguishing between backups. We can manage this using the name of the subfolder we create to store the backups, as in listing 13.20.

Listing 13.20   Backup IIS configuration

```
$d = Get-Date
$folder = "PIP-IIS-Backup-$($d.Year)-$($d.Month)-$($d.Day)"
Backup-WebConfiguration -Name $folder
```

DISCUSSION

The easiest (and probably best) distinguisher is date-based as shown in the script. We start by retrieving the current date with Get-Date. A folder name is created using the year, month, and day portions of the date. A prefix has been supplied. This is useful if backups are taken for specific reasons. The final step is to call Backup-WebConfiguration with the name of the folder as the argument.

> **MULTIPLE DAILY BACKUPS** Multiple backups taken in the same day will overwrite each other with this naming convention. Add seconds to the name if more than one backup per day is required.

The results of the backup are shown in the following directory listing:

```
PS> Get-ChildItem $env:windir\system32\inetsrv\backup -Recurse

    Directory: C:\Windows\system32\inetsrv\backup

Mode              LastWriteTime      Length Name
----              -------------      ------ ----
d----      29/05/2009    21:28              PIP-IIS-Backup-2009-5-29
```

```
    Directory: C:\Windows\system32\inetsrv\backup\PIP-IIS-Backup-2009-5-29

Mode                LastWriteTime      Length Name
----                -------------      ------ ----
-a---         19/04/2008     16:44      14256 administration.config
-a---         29/05/2009     21:12      56057 applicationHost.config
-a---         03/10/2007     21:31        490 redirection.config
```

These files are backed up as a set and restored as a set. It's not possible to restore only one of the files, for instance. The backup sets that are available can be viewed using:

```
Get-ChildItem "$($env:windir)\system32\inetsrv\backup"
```

A restore can be performed using the name of the folder as follows:

```
Restore-WebConfiguration -Name "PIP-IIS-Backup-2009-5-29"
```

Old backups can be pruned using `Remove-Item`. Thinking about what we've discussed throughout the book, how could we remove backup folders that were more than three months old? As a clue, remember the `PSIsContainer` and `CreationTime` properties of folders, and that `Get-Date` has an `AddMonths` method.

We can protect our configuration files (from ourselves if required); now we can look at reading the files and then at modifying them.

TECHNIQUE 168   **Reading web configuration files**

Before we can do anything with the web configuration files, we need to know where they're located. This can be achieved by using the `Get-WebConfigFile` cmdlet:

```
PS> Get-WebConfigFile

    Directory: C:\Windows\system32\inetsrv\config

Mode                LastWriteTime      Length Name
----                -------------      ------ ----
-a---         29/05/2009     21:12      56057 applicationHost.config
```

Note that this is one of the files we saw when we were looking at the results of backing up the configuration file. `Get-WebConfigFile` only returns the filesystem path to the configuration; it doesn't display the contents.

PROBLEM

We need to view the contents of a web configuration file.

SOLUTION

We can either display the file onscreen or we can open it in an editor, as shown in listing 13.21. `Get-Content` ❶ is the standard PowerShell method of accessing the contents of a file. This will display the contents of the file on screen. These files are too big for this to be viable.

`Get-WebConfigFile` without a path returns the server configuration file. We can use a simple editor, such as Notepad, to display the file ❷. Note that we use a path in the IIS provider to determine the location of the file.

Listing 13.21 Read a configuration file

```
Get-Content -Path (Get-WebConfigFile)        ◁──❶ Display onscreen

notepad (Get-WebConfigFile "iis:\sites\testnet")    ◁──❷ Open in editor
```

DISCUSSION

The file can then be searched. We can also scroll through the file using the normal controls.

Alternatives include using:

```
Select-String -Path (Get-WebConfigFile "iis:\sites\default web site")
-Pattern "Authentication" -SimpleMatch
```

or the XPath queries we saw in section 13.4.2. Both of these alternatives rely on our understanding the structure of the file, which we can learn from the techniques in this section. Start by using the generic techniques, and as we develop a greater understanding of the configuration files, we can be more specific in our searches.

Reading the files is only half the problem. We also need to know how to modify them.

TECHNIQUE 169 Modifying web configuration files

The scripts we created in the earlier parts of the chapter will modify the IIS configuration. When we change the bindings for a website, for instance, the changes will be stored in the configuration file. In many cases, it's better to make the changes at the object level rather than change the configuration file. This ensures that the configuration file is updated correctly. But not all changes can be performed in this way.

PROBLEM

The authentication settings need to be modified on our IIS server. We need to enable basic authentication.

SOLUTION

We can modify the server-level configuration file to accomplish this change, as in listing 13.22. We don't want to spend time performing tasks that are unnecessary, so we'll start by checking the authentication configuration of our server ❶. The -Filter parameter accepts an XPath query to enable the information to be retrieved from the file. If you've examined the configuration file as suggested in the previous example, you'll realize why we used a simple file to investigate XPath earlier in the section. There's a method to our madness after all.

The -Path parameter uses IIS provider paths to find the configuration file. We select the properties we need and display the data in a table.

Listing 13.22 Modify a configuration file

```
Get-WebConfiguration
-Filter system.webServer/security/authentication/*[@enabled]
-PSPath iis:\ |
select ItemXPath,enabled | Format-Table -AutoSize    ◁──❶ View authentication
```

```
Get-WebConfiguration
-Filter system.webServer/security/authentication/*[@enabled]
-PSPath iis:\sites\testprov |
select ItemXPath,enabled | Format-Table -AutoSize      <-- 2  Check at site level

Get-WebConfiguration                                          3  View
-Filter system.webServer/security/authentication/*[@enabled] |   configuration
Get-Member                                                <-- properties

Set-WebConfiguration                                 Enable basic authentication  4
-Filter system.webServer/security/authentication/basicAuthentication
-Value @{enabled="True"} -PSPath iis:\                     <--
```

DISCUSSION

There are configuration files at a number of levels on our IIS server. We can also examine the same information on the website ❷ rather than the server. Note that the configurations such as authentication do flow down from the server to the site.

The properties we're selecting in ❶ and ❷ aren't obvious, so how do we know what to use? Get-Member ❸ enables us to view the properties of the object. We can then select the ones we're interested in. The examples in the help files are also a good place to find this type of information.

So far we've been reading using Get-WebConfiguration. Now we make the modification using Set-WebConfiguration ❹. Note that we take the filter down a level to the basicAuthentication node. The new value is supplied as a hash table. It's possible to make multiple changes in one hash table. The hash table key is the property we're changing, and the value is its new value as shown. We still need to supply the path to the configuration file. We could repeat ❶ to view the configuration changes.

> **PRIVILEGES**   PowerShell needs to be started with elevated privileges to modify the web configuration files on Windows Server 2008, but not on Windows Server 2008 R2

We've seen how to create and administer websites, but these sites need content. We can create that content directly from PowerShell if required.

TECHNIQUE 170   **Creating HTML**

There's always a need to store information about the computers we administer. In the next chapter, we'll look at using SQL Server as the storage mechanism. An alternative is to create web pages holding the information. Creating these pages by hand would be tedious and time consuming, so we need to think about automating the process.

PROBLEM

We need to create web pages to store information about the machines in our environment.

SOLUTION

This problem can be solved using ConvertTo-Html. There's a simple three-stage process to solving this problem. We start by generating information—in this case we're using Get-Process. With PowerShell v2, we can use the computername parameter and generate results for remote machines. In PowerShell v1, we can use WMI

(Win32_Process class). Other information sources include Get-Service and the WMI-based scripts we saw in chapters 7 and 8.

The second stage of our process is to convert the data into HTML that we can display in our web pages, as in listing 13.23. We can use the parameters of ConvertTo-Html to select object properties, to specify a table or list format, to specify the HTML page title, to add text before and after the object, and to return only the table or list fragment, instead of a strict DTD page.

Listing 13.23 Creating a web page

```
Get-Process | ConvertTo-Html -As TABLE | Out-File -FilePath t2.html
```

DISCUSSION

This cmdlet has been enhanced in PowerShell v2; for instance the -As parameter enables us to format the data as a table or as a list. Choosing table produces an output similar to that produced by Format-Table, whereas choosing list produces an output that generates a two-column list (property name and value) similar to Format-List. In PowerShell v1, we can only produce an HTML table.

ConvertTo-Html outputs to the screen. We need the third stage of our process to produce a file we can put into our website. In this case, we use out-file. We could use Set-Content (or even Add-Content) as an alternative.

If we want to view the results of this script, we can open the file in our favorite web browser using:

```
Invoke-Item t2.html
```

We can view multiple HTML files by using Get-ChildItem and piping into Invoke-Item. This will open each file in a separate browser tab. If we want to view the whole site, we can do that by using:

```
Start-Process www.microsoft.com
```

This only works with the release version of PowerShell v2.

13.5 *Summary*

There are a number of PowerShell tools available for administering IIS. It's recommended that the IIS provider and PowerShell remoting be used to give the best experience. This means adopting PowerShell v2 as soon as is practical.

Websites, application pools, virtual directories, and web applications can all be administered using PowerShell. The provider supplies functionality to support the whole lifecycle.

IIS configuration files are XML. The techniques, such as XPath, that are used for working with these configuration files can be applied to other non-IIS XML files.

Many of our applications, including those hosted in IIS, require a database to store the associated data. Now it's time to turn our attention to administering SQL Server with PowerShell.

This chapter covers

- Configuring SQL Server
- Creating and administering databases
- Creating and managing database objects such as tables and indexes
- Manipulating data in a SQL Server database

Any Windows-based environment is more than likely to have SQL Server installed somewhere. In addition to being used as a database in its own right, it also appears as a data store for a number of other Microsoft products including SharePoint, Operations Manager, and Configuration Manager.

SQL Server has a powerful scripting language in the shape of *T-SQL*. Many SQL Server experts will say they don't need PowerShell, as they can administer SQL Server quite happily using T-SQL.

Unfortunately, in many organizations the opportunity to specialize in one product, such as SQL Server, is disappearing. The phrase "Do more with less" seems to crop up frequently. I've even been known to use it myself when talking about PowerShell. Chad Miller discussed this in a blog posting "The Value Proposition of PowerShell to DBAs." The following was one of my comments in the follow-up discussion:

> *Chad gives a number of benefits of learning PowerShell. I think that one of the most compelling reasons is that it'll be a part of all future Microsoft server products—look what is happening with Windows 2008 R2—and provides a common automation platform across your Microsoft estate. PowerShell gives us the possibility of integrated, automated administration across your servers and applications.*

In other words: the theme of this book. PowerShell shouldn't be thought of as a replacement for T-SQL, but for the generalist administrator who has a number of servers and applications to administer, it's the way forward. It has a lot to offer the pure DBA in terms of automation especially in SQL Server 2008.

Having said all that, what are we going to learn regarding PowerShell and SQL Server? We'll start by looking at SQL Server Management Objects, which is the .NET object model for administering SQL Server. This will lead into server administration and database administration. We'll create a configuration database together with the tables to hold the data. This was discussed in chapter 7. We'll examine methods of working with data held in SQL Server, including creating, reading, and deleting. We'll also discover how to back up our databases.

WINDOWS SERVER 2008 R2 AND POWERSHELL V2 SQL Server 2008 will install on R2 with PowerShell v2. It needs SQL Server 2008 SP1 to complete the install. The install will also work on Windows Server 2008 if PowerShell v2 is installed first. I wouldn't recommend installing PowerShell v2 over a PowerShell v1 on a production machine. I've heard of issues when this happens.

Our starting point will be how we automate SQL Server administration.

14.1 Automating SQL Server administration

SQL Server has a number of tools such as T-SQL and SQL Server Agent jobs that can be used to automate administration. The Policy-Based Administration introduced in SQL Server 2008 adds another strand.

PowerShell can be used to augment or replace these tools. Not a lot of SQL Server material is available compared to some other products. Idera (http://www.idera.com) has some scripts available for download from its website and CodePlex (http://www.codeplex.com) has the SQL Server PowerShell Extensions. After a few blog posts, we start to run out. This chapter aims to plug some of that gap. Our starting point is discovering more about SMO.

14.1.1 SMO

SQL Server Management Objects (*SMO* to its friends) is a .NET management interface introduced with SQL Server 2005. It's a hierarchical object model in that servers contain databases, which contain tables, which contain columns, and so on. SMO can be used to programmatically manage SQL Server 2000 and later. We can use it in PowerShell, but there's one slight snag in that it's not loaded into PowerShell by default.

We overcome this by loading the SQL Server client tools on the machine we're going to use for administration. If you load the latest version of the tools (SQL Server 2008), you should be able to administer SQL Server 2000, 2005, and 2008 with them. The SMO .NET assemblies are installed with the tools and we can then load them into PowerShell, as in listing 14.1.

Listing 14.1   Load SQL 2005 SMO assemblies

```
$null = [reflection.assembly]::
LoadWithPartialName("Microsoft.SqlServer.ConnectionInfo")

[void][reflection.assembly]::
LoadWithPartialName("Microsoft.SqlServer.SmoEnum")

[reflection.assembly]::
LoadWithPartialName("Microsoft.SqlServer.Smo") | Out-Null
```

With SQL Server 2005, we have three assemblies to load as shown. They all use the LoadWithPartialName static method to perform the load. The full name of the assembly could be discovered and used instead if preferred. Three different techniques are used to suppress the messages produced by loading the assemblies. We can use $null to absorb the messages; we can use the .NET [void], which serves the same purpose (but might seem too developer-like), or we can pipe the results to Out-Null. Pick whichever you prefer, as they work equally well. In PowerShell v2, I'd use Add-Type to load the assembly.

We could put these three lines in each script that uses SMO, but it's more efficient to execute them as part of the PowerShell profile or in a specific script that we dot-source to perform the load. A similar technique can be used with SQL Server 2008, but it's more complicated, as we'll see.

14.1.2   *SQLPS*

SQL Server 2008 brings us PowerShell by default. It's a prerequisite for installation. The way PowerShell has been implemented in SQL Server 2008 is different from the other applications we've examined. The SQL Server team has created a separate implementation of PowerShell known as sqlps.exe. In the early beta version of Power-Shell (back when it was called *Monad*), the only way to extend PowerShell was to recompile the shell, incorporating your DLL in the process. This is how SQL Server implements PowerShell.

One other major difference is that sqlps is a closed shell. This means we can't add any snapins to it. In fact, the *-PsSnapin cmdlets aren't available in sqlps. PowerShell in SQL Server 2008 gives us a provider and a few cmdlets. One issue with the provider is that New-Item doesn't work, so it can't be used for creation. The other *-Item cmdlets do work. We'll see a little of the provider in this section, but I'm going to concentrate on using SMO.

There's one exceptional aspect of the PowerShell functionality in SQL Server 2008. If you right-click an object such as a database, table, or job in SQL Server Management

Studio (GUI), the context menu includes the option to open PowerShell at that point. We can jump straight into the provider without navigating down the tree. The GUI enables us to work with local and remote servers. This extends to PowerShell as well. We can use the provider against remote machines, but we have to type in the machine name rather than it being automatically available. This is another way of working remotely.

One thing we can do is load the SQL Server 2008 functionality into a standard PowerShell session. Normally, with something like Exchange 2007 or IIS 7, it's a simple matter of loading the appropriate snapins. With SQL Server 2008, it's more complicated. The script in listing 14.2 is adapted from that shown on Michiel Worie's blog http://blogs.msdn.com/mwories/archive/2008/06/14/SQL2008_5F00_Powershell.aspx.

Listing 14.2 Load SQL 2008 SQL server provider

```
$ErrorActionPreference = "Stop"

$sqlpsreg = "HKLM:\SOFTWARE\Microsoft\PowerShell\1\
ShellIds\Microsoft.SqlServer.Management.PowerShell.sqlps"

$item = Get-ItemProperty $sqlpsreg
$sqlpsPath = [System.IO.Path]::GetDirectoryName($item.Path)

$assemblylist =
"Microsoft.SqlServer.ConnectionInfo ",
"Microsoft.SqlServer.SmoExtended ",
"Microsoft.SqlServer.Smo",
"Microsoft.SqlServer.Dmf ",
"Microsoft.SqlServer.SqlWmiManagement ",
"Microsoft.SqlServer.Management.RegisteredServers ",
"Microsoft.SqlServer.Management.Sdk.Sfc ",
"Microsoft.SqlServer.SqlEnum ",
"Microsoft.SqlServer.RegSvrEnum ",
"Microsoft.SqlServer.WmiEnum ",
"Microsoft.SqlServer.ServiceBrokerEnum ",
"Microsoft.SqlServer.ConnectionInfoExtended ",
"Microsoft.SqlServer.Management.Collector ",
"Microsoft.SqlServer.Management.CollectorEnum"

foreach ($asm in $assemblylist)
{ [void] [Reflection.Assembly]::LoadWithPartialName($asm) }

Set-Variable -scope Global -name SqlServerMaximumChildItems -Value 0
Set-Variable -scope Global -name SqlServerConnectionTimeout -Value 30
Set-Variable -scope Global -name SqlServerIncludeSystemObjects -Value $false
Set-Variable -scope Global -name SqlServerMaximumTabCompletion -Value 1000

Push-Location
cd $sqlpsPath
Add-PSSnapin SqlServerCmdletSnapin100
Add-PSSnapin SqlServerProviderSnapin100
Update-TypeData -PrependPath SQLProvider.Types.ps1xml
Update-FormatData -prependpath SQLProvider.Format.ps1xml
Pop-Location
```

I put this into a script that I call from my profile. That way, it's always loaded when I start PowerShell. The script starts by ensuring that the script will stop in the event of an error. We then read the registry key that gives us the path to sqlps.exe and use it to derive the path.

There are a large number of assemblies loaded in this script. The names are defined, and then a `foreach` is used to perform the load. The first three assemblies on the list are the direct equivalents of the SQL Server 2005 SMO assemblies. If only the SMO functionality is required, just load the three assemblies.

A few variables are set that control how the provider works, and then we load the SQL Server 2008 snapins and update the type data. The provider has a few odd ideas on formatting and the default data to display, so be prepared to override with `Select-Object` and `Format-Table` as required.

> **ASSUMPTION**   All of the scripts in this chapter will be shown in an environment where either listing 14.1 or listing 14.2 has been run prior to execution. In other words, SMO and/or the PowerShell provider is loaded into my PowerShell session before I run any of the scripts. The default environment for my scripts is SQL Server 2008, though they were originally developed on SQL Server 2005.

The scripts in the bulk of the chapter will show alternative solutions using the SQL Server provider and SMO where possible. Database systems don't get refreshed as often as other systems in many organizations. I know of organizations that are still in the process of upgrading to SQL Server 2005, or can't upgrade to SQL Server 2008 because the applications aren't supported on that platform. There will be a need for the SMO scripts for a good while yet.

We've seen that SMO and the provider are both hierarchical in nature. The server object is at the pinnacle of that hierarchy, so that's where we'll start.

14.2   Server administration

When we think about administering servers, whatever the application, we tend to concentrate on a few basic questions:

- Are the correct services running?
- Are we running the right versions of the software?
- Have we configured our applications correctly?

We might also consider checking particular performance counters if we suspect a particular problem and need to investigate further. We also need to consider recording performance counter data for baselining server performance.

TECHNIQUE 171   Checking service health

Service health is the basic question of whether the services our application needs are running. If they aren't, we know at least part of one problem we have to solve before we can restore user access.

PROBLEM

The SQL Server services must be checked to see whether they're running. Any dependencies must also be checked.

SOLUTION

We don't have a specific cmdlet for this as we do with Exchange, but we can use `Get-Service` to solve this problem, as shown in listing 14.3. This script breaks down into two nested calls to `Get-Service`. The first call ❶ performs a `Get-Service` using `*sql*` as a filter to catch all of the SQL Server services. A sort is performed on the display names to produce an ordered output. The example shows it being run on the local machine, but with PowerShell v2 we could make this work on a remote machine.

> **WMI** An alternative would be to use the `Win32_Service` class, which would also allow us to work with remote machines.

The status is checked and a message is written ❷ to give the service name and its status. `Write-Host` gives us the option to set the foreground and background colors. I've been told many times that I have no color sense, so if this choice isn't suitable the colors can be altered. The help file for `Write-Host` should be checked for the allowable color names.

Listing 14.3 View SQL Service Health

```
Get-Service *sql* |sort -property Displayname | foreach{      ◁──❶ Get services

    If ($_.Status -eq "Stopped") {
        Write-Host `n $_.DisplayName, "is" $_.Status
            -foregroundcolor Red  -backGroundColor White}        ❷ Check
    Else {                                                          status
        Write-Host `n $_.DisplayName, "is" $_.Status }

    Get-Service $_.Name |
    select -ExpandProperty ServicesDependedOn |      ◁──❸ Get dependencies
    foreach{
    If ($_.Status -eq "Stopped") {
        Write-Host `t "is dependent on",
            $_.DisplayName, which is",
            $_.Status
            -foregroundcolor Red `
            -backGroundColor White}             Check status ❹

    Else {Write-Host `t "is dependent on", $_.DisplayName, "which is",
            $_.Status }
    }
}
}
```

DISCUSSION

A second call to `Get-Service` is performed ❸. This uses the name of the individual service to restrict the output. This time, though, we use the `ExpandProperty` parameter of `Select-Object` to get the services SQL Server depends on. This will show us whether our services have a problem because of a dependency. The status of each of the services we're dependent on is displayed ❹ with suitable coloring of the text.

There are often multiple versions of SQL Server running in an organization. It's important that we know which one is running on which server.

Viewing the server version

The version of SQL Server that's in use on our systems can become a vital piece of information:

- Does the application we need to install work with the versions of SQL Server we have installed?
- Are we up-to-date with service packs?
- Do we need to upgrade or replace any of our current systems because that version is no longer supported?

For a small number of systems, we might remember this information. If there are a larger number of SQL Server instances, we may have it written down. Alternatively, we can go and find the information.

PROBLEM

We need to determine the version of SQL Server installed on our systems so that we can determine which machines would be suitable for installing a new application our manager is keen to introduce.

SOLUTION

This information is stored in the `VersionString` property of the server object. Our first SMO script, shown in listing 14.4, starts by getting the server object that represents our SQL Server. The hierarchical nature of SMO means that you'll be seeing lines similar to this all through the chapter. The time to worry is when you start dreaming in SMO!

Listing 14.4   View server version

```
$Server = New-Object Microsoft.SqlServer.Management.Smo.Server("SQL08")

$ver = $Server.Information.Properties | Where {$_.name -eq "VersionString"}
 switch ($ver.Value.SubString(0,9))
  {
    "8.194.0"   {Write-Host $svr "SQL Server 2000 RTM"; break}
    "8.384.0"   {Write-Host $svr "SQL Server 2000 SP1"; break}
    "8.534.0"   {Write-Host $svr "SQL Server 2000 SP2"; break}
    "8.760.0"   {Write-Host $svr "SQL Server 2000 SP3"; break}
    "8.00.2039" {Write-Host $svr "SQL Server 2000 SP4"; break}
    "9.00.1399" {Write-Host $svr "SQL Server 2005 RTM"; break}
    "9.00.2047" {Write-Host $svr "SQL Server 2005 SP1"; break}
    "9.00.3042" {Write-Host $svr "SQL Server 2005 SP2"; break}
    "9.00.4035" {Write-Host $svr "SQL Server 2005 SP3"; break}
    "10.0.1300" {Write-Host $svr "SQL Server 2008 CTP6"; break}
    "10.0.1600" {Write-Host $svr "SQL Server 2008 RTM"; break}
    "10.0.2531" {Write-Host $svr "SQL Server 2008 SP1"; break}
    default     {Write-Host $svr "version cannot be determined"; break}
  }
```

DISCUSSION

The only parameter we need to give is the server name—the hostname. Our example is a default instance. If we need to access a named instance we can use:

```
Server_name\instance_name, port_number
```

instead of the server name, where the port_number is the TCP port used by the particular instance of SQL Server. The version string can be found on the information properties. We'll see the different property groupings in the next section. The first nine characters of the version string are sufficient for our purposes.

A `switch` statement is used to test the value of the version string. Note the use of `break` to force the `switch` statements not to test other options. It makes this code slightly faster, and will avoid ambiguous answers in other switch statements. The default statement is useful to find any versions you have missed and as a reminder to upgrade the script when new service packs are released.

The version numbers can be found in Microsoft KB article 321185, (http://support.microsoft.com/kb/321185) which is updated as new service packs and versions are released. I haven't gone further back than SQL Server 2000, as previous versions don't support SMO.

This script may seem like a lot of work for one property, but if we parameterize the server name, we can use our usual trick with CSV files to determine this information for all our servers. The script should be modified to output the server name as well.

We've seen how to access one server-level property. How can we access the others?

TECHNIQUE 173   Viewing server configuration

In one respect, SQL Server doesn't have many moving parts. There isn't a lot of configuration tuning required. The defaults mostly work well. But there are a lot of properties that can be configured if required. If we use the GUI to examine the properties, we're talking about several tabs' worth on the dialog.

I recently had to examine some SQL Server machines to determine their configuration properties. The total listing was quite a few pages, using a small font. Did I type all of that? Of course I did, boss; how else do you think I could do it?

PROBLEM

We need to determine the configuration properties of our SQL Server systems.

SOLUTION

This information is available in the property collections on the `server` object, as shown in listing 14.5. Create the server object ❶. We have four sets of properties to discover. Each of them is preceded by `n (new line—though you may get two as a bonus) and a label. The server information ❷ includes things such as the SQL Server version, paths to the master database and logs, language, and the collation.

Listing 14.5 View server configuration

```
$Server =
New-Object Microsoft.SqlServer.Management.Smo.Server("SQL08")    ❶ Server
                                                                    object
"`n"
"Server Information"
$Server.Information.Properties | Select-Object Name, Value |    ❷ Server
Format-Table -auto                                                 information

"`n"
```

```
"Server Settings"
$Server.Settings.Properties | Select-Object Name, Value |
Format-Table -auto
```

❸ Server settings

```
"`n"
"User Options"
$Server.UserOptions.Properties | Select-Object Name, Value |
Format-Table -auto
```

❹ User options

```
"`n"
"Server Configuration"
$Server.Configuration.Properties |
Select-Object DisplayName, ConfigValue, RunValue, Description |
Format-Table -auto
```

Server configuration ❺

DISCUSSION

The properties under server settings ❸ include auditing, default data file and log file locations, and the login modes. User options ❹ brings us to the defaults for the ANSI settings such as nulls, padding, and abort settings for exceptions. These settings can be overridden in individual queries, but it makes more sense to configure the default to match expected usage. By default, all of these are set to false.

The server configuration properties ❺ are the most extensive. These properties have both a configured value and a running value. Keep this section in mind when we start discussing the configuration database and think how we could get this information into the database.

Discovering the information is one thing, but sometimes we need to change it.

TECHNIQUE 174 **Modifying the server configuration**

Once SQL Server is running, we don't need to make changes that often. But if different people configure the servers without there being any defined standards, it's possible for the systems to have different configurations.

PROBLEM

We need to alter our server so that all of our SQL Server instances have a consistent configuration.

SOLUTION

We can access the server properties to perform our alterations. We saw in the previous example how to access the server and properties. The property collections are accessed as a collection. We can read the value of an individual property by using its name:

```
$Server.UserOptions.Properties["AnsiNulls"]
```

Substitute the name of the appropriate property for "AnsiNulls". The quotes are required. The value of a property can be modified by using the value property of the property:

```
$Server.UserOptions.Properties["AnsiNulls"].Value = $false
```

Confusing but logical.

The change is saved using the Alter() method, as shown in listing 14.6. This is consistent with SQL Server usage as in ALTER DATABASE and so forth, but means that across .NET we've now seen `Save()`, `CommitChanges()`, and `Alter()` all doing the same job. This will cause errors until we get used to it. If in doubt, check the documentation on MSDN.

Listing 14.6   Modify configuration

```
$Server = New-Object Microsoft.SqlServer.Management.Smo.Server("SQL08")
$Server.UserOptions.Properties["AnsiNulls"].Value = $false
$server.Alter()

$Server = new-object Microsoft.SqlServer.Management.Smo.Server("SQL08")
$Server.UserOptions.Properties | Select-Object Name, Value |
Format-Table -auto
```

DISCUSSION

This script could be modified by adding more properties to change so that it sets every property on the server to your organization's requirements. This would be a good way of enforcing consistency on a server estate. The script could even check the actual value and only perform changes if the value had deviated from the standard. I'll leave that as an exercise for you; I don't have the space to cover it here.

There are other configuration options concerning the network that aren't included in the property sets we've been working with. These control the server's network communication and are vital to SQL Server's usability.

TECHNIQUE 175   ## Network configuration

SQL Server is useless without a network. Just try pulling the network cable and see how long it is before your users start shouting. Communication obviously depends on the networking components in the Windows OS. It also depends on SQL Server's network configuration. There isn't much to configure. There are the protocols to use, together with the IP addresses and ports SQL Server is listening on.

This is the information we want to know about. There's a GUI tool for this, but it isn't accessible remotely. We must either visit the machine, `remote desktop` into it, or try scripting.

Unfortunately, SMO doesn't give us a way to getting at this information. As with many other areas of administering a Windows environment, WMI comes to the rescue. Microsoft has made a huge effort with WMI, and I suspect that it's one of the most underappreciated and underrated technologies in the Windows infrastructure. Power-Shell has given it a new lease on life, and now we apply it to SQL Server.

PROBLEM

Having inherited a number of SQL Server machines, and incomplete documentation (nonexistent in many cases), we need to discover the network settings to ensure that clients and servers are using the same protocols for communication.

SOLUTION

We can access the information remotely through the WMI provider, as in listing 14.7. Our earlier looks at WMI showed us that WMI is organized into namespaces under the root. The SQL Server WMI provider (automatically installed in SQL Server 2005 and 2008) adds the namespace ❶. In SQL Server 2005, it's Microsoft\SqlServer\ ComputerManagement, and in SQL Server 2008, it's Microsoft\SqlServer\Computer-Management10, just to be confusing.

We can find the classes available by using the -List parameter. Best of all, we can do this remotely by supplying a computer name.

When we look at the available classes, those to do with protocols are quickly apparent. SQL Server has two sets of protocols—client and server. The client and server protocols are configured on their respective machines. The server also has a client protocol for local access. There must be a protocol in common for communication to occur.

Listing 14.7 Network Protocols

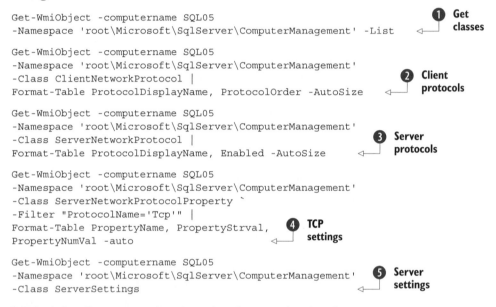

```
Get-WmiObject -computername SQL05
-Namespace 'root\Microsoft\SqlServer\ComputerManagement' -List        ❶ Get
                                                                        classes

Get-WmiObject -computername SQL05
-Namespace 'root\Microsoft\SqlServer\ComputerManagement'
-Class ClientNetworkProtocol |                                        ❷ Client
Format-Table ProtocolDisplayName, ProtocolOrder -AutoSize              protocols

Get-WmiObject -computername SQL05
-Namespace 'root\Microsoft\SqlServer\ComputerManagement'
-Class ServerNetworkProtocol |                                        ❸ Server
Format-Table ProtocolDisplayName, Enabled -AutoSize                    protocols

Get-WmiObject -computername SQL05
-Namespace 'root\Microsoft\SqlServer\ComputerManagement'
-Class ServerNetworkProtocolProperty `
-Filter "ProtocolName='Tcp'" |                                        ❹ TCP
Format-Table PropertyName, PropertyStrval,                             settings
PropertyNumVal -auto

Get-WmiObject -computername SQL05
-Namespace 'root\Microsoft\SqlServer\ComputerManagement'             ❺ Server
-Class ServerSettings                                                  settings
```

We find the client protocol settings (on the server) using the ClientNetworkProtocol WMI class ❷. We only need to consider the ProtocolDisplayName and Protocol-Order properties. A protocol order of zero (0) means that the protocol is disabled.

The server protocols are discovered using the ServerNetworkProtocol class ❸. This time we need the ProtocolDisplayName and Enabled properties, to be consistent. If we drill deeper into the namespace, we'll find the ServerNetworkProtocolProperty class. We can use this to discover the properties associated with the protocols. Using a filter ❹, we restrict our information to the TCP/IP settings by using the protocol name. Properties either have numeric or string-based values, so we can display both as well as the property name. Just be aware that some values will be blank (null). Of particular interest are the properties named IP address, which stores the IP addresses associated with the server, and the TcpPort property. The port is especially important on a named instance or multi-instance server. as it will vary from the default 1433.

We also have a class ❺ to retrieve the server settings.

DISCUSSION

Running this as a single script may cause formatting errors due to the interaction of multiple calls to `Format-Table` and the default formatter. The commands can either be run from the command line, or the `Format-Table` calls could be replaced by a `Select-Object` cmdlet. If the information is destined for a file of some kind, the `select` is probably a better choice.

There's a lot of documentation available about wrapping these WMI classes in SMO code, but with PowerShell that's an unneeded complication. I recommend accessing the WMI classes directly through PowerShell.

> **SQL SERVER 2000** There's a WMI provider for SQL Server 2000—root/Micro-softSQLServer—but it has to be installed separately. The installation files are on the CD. I haven't investigated it, given the age of SQL Server 2000 and its lifecycle position.

Server performance always needs to be monitored.

TECHNIQUE 176 Viewing performance counters

"The server is running slow." How many times is a problem introduced to us this way? An even worse version is, "Mr. X says the server is running slow" where we don't even get to talk to the user directly.

The problem is knowing where to start with solving this issue. Often, it isn't a server problem but an application issue. We still need to check the server to rule it out potential problems. One if the best ways is to use performance counters.

Windows has a lot of performance counters covering every aspect of the server operation including processor, memory, disk, and network. Applications such as SQL Server add another layer of counters. Any long-term benchmarking may be better done through the performance monitoring tools, but ad-hoc investigations can be performed easily using the PowerShell v2 `Get-Counter` cmdlet.

PROBLEM

Our server's performance counters need to be accessed and displayed to monitor processor usage.

SOLUTION

PowerShell v2 introduces the `Get-Counter` cmdlet for this. Our first example, listing 14.8, displays the total processor utilization on the system ❶. There's a `-ComputerName` parameter so we can access remote machines. This syntax will produce a single sample, because we've limited ourselves using the `-Maxsamples` parameter. We can keep producing values by using the `-Continuous` parameter, and we can also modify the sampling interval from the default once per second.

Listing 14.8 View performance counters

```
PS> Get-Counter   -Counter "\Processor(_total)\% Processor Time"
      -MaxSamples

Timestamp                 CounterSamples
```
 ❶ **Default display**

```
- - - - - - - - -              - - - - - - - - - - - - - -
30/06/2009 15:44:46            \\rslaptop01\processor(_total)\
                              % processor time :
                              1.53783037475346
```

```
PS> (Get-Counter -Counter "\Processor Information(_total)\
% Processor Time" -MaxSamples 1 ).CounterSamples |
Select *
```
❷ **Property list**

```
Path             : \\rslaptop01\processor information(_total)\
                   % processor time
InstanceName     : _total
CookedValue      : 0.76859960552268
RawValue         : 269354602620
SecondValue      : 128908467546756000
MultipleCount    : 1
CounterType      : Timer100NsInverse
Timestamp        : 30/06/2009 15:45:54
Timestamp100NSec : 128908503546756000
Status           : 0
DefaultScale     : 0
TimeBase         : 10000000
```

```
PS> (Get-Counter -Counter "\Processor Information(_total)\
% Processor Time" -MaxSamples 1 ).CounterSamples |
Select CookedValue |
Out-Gauge -Type Digital -Refresh 00:00:01
```
❸ **Graphical display**

DISCUSSION

The main problem with using this cmdlet is getting the counter names correct. We can use:

```
Get-Counter -ListSet * | Select CounterSetName
```

to display the list of counters available. If we're only interested in a particular subset, then we can filter further using

```
Get-Counter -ListSet processor
```

The actual counter paths are found using:

```
(Get-Counter -ListSet processor).Paths
```

It's worth the time investigating how the parameters are named, as it's not always intuitive. The default display gives us more (and less) information than we require. We can find the properties we really need by looking at the CounterSamples properties ❷. This shows that the data value we want is in the CookedValue property.

Selecting this value and piping into Out-Gauge (from PowerGadgets) gives a nice digital counter ❸ that can tick along, being refreshed every second showing the state of the processor on our server. If PowerGadgets isn't available, we could just display the numeric values at a PowerShell prompt using the -Continuous parameter.

There are a large number of SQL Server-specific counters that can be accessed via this method. These include:

- Buffer Management Object\Buffer Cache Hit ratio
- Databases Object\Log Flush Waits/sec
- Locks Object\Lock Waits/sec

Server administration tends to be intermittent. The real fun lies when we get down to the databases.

14.3 Database administration

A SQL Server installation isn't much use without databases. This section will look at how we can use PowerShell to administer our databases. Creating databases and how to work with the data inside a database is covered in the next section.

Our starting point is discovering the databases that are actually on the system.

TECHNIQUE 177   Finding databases

There are two things we need to know immediately about our SQL Server. First, we need to know what databases are installed on the system, and second, if they're available to the users. If the databases are available, that means the users are working and not phoning us. Important point—keep the users working; it's quieter that way.

PROBLEM

Having just inherited a number of SQL Server systems, we need to discover the status of the installed databases.

SOLUTION

We can find the databases using SMO or the provider. SMO objects need to be created each time we want to use the functionality. That means we have to spend a lot of effort typing in the names of the objects we want to create. One possible solution is to use a variable to store the bulk of the object name, as in listing 14.9. This variable ❶ can then be used whenever we need to create an SMO object ❷ such as a SQL Server object.

Listing 14.9   List databases

```
$Smo = "Microsoft.SqlServer.Management.Smo."          ❶
$server = New-Object ($Smo + 'server') "sql08"        ❷
$server.databases          ◄──❸  View databases

Get-ChildItem SQLSERVER:\sql\SQL08\Default\databases          ◄── ❹ View through provider

Get-ChildItem sqlserver:\sql\sql08\default\databases -Force          ◄── ❺ View system databases
```

DISCUSSION

Once we have the server object, we can then access the databases collection ❸ to produce the display shown in figure 14.1.

In this example, we're using the name of the SQL Server as the parameter. It's possible to have multiple instances of SQL Server on a system. In this case, only the default instance will be using port 1433 (the default TCP port for SQL Server). The other instances require us to change the way we connect, either by using the server name, the instance name, or the TCP port:

```
$server = New-Object ($Smo + 'server') "SQLXX\InstanceYY,Port_Number"
```

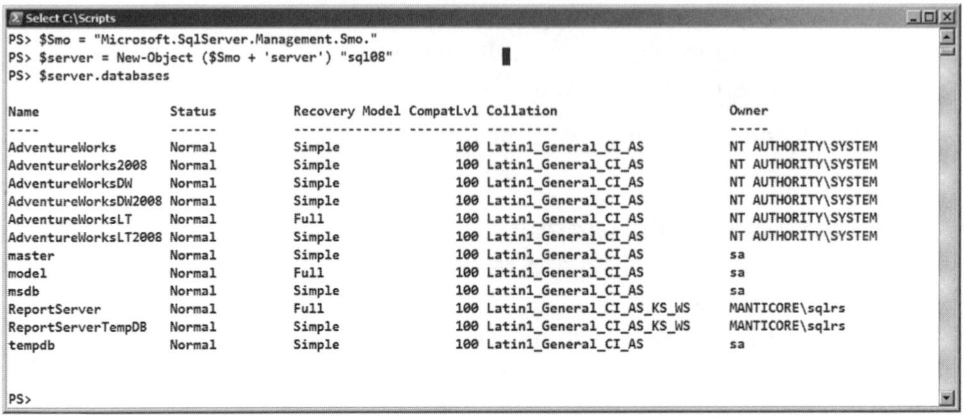

Figure 14.1   Viewing the databases using PowerShell and SMO

Or by using the IP address of the instance:

```
$server = New-Object ($Smo + 'server') "10.10.10.10,Port_Number"
```

Once the connection to the server is made, the other SMO objects behave as normal.

> **SQL SERVER 2000**   If we're connecting to SQL Server 2000, the default for-
> matting may not work properly when objects are returned. In this case,
> pipe into a `foreach-object` cmdlet or use `select` to choose the properties
> to display.

An alternative method is to use the provider ❹. `Get-ChildItem`, used against the
SQL Server provider, will return similar information to figure 14.1. One major difference is that the system databases won't show on the display. The provider doesn't display the system databases by default. This means we don't get a full view of our
server. How can we get around this? "Use the force, Luke." Adding a `-Force` parameter to `Get-ChildItem` ❺ will override the providers default behavior and display the
system databases.

The status column will show if database is offline. A status of `Normal` means that it's
up and available for use. We can bring a database back online by using the provider:

```
$db = Get-Item sqlserver:\sql\sql08\default\databases\AdventureWorksLT
$db.SetOnline()
```

We can access the object through the provider and `Get-Item`. The `SetOnline()`
method will then bring the database back online. Alternatively, we can use SMO:

```
$server = New-Object ($Smo + 'server') "sql08"
$db = $server.Databases["AdventureWorksLT"]
$db.SetOnline()
```

A server object is created as before. We then need to access a particular database via
the databases collection. This is best done by using the database name, as shown. We

can then call the SetOnLine() method. In case you were wondering, there's a SetOf-
fline() method to take a database offline.

> **CAUTION** The status of the database doesn't always refresh correctly in Power-
> Shell. If in doubt, try another way of viewing or open another instance of Pow-
> erShell or SQLPS and view.

Now that we know what databases are available, our next task is to discover how much
disk space these databases are using.

TECHNIQUE 178 Viewing space used

Databases tend to keep getting bigger over time. It's a rare database that actually
shrinks. One task we need to perform on a regular basis is monitoring the available
disk space on the server and checking our database sizes so we don't run out of disk
space. That would be bad.

    I recently had to determine this information for a number of SQL Server instances.
Unfortunately, I didn't have PowerShell available so I had to check each database individually. There isn't an easy way to get this information, as it's stored with each database rather than centrally. As you can imagine, this caused a lot of muttering and
unhappiness because I wasn't able to do this in an efficient manner.

PROBLEM
We have to discover the size of the individual databases on our server so that we can
assign the correct amount of storage on a new server.

SOLUTION
The size of the data files and log files can be discovered on the database object, as in
listing 14.10. In the later versions of SQL Server, when we look at the front tab of a
database's properties sheet we see the size and free space. Those numbers combine
the sizes of the data files and the log files. In this example, I've only considered a single data file and log file for simplicity, but the scripts can be readily adapted to cope
with more complicated scenarios. We already access the log files via the collection as
we have to use LogFiles[0] to access the first log file.

Listing 14.10 View space used by databases

```
Get-ChildItem sqlserver:\sql\sql08\default\databases | Format-Table Name,
    @{Label="Size";Expression={($_.Size).ToString("F")}},
    @{Label="Available";
Expression={($_.SpaceAvailable/1KB).ToString("F")}},
@{Label="LogSize";                                              ❶ Provider and
Expression = {($_.LogFiles[0].Size/1KB).ToString("F2")}}    ◁──  Format-Table
,@{Label="LogUsed";
Expression={($_.LogFiles[0].UsedSpace/1KB).ToString("F")}}

$Smo = "Microsoft.SqlServer.Management.Smo."
$server = New-Object ($Smo + 'server') "sql08"    ◁──❷ Server object

"`n   {0,20} {1,15} {2,15} {3,15} {4,15}" -f
"Name", "Size", "Available", "Log size", "Log Used"    ◁──❸ Header
```

```
foreach ($db in $Server.Databases)
{"`n   {0,20}  {1,15:n} {2,15:n}  {3,15:n} {4,15:n}" -f
$db.Name, $db.Size, $($db.SpaceAvailable/1KB),
$($db.LogFiles[0].Size/1KB), $($db.LogFiles[0].UsedSpace/1KB)}
```

 ❹ **Data display**

Our first example uses the provider to access the database information ❶. We then use Format-Table to display the data. The name of the database is used directly, and then we use a number of calculated fields to display the size and free space data. We've seen calculated fields used in earlier chapters, but a brief recap may be useful-especially if you aren't reading the book cover to cover.

We use a hash table to create the field. The key provides a name (in PowerShell v2 we can use Name as well as Label so the usage is consistent with Select-Object) and the value is supplied as a script block via the Expression field. In this case, we're taking the relevant property of the database or log file and dividing by 1KB where appropriate to convert everything to megabytes. The value is then converted to a string; use the "F" formatter to restrict the display to two decimal places.

DISCUSSION

In PowerShell v2, we can be slightly more sophisticated, in that we can control the alignment of the calculated fields. The default is to left align the fields but we can change that by using:

```
@{Label="Size";Expression={($_.Size).ToString("F")};Alignment="Right"}
```

The alignment parameter can be used to right-align the fields and give a neater display. Check the -Property parameter in Format-Table help for full details of this and the other changes to calculated fields.

If we don't have the provider available, we can use SMO. Our starting point is the server object ❷. We then have to print our own header using the -f operator. The values on the right are substituted into their respective fields in the string on the left side of the operator ❸. A foreach statement enables us to loop through the databases. The same calculations to convert the values to megabytes are performed, but we don't need to worry about converting to strings and formatting when we substitute into the display string ❹, as our clever friend -f does all that for us.

An alternative approach would be to create an object with the appropriate values for each property and use Format-Table to display.

We can use listing 7.7 to get a report of free space on the appropriate volumes. This together with the display from this example will provide the information we need if we have to move a database to another volume or server.

Databases, like all things, need regular maintenance. This is achieved by creating SQL Server Agent jobs.

TECHNIQUE 179   **Creating a job**

SQL Server has a large number of features. One of the most useful from an administrator's view is the SQL Server Agent service, which manages jobs, alerts, and associated tasks. SQL Server jobs are scheduled tasks that are managed by the SQL Server

Agent. They can have one or more steps, be run on demand or to a schedule, and can use T-SQL, command-line utilities, and a number of other facets of SQL Server. In SQL Server 2008, the job engine gained the ability to use PowerShell job steps.

PROBLEM

We need to create a number of jobs on our SQL Server system.

SOLUTION

We need to use the SMO classes that administer the SQL Server agent service for this task, as shown in listing 14.11. Create a server object and then use that as a parameter when creating the object for the job ❶. The other parameter is the job name. We can add a description and a category. Jobs that we'll create are usually in the [Uncategorized (Local)] category. A job owner is established, and then we can create the job on the server ❷. At this point, the job is a container that we need to fill with the working parts.

Listing 14.11   Create job

```
$Server =
New-Object Microsoft.SqlServer.Management.Smo.Server("SQL08")

$job =
New-Object Microsoft.SqlServer.Management.Smo.Agent.Job `
-ArgumentList $Server.JobServer, "Pip14"          ◁─❶ Job object

$job.Description = "PowerShell - populate ConfigDB"
$job.Category = "[Uncategorized (Local)]"
$job.OwnerLoginName = 'MANTICORE\Richard'
$job.Create()                          ◁─❷ Create job

$step = New-Object Microsoft.SqlServer.Management.Smo.Agent.JobStep
($job, "Get-data")                     ◁─❸ Step object

$step.SubSystem = [Microsoft.SqlServer.Management.`
Smo.Agent.AgentSubsystem]::PowerShell          ◁─❹ PowerShell
$step.Command = "get-service | out-file c:\scripts\serv.txt"   step

$step.OnSuccessAction =
[Microsoft.SqlServer.Management.Smo.Agent.`
StepCompletionAction]::QuitWithSuccess
$step.OnFailAction =                   ◁─❺ Work flow
[Microsoft.SqlServer.Management.Smo.Agent.`
StepCompletionAction]::QuitWithFailure
$step.Create()                         ◁─❻ Create step

$job.ApplyToTargetServer($Server.Name)
$job.StartStepID = $step.id
$job.Alter()                           ◁─❼ Set starting step

$sched = New-Object Microsoft.SqlServer.`
Management.Smo.Agent.JobSchedule ($job, 'Schedule1')  ◁─❽ Schedule object

$sched.FrequencyTypes =
[Microsoft.SqlServer.Management.Smo.Agent.`
FrequencyTypes]::Daily                 ◁─❾ Schedule frequency

$sched.FrequencySubDayTypes =
```

```
[Microsoft.SqlServer.Management.Smo.Agent.`
FrequencySubDayTypes]::Once                    ◁──9  Schedule frequency

$schedstart = New-Object System.Timespan(22, 0, 0)
$sched.ActiveStartTimeOfDay = $schedstart
$schedend = new-object System.Timespan(23, 59, 59)
$sched.ActiveEndTimeOfDay = $schedend          ◁──10  Timing

$sched.FrequencyInterval = 1
$sched.ActiveStartDate = Get-Date     ◁──11  Start date
$sched.Create()                 ◁──12  Create schedule
```

A job must have at least one job step, and can have multiple job steps. The job step object is created using the job and a name as parameters ❸. Now we can add what type of job step we're creating ❹. In this case, it's a PowerShell step.

> **SQL SERVER 2008 ONLY** PowerShell job steps can only be used in SQL Server 2008. If we need to run PowerShell on SQL Server 2005, we need to use a command-line step and call PowerShell and the script we want to run.

Other types include `TransactSql` for running SQL commands and `CmdExec` for running command-line programs. The command we're running is added together with simple workflow commands ❺ regarding success and failure. The command in this example is simple, but we can add multiple lines of PowerShell or call a PowerShell script.

The step is saved ❻ and set as the first step in the job. The alteration ❼ is then saved. Creating job steps may be repeated as many times as required. This is a prime example of where a function would be useful.

The last part of this script creates a schedule. We don't want to keep running things manually. There are no prizes for guessing that we start by creating a schedule object ❽ using the job and a schedule name as parameters. We set the schedule to run once per day ❾ and use `timespan` objects ❿ to define the start and end of the period in which it can run. We can set how many times the job runs in that period and when it'll start to run ⓫. The schedule is saved ⓬ using the `Create()` method.

DISCUSSION

We now have a SQL Server job that can run PowerShell scripts. PowerShell itself doesn't have a scheduling system. Even if one appears in PowerShell v3, it'll be a few years away. In the meantime, we could install SQL Server Developer Edition on a workstation and use that to provide our scheduling capability. The existing jobs can be viewed using:

```
ls sqlserver:\sql\sql08\default\jobserver\jobs
```

Remember that sql08 is the server name. One issue is accessing remote machines. We overcome this by creating a SQL Server credential using a Windows account with permissions to access remote machines. We then create a SQL Server Agent Proxy that has permission to run PowerShell jobs. Both tasks are detailed in SQL Server documentation. Our PowerShell jobs can then access remote machines using WMI or .NET.

Alternatively, with Windows Server 2008 R2 we can use the PowerShellPack from the Windows 7 Resource Kit (also available as a separate download from http://code.msdn.microsoft.com/PowerShellPack). It has a module for working with the Windows Task Scheduler.

This could even be used to schedule data collection for the configuration database we'll be discussing next.

14.4 Configuration database

In this section, we'll create the skeleton on a configuration database. We first mentioned this idea in chapter 7 when we looked at retrieving configuration information. We'll look at creating and populating the database, working with the data, and taking a backup of our data. The scripts in this section can be easily modified to work in other database scenarios.

One aspect of the lifecycle I won't cover is deleting objects such as databases or tables. We can manage that using the provider and `Remove-Item` or we can use SMO and the `delete` method on the various objects

Our objective in this section is to provide an outline of how we can use PowerShell to manage our configuration database. I'll only be providing a couple of examples of the sort of data we'd want to install, but it should be possible to extrapolate to cover other sets of information.

> **DATABASE DESIGN** I'm not providing any information on database design in this section. The examples I'm using are designed to be a practical use of PowerShell that shows how to use it with SQL Server.

The first step in this is to create a database.

TECHNIQUE 180   Creating a database

Databases can be created using the SQL Server GUI tools or T-SQL. Using PowerShell, we can create the database on remote machines and we also have a consistent, repeatable process that we can use against multiple machines.

PROBLEM

Our configuration database has to be created on the SQL Server system so that we have a storage area for our configuration data.

SOLUTION

The SMO database object has a create method that we can use for this purpose. We'll discuss variations on creating our database. The first is quick and dirty—the scripter's ideal. The second extends the first by explicitly defining the database properties rather than using the defaults.

> **TWO OPTIONS** The following script contains *two* separate options for creating the database. Use one option or the other. Running the whole script will cause an error on the final `create` statement, as the database will already exist.

We're using SMO for this, so our first act is to create an object to represent the SQL Server we'll use to create the database. In listing 14.12, I'm using the full SMO class name rather than putting part into a variable as I've done earlier. We follow this by creating a database object on the server. Our parameters are the server object and the database name. Do you like the imaginative name for the database? That was a major decision point for the chapter. Finally, we call the `Create()` method ❶ to create the database.

That was easy. Too easy. We don't know where our database is located or even how big it is, as it's created with all default parameters. The database will be 1MB in size by default and the data file and log file will be situated on the paths indicated by the following properties:

```
$server.Information.MasterDBPath
$server.Information.MasterDBLogPath
```

Other properties such as growth factors will also take the default values. If all we need is a quick test database, this is great. Usually we want to be able to control these properties, so we need to be a bit more complicated in our approach:.

Listing 14.12   Create database

```
## Using defaults
$Server = New-Object Microsoft.SqlServer.Management.Smo.Server("SQL08")
$db =
New-Object Microsoft.SqlServer.Management.Smo.Database($server, "ConfigDB")
$db.Create()                        ⬅──── ❶ Create with defaults

## Setting options
$Server =
New-Object Microsoft.SqlServer.Management.Smo.Server("SQL08")

$db =
New-Object Microsoft.SqlServer.Management.`
Smo.Database($server, "ConfigDB")    ⬅──❷ Create database object

$fg =
New-Object Microsoft.SqlServer.Management.`
Smo.FileGroup ($db, 'PRIMARY')
$db.Filegroups.Add($fg)              ⬅──❸ Add filegroup

$mdf =
New-Object Microsoft.SqlServer.Management.`
Smo.DataFile($fg, "ConfigDB_Data")
                                        ❹ Add file
$fg.Files.Add($mdf)                  ⬅
$mdf.FileName = "C:\SQLdata\ConfigDB_Data.mdf"
$mdf.Size = 25.0 * 1KB
$mdf.GrowthType = "Percent"             ❺ File
$mdf.Growth = 25.0                        properties
$mdf.IsPrimaryFile = "True"

$ldf =
New-Object Microsoft.SqlServer.Management.`
Smo.LogFile($db, "ConfigDB_Log")
```

```
$db.LogFiles.Add($ldf)                    ← 6 Add log file
$ldf.FileName = "C:\SQLlog\ConfigDB_Log.ldf"
$ldf.Size = 20.0 * 1KB                       7 Log
$ldf.GrowthType = "Percent"                    properties
$ldf.Growth = 20.0

$db.Create()          ← 8 Create database
```

DISCUSSION

We can start by creating the server and database objects as before ❷. Our next job is to create the data file, which we start by creating a file group and adding it to the file group collection ❸. The first file group is named PRIMARY, as in the example. A file group is a logical collection of database files. One use is that database tables are created on file groups rather than on files. You need to read a good SQL Server book if you want more on the physical structure of SQL Server databases (for example, *SQL Server 2008 Administration in Action* by Rodney Colledge, published by Manning).

The next step is to create the data file. The filename we give here is the logical name that's used by SQL Server. We can then add it to the files collection of the file group ❹. Now we can configure the file properties ❺. The filename is the full path to the file. An .mdf file is a primary data file (one per database). If we create additional files, they'll be secondary files with the extension of .ndf.

The file size is a bit awkward to define. It should be in megabytes according to the documentation, but that doesn't actually work. We need to supply a size greater than (or equal to) 1MB, but it has to be input as kilobytes. This is as bad as defining Exchange mailbox limits in the GUI! Luckily, PowerShell makes this easier, because we can take our number of megabytes, 25.0 in this case, and multiply by 1KB (1024) to get the correct value. Treating it in this way also makes using parameters with the script a lot easier. The data file is set to grow by 25% when required.

We're nearly finished. We complete our database by creating a file ❻ for the transaction logs. Just to keep things interesting, log files don't exist in file groups. We set the log file properties ❼ in a similar way to the data file and then create the database ❽ as before.

Most databases on SQL Server will have a single data file and log file, though the script can be adapted to create multiples of both, and multiple file groups, if required. The database is the container for our data, roughly analogous to a folder in the filesystem. If we want to do anything with the database, we need to create some tables.

TECHNIQUE 181 Creating a table

A database table is a two-dimensional, tabular arrangement of data. The horizontal dimension is called a *row* and the vertical is called a *column*. There is a lot of theory around relational databases such as SQL Server, which we're going to cheerfully ignore in this example. If you do decide to extend this database, I'd recommend designing it properly before creating additional tables.

PROBLEM

Our database needs a table to store the data from listing 7.1

SOLUTION

We can use the SMO database object to execute a script that'll create the table, as in listing 14.13. In some respects this is the best and easiest way to create a table, but it involves PowerShell, SMO, and T-SQL. If this is too much SQL, then try listing 14.14, which is an SMO-only version.

Listing 14.13   Create table via a script

```
$Server =
New-Object Microsoft.SqlServer.Management.`
Smo.Server("SQL08")                            ◁──❶ Create server

$script =                                                        ❷ Create
New-Object -Type System.Collections.Specialized.StringCollection  ◁─┘ script
$script.Add("SET ANSI_NULLS On")           ❸ Set execution
$script.Add("SET QUOTED_IDENTIFIER ON")    ╱  options

$script.Add("
CREATE TABLE [dbo].[Computers](
[ComputerID] [int]IDENTITY(1,1) NOT NULL,
[Computer] [char](12) NOT NULL,
[Manufacturer] [char](30) NOT NULL,
[Model] [char](25) NOT NULL,
[Timezone] [int] NOT NULL,
[RAM] [bigint] NOT NULL,
CONSTRAINT [PK_ComputerID] PRIMARY KEY CLUSTERED ([ComputerID] ASC))
ON [PRIMARY]")                    ◁──❹ Table script
                                                    Create  ❻
$db = $server.Databases["ConfigDB"]   ◁──❺ Set database    table
$extype =
[Microsoft.SqlServer.Management.Common.ExecutionTypes]::ContinueOnError
$db.ExecuteNonQuery($script, $extype)                       ◁──
```

The server object is created ❶. We then create a `StringCollection` ❷, which is best thought of as a multiline string for this purpose. The execution options ❸ define how SQL Server will react to null values and putting quotes around names.

The table creation is performed using a T-SQL `CREATE TABLE` statement ❹. The table will be called Computers. Each column in the table is defined with a name, a data type, size where appropriate, and whether the column can accept null values. Compare this to listing 7.1. The first column, ComputerID, is used to uniquely identify the row (IDENTITY). The value is automatically generated when the field is created. It may seem odd to put [] around many of the values, but it's SQL Server's method of dealing with nonstandard identifiers (for example, if we used [Computer Name] instead of [Computer]).

The primary key is an index used to ensure that the identities remain unique. The table is ordered by this key. `ON [PRIMARY]` refers to the file group on which we'll create the table.

The database is defined ❺ and after setting the error action to continue, we execute the script against the database ❻. A nonquery means that there won't be any results returned by the query.

DISCUSSION

There are a couple of real advantages to using this method. First, we can add more members to the `StringCollection`, which means that we could create multiple tables in the same script. Second, we're using T-SQL, which means we can take the output of scripting out a database and turn it into a PowerShell script. This process could be automated. The drawback is that we need to know enough T-SQL to work with the `CREATE TABLE` command. Listing 14.14 shows an alternative, in that we can use a purely SMO approach.

Listing 14.14   Create table with SMO

```
$Server = New-Object Microsoft.SqlServer.Management.Smo.Server("SQL08")
$db = $server.Databases["ConfigDB"]

$table =
New-Object Microsoft.SqlServer.Management`
.Smo.Table($db, "OS")                        ◁──❶ Table object

$col1 =
New-Object Microsoft.SqlServer.Management.`
Smo.Column ($table, "OSID")                  ◁──❷ Column object

$col1.DataType = [Microsoft.SqlServer.Management.Smo.Datatype]::Int
$col1.Nullable = $false
$col1.Identity = $true
$col1.IdentitySeed = 1
$col1.IdentityIncrement = 1
$table.Columns.Add($col1)                                     ◁─┐

$col2 =
New-Object Microsoft.SqlServer.Management`
.Smo.Column ($table, "Computer")

$col2.DataType =
[Microsoft.SqlServer.Management.Smo.Datatype]::Char(12)

$col2.Nullable = $false
$table.Columns.Add($col2)                                    ◁─┤

$col3 = New-Object Microsoft.SqlServer.Management.`
Smo.Column ($table, "Name")

$col3.DataType = [Microsoft.SqlServer.Management.`       ❸  Add
Smo.Datatype]::Char(100)                                    column

$col2.Nullable = $false
$table.Columns.Add($col3)                                    ◁─┤

$col4 =
New-Object Microsoft.SqlServer.Management.`
Smo.Column ($table, "Version")

$col4.DataType = [Microsoft.SqlServer.Management.`
Smo.Datatype]::Char(10)

$col2.Nullable = $false
$table.Columns.Add($col4)                                    ◁─┘
```

```
$col5 =
New-Object Microsoft.SqlServer.Management.`
Smo.Column ($table, "ServicePack")

$col5.DataType = [Microsoft.SqlServer.Management.`
Smo.Datatype]::Int

$col5.Nullable = $false
$table.Columns.Add($col5)

$col6 =
New-Object Microsoft.SqlServer.Management.
Smo.Column ($table, "WinDir")

$col6.DataType = [Microsoft.SqlServer.Management.`
Smo.Datatype]::Char(20)

$col6.Nullable = $false
$table.Columns.Add($col6)                          Add column  ⟵ ❸

$col7 =
New-Object Microsoft.SqlServer.Management.`
Smo.Column ($table, "TotalVM")

$col7.DataType = [Microsoft.SqlServer.Management.Smo.Datatype]::Int
$col7.Nullable = $false
$table.Columns.Add($col7)

$table.Create()     ⟵ ❹  Create table
```

Examining the script shows that we start by creating the server and database objects. A table object is created ❶ using the database and table name as parameters. This is followed by a series of code blocks that create a column object ❷; set the data type, nullability, and any other options; and then add it to the table ❸. The Create() method ❹ is used to finally create the table in the database.

This script could be improved by using a function to create the columns. Awkward items would include data type handling and the identity properties on the first column.

However we create our table, at some stage we'll need to modify it.

TECHNIQUE 182 **Modifying a table**

The two tables we've created need to be linked so that the operating system information in one table can be directly related to the computer information in the other table. It's at this point that database design gets complicated due to the number of links. That's a problem for another book.

PROBLEM

We need to create an index on a column in our table so that the values are unique.

SOLUTION

SMO supplies an object to work with indexes that we can use to solve this problem, as shown in listing 14.15. After quickly creating a server and database object, we create an object for the table to which we'll add an index ❶. Indices aren't standalone objects; they belong to tables. The index is created in the usual way with the table and name ❷ as parameters. The index type is then defined ❸. In this case, it's a unique constraint, which means that no two values in the column can have the same value.

Listing 14.15 Add a unique key

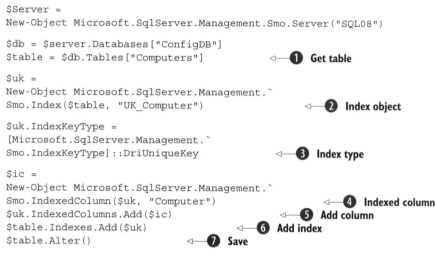

```
$Server =
New-Object Microsoft.SqlServer.Management.Smo.Server("SQL08")

$db = $server.Databases["ConfigDB"]
$table = $db.Tables["Computers"]          ◁—❶ Get table

$uk =
New-Object Microsoft.SqlServer.Management.`
Smo.Index($table, "UK_Computer")          ◁—❷ Index object

$uk.IndexKeyType =
[Microsoft.SqlServer.Management.`
Smo.IndexKeyType]::DriUniqueKey            ◁—❸ Index type

$ic =
New-Object Microsoft.SqlServer.Management.`
Smo.IndexedColumn($uk, "Computer")         ◁—❹ Indexed column
$uk.IndexedColumns.Add($ic)                ◁—❺ Add column
$table.Indexes.Add($uk)            ◁—❻ Add index
$table.Alter()                 ◁—❼ Save
```

DISCUSSION

We have to decide which column will be affected by the index ❹ and add it to the list of columns in the index ❺. The index is added to the table's collection of indices ❻ and saved using the Alter() method ❼. If at this point you think that SMO is like one of those Russian dolls with objects inside objects inside objects, you're probably not wrong.

Constraining the computers column so that it can only have unique values means that we can link to it and know we'll get the correct machine.

TECHNIQUE 183 **Adding keys**

Building on the previous example, we need to create a foreign key from the OS table to the Computer table. This enforces the referential integrity between the tables. Simplistically, referential integrity keeps the data and links correct. We do this by adding some more keys.

PROBLEM

We need to add a primary key and a foreign key to our OS table.

SOLUTION

We can adapt the script from the previous example to add a primary key. The foreign key is added using the ForeignKey object, as shown in listing 14.16.

We can skip through creating the server, database, and table objects ❶, which we've seen before. The primary key object is created as an index with the table and its name as parameters. We set the index type, in this case a primary key, and we add the column on which we'll create the index ❷. This column must already exist in the table. The next job is to add the column to the index, add the index to the table, and remember to alter the table ❸ so that we save the changes.

Listing 14.16   Add a primary and foreign key

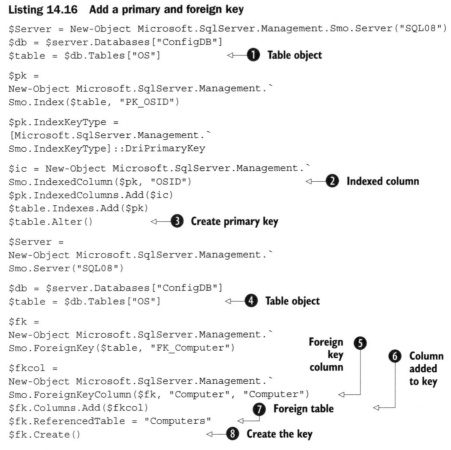

```
$Server = New-Object Microsoft.SqlServer.Management.Smo.Server("SQL08")
$db = $server.Databases["ConfigDB"]
$table = $db.Tables["OS"]                  ◄──❶ Table object

$pk =
New-Object Microsoft.SqlServer.Management.`
Smo.Index($table, "PK_OSID")

$pk.IndexKeyType =
[Microsoft.SqlServer.Management.`
Smo.IndexKeyType]::DriPrimaryKey

$ic = New-Object Microsoft.SqlServer.Management.`
Smo.IndexedColumn($pk, "OSID")              ◄──❷ Indexed column
$pk.IndexedColumns.Add($ic)
$table.Indexes.Add($pk)
$table.Alter()              ◄──❸ Create primary key

$Server =
New-Object Microsoft.SqlServer.Management.`
Smo.Server("SQL08")

$db = $server.Databases["ConfigDB"]
$table = $db.Tables["OS"]                  ◄──❹ Table object

$fk =
New-Object Microsoft.SqlServer.Management.`
Smo.ForeignKey($table, "FK_Computer")

$fkcol =
New-Object Microsoft.SqlServer.Management.`
Smo.ForeignKeyColumn($fk, "Computer", "Computer")   ◄──
$fk.Columns.Add($fkcol)
$fk.ReferencedTable = "Computers"   ◄──
$fk.Create()              ◄──❽ Create the key
```

❺ Foreign key column

❻ Column added to key

❼ Foreign table

DISCUSSION

Adding a foreign key is a bit different. We still start by creating the same server, database, and table objects ❹ Now, though, we create a specific foreign key object with the usual parameters. Remember our discussion on patterns in earlier chapters. The foreign key needs a foreign key column ❺ whose parameters are the foreign key, the column in the table it applies to, and the column in the table that'll be referred to by the key.

The column is added to the key ❻, and we remember to add the table we'll be referencing ❼. The final act is to create the key ❽. Once created, we can't create a value in the computers column of the OS table that doesn't exist in the computers column of the computers table. In other words, we have to have a computer before we can have an operating system.

Our database is finished but empty. A database without data isn't much use to us, so our next step is to learn how to populate these tables with data.

TECHNIQUE 184   **Populating a table**

PowerShell has the `*-Csv` and `*-Content` cmdlets for working with files. It doesn't have any cmdlets for working with the data in SQL Server databases. PowerGadgets has a cmdlet, `Invoke-SQL`, that can be used to access databases. There's also a cmdlet supplied with SQL Server 2008. We'll start by learning how to work with databases by scripting.

PROBLEM

The data that we receive from our configuration scripts has to be written into our database.

SOLUTION

We can use the ADO.NET classes to execute a T-SQL `insert` command to populate the tables, as in listing 14.17. The idea behind this script is that we run some WMI commands against a remote machine and write the results into our database tables. The WMI statements ❶ are based on those from listing 7.1 and find information about the computer, make and model, and about the operating system. Not all of the data will be written to the database. If you wish to extend the tables, the opportunity is available.

> **ADO.NET ALTERNATIVES** You'll find many different ways of using the ADO.NET classes to work with databases. They all use the same classes and achieve the same goals, but have syntax variations. I use this format because I'm comfortable with it and I know it works. Experimentation is encouraged if you want to try a different format.

We need to create a connection to the database ❷ so that we can insert the data. The connection uses a connection string with the server, database, and security type as the parameters. The connection must then be opened before we can use it.

Listing 14.17 Insert data

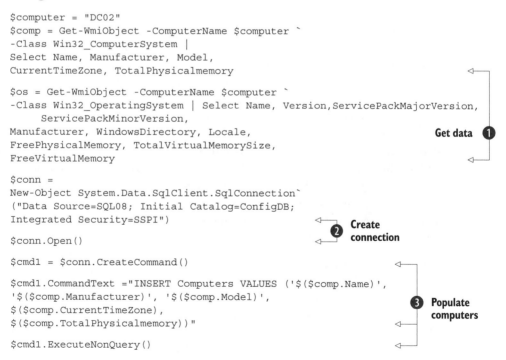

```
$computer = "DC02"
$comp = Get-WmiObject -ComputerName $computer `
-Class Win32_ComputerSystem |
Select Name, Manufacturer, Model,
CurrentTimeZone, TotalPhysicalmemory                                    ◁─┐

$os = Get-WmiObject -ComputerName $computer `
-Class Win32_OperatingSystem | Select Name, Version,ServicePackMajorVersion,
     ServicePackMinorVersion,
Manufacturer, WindowsDirectory, Locale,                        Get data ❶
FreePhysicalMemory, TotalVirtualMemorySize,
FreeVirtualMemory                                                       ◁─┘

$conn =
New-Object System.Data.SqlClient.SqlConnection`
("Data Source=SQL08; Initial Catalog=ConfigDB;
Integrated Security=SSPI")                     ◁─┐   Create
                                               ❷   connection
$conn.Open()                                   ◁─┘

$cmd1 = $conn.CreateCommand()                                   ◁─┐

$cmd1.CommandText ="INSERT Computers VALUES ('$($comp.Name)',
'$($comp.Manufacturer)', '$($comp.Model)',                ❸ Populate
$($comp.CurrentTimeZone),                                    computers
$($comp.TotalPhysicalmemory))"                                 ◁─┘

$cmd1.ExecuteNonQuery()                                         ◁─┘
```

```
$cmd2 = $conn.CreateCommand()
$cmd2.CommandText =
"INSERT OS VALUES ('$($comp.Name)', '$($OS.Name)',
'$($OS.version)', $($OS.ServicePackMajorVersion),
'$($OS.WindowsDirectory)',
$($OS.TotalVirtualMemorySize))"

$cmd2.ExecuteNonQuery()

$conn.Close()
```

4 Populate OS

5 Close connection

DISCUSSION

The `CreateCommand()` method of the connection object is used to create the command object we need. The text property holds the T-SQL query we'll execute to insert the data into the table. The `ExecuteNonQuery()` method is used to perform the query **3**. This method is used because we're not expecting any results to be returned.

Data has been inserted into the Computers table. The process can be repeated to insert data into the OS table **4**. The last line of the script closes the connection **5**. This is important to conserve resources on the server.

This script is used to insert data into the database. We can use a similar pattern to read the data in the database.

TECHNIQUE 185   **Reading data**

A T-SQL `SELECT` statement is used to read data from a database.

PROBLEM

We need to report on the computers and their operating systems held in our configuration database.

SOLUTION

The ADO.NET solution we saw when inserting data can be modified to extract data, as in listing 14.18. We start by creating and opening a connection to the database **1**. The connection string is identical to the one used previously. Incidentally, if you find yourself having trouble with connection strings, look at http://connectionstring.com. The site has more connection strings than you ever want to see.

The command we'll run is created as before **2**. This time we're running a `SELECT` statement because we want to read data from the database **3**. The query joins our two tables using the foreign key we established earlier (I knew that would come in useful) and picks out a number of columns across the two tables. We use the `Exe-cuteReader()` method to execute the query and put it into a `datareader` object **4**. The `datareader` objects give us a method of working with the results by iterating on a row by row basis, but we really want to be dealing with objects.

Listing 14.18   Read data

```
$conn =
New-Object System.Data.SqlClient.SqlConnection`
("Data Source=SQL08; Initial Catalog=ConfigDB;
Integrated Security=SSPI")

$conn.Open()
```

1 Open connection

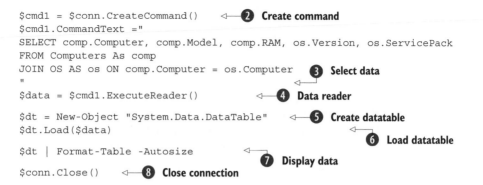

```
$cmd1 = $conn.CreateCommand()          ← ❷ Create command
$cmd1.CommandText ="
SELECT comp.Computer, comp.Model, comp.RAM, os.Version, os.ServicePack
FROM Computers As comp
JOIN OS AS os ON comp.Computer = os.Computer    ❸ Select data
"                                          ←
$data = $cmd1.ExecuteReader()          ← ❹ Data reader

$dt = New-Object "System.Data.DataTable"    ← ❺ Create datatable
$dt.Load($data)                            ←
                                              ❻ Load datatable
$dt | Format-Table -Autosize             ←
                                            ❼ Display data
$conn.Close()     ← ❽ Close connection
```

There's a `datatable` object that we can use. Think of it as an in-memory representation of a SQL Server table that we've created. We can use `New-Object` ❺ to make one of these and then use the `Load()` method to get the data from our data reader ❻. A quick trip to `Format-Table` and we have our display ❼, and then we can close the connection ❽. In PowerShell v2, we could think about using the `Out-GridView` cmdlet to display the data.

DISCUSSION

The PowerShell snapin in SQL Server 2008 provides an `Invoke-SQLcmd` cmdlet that we could use instead of a script. The parameters supply the server, database, and the query to execute:

```
Invoke-Sqlcmd -ServerInstance "SQL08" -Database "ConfigDB"
-Query "SELECT comp.Computer, comp.Model, comp.RAM, os.Version,
os.ServicePack
FROM Computers As comp
JOIN OS AS os ON comp.Computer = os.Computer"
```

It's often a bad idea to let users write their own queries. Raise your hands if you've seen an end user query that tries to extract all the data in a gigantic set of joins that grind the server to a halt. One way around this is to use *stored procedures*, which are prewritten queries that we know will work properly. Often parameters will be used to make the procedure more flexible (use the `parameters` property of our `$cmd1` variable). Listing 14.19 rewrites our example to use a stored procedure. The stored procedure can be created using pip14.sql in the accompanying scripts collection to create the stored procedure.

Listing 14.19 Read data using a stored procedure

```
$conn =
New-Object System.Data.SqlClient.SqlConnection`
("Data Source=SQL08; Initial Catalog=ConfigDB;
Integrated Security=SSPI")

$conn.Open()

$cmd1 = $conn.CreateCommand()
$cmd1.CommandType = [System.Data.CommandType]::StoredProcedure
$cmd1.CommandText ="pip14"
```

```
$data = $cmd1.ExecuteReader()

$dt = new-object "System.Data.DataTable"
$dt.Load($data)

$dt | Format-Table -Autosize

$conn.Close()
```

The main change is that we use a different command type, in this case a stored procedure rather than the default Text that we used earlier. The CommandText is much shorter, as we use exec with the name of the procedure. Stored procedures can be used with Invoke-SQLcmd:

```
Invoke-Sqlcmd -ServerInstance "SQL08" -Database "ConfigDB"
-Query "exec pip14"
```

```
C:\Scripts\PIP14                                                    _ □ X
PS> . ./get-sqlsp.ps1

Computer    Model                        RAM Version   ServicePack
--------    -----                        --- -------   -----------
SQL08       Virtual Machine         536322048 6.0.6001           1
DC02        Virtual Machine         536322048 6.0.6001           1


PS> $dt.Rows[0] | Format-Table -AutoSize

Computer    Model                        RAM Version   ServicePack
--------    -----                        --- -------   -----------
SQL08       Virtual Machine         536322048 6.0.6001           1


PS> foreach ($row in $dt.Rows){$row.Computer}
SQL08
DC02
PS>
```

Figure 14.2   Accessing the rows and columns of a data table object

Figure 14.2 shows the results of running our script to read the data. It also shows how we can access the rows and columns of the data table we've created.

Data isn't cast in concrete; sometimes we need to modify it.

TECHNIQUE 186   Modifying data .

Data modification is a task that becomes necessary when things change. In terms of our configuration database, we may want to change the way we group things or even correct data if it has been entered manually and mistakes have crept in.

PROBLEM
The values in the model column of our Computers table need to be modified.

SOLUTION

We use the standard ADO.NET pattern with a T-SQL UPDATE command. The script in listing 14.20 is a variation on the one we used to put the data into the database in the first place. ADO.NET is a great example of reuse. If we examine the scripts, the only changes are the command type and the actual query.

Listing 14.20   Update data

```
$conn =
New-Object System.Data.SqlClient.SqlConnection`
("Data Source=SQL08; Initial Catalog=ConfigDB;
Integrated Security=SSPI")

$conn.Open()

$cmd1 = $conn.CreateCommand()
$cmd1.CommandType = [System.Data.CommandType]::Text
$cmd1.CommandText ="
UPDATE Computers
SET Model = 'Virtual'
WHERE Model = 'Virtual Machine'
"
$cmd1.ExecuteNonQuery()
$conn.Close()
```

We need to use a Text command type for this solution. It's the default, but it's shown here for completeness. The other point is that we use the NonQuery() method because we're not expecting any results to be returned.

The last aspect of our data manipulation is deleting data.

TECHNIQUE 187   **Deleting data**

Everything in IT has a lifecycle, and eventually we'll need to remove data from our database. This could be because the machine has been decommissioned or we've decided that we don't need to store a particular type of data. One thought would be to link removal from the database to removal from Active Directory when a machine is decommissioned. Computer accounts are a variation of user accounts, so the information in chapter 5 can be modified to work with the information in this chapter. That is true automation!

PROBLEM

A server has failed and won't be repaired. We need to remove the entry for that machine from the database.

SOLUTION

We can use a delete T-SQL statement, as in listing 14.21. The connection to the database follows our normal pattern. The learning point is how we deal with the links between the tables.

Listing 14.21   Delete data

```
$conn =
New-Object System.Data.SqlClient.SqlConnection`
("Data Source=SQL08; Initial Catalog=ConfigDB;
```

```
Integrated Security=SSPI")

$conn.Open()

$cmd1 = $conn.CreateCommand()
$cmd1.CommandType = [System.Data.CommandType]::Text
$cmd1.CommandText ="
DELETE FROM OS WHERE Computer = 'DC02';
DELETE FROM Computers WHERE Computer = 'DC02'
"
$cmd1.ExecuteNonQuery()
$conn.Close()
```

DISCUSSION

We created a foreign key so that we couldn't have a computer in the OS table that didn't exist in the Computers table. If we delete from the Computers table first, we'll get an error. Delete from the OS table and then from the Computers table.

The semicolon is an end-of-line marker for T-SQL.

> **FOREIGN KEYS AND DELETE** It's possible to create the foreign key such that a deletion in the parent table will cascade into the child table. I thought that was too much of a digression into database theory for a PowerShell book. More information can be found at http://msdn.microsoft.com/en-us/library/aa933119(SQL.80).aspx.

We've created a database and populated it with data. We've seen how to manipulate that data. The last thing we need to learn is how to back up the database.

TECHNIQUE 188   Backing up a database

Data! Protect! The concept is drummed into us from day one at admin school. Databases must be backed up, and our configuration database is no exception.

PROBLEM

We need to create a backup of our configuration database in order to protect the data.

SOLUTION

SMO has a backup class we can use for this task, as shown in listing 14.22. I've used this script in a number of demonstrations when talking about PowerShell, so I know it works exactly as advertised. We start with a server object ❶ and then create an SMO backup object ❷. The database we want to back up is given as a property rather than a parameter.

Listing 14.22   Back up a database

```
$Server = New-Object Microsoft.SqlServer.Management.Smo.Server("SQL08")      ❶

$bkup = New-Object Microsoft.SQLServer.Management.Smo.Backup          ❷
$bkup.Database = "ConfigDB"

$date = Get-Date
$date = $date -replace "/", "-"
$date = $date -replace ":", "-"          ❸
$date = $date -replace " ", "--Time-"
```

```
$file = "C:\Backups\ConfigDB" + "--" + $date + ".bak"   ❹

$bkup.Devices.AddDevice($file,
[Microsoft.SqlServer.Management.Smo.DeviceType]::File)   ❺
$bkup.Action =
[Microsoft.SqlServer.Management.Smo.BackupActionType]::
Database                                                 ❻

$bkup.SqlBackup($server)       ❼
```

DISCUSSION

I like to include the date in the backup file name because it makes finding the correct data to restore so much easier ❸. Start with Get-Date and then replace the / and : characters, which are illegal characters in filenames. There are more elegant ways of performing this, but this way has the advantage of being obvious, so the script needs fewer comments.

The date is used as part of the filename ❹. The filename is used to create the backup device ❺ and we define the type of backup we need ❻—in this case, a full database backup.

The last action of the script is to start the backup ❼. Note that the server is used as the parameter, rather than the database.

In section 14.3.3, we looked at creating a SQL Server Agent job and stated that we could run PowerShell scripts as a job step. By creating our backups using Power-Shell scripts, we can run them through SQL Server Agent as a scheduled task. We can also run them manually if required. We get multiple uses from the same piece of scripting. Excellent.

14.5 Summary

SQL Server has many facets that can be administered with PowerShell. We've seen how to administer our servers and databases. The configuration database can form the basis of any application based on SQL Server and controlled by PowerShell. Within that context, we've seen how to create databases, tables, and other objects. The ability to use the data in our databases via PowerShell gives us a powerful reporting tool, in that we now know how to extract the data, and by using chapter 7 we know how to write it to a spreadsheet. Script this and it can be run whenever needed. We could even schedule it from within SQL Server.

The ability to run PowerShell in SQL Server Agent job steps provides a level of flexibility and sophistication that opens up many possibilities for scheduling and automation. Built-in PowerShell support in SQL Server 2008 brings a provider that gives direct access through PowerShell as well as extending the GUI tools.

SQL Server is the last of the major applications we'll cover in the book. But we're not finished with PowerShell just yet. The PowerShell world is continually evolving and innovating. As administrators, we've seen how we can achieve more with less effort by using PowerShell. In chapter 15 we'll look at some of the cutting edge areas that we need to be aware of so that we can increase our knowledge and versatility.

PowerShell innovations

15

This chapter covers

- PowerShell jobs
- Windows Server 2008 R2
- Active Directory provider
- PowerShell Hyper-V library

This chapter is a collection of topics that represent leading-edge technologies and recent innovations in the PowerShell world. Some are still be in beta. The topics are those we need to consider to round out our PowerShell knowledge and to position us for the future. PowerShell is evolving internally and in the breadth and depth of applications that have PowerShell support. We need to be aware of these changes to ensure we stay on top of automating our administration tasks.

The chapter starts with an examination of how we can use PowerShell jobs to make ourselves more productive...without doing any more work. We can use background jobs to run PowerShell asynchronously, meaning we can start a set of jobs, go do other things, and come to our results.

Windows 2008 R2 and Windows 7 install PowerShell v2 by default. A huge amount of extra PowerShell functionality is available between v2 and Windows 2008 R2. We've seen a lot of the PowerShell v2 functionality in various chapters of the book.

In this chapter, we'll briefly peek at Windows 2008 R2 and some of the good PowerShell things that it brings to us.

Virtualization is a big topic in IT at the moment. PowerShell is there, helping to administer our virtual machines. This is true for VMware, which has a PowerShell toolkit available, and Hyper-V, which can be managed from PowerShell via System Center Virtual Machine Manager and/or the PowerShell Hyper-V library.

Cloud computing is probably the "next big thing." As a heads-up for the future, we'll look at how PowerShell is already working in this environment. Our investigation of these topics starts with PowerShell jobs.

15.1 PowerShell jobs

Much of the discussion around PowerShell v2 is concerned with the ability to administer remote machines. We discussed this in chapter 13 when we looked at administering IIS as an example. In chapter 1 we discovered that PowerShell v2 has the capability of running PowerShell tasks as background jobs. In my opinion, the ability to run background jobs will have at least as big an impact on administering our systems as remoting.

What's a background job?

When we start a PowerShell script, the prompt is locked up until the script has finished. If this is a few seconds, it isn't much of a problem. But if it's a few minutes, or longer, it can be a pain. We could of course have multiple PowerShell windows open, but that can get messy and invariably an instance of PowerShell will be closed before the results have been examined. That is a major source of frustration. These scenarios describe PowerShell running synchronously—the task is running in the foreground and takes over the PowerShell instance.

What we need is a way to get the prompt back so we can carry on working while our task churns away in the background. This is a background job. A job can be started using the job-related cmdlets.

- `Get-Job`
- `Receive-Job`
- `Remove-Job`
- `Start-Job`
- `Stop-Job`
- `Wait-Job`

Alternatively, there are a number of cmdlets that can start jobs in their own right. We can discover these cmdlets using `Get-Help`:

```
PS> Get-Help * -Parameter AsJob | Format-Wide Name -Column 3

Invoke-Command      Get-WmiObject      Invoke-WmiMethod
Remove-WmiObject    Set-WmiInstance    Test-Connection
Restart-Computer    Stop-Computer
```

`Get-Help`'s `-Parameter` parameter is useful for discovering which cmdlets can perform which tasks. Replace `AsJob` with `ComputerName` to see how many cmdlets have built-in remoting capability. I counted 35 in Windows 7. It's an interesting mix. Format-Wide we haven't seen much, but it's useful when we need to produce a more compact display.

PowerShell jobs can be run against the local machine, or we can use the remoting functionality to run against remote machines. As an example, we'll consider this task:

```
Get-ChildItem -Path c:\ -Filter "*.txt" -Recurse
```

This will iterate through the whole of our C: drive to find all of the text files. On any machine that has a reasonable number of applications installed, this will take a while to run. So how can we run this task in the background?

TECHNIQUE 189   Creating a job

Before we can do anything with our jobs, we have to create them.

PROBLEM
A long-running task has to be run in the background so that we can continue working.

SOLUTION
The task can be run as a job. We use Start-Job to create a new job, as shown in listing 15.1. This may seem odd, as we've used New-* everywhere else, and it does cause the odd error message when we forget.

Listing 15.1   Create a PowerShell job

```
$job1 = Start-Job -Name j1
-ScriptBlock {Get-ChildItem -Path c:\ -Filter "*.txt" -Recurse}

$job2 = Start-Job -Name j2 -ScriptBlock {Get-Service}
```

I usually give my jobs names. The system will allocate names such as Job1, Job3, and so on, but giving the jobs descriptive names can help you distinguish between them. The commands the job will run are presented in the script block. This can contain a simple command, as in these examples, or can call a script.

DISCUSSION
Cmdlets that have the -AsJob parameter are used as follows. Using this parameter causes the command to be added to the job queue and to function as a job:

```
$job4 = Get-WmiObject -Class Win32_Service -AsJob
```

Once our job has started, the prompt is returned to us and can perform other tasks, such as creating more jobs or viewing the status of our current jobs, as is shown in figure 15.1.

TECHNIQUE 190   Viewing jobs

Submitting tasks to run in the background is a good way of multitasking. You can even sit with your feet on the desk and tell the boss you're working hard because you have all these jobs running. He might even believe you.

PROBLEM
The status of our jobs needs to be viewed so that we can determine when we can access the data.

SOLUTION

There's a standard PowerShell answer to this question. We need to look at some data, so we need a Get-Job cmdlet, as shown in listing 15.2.

Listing 15.2 View the running jobs

```
Get-Job

Get-Job -Name j1

$job1
```

There are a number of ways of viewing the job data. The easiest way is to view all the jobs that are on the system using Get-Job. Figure 15.1 illustrates the data returned from Get-Job. The state property shows how the job is progressing. States of Running or Completed are good and have the meanings you'd expect. A state of Failed is bad and means something has gone wrong. The usual culprit is a typo in the command. Scripts should be tested manually before using in jobs, so look at the data being input as a possible cause.

DISCUSSION

The other property of interest is HasMoreData. A value of true means that the job has results sitting on the job queue waiting for us to do something with them. A value of false means that no data is associated with the job. If you want to see what a failed job looks like, try:

```
Start-Job -ScriptBlock {get-srvice}
```

No prizes for guessing the reason why the job failed!

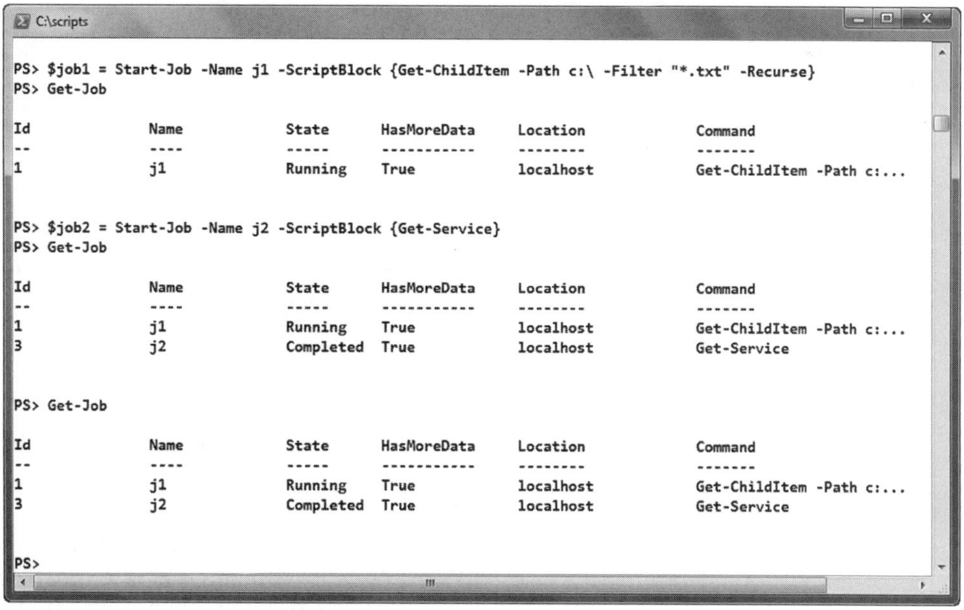

Figure 15.1 Viewing the current jobs on a system

If we only want to view the status of a single job, we can use its name with Get-Job. Alternatively, we can use the variable we assigned to the job when we created it.

> **SCHEDULING AND NOTIFICATION**   PowerShell v2 doesn't have a scheduling mechanism for jobs or a system of notifying us of a completed job. Hopefully, these will be made available in future versions.

At some time after our job has completed, we'll need to access the data associated with the job.

TECHNIQUE 191   Viewing data

Jobs produce data unless they fail, and then they produce headaches. The data is what we're really interested in. We may just want to look at the data the job produced, or we may need to do some further analysis.

PROBLEM

Our job has completed and we need to view the results.

SOLUTION

The simplest way to access the job results is to use Receive-Job. Supply the name of a job, as in listing 15.3, and the data appears. The -Keep parameter ensures that the data is left with the job on the queue.

-Keep is an important parameter. If we don't use -Keep, the data is stripped off the job and will no longer be accessible. The HasMoreData property is set to false. I recommend using -Keep as a standard part of your processing. It really should've been the default setting.

Listing 15.3   Retrieve results from a job

```
Receive-Job -Name j2 -Keep

$job2 | Receive-Job -Keep

$job2 | Receive-Job -Keep | where{$_.Status -eq "Stopped"}

$srv = $job2 | Receive-Job -Keep | where{$_.Status -eq "Stopped"}
```

DISCUSSION

If we don't use -Keep, only the shell of the job remains, which we have to remove manually. The job data can be treated as any other dataset in PowerShell. We can pipe the job variable into Receive-Job instead of using the name. The data from the job can be put onto the pipeline for further processing, or we can even read the data into a variable so we can perform further manipulations.

Eventually we'll no longer need the data in our jobs and we can delete them.

TECHNIQUE 192   Deleting a job

We can delete the contents of the job queue by closing PowerShell. That's an inelegant way of performing the task, and runs the risk of deleting data we need. It's better to manually clean the job queue before closing PowerShell. This also helps ensure that we don't inadvertently delete data we want.

PROBLEM

The job queue isn't self-cleaning. We need to manually remove the jobs from the queue.

SOLUTION

`Remove-Job` will be our cmdlet of choice for this task, as in listing 15.4. We need to identify which jobs we want to remove. The "big hammer" approach is to use `Get-Job` to pipe the jobs into `Remove-Job`.

Listing 15.4   Delete a job

```
Get-Job | Remove-Job

$job1 | Remove-Job

Remove-Job -State Failed

Get-Job -State Failed
Get-Job -State Failed | Remove-Job

Get-Job | where{!$_.HasMoreData}
Get-Job | where{!$_.HasMoreData} | Remove-Job
```

This will empty the job queue and remove all of the data. It's a good way to ensure that the queue is empty before we close PowerShell, but we probably need a bit more finesse most of the time.

> **WHATIF** `Remove-Job` has a `-WhatIf` parameter. It can be used in these examples to double-check that we're deleting the correct jobs.

We can identify individual jobs to `Remove-Job` by using the job name, piping in the results of a `Get-Job` that selects a job, or using the variable to represent the job. This gives us the option of picking out and eliminating individual jobs.

DISCUSSION

There are two properties we can use to filter jobs. We can work with the state of the job (`Remove-Job` can work directly with the state) or we can use `Get-Job` to check on the state and then remove. We need to make sure that we know why the job failed before deleting it. If it's just our miserable typing, that's okay, but if there's a flaw in the script logic, we should get to the bottom of it before deleting the job.

The other property we should consider is `HasMoreData`. If a job doesn't have any data for us, we don't need it, so it's time for it to go. Unfortunately, we can't work directly with this property in the `*Job` cmdlets, but we can use `Where-Object` as a filter. We can check which jobs don't have any data then pipe those results into `Remove-Job`. Instant clean up!

PowerShell jobs will become an important part of the administrator's tool kit now that v2 is fully available. This will be especially true on Windows 2008 R2.

15.2   *Windows 2008 R2*

Windows 2008 R2 and Windows 7 have PowerShell v2 installed and enabled by default. Server Core has PowerShell v2 as an optional feature. PowerShell ISE is installed by default on Windows 7, but is an optional feature on the server.

According to TechNet, the following areas of Windows administration get direct PowerShell support:

- Active Directory Domain Services cmdlets
- Best Practice Analyzer cmdlets
- BITS cmdlets
- Failover Clustering cmdlets
- Web Server (IIS) cmdlets
- Server Manager cmdlets
- Remote Desktop Services cmdlets
- WS-Management cmdlets

- Active Directory Rights Management Services cmdlets
- Windows BitLocker Drive Encryption cmdlets
- Diagnosis and Supportability cmdlets
- Group Policy cmdlets
- Network Load Balancing cmdlets
- Server Migration cmdlets
- Windows Server Backup cmdlets

This is in addition to the extra Windows PowerShell cmdlets and the Windows Power-Shell *Integrated Scripting Environment (ISE)* that come with PowerShell v2. Active Directory Federation Services 2.0 will also be manageable by PowerShell. We took an in-depth look at the IIS provider in chapter 13 and the AD cmdlets in chapters 5 and 10. In this section we'll examine highlights of PowerShell in Windows Server 2008 R2.

TECHNIQUE 193   **Modules**

In PowerShell v2, the snapin has been superseded by the module. A module can be either a compiled DLL (effectively a snapin) or can be written in PowerShell. Using the advanced function capabilities enables us to create modules where the functions can behave as cmdlets. PowerShell functionality is delivered as modules. We'll look at creating our own modules in appendix B. When the appropriate administration tools such as Active Directory are installed, the matching PowerShell module is installed in the Modules folder in the PowerShell home directory. The discovery method for the installed modules is shown in listing 15.5; alternatively a simple `ls $pshome\modules` will show the modules installed in the PowerShell folder.

> **64 OR 32**   Some modules are installed in 64-bit and 32-bit versions whereas others only seem to be installed in 32-bit flavors. Check PowerShell carefully so you access in the right way.

The modules can then be installed as required.

PROBLEM

We need to determine which modules are installed and which are available to us.

SOLUTION

A cmdlet called `Get-Module` is available to do this, as in listing 15.5.

Listing 15.5   Discover available modules

```
PS> Get-Module -ListAvailable

ModuleType Name                        ExportedCommands
---------- ----                        ----------------
```

```
Manifest   ActiveDirectory          {}
Manifest   ADRMS                    {}
Manifest   AppLocker                {}
Manifest   BestPractices            {}
Manifest   BitsTransfer             {}
Manifest   GroupPolicy              {}
Manifest   PSDiagnostics            {}
Manifest   ServerManager            {}
Manifest   TroubleshootingPack      {}
```

DISCUSSION

Get-Module used by itself will display a list of the installed modules. Those modules that are available for install can be found by using the -ListAvailable parameter. The important part of the display is the name used to install the module. When installing from the prompt, it's worth using Get-Module to display the names. We can then use cut and paste to save typing.

Modules can be installed from a script or by a call from the profile. If a module is already installed and another attempt is made to install it, an error is issued but the original install is unaffected. How can we use these modules now that we've found them?

TECHNIQUE 194   ## Server Manager

Server Manager is used to add or remove roles and features from a Windows 2008 server. In the RTM version, we have a GUI tool and a command-line tool. In R2, we also get access to this functionality through PowerShell.

PROBLEM

The DHCP role must be added to our server.

SOLUTION

The ServerManager cmdlets need to be loaded to do this. We can start by loading the module into PowerShell using Import-Module, as in listing 15.6. The parameter is the name of the module we discovered using Get-Module in the previous example. If we try Get-Module again without any parameters, we'll see the modules we've loaded. The ExportedCommands column, in this case, shows the cmdlets that the module adds to PowerShell. If our module consists of advanced PowerShell functions, we can restrict which functions are exported (exposed) to PowerShell and which are kept in the background as unseen functionality.

Listing 15.6   Adding DHCP role to server

```
PS> Import-Module ServerManager
PS> Get-Module

ModuleType Name                      ExportedCommands
---------- ----                      ----------------
Manifest   ServerManager             {Remove-WindowsFeature,
                                       Get-WindowsFeature,
                                       Add- WindowsFeature}

PS> Get-Command -Module ServerManager

CommandType     Name
```

```
-----------        ----
Cmdlet             Add-WindowsFeature
Cmdlet             Get-WindowsFeature
Cmdlet             Remove-WindowsFeature

PS> Add-WindowsFeature -Name DHCP, RSAT-DHCP -Concurrent

Success Restart Needed Exit Code Feature Result
------- -------------- --------- --------------
True    No                       Success   {DHCP Server, DHCP Server Tools}
```

The cmdlets from the module can be checked using `Get-Command`. The parameter `-Module` has replaced `-Pssnapin`, though `-Pssnapin` can be used an alias if required. The results show the same three cmdlets shown in the `ExportedCommands` output earlier.

DISCUSSION

`Get-WindowsFeature` displays the roles and features currently installed on the server. We can add features and roles using `Add-WindowsFeature`. In this case, we're adding the DHCP server role and the DHCP administration tools. Unless it's a feature you're dealing with a lot, it's worth using `Get-WindowsFeature` to check the names before running the add command. Alternatively, we can have the fun of trying out `Remove-WindowsFeature` to get rid of the mistakes.

DHCP TechNet states that there are cmdlets for the DHCP server. This appears to be incorrect.

One task that comes around periodically is troubleshooting. We don't want to see this one too often, as it means something is very wrong with our infrastructure, but when it does occur, it'd be nice to have some help.

TECHNIQUE 195   **Troubleshooting**

Windows 7 and Windows Server 2008 R2 introduce the PowerShell-based troubleshooting packs.

PROBLEM

Our users are having problems connecting to a server. We need to check the networking.

SOLUTION

We can run the networking trouble shooting pack, as in listing 15.7.

Listing 15.7   Using the TroubleshootingPack module

```
Import-Module TroubleshootingPack

Get-TroubleshootingPack c:\windows\diagnostics\system\networking

Get-TroubleshootingPack c:\windows\diagnostics\system\networking |
Invoke-TroubleshootingPack
```

The first step is to import the `TroubleshootingPack` module. We can then get the networking pack. This gives us a bit of information about the pack. Pipe into `select *` for all its guilty secrets.

DISCUSSION

Wait a minute! How do we know what packs are available? Unfortunately, we don't get this information directly through the troubleshooting cmdlets. It's easy to discover, as we know where the packs are stored, so we can perform a directory listing:

```
PS> Get-ChildItem -Path "C:\Windows\diagnostics\system" |
Format-Wide -Property Name -Column 3
```

On my Windows 7 machine I got these results:

- AERO
- Device
- HomeGroup
- IESecurity
- PCW
- Power
- Search
- WindowsMediaPlayerMediaLibrary
- WindowsUpdate

- Audio
- DeviceCenter
- IEBrowseWeb
- Networking
- Performance
- Printer
- WindowsMediaPlayerConfiguration
- WindowsMediaPlayerPlayDVD

The pack can be started by piping the results of the get action into Invoke-Trouble-shootingPack. The pack will then step through a series of interactive questions to help you determine the problem and get advice on how to fix it.

> **PRIVILEGES**   The troubleshooting packs have a property RequiresElevation which indicates whether the cmdlet needs to run in a PowerShell instance with elevated privileges.

It's possible to create answer files for common scenarios to speed the process. One way to avoid a lot of troubleshooting is to ensure we adhere to the recommended best practices.

TECHNIQUE 196   **Best practice**

Best practice covers a multitude of configuration points for the particular technology. Starting with checklists, the application of best practice has become more sophisticated with the development of analyzers that examine our environment and make recommendations based on the information they hold. The best of them have models that are updatable to ensure that the analysis keeps track of any changes to recognized best practice.

PROBLEM

We need to apply best practices to our environment.

SOLUTION

The BestPractices module answers our need. We can start by importing the module, as shown in listing 15.8. The use of Get-Command shows that we have four cmdlets in the module dealing with models and results.

Listing 15.8   Discovering best practice models

```
PS> Import-Module BestPractices
PS> Get-Command -Module BestPractices

CommandType     Name
-----------     ----
Cmdlet          Get-BpaModel
Cmdlet          Get-BpaResult
Cmdlet          Invoke-BpaModel
Cmdlet          Set-BpaResult

PS> Get-BpaModel

Id                                          LastScanTime
--                                          ------------
Microsoft/Windows/DirectoryServices         Never
Microsoft/Windows/DNSServer                 Never
```

The models will show us what we can work with—in this case DNS or Directory Services. Note that the last scan time is recorded. Other models are available for AD Certificate Services, IIS, and Remote Desktop Services (Terminal Services). Presumably other aspects of Windows servers will be covered in due time.

DISCUSSION

Using the analyzer is shown in listing 15.9. We invoke the particular model and it'll generate the results. `Invoke-BpaModel` doesn't directly display the results; we need to use `Get-BpaResult` to show the data. I recommend outputting the results to a file possibly for future comparisons because there's a lot of data to display that may overflow the PowerShell screen buffer, resulting in data loss.

Listing 15.9   Analyze DNS for best practice

```
PS> Invoke-BpaModel -BestPracticesModelId Microsoft/Windows/DNSServer

ModelId                       Success Detail
-------                       ------- ------
Microsoft/Windows/DNSServer   True    (InvokeBpaModelOutputDetail)

PS> Get-BpaResult `
-BestPracticesModelId Microsoft/Windows/DNSServer |
 Out-File dnsbpa.txt
```

There are 59 results for DNS. The following is an example of one item:

```
ResultNumber : 1
ModelId      : Microsoft/Windows/DNSServer
RuleId       : 0
ResultId     : 2049755913
Severity     : Information
Category     : Other
Title        : DNS: IP addresses must be configured on Local Area
               Connection - Virtual Network
Problem      :
Impact       :
Resolution   :
```

```
Compliance    : The DNS Best Practices Analyzer scan has determined that you
                are in compliance with this best practice.
                For additional information about this best practice and its
                configuration steps, click the More information link.
Help          : http://go.microsoft.com/fwlink/?LinkId=121988
Excluded      : False
```

To see the categories, we could use `Select-String` to filter on the title field. The analyzer gives a clear indication as to whether our systems are in compliance with best practice. You didn't think I'd show a category that was out of compliance, did you? This is a good tool for showing auditors that our systems are configured correctly. If the analysis is performed on a regular basis, it can help keep our systems compliant.

The best practice cmdlets don't have a `ComputerName` parameter, but we can easily use PowerShell remoting to access this functionality on other servers.

One of the big moans about PowerShell v1 was that there were no native cmdlets for Active Directory. This has been remedied in Windows 2008 R2, with a set of cmdlets and an Active Directory provider.

TECHNIQUE 197   **Active Directory provider**

In chapters 5 and 10, we took a good look at administering Active Directory using scripts and a mixture of the Quest and Windows Server 2008 R2 cmdlets. A provider for Active Directory is installed as well as the cmdlets. An AD provider is available as part of the PowerShell Community Extensions (PSCX). I've used it extensively, and used to include it in demos of PowerShell. It worked well and I didn't have any problems with it. The only real issue is that it wasn't from Microsoft, so many organizations wouldn't use it.

Providers versus cmdlets is an interesting and often heated debate. A good, well-written provider can reduce the learning curve, because we already know how to navigate and access the data. It comes down to how you like to work. I've used various scripting languages over the years and prefer to work that way. I know others who really like the provider concept. As long as we can get the job done, it doesn't matter how we have to do it. If you're relatively new to scripting and/or PowerShell, investing time in learning the providers would definitely be beneficial.

PROBLEM

How can we check the schema version using the provider?

SOLUTION

This AD provider and the core commands can be used to perform this task, as in listing 15.10. A provider makes a data store accessible in the same way as the filesystem—by a drive. In this case, we have a drive called AD ❶. Possibly not the most imaginative of names, but it's obvious what it is. We can use the core commands to navigate and work with the provider.

Listing 15.10   Schema version by AD provider

```
PS> cd ad:              ⊲──❶ Enter provider

PS> Get-ChildItem              ⊲──❷ Display top-level items
```

```
PS> Get-ItemProperty `
-Path "CN=Schema,CN=Configuration,DC=sphinx,DC=org" `     ③ Access
-Name ObjectVersion                                          schema

                                                  ④ Enter Users
PS> cd "CN=Users,DC=sphinx,DC=org"                  container
                                                                ⑤ Access user
PS> Get-ADUser "CN=Richard,CN=Users,DC=sphinx,DC=org"              information
```

DISCUSSION

If we perform a `Get-ChildItem` on the root of the AD drive ❷, we see a number of containers:

- Sphinx
- Configuration
- Schema
- DomainDnsZones
- ForestDnsZones

The good news about this is that we can access the Schema, Configuration, and DNS partitions directly through the provider as well as the data we normally see in ADUC. By contrast, the PSCX provider only shows the latter. The distinguished name ❸ can used to access the object directly.

We need to access the `ObjectVersion` property of the schema ❸. As it's a property, we can use `Get-ItemProperty`. The results show that we're using version 47, which is the Windows 2008 R2 value.

The distinguished name can be used directly to navigate to a container ❹. The AD cmdlets can be used to access the AD objects in the container ❺ when working in the provider. It'll be worth spending time getting to know the provider. The following examples illustrate how to perform a number of the common AD administrative tasks via the provider.

We can start by navigating into the provider and then into the domain:

```
cd ad:
cd "DC=Manticore,DC=org"
```

We can navigate into and out of OUs as easily as we can folders in the filesystem:

```
cd ou=England
cd ..
```

One thing we have to be careful about is supplying the name of the OU correctly. We can't just supply the name:

```
PS> ls england
Get-ChildItem : Cannot find path
//RootDSE/england,DC=Manticore,DC=org' because it does not exist.
```

This can be frustrating, because we can see the OU. We need to identify it correctly to the provider; for example:

```
ls ou=england

Get-Item -Properties * '.\CN=SORBY Henry'
```

A huge bonus is that tab completion works on the items in the folder—type cn=s and tab through choices. Similarly, in the root of the domain, we can type ou=E and use tab completion to complete the name. This is a handy speed boost to navigation.

We have to be aware that the Windows Server 2008 R2 cmdlets, and the provider, don't work with the DirectoryEntry class we saw in chapter 5. If we modify our earlier Get-Item so that we create a variable and then put it through Get-Member:

```
PS> Get-Item -Properties * '.\CN=SORBY Henry'
PS> $user | gm

    TypeName: Microsoft.ActiveDirectory.Management.ADObject
```

we can see that it uses a completely different type. The AD provider and cmdlets work through a web service running on the domain controllers. This web service is available for download to run on Windows Server 2008 or Windows Server 2003 domain controllers, but a Windows Server 2008 R2 or Windows 7 machine is required to run the cmdlets.

Be aware that not all properties are returned as with the cmdlets. If we want properties beyond the default, we have to explicitly include them or tell it to bring back everything by using *. I tend to bring back everything, on the principle that I never know how scripts will be modified in the future, so removing ambiguity about the properties available works best for me. If you prefer a neat and tidy existence and only want to work with a subset of properties, feel free.

Changing the attributes of an object is a common administrative task. The *-Item-Property cmdlets perform this task for us. We can view the value of a particular property:

```
Get-ItemProperty -Path '.\CN=SORBY Henry' -name department
```

It's a simple matter to change values:

```
Set-ItemProperty -Name department -Value "Geology Sheffield"
-Path '.\CN=SORBY Henry'
```

The previous example assumes that we've navigated to the OU containing the particular user to be modified. We can perform this action from any location when using the PowerShell prompt. I don't recommend it as a practice, but it'd be possible to navigate into the registry and then make a change in Active Directory!

One point to be careful about is that the common cmdlets used in providers (for example the *-Item and *-ItemProperty cmdlets) can be changed by the provider. As an exercise, compare the help information for New-Item when in the filesystem provider and in the Active Directory provider:

```
Get-Help New-Item -Full
```

These dynamic parameters can be a source of confusion if you aren't aware of the changes. When we use New-Item in the filesystem, we can create folders and files. These change to groups, users, and organizational units in the Active Directory provider:

```
New-Item -Path "ou=england,DC=Manticore,DC=org"
-Name "CN=ProvUser" -ItemType user
-Value @{samAccountName='provuser';description='test user'}
```

Other attributes can be added to the -Value parameter as required or can be modified later via the *-ItemProperty cmdlets. One interesting quirk of the Active Directory provider is that if we use directory for the item type an OU is created:

```
md ou=test
```

It really works and creates an OU!! If we create objects, then we'll have occasion to delete objects. When using Remove-Item in the AD provider, we're automatically prompted to confirm the deletion:

```
PS> Remove-Item '.\CN=ProvUser'

Are you sure you want to remove?
CN=ProvUser,OU=England,DC=Manticore,DC=org
[Y] Yes  [N] No  [S] Suspend  [?] Help (default is "Y"): y
```

This can be bypassed by using the -Force parameter:

```
PS> Remove-Item -Force .\OU=test
Remove-Item : Access is denied
```

In both cases, we'll fail miserably in our attempt to delete the offending object. We need to remove the Protected from Accidental Deletion setting:

```
PS> Set-ADObject -ProtectedFromAccidentalDeletion $false
-Identity "OU=test,OU=England,DC=Manticore,DC=org"
PS> Remove-Item .\OU=test

Are you sure you want to remove?
OU=test,OU=England,DC=Manticore,DC=org
[Y] Yes  [N] No  [S] Suspend  [?] Help (default is "Y"): y
```

Now it goes away. Group administration is just as straightforward:

```
New-Item -ItemType group -Name "cn=English"
-value @{samAccountName='English';description='English users'}
```

The properties are supplied as a hash table in a similar manner to when we created a user account earlier. We can also work with group memberships. In this case, I want to add all of the users in the current OU into the group we just made:

```
Get-ChildItem | where{$_.objectclass -eq 'user'} |
foreach {Add-ADGroupMember
-Identity "CN=English,OU=England,DC=Manticore,DC=org"
 -Members $_.DistinguishedName
}
```

We use Get-ChildItem to iterate through the objects in the OU. The Where-Object cmdlet is used to only accept those objects that are users. Within a loop created by the foreach-object cmdlet, Add-GroupMember adds each user in turn to the designated group. We can test the membership of a group using Get-Item:

```
Get-Item -Properties *  .\CN=English |
select -ExpandProperty Member
```

The -ExpandProperty parameter on the select-object cmdlet enables us to view the whole membership list.

Many of the Active Directory cmdlets have a `-Filter` parameter and an `-LDAPFil-ter` parameter. Both of these parameters are used to filter the data. It's usually more efficient to perform the filtering when originally getting the data, rather than using `Where-Object` as the next step on the pipeline. The two parameters produce similar results but have different syntax:

```
Get-ADUser -Filter {title -eq 'scientist'} |
select distinguishedname
```

The `Filter` parameter uses PowerShell operators for the comparison as illustrated here. LDAP filters are used in the `LDAPFilter` parameter. We saw these filters in chapter 5, and there's a full explanation in appendix D.

```
Get-ADUser -LDAPFilter "(Title=scientist)" |
select distinguishedname
```

We have two ways to filter this data. Which should we use? My answer, as always, is whichever works best for you. If you're used to writing LDAP filters, keep using them, but if you're new to all this then try the PowerShell filters, as you can build on what you already know.

When I first saw this AD provider in the beta versions of Windows Server 2008 R2, I wasn't that impressed, but I have to say that it's growing on me. I still tend to think of scripting first, but there are some actions that are easier in the provider, which is always a plus for me. Navigation in the provider is a bit cumbersome, but there's a way to make life easier for ourselves.

TECHNIQUE 198   Creating an AD drive

PowerShell providers are exposed as drives. We've seen the use of `Get-PSDrive` to dis-cover drives. Most providers will create a single drive, though the registry creates two. One excellent addition to the information shown by `Get-PSDrive` in Windows 7/Win-dows 2008 R2 (PowerShell v2) is that the filesystem drives now show the used and free space on the drives.

In Windows we've always been able to map additional drives to position us at a par-ticular point in the filesystem. This concept extends to the drives exposed by providers as well.

PROBLEM

We need to make a shortcut to the Users container.

SOLUTION

We can create a PowerShell drive using the provider, as in listing 15.11. Many organi-zations will group their AD user accounts into a small number of OUs or containers. We can create a shortcut to those OUs by creating a PowerShell drive. The new-PSDrive cmdlet requires a name for the drive, which provider we're using, and the root of the drive.

This drive can be accessed as any other, and enables us to navigate directly to the data we need to work with. A number of drives could be created for the common loca-tions in AD and the definitions placed into the profile so that they're always available.

Listing 15.11   Create an AD drive as a shortcut

```
New-PSDrive -Name Users -PSProvider ActiveDirectory
-Root "AD:\CN=Users,DC=sphinx,DC=org"

PS> cd users:
PS> ls
```

DISCUSSION

More information on how to work with Active Directory objects can be found in the help files. Use:

```
get-help about_ActiveDirectory_ObjectModel
```

This concludes our look at Windows 2008 R2. There's a lot more to discover, but by concentrating on the new functionality, we get a good flavor of the benefits it brings to our administration efforts using PowerShell. The last major topic in this chapter is virtualization, which brings its own administrative challenges.

15.3   *Virtualization*

Virtualization is the technique of hosting a number of virtual servers on a single physical machine. Introduced into the mainframe world more than 40 years ago, it has become a major component of Windows-based infrastructures in the last few years. Virtualization reduces the number of physical machines we need to administer, but can increase the overall total of machines, as we now have to administer the host machine as well as the virtual machines. PowerShell becomes even more necessary.

A number of virtualization technologies are available. What's even better is that we can use PowerShell with most of them. VMware is the one most people think of first. VMware has released a PowerShell snapin for managing their environment. Some excellent information on using PowerShell with VMware can be found on the blogs of Hal Rottenberg, Alan Renouf, and Jonathan Medd. A PowerGUI power pack is also available that uses the VMware cmdlets.

Microsoft has Virtual Server, for which Ben Pearce has posted a number of PowerShell scripts. Windows 2008 introduced Hyper-V. These can be managed with System Center Virtual Machine Manager.

An alternative for Hyper-V is to use the Hyper-V PowerShell library of functions that can be found on http://www.codeplex.com. Written by James O'Neill, it's a free download. The zip file will need to be unblocked before extraction; otherwise PowerShell will keep asking for permission to run the scripts. Unblock a file by opening the properties and clicking on Unblock. The zip file contains two files:

- hyperv.format.ps1xml
- hyperv.ps1

Hyperv.ps1 is a library of functions that's based on WMI. It would be possible to use WMI directly, but it would involve a lot more work and effort to create your own scripts. Use what's available.

Run PowerShell with elevated privileges and dot-source the file:

```
. ./hyperv.ps1
```

This will load the functions and update the format data using the hyperv.format.
ps1xml file. This is a good example of a format file if you need to create your own.

> **FUNCTIONS VERSUS MODULES**   The Hyper-V library is currently a set of func-
> tions. This makes it usable with PowerShell v1 and v2. PowerShell v2 intro-
> duces the concept of modules, which make the use of function libraries more
> dynamic. The library is being updated to a module that should be available by
> the time you read this.

Now that we've loaded the functions, let's see how to use them.

TECHNIQUE 199   Discovering Hyper-V functions

The first thing we need to know is what functions are available. A help file is available
for download in PDF format, but it may not always be accessible. Often we only need a
reminder of the name. PowerShell v2 includes function names in tab completion.

PROBLEM

We need to know which functions have been loaded by the Hyper-V library.

SOLUTION

The function provider can be used to access the information, as shown in listing 15.12.

Listing 15.12   Discover Hyper-V functions

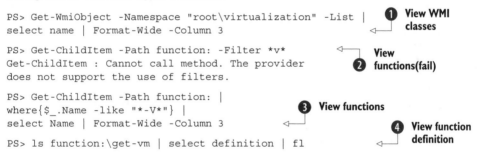

```
PS> Get-WmiObject -Namespace "root\virtualization" -List |      ❶ View WMI
select name | Format-Wide -Column 3                                classes

PS> Get-ChildItem -Path function: -Filter *v*            View
Get-ChildItem : Cannot call method. The provider       ❷ functions(fail)
does not support the use of filters.

PS> Get-ChildItem -Path function: |
where{$_.Name -like "*-V*"} |                        ❸ View functions
select Name | Format-Wide -Column 3
                                                          ❹ View function
PS> ls function:\get-vm | select definition | fl            definition
```

The Hyper-V library is based on WMI. We can view the WMI classes ❶. It's sometimes
useful to use WMI directly, but the functions make life easier. The obvious way to
access the function names is to interrogate the function provider using `Get-
ChildItem` ❷. But we can't use a filter on the function provider. If we take a step side-
ways, we can use `where` instead of a filter ❸. If we just select the name, we can reduce
the output to an amount that's easily viewable.

DISCUSSION

There are some 80 functions in total. In PowerShell v2, `Get-Verb` creeps in just to be
confusing. If we want to see the code for a particular function, we can view the definition property ❹, which holds the code. If you want to see more than one function's
worth then open the library file in an editor.

Let's start by using the functions to view the status of our virtual machines.

Virtual machine status

Before we can do any work with our virtual machines, we need to know their status. Are they running? Can we switch them on from PowerShell? PowerShell takes fewer resources than the Hyper-V manager, and using a Remote Desktop Connection provides a better experience than connecting from the GUI.

PROBLEM
The status of virtual machines has to be changed—stopped and started. In addition, we need to be able to view the status of our VMs.

SOLUTION
We can test the status using two functions from the Hyper-V library, as shown in listing 15.13.

Listing 15.13 Test virtual machine status

```
PS> Start-VM -VM DC08                        ◁── ❶ Start

PS> "dc08", "exch10" | Ping-VM |
Format-Table VMName, ResponseTime, Status -auto    ◁── ❷ Ping

VMName ResponseTime Status
------ ------------ ------
DC08            194 Success
Exch10              VM Stopped

PS> Get-VM            ◁── ❸ Check status

Host          VMElementName        State      Up-Time (mS) Owner
--------      -------------        -----      ------------ -----
SERVER01      Exch10               Stopped    0
SERVER01      DC08                 Running    298568

PS> Shutdown-VM -VM dc08    ◁── ❸ Stop
```

DISCUSSION
Starting a virtual machine under Hyper-V involves Start-VM ❶. The name of the VM is provided as a parameter. A server parameter can be supplied to all of the functions to work with a remote system. Remember that the library is based on WMI, so remote administration is built in.

> **FIREWALL** Using Netsh to configure the firewall on our servers, to allow remote administration via WMI, is probably the quickest and easiest way to perform the task. See listing 9.1 for details

Ping-VM can be used as a quick check on our VMs ❷. If we need to check more servers, the name and server could be put into a CSV file. One thing that isn't shown is the uptime, which is a statistic that seems to fascinate managers for some reason. We can access this through Get-VM ❸, which also shows the state of the VM.

I use virtual machines a lot for experimenting with technologies and preparing demos. It's useful to be able to stop and start machines. We can use Shutdown-VM ❹ to cleanly close down the virtual machine.

In addition to using the functions from the command line, we can incorporate them into our scripts.

TECHNIQUE 201   VM uptime

Formatting of output has been an issue since the earliest days of computing. Power-Shell gives us access to the properties of an object so that we can easily modify how we display the data.

PROBLEM

The uptime reported by Get-VM is in milliseconds. Working at this scale isn't intuitive, so I want to view the uptime in a more easily understood format.

SOLUTION

We can write a function that displays the uptime in a more easily understood format, as shown in listing 15.14.

Listing 15.14   Determine uptime of a virtual machine

```
function get-uptime{
param ([string]$name = "")
    $vm = Get-VM -Name $name
    $time = New-TimeSpan -Seconds $($vm.OnTimeInMilliseconds/1000)
    Write-Host "Uptime for $name =
      $($time.Hours):$($time.Minutes):$($time.Seconds)"
}

PS> . .\get-uptime.ps1
PS> get-uptime dc08
Uptime for dc08 = 0:15:21
```

DISCUSSION

We'll do this as a function so that it's always available. The function accepts a server name as a parameter. It then uses Get-VM to retrieve the information about the virtual machine. We can create a timespan object using the using the OnTimeInMilliseconds (uptime) property. Write-Host is used to display the data as *hours:minutes:seconds.*

The function is loaded by dot-sourcing it and can be accessed from the command line or within a script by passing the name of a virtual machine. If required, the format file that ships with the library could be modified to output the uptime in this format.

Virtual machines have virtual hard disks. Though it sounds like the beginning of a nursery rhyme, this means that we have another object to investigate and test.

TECHNIQUE 202   Checking disk status

One of PowerShell's strengths is its composable nature. This means we can take pieces of functionality and easily combine them to provide a more sophisticated outcome. We can use Get-VMDisk to view all the virtual hard disks associated with our Hyper-V server. The status of individual disks can be checked using Test-VHD.

PROBLEM

We need to view the status of all the virtual hard disks known to our Hyper-V server.

SOLUTION

We have to combine a couple of functions to do this, as shown in listing 15.15.

Listing 15.15   Check virtual disk status

```
$disks = Get-VMDisk
foreach ($disk in $disks) {
    $test = Test-VHD -vhdPath $disk.DiskPath
    Add-Member -InputObject $disk -MemberType NoteProperty
            -Name disktest -Value $test
}
$disks | Format-Table VMElementName, DriveLUN, DiskPath, disktest -AutoSize
```

DISCUSSION

Start by reading all of the disk information in an array using Get-VMDisk. We can then iterate through the disks, testing each in turn. The results are added to the disk object as a NoteProperty. We can then use Format-Table to display the data.

Adding a property in this manner is a simple way to carry data through the rest of the script for future display or processing. It's especially useful because we don't need to worry about keeping track of extra variables.

In a similar way, we can test the disk sizes.

TECHNIQUE 203   **Checking disk usage**

Disk space is always an issue. We need to be able to monitor the size of the virtual hard drives. If they become too large, we may need to investigate, as running out of disk space on the volumes that host the VHD files would be generally considered a bad thing to happen.

PROBLEM

We need to examine the space used by our VHD files.

SOLUTION

This time we combine Get-VHDInfo with Get-VMDisk, as in listing 15.16.

Listing 15.16   Check virtual disk capacity

```
Get-VMDisk | foreach {
    Get-VHDInfo -vhdPath $_.Diskpath
} | Format-Table Path, FileSize, MaxInternalSize -AutoSize
```

DISCUSSION

Use Get-VMDisk to retrieve the list of disks. A foreach-object cmdlet is used to pass the disk path of each disk into Get-VHDInfo. Format-Table displays the disk and size information.

TECHNIQUE 204   **Compacting disks**

Virtual hard disks can be compacted to reclaim unused disk space. Ideally, we'd combine this with defragmenting. We can mount the VHD file in the filesystem of the Hyper-V server. We can use the standard Windows defragmentation tool to remove the file fragmentation. Compacting the disks has to be performed when the virtual machine is switched off. If this is a production machine, we need to schedule this as part of the standard maintenance window. Doing this during business hours won't win many friends.

PROBLEM

We need to compact the hard disks of virtual machines.

SOLUTION

Compact-VHD provides the answer, as shown in listing 15.17.

Listing 15.17   Compact a virtual disk

```
PS> Get-VMDisk | foreach {Compact-VHD -vhdPath $_.diskPath}
Job Started
\\SERVER01\root\virtualization:`
Msvm_StorageJob.InstanceID=`
'9c77237c-3a08-4c21-9086-4e3e5730a2fe'

Job Started
\\SERVER01\root\virtualization:`
Msvm_StorageJob.InstanceID=`
'10be0cf1-b295-4690-9d82-a9fe44be7017'
```

DISCUSSION

Get-VMDisk supplies a list of disks that we pipe into a foreach. Compact-VHD takes the path to the disk as a parameter and starts a job (not a PowerShell job) to perform the compaction. We can check status with:

```
Get-WmiObject -NameSpace root\virtualization msVM_storagejob |
 ft jobStatus, description, percentcomplete -auto
```

We can perform a large number of other tasks to manage our Hyper-V environment. We can combine other functions from the Hyper-V library to complete these tasks.

Our final topic is looking ahead to cloud computing and what this may mean for using PowerShell.

15.4   *PowerShell in the cloud*

Cloud computing delivers resources over the internet. These resources may be virtualized, they may be dynamically scalable, but they're delivered as a service rather than your organization investing in the infrastructure. This could take a number of forms:

- Partially hosting applications—some data is held in the cloud and other data is stored on-premises
- Hosting applications such as SQL Server, Exchange, or SharePoint and making them available across the Web
- Providing a platform for the development of applications based in the cloud

My examples will concentrate on Microsoft offerings for two reasons. One, I'm most familiar with the Microsoft product stack, and two, the examples fit better with the topics we've already discussed in the book.

The question of where an application is administered is an interesting one and often will be resolved by the commercial agreement for the service. The options are:

- By the provider
- By the customer
- Mixed management

The management tools need to be applicable from the customer's premises, the supplier's premises, or another location that accesses the data across the web.

Exchange 2010 provides an example of our first category. It provides for a mixture of on- and off-premise data which needs to be managed regardless of its location. With Exchange, it's relatively straightforward to move mailboxes or even whole databases between servers and therefore between locations. We've already seen how Exchange 2010 supplies a method to use PowerShell against remote servers. This capability is web-based so there's no reason it can't translate to the cloud. This means our knowledge, skills, and scripts transfer directly into the new environment. We're up and running and ready to go.

We've already seen how we can manage Exchange 2007 and SQL Server 2005/8 with PowerShell. SharePoint 2007 and earlier don't have PowerShell, but the 2010 version does. It's currently possible to use the SharePoint .NET classes to perform administrative tasks. This means that we can administer the applications in our second category using PowerShell. It gets even easier when SharePoint 2010 is available.

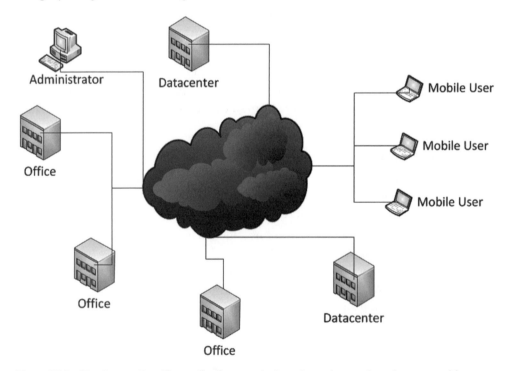

Figure 15.2 Cloud computing. The applications can be based anywhere and can be accessed from anywhere. Our administrator can be anywhere.

The third category is covered by the Microsoft Azure platform. The management tools for this include PowerShell. In addition, some of the examples include PowerShell cmdlets for managing the applications or even working directly with the applications. For instance, the Cloud Drive sample provides a PowerShell interface in the form of a provider that gives access to Blob (named files and metadata) and Queue (storage and delivery of messages) data as if they were a network drive. It's possible to get access to a test environment and experiment with managing Azure with PowerShell.

Cloud computing (see figure 15.2) isn't going to remove the need to manage our applications. It's probable that as administrators, we're going to be asked to do more rather than less. Automation will still be required, and probably in larger amounts. PowerShell is only on its second version and is a young product. There's much more to come in this story.

15.5 *Summary*

PowerShell is still evolving, with new functionality appearing in PowerShell v2, Windows 7/Windows 2008 R2, and applications being PowerShell-enabled. One of the new features in PowerShell v2 is background jobs. These can be run asynchronously, so we can set the task running and come back when it's complete. Though not as glamorous as the remoting functionality, background jobs have the capability to significantly increase our productivity.

Windows Server 2008 R2 will install PowerShell v2 as part of the base operating system install. In addition, a significant number of features now come with PowerShell modules including Active Directory, Server Manager, and the Troubleshooting packages. Some functionality such as Windows Backup is still supplied as a snapin. This functionality is installed when the appropriate administration tools are installed and is also available for remote administration via the RSAT download.

Virtualization is becoming a mainstream component in the infrastructure of many organizations. PowerShell is able to manage VMware and Hyper-V. The Hyper-V PowerShell library from Codeplex provides many functions we can use directly or incorporate into our scripts.

Cloud computing increases the reach of our PowerShell administration. The systems we're managing may not be in our data center but will be found via the Web. This adds complexity, but with PowerShell built into the applications and the management tools, we're well placed to ride the computing wave of the future.

afterword
PowerShell is for you

We've seen a lot of PowerShell by this point. Is this the end of it? Have we learned all there is to know about PowerShell?

The short answer is no, but I have to stop; otherwise the book will never be finished. I've learned a lot about PowerShell while writing this book. Most of it's in the book but there are some bits that didn't make it for space reasons. The PowerShell team likes to say, "To ship is to choose." That has been driven home by the choices I've had to make regarding what to include. These topics will appear somewhere, even if it's a blog post. PowerShell is a completely open topic. There's always something new to learn, whether it's a new set of cmdlets or a new technique. PowerShell is still evolving, and while we don't know where it's going, it'll be fun getting there.

The techniques we've learned so far mean we can start experimenting with PowerShell to solve our own unique problems. We'd need a book of infinite length to cover all possible scripts, and my fingers would be even more worn down from all that typing. It's time to fly the nest and write your own scripts.

The enjoyment produced by writing a script to solve your unique problem is very real. Savor it and look for the next problem. PowerShell, like all skills, needs constant practice. Don't be too upset looking back on scripts you created six months ago. Think instead of the things you've learned.

I said at the beginning of the book that there's a fantastic PowerShell community. Join it. Bring your scripts and problems, and share with that community. If you get really excited about something you've discovered, I'm always looking for speakers for User Group meetings. Help build a bigger and better PowerShell community.

The closing words belong to Jeffrey Snover, the man who invented PowerShell: "Experiment! Enjoy! Engage!"

appendix A:
PowerShell reference

This isn't designed to be a full PowerShell reference, as that would duplicate the help system and possibly double the length of the book. I'm including the information that I tend to look up and forget where it can be found, some useful definitions, and a few pieces that aren't in the documentation.

A.1 About files

The help files supplied with PowerShell contain information on the cmdlets as well as the about files. These are files that contain help information about PowerShell. The topics covered include:

- Keywords such as if, for, and do
- Advanced functions
- Remoting
- Operators

To view the available about files, access them as follows:

```
Get-Help about | select Name | Format-Wide -Column 3
```

The individual files can then be accessed using Get-Help.

A.2 Add-Type

We've seen, over the course of 15 chapters, how to manipulate various types of .NET objects with PowerShell. This section covers how to create our own objects. Add-Member was available in PowerShell v1. Using it, we can create an object and add properties to the object. We can work with that object in the same way as any other PowerShell object.

The drawback to Add-Member is that we can't define types for the property—we can't restrict the property to only accepting an integer or a string value. Add-Member is great if we only want to add a property or two to an existing object, but the whole approach looks messy and seems like more work than is required if we need to create a completely new object.

Add-Type is introduced in PowerShell v2 and allows us to use .NET code to create a new class from which we can create objects. It sounds like this is something for developers, but the code is simple, as shown in listing A.1.

Listing A.1   Using Add-Type to create a class

```
function Get-RouteTable {
param (
    [parameter(ValueFromPipeline=$true)]     ◁──❶ Computer parameter
    [string]$computer="."
)

$source=@"                                    ◁─┐
public class WmiIPRoute
{
    public  string Destination  {get; set;}
    public  string Mask     {get; set;}
    public  string NextHop {get; set;}        ❷ C# code
    public  string Interface {get; set;}
    public  int Metric  {get; set;}
}
"@                                            ◁─┘
Add-Type -TypeDefinition $source -Language CSharpversion3   ◁──❸ Create class

    $data = @()
    Get-WmiObject -Class Win32_IP4RouteTable -ComputerName $computer|
     foreach {
        $route = New-Object -TypeName WmiIPRoute -Property @{   ◁──❹ Use class
            Destination = $_.Destination
            Mask        = $_.Mask
            NextHop     = $_.NextHop
            Metric      = $_.Metric1
        }

        $filt = "InterfaceIndex='" + $_.InterfaceIndex + "'"
        $ip = (Get-WmiObject -Class Win32_NetworkAdapterConfiguration
            -Filter $filt -ComputerName $computer).IPAddress

        if ($_.InterfaceIndex -eq 1) {$route.Interface = "127.0.0.1"}
        elseif ($ip.length -eq 2){$route.Interface = $ip[0]}
        else {$route.Interface = $ip}

        $data += $route     ◁──❺ Add to array
    }
    $data | Format-Table -AutoSize   ◁──❻ Display data
}
```

Our function takes a computer name as a parameter ❶. An IP address would work equally well. The C# code is defined in a here string ❷. The new class is given a name, in this case WmiIPRoute, and we define a set of properties for the class. I've not defined any methods—that's getting a bit advanced. Each property has a name, a data type and a code block to get and set the property. When we create objects from the class, we can use the properties because we defined the class and properties as public.

Other data types are available beyond integer and string. A full list is available on MSDN. Be aware that C# is case sensitive. Ensure that the correct case is used for the C# keywords or your code won't compile. Add-Type takes the source code as an input parameter ❸. We set the language type to C# 3.0 so that we can keep the syntax for defining the properties as simple as possible.

The rest of the script is pure PowerShell. We can use WMI to get a list of IP routes defined on the machine. A foreach loop creates an object from our new class for each route ❹. One of the improvements to New-Object is that we can set the property values at the same time as we create the object. This creates neater-looking code and involves less coding.

A filter string is created using the IP route's InterfaceIndex and used with the Win32_NetworkAdapterConfiguration class to get the IP address associated with the adapter.

There are normally a number of routes associated with a machine, so we store the result from each iteration of the loop in an array ❺. The script finishes ❻ by displaying the data using Format-Table.

A.3   Alias

The full list of built-in aliases for PowerShell v2 is supplied in table A.1.

Table A.1   Standard aliases

Name	Definition	Name	Definition	Name	Definition
%	ForEach-Object	gi	Get-Item	ps	Get-Process
?	Where-Object	gjb	Get-Job	pushd	Push-Location
ac	Add-Content	gl	Get-Location	pwd	Get-Location
asnp	Add-PSSnapIn	gm	Get-Member	r	Invoke-History
cat	Get-Content	gmo	Get-Module	rbp	Remove-PSBreakpoint
cd	Set-Location	gp	Get-ItemProperty	rcjb	Receive-Job
chdir	Set-Location	gps	Get-Process	rd	Remove-Item
clc	Clear-Content	group	Group-Object	rdr	Remove-PSDrive
clear	Clear-Host	gsn	Get-PSSession	ren	Rename-Item
clhy	Clear-History	gsnp	Get-PSSnapIn	ri	Remove-Item
cli	Clear-Item	gsv	Get-Service	rjb	Remove-Job

Table A.1   Standard aliases *(continued)*

Name	Definition	Name	Definition	Name	Definition
clp	Clear-ItemProperty	gu	Get-Unique	rm	Remove-Item
cls	Clear-Host	gv	Get-Variable	rmdir	Remove-Item
clv	Clear-Variable	gwmi	Get-WmiObject	rmo	Remove-Module
compare	Compare-Object	h	Get-History	rni	Rename-Item
copy	Copy-Item	history	Get-History	rnp	Rename-ItemProperty
cp	Copy-Item	icm	Invoke-Command	rp	Remove-ItemProperty
cpi	Copy-Item	iex	Invoke-Expression	rsn	Remove-PSSession
cpp	Copy-ItemProperty	ihy	Invoke-History	rsnp	Remove-PSSnapin
cvpa	Convert-Path	ii	Invoke-Item	rv	Remove-Variable
dbp	Disable-PSBreakpoint	ipal	Import-Alias	rvpa	Resolve-Path
del	Remove-Item	ipcsv	Import-Csv	rwmi	Remove-WMIObject
diff	Compare-Object	ipmo	Import-Module	sajb	Start-Job
dir	Get-ChildItem	ipsn	Import-PSSession	sal	Set-Alias
ebp	Enable-PSBreakpoint	ise	powershell_ise.exe	saps	Start-Process
echo	Write-Output	iwmi	Invoke-WMIMethod	sasv	Start-Service
epal	Export-Alias	kill	Stop-Process	sbp	Set-PSBreakpoint
epcsv	Export-Csv	lp	Out-Printer	sc	Set-Content
epsn	Export-PSSession	ls	Get-ChildItem	select	Select-Object
erase	Remove-Item	man	help	set	Set-Variable
etsn	Enter-PSSession	md	mkdir	si	Set-Item
exsn	Exit-PSSession	measure	Measure-Object	sl	Set-Location
fc	Format-Custom	mi	Move-Item	sleep	Start-Sleep

Table A.1   Standard aliases *(continued)*

Name	Definition	Name	Definition	Name	Definition
fl	Format-List	mount	New-PSDrive	sort	Sort-Object
foreach	ForEach-Object	move	Move-Item	sp	Set-ItemProperty
ft	Format-Table	mp	Move-ItemProperty	spjb	Stop-Job
fw	Format-Wide	mv	Move-Item	spps	Stop-Process
gal	Get-Alias	nal	New-Alias	spsv	Stop-Service
gbp	Get-PSBreakpoint	ndr	New-PSDrive	start	Start-Process
gc	Get-Content	ni	New-Item	sv	Set-Variable
gci	Get-ChildItem	nmo	New-Module	swmi	Set-WMIInstance
gcm	Get-Command	nsn	New-PSSession	tee	Tee-Object
gcs	Get-PSCallStack	nv	New-Variable	type	Get-Content
gdr	Get-PSDrive	ogv	Out-GridView	where	Where-Object
ggh	Get-GuiHelp	oh	Out-Host	wjb	Wait-Job
ghy	Get-History	popd	Pop-Location	write	Write-Output

This will be of use when trying to unravel a highly aliased script you've found on the web.

A.4   Computer name

A number of cmdlets have a computer name parameter that allows them to access remote machines without using the full PowerShell remoting infrastructure. This number is greatly expanded in PowerShell v2.

We can use PowerShell to discover this information:

```
Get-Help * -Parameter computername | Format-Wide -Column 4
```

- Get-WinEvent
- Get-Counter
- Test-WSMan
- Invoke-WSManAction
- Connect-WSMan
- Disconnect-WSMan
- Get-WSManInstance
- Set-WSManInstance
- Remove-WSManInstance
- New-WSManInstance
- Invoke-Command
- New-PSSession
- Get-PSSession
- Remove-PSSession
- Receive-Job
- Enter-PSSession
- Get-EventLog
- Clear-EventLog
- Write-EventLog
- Limit-EventLog
- Show-EventLog
- New-EventLog
- Remove-EventLog
- Get-WmiObject

(continued)

- Invoke-WmiMethod
- Get-Process
- Remove-WmiObject
- Register-WmiEvent
- Get-Service
- Set-Service
- Set-WmiInstance
- Get-HotFix
- Test-Connection
- Restart-Computer
- Stop-Computer

A similar syntax can be used to discover other common parameters.

A.5   *Functions*

The syntax for functions is:

```
function Name {
    param(
        [type]$ParameterA = default_value,
        [type]$ParameterB = default_value
    )
    begin {< PowerShell code> }
    process {< PowerShell code> }
    end {< PowerShell code> }
}
```

The syntax for advanced functions is dealt with in appendix B. If the begin, process, and end blocks aren't supplied, the code is treated as a process block.

A.6   *Format files*

If we look in the PowerShell install folder, we'll find a number of files with an extension of .ps1xml. We can see discover them with:

```
Get-ChildItem -Path $pshome -Filter "*.ps1xml" | sort name
```

This will generate the following list of files:

```
Certificate.format.ps1xml
Diagnostics.Format.ps1xml
DotNetTypes.format.ps1xml
FileSystem.format.ps1xml
getevent.types.ps1xml
Help.format.ps1xml
PowerShellCore.format.ps1xml
PowerShellTrace.format.ps1xml
Registry.format.ps1xml
types.ps1xml
WSMan.Format.ps1xml
```

$pshome is a PowerShell automatic variable that contains the path to the PowerShell install folder. There are a number of automatic variables. They can be found using Get-Variable on a newly opened instance of PowerShell. These files control the default output when an object is displayed. We can demonstrate this by creating and displaying an arbitrary timespan object:

```
PS> $ts = (get-date) - (get-date).AddDays(`
$(get-random -Minimum -57 -Maximum -3))
PS> $ts
```

```
Days               : 39
Hours              : 0
Minutes            : 0
Seconds            : 0
Milliseconds       : 0
Ticks              : 33696000000000
TotalDays          : 39
TotalHours         : 936
TotalMinutes       : 56160
TotalSeconds       : 3369600
TotalMilliseconds  : 3369600000
```

There are default displays for table, list, and wide formatting. Table is usually first, which is why we see tabular data by default. These files are XML-based. We can export the XML using:

```
Get-FormatData -TypeName System.TimeSpan |
Export-FormatData -Path demo.ps1xml -IncludeScriptBlock -Force
```

After producing a pretty-printed version of the XML, we see:

```
<?xml version="1.0" encoding="utf-8"?>
<Configuration>
  <ViewDefinitions>
    <View>
      <Name>System.TimeSpan</Name>
      <ViewSelectedBy>
        <TypeName>System.TimeSpan</TypeName>
      </ViewSelectedBy>
      <ListControl>
        <ListEntries>
          <ListEntry>
            <ListItems>
              <ListItem>
                <PropertyName>Days</PropertyName>
              </ListItem>
              <ListItem>
                <PropertyName>Hours</PropertyName>
              </ListItem>
              <ListItem>
                <PropertyName>Minutes</PropertyName>
              </ListItem>
              <ListItem>
                <PropertyName>Seconds</PropertyName>
              </ListItem>
              <ListItem>
                <PropertyName>Milliseconds</PropertyName>
              </ListItem>
              <ListItem>
                <PropertyName>Ticks</PropertyName>
              </ListItem>
              <ListItem>
                <PropertyName>TotalDays</PropertyName>
              </ListItem>
              <ListItem>
```

```xml
                <PropertyName>TotalHours</PropertyName>
              </ListItem>
              <ListItem>
                <PropertyName>TotalMinutes</PropertyName>
              </ListItem>
              <ListItem>
                <PropertyName>TotalSeconds</PropertyName>
              </ListItem>
              <ListItem>
                <PropertyName>TotalMilliseconds</PropertyName
              </ListItem>
            </ListItems>
          </ListEntry>
        </ListEntries>
      </ListControl>
  </View>
  <View>
    <Name>System.TimeSpan</Name>
    <ViewSelectedBy>
      <TypeName>System.TimeSpan</TypeName>
    </ViewSelectedBy>
    <TableControl>
      <TableHeaders />
      <TableRowEntries>
        <TableRowEntry>
          <TableColumnItems>
            <TableColumnItem>
              <PropertyName>Days</PropertyName>
            </TableColumnItem>
            <TableColumnItem>
              <PropertyName>Hours</PropertyName>
            </TableColumnItem>
            <TableColumnItem>
              <PropertyName>Minutes</PropertyName>
            </TableColumnItem>
            <TableColumnItem>
              <PropertyName>Seconds</PropertyName>
            </TableColumnItem>
            <TableColumnItem>
              <PropertyName>Milliseconds</PropertyName>
            </TableColumnItem>
          </TableColumnItems>
        </TableRowEntry>
      </TableRowEntries>
    </TableControl>
  </View>
  <View>
    <Name>System.TimeSpan</Name>
    <ViewSelectedBy>
      <TypeName>System.TimeSpan</TypeName>
    </ViewSelectedBy>
    <WideControl>
      <WideEntries>
        <WideEntry>
          <WideItem>
```

```
            <PropertyName>TotalMilliseconds</PropertyName>
          </WideItem>
        </WideEntry>
      </WideEntries>
    </WideControl>
  </View>
 </ViewDefinitions>
</Configuration>
```

The file is included as pretty.xml in the book's download file (in the appendix A folder). In this case, the default display is a list including the following properties:

```
Days
Hours
Minutes
Seconds
Milliseconds
Ticks
TotalDays
TotalHours
TotalMinutes
TotalSeconds
TotalMilliseconds
```

Under some circumstances, we may just want the total values. This can be achieved by using a select statement (good if it's only now and again), or we can change the default display if we want to use the new format all of the time.

> **WARNING** Don't modify the files in the PowerShell folder. They'll be over-written when new versions of PowerShell are released and the changes will be lost.

We can create a new format file (AppB_new_timespan_format.ps1xml in the download):

```
<?xml version="1.0" encoding="utf-8"?>
<Configuration>
  <ViewDefinitions>
    <View>
      <Name>System.TimeSpan</Name>
      <ViewSelectedBy>
        <TypeName>System.TimeSpan</TypeName>
      </ViewSelectedBy>
      <ListControl>
        <ListEntries>
          <ListEntry>
            <ListItems>
              <ListItem>
                <PropertyName>TotalDays</PropertyName>
              </ListItem>
              <ListItem>
                <PropertyName>TotalHours</PropertyName>
              </ListItem>
              <ListItem>
                <PropertyName>TotalMinutes</PropertyName>
              </ListItem>
```

```
                <ListItem>
                  <PropertyName>TotalSeconds</PropertyName>
                </ListItem>
                <ListItem>
                  <PropertyName>TotalMilliseconds</PropertyName>
                </ListItem>
              </ListItems>
            </ListEntry>
          </ListEntries>
        </ListControl>
      </View>
    </ViewDefinitions>
</Configuration>
```

This file will only display the total values. We can load our format file into PowerShell using:

```
Update-FormatData -PrependPath AppB_new_timespan_format.ps1xml
```

This forces our format to be loaded and used ahead of the standard PowerShell formatting. When we display our `timespan` object, we now see just the total times:

```
PS> $ts

TotalDays         : 39
TotalHours        : 936
TotalMinutes      : 56160
TotalSeconds      : 3369600
TotalMilliseconds : 3369600000
```

Any time you create an object to display, or you need to control an object's formatting on a frequent basis, think about creating a format file to do the work. They can be loaded from the PowerShell profile to be always available.

A.7   Loops

We've seen how loops are used throughout the book. This gives a quick syntax reference. The use of each individual style of loop is given in chapter 2.

A.7.1   Foreach

Use the following syntax for a `foreach` loop:

```
foreach ($item in $collection_of_items) {
    < PowerShell code>
}
```

A.7.2   For

Use the following syntax for a `for` loop:

```
for ($i = 0; $i -lt somevalue; $i++) {
    < PowerShell code>
}
```

A.7.3 *While*

Use the following syntax for a while loop:

```
while (<condition>) {
    < PowerShell code>
}
```

A.7.4 *Do*

The syntax of the do loop has two versions:

```
do {
    < PowerShell code>
} until (<condition>)

do {
    < PowerShell code>
} while (<condition>)
```

A.8 *Operators*

In PowerShell, operators are used to perform some operation on data. This can be a comparison, arithmetic, or a logical operation. It's probable that some operators will be used more frequently than others. The operator information is spread across a number of help files. It's gathered here for completeness.

A.8.1 *Arithmetic operators*

The arithmetic operators +, -, *, and / mean plus, subtract, multiply, and divide as normal when dealing with numbers.

Strings are concatenated using a + sign.

Modulo arithmetic is performed using a % sign. It returns the remainder of a division:

```
PS> 28 % 5
3
```

Be careful not to confuse the modulo operator with % when it's used as an alias of Foreach-Object. Further information can be found using:

```
Get-Help about_arithmetic_operators
```

ARITHMETIC PRECEDENCE

Arithmetic operators are computed in the following order:

1. Parentheses ()
2. - (negative number)
3. *, /, %
4. +, - (subtraction)

A.8.2   Assignment operators

Table A.2 lists the available assignment operators.

Table A.2   Assignment operators

Operator	Meaning	Example
=	Sets the value of a variable	`$x = 5`

+=	Increases variable by given value	`PS> $x = 5`
		`PS> $x += 4`
		`PS> $x`
		`9`
		
		`PS> $y = "aa"`
		`PS> $y += "bb"`
		`PS> $y`
		`aabb`

-=	Decreases variable by given value	`PS> $x -= 3`
		`PS> $x`
		`6`

*=	Multiplies variable by given value	`PS> $x *= 3`
		`PS> $x`
		`18`

/=	Divides variable by given value	`PS> $x /= 6`
		`PS> $x`
		`3`

%=	Divides variable by given value and assigns remainder to the variable	`PS> $x = 28`
		`PS> $x %= 5`
		`PS> $x`
		`3`

For more information, run the following command:

```
Get-Help about_assignment_operators
```

A.8.3   Bitwise operators

Bitwise operators work on the binary version of a number. They see extensive use when working with the `useraccountcontrol` flags in Active Directory—see appendix D and chapter 5. In PowerShell v2, the bitwise operators work with 64-bit integers. Table A.3 lists the bitwise operators.

I'll leave it as an exercise for the reader to work through the binary versions of the examples!

Table A.3 Bitwise operators

Operator	Meaning

`-band`	Bitwise AND. The resultant bit is set to 1 when both input bits are 1.
	`PS> 15 -band 5`
	`5`

`-bor`	Bitwise OR (inclusive). The resultant bit is set to 1 when either or both input bits are 1. If both bits are 0, the result is 0.
	`PS> 15 -bor 5`
	`15`

`-bxor`	Bitwise OR (exclusive). The resultant bit is set to 1 only if one input bit is equal to 1.
	`PS> 15 -bxor 5`
	`10`

A.8.4 Comparison operators

There are two flavors of comparison operators: equality and containment.

EQUALITY OPERATORS

The equality comparison operators compare two values and decide whether they're equal, or whether one is greater than or less than the other. These are shown in table A.4.

A common typing error is to type -neq for not equal to. Another common mistake is to use = instead of -eq. These don't work!

There was a lot of discussion about the comparison operators in the early Power-Shell (Monad) betas, with many people preferring the symbol approach: > rather than -gt. The final decision was not to use symbols. These operators may seem familiar if you've seen Fortran in the past.

The default mode of comparison is that the operators are implicitly case insensitive. PowerShell as a whole is case insensitive. The comparison can be forced to be case sensitive by adding a c as a prefix; for example –eq becomes –ceq. Case insensitivity can be made explicit by adding an i as a prefix. These prefixes also apply to the replace operator (see string operators).

Table A.4 Equality comparison operators

Operator	Meaning
`-eq` `-ceq, -ieq`	Equal to. Returns `true` if both sides are equal. `8 -eq 8, "me" -eq "you"`
`-ne` `-cne, -ine`	Not equal to. Returns `true` if the two objects are different. `8 -eq 8, "me" -eq "you"`
`-gt` `-cgt, -igt`	Greater than. Returns `true` if left side is greater than right side. `8 -gt 7`
`-ge` `-cge, -ige`	Greater than or equal. Returns `true` if left side is greater than or equal to right side. `8 -ge 7, 8 -ge 8`

Table A.4 Equality comparison operators *(continued)*

Operator	Meaning
`-lt` `-clt, -ilt`	Less than. Returns `true` if left side is less than or equal to right side. `7 -lt 8`
`-le` `-cle, -ile`	Less than or equal to. Returns `true` if left side less than or equal to right side. `7 -le 8, 8 -le 8`

CONTAINMENT OPERATORS

These could also be called matching operators because we're trying to get a match to a pattern of some sort. The operators are shown in table A.5.

Table A.5 Containment equality operators

Operator	Meaning
`-like, -clike,` `-ilike`	Returns values that match strings based on wildcards * or ? `Get-Process	where {$_.Name -like "win*"}`

`-notlike,`
`-cnotlike,`
`-inotlike`
	Returns values that don't match strings based on wildcards * or ?
	`Get-Process
		where {$_.Name -notlike "w*"}`

`-match, -cmatch,` `-imatch`	Returns values that match strings based on regular expressions. In the following example, two characters, an n, a character, an n, and then one or more characters `Get-Process	where {$_.Name -match "\w\w[n]\w[n]."}`

`-notmatch,`
`-cnotmatch,`
`-inotmatch`
	Returns values that don't match strings based on regular expressions.
	`Get-Process
		where {$_.Name -notmatch "\w\w[n]\w[n]."}`

`-contains`
`-ccontains,`
`-icontains`
	Returns `true` if the right side is contained in the set on the left side
	`"red", "blue", "green" -contains "red"`

`-notcontains`
`-cnotcontains,`
`-inotcontains`
	Returns `true` if the right side isn't contained in the set on the left side
	`"red", "blue", "green" -notcontains "purple"`

A.8.5 *Logical operators*

The logical operators connect expressions or statements. Multiple conditions can be tested. Expect to use them in:

- `If` statements
- `Where` filters
- `Switch` statements

The logical operators are listed in table A.6.

Table A.6 Logical operators

Operator	Meaning
-and	Logical AND. Returns `true` when both statements are true. `get-process	where{ ($_.Name -like "w*") -and ($_.CPU -gt 100.0)}`
-or	Logical OR. Returns `true` when either statement is true. `get-process	where{ ($_.Name -like "w*") -or ($_.Name -like "a*")}`

-xor	Logical exclusive OR. Returns `true` when one statement is true and the other is false.
	`PS> (1 -eq 1) -xor ("a" -eq "b")`
	`True`
	`PS> (1 -eq 1) -xor ("a" -eq "a")`
	`False`

-not !	Logical NOT. (Two ways of writing). Negates the following statement. `get-process	where{-not($_.Name -like "w*") }` `get-process | where{!($_.Name -like "w*") }`

A.8.6 Range operator

The range operator can be used to identify a contiguous set of values:

```
PS> $a = 1..10
PS> $a[0]
1
PS> $a[9]
10
```

A.8.7 String operators

The string operators are listed in table A.7. The `replace` operator is included in the comparison operators in the help files.

Table A.7 String operators

Operator	Meaning

-replace
-creplace
-ireplace
	Replaces the specified part of a string with another string.
	`PS> "abcdef" -replace "B", "X"`
	`aXcdef`
	`PS> "abcdef" -ireplace "B", "X"`
	`aXcdef`
	`PS> "abcdef" -creplace "B", "X"`
	`abcdef`
	`compare with`
	`"My name is Joe".Replace("Joe", "Richard")`

Table A.7   String operators *(continued)*

Operator	Meaning

-split	Splits single string into one or more strings.
	```PS> "PowerShell is great" -split " "```
	```PowerShell```
	```is```
	```great```

-join	Joins multiple strings into a single string. The elements are separated by the supplied delimiter. Will also join contents of an array into a single string.
	```PS> "PowerShell", "is", "great" -join " "```
	```PowerShell is great```

A.8.8   Type operators

The type operators, shown in table A.8, can be used to test the .NET type of an object or to perform a type conversion.

Table A.8   Type operators

Operator	Meaning

-is	Returns true when the left side is an instance of the .NET type given on the right side.
	```2.0 -is [System.Double]```
	```2 -is [System.Double]```

-isnot	Returns true when the left side isn't an instance of the .NET type given on the right side.
	```2 -isnot [System.Double]```
	```2.0 -isnot [System.Double]```

-as	Converts the input on the left side into the type given on the right side.
	``2
		gm```
		``(2 -as [System.Double])
			gm```
			```Compare with direct casting```
			``[double]2
				gm```

A.8.9   Unary operators

The unary operators are listed in table A.9.

Operator	Meaning

-	Sets to negative; i.e., multiplies by -1
	```PS> $x = -4```
	```PS> $x```
	```-4```

++	```Attempts cast to a number```
	```PS> $x = +"12"```
	```PS> $x```
	```12```
	```PS> $x.GetType() - returns Int32```

Table A.9   Unary operators

Operator	Meaning

`--`	Decrements the variable
	`PS> $x = 5`
	`PS> $x--`
	`PS> $x`
	`4`

`++`	Increments the variable
	`PS> $x = 5`
	`PS> $x++`
	`PS> $x`
	`6`

`[<type>]`	Type cast. Sets the .NET type of the variable
	`PS> $x = [string]1`
	`PS> $x.GetType() - returns String`

Table A.9   Unary operators (continued)

A.8.10 *Special operators*

There are a number of special operators within PowerShell that we need to consider to complete this section, as shown in table A.10.

Table A.10   Special operators

Operator	Meaning

`&`	Call or invocation operator. Used to execute commands contained within a string.
	`$e = "Get-Process"`
	`& $e`

`.`	Used to indicate a property and for dot-sourcing a script when the variables are to be kept in memory.
	`$str.Length`
	`. ./myscript.ps1`

`::`	Used to execute a static method of a class. Static methods are explained in chapter 3.
	`PS> [Math]::PI`
	`3.14159265358979`
	`PS> [Math]::SQRT(16)`
	`4`

`-f`	Format operator. Used to format strings.
	`PS> "{0:F2}" -f 5.678890`
	`5.68`

`$( )`	Subexpression. The commands in the braces are executed and returned as the value of the "variable."

Table A.10   Special operators *(continued)*

Operator	Meaning

@ ( ), @{ }	Return an array or hash table, respectively. Array elements are separated by commas; the elements in a hash table are separated by semicolons.
	`$a = @(1,2,3,4,,5)`
	`$h = @{"a"=1; "b"=2; "c"=3; "d"=4; "e"=5}`

,	Creates an array.
	`PS> $a1 = ,1`
	`PS> $a1`
	`1`
	`PS> $a2 = 1,2,3`
	`PS> $a2`
	`1`
	`2`
	`3`
	Note that the first example creates an array with a single member.

The difference between the call (invoke) operator and `Invoke-Expression` isn't immediately obvious. These examples should help to clear the ambiguity:

```
$bk = "Get-Process"
&$bk
Invoke-Expression $bk
```

Both statements work, so either method can be used for a single command. If we want to extend our expression to multiple commands on the pipeline:

```
$bk = "Get-Process | sort cpu"
&$bk
```

using the call operator fails, but we can successfully use `Invoke-Expression`:

```
Invoke-Expression $bk
```

But if we try to use a script block instead of encapsulating the commands as a string:

```
$bk = {Get-Process | sort cpu}
& $bk
```

the call operator fails but `Invoke-Expression $bk` works. Life doesn't stay simple unfortunately, because if we put multiple commands in a script block:

```
$x = {$a=2+2; $a}
&$x
```

we find that the call operator works, but the following fails:

```
Invoke-Expression $x.
```

Just in case you thought to try multiple commands in a string:

```
$x = "$a=2+2; $a"
&$x
Invoke-Expression $x
```

both options fail.

There are ways to invoke any expression, as we've seen. Use these examples as templates when invoking commands.

A.9 Special characters

Special characters are listed in table A.11.

Character	Meaning
`` `0 ``	Null
`` `a ``	Alert
`` `b ``	Backspace
`` `f ``	Form feed
`` `n ``	New line
`` `r ``	Carriage return
`` `t ``	Horizontal tab
`` `v ``	Vertical tab

Table A.11   Special characters

A.10 Standard names

In PowerShell, a cmdlet is always given a name that consists of a verb-noun pair with the two words separated by a hyphen. It's good practice to use this convention for functions and scripts as well.

Capitalization seems to be a huge issue for some folks. I tend to follow the PowerShell team's lead and capitalize the first letter of the verb and noun unless I'm using a prefix on the noun, in which case that's also capitalized. This isn't set in stone, and I often use lowercase for functions. Even the PowerShell team don't always follow these conventions (as shown by ls function:).

A.10.1 Verb

The verb should be drawn from the list of standard verbs. PowerShell doesn't check whether the verb is part of the standard set, but expect loud comments from the PowerShell community if you step outside the standards. The list of standard verbs can be found by using the Get-Verb function in PowerShell v2.

```
Get-Verb | Sort verb | Format-Wide -Property Verb -Column 5
```

The standard verbs are:

- Add
- Approve
- Assert
- Backup
- Block
- Checkpoint
- Clear
- Close
- Compare
- Complete
- Compress
- Confirm
- Connect
- Convert
- ConvertFrom
- ConvertTo
- Copy
- Debug
- Deny
- Disable

(continued)

- Disconnect
- Dismount
- Edit
- Enable
- Enter
- Exit
- Expand
- Export
- Find
- Format
- Get
- Grant
- Group
- Hide
- Import
- Initialize
- Install
- Invoke
- Join
- Limit
- Lock
- Measure
- Merge
- Mount
- Move
- New
- Open
- Out
- Ping
- Pop
- Protect
- Publish
- Push
- Read
- Receive
- Redo
- Register
- Remove
- Rename
- Repair
- Request
- Reset
- Resolve
- Restart
- Restore
- Resume
- Revoke
- Save
- Search
- Select
- Send
- Set
- Show
- Skip
- Split
- Start
- Step
- Stop
- Submit
- Suspend
- Switch
- Sync
- Test
- Trace
- Unblock
- Undo
- Uninstall
- Unlock
- Unprotect
- Unpublish
- Unregister
- Update
- Use
- Wait
- Watch
- Write

The verbs are grouped by function. The groups and the number of verbs in each group are shown in table A.12. The content of the table can be generated by this piece of PowerShell:

```
Get-Verb | Group group
```

Count	Group Name
32	Common
24	Data
20	Lifecycle
7	Diagnostic
6	Communications
6	Security
1	Other

Table A.12   Verb groups

The names of the groups refer to the their purpose. Examining the group contents will help explain the group's purpose; for example:

```
Get-Verb | where {$_.group -eq 'Security'}
```

We can test whether a verb is part of the standard list:

```
$verbs = @()
get-verb | foreach {$verbs += $_.verb.ToString()}
$verbs -contains "grant"
$verbs -contains "choose"
```

This is also a nice demonstration of the -contains operator.

In PowerShell v1, we don't have a Get-Verb function, but we can find the verbs that are currently in use:

```
get-command | sort verb | group verb
```

A.10.2 Nouns

Nouns should be singular and should relate exactly to the object being accessed.

A.11 Type shortcuts

A number of type shortcuts or accelerators have been mentioned throughout the book. They're used as a shortcut for a .NET type. We can use the shortcut instead of typing the whole name of the type. The most commonly used are probably [adsi] for System.DirectoryServices.DirectoryEntry and the data type short cuts [int] and [string] for integer and string, respectively.

A full list doesn't seem to have been published but, Oisin Grehan, a PowerShell MVP, has shown how to obtain the list from PowerShell itself on his blog (search for "nivot ink"). The full list for PowerShell v2 is shown in table A.13.

Table A.13 Type shortcuts or accelerators

Shortcut	.NET type
adsi	System.DirectoryServices.DirectoryEntry
adsisearcher	System.DirectoryServices.DirectorySearcher
array	System.Array
bool	System.Boolean
byte	System.Byte
char	System.Char
decimal	System.Decimal
double	System.Double
float	System.Single
hashtable	System.Collections.Hashtable
int	System.Int32
ipaddress	System.Net.IPAddress
long	System.Int64

Table A.13 Type shortcuts or accelerators *(continued)*

Shortcut	.NET type
powershell	System.Management.Automation.PowerShell
pscustomobject	System.Management.Automation.PSObject
psmoduleinfo	System.Management.Automation.PSModuleInfo
psobject	System.Management.Automation.PSObject
psprimitivedictionary	System.Management.Automation.PSPrimitiveDictionary
ref	System.Management.Automation.PSReference
regex	System.Text.RegularExpressions.Regex
runspace	System.Management.Automation.Runspaces.Runspace
runspacefactory	System.Management.Automation.Runspaces.RunspaceFactory
scriptblock	System.Management.Automation.ScriptBlock
single	System.Single
string	System.String
switch	System.Management.Automation.SwitchParameter
type	System.Type
wmi	System.Management.ManagementObject
wmiclass	System.Management.ManagementClass
wmisearcher	System.Management.ManagementObjectSearcher
xml	System.Xml.XmlDocument

This gets confusing, because we can also do this:

```
$d = [datetime]"1 january 2010"
$d | gm
```

In this case, we aren't using an accelerator; we're using the fact that we can drop the System part off the type name. We've actually written:

```
$d = [System.DateTime]"1 january 2010"
$d | gm
```

Remember, too, that these shortcuts are in themselves shortcuts for using New-Object.

appendix B:
Modules and
advanced functions

Functions have been a useful part of PowerShell v1, in that they allow us to reuse code and cut down the size of our scripts by avoiding repetition. We can also save the functions into memory so that they're available from within our PowerShell session. It's possible to organize functions into libraries and perform a bulk load. These functions can be used from the command line or within scripts. The structure of functions was discussed in section 2.4.5.

PowerShell v2 provides a new way of organizing functions into modules. A module can be a collection of functions or even a compiled DLL. Windows 7 and Windows Server 2008 supply their PowerShell functionality as modules, as we saw in chapter 15. We'll discover how to write our own modules and how we can use this functionality.

If we want to use our PowerShell v1 functions on the pipeline, we have to create them as filters because a function only runs once. A filter will run once for every object on the pipeline. Advanced functions in PowerShell v2 enable us to write our functions and use them as if they were cmdlets—on the command line, in scripts, and on the pipeline.

B.1 Modules

Modules are stored, by default, in two places—a modules folder in the WindowsPowerShell folder of the user's documents and the modules folder within the PowerShell install folder. An x64 machine will add an additional folder in the 64-bit PowerShell install folder. The current paths to the modules are stored in a PowerShell variable:

```
PS> $env:psmodulepath -split ";"
C:\Users\Richard\Documents\WindowsPowerShell\Modules
C:\Windows\system32\WindowsPowerShell\v1.0\Modules\
```

It's possible to add other folders to that path if required.

The list of currently available modules can be seen:

```
PS> Get-Module -ListAvailable

ModuleType Name                          ExportedCommands
---------- ----                          ----------------
Manifest   FileFunctions                 {}
Script     MathFunctions                 {}
Script     ServiceFunctions              {}
Manifest   UserFunctions                 {}
Manifest   AppLocker                     {}
Manifest   BitsTransfer                  {}
Manifest   PSDiagnostics                 {}
Manifest   TroubleshootingPack           {}
```

This is the list on my Windows 7 RTM system. There are two types of module:

- *Manifest* which may contain scripts or a DLL. It has a manifest file that controls how the module is loaded. We'll see a manifest file later.
- *Script* which contains scripts and loading is controlled by the module.

The first four modules are loaded from my WindowsPowerShell folder, and the second four are modules that PowerShell supplies. Each modules folder contains a series of subfolders, each of which contains a module, which is a file of PowerShell functions with a .psm1 extension. The manifest file, if present, will have a .psd1 extension.

Modules are a good way of storing and loading scripts that are functionally related. As an example, let's consider the script we saw in listing 5.1 (creating an account on the local machine). We'll take that concept and extend it by adding the functions needed to create a random password for the account. This gives us a total of four functions:

- new-user—Creates the user account. This is essentially the same as listing 5.1 except we are generating a strong random password within the script.
- new-password—Generates the random password.
- get-randchar—Generates a random character from a defined set.
- add-character—Controls the adding of new characters into the password.

Listing B.1 incorporates the four functions that comprise our module. The code is a mixture of functions that we use directly and background helper functions that aren't directly exposed.

Listing B.1 UserFunctions module

```
#Requires -version 2.0                    ❶ Set requirements
## acceptable symbols (23 symbols)
$symbols = "(", "!", "@", "#", "$", "%", "^", "&", "*", "_", "+", "=", "?",
    "/", "~", ";", ":", ",", "<", ">", "\", ")", "."
function get-randchar {                                      ❷ Generate
    param ([int]$value)                                        character
    switch ( $value) {
        ## number
0 {[string][char](Get-Random -Minimum 48 -Maximum 58)}
```

```
          ## upper case
1 {[string][char](Get-Random -Minimum 65 -Maximum 91)}
          ## lower case
2 {[string][char](Get-Random -Minimum 97 -Maximum 123)}
          ## symbol
3 {$symbols[$(Get-Random -Minimum 0 -Maximum 23)]}
      }
}
function add-character{                    ←───❸ Add characters
    param (
        [int]$count,
        [int]$type
    )

    while ($count -gt 0) {
        $index = Get-Random -Minimum 0 -Maximum $length    ←───❹ Set position
        if ($characters[$index] -eq "") {
            $characters[$index] = get-randchar $type
            $count --
        }
    }
}
function new-password {                    ←───❺ Create new password
    [CmdletBinding()]
    param (
        [Parameter(Position=0,HelpMessage=
          "The length of password. Default is random between 8 and 12")]
        [int]$length = (Get-Random -Minimum 8 -Maximum 13),

        [Parameter(Position=1,HelpMessage=
        "The number of numeric characters the password should contain.
          Minimum is 1")]
        [int]$number = 1,

        [Parameter(Position=2,HelpMessage=
        "The number of upper case characters the password should contain.
          Minimum is 1")]
        [int]$upper = 1,

        [Parameter(Position=3,HelpMessage=
          "The number of lower case characters the password should contain.
          Minimum is 1")]
        [int]$lower = 1,

        [Parameter(Position=4,HelpMessage=
        "The number of punctuation characters the password should contain.
          Minimum is 1")]
        [int]$punc = 1
    )
    ## test password length
    $sumchars = $number + $upper + $lower + $punc    ←───❻ Check length
    if ($sumchars -gt $length){
        Write-Host "Password complexity will be preserved"
        Write-Host "Resetting password length to sum of input characters =
            $sumchars"
        $length = $sumchars
    }
```

```
    $characters = New-Object string[] $length
    for($i=0;$i -le ($length-1);$i++){$characters[$i] = ""}
    ## requirements                                          ←─❼ Add characters
    for($i=1;$i -le 4;$i++){
        switch ($i){
            1 {add-character $number 0}  ## numbers
            2 {add-character $upper 1}   ## upper case
            3 {add-character $lower 2}   ## lower case
            4 {add-character $punc 3}    ## punctuation
        }
        Write-Debug "$characters"
    }

    ## complete password                         ←─❽ Complete password
    for ($i=0;$i -le ($length-1);$i++){
        if ($characters[$i] -eq "") {
          $characters[$i] = get-randchar ($i % 4)
        }
    }
    $characters -join ""                          ←─❾ Join characters
}
function new-user {                               ←─❿ New user function
    [CmdletBinding()]
    param (
        [Parameter(Position=0,HelpMessage="The loginid")]
        [string]$id ,

        [Parameter(Position=1,HelpMessage="The Display name")]
        [string]$name
    )
    ## create a password                         ←─⓫ Create password
    $password = ConvertTo-SecureString
            -String $(new-password 8) -AsPlainText -Force
    $cred =
     New-Object -TypeName System.Management.Automation.PSCredential
            -ArgumentList "userid", $password

    ## get the machine                            ←─⓬ Get machine
    $pc = $env:computername
    ## create the context i.e. connect to the domain
    $ctype =
    [System.DirectoryServices.AccountManagement.ContextType]::Machine
    $context = New-Object
    -TypeName System.DirectoryServices.AccountManagement.PrincipalContext
    -ArgumentList $ctype, $pc

    ## create the user object                     ←─⓭ Create user object
    $usr = New-Object
    -TypeName System.DirectoryServices.AccountManagement.UserPrincipal
    -ArgumentList $context

    ## set the properties                         ←─⓮ Set properties
    $usr.SamAccountName = $id
    $usr.SetPassword($cred.GetNetworkCredential().Password)
    $usr.DisplayName = $name
    $usr.Enabled = $true
```

```
    $usr.ExpirePasswordNow()

    ## save the user
    $usr.Save()
}
```

The important point to remember about these function is the order in which they're used. We'll normally use them in this order:

1 new-user
2 new-password
3 add-character
4 get-randchar

Functions 1 and 2 can be used directly. We normally wouldn't call 3 or 4 directly. In fact, we'll hide them when we come to look at manifests.

Our module starts with a Requires statement ❶. This is used to ensure that we only run the script on PowerShell v2. We also set the symbol list. This contains the symbols we can use in our passwords. The password is created as an array of characters to begin with so that we can randomize the position of characters. We want to be able to create a strong password that consists of at least one of each of the following:

- Uppercase characters
- Lowercase characters
- Numbers
- Symbols

The function get-randchar ❷ is used to generate the individual characters. It accepts a type (0-4) as input and generates a random character of the appropriate type; for example, numbers are ASCII characters 48-57. The number 9 is generated by [char]57, for instance. Get-Random uses a maximum and minimum value when producing a random number. The cmdlet always produces a value less than the value supplied to the maximum parameter!

Our next function is add-character ❸. It accepts two integers as parameters. $count dictates how many characters to create, and $type controls the type of character. The function runs through a loop ❹, picking a random position in the array of characters that represents the password. If that position is empty, a character of the appropriate type is generated using get-randchar and the counter is decremented. The loop runs until the counter reaches zero.

These two functions are used by new-password ❺. This can accept a number of parameters, including:

- *Password length*—Default is 8-12.
- *Number of numeric characters*—Default is 1.
- *Number of uppercase characters*—Default is 1.
- *Number of lowercase characters*—Default is 1.
- *Number of symbols*—Default is 1.

The defaults ensure that a strong password is created that'll meet the Active Directory password complexity requirements. The number of characters defined for each type is summed, and if the total is greater than the stated length then the length is increased to match that value ❻. I always assume that I want to strengthen pass words, not weaken them. The defaults can be altered to suit your requirements if different.

An array of characters is created and we loop through the four character types, calling add-character to supply the contents ❼. If we use the –debug parameter when calling new-password, we'll see the characters being assigned after each pass. Once we have the stated requirements in place, we can fill in the rest of the characters randomly ❽. We loop through the array of characters and if a character is empty (""), we fill it using get-randchar. The type of character assigned is determined by taking the modulus of its position. As the preset character types are positioned randomly, this is a pseudorandom way of filling in the rest. If desired, get-random could be used instead. The final act of this function is to create a character string ❾ from the character array using the join operator.

The new-user function takes the login ID and user name as parameters ❿. A password is generated using new-password ⓫ and used to create a credential object. The machine we want to create the user account on is defined ⓬ and the user is created ⓭. The appropriate properties are set ⓮, including the password with a final save operation.

One thing to note is that we never see the password. This means that the account can be created ahead of time and the password reset when it's needed.

In its present form, the module exports all of the functions—makes them available for use. We can control which functions are exported by using:

```
Export-ModuleMember -function new-password, new-user
```

as the last line of the module. Alternatively, we can create a manifest for the module, which gives more flexibility.

A module manifest can be created using New-Modulemanifest. This cmdlet will step through asking for the information to complete the manifest. The other option is to copy one and hand-edit it, but you'll need to create a GUID.

If a manifest is present, it's executed in preference to the module file. It can load multiple modules using the NestedModules section. The lines dealing with versioning, ownership, copyright, and descriptions are self-explanatory. The GUID is created by New-ModuleManifest and uniquely identifies the module.

The manifest controls the functions, aliases, variables, and cmdlets that can be exported. It's conceivable that a situation could arise in which different functions were exported by different manifests. The manifest also organizes the scripts, type files, modules, and assemblies that must be loaded for the functions in the module to work. The manifest that accompanies the module discussed in listing B.1 is shown in listing B.2.

Listing B.2 Module manifest

```
#
# Module manifest for module 'userfunctions'
#
# Generated by: Richard Siddaway
#
# Generated on: 22/02/2009
#

@{
# These modules will be processed when the module manifest is loaded.
NestedModules = 'userfunctions.psm1'

# This GUID is used to uniquely identify this module.
GUID = 'b55021a4-5a21-4cf6-9b76-29eef95db0cf'

# The author of this module.
Author = 'Richard Siddaway'

# The company or vendor for this module.
CompanyName = 'Macdui'

# The copyright statement for this module.
Copyright = '(c) Richard Siddaway'

# The version of this module.
ModuleVersion = '1.0'

# A description of this module.
Description = 'Module of scripts for working with local user accounts'

# The minimum version of PowerShell needed to use this module.
PowerShellVersion = '2.0'

# The CLR version required to use this module.
CLRVersion = '2.0'

# Functions to export from this manifest.
FunctionsToExport = 'new-password', 'new-user'

# Aliases to export from this manifest.
AliasesToExport = '*'

# Variables to export from this manifest.
VariablesToExport = '*'

# Cmdlets to export from this manifest.
CmdletsToExport = '*'

# This is a list of other modules that must be loaded before this module.
RequiredModules = @()

# The script files (.ps1) that are loaded before this module.
ScriptsToProcess = @()

# The type files (.ps1xml) loaded by this module.
TypesToProcess = @()

# The format files (.ps1xml) loaded by this module.
FormatsToProcess = @()
```

```
# A list of assemblies that must be loaded before this module can work.
RequiredAssemblies = @()

# Module specific private data can be passed via this member.
PrivateData = ''
}
```

The module is loaded using `Import-Module` as shown in figure B.1. `Get-Module` will display the modules currently loaded and the functions that are exported. We can test that the functions are present by testing the function drive for the exported functions.

An example of using `New-Password` is also shown in figure B.1. Tab completion also works on the functions for the name and the parameters.

The module can be removed from use by using `Remove-Module UserFunctions`, which also removes the functions.

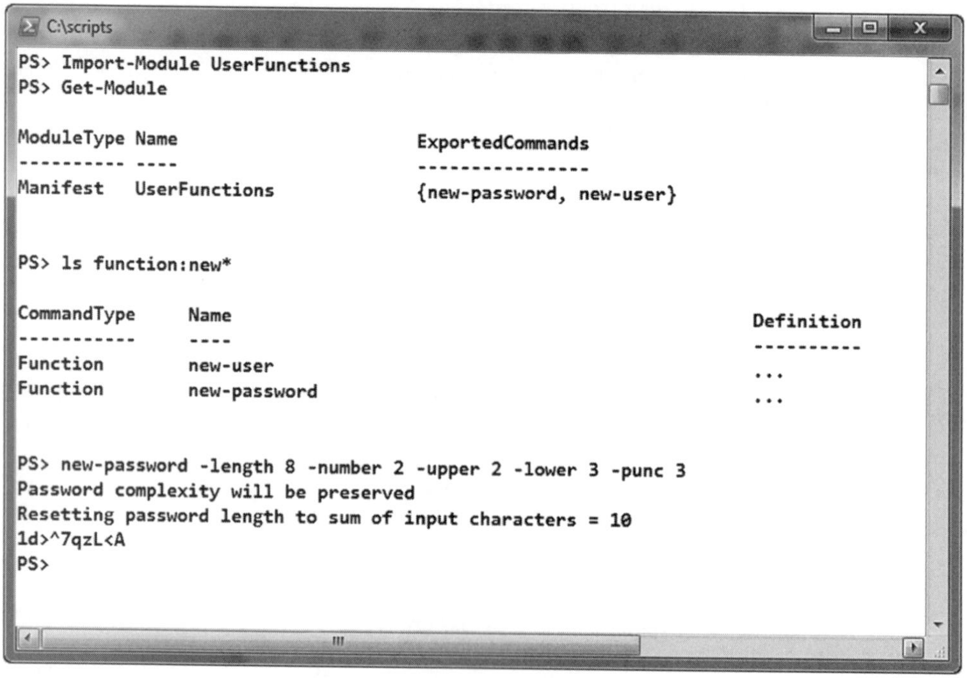

```
PS> Import-Module UserFunctions
PS> Get-Module

ModuleType Name                            ExportedCommands
---------- ----                            ----------------
Manifest   UserFunctions                   {new-password, new-user}


PS> ls function:new*

CommandType    Name                                                Definition
-----------    ----                                                ----------
Function       new-user                                            ...
Function       new-password                                        ...


PS> new-password -length 8 -number 2 -upper 2 -lower 3 -punc 3
Password complexity will be preserved
Resetting password length to sum of input characters = 10
1d>^7qzL<A
PS>
```

Figure B.1   Loading and using a module.

PowerShell v2 also allows us to write cmdlets in PowerShell. These were known as *script cmdlets* in the early beta versions but are now called *advanced functions*.

B.2   *Advanced functions*

Advanced functions enable us to write functions that act as first-class citizens on the pipeline. The `cmdletbinding` attribute is used to identify a function as an advanced function. The `$args` parameter doesn't work in advanced functions, so we have to define all parameters. A positional parameter that doesn't match with the defined parameters will cause the function to fail. In other words, you can't pass three parameters if you've only defined two!

Another innovation for functions (advanced or normal) is the ability to provide help information. This can be through comment-based help as we'll see in the example, or by a link to an external help file.

These concepts are illustrated in listing B.3 using a function that provides a colorized output for Get-ChildItem.

Listing B.3 Advanced function

```
function Format-Colorfile {
<#                                                                    1
.SYNOPSIS
    Creates a colored listing of a folders files
.DESCRIPTION
    Uses [System.Console]::ForegroundColor to control
    the color used to write out the file name.
    This is based on a PowerShell filter from
    the very first Monad book.
.NOTES
    Author:   Richard Siddaway
    File:     variable
    Requires: PowerShell V2
    Modifications:
            Several
.LINK
.EXAMPLE

    "Get-ChildItem c:\windows | Format-Colorfile"
.INPUTS
    output of Get-ChildItem
.OUTPUTS
    None
.PARAMETER file
#>
[CmdletBinding(SupportsShouldProcess=$True)]
param (
[Parameter(ValueFromPipeline=$true)] $file
)
    begin {
    $colors=@{ps1="Cyan"; exe="Green"; cmd="Green"; directory="Yellow"}
    $defaultColor = "White"
    }
    process{
        if ($file.Extension -ne "") { $ext = $file.Extension.Substring(1) }
        if ($file.Mode.StartsWith("d")) { $ext = "directory" }
        if ($colors.ContainsKey($ext)) {
        [System.Console]::ForegroundColor = $colors[$ext] }

        $file
          [System.Console]::ForegroundColor = $defaultColor
    }
```

1 Comment-based help

2 cmdletbinding

3 Parameter from pipeline

4 Set colors

5 Display file

```
    end {
        [System.Console]::ForegroundColor = $defaultColor
    }
}
```

6 **Set default color**

Everything starts off normally with a function keyword and the name of the function. We then meet our first new item **1**. The comment-based help uses a block comment that defines all lines between the opening defined by <# and the closing defined by #>. Block comments can be used anywhere in your scripts and functions. They look a lot more elegant than commenting every line and are easier to type. Block comments are especially useful if you need to comment out a bunch of code while testing.

The comment-based help can be placed at the beginning or the end of a function or script. I prefer to put it at the front because I can use it to document the script and it's immediately viewable when the script or function is opened in an editor.

There are a number of keywords used in comment-based help. They're always preceded by a full stop, as shown. My experience with using comment-based help suggests that if you get one of the keywords wrong then the comment-based help stops working. This means that any script acquired from the internet, or other third party, containing comment-based help should be carefully checked. The syntax for comment-based help changed a number of times over the evolution of PowerShell v2.

The keywords should be recognizable from the using the PowerShell help system. Comment-based help is accessed in exactly the same way as any other PowerShell help file, as shown in figure B.2.

The name, syntax, parameter list, parameter attribute table, common parameters, and remarks are automatically generated by the Get-Help cmdlet. There's also the possibility of using the Get-Help parameters such as -examples or -full with this system. The full list of keywords for the comment based-help can be found with:

```
Get-help about_comment_based_help
```

Now we get into the function **2**. The important attribute is:

```
[CmdletBinding(SupportsShouldProcess=$True)]
```

This causes the function to behave in the same way as a compiled cmdlet. The SupportsShouldProcess=$True part causes the automatic addition of the -whatif and -confirm parameters for when system changes are being made. This isn't essential for this particular function, but it's a good habit to get into. Other parameters are described in the about_functions_cmdletbindingattribute help file.

Our function accepts a single parameter **3**, which is file information. The way the function is written, it only accepts input from the pipeline, which is fine for what we want to achieve. The attribute ValueFromPipeline=$true on the parameter indicates that input can be accepted from the pipeline. Other parameters are available. See about_functions_advanced_parameters for details. These parameters are another place where syntax has changed over PowerShell v2's evolution. Check scripts carefully for the correct syntax.

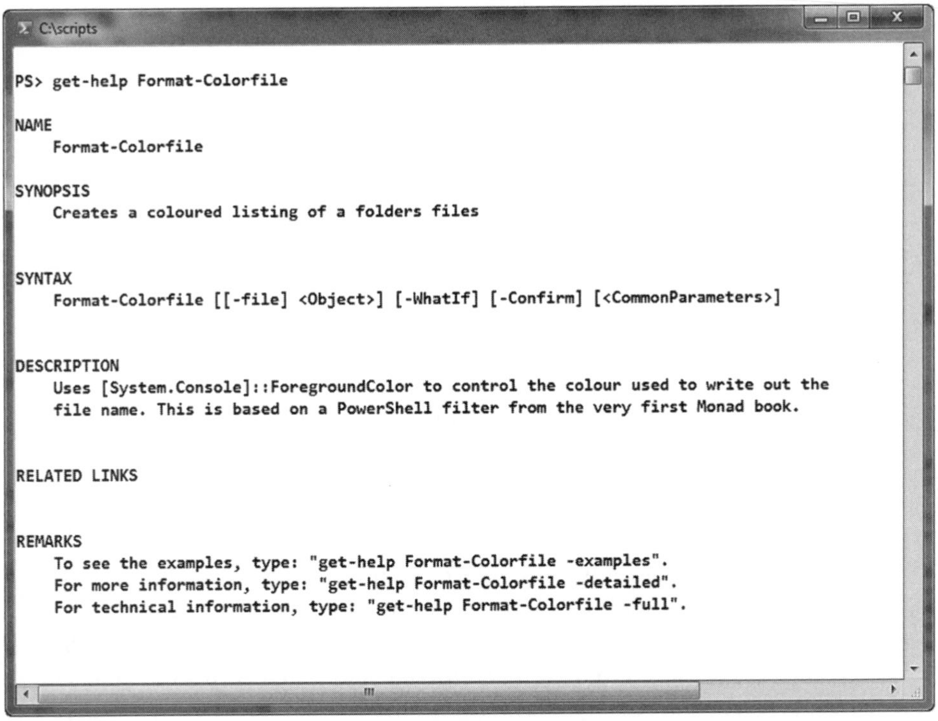

```
C:\scripts                                                    ─ □ X

PS> get-help Format-Colorfile

NAME
    Format-Colorfile

SYNOPSIS
    Creates a coloured listing of a folders files


SYNTAX
    Format-Colorfile [[-file] <Object>] [-WhatIf] [-Confirm] [<CommonParameters>]


DESCRIPTION
    Uses [System.Console]::ForegroundColor to control the colour used to write out the
    file name. This is based on a PowerShell filter from the very first Monad book.


RELATED LINKS

REMARKS
    To see the examples, type: "get-help Format-Colorfile -examples".
    For more information, type: "get-help Format-Colorfile -detailed".
    For technical information, type: "get-help Format-Colorfile -full".
```

Figure B.2 Comment-based help being displayed by `Get-Help`

The function is split into three script blocks labeled begin, process, and end. These run once before the pipeline enters the cmdlet, once for each object on the pipeline, and once after the last item on the pipeline has been processed respectively.

The begin script block **❹** defines the hash table of the colors that'll be used for each different type of file and sets a default color. The process block **❺** checks the file extension (or determines whether it's a directory) and uses the hash table to set the foreground color. The file information is printed to screen and the default color applied.

The end script block ensures that the default color is applied. **❻**

B.3   Recommendations

Is this new functionality worth the effort of learning it? Modules are a great way to organize our scripts. I definitely recommend using them if you'll be working in a PowerShell version 2 environment.

Advanced functions aren't necessary for everyone. If the task you're working on benefits from treating the function as a cmdlet then use it; otherwise it's extra effort for no gain. I won't be converting all of my functions to advanced functions, but I see a lot of places where it's worth doing, and will no doubt find more as time progresses.

appendix C:
PowerShell events

The Windows OS and everything you do in it is based on events:

- Start a program and an event occurs.
- Deleting a file records another event.
- Changing a configuration is yet another event.

Some of these events we're interested in, and others can be treated as noise we can ignore. PowerShell v2 provides the functionality to access these events, which provides another way to monitor system activity in real time. "Yes, I do want to know if xyx.exe is started on that machine during the day or if someone changes a file in a particular folder."

This material is somewhat advanced, which is why it's in an appendix. Not all administrators will need access to this, but if you do, it'll be really useful. The PowerShell isn't too bad, but the underlying concepts and the interaction with .NET and WMI can be a bit much.

The eventing system works as follows:

1 We define something that we want to track. This can be a new process starting to show when applications are started, or a watch on a particular folder so that we're notified if one of its files is changed.

2 We register this object with the event system and define the actions we want to happen when the event occurs. This can range from the default of adding information to the event queue to running a script that'll write a message to the screen, put an entry in a log file, or do something to negate the action. For example, we can make it so that if a particular application is started during the working day, the process is immediately killed.

3 The events raised by our object are put on to the event queue, or the defined actions are performed, when event occurs.

4 We can act on the information supplied by the event.

5 When we've finished with the object, we can unregister it and the system stops reacting to that event.

The event registrations and the event queue only exist in the session in which they're created. If PowerShell is closed, the registrations and any data on the event queue are lost. The events won't automatically be registered when PowerShell restarts unless there's a call in the profile to perform this action.

PowerShell v2 supplies a number of cmdlets to work with the event system. Full details and examples can be found in the help files:

```
PS> get-command *event | where {$_.Name -ne "Get-WinEvent"}

CommandType     Name
-----------     ----
Cmdlet          Get-Event
Cmdlet          New-Event
Cmdlet          Register-EngineEvent
Cmdlet          Register-ObjectEvent
Cmdlet          Register-WmiEvent
Cmdlet          Remove-Event
Cmdlet          Unregister-Event
Cmdlet          Wait-Event
```

GET-WINEVENT Get-Winevent doesn't belong with the eventing cmdlets, which is why it's deliberately excluded from the list. It's used to access the new style of event logs introduced in Windows Vista/2008 and subsequent versions.

The three Register* and New-Event cmdlets are used to create event registrations (also known as *subscriptions*). Unregister-Event deletes an event subscription. The other *Event cmdlets are used to manage the events on the event queue as their verbs suggest.

If we start by looking at application startup, we know that WMI can be used to access the process information on a system. An event to monitor creation of a new Win32_Process object—a new process—can be created like this:

```
PS> Register-WmiEvent -Query "select * from __InstanceCreationEvent
    within 3 where targetinstance isa 'Win32_Process'"
        -SourceIdentifier "WMI Process Start"
    -MessageData "WMI Process Started"
```

A WMI system class, __InstanceCreationEvent, is used to access the creation of a new process. The number 3 refers to the number of seconds between checks for new processes. We can see the event subscriber information:

```
PS> Get-EventSubscriber

SubscriptionId    : 1
SourceObject      : System.Management.ManagementEventWatcher
EventName         : EventArrived
SourceIdentifier  : WMI Process Start
Action            :
HandlerDelegate   :
SupportEvent      : False
ForwardEvent      : False
```

We can start a process from within our PowerShell session, from another session, or from Windows Explorer. The event information recorded can be accessed using `Get-Event`. If multiple event subscriptions exist, use the `EventIdentifier` property to access individual events or the `SourceIdentifier` to access a group of events from the same source:

```
PS> Start-Process notepad
PS> Get-Event

ComputerName     :
RunspaceId       : 3c4a9b12-5ee4-456c-85e7-87c2ec6c31aa
EventIdentifier  : 1
Sender           : System.Management.ManagementEventWatcher
SourceEventArgs  : System.Management.EventArrivedEventArgs
SourceArgs       : {System.Management.ManagementEventWatcher,
                     System.Management.EventArrivedEventArgs}
SourceIdentifier : WMI Process Start
TimeGenerated    : 08/11/2009 16:57:25
MessageData      : WMI Process Started
```

This gives us the ability to know when a new process has started, but unfortunately we can't discover what that process is from the information supplied by the event. In addition, we don't get information about processes stopping. There are three properties that could hold information:

- `Sender`
- `SourceEventArgs`
- `SourceArgs`

Investigating these doesn't give us what we need, but don't forget them because we'll return to them later. We need to remove this subscription and try something different:

```
PS> Unregister-Event -SourceIdentifier "WMI Process Start"
```

There are two WMI classes that trace the stopping and starting of processes:

- `Win32_ProcessStartTrace`
- `Win32_ProcessStopTrace`

We can use them to monitor the process activity on our systems. The script in listing C.1 logs the event information to a file for easy access and analysis. Our script starts by requiring PowerShell 2.0. We then define a header string ❶ that'll be used in the log file. If the log file exists, we remove it and then create the log file ❷ for this session by using `Add-Content` to write the header into the file.

Listing C.1   Log process start and stop events to a file

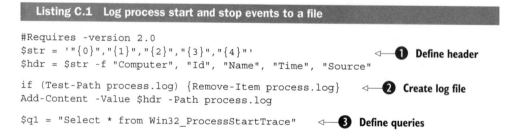

```
#Requires -version 2.0
$str = '"{0}","{1}","{2}","{3}","{4}"'                    ◁─❶ Define header
$hdr = $str -f "Computer", "Id", "Name", "Time", "Source"

if (Test-Path process.log) {Remove-Item process.log}      ◁─❷ Create log file
Add-Content -Value $hdr -Path process.log

$q1 = "Select * from Win32_ProcessStartTrace"   ◁─❸ Define queries
```

```
$q2 = "Select * from Win32_ProcessStopTrace"

$a = {                                              ←——④ Define script block
    $eSEANE = $Event.SourceEventArgs.NewEvent
    $str = '"{0}","{1}","{2}","{3}","{4}"'
    $data = $str -f $Event.Sender.Scope.Path.Server, $eSEANE.ProcessId,
    $eSEANE.ProcessName, $Event.TimeGenerated, $Event.SourceIdentifier
    Add-Content -Value $data -Path process.log
}                                                   Register events ⑤
Register-WmiEvent -Query $q1 -SourceIdentifier "Process Start" -Action $a
Register-WmiEvent -Query $q2 -SourceIdentifier "Process Stop " -Action $a
```

Two queries are defined to retrieve the information from the WMI classes ❸. An action block is created to process the event information and add records to the log file ❹. The action block starts by creating a variable representing a new event. $Event is an automatic PowerShell variable that represents an event that's being processed. It only exists in the action blocks of event registration commands!

A template for the record is created and populated with the required information. Refer to the following dump of the process log file to fully understand the contents. The final actions of the script are to register our two WMI Event subscriptions. ❺

The registration creates PowerShell jobs to monitor process start and stop events. The jobs can be viewed using Get-Job:

```
Id      Name            State       HasMoreData   Location   Command
--      ----            -----       -----------   --------   -------
1       Process Start   NotStarted  False                    ...
2       Process Stop    NotStarted  False                    ...
```

If you're in a hurry to see the results, we can get our machine to stop and start a few processes to generate some activity:

```
PS> 1..3 | foreach {start-process notepad; start-process calc}
PS> 1..3 | foreach {stop-process -Name calc; stop-process -name notepad}
```

Alternatively, we can be patient and leave the jobs running in the background while we do some work. The log file can be viewed as shown. It clearly shows when individual processes stop and start:

```
PS> cat process.log
"Computer","Id","Name","Time","Source"
"localhost","4916","SearchProtocol","08/11/2009 20:28:31","Process Stop "
"localhost","4588","SearchFilterHo","08/11/2009 20:28:31","Process Stop "
"localhost","4940","notepad.exe","08/11/2009 20:29:01","Process Start"
"localhost","5500","calc.exe","08/11/2009 20:29:01","Process Start"
"localhost","4704","ielowutil.exe","08/11/2009 20:29:59","Process Stop "
"localhost","5508","Solitaire.exe","08/11/2009 20:30:09","Process Start"
"localhost","4732","audiodg.exe","08/11/2009 20:30:09","Process Start"
"localhost","5508","Solitaire.exe","08/11/2009 20:32:33","Process Stop "
"localhost","5500","calc.exe","08/11/2009 20:32:57","Process Stop "
"localhost","2728","notepad.exe","08/11/2009 20:32:57","Process Stop "
```

The contents of this file could be analyzed to match process start and stop events to determine for how long each individual process was active.

When we've finished with our event monitoring, we can unregister the subscriber and delete the jobs:

```
Get-EventSubscriber | Unregister-Event
Get-Job | Remove-Job
```

Make sure that you close down in this order; otherwise it'll be difficult to remove the subscriptions unless you close down PowerShell. Other types of events are available. We can also monitor .NET events.

One useful .NET event to monitor is the filesystem watcher event. We can use it to discover when things happen to our files, as in listing C.2.

Listing C.2   Capture filesystem events

```
$folder = "C:\test"                                                    ❶  ┐ Define
$filter = "*"                                                          ❷  ┤ events
$events = @("Changed", "Created", "Deleted", "Renamed")               ❸  ┘

$fsw = New-Object -TypeName System.IO.FileSystemWatcher               ❹
-ArgumentList $folder, $filter
$fsw.IncludeSubDirectories = $true                                        Register
                                                                          subscriptions
foreach ($event in $events){                                          ❺
    Register-ObjectEvent -InputObject $fsw -EventName $event
        -SourceIdentifier "File System $event"
}
```

The folder ❶ and files ❷ to monitor are defined. A value of * means that all files will be monitored. There are a number of events that can occur in the filesystem ❸. In this case we're interested in all changes, deletions, creations, and file rename actions.

An object of `System.IO.FileSystemWatcher` type is created ❹ using the folder and file filters as arguments. We then ensure that the subfolders are monitored as well by setting the `IncludeSubDirectories` property to `true`.

We register an `ObjectEvent` ❺ for each of the event types we defined earlier. The event type is used to individualize the source identifier and the event name.

If we examine the whole list of events, we'll see that for each creation, deletion, and rename event, a change event is also raised. We can ignore this in most cases. Accessing the events for the creation, deletion, and rename events is straightforward, as these examples indicate:

```
Get-Event -SourceIdentifier "File System Created" | foreach {
    "{0}, {1}, {2}" -f  $_.SourceIdentifier,
     $_.SourceEventArgs.FullPath, $_.TimeGenerated

}

Get-Event -SourceIdentifier "File System Deleted" | foreach {
    "{0}, {1}, {2}" -f  $_.SourceIdentifier, $_.SourceEventArgs.FullPath,
    $_.TimeGenerated

}

Get-Event -SourceIdentifier "File System Renamed" | foreach {
```

```
"{0}, {1}, {2}, {3}" -f   $_.SourceIdentifier,
 $_.SourceEventArgs.OldFullPath, $_.SourceEventArgs.FullPath,
 $_.TimeGenerated
```

}

The change event is slightly more problematic, in that it generates two event records each time the event occurs, both labeled with a source identifier of File System Changed. The following example shows how we can deal with this.

We use Get-Event to retrieve the events for the changes. These events are grouped based on the time the events were generated. A filter is applied to only accept groups where there are two members. (We're accepting true change events and filtering out the secondary change event raised by creation, deletion, and rename events.)

The accepted events are used to supply the information we use to retrieve the first of the pair of events:

```
Get-Event -SourceIdentifier "File System Changed" |
Group TimeGenerated | where {$_.Count-eq 2} |
foreach {$time = $_.Name; Get-Event |
     where {$_.TimeGenerated.ToString() -eq $time}| select -First 1}
```

This look at PowerShell events has only scratched the surface of what we can do with this functionality. As administrators get more familiar with this concept, I expect to see a lot more examples appearing in the PowerShell community.

appendix D: Reference data

This appendix contains a collection of reference data that I've found useful. This information is available on the web, but can some of it can be awkward to track down.

D.1 Active Directory: user account control

The user account control flags are used to set the properties on a user account, including whether it's enabled or disabled. The attribute is a 32-bit integer where various bits have a particular meaning, as shown in table D.1.

Table D.1 User account control flags

Property	Decimal value	Hexadecimal value
Script (logon script will run)	1	0x01
Account Disabled	2	0x02
Home Directory Required	8	0x08
Account Locked Out	16	0x10
Password Not Required	32	0x20
Password Cannot Change	64	0x40
Encrypted Text Password Allowed	128	0x80
Temporary Duplicate Account	256	0x100
Normal Account	512	0x200
Interdomain Trust Account	2048	0x800
Workstation Trust Account	4096	0x1000
Server Trust Account	8192	0x2000

Table D.1   User account control flags *(continued)*

Property	Decimal value	Hexadecimal value
Do not Expire Password	65536	0x10000
MNS Logon account	131072	0x20000
Smartcard Required	262144	0x40000
Trusted for delegation	524288	0x80000
Not Delegated	1048576	0x100000
Use DES Key Only	2097152	0x200000
Do Not Require Kerberos Preauthentication for Logon	4194304	0x400000
Password Expired	8388608	0x800000
Trusted to Authenticate for Delegation	16777216	0x1000000

NOTE   Account Locked Out, Password Cannot Change, and Password Expired are *not* controlled through the useraccountcontrol attribute in Windows 2003 and later.

The expected values for a user, computer, and domain controller are given in table D.2. These values are applied to accounts in a normal usable state. Expect to see the values of 2 and 16 on a regular basis, as they represent disabled and locked out accounts, respectively.

Table D.2   Normally expected values

Object	Decimal value	Hexadecimal value
Normal user	512	0x200
Workstation or server	4096	0x4096
Domain Controller	532480	0x82000

Further information can be found at http://support.microsoft.com/kb/305144.

The final value of the useraccountcontrol attribute is the sum of the individual flags. A disabled normal account would have a value of 514 (512 + 2). These values can become difficult to unravel.

TECHNIQUE 205   Understanding the user account control values

As we have seen the useraccountcontrol attribute cannot be be directly understood. It is a bitmap that needs to be picked apart for full understanding. This technique acan be applied to any other bitmap attribute that is present in Active Directory or any other application.

PROBLEM

We need to understand the meaning of the useraccountcontrol attribute on an Active Directory object.

SOLUTION

The function in listing D.1 will take the value of the useraccountcontrol attribute as input and compare each of the possible settings to determine the full meaning of the value. The domain controller setting isn't part of the useraccountcontrol settings but is a useful test in its own right.

Listing D.1   User account control listing

```
function get-uac{                          ❶  Must be
param([int]$uac)                               integer

$flags = @(1,2,8,16,32,64,128,256,512,2048,4096,8192,
65536,131072,262144,524288,532480,1048576,2097152,      ❷  Array of
4194304,8388608,167772160)                                  possible values
$uacflags = @{1="Script (logon script will run)";       ❸  Hash table
2="Account Disabled";                                        of meanings
8="Home Directory Required";
16="Account Locked Out";
32="Password Not Required";
64="Password Cannot Change";
128="Encrypted Text Password Allowed";
256="Temporary Duplicate Account";
512="Normal Account";
2048="Interdomain Trust Account";
4096="Workstation Trust Account";
8192="Server Trust Account";
65536="Do not Expire Password";
131072="MNS Logon account";
262144="Smartcard Required";
524288="Trusted for delegation";
532480="Domain Controller";
1048576="Not delegated";
2097152="Use DES Key only";
4194304="Does not require Kerberos PreAuthentication for logon";
8388608="Password Expired";
167772160="Trusted to Authenticate for Delegation"}
                                           ❹  Loop through
foreach($flag in $flags){                      possible values

    if($uac -band $flag){Write-Host $uacflags[$flag]}   ❸  List meanings
    }
}
```

DISCUSSION

This is presented as a function for maximum flexibility in using. You can include it in your scripts, load it as required, or have it as a permanently available utility by loading it in your profile.

The function accepts an integer as the input parameter ❶. If you input a string or any other data type, it'll throw an error. The first task is to create an array of values that we want to test against ❷. These values are taken from tables D.1 and D.2. A hash table ❸ is used to hold the meanings of the values, with the value forming the key.

A foreach loop is used to iterate through the possible values in our initial array ❹. A comparison is perfomed using a bitwise AND operation ❺. If the corresponding bits in $flag and $uac are both 1, the resultant bit is 1; in other words we're checking to see whether $flag is contained within $uac. If we match at the bit level then the appropriate meaning is written out by a call to the $uacflags hash table using $flag as the key.

D.2   Local user accounts: userflags

We saw the userflags attributes in chapter 5 when dealing with local accounts. Table D.3 lists the common userflags values. They're a subset of the useraccountcontrol flags seen earlier.

Table D.3   User account control flags

Property	Decimal value	Hexadecimal value
Script (logon script will run)	1	0x01
Account Disabled	2	0x02
Home Directory Required	8	0x08
Account Locked Out	16	0x10
Password Not Required	32	0x20
Password Cannot Change	64	0x40
Encrypted Text Password Allowed	128	0x80
Do Not Expire Password	65536	0x10000
Smartcard Required	262144	0x40000
Password Expired	8388608	0x800000

D.3   LDAP Filters

In listings 5.12 and 5.13, we used a filter to limit the results returned by an Active Directory search, like so:

```
$search.Filter = "(cn=$struser)"
```

The filter is in effect performing an LDAP query to determine which accounts to return. The LDAP filter takes the form of a string with the following syntax:

```
"(<attribute> <operator> <value>)"
```

The parentheses () are required. A search can be performed on any attribute that's valid for the object for which you're searching. If an Active Directory object doesn't have an attribute set then in effect the attribute doesn't exist and we can't search on it.

There are a limited number of operators available to an LDAP filter, as shown in table D.4.

Table D.4   LDAP filter operators

Symbol	Name	Meaning
=	Equal	Simple equality check: `"(sn=Jones)"`
~=	Approximately equal	This can produce unpredictable results and should be avoided.
>=	Equal or greater than	Returns values greater than or equal to the given value: `"(badpwdCount>=1)"`
<=	Equal or less than	Returns values less than or equal to the given value: `"(badpwdCount<=2)"`
`Attrib:rule`	Extensible	Enable provider-specific matching rules. Most common use is for bitwise operations.
=*	Presence	This checks whether an attribute is present: `"(sn=*)"`

= [start] any [final]	Substring	A match is performed on part of the string. We can supply the start and/or the end of the string and the match will be performed against that portion of the string. We don't use the word *any* it's represented by the *symbol.
		`"(sn=Smi*)"`
		`"(sn=S*th)"`
		`"(sn=*h)"`

Note that > and < ("greater than" and "less than") aren't supported as operators.

The extensible matching rule is used to perform and/or operations on bit flags. The AND rule is 1.2.840.113556.1.4.804 whereas the OR rule is 1.2.840.113556.1.4.803. These examples show how to use them.

`"(useraccountcontrol: 1.2.840.113556.1.4.803:=2)"` finds all `useraccountcontrol` attributes with the 2 bit set—all disabled accounts.

Filters can be combined using three operators:

- AND (`&`)
- OR (`|`)
- NOT (`!`)

To find users with surname of Smith and given names of John:

`"(|(givenname=John)(sn=Smith))"`

To find all users with surnames of Smith or Jones:

`"(|(sn=Jones)(sn=Smith))"`

To find users not called Smith:

`"(!(sn=Smith))"`

Both the Microsoft and Quest AD cmdlets have a parameter that accepts an LDAP filter when searching—Get-*.

D.4 Identity in Active Directory cmdlets

The Active Directory cmdlets (Quest and Microsoft) have a parameter that gives the identity of the object to be returned or manipulated.

The Microsoft cmdlets accept:

- Distinguished name
- GUID
- SID
- SAM account name

The Quest cmdlets accept the following values where appropriate:

- Distinguished name
- Canonical name
- GUID
- 'domain_name\name'
- UPN
- SID

There are differences between these lists that can make moving between the two sets of cmdlets difficult. As stated earlier, it's better to pick one if possible, though the combination does give better functionality.

D.5 PowerShell filters in Active Directory cmdlets

Instead of using LDAP filters, it's possible to use a PowerShell-based filter. This is handled slightly differently in the two sets of cmdlets. A standard LDAP filer would be:

```
"(sn=Jones)"
```

In the Microsoft cmdlets, the LDAP filter would be:

```
Get-ADUser -LDAPFilter "(sn=Jones)"
```

Using a PowerShell filter, we'd have:

```
Get-ADUser -Filter {sn -eq "Jones"}
```

The Quest cmdlets would handle this as:

```
Get-QADUser -LDAPFilter "(sn=Jones)"
Get-QADUser -SearchAttributes @{sn='Jones'}
```

It's also possible to use a large number of names attributes with either system.

D.6 Special folders

Windows special folders were discussed in chapter 7. They're folders that the OS creates and manages; for example, the desktop and the recycle bin. The full list of special folders is presented in table D.5.

Table D.5   Windows special folders

Value	Variable	Meaning
0	$Desktop = 0x0	Desktop
1	$ie = 0x1	Internet Explorer
2	$progs = 0x2	Programs
3	$cp = 0x3	Control Panel
4	$printers = 0x4	Printers and Faxes
5	$mydocs = 0x5	My Documents
6	$favs = 0x6	Favorites
7	$startup = 0x7	Startup
8	$myrecdocs = 0x8	My Recent Documents
9	$sendto = 0x9	SendTo
10	$recycle = 0xa	Recycle Bin
11	$start = 0xb	Start Menu
13	$music = 0xd	My Music
13	$videos = 0xe	My Videos
16	$desktop = 0x10	Desktop
17	$mycomp = 0x11	My Computer
18	$mynet = 0x12	My Network Places
19	$nethood = 0x13	NetHood
20	$fonts = 0x14	Fonts
21	$templates = 0x15	Templates
22	$allsm = 0x16	All Users Start Menu
23	$allprogs = 0x17	All Users Programs
24	$allstart = 0x18	All Users Startup
25	$alldesk = 0x19	All Users Desktop
26	$appdata = 0x1a	Application Data
27	$printhood = 0x1b	PrintHood
28	$lsapps = 0x1c	Local Settings\Application Data
32	$lstempie = 0x20	Local Settings\ Temporary Internet Files
33	$cookies = 0x21	Cookies

Table D.5   **Windows special folders** *(continued)*

Value	Variable	Meaning
34	`$lshist = 0x22`	Local Settings\History
35	`$allappdata = 0x23`	All Users Application Data
36	`$windows = 0x24`	Windows
37	`$system32 = 0x25`	System32
38	`$progfiles = 0x26`	Program Files
39	`$mypics = 0x27`	My Pictures
40	`$profile = 0x28`	User Profile
43	`$common = 0x2b`	Common Files
46	`$alltemplates = 0x2e`	All Users Templates
47	`$admintools = 0x2f`	Administrative Tools
49	`$netconn = 0x31`	Network Connections

appendix E: Useful links

These are the links that I've found useful during my investigations of PowerShell and while writing this book.

E.1 PowerShell downloads

.NET 2.0

32-BIT

http://www.microsoft.com/downloads/details.aspx?FamilyID=0856EACB-4362-4B0D-8EDD-AAB15C5E04F5&displaylang=en

64-BIT

http://www.microsoft.com/downloads/details.aspx?familyid=B44A0000-ACF8-4FA1-AFFB-40E78D788B00&displaylang=en

.NET 3.5

http://www.microsoft.com/downloads/details.aspx?FamilyId=AB99342F-5D1A-413D-8319-81DA479AB0D7&displaylang=en

Also download and install the hotfixes from:

http://support.microsoft.com/kb/959209
http://www.microsoft.com/downloads/details.aspx?FamilyID=c411b91e-4dab-4550-915c-e119204d0732&displaylang=en

PowerShell v1

http://www.microsoft.com/windowsserver2003/technologies/management/powershell/download.mspx

PowerShell v2

http://support.microsoft.com/kb/968929

Microsoft MSDN

http://msdn.microsoft.com/en-us/library/w0x726c2.aspx

.NET class library

http://msdn.microsoft.com/en-us/library/ms229335.aspx

.NET CLASSES
System.Random-random numbers:
http://msdn.microsoft.com/en-us/library/w0x726c2.aspx

SYSTEM.MATH—MATH FUNCTIONS
http://msdn.microsoft.com/en-us/library/system.math.aspx

SYSTEM.DIRECTORYSERVICES.ACCOUNTMANAGEMENT
http://msdn.microsoft.com/en-us/magazine/cc135979.aspx

WMI CLASSES
System.Management.Management Object:
http://msdn.microsoft.com/en-us/library/system.management.managementobject.aspx
System.Management.ManagementClass:
http://msdn.microsoft.com/en-us/library/system.management.managementclass.aspx
System.Management.ManagementObjectSearcher:
http://msdn.microsoft.com/en-us/library/system.management.managementobjectsearcher.aspx

WQL
http://msdn.microsoft.com/en-us/library/aa394606(VS.85).aspx

PowerShell

POWERSHELL OBJECTS, - PSBASE, AND SO ON
http://blogs.msdn.com/powershell/archive/2006/11/24/what-s-up-with-psbase-psextended-psadapted-and-psobject.aspx.

WINDOWS SCRIPTING GUIDE
http://www.microsoft.com/technet/scriptcenter/guide/sas_ent_qpyo.mspx?mfr=true

ADSI SDK
http://msdn.microsoft.com/en-gb/library/aa772170.aspx

WMI SDK
http://msdn2.microsoft.com/en-us/library/aa394582.aspx

WMIEXPLORER
http://thepowershellguy.com/blogs/posh/archive/2007/03/22/powershell-wmi-explorer-part-1.aspx

OPENXML POWER TOOLS
http://staffdotnet.com/services/powertools.html

OPEN XML SDK
http://go.microsoft.com/fwlink/?LinkId=120908

.NET 3.5 is also required. See the .NET 3.5 download link supplied earlier.

PowerShell blogs

This isn't meant to be an exhaustive list, but it represents a good cross section of the PowerShell community. These blogs will include links to many other areas of the PowerShell community.

RICHARD SIDDAWAY
My primary blog

http://msmvps.com/blogs/RichardSiddaway/Default.aspx

The next one concentrates on PowerShell and WMI:

http://itknowledgeexchange.techtarget.com/powershell/

Many of the code examples from my blogs will be published as PowerShell modules

http://psam.codeplex.com/

POWERSHELL TEAM BLOG
http://blogs.msdn.com/PowerShell/

JAMES O'NEILL
http://blogs.technet.com/jamesone/

DMITRY SOTNIKOV
http://dmitrysotnikov.wordpress.com/

LEE HOLMES
http://www.leeholmes.com/blog/

MARCO SHAW
http://marcoshaw.blogspot.com/

THOMAS LEE
http://tfl09.blogspot.com/

THE POWERSHELL GUY (MoW)
http://thepowershellguy.com/blogs/posh/

SHAY LEVY
http://blogs.microsoft.co.il/blogs/ScriptFanatic/
Shay also has a PowerShell IE toolbar download available with many useful links.

JONATHAN MEDD
http://www.jonathanmedd.net/

ACTIVE DIRECTORY POWERSHELL
http://blogs.msdn.com/adpowershell/default.aspx

Other PowerShell downloads

POWERSHELL COMMUNITY EXTENSIONS
http://www.codeplex.com/Wiki/View.aspx?ProjectName=PowerShellCX

POWERGUI

http://www.powergui.org

Check on a regular basis for new power packs.

QUEST AD CMDLETS

http://www.quest.com/powershell/activeroles-server.aspx

POWERSHELL PLUS

http://www.idera.com/Products/PowerShell/

SDM GPO CMDLETS

http://www.sdmsoftware.com/freeware.php

POWERSHELL MANAGEMENT LIBRARY FOR HYPER-V

http://pshyperv.codeplex.com/

Code Sources

Check codeplex on a regular basis for new projects.

Code examples can be found at:

The TechNet script center

http://technet.microsoft.com/en-gb/scriptcenter/default.aspx

www.poshcode.org

Podcasts

http://powerscripting.wordpress.com/

http://get-scripting.blogspot.com/

User Groups

http://powershellgroup.org/

index

MORE TITLES FROM MANNING

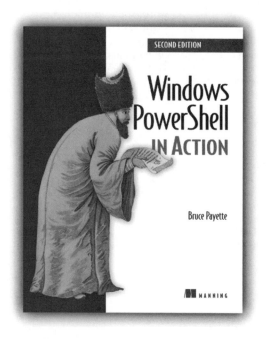

Windows PowerShell in Action,
Second Edition

by Bruce Payette

ISBN: 978-1-935182-13-9
700 pages
$49.99
July 2010

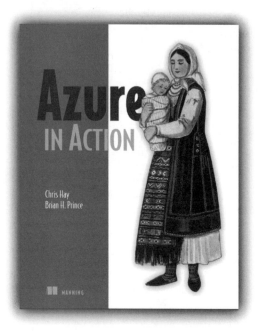

Azure in Action

by Chris Hay and
   Brian H. Prince

ISBN: 978-1-935182-48-1
425 pages
$44.99
August 2010

For ordering information go to www.manning.com

Brownfield Application Development in .NET

by Kyle Baley and Donald Belcham

> ISBN: 978-1-933988-71-9
> 416 pages
> $49.99
> April 2010

DSLs in BOO

by Ayende Rahien

> ISBN: 978-1-933988-60-3
> 352 pages
> $49.99
> January 2010

For ordering information go to www.manning.com

MORE TITLES FROM MANNING

SQL Server 2008 Administration in Action

by Rod Colledge

ISBN: 978-1-933988-72-6
464 pages
$44.99
August 2009

SQL Server MVP Deep Dives

Contributions from 53 SQL Server MVPs
Edited by Paul Nielsen,
Kalen Delaney, Greg Low,
Adam Machanic, Paul S. Randal,
and Kimberly L. Tripp

ISBN: 978-1-935182-04-7
848 pages
$59.99
November 2009

For ordering information go to www.manning.com